THE ACCOUNTING HALL OF FAME

The Ohio State University

Thomas J. Burns Series in Accounting History

VOLUME 2
T. Coleman Andrews: A Collection of His Writings

T. Coleman Andrews
1899 – 1983

T. COLEMAN ANDREWS
A Collection of His Writings

Edited by

Edward N. Coffman
Virginia Commonwealth University

Daniel L. Jensen
The Ohio State University

The Accounting Hall of Fame
THE OHIO STATE UNIVERSITY
Max M. Fisher College of Business
1996

TABLE OF CONTENTS

Administration of the Internal Revenue Service

Political and Personal Philosophies

EDITORS' PREFACE

This volume brings together the writings of Mr. T. Coleman Andrews in recognition of his contributions to the profession of accounting and his devotion to public service. Through the years, many individuals have made significant contributions to the growth and development of the accounting profession. Fifty-five such individuals, including T. Coleman Andrews, have been elected to The Accounting Hall of Fame at The Ohio State University since the Hall was established in 1950. The scholarly contributions of some of these important accountants—particularly those in academe—have been collected and published in special volumes, as a way of documenting and preserving a written record of contributions. But the contributions of many others remain dispersed in difficult to access periodicals, books, and manuscripts. These are in danger of being forgotten. The record of contributions by accountants who, like T. Coleman Andrews, made their careers outside academe are particularly vulnerable to being lost. For those who wrote and published little, one hopes that writers of history and biography will capture their contributions. But for those who wrote significantly, as did T. Coleman Andrews, published collections of their works have an important role to play in preserving unpublished materials and in collecting published materials that are difficult to locate.

This volume is the second in a series presenting the collected works of Hall of Fame members whose works have not been collected and published elsewhere. The series was established in 1992 and named the Thomas J. Burns Series in Accounting History in recognition of his twenty-five years of administrative service to The Accounting Hall of Fame. With Tom Burns' passing on January 10, 1996, those associated with the Hall of Fame will greatly miss his dedication to and involvement in its activities.

A chronological bibliography of Mr. Andrews' writings and speeches appears at the end of this volume. The bibliography includes the writings and speeches that we were able to locate through searches of bibliographic sources including *The Accountants' Index* as prepared by the American Institute of Certified Public Accountants and an inventory of Andrews' papers in Special Collections at the University of Oregon Library. Copies of all items in our bibliography were located.

In selecting the works to appear in this volume, we have attempted to present items that reveal Mr. Andrews' views on accounting and auditing as practiced in both the private and public sectors. In addition, we present several papers that are representative of his political and personal philosophies, although a complete presentation of his political writings and speeches is beyond the scope of this volume. We have attempted to minimize redundancy by reproducing just one version of similar papers or speeches. The editors' footnote to each item identifies the source of the item reproduced and cites duplicate or nearly duplicate items that are omitted from the collection.

We have endeavored to reproduce Mr. Andrews' writings as they originally appeared. Typewritten manuscripts are printed as they appear with only minor editorial changes and typographical corrections. Similarly, published materials are reproduced using Mr. Andrews' complete text; however, some editorial and stylistic elements of the book or journal are omitted in the interests of a uniform style. Occasionally, we have made comments and explanations in footnotes to the articles and speeches reproduced here. These are identified as "editors' notes" and printed in italics.

Mr. Andrews' works are arranged in seven groups of related articles: (1) accounting and auditing practice, (2) state and local government accounting reforms, (3) federal government accounting reforms: the general accounting office, (4) federal government accounting reforms: the Hoover commission, (5) professional leadership: the American Institute of Accountants, (6) administration of the internal revenue service, and (7) political and personal philosophies. With a few exceptions, each group presents work from a different segment of Mr. Andrews' career. Further, the groups are presented in an order that preserves their approximate chronology as the best means of tracing the development of his thinking and philosophy.

We are grateful to the Department of Accounting and Management Information Systems at The Ohio State University, to the School of Business and the Department of Accounting at Virginia Commonwealth University, and to Ray J. Groves and Ralph E. Kent for their financial support of this volume. We are also grateful for the invaluable assistance of Susan Morecroft and Barbara Eide, doctoral candidates at Virginia Commonwealth University, and Jeanne Scott, Interlibrary Loan Borrower, also at Virginia Commonwealth University, and to Vicky Jones in Special Collections at the University of Oregon Library which houses a collection of Andrews' papers. We wish to thank Wilson P. Andrews for his valuable comments and for his approval to reprint and publish these writings and speeches of his father. Finally, in addition to acknowledgments elsewhere, we wish to acknowledge the American Institute of CPAs, Baruch College (Accountancy Department), Hearst Corporation, Illinois Society of CPAs, Institute of Chartered Accountants in England & Wales, International Newspaper Financial Executives (formerly the Institute of Newspaper Controllers and Finance Officers), National Tax Association, Norfolk Southern Corporation, Pennsylvania Institute of CPAs, Penton Publishing, Richmond Newspapers, Inc., Society of Louisiana CPAs, University of

Alabama (Center for Business and Economic Research), Virginia Society of CPAs for permissions to reproduce Mr. Andrews' writings in this volume.

May 1996   Edward N. Coffman
                                    Virginia Commonwealth University

                                            Daniel L. Jensen
                                    The Ohio State University

A BIOGRAPHY
of
T. COLEMAN ANDREWS

THOMAS COLEMAN ANDREWS, the son of Cheatham William and Dora Lee Pittman Andrews, was born on February 19, 1899, in Richmond, Virginia.[1] After graduating from John Marshall High School in 1916, Andrews was employed in Richmond at a series of businesses. His first jobs were clerical in nature, but within two years, he had advanced to office manager. For a time, Andrews subscribed to business correspondence courses of Pace Institute in New York. Impatient with the slow speed of the process, he purchased all of the required texts, and completed his accounting education on his own.[2] During World War I, he studied and served as a sergeant-major at the Richmond College unit of the Army's Student Army Training Corps. He was married October 18, 1919 to Rae Wilson Reams; they had two children.

T. Coleman Andrews, as he was known, began his public accounting career in 1918, when he joined the Richmond office of F.W. Lafrentz & Company as a junior accountant. In 1921, he became a CPA in Virginia; at the time, he was the youngest individual ever to have passed the test. He left F.W. Lafrentz & Company in 1922, having achieved the status of chief accountant, to establish his own public accounting firm, T. Coleman Andrews & Company.[3] From 1922 to 1925, Andrews was an instructor of accountancy and business administration at the Virginia Mechanics' Institute at Richmond.[4] During the 1920s, he was an active member of the American Society of Certified Public Accountants, representing that Society at the Second International Congress of Accountants in Amsterdam, Holland

---

[1]This biographical profile builds upon information contained in Thomas J. Burns and Edward N. Coffman, eds., *The Accounting Hall of Fame: Profiles of Fifty Members* (Columbus, OH: College of Business, The Ohio State University, 1991).

[2]Dorothy Ulrich Troubetzkoy, "T. Coleman Andrews Commissioner of Internal Revenue," *Virginia and the Virginia County* 7 (August 1953): 5-6, 23, 26-27.

[3]Andrews' Richmond practice was eventually merged with Arthur Young, becoming Ernst & Young in 1989.

[4]Philip Alexander Bruce, *Virginia: Rebirth of the Old Dominion*, Vol. IV (Chicago: The Lewis Publishing Company, 1929): 473-474.

(1926),[5] and serving as Treasurer (1926-27), and as a member of the Board of Directors (1927-28).[6]

In 1931, Andrews took temporary leave of absence from his firm to serve as Auditor of Public Accounts of the Commonwealth of Virginia, a position he held until 1933. During the course of auditing the existing accounting systems, he uncovered shortages in the accounts of forty-two of the state's 100 county treasuries and found evidence leading to the convictions of six county officials. The greatest accomplishment of his tenure, however, was the development and installation of a state-wide uniform system of accounting. Andrews' new system for county accounts resulted in a dramatic reduction in bonding premiums for public officials—one indication of his reforms' effectiveness.[7]

From July 1, 1938 through June 30, 1940, Andrews again took temporary leave of his firm to serve as Comptroller and Director of Finance of his home town, Richmond. He was determined to improve the efficiency of city government administration. The cornerstone of his program was a reorganization of the city finance department.[8] Andrews successfully implemented many of the reforms he had planned, including the installation of a modernized system of financial accounting. He also dramatically increased the collection rate on delinquent personal property taxes. In this position, Andrews developed a reputation for "impartiality [which] perturbed politicians, but brought order to the system and money to the city."[9]

During the late 1930s, Andrews also became actively involved with the Municipal (now Government) Finance Officers Association of the U.S. and Canada and served on the advisory group of its National Committee on Municipal Accounting. This committee was organized to improve public administration by introducing "modern standards of accounting, auditing, and reporting suitable to the requirements of government."[10] His involvement with the American Institute of Accountants (AIA) also

---

[5]Andrews was elected a member of the Presiding Council of the Congress.

[6]The American Society of Certified Public Accountants merged with the American Institute of Accountants (AIA) in 1936. In 1957, the AIA became known as the American Institute of Certified Public Accountants (AICPA).

[7]"Taxes," *Time* 62 (August 31, 1953): 11.

[8]"Miller to Seek Andrews' Post," *The Richmond News Leader* (December 14, 1939): 1, 2.

[9]"New Revenue Head a Trouble-Shooter," *The New York Times* (January 18, 1953): 22.

[10]T. Coleman Andrews, "Accounting—the Eye of Management," *Municipal Finance* 7 (February 1935): 2-3.

increased; he became Chairman of its Special Committee on Bankruptcy in 1939.

In 1941, Andrews' commitment to public service and the events of World War II led him to Washington, D.C., where, as a civilian, he worked on the staff of the Director of the Fiscal Division of the War Department in the Office of the Undersecretary of War. His professional activities at the same time included chairing the AIA Committee on Governmental Accounting. In 1942, he joined the staff of the Contract Renegotiation Division of the Navy Department in the Office of the Undersecretary of the Navy, where he worked until he joined the U.S. Marine Corps later that year.

Andrews served during the war years 1942 to 1945 as an officer in the U.S. Marine Corps. From 1942 to 1944, he was assigned to the Department of State as Chief Accountant and Transportation Director of the North African Economic Board in Algiers.[11] During the latter part of the war, he served 30 months overseas as an officer on the general staff of the Fourth Marine Aircraft Wing in the Central Pacific and Africa. He received the Bronze Star and a presidential citation during his tour of duty as a Marine. In the spring of 1945, he was called back from the Pacific and was released from active duty, having attained the rank of major, in order to serve as organizer and initial director of the newly created Corporation Audits Division of the General Accounting Office (GAO). Andrews was recommended for this position by John L. Carey, who was at the time executive secretary of the AIA.[12]

The Corporation Audits Division of the GAO had been created to carry out the provisions of the George Bill, which required the 101 government corporations then in existence to be audited by the GAO "in accordance with principles and procedures applicable to commercial corporate transactions,"[13] and that audit reports be transmitted to Congress.[14] For

---

[11]In this position, Andrews was on the staff of General Eisenhower, who as President was to appoint Andrews to the position of Commissioner of Internal Revenue.

[12]Dale L. Flesher and Tonya K. Flesher, "T. Coleman Andrews Contributions to Governmental Accounting," in Imogene A. Posey, ed., *Collected Papers of the Fortieth Annual Meeting, Southeast Region, American Accounting Association* (Knoxville, TN: The University of Tennessee, April 21-23, 1988): 176-180.

[13]John L. Carey, "Audits of Government Corporations," *The Journal of Accountancy* 80 (August 1945): 81.

[14]The George Bill was enacted in February of 1945 and applied to fiscal years ending June 30, 1945 and 1946. The Government Corporation Control Act, enacted in December 1945, contained similar auditing requirements but applied to subsequent fiscal years (T. Coleman Andrews, "The Work of the Corporation Audits Division of the GAO," in *New Developments in Accounting* (New York: American Institute of Accountants, 1946): 165-170). These laws
(continued...)

the first time, these government corporations, such as the Tennessee Valley Authority and the Reconstruction Finance Corporation, were to be subject to audits that considered the efficacy of management and internal controls, in addition to the traditional focus of legal compliance. Soon after tackling the assignment, Andrews produced a report, which led to testimony before Congress (on July 2, 1946), lambasting the Reconstruction Finance Corporation's accounting methods and recommending basic changes in its over-all management.[15]

Andrews completed his service at the GAO in October 1947, after achieving the goal of establishing a professional audit division in the federal government that would operate in a manner similar to that of a public accounting firm. Andrews had "made it plain, when he accepted the job of organizing the newly created Corporation Audits Division ... that he did not regard the position as a permanent one. He accepted it ... as a service to the public and to his own profession."[16] The GAO's position as the investigative arm of congress was made possible by Andrews' work; he is considered by some to be the father of operational auditing in the federal government.[17] To recognize Andrews' organization and operation of the Corporation Audits Division, the AIA awarded Andrews its 1947 Gold Medal Award for distinguished service to the profession of accountancy.[18]

Andrews' experiences with the federal government helped to convince him of the need for "a thorough overhaul of the Federal Government's financial and accounting policies,"[19] a conviction he strongly advocated. Upon leaving the GAO, Andrews took on the chairmanship of the Accounting Policy Committee (or "Accounting Phase") of the task force on Fiscal, Budgeting and Accounting Activities for the Commission on Organization of the Executive Branch of the Government (the Hoover Commission). The Hoover Commission was to study and make recommendations for reforming the accounting, auditing, and financial

---

[14](...continued)
emerged as part of a compromise measure between the Congress and President F.D. Roosevelt, then in his fourth term, and served to increase congressional oversight ("Audit Crackdown," *Business Week* (July 21, 1945): 17-18).

[15]"T.C. Andrews Blasts RFC, Asks Changes," *The Richmond Times Dispatch* (July 3, 1946): 8.

[16]"T. Coleman Andrews Leaves Corporation Audits Division," *The Journal of Accountancy* 84 (October 1947): 269.

[17]Dale L. Flesher and Tonya K. Flesher, "T. Coleman Andrews and the GAO Corporation Audits Division," *The Government Accountants Journal* 38 (Spring 1989): 23-28.

[18]"Institute Award to Andrews," *The Journal of Accountancy* 84 (December 1947): 448.

[19]"New Revenue Head a Trouble-Shooter," 22.

reporting procedures of the federal government. The membership of the AIA's Committee on Federal Government Accounting (of which Andrews was chair) served as the Advisory Committee for this Accounting Phase. Andrews submitted his committee's report to the task force in October of 1948; the task force released its report to the Commission in January of 1949;[20] and the Commission made its report to Congress in February of 1949.[21] The recommendations contained in the final Commission report differed in several respects from those made by the Accounting Policy Committee.[22]

Although Andrews' official work with the Hoover Commission essentially ended with the submission of the task force report, Andrews continued to advocate enactment of the executive branch changes recommended by his committee and some of the recommendations contained elsewhere in the Commission Report. He was Chairman of the Virginian Citizens' Committee for the Hoover Report, which was organized as part of a nationwide effort to provide popular support for the Hoover Commission recommendations. Andrews was to be disappointed by the accounting-related provisions in the resulting Act, which passed Congress as The Budget and Accounting Procedures Act of 1950: as he put it, "for want of observance of some of the most fundamental principles that should be observed ... this Act becomes a good example of noble intentions rendered doubtful of achievement by another triumph of expediency over forthrightness."[23] The heads of federal fiscal agencies, however, praised the act as "the most progressive step forward in the improvement of the federal government's financial system since the Budget and Accounting Act of 1921."[24]

In addition to pursuing his interest in the Hoover Commission report during the period immediately following his return to private practice in 1948, Andrews was active in business, professional and civic activities. In 1948, he co-founded Bowles, Andrews and Towne, actuaries and insurance

---

[20]The Report of the Accounting Policy Committee of the Fiscal, Budgeting and Accounting Project is reprinted in this collection under the title "The Accounting Needs of the Federal Government."

[21]The accounting-related recommendations of the Commission on Organization of the Executive Branch of the Government in its final report to Congress are reprinted in the appendix to this collection under the title, "Reorganization of Accounting in the Government."

[22]T. Coleman Andrews, "Hoover Commission Disagrees on Changes in Government Accounting," *The Journal of Accountancy* 87 (March 1949): 192-199.

[23]T. Coleman Andrews, "The Budget and Auditing Procedures Act of 1950," *The Michigan Certified Public Accountant* 2 (February 1951): 12.

[24]John L. Carey, *The Rise of the Accounting Profession to Responsibility and Authority 1937-1969* (New York: American Institute of Certified Public Accountants, Inc., 1970): 429.

and pension fund consultants. He took on the vice-presidency (1948-1949) and then presidency (1950-1951) of the AIA. He lectured at the summer course at Christ Church, Oxford University (1949), sponsored by the Institute of Chartered Accountants in England and Wales. In 1952, Andrews co-founded Andrews and Howell, management-engineering consultants. He was on the board of directors and executive committee (1951-53) of the Panama Canal Company, a government-owned corporation operating in the Canal Zone.

In 1953, Andrews was inducted into the Accounting Hall of Fame for his "distinctive service to his country and to the advancement of Accounting as a profession and his high devotion to public service."[25] Also in 1953, Andrews was awarded a life membership in the Municipal Finance Officers Association.

Andrews returned to public service as the first CPA to become Commissioner of the Federal Bureau of Internal Revenue.[26] The Bureau was renamed the "Internal Revenue *Service*," reflecting his philosophy about the role of government. Appointed as a member of President Eisenhower's original (Republican) administration in 1953, Andrews held the position from February 4, 1953 through October 31, 1955. He was nominated for the position by Eisenhower's Secretary of the Treasury, George M. Humphrey;[27] and urged to accept the post by Senator Harry F. Byrd, Sr. of Virginia, another conservative Democrat from Virginia who, like Andrews, had supported Eisenhower over the Democratic nominee, Aldai E. Stevenson.[28] Although long regarded as one of the nation's top accounting experts,[29] Andrews' appointment was not welcomed by leaders of Virginia's regular Republican organization and he

---

[25]"Presentation of Distinguished Accountants to the Accounting Hall of Fame," *Proceedings of the Fifteenth Annual Institute on Accounting* (Columbus, OH: College of Commerce and Administration, The Ohio State University, 1953): 61.

[26]Andrews' selection for the Commissioner position was welcomed by the accounting profession as a tribute to the profession of accounting. In recognition of this "outstanding event in the history of the accounting profession," the AIA gave a reception and testimonial dinner honoring Andrews and attended by many prominent Washingtonians ("CPA Appointed Commissioner," *The Journal of Accountancy* 95 (February 1953): 165; "Testimonial Dinner to the Honorable T. Coleman Andrews by the American Institute of Accountants," *L.R.B.&M. Journal* 34 (April 1953): 15-16).

[27]"Appointment of Andrews is Applauded," *The Richmond News Leader* (January 14, 1953): 1, 4.

[28]"Battle of the Tax Returns: Congress vs. Collector," *U.S. News & World Report* 36 (October 2, 1953): 62, 64-65.

[29]"Ike, Top Aides Scan Strategy, Security," *The Washington Post* (January 15, 1953): 2.

was to face continued congressional opposition.[30] For instance, as part of Andrews' decentralization program, a division for post-audit review had been dispersed to the field. Members of congress opposed this reform because it made it more difficult for them to get information and "perhaps exercise their influence."[31] Given Andrews' reputation for indifference to political pressure, such conflicts should not have been surprising. Upon Andrews' appointment, *Time* had described Andrews as "blunt and hard-driving," a man who "trod on many a toe as Richmond city comptroller and Virginia state auditor," and one predicted to "spare no toes as the nation's chief tax collector."[32]

As Commissioner of Internal Revenue, Andrews had a clear mandate to restore public confidence in and the prestige of the Service,[33] which had suffered from the tax scandals of the Truman Administration.[34] Andrews' reorganization of the Service included decentralizing authority from Washington to regional offices, reducing the number of regional offices from seventeen to nine,[35] reducing the number of employees in Washington, giving greater freedom of action to field agents, reducing the backlog of unaudited returns and contested cases, and introducing programs to improve public relations.[36] One high-profile reform introduced by Andrews was a door-to-door canvass, named "Operation Snoop" by the press, that sought proof that citizens had paid their federal taxes. The "violent reaction" by the public against this tactic was reportedly defused as the public began to understand Andrews' view that only tax-evaders need fear the intrusion.[37] Public opinion of Andrews may also have been helped by Andrews' pro-taxpayer efforts to simplify many aspects of tax paying and to reduce conflicts between taxpayers and their government.[38] Other reforms, such as the establishment of the IRS Advanced Training

---

[30]"Battle of the Tax Returns: Congress vs. Collector," 64.

[31]*Ibid.*, p. 65.

[32]"National Affairs," *Time* 61 (January 26, 1953): 17-25.

[33]"The Taxpayers' Debt to a Public Servant," *The Journal of Accountancy* 100 (December 1955): 28.

[34]"Taxes," *Time* 62 (August 31, 1953): 11.

[35]*Ibid.*, p. 11.

[36]"The Commissioner Completes His First Year," *The Journal of Accountancy* 97 (April 1954): 417-418.

[37]"Taxes," 11.

[38]"Taxpayer May Be Right—New Line at the Treasury," *U.S. News & World Report* 34 (February 13, 1953): 84-87.

Center at the University of Michigan, were less controversial, but were advanced by Andrews with equal determination.

Andrews was widely regarded as successful in his pursuit of decentralization, efficiency, and simplification for the Service. His performance as commissioner reinforced his reputation for resisting political pressure and emphasizing efficiency and fairness;[39] his success in restoring public confidence in the Service was attributed to his "courage" and "unimpeachable character."[40] President Eisenhower awarded Andrews the Alexander Hamilton Award of the U.S. Treasury Department in 1955 for outstanding service to the federal government in recognition of Andrews' work as IRS Commissioner.[41] Andrews also earned the first award of the Tax Executives Institute for outstanding service in the field of tax administration (1955) and the Silver Medallion of Virginians of Maryland for outstanding public service (1955). Upon Andrews' resignation, President Eisenhower commended Andrews, writing, "The work you have done in the reorganization of the Internal Revenue Service, as well as improving its over-all efficiency and relations with the public, has been outstanding. You have my personal thanks, and, I am sure, the appreciation of the entire nation."[42]

Andrews had resigned from all three of his firms in 1953, prior to taking the position of Commissioner of the Internal Revenue Service.[43] Upon leaving government service in 1955, he returned to Richmond as Chairman of the Board and Chief Executive Officer of American Fidelity & Casualty Company. He was affiliated with the University of Virginia's Graduate School of Business Administration, where he was a member of the Sponsoring Committee and a visiting lecturer (1955-56).

In 1956, Andrews campaigned as an independent, states' rights party candidate for President of the United States. He advocated an end of the federal income tax system and limits on government spending. A large number of conservative splinter groups supported Andrews and his running

[39]Tris Coffin, "Firm, Fair and Prompt—Taxwise," *Nation's Business* 41 (September 1953): 52, 54, 56, 58.

[40]Comments made by William A. Sutherland in introducing T. Coleman Andrews, in *1953 Proceedings of the Forty-Sixth Annual Conference on Taxation*, Ronald B. Welch, ed. (Sacramento, CA: National Tax Association, 1954): 539.

[41]"Ex-commissioner's Funeral is Tomorrow," *The Richmond News Leader* (October 17, 1983): 4.

[42]"The Taxpayers' Debt to a Public Servant," 28.

[43]"T. Coleman Andrews," *Wisconsin Society of Certified Public Accountants Newsletter* (March 1954): 1, 4.

mate for vice-president, Thomas H. Werdel.[44]   After the election, he continued to be active politically. He was one of the twelve men present at the founding meeting of the John Birch Society in 1958 and was active with that group.[45] He assumed leadership positions with the Richmond Chamber of Commerce, including its Presidency in 1958. He was also an active member of the Virginia State Chamber of Commerce and of the United States Chamber of Commerce. In 1958, American Fidelity & Casualty Company was reorganized, and Andrews was elected President; he continued as board chairman.

Andrews retired from his position as president of American Fidelity & Casualty Company in 1963. He continued as Chairman of the Board until 1965. From 1965 to 1967, he was Chairman of the Board of National Liberty Life Insurance Company of Valley Forge, Pennsylvania. A nationally known horticulturist, he devoted some of his retirement to developing strains of rhododendrons and azaleas.

Throughout his career, T. Coleman Andrews had been active in many professional organizations in addition to those already mentioned. His affiliation with the AIA included memberships on the Council and the Executive Committee, and various positions on the following committees: Government Accounting, Budget and Finance, Cooperation with the Securities and Exchange Commission, National Defense, and Cooperation with the Bar. He was also a member of the American Accounting Association and the Association of Government Accountants. He served the Virginia Society of CPAs as secretary/treasurer (1925), as a member of the Cooperation with the Bar Committee (1948) and the Legislative Committee (1948-53; chairman 1948, 1951-53), and as a member of the Board of Directors (1952).

He was awarded honorary memberships in Beta Alpha Psi, Beta Gamma Sigma, and Omicron Delta Kappa, as well as a membership in Pi Kappa Alpha. He received honorary Doctor of Laws degrees from the University of Michigan (1955) and Grove City College (1963), an honorary Doctor of Commercial Science from Pace College (1954), and an honorary Doctor of Science degree from the University of Richmond (1955).

---

[44]Flesher and Flesher, "T. Coleman Andrews Contributions to Governmental Accounting," 179.

[45]One of the allegations made by Robert Welch, founder of the John Birch Society, was that Dwight D. Eisenhower (who had appointed Andrews to the IRS) had actively aided the "communist conspiracy." Andrews made it clear that he did not agree with Welch's conclusions about Eisenhower ("Differed with Welch: Andrews Cites Group's Aims," *The Richmond Times Dispatch* (April 1, 1961): 17). Andrews resigned from the executive council of the John Birch Society in late 1965 ("Andrews, 2 Others Quit Birch Council," *The Richmond Times Dispatch*, (September 12, 1966): 2). See also, G. Edward Griffin, *The Life and Words of Robert Welch* (Thousand Oaks, CA: American Media, 1975).

T. Coleman Andrews had affiliations with a number of other civic and educational interests; these included positions on the advisory board of the University of Richmond School of Business Administration, and on the advisory board of the Richmond Memorial Hospital.[46]

T. Coleman Andrews is remembered for a long and distinguished career in business and public service built upon a personal philosophy of self-reliance, hard-work and personal integrity. He was a skillful public speaker, who lectured widely and authored many articles and monographs. The substantive reforms he introduced to public administration, public finance, and government accounting earn T. Coleman Andrews a place as a major contributor to these fields. He died October 15, 1983, at the age of 84.

---

[46]*Current Biography Yearbook 1954,* (New York: H.W. Wilson Co., 1954): 25-27.

ACCOUNTING AND AUDITING PRACTICE

THE PROFESSION OF ACCOUNTANCY
Its Problems and Its Ideals[†]
by
T. Coleman Andrews

A little over a quarter century ago the legislature of the State of New York enacted the first law defining a Certified Public Accountant and specifying the requirements which one must satisfy in order to earn the right to hold oneself out as such. The recognition of accountancy as a profession in this country may, therefore, be said to date from the passage of that act. On account of the accountant's peculiar relationship to the science of business, it is quite natural that he first become recognized in the centre of greatest business activity. Since the passage of the New York statute every other state, the District of Columbia, and the Philippine Islands have enacted C.P.A. laws.

However, the enactment of C.P.A. laws has not in all cases been an aid to the growth of the profession. Quite the contrary has been true of several of the statutes. Investigation seems to indicate that persons responsible for the enactment of C.P.A. laws in many states have been men not engaged in accounting, who had no thought for the standards of the profession, but who sought personal gain through the acquisition of an official designation. In such cases the interested parties saw to it that they would immediately be designated Certified Public Accountants without any test of their worthiness other than that they present evidence of a given period of experience as a bookkeeper.

Then we find that the requirements of some of the statutes are woefully inadequate. Only a few years ago one of the state legislatures enacted a law whereby the only requirement that one had to meet in order to be designated a Certified Public Accountant was that he or she present evidence of a least ten years' experience as a bookkeeper.

Not very long ago a company was organized in the District of Columbia, and did a flourishing business selling certificates declaring the holders thereof Certified Public Accountants. A half dozen other certificate-selling schemes of almost equal brazenness could be mentioned. However, we shall pass on to other phases of the situation.

Another problem of the profession is the school which advertises that its course of study will make one a finished accountant within a year, after

---

[†]Reprinted with permission from *The Accounting and Business Quarterly*, September 1923, pp. 3-5.

which the passage of the state board examinations will be a comparatively simple matter. Such schools usually point out in their advertisements that accountants generally draw large salaries, one of them implying in a recent newspaper ad. that anyone completing its course might reasonably expect a salary of $10,000 per annum. With such alluring enticements it is almost hard to understand why there hasn't been such a rush to the field of public accounting as to leave other fields of endeavor virtually deserted. It is a tribute to the common sense and good judgment of the average American that such a calamity has not befallen us. The increase of students taking courses in accounting and kindred subjects has been enormous during the last few years, but there are still more good positions than there are men to fill them.

Now, it is not intended that anyone should infer from the foregoing remarks that everyone who has become a Certified Public Accountant under a waiver clause or law containing inadequate requirements is unworthy of the title. Such is not the case. There are many such Certified Public Accountants who stand high in the profession and who have built up large practices on services well rendered. On the other hand there are persons holding certificates who could not meet the first requirement of what is considered a fair test of a person's worthiness of the title of Certified Public Accountant.

Furthermore, this article is not intended as a brief for the Certified Public Accountant to the exclusion of those reputable practitioners who, for various reasons, have never obtained certificates. The designation "Certified Public Accountant" is looked upon by members of the profession as a badge of the qualified practitioner. It is a state-granted privilege, and the idea that one becomes a Certified Public Accountant by the mere purchase of a certificate stating that he is such is absurd.

There was a time when public accountants were generally regarded as useful only for checking up defalcations. Such is not the case now. Mere checkers of figures are of little use in the modern accounting organization. To be a successful public accountant today one must have a thorough understanding of the principles of economics, public finance, taxation, business administration, organization, banking, business law, and other kindred subjects; and he should be somewhat familiar with business tendencies and the politico-economic condition of his country. Behind all this there must be years of practical experience. It is therefore apparent that it takes years and not months for one to equip himself—or herself for public practice. There is no better proof of this fact than the large percentage of applicants for the title of Certified Public Accountant who yearly fail to satisfy the prescribed requirements of the various state laws.

It has been truly said that a profession puts service above all else. The professional man does not blatantly advertise his accomplishments; neither does he urge his services unduly upon those who may have need of them. The accounting profession frowns upon the practices of those so-called professional accountants who go from office to office hawking their wares, even resorting to the use of such baits as offering to do the work cheaper than it is already being done in order to obtain an engagement. It is perhaps quite natural that the business man, in his desire to save wherever possible, is attracted by such propositions. He is probably not aware that accountants with high ideals regard their work as a profession, and being accustomed to competitive practices, he does not regard the tactics of the solicitor as unprofessional. However, he invariably finds later that the first price was only a scheme to obtain the engagement, and that he would have in all probability been better served had he made no change.

Just as a man's character is judged by his daily acts so also is a public accountant's ability gauged by the quality of service which he renders. Whenever he fails to put his very best efforts into an engagement he has hurt no one so much as himself. His reports must state facts in an unbiased manner. He must not be influenced by the interest of anyone. He stands in the midst of all the parties at interest. His relation to the client is a very confidential one. He does not enter the coveted realm until he reaches the stage wherein satisfaction in the performance of work well done means more to him than financial reward. The latter is the natural sequence of the former.

There is nothing wrong with the profession. True, mistakes have been made. It would be a fallacy to say that they have not, but each mistake has been a stepping-stone to greater and higher accomplishments. The business man will understand better the ideals of the accountant and the accountant will grow in his ability to grasp the view-point of the business man. The result will be that the business man will find the accountant more and more indispensable in working out his daily problems and the accountant will enjoy a greater usefulness to the science of business.

CONSTRUCTIVE ACCOUNTING†
by
T. Coleman Andrews

FOR many years, in fact, ever since public accounting and auditing emerged from the "shortage checking" stage, there has been a tendency on the part of accountants and auditors to regard their profession as having two broad aspects. The first aspect never has been named; it may only be inferred from the word that has been pretty generally, although perhaps not altogether appropriately, used to define the second. But since the first isn't particularly important to the purpose of this article, we won't attempt to define or explain it.

The second aspect usually is called the "constructive" side of accounting. In the narrow sense, this term alludes to the designing and installing of systems; in the broad sense it alludes to the studying and appraising of "office" organization and routine. Academicians have coined impressive terms for such studies and appraisals; they call them "administrative surveys" or "administrative management studies." The average general manager who isn't satisfied with the way his concern's office is running, or who just wants to be sure that it is being kept up to date in both organization and methods, doesn't have a name for it; he just says, "While you're here look around a bit and let me know whether our system is adequate and the office is being run the way it should be."

No matter what you call it, it all adds up to the same thing; business people expect accountants and auditors to be "office engineers," to be able to do in the "office end" of a business what the production engineer does in the "manufacturing end" and the "sales engineer" does in the "sales end." Consequently, and because there was no other group better or as well prepared to meet the demand for such service, or to whom business could more logically turn for it, accountants and auditors were tagged and became "it," just as it fell to them to assume the primary burden—and take some of the benefits, of course—of handling income tax matters.

And so, accounting and auditing practice has acquired a "constructive" side. This is the side in which the profession's greatest and most frequent opportunities for creative effort arise, and from which, because of these opportunities, members of the profession get the greatest "kick." The sensation of creating, or building, undoubtedly explains the word "constructive." And constructive it probably is, for certainly nothing is

---

†Reprinted with permission from *The Accounting Forum*, June 1941, pp. 52-55, 62.

7

more conducive than constructive accomplishment to that most pleasant of all sensations—the pride and satisfaction one experiences upon having done something really worth while. Making anything better than it is, is constructive accomplishment and is bound to give the maker a "kick."

PERSONAL REQUISITES

Now, what does this business of looking around, seeing whether things are as they should be, and recommending changes involve? First of all, it involves ability on the part of the person who does it to "size up" the situation and determine just what clerical routines are necessary in order to properly dispatch the business of the office under observation. Incidentally, whether this ability can be acquired is a debatable question. There are strong indications that it is an inherent trait, but persuasive argument can be given to show that it may also be a product of academic and practical training for, and experience in, management. Space does not permit development of the question here; indeed this is not the place for an attempt at development of it at all. Mention of it is desirable, however, as a suggestion to any reader aiming at an accounting and auditing career that perhaps it might be well for him to determine how broad he should make his academic preparation.

Second, no matter how much natural aptitude one has for this sort of thing, he should supplement and enrich it with thorough study of the principles of organization and management.

And third, this study should include: (1) at least enough instruction and practice in drafting to assure ability to turn out accurate drawings of forms and make scale drawings of office layouts, and (2) a thorough study of accounting machines and other office devices and equipment. The latter is especially important, since so much of the work of modern offices is done with the aid of office machines and appliances of one kind or another. The study of these devices should include not only what they *will* do but also what they *will not* do, because it is the business of the machine and appliance manufacturers to sell what they make, and it is as natural for them to overestimate the applicabilities of their products as it is for parents to overestimate the virtues of their children. Many a good set-up has gone awry because the wrong appliances were chosen for use in it.

Also, the accountant and auditor should be particularly careful not to limit his study of appliances to the so-called "accounting" or "bookkeeping" machines. He is apt to do this because he naturally tends to overemphasize the importance of those appliances that are of particular usefulness as aids to accounting and bookkeeping. But there are any number of appliances not directly applicable to accounting and bookkeeping routines which afford opportunities to effect some of the most substantial savings obtainable from the use of modern devices.

SYSTEM FUNCTIONS

Accountants and auditors should avoid getting the idea that an accounting system will do things that it simply cannot do. Many a system has been introduced because the purchaser was sold on the idea that once it was in full operation all his problems would be solved. As if the system could be capable of managerial judgement! Accounting systems can't see or think or form conclusions; they merely reveal direction and position. They show management whether its performance has been financially good, bad or indifferent, and what results its performance, whatever its quality, has wrought. An accounting system produces nothing but a record of financial facts. It is a chronicle of financial events, management's most valuable tool perhaps, but never its proxy.

Nor is even a very good system an effective solution for poor office organization and management. A personal recollection will illustrate this point. In the particular instance, something obviously was wrong; the bookkeeping was behind; financial statements came so late that they were of little current value, and when they did come they were inadequate; collections were bad; salesmen were complaining that their orders were not being filled and their correspondence was not being attended to properly; cash discounts were being lost because bills were not audited and paid on time; the preparation of payrolls was little short of a nightmare; and...well, that's enough. The company's accountants were called in. Many circumstances indicated that the accounting system was the root of the trouble. At any rate, everyone agreed that it was. A fine new system was installed. But it wasn't the full answer; it was only a part of it.

The fundamental difficulty lay in the manner in which the office was organized and managed. The business had grown very rapidly. Considerable attention had been paid to production and sales, but the office had just "growed up" like Topsy, without planning of either its organization or management. When it became obvious that the new system was not the solution to the problem, an "office engineer," a "constructive" accountant was called in. He studied the organization and management of the office and submitted his recommendations. These involved, among other things, a reduction of almost 30% in the personnel of the office. Needless to say, this and the other changes made afforded a substantial saving in expenses, to say nothing of the improvement that the reorganization wrought in the effectiveness of the office generally as an important part of the general pattern of the business. The company's accountants failed to see the whole picture, and they were oversold on the virtues of accounting.

Reorganizations almost invariably encounter strong resistance from some of those who will be affected by them. People naturally tend to resist change from something they do understand to something they don't, particularly people who lack imagination and who are slow to learn new ways of doing things. This is the most serious problem the reorganizer has to deal with. Consequently, it is a good idea for him to avoid being mysterious or unduly secretive as he goes about his task. His chance of "putting his ideas across" will be greatly enhanced if he will, first, recognize the fact that understanding promotes cooperation and second, put this understanding to practical use by explaining to a few key people, as his study progresses, what he seeks to accomplish and how he proposes to do it. Even people who are doing a thing the hard way will shy off from changing to the easy way until the easy way is explained to them and they are made to understand that if they learned to do it the hard way they certainly can learn to do it the easy way.

AN ILLUSTRATIVE SURVEY

As an illustration of what an office organization and management survey, or so-called "constructive" engagement, may amount to, let us summarize a study made of what, for lack of a more descriptive term, we will call the "front office" of a utility company.

This office is responsible for making contracts with customers; reading meters; preparing, delivering and collecting bills; receiving and attending to complaints; making rebates and other adjustments; and keeping the customers' accounts.

Let us say that there are 100,000 connected customers and that they are billed monthly. This means that 100,000 bills have to be rendered and collected every month. 100,000 accounts to be serviced; that's the "milk in the coconut." If an accounting system were all that were needed here the job would be a comparatively simple one. But the case is not just one of accounting. It is one of organization and management. Some of the vital matters that arise and have to be decided in a case of this kind are stated and briefly explained in the paragraphs that follow.

Assuming that this company renders a metered service, it is obvious that the meter for each of the 100,000 connections has to be read every time a bill is rendered; and every bill that is rendered has to be collected, of course. To be sure, it would not be economical to organize for the reading of 100,000 meters and the making of 100,000 bills all at one time. This not only would be uneconomical from the standpoints of the reading of meters and preparing of bills, but also from the standpoints of both the delivering and collecting of bills. Hence, one of the first things that has to be decided is what the billing procedure shall be.

Assuming that it is decided that each account shall be billed monthly, then in order to keep the costs of billing and collecting down and assure an even flow of work in the meter reading, billing and collecting departments, it becomes desirable to spread the work over the month in such a way as to provide for the reading of about the same number of meters each day. This will, in turn, similarly spread the preparing, delivering and collecting of bills.

However, this process also involves the question of the determination of what meters shall be read each day. This in itself is an analytical and planning job of considerable proportions. After this is all worked out, the reading of meters and the preparing, delivering and collecting of bills becomes a routine matter. It is a very important routine, however, since these four operations must be scheduled in advance, taking into account holidays and other interruptions, so as to assure the billing of every account on or about the same date each month.

Then there is the question of what kind of bill to use. Although this sounds like a simple matter, in reality, because of numerous other considerations that are tied up with it, it is an extremely complex problem. There are, generally speaking, three types of utility billing and customer accounting plans: the bill and ledger plan, the register sheet plan and the bill and stub plan. Each of them is good in its place.

Closely connected with the matter of the type of bill to be used is the matter of what billing machines shall be used, for, with possibly one exception, no single billing machine will do equally as good work on all three of the billing and customer accounting plans.

Moreover, public utilities have a large number of complaints. This is not due to any lack of effort on the part of these enterprises to reduce the causes of complaints—indeed, the progress that has been made in this direction has been almost phenomenal—but public utilities touch intimately the daily lives of the consumers. Consequently, there are many complaints, perhaps not relatively but quantitatively. For instance, a few complaints relatively from 100,000 customers could run into a large number of complaints quantitatively. Moreover, customers frequently lose their bills and demand duplicates, or they just want to ask questions. Thus, it is important that the "front office" be so organized that the customer gets "prompt attention." This involves the use of the most modern types of communicating systems and the use of tho most efficient methods in the cashiers' cages. It also necessitates the greatest possible accessibility to the ledger accounts, account histories, customers' names and addresses, street indices, etc.

Also, there is the matter of collection. This is a particularly delicate problem with utilities, but such enterprises, like all others, have to collect their charges if they want to make money and stay in business. So there has to be a tactful, yet effective, collection system.

It is especially important that the keeping of the customers' accounts be accurately done, because nothing irks a customer so much as a mistake in his bill or account. He just doesn't think that utilities have any right to make mistakes. And, as a matter of fact, there shouldn't be very many if the proper pre-auditing of meter readings and post-proving of billings is done and the accounts are properly controlled. The writer has seen in one utility company 275 ledgers containing nearly 75,000 accounts kept in uninterrupted balance with the controls ever since a reorganization was made over two years ago. In this same office errors in bills are practically unheard of.

A utility must know its customers' consumption habits too. This is of vital importance for rate purposes. Full statistics on consumption enable the utility to intelligently combat unfair rate proposals. Thus, it is imperative that there be a reliable system for the gathering of consumption statistics.

What has been told about the reorganization of the "front office" of a utility company was not intended, of course, as a treatise on how to reorganize such an office. Indeed, the matters stated and explained were only a few of the many that are encountered in such an undertaking, and were presented to show how broad the "constructive side" of accounting really is. It is obvious that such a reorganization is not just an accounting job, that, on the contrary, it is a job that involves and requires, in addition to a knowledge of accounting, a thorough knowledge of office organization, methods, clerical routines, human psychology, and management generally.

COOPERATION WITH BAR ASSOCIATION[†]

by

T. Coleman Andrews

I have deemed it perhaps best to discuss this matter informally rather than to bring you a formal paper on the subject primarily because I think that perhaps we may get more out of it if we do discuss it rather than my reading a paper.

I rather regret that I was not here for the discussion on restrictive legislation. I heard a part of it but not all of it. I think if I had heard all of it, I would have been better able to address you more currently on this subject, because that subject and the subject of cooperation with the bar are two that are very closely related. As a matter of fact, I think one grows out of the other and they both have the same origin.

There is one thing that I think we must keep in mind as far as this matter of cooperation with the bar associations is concerned and that is that at least we must believe that the bar associations have not singled us our for special attack. We are merely a phase or a part of a general situation which confronts the bar associations. I believe that that attitude is essential. If we get the contrary attitude firmly fixed in our minds, we are apt to feel that personal resentment which one naturally feels when he thinks he is being individually attacked and are, therefore, apt to have our point of view a bit distorted when we come to deal with the situation.

I am convinced, and I think our committee is convinced, that the bar associations are not just after us. Let me review just very briefly some of the problems with which they are faced so that we may understand why they are trying to proscribe others.

There was a time when practically all wills were written by lawyers. The situation developed to a point, in our community at least, where lawyers rarely ever wrote a will. Most of them were written by trustees. There was a time when all contracts for the sale of real estate were written by lawyers and when all title certificates were made by lawyers and when all deeds were drawn by lawyers. There was a time when the situation reached a point in most communities where it was almost rare for a lawyer to draw any of these documents.

[†]Presented at the meeting of the Advisory Council of State Society Presidents, Detroit, Michigan, September 15, 1941. Reprinted with permission from the files of the American Institute of Certified Public Accountants.

13

Now, I might go on and mention a great many things that lawyers used to do but which they no longer do. When you understand that and when you understand further how many people have embraced the law profession as a vocation, you understand how very difficult it is for a man in the legal profession to make a living and you understand further the statistics as to the earnings of members of the legal profession.

Now, that is a very practical question which the legal profession faces, and that is a problem which we must recognize in order to deal with this whole question objectively.

We say to ourselves, of course, that some of the things the lawyers apparently are trying to do to us are not sought by the better lawyers. Well, that probably is true and that probably is a reasonable position to take. But the fact of the matter is that in law, as in accounting and in medicine and in all professions, the level of income follows a very erratic curve and the profession as a whole is made up of all types of individuals. The legal profession cannot look after one type any more than we would consent to have the American Institute look after one type or one branch or one segment of the membership of the accounting profession. And so while the well-to-do, affluent attorney would not be particularly interested in this question, you will find him very definitely unwilling to enter into an opposition, an active opposition, against those who are trying to do it.

Now, that is the background of your problem and it is a background that we must understand.

I have always felt that the best way in the world to be prepared for offensive action is to be in a position where the other fellow doesn't dare attack you. Now, that is more or less of a trite thing to say today when all of us have seen more or less tangible proof of the validity of that point of view in international affairs when we are spending so many billions that we as accountants cannot even comprehend in order to put ourselves in a position where no one dares to attack us. But as it is true in large affairs, it is true also in smaller affairs. It is true in individual affairs.

And that brings me to this second point. The accounting profession, after all, is not a particularly old profession. I think we must admit that we are to some extent still emerging from the chrysalis, and that puts us in the position where we have not yet attained the strength that we should like to have. I don't think we are weak but as some gentleman said a few minutes ago in his state there are less then one hundred accountants and nearly eight thousand lawyers, it is obvious that from the point of view of numbers, we have a pretty tough road to hoe.

In addition to that, we must not overlook the fact that the average state legislature in this country is composed to the extent of more than fifty percent of lawyers. In my state the General Assembly is the training ground for young lawyers. They get out of school and then they go to their communities, small towns, counties or cities, and they want to get started. And the way to attract attention, a legitimate way to attract attention, is to

14

go around to all their childhood friends and friends of the family and say, "Now, look here, Mr. Jones, I have got to make a living and I am going to run for the Assembly. I want you to vote for me. Papa says he thinks you ought to vote for me and Mama would appreciate it." He gets elected and he goes down there.

The result is that if you walk into the Legislature of Virginia—and it is a distinguished body if I do say so myself, despite all its deficiencies—you will see any number of young men who are getting their training and whose voices are important in the affairs of Virginia, whether you like it or not.

And those are the boys we have to deal with and they are the boys you have to deal with, because they are members of the profession that is seeking to entrench itself, and I am willing to say seeking perhaps legitimately to entrench itself.

Looking at it more or less subjectively and being not particularly interested in the problems of the trust companies and the real estate agents and the claim adjusters and others who have been the object of the attention of the Bar Association's Committee on Unauthorized Practice, looking at it, as I say, selfishly, as long as we can take care of ourselves, I am willing to let the other fellow work out his own salvation, and it is ourselves that I want to talk to you about today as far as dealing with bar associations is concerned.

As I say, you have these men entrenched in the legislatures who are naturally sympathetic and particularly sympathetic in view of the fact that most of them are getting started and they are the type of people to whom this type of legislation appeals, so you have a very practical political problem with which you have to deal. You have a problem in connection with which a certain segment of the bar will listen attentively and agree with you but not necessarily get out and work for you; as a matter of fact, they will not. And so you have to sit around the conference table with these younger men, sometimes middle-aged, rarely ever the older men of the legal profession, and work out this problem of cooperation.

Now, there have been indications of considerable success in various states in dealing with this problem. Therefore, I ask you not to look upon me as coming here to tell you how to do it, because I am not so sure that but each of you in your own state cannot handle your own situation as well as anybody can. The national committee can act as a clearing house; that is, a committee of the Institute can act as a clearing house for what has been done in this state or that state or the other. They can adopt certain principles which they would suggest as a matter of procedure and then rely upon you to use your own judgment. We recognize the fact that it would be utterly foolish for an outsider to go into a state with which he is not familiar and attempt to help solve this problem, except in the background and then only when asked.

I remember not so long ago one of the great national organizations that seeks to improve the quality of public employment wrote down to our state and wanted to come down and put on a campaign to carry their ideas into effect in Virginia, and they were all ready to come down there and spend a lot of money to put on this campaign when somebody reminded them that we had just had a Democratic nomination for Governor down there. And as far as we are concerned, that is the end of the ballot. There just "ain't" no use in anybody running after that because if a man is nominated on the Democratic ticket he is elected.

Now, this organization was willing to came down with money and with influence and try to tell us how to do this job when every man in the State Capitol who is in there today probably will not have a job on the second of January. The chances are that there will be an exodus right after New Year's that will be worse than the headache from the New Year's party.

And so we recognize the fact that we cannot solve these problems for you.

In Missouri in the St. Louis chapter—Mr. Charles spoke of it—they handled their problem adroitly. I saw a letter about it, but I don't know if I would be betraying any confidence if I told you about it. Mr. Charles and his committee got rid of the problem by reaching an agreement with the Bar Association of St. Louis. They got along all right.

In my own state, if you will pardon me for speaking about ourselves, we follow about the same procedure—sitting down with the lawyers and talking it over with them, giving them an understanding of our position and agreeing with them that we will not do certain things if we think they have a perfect right in asking us not to do them. For instance, they object to our drawing charters, filing charters, and in some cases drawing contracts and other legal documents, all of which certain members of our profession in our state had been doing. Our Society met and considered these things and we determined that certain members were doing things that they had no right to do. So we came out in resolution and we handed it to them and said, "We don't think our members ought to do certain things. If you find any member doing any of these things, you come to us and we shall be glad to talk the matter over." We have got it on a case basis, in other words.

In all of our dealings with the American Bar Association there has been that fundamental idea proposed and agreed upon at Cleveland, I believe, several years ago, that we would deal with situations involving the unauthorized practice of law by accountants on the case basis. If we keep it on that basis that they will cite the cases wherein we transgress their territory or trespass upon that territory and let us jointly with them deal with those cases, we can most quickly achieve the situation that we want to create between them and ourselves.

We strongly warn every member of every State Society or of every committee to stay away from agreements as to what is the practice of law and what is the practice of accounting. We don't think that anybody as yet is smart enough to determine exactly where the line should be drawn. We, therefore, suggest to you gentlemen in your State Societies that you do not agree upon such a basis as that. We suggest that you say, as other State Societies have said, "Certainly, gentlemen, we won't want to practice law and if you will give us the cases where you think we have been practicing law, we shall be perfectly willing to sit down and review the matter with you and come to a conclusion which we believe will be satisfactory to everybody, and assist you in taking appropriate steps."

Now, those are the principles that the committee has worked out.

We have, of course, followed national legislation in the course of time. I am not going to attempt to review the entire national picture, because it has been reviewed in at least two issues of *The Journal of Accountancy*, first in March and then later the statement which President Wellington made to one of the committees of Congress with regard to these pending bills, which statement was published, I believe, in July.

So I suggest that if you want to bring yourselves right up to date on these Congressional bills, two Congressional bills and three Senate bills, that you read the digest or the review in the March issue of *The Journal* and that you read the President's statement to the Senatorial committee in the July issue. If you do that, you will be as nearly up to date as we are.

I might say that as far as we know now none of these five bills is being seriously considered by the committee for reporting out. Apparently the situation, as far as that is concerned, is in status quo.

I might point out to you, of course, that two of these bills are sponsored by the American Bar Association. One of those is H. R. 2526 and the companion bill in the Senate is Senate Bill 918.

Two other bills, Senate Bills 674 and 675 were sponsored by the Attorney General's Committee on Administrative Procedure. One bill embodies the ideas of the majority of the committee. The other bill embodies the ideas of the minority.

As I say, you can get all of the dope on these bills from *The Journal*.

Now, I have talked at some length, but there is one other matter that I should like to leave with you or tell you about so that you may get what comfort you can from it, and this is with particular reference to tax practice. It has to do with two cases, one of them a very important case, reported to us by our Counsel in Washington in a letter to Mr. Carey from our Counsel on February 26th.

I am going to read that letter if I may, Mr. Chairman, because it gives us the full information on those cases and I think it is heartening.

In the case of Blair vs. the Motor Carriers' Service Bureau, decided by the Court of Common Pleas in Philadelphia and reported in the Legal Intelligencer of February 24, 1939, the court held:

"The preparation by defendants of tax reports and tax returns and the filing thereof with governmental bureaus, the construction of accounting systems and the preparation of record forms do not constitute the practice of law. Furnishing of advice concerning tax laws and methods of business organization and operation likely to reduce the amount of tax liability does not constitute the unauthorized practice of law."

The Court said: "An accountant broker is frequently called upon to discuss with clients the advantages from a business point of view of forming a partnership, of purchasing or selling a business, of organizing or dissolving a corporation, of merging corporations, of increasing or decreasing capital stock. Furnishing business counsel of this character does not of itself constitute the practice of law even though incidentally legal questions may be involved."

We recently had a case in the District of Columbia which caused a great deal of comment. The Bar Association objected to a good many things that the trust companies were doing. The final decision was by the United States Court of Appeals for the District of Columbia on the ninth of October, 1939. The Supreme Court denied application for certiorari on January 2, 1940. The case is Merrick vs. American Security and Trust Company.

At the conclusion of the opinion the Court said:

"Appellants do not emphasize the fact that defendants employ laymen to prepare tax returns and advise organization on tax figures. Such work may properly be done by lawyers or laymen."

This is a clear-cut recent statement by an important court in an important case which may be helpful in this situation. The findings of the Court, showing exactly what was done in tax matters, appears on page 86 of the review.

I shall not read that but I give you those two cases, one from a court which admittedly is not a court of last resort but the other from a court whose opinion was appealed to the Supreme Court of the United States, which appeal was denied.

Personally, I feel rather optimistic about this question provided we continue in the various states to deal with it with the intelligence with which it has already been dealt. I think that we must bear in mind that to the extent that we have a commanding position in our communities, we have that much better chance of defeating legislation of that kind.

In other words, our defense is a good deal more fundamental than the mere matter of objection to what the legal profession is trying to do. We must attempt to understand the legal profession and we must attempt to deal with them in a reasonable sort of way. But in addition to that, and more important than that, we must constantly place more emphasis upon raising ourselves actually to a professional status. We cannot hope, if we allow the profession to sink down to a bookkeeper's status or to a mere clerical status, to have these members of the legal profession with us on a basis of parity with themselves.

So, therefore, the fundamental defense to this whole question is a matter of how good are we? Where do we stand in our communities as professional men?

I believe that if we keep that in mind and remember that the legal profession has a problem with which to deal, that we have got to help them solve it and at the same time help ourselves, and continue to go along the lines of the general principles which the committee of the Institute has adopted not as its own ideas but as the ideas which have come to it from

State Societies all over the country—I believe that if we pursue that policy with understanding, with a reasonable attitude of proper self-defense, not yielding any point of important principle but being willing to give way to details that are not important to the main issue involved, and at the same time continue to lay emphasis on the elevation of our profession to a true professional level, we can look forward to the solution of this problem, not just an ordinary solution that we can chalk up as a successful accomplishment but something more important than that—I think that we can come out of that question with an acknowledged parity with one of the great professions of the day, working side by side and shoulder to shoulder with the legal profession.

Thank you.

THE ACCOUNTANT IN PRACTICE AND IN PUBLIC SERVICE[†]

by

T. Coleman Andrews

IT is essential to accurate understanding of public accounting practice in the United States that the source of the practitioner's professional status there be clearly understood.

Contrary to the situation here in the country of our hosts, where an accountant gets his professional recognition from the profession itself, it is traditional in the United States that public practice of accounting is deemed to be an activity affected with the public interest and, therefore, a proper subject of state regulation. Hence, those who engage in public accounting practice get their recognition from one of the forty-eight states, the District of Columbia, or one of the territories or insular possessions. In other words, the public practitioners in my country are "certified" pursuant to law.

The common title of the public practitioner is "Certified Public Accountant." However, in some states there is another class known simply as "Public Accountants." In both cases, however, the designation is a legal one.

In general, the designation "Certified Public Accountant" has been granted only to those who have taken a written test of their knowledge of accounting theory, accounting practice, auditing, and commercial law, although a few states include one or more other subjects.

To explain generally how there came to be two designations, I will illustrate by reviewing the situation in my own State of Virginia, which is fairly typical.

Virginia first adopted legislation regulating public practice of accounting in 1910. This legislation provided that those who satisfied its requirements would be designated "Certified Public Accountants," but since

---

[†]Reprinted with permission from *The Sixth International Congress on Accounting* (London, England: Institute of Chartered Accountants in England and Wales, 1952), pp. 402-418. This article was also published in *The Accountant* (Eng.), September 27, 1952, pp. 346-355, and under the title, "The American Accountant in Practice," in *The Canadian Chartered Accountant*, December 1952, pp. 229-242 (excludes Appendix A). An article covering similar topics was published under the title "The History, Growth and Organization of Public Accounting in America," in *Memoria de la Primera Conferencia Interamericana de Contabilidad, Mayo 17 al 22, 1949* (San Juan, Puerto Rico: Instituto de Contadores de Puerto Rico, 1950), pp. 137-149.

there were no certified public accountants prior to that time, the initial legislation waived the examination for those who were deemed to be qualified by experience. Hence, the first Virginia C.P.A.s received what we call waiver certificates. These certificates were unqualified and entitled those who held them to full recognition as certified public accountants. The certificates initially issued by most of the states were waiver certificates.

It might be of interest to note in passing that each of the members of Virginia's first Board of Accountancy voluntarily submitted to examination by the other members. Thereafter, only those who took and satisfactorily passed written examinations were to receive the right to call themselves certified public accountants, and the Virginia State Board of Accountancy, which had been created by the Accountancy Act, was charged with giving the annual examinations and otherwise administering the Act. This initial law did not prevent anyone from practicing public accounting. It only prohibited anyone from calling himself a certified public accountant if he had not acquired the right to do so as provided by the law.

This procedure prevailed until 1926, when strong protest was made to the General Assembly of the Commonwealth by the uncertified practitioners that their ability to earn a livelihood was seriously impaired by their lack of legislative recognition. The Accountancy Act was then changed to what is commonly called in my country "two-class legislation." Under the revised Act those uncertified practitioners who were engaged in practice at the time of the revision were recognized and registered as "public accountants," but the revised Act closed the door to future registrations and also limited practice thereafter to those holding C.P.A. certificates and those registered as public accountants. Thus the uncertified practitioner became what we call a "dying class" and the way was cleared for ultimate restriction of practice to those holding C.P.A. certificates. Hence, while Virginia presently has two-class legislation, this legislation will in time become one-class legislation.

At the time of the revision, about sixty practitioners were registered as public accountants. Since then, many of these have passed the examination and become certified, some have died, and others have retired from practice, so that at the present time only a few public accountants are registered and practicing. Virginia, therefore, is approaching the time when all of its practitioners will be C.P.A.s.

So much for the difference generally between certified public accountants and public accountants, except to say that some states recognize public accountants as a continuing class.

For several years the examination has been uniform in all but one of the fifty-odd state and other jurisdictions and is taken at the same time in each of these jurisdictions. The one state which holds its own examination has been unable to adopt the uniform examination because of a difficulty presented by this state's accountancy law. It is expected, however, that this difficulty will be overcome shortly and that this state will adopt the uniform examination, so making its use universal.

It should be pointed out, however, that, since public practice of accounting is regulated by state law, each state, the District of Columbia, and each of the territories and insular possessions has its own Board of Accountancy and the decision of each of these boards is final as to whether a candidate who appears before it satisfactorily passes the examination that he or she takes, subject to appeal, in some states, to the courts of those states. The uniform examination is prepared under the direction of the Board of Examiners of the American Institute of Accountants, and is held in each of the fifty-odd jurisdictions in the fall and in some of them also in the spring. In general, each applicant for the C.P.A. certificate files with the Board of Accountancy of the jurisdiction in which he resides, but the laws of some states permit examination and certification of applicants from other states.

HISTORY AND GROWTH OF THE PROFESSION

As is generally known, the origin of public accounting in the United States was British. The investment of British funds in American enterprise was considerable in the last half of the nineteenth century and the British practitioners followed British capital. This, together with the obviously favorable outlook for accounting practice in the States, naturally led to the establishment of offices in the United States by the leading British firms.

However, it was not long before our own people began to develop an interest in practice and to establish offices, and in 1896 the legislature of the State of New York enacted the first accountancy law. Schools for the giving of courses in accounting soon came into being, the teaching of accounting quickly developed into quite a profession itself, and one by one the state legislatures enacted accountancy laws. By 1921 such laws had been enacted by all the states. However, as recently as 1920 there were only 5,000 certified public accountants in the entire country. But from that point on the number increased rapidly. By 1940 there were 17,500. By 1948 there were 35,000. Today there are close to 42,000.

ORGANIZATION OF THE PROFESSION

The organization of the profession starts at the state level, each state having its own state society, institute or association; in recent years many of the state organizations have also organized local chapters. To illustrate, the Virginia Society of Public Accountants has chapters at Richmond, the capital city of the Commonwealth; in the Arlington-Alexandria area, across the river from the nation's capital; in the Hampton Roads area, embracing the cities of Norfolk, Portsmouth and Newport News; in the southwestern part of the state, with headquarters at Roanoke; and in the upper Piedmont section, at Charlottesville, where the State University is situated.

The membership of the state societies varies from less than a hundred in the states of relatively small population to several thousand in the states having large populations. The New York State Society, for instance, has more than 6,000 members.

Nationally, the organization of the profession follows to some extent the pattern of the organization of the government of the United States, in that each of the state organizations is autonomous. The American Institute of Accountants, which is the national organization, co-operates closely with the state organizations and maintains continuous liaison with them, but it does not attempt to control them. In other words, the state organizations as such are not members of the Institute. Indeed, not all of their members are. Membership in the American Institute and the state societies is open only to individuals.

In general, membership in the American Institute of Accountants is open to all holders of C.P.A. certificates who are in good standing in their respective states. The Institute is governed by a Council consisting of seventy-two members chosen from the states generally on the basis of the distribution of the Institute's membership; nine members at large; the past presidents of the American Association of Public Accountants (which was the former name of the American Institute); the past presidents of the American Society of Certified Public Accountants (which merged with the American Institute in 1936); and the presidents of the state societies. The Council holds an annual meeting and a spring meeting, the annual meeting at the same time as the annual membership meeting, and the spring meeting usually in late April or early May.

To facilitate the work of the Council, there is an Executive Committee which consists of the officers—President, four Vice-Presidents and Treasurer—and seven members of the Council. The Executive Committee meets as often as the volume or urgency of matters calling for its attention requires. Usually there are five or six meetings a year.

The membership of the American Institute at present is just a little short of 19,000, and because of the Institute's overall representation of the profession and its consequent ability to finance the greatest possible scope of activities, it has taken the lead in dealing with matters which, for the sake of uniformity, or for other reasons, can be best dealt with at the national level, such as research; formalization of accounting and auditing procedures; public relations; co-operation with bankers, lawyers and the Securities and Exchange Commission; and the role of the certified public accountant in federal taxation and national defense. That is not to say that important and effective activity is not engaged in with respect to these matters by the state societies. A number of the state societies do, in fact, engage in activities which are closely parallel to those of the American Institute.

24

Then, as previously indicated, the role of the American Institute in the matter of developing and making available the uniform examinations, and in grading the candidates' papers when requested to do so, is of itself a major undertaking. This work is carried on under the direction of a group known as the Board of Examiners and involves the employment of a staff of considerable proportions.

The American Institute also concerns itself extensively with the matter of education for the profession, and in this field not only combines with the teachers of accounting and their respective institutions to improve the choice of academic subject matter and the organization of courses, but also seeks to develop positive means of identifying the outstanding characteristics of accountants and discovering those who have these characteristics, and of checking the progress of students and helping them find satisfactory employment upon completion of their studies. The program of finding positive tests of accounting aptitude, checking the progress of students, and finding employment for graduates has been intensively carried out and has resulted in great benefit to the profession as well as to students.

The American Institute is mindful that, since membership in it is individual, it has a clear obligation to do whatever it can to improve the material status of its individual members. In pursuance of this obligation, the Institute has made available to its members opportunity to participate in a group insurance plan, under which coverage is available up to the amount of $10,000. This opportunity is extended not only to the Institute's members but also to its members' employees, even those who may not be members of the Institute. At the end of 1951 a total of 1,232 firms were participating in this plan with 8,031 persons covered and $41,606,000 of insurance in force.

OTHER ORGANIZATIONS

In addition to the American Institute of Accountants, there are other organizations which provide focal points of activity for accountants not engaged in public practice, although the membership of each of these organizations includes many public practitioners. Without any implication as to relative rank, these organizations are: American Accounting Association, Controllers' Institute of America, National Association of Cost Accountants.

The American Accounting Association is the national organization of teachers of accounting.

The Controllers' Institute of America is the national organization of the controllers and finance officers of the nation's enterprises.

The National Association of Cost Accountants is the national organization of cost accountants and those who are primarily interested in cost accounting.

Both the Controllers' Institute of America and the National Association of Cost Accountants have great numbers of local chapters which, in each case, are directly affiliated with the national organization.

At the end of 1951, the approximate memberships of these three organizations were: American Accounting Association, 4,000; Controllers' Institute of America, 3,600; National Association of Cost Accountants, 25,000.

EDUCATION FOR THE PROFESSION

In the early days of the profession in my country, the principal source of education for the profession seems to have been the correspondence school; that is, the school which operates from a central location, enrolls students throughout the country, distributes its text material to its students by mail, requires the students to submit written examinations, and grades the papers submitted at the central headquarters. These schools have made a great contribution to the advancement of the profession.

Later the colleges and universities put in courses, often, in the early days, integrating these courses with their schools of economics, though sometimes integrating them with their schools of liberal arts. More recently, there has been a strong trend at the college and university level toward the establishment of schools of business administration and the integration of instruction in accounting with these schools. There already are many such schools.

In recent years, based upon the theory that modern conditions require that an accountant should have something more than a mere vocational education, there has been a strong trend toward the requirement that accounting students precede their specialized study of accounting with some period of basic instruction in the liberal arts, usually for two years. This theory has much to recommend it and it has strong advocates.

If I were to hazard a guess, I would say that this pattern of preparation will in time become the prevailing one. At any rate, from my own observations and experience with staff personnel, and judging from opinions expressed to me by many of my colleagues, I would say that the beginner in the profession who based his study of accounting and related subjects upon a foundation of at least two years of liberal arts education comes to the profession with superior preparation. Such an entrant has the best chance of progressing rapidly and of developing the comprehensive understanding of economic affairs which is rapidly coming to be expected of professional practitioners.

I have no exact data on the subject, but a very large proportion of the colleges and universities of the country now offer varying degrees of instruction appropriate for those who desire to make a career of accounting.

Following World War II, the country embarked upon an extensive program of education for ex-servicemen, and some idea of the popularity of business administration and accounting can be gained from the fact that I am told that the number of G.I.s who enrolled as business administration and accounting students was greater than the number enrolled for any other course. One would have thought that this would have flooded the accounting profession with a surplus of talent, but it didn't. The G.I. program has about run out, but in spite of the number of accounting graduates turned out under this program, and in spite of the fact that the business and accounting schools still are experiencing heavy enrollments, there continues to be a very considerable shortage of personnel trained for the profession. This condition undoubtedly is largely attributable to the high level of economic activity which has resulted from the current defense program, but the demand for accounting personnel continues to grow, and the time when balance between demand and supply will be reached is not yet in sight.

FACTORS CONTRIBUTING TO THE GROWTH OF PUBLIC ACCOUNTING PRACTICE

Public practitioners and laymen alike are inclined to ascribe the growth of public accounting practice largely to adoption by my country of income-tax legislation. The first federal tax based upon income was passed in 1909, but we did not get down to income taxation in its present form until 1st March, 1913. It cannot be denied that the adoption of the income-tax and the almost annual extension of the base of this tax created expanding demand for accounting services, and it is a fact, of course, that a good portion of every practitioner's time is devoted to engagements directly or indirectly related to the income-tax. However, I think that the influence of this tax has been greatly overstated.

It is my opinion that fundamentally the profession's almost phenomenal growth has been due to the intensive development of natural resources and the equally intensive extension of industrial activity which has characterized the economy of my country, especially since the turn of the century. It seems to me that this becomes crystal clear when one stops to recall the number of our major industries which have come into being during the last forty years and the proportions of the contribution of these industries to our gross national product.

These industries include such giants as electric power; electrical equipment and appliances; the automobile; truck transportation; radio; industrial chemistry; plastics; rayon; motion pictures; the airplane; air transportation; frozen food; television; and synthetic rubber—not to mention the enormous expansion that has taken place in the production of metals, notably steel, copper and aluminum. A good idea of the country's industrial growth can be obtained from the fact that its productive capacity has been far more than doubled since 1939. It was increased about 90 percent in the three-year period from 1949 to 1951 alone.

27

The automobile industry alone directly and indirectly affords employment to 9 million workers, or about one-seventh of the country's entire labor force. The trucking industry, which carries 80 percent of all the country's inter-state passengers, transports more than 50 percent of all workers to their jobs, carries 90 percent of all the nation's food to market, and hauls 75 percent of all general freight, employs more people than all other forms of transportation combined.

Fundamentally, therefore, while such developments as income taxation, bankruptcy legislation, the control of security exchanges and the issuing of securities, the regulation of public utility rates, and economic controls generally, each has created a large demand for accounting services, the main driving force behind the growth of the accounting profession undoubtedly has been the unparalleled expansion of industry.

TYPES OF ENGAGEMENTS UNDERTAKEN BY PUBLIC ACCOUNTANTS

The backlog of every practitioner's concern is auditing of the books of the country's enterprises and institutions. This is heavily supplemented by tax practice and by engagements involving the installation or revision of accounting systems and procedures. I would say, however, that these other engagements, though many of them are highly important and call for the very highest level of technical judgment and skill, still rank second, even in the aggregate, to auditing.

There has been a recent development, however, that should not be overlooked. The growing complexity of our economic structure, and the burden of complying with an ever-increasing number of government regulations designed to control economic activity, and the exceptional manner in which the public practitioner has met the challenges of practice, naturally have caused clients to look to their certified public accountants for assistance in solving a growing list of problems not originally deemed to be within the scope of the public practitioner's training and experience.

Over the years, business management has found it increasingly difficult to keep costs and expenses down to the point where there would be a reasonable return on investment after the payment of taxes. More and more management has turned to the certified public accountant for help in meeting this problem. As a consequence, many accounting firms have established divisions of their practices to render this kind of service; and be it said to their credit that they have in many situations distinguished themselves highly in this field.

This development is growing and undoubtedly will grow to larger and larger proportions as the years go by, and the certified public accountant will find himself not only an accountant and auditor but also something akin to a business doctor. This is inevitable, because it is a natural evolution.

28

The constantly broadening base of the public practitioner's academic training and experience make it so.

LITERATURE OF THE PROFESSION

The most widely distributed publication of the profession is *The Journal of Accountancy,* which is published by the American Institute of Accountants. Its present circulation is approximately 67,500. It goes to every member of the American Institute as a part of his membership fee. Thus you will see that there is a circulation of close to 50,000 among others. The other subscribers include, for the most part, business executives, treasurers, controllers and educators.

The American Institute also sponsors from time to time books and other publications on various phases of accounting, one of the most widely circulated of which is the annual publication entitled *Accounting Trends and Techniques.* This is an annual survey by the Institute's Research Department of the published annual reports of corporations. In it are particularly analyzed and reported the handling of various elements of corporate financial statements, thus pointing up what is being done in practice about the problems of accounting with which business and the profession, particularly the Institute's Committee on Accounting Procedure and Auditing Procedure, are especially concerned.

Specific technical problems are dealt with from time to time by the Institute's Committee on Accounting Procedure and its Committee on Auditing Procedure. After being thoroughly discussed and reviewed, not only by the respective Institute committees but also by other interested parties and organizations, these problems are reported in the form of Accounting Research Bulletins by the Committee on Accounting Procedure and in the form of Statements on Auditing Procedure by the Committee on Auditing Procedure. Up to this time, forty-one Accounting Research Bulletins and twenty-four Statements of Auditing Procedure have been issued. These statements and bulletins go to all members of the American Institute without charge and are available to other interested persons at nominal prices.

At the moment, the American Institute is engaged in the writing and compiling of what will be called the *Manual of Accounting Practice.* This is perhaps the most ambitious single publication yet undertaken by the Institute and will provide for its members information written by carefully chosen authors concerning every phase of public practice. It undoubtedly will constitute the most valuable of all the many aids to its members that the Institute thus far has developed.

In addition to the publications of the Institute, many of the state societies publish monthly or quarterly reviews of accounting papers and, of course, a great many original papers as well.

Another valuable publication is *The Accounting Review*, which is published monthly by the American Accounting Association. This publication is turned out primarily for the benefit of that Association's members, many of whom are members of the American Institute of Accountants, but, like *The Journal of Accountancy*, it also enjoys substantial circulation among business executives, treasurers, controllers and others.

Further, both the Controllers' Institute of America and the National Association of Cost Accountants put out regular publications dealing primarily with matters of particular interest to their members, many of whom, again, are members of the American Institute of Accountants. Finally, never a month goes by without independently published books on some phase of accounting, auditing, taxes and other subjects of interest to the profession. Altogether, therefore, the literature of the profession in my country is prodigious, to say the least.

STAFF TRAINING

There has not been, so far as I know, any nationwide, or even any statewide, survey and report on the extent to which staff training is conducted, the kind of training given and the manner in which it is given. However, I have discussed this problem with a great many of my colleagues, and I believe that I can make a fairly accurate statement concerning it.

First, I would say that there is hardly a practitioner in my country who does not recognize the need for staff training, not only as affording the best assurance of establishing and maintaining the highest possible level of competence but also, particularly at this time, as the best possible means of getting beginners up to an adequate level of earnings as rapidly as possible. This is especially important right now, because public practice has been traditionally the training camp from which private industry has drawn much of its accounting personnel. With taxes at their present levels, with the supply of accounting personnel almost acutely short of demand and with salaries subject to strict control, the public accounting profession recently has become the victim of extensive pirating of its personnel by private industry.

Notwithstanding the fact that beginners generally now start in the profession with increasingly better academic training, everyone agrees, including the educators, that there is no substitute for experience. Even the best apprenticeship training during the course of a student's academic work (which is being tried with varying degrees of success, but which is growing) is not now, and is not likely to become, a complete substitute for experience. Consequently, the progressive firm must do everything practicable to hasten acquisition of experience by its junior staff members. Staff training, therefore, is essentially an effort to accelerate the beginner's progress.

Such training varies all the way from relying upon juniors to get the most out of the engagements to which they are assigned, supplemented by study of current papers and articles, to carefully conceived programs of study and instruction.

For obvious reasons, the extent of in-service training usually is in proportion to the size of the practice enjoyed by the beginner's employer or employers and to his employer's attitude concerning his or their responsibility for the progress of staff members. Some firms, particularly the larger ones, give the instruction themselves. Others arrange to have their staff members attend available extracurricular classes. Still others, of course, do nothing at all. Some of the larger firms go so far as to put a beginner, regardless of his academic training, through a considerable period of instruction before he is assigned to his first engagement.

There is no question but that staff training is destined, probably very soon, to be extended far beyond its present proportions. In my opinion, this is going to be necessary if the growing firms are to have any hope of keeping the sizes of their staffs equal to the demand for their services. Indeed, I will go even further and venture the opinion that if this is not done, if beginners are not more quickly brought to the point where higher charges can be made for their time and skill, with consequent acceleration of salary increases, the time soon will come, if our economy continues to expand as it has in recent years, when there will not be any but partners left to render the services required by the profession's clients. If this happens, reduction in the size of some firms and increase in the number of so-called small practitioners will be inevitable.

Personally, I should regard this eventuality as being not only unfortunate but also highly undesirable from the standpoints of clients, practitioners and staff members, all three, for the simple reason that the present demand for the services of public accounting firms is so varied that it is next to impossible for an individual practitioner without a fairly numerous staff to render satisfactorily all the different kinds of services now expected of certified public accountants. I do not think it would be good for the profession, for those who require the profession's services, or for staff members for practice to become highly specialized. I believe that if this happens we would find ourselves in the position that the medical profession has reached in my country, where the gradual disappearance of the general practitioner is regarded as a serious problem.

This is not to say that a certain amount of specialization is not desirable, for such a position could not be justified. However, there is such a thing as overspecialization, and in my opinion that is more undesirable than no specialization at all.

PROFESSIONAL ETHICS

The recognized authority on ethics in the public accounting profession in the United States is the Executive Director of the American Institute of Accountants, Mr. John L. Carey, who is here at this congress. In 1946, the American Institute published a book on ethics written by Mr. Carey and entitled *Professional Ethics of Public Accounting*. Prior to and since that time, Mr. Carey has spoken extensively on ethics. Mr. Carey believes, as I do, that no profession in our country has a higher code of ethics than the public accounting profession and that the members of no profession are more faithful in their compliance with the rules that they voluntarily have adopted to control their conduct towards the public and themselves.

In a paper read at the Second Inter-American Accounting Conference at Mexico City in November, 1951, Mr. Carey classified and reviewed the rules of ethics that generally prevail in the United States. In this address Mr. Carey divided the rules of ethics into three categories: first, those that are designed to assure and preserve independence and impartiality on the part of the public practitioners; second, those that are designed to safeguard the legitimate interests of clients of the profession; and, third, those that are designed to guide the members of the profession in their relations with each other.

As to the first category, Mr. Carey said:

... the most important rule in a code of ethics for the public accounting profession should be a rule that serves as a guide to right action to the professional accountant in preserving his independence and impartiality and at the same time as a declaration to the public that he will not place himself in positions in which his independence is liable to be impaired.

Such a rule may be broken down into several parts covering the following points:

(1) The professional accountant acting as an independent auditor accepts the obligation of maintaining independent and impartial judgment in his examination of accounts and in expressing his opinion on financial statements.

(2) He will disclose all material facts which he discovers that have a bearing on the financial position or the results of operations.

(3) He will conduct his examination of accounts in accordance with generally accepted auditing procedures and not express an opinion on financial statements unless he has made an adequate examination.

(4) He will not have any substantial financial interest in the affairs of a company on whose financial statements he is reporting without fully disclosing that interest.

(5) He will not render an opinion on financial statements under circumstances in which the amount of his fee depends on the successful outcome of any venture in which those financial statements may play a part, such as the issuance of securities.

(6) He will not engage in any other occupation simultaneously with the practice of public accounting which might impair his impartiality or objectivity in reporting on financial statements.

As to the second category, Mr. Carey said:

> ... the second most important rule of a code of professional ethics for the accounting profession is a rule designed to safeguard the legitimate interests of clients of members of the profession.
>
> This rule may be broken down into parts to cover the following points:
>
> (1) A practitioner will not violate the confidential relationship between himself and his client.
>
> (2) He will not exploit his professional relationship with the client by accepting commissions, brokerages or other compensation from suppliers whose products or services he may influence the client to purchase.
>
> (3) He will not seek to shield himself behind the corporate form of organization, but will conduct his practice as an individual or member of a partnership.
>
> (4) He will not allow others to practice in his name unless they are in partnership with him or in his employ as an accredited member of the profession and thus subject to his control and supervision. Likewise, he will not sign his name to reports on financial statements which have been prepared by others who are not in his employ or in partnership with him or who, as his representative, are not accredited members of his profession who accept responsibility to him.

As to the third category, Mr. Carey said:

> ... the third most important rule in a code of professional ethics for the public accounting profession is a rule to serve as a guide to right action in relations of the practitioner with his colleagues and with his profession as a whole.
>
> Such a rule might be broken into parts covering the following points:
>
> (1) The professional public accountant will not advertise his professional attainments or services, except as appropriate announcements may be permitted by the rules of his society.
>
> (2) He will not solicit the clients or encroach upon the practice of another professional accountant, although he may properly respond to any request for service and advice which comes without solicitation.
>
> (3) He shall not offer employment to an employee of another public accountant without first informing that accountant, although he may properly employ anyone who of his own initiative applies for such employment.

Mr. Carey then pointed out that his paper was not intended as an outline of "a complete code of professional ethics for the accounting profession, but only to suggest the fundamental rules which it is believed should be an essential part of any such code. There are many other aspects of professional accounting practice on which rules or precepts might usefully be written, but the ones mentioned here, in my opinion, are basic and indispensable."

Finally, Mr. Carey concluded: "All the points I have mentioned in this paper are now covered, explicitly or implicitly, in the rules of the American Institute as well as some other points which do not seem sufficiently fundamental to warrant consideration at this time," reminding his audience that "these rules were not all put into effect at one time but have been developed over a long period of time out of the experience of the membership" and suggesting the certainty that "they will undoubtedly be modified and elaborated further in the future as additional experience may indicate desirable changes."

Such rules have been adopted by all the state societies, institutes and associations. In some states, the rules of professional ethics have been written into the accountancy laws, either specifically or by reference.

The American Institute enforces its rules continually through its Committee on Professional Ethics, which receives and considers complaints of violations and refers to a trial board those complaints that require disciplinary action. The trial board may admonish, suspend or expel a member who is found guilty after a hearing of the charges made against him. Somewhat the same procedure is followed in one form or another by the state organizations.

SOME CURRENT PROBLEMS

This paper would not be complete without some reference to at least two problems that currently confront the profession in the United States: first, the question whether it is desirable to define accounting practice; and, second, the question whether those who do not intend to engage in the practice of public accounting should be given C.P.A. certificates.

The first of these questions has been plaguing the profession for years. The second is only beginning to emerge. As to each of them, I desire to make it clear that what I shall say concerning it must be regarded as indicating my own thoughts alone and should not be regarded as indicative of any opinion or conclusion by the American Institute or of any state organization.

For several years, there has been a growing insistence by certain members of the Bar that certified public accountants, in their practice, particularly in their handling of tax matters, frequently get over into the realm of the lawyer. Some of these gentlemen even go so far as to take the position that certified public accountants are practicing law when they do no more than prepare a tax return, and the American Bar Association itself, and some of the state Bar associations, have, through their Committees on Unauthorized Practice of the Law, sought to exclude the certified public accountants from tax practice in one degree or another.

Recently, however, the two professions have agreed upon a tentative statement on this troublesome question through a group consisting of representatives of both professions and known as the National Conference of Lawyers and Certified Public Accountants. A copy of this tentative statement accompanies this paper as Appendix A.

I do not intend to discuss the position taken by the lawyers. I must admit, however, that on occasion, and in varying degrees, members of the accounting profession undoubtedly have gotten over into the lawyers' field. However, I hasten to point out that I have never heard of a single case where the transgression was deliberate and intentional: in every case the accountant has averred (honestly, I believe) that he did not intend to invade the lawyers' province and would be especially careful to avoid repetition of the offense.

The difficulty up to this time has been that the accountants have always been on the receiving end of the complaints, whereas it is perfectly obvious that lawyers frequently invade the province of the certified public accountant. Moreover, lawyers not infrequently (especially where they act as secretary, director or in other close relationships to business enterprises) seek to impose views, not to say orders on occasion, upon the certified public accountant which, if yielded to, would make the certified public accountant guilty of utter and complete violation of his obligation of independence.

It may well be that this problem can be worked out by negotiation, but the lawyers are numerous in our country; it is well known that they are in control of the Congress and practically all state and local legislative bodies. It is entirely possible, therefore, that the lawyers' infringements upon the province of the certified public accountants cannot be solved except by including in the state accountancy laws some definition of what constitutes the practice of accounting, although, recognizing that the lawyers are in virtual control of our legislative bodies, this obviously might be a very difficult, if not impossible, undertaking.

However, it is my opinion that if the problem cannot be solved by negotiation, then public interest demands that an effort be made to settle it by legislation. At any rate, I am not willing to concede that the lawyers are Simon Pures and that the accountants alone are sinners, and I think that the accounting profession is too grown-up, and the essentiality of its position in the scheme of things is too well recognized, to warrant its members' allowing it to be picked on, bullied, pushed around and interdicted by another group, no matter how exalted that group may be or in what esteem it may be held by itself and others, including the members of the public accounting profession—and I assure you that we of the public accounting profession yield to no one in our admiration of and respect for our brothers of the Bar individually and as members of a great and most useful profession.

The probable need for defining what constitutes the practice of accounting is not suggested by the encroachment of the lawyers alone, however. We have another group in our country, generally described as public bookkeepers, who are not subject to regulation, though there is no good reason why they should be. This group frequently gets over the line into accounting practice, and sometimes with tragic results. For instance, I have seen numerous cases where business people have got into serious financial difficulties, and into such difficulties with the tax authorities as to cause these authorities to assert fraud, because some fellow who fancied himself to be an accountant gave faulty advice as to how books should be kept.

Considering the importance that accounting assumes in a society that is so highly industrialized as that of my country, it seems to me that the giving of advice as to how accounts should be kept is an activity which, like the independence and impartiality of the certified public accountant, acting in the capacity of auditor, is affected with the public interest. I am inclined to believe, therefore, that the time has come for us to insist that the right to give such advice be limited to those who have proven themselves qualified by training and experience to give it.

The question whether C.P.A. certificates should be issued to those who do not intend to follow public accounting as a career is beset with difficulties of equal magnitude, although I do not believe that these difficulties are insurmountable.

The principal difficulty lies in the question what is to be done about those who become certified public accountants and later leave the profession to accept other employment. I would not be so foolish or so unfair as to suggest that in such cases the C.P.A. certificate should be recalled. I do suggest, however, that perhaps the granting of C.P.A. certificates should be conditioned upon demonstration of sincere intention to follow public accounting as a career. It may well be that what I have in mind as a demonstration of this sincerity will not work out in practice, but I believe it will. In any event, I think that the time has come for serious consideration of the problem.

Most of our state laws are founded upon the theory that C.P.A. certificates should not be granted until those who apply for them have acquired some amount of experience, usually from two to three years, on the staff of a C.P.A. or firm of C.P.A.s. But there are many who feel—and this is true of the members of many state legislatures—that anyone who completes a satisfactory course of academic instruction and is of good character should be permitted to take the examination and be given a certificate if he passes. In fact, there are some states that do not impose any experience requirement, and that is exactly what happens in those states.

Based upon my observations and experience over thirty-five years of practice, I think that this is an utterly fallacious view. My own proposition is that anyone of good character who is academically qualified to take the examination should be permitted to do so and that his papers should be graded without regard to whether he has had experience or not. However, I would withhold the issuing of the C.P.A. certificate where the examinee had not had any experience until such time as he gains it, and I would recognize only experience gained under the direction of a C.P.A. or firm of C.P.A.s.

Just how much experience one should have before receiving the certificate need not be discussed at this time. I would say, however, that it ought to be a minimum of three years and perhaps as much as five years, since under such a policy as I have suggested the waiting period ought to be sufficient not only to assure the acquisition of requisite experience, but also sufficient to give reasonable assurance of the applicant's intention to make public accounting his career.

Under the plan that I propose that we should consider, a person who successfully passes the examination and completes the required number of years of experience would be deemed to have demonstrated intention to make public accounting his career and would be given his certificate regardless of whether or not he continues in the accounting profession thereafter.

The C.P.A. certificate was originally conceived as an attestation of fitness to engage in the *public* practice of accounting, and the reasons for this distinction are more compelling to-day than ever. Those accountants who do not choose to go into public practice do not need C.P.A. certificates, and it is a distortion of the purpose of the accounting laws to give them certificates. I know of no surer way to make certain that the designation certified *public* accountant means what it clearly implies than to make the C.P.A. certificate available only to those who demonstrate that they intend to make their careers in public practice.

CONCLUSION

The outline that was sent to me as a guide for this paper indicated that my subject was to be "The Accountant in Practice and Public Service." I have not dealt with the accountant in public service, because that is a separate subject in itself and the problems of governmental accounting are quite different from those encountered by the professional public accountant. True enough, governmental accounting involves the application of special techniques and procedures, but in this respect governmental accounting is no different from many categories of enterprise accounting.

I might say, however, that tremendous advances have been made in governmental accounting in my country during the past twenty-five years, and I think that the professional accountants can claim a great deal of the credit for this, because undeniably it has been the progress of accounting generally that has forced improvement in governmental accounting, and much of this progress has been wrought by professional public accountants who have either temporarily or permanently entered the public service to apply the techniques and procedures that they learned and helped develop in the course of their professional practices.

For instance, our national government has made tremendous improvement in its accounting, especially since World War II, and the leadership in this improvement has been, and is being, furnished without exception by men recruited from the public accounting profession.

APPENDIX A

Statement of Principles Relating to Practice in the Field of Federal
Income Taxation

Promulgated by the
National Conference of Lawyers and Certified Public Accountants

1. *Collaboration of Lawyers and Certified Public Accountants Desirable.* It is in the best public interest that services and assistance in federal income-tax matters be rendered by lawyers and certified public accountants, who are trained in their fields by education and experience, and for whose admission to professional standing there are requirements as to education, citizenship and high moral character. They are required to pass written examinations and are subject to rules of professional ethics, such as those of the American Bar Association and American Institute of Accountants, which set a high standard of professional practice and conduct, including prohibition of advertising and solicitation. Many problems connected with business require the skills of both lawyers and certified public accountants and there is every reason for a close and friendly cooperation between the two professions. Lawyers should encourage their clients to seek the advice of certified public accountants whenever accounting problems arise and certified public accountants should encourage clients to seek the advice of lawyers whenever legal questions are presented.

2. *Preparation of Federal Income Tax Returns.* It is a proper function of a lawyer or a certified public accountant to prepare Federal income-tax returns.

When a lawyer prepares a return in which questions of accounting arise, he should advise the taxpayer to enlist the assistance of a certified public accountant.

When a certified public accountant prepares a return in which questions of law arise, he should advise the taxpayer to enlist the assistance of a lawyer.

3. *Ascertainment of Probable Tax Effects of Transactions.* In the course of the practice of law and in the course of the practice of accounting, lawyers and certified public accountants are often asked about the probable tax effects of transactions.

The ascertainment of probable tax effects of transactions frequently is within the function of either a certified public accountant or a lawyer. However, in many instances, problems arise which require the attention of a member of one or the other professions, or members of both. When such ascertainment raises uncertainties as to the interpretation of law (both tax law and general law), or uncertainties as to the application of law to the transaction involved, the certified public accountant should advise the taxpayer to enlist the services of a lawyer. When such ascertainment involves difficult questions of classifying and summarizing the transaction in a significant manner and in terms of money, or interpreting the financial results thereof, the lawyer should advise the taxpayer to enlist the services of a certified public accountant.

In many cases, therefore, the public will be best served by utilizing the joint skills of both professions.

4. *Preparation of Legal and Accounting Documents.* Only a lawyer may prepare legal documents such as agreements, conveyances, trust instruments, wills, or corporate minutes or give advice as to the legal sufficiency or effect thereof, or take the necessary steps to create, amend or dissolve a partnership, corporation, trust, or other legal entity.

Only an accountant may properly advise as to the preparation of financial statements included in reports or submitted with tax returns, or as to accounting methods and procedures.

5. *Prohibited Self-designations.* An accountant should not describe himself as a "tax consultant" or "tax expert" or use any similar phrase. Lawyers, similarly are prohibited by the canons of ethics of the American Bar Association and the opinions relating thereto, from advertising a special branch of law practice.

6. *Representation of Taxpayers before Treasury Department.* Under Treasury Department regulations lawyers and certified public accountants are authorized, upon a showing of their professional status, and subject to certain limitations as defined in the Treasury rules, to represent taxpayers in proceedings before that department. If, in the course of such proceedings, questions arise involving the application of legal principles, a lawyer should be retained, and if, in the course of such proceedings accounting questions arise, a certified public accountant should be retained.

7. *Practice before the Tax Court of the United States.* Under the Tax Court rules non-lawyers may be admitted to practice.

However, since upon issuance of a formal notice of deficiency by the Commissioner of Internal Revenue a choice of legal remedies is afforded the taxpayer under existing law (either before the Tax Court of the United States, a United States District Court or the Court of Claims), it is in the best interests of the taxpayer that the advice of a lawyer be sought if further proceedings are contemplated. It is not intended hereby to foreclose the right of non-lawyers to practice before the Tax Court of the United States pursuant to its rules.

Here also, as in proceedings before the Treasury Department, the taxpayer, in many cases, is best served by the combined skills of both lawyers and certified public accountants, and the taxpayers, in such cases, should be advised accordingly.

8. *Claims for Refund.* Claims for refund may be prepared by lawyers or certified public accountants, provided, however, that where a

controversial legal issue is involved or where the claim is to be made the basis of litigation, the services of a lawyer should be obtained.

9. *Criminal Tax Investigations.* When a certified public accountant learns that his client is being specially investigated for possible criminal violation of the income-tax law, he should advise his client to seek the advice of a lawyer as to his legal and constitutional rights.

Conclusion. This statement of principles should be regarded as tentative and subject to revision and amplification in the light of future experience. The principal purpose is to indicate the importance of voluntary cooperation between our professions, whose members should use their knowledge and skills to the best advantage of the public. It is recommended that joint committees representing the local societies of both professions be established. Such committees might well take permanent form as local conferences of lawyers and certified public accountants patterned after this conference, or could take the form of special committees to handle a specific situation.

STATE AND LOCAL GOVERNMENT ACCOUNTING REFORMS

REORGANIZATION OF VIRGINIA ACCOUNTS†

by

T. Coleman Andrews

Richmond, April 29, 1933

Honorable John Garland Pollard,
Governor, Commonwealth of Virginia,
Richmond, Virginia.

Your Excellency:

WHEN I tendered my resignation recently, I stated that upon my retirement from office I would submit a review of and report on the activities of my department for the period of my incumbency. Having retired from office today, I now submit the promised review and report.

I was appointed on February 1, 1931, to complete the unexpired term of my predecessor, and at the 1932 session of the General Assembly my appointment was confirmed, and I was reappointed for a term of four years beginning March 1, 1932.

I understood that it was expected that I should address myself primarily to the accomplishment of the following objectives:

1. The development and installation of a uniform system of accounting for the counties of the Commonwealth as required by section 552 of the Code of Virginia;

2. The establishment of the department of the Auditor of Public Accounts on a basis that would afford to the Commonwealth and its political subdivisions a high standard of accounting and auditing service; and

3. Improvement, where needed, and in so far as the statutes would permit, of the fiscal methods and procedures employed in the administration of the affairs of the counties.

†This article reproduces Andrew's report upon leaving the position of Auditor of Public Accounts of Virginia. Reprinted with permission from *The Certified Public Accountant*, November 1933, pp. 677-689.

As soon as I felt that these objectives had been accomplished, or were shortly to be accomplished, I tendered my resignation and proceeded at once to conclude the unfinished business of the office which I felt I should dispose of before retiring, and have today turned over the affairs of the office to my successor.

DEVELOPMENT AND INSTALLATION OF UNIFORM SYSTEM OF ACCOUNTING

There isn't a great deal to be said about the development and installation of the uniform system of accounting for the counties, except that it was developed and installed. Shortly after I took office the Auditing Committee of the General Assembly met, and at this meeting it was concluded to try to have the uniform system ready for installation by the beginning of the next fiscal year, which at that time was less than five months away. This was no more time than we needed to familiarize ourselves with the duties of the office, dispose of the routine business thereof, develop the uniform system, formulate a reliable code of auditing procedures, and do the many other things that were necessary in order to be ready to institute the new order at the beginning of the new year. However, everything worked smoothly, and installations of the uniform system were begun according to schedule. And the final installation was made about sixty days ago.

The uniform system represents our conception of the accounting requirements of the counties, based upon the statutory requirements as to the administration of county affairs, field observations of the manner in which the affairs of a representative group of counties were being conducted, discussion of accounting requirements and administrative policies and practices with a number of county officers, and the application, of course, of established principles of accounting. In our judgment it is about as simple as it can be made without sacrificing the accumulation of essential information. And experience up to this time indicates that it meets the elaborate requirements of the larger counties without burdening the smaller counties with unnecessary record-keeping.

With the uniform system now installed in every county of the Commonwealth, we have a situation which probably is unique in the annals of the administration of the affairs of local governments, in that the revenues, expenditures, assets and liabilities of each county are recorded and presented in the same manner as those of every other county—a fact which, I believe, is not true of any other State in the Union. The advantages of this are obvious, I think, and so need not be recited here.

Before leaving the subject of the development and installation of the uniform system, I should like to say a word about the attitude of the county treasurers with respect thereto. A very few of these officials took an antagonistic attitude toward the new system, and since opposition usually is much more noisy than favor, the public generally gained the impression, I believe, that the county treasurers as a class were opposed to the system. Such was not the case, however. On the contrary, the vast majority of the county treasurers welcomed it. And I am very happy to say that those who objected to it in the beginning now appear to be well satisfied with it. As a matter of fact, some of those who objected are now among those who are loudest in their praise.

ORGANIZATION OF THE DEPARTMENT

For reasons which no doubt will be obvious to you, I prefer to pass over the matter of the status of the department at the time I took office without making any statement other than that it was woefully under-staffed and otherwise unqualified to execute in an acceptable manner the number of audits that were required of it by the statutes, and that consequently it was necessary to reorganize it completely and add materially to the field staff.

In reorganizing the department, I endeavored to fill each position with one qualified to hold it. The unemployment situation, of course, made this much easier of accomplishment than would have been the case under ordinary conditions. At any rate, appointments were made upon the basis of merit alone, and I leave to my successor a staff which, in my judgment, are without peers in efficiency, integrity, loyalty, and qualifications generally for the work which they have to do. Indeed, I sincerely feel that the staff of the office today are as well qualified for their work as any group of accountants and auditors with which I ever have been associated. Your appointment of one of the field supervisors of the department as my successor was both a tribute to the character of the organization of the department, which I sincerely appreciate, and an act of assurance of opportunity to worthy employees of the Commonwealth, which I am certain has had a tremendously helpful effect upon the morale of the employees of the Commonwealth.

AUDITS FOR THE YEAR ENDED JUNE 30, 1931

When I took office the staff was engaged in the auditing of the accounts and records of the counties for the year ended June 30, 1930. As a matter of fact, more than half the county audits for this period had been completed. We concluded, therefore, the Auditing Committee of the General Assembly concurring, to complete the work program of the office for the fiscal year ending June 30, 1931, without any change in the then existing auditing procedures. This was particularly desirable since we could not very well adopt a definite code of auditing procedures until the form of the new system had been definitely determined, and since it was obvious that it would be necessary to make a thorough audit of the accounts and records of each county before installing the new system.

I believe that almost every one knows what the situation with respect to the account- and record-keeping in the counties was when I took office. Therefore I shall not undertake to describe it. Suffice it to say that we found very few complete systems in use; that as a rule accountings were not made oftener than annually; that it was not the custom to keep any chronological record of receipts and expenditures, and that consequently the authorities of the counties generally had not been informed as to the exact status of the separate funds and the financial condition of their counties as a whole oftener than once each year.

On account of these facts, it was necessary that the scope of the initial audits be very comprehensive and the auditing procedures very detailed. As a matter of fact, in almost every case we had to review and classify each transaction and construct a record of the county's affairs in order to obtain accurate statements of receipts and expenditures and financial condition. Consequently the initial audits took a considerable amount of time, and necessarily cost quite a good deal more than they would have had adequate and correctly kept records been found. I shall not undertake to describe the difficulties which we encountered in making the initial audits, because it would require a great deal of space just to outline these difficulties. Instead, I shall pass on to the results.

The results of the initial audits showed, of course, all sorts of financial conditions, ranging from very bad to very good. These results are hardly susceptible of reduction to a general statement; besides, they will be shown in more or less detail in our report on the comparative cost of local government for the period covered by the initial audits, which report is now being compiled. So I shall not undertake to summarize them here.

SHORTAGES OF $1,138,875.02 DISCLOSED

These initial audits disclosed also the fact that at June 30, 1931, forty-six treasurers, one county clerk, one school board clerk, and one school superintendent's secretary were short in the aggregate amount of $1,119,300.56. This amount, plus a shortage of $19,574.46 on the part of the treasurer of Virginia Military Institute, made a total of $1,138,875.02, which amount, without adding interest thereto, is approximately fourteen times the annual appropriation of the department of the Auditor of Public Accounts in the budget for the biennium ending June 30, 1934. Subject to compromises made and probably to be made to facilitate the settlements of these shortages, this amount, of course, is recoverable. As a matter of fact, a large part of it already has been recovered. This, I think, demonstrates the necessity for a strong auditing department and justifies the cost thereof. In this connection, it is highly significant that in over sixty audits for the year ended June 30, 1932, we have not found a single new shortage.

Due to the inadequacy and inaccuracy of the accounts and records encountered by us, I have to report that we could not identify the causes of the shortage in each case. However, we are satisfied that in all but a few cases the shortage arose from the carrying or holding out of tax tickets. On the other hand, of the total amount of these shortages, approximately $700,000.00, or well over 50% was due to misappropriation of funds. Parenthetically, it should be remembered that I am speaking now of the situation at June 30, 1931. Some of the initial audits, especially those where shortages were involved, were brought down to the dates on which the audits were made, so that the aggregate amount of misappropriation at June 30th does not represent the entire amount of misappropriation discovered. The final amount of these items was approximately $800,000.00.

In every case except one, where there was positive evidence of misappropriation—and there were six such cases—criminal proceedings were instituted. The criminal action was instituted by the local authorities in each case, but you will recall that the number of officials and the amount of money involved in the situation in Arlington County were such that, with the approval and concurrence of the Commonwealth's attorney of that county, I requested you to direct the Attorney General to assist in the prosecutions there. Four of the five criminal proceedings instituted have been concluded with convictions, and the trial of the fifth case will be held shortly.[1] We do not know why proceedings were not instituted in the sixth case, which was that of the secretary of the school superintendent of Fairfax County.

On account of the situation disclosed by the initial audits the surety companies who were on the bonds of the treasurers of the counties notified us late in 1931 that they were not inclined to continue to write county treasurers' bonds after the end of that year. Since the statutes required the treasurers to give either corporate or personal surety as a prerequisite to qualification for office, and since personal bond could not be obtained except in very few cases, the withdrawal of the bonding companies would have had very serious consequences.

Therefore we took steps immediately to meet the situation, and, through the cooperation of the surety companies, arranged for a discussion of the situation with the Public Official Bond Committee of the Surety Association of America. As a result of the meeting with the committee, the Association expressed confidence in the demonstrated intention of the Commonwealth to improve the accounting systems of the counties and make more thorough audits, and agreed to continue on the bonds of the treasurers, subject to demonstration of the effectiveness of the new system and the revised auditing procedures and the passage of legislation at the

---

[1]Editor's Note: The fifth trial was successful.

1932 session of the General Assembly that would so define the responsibilities of the treasurers and their sureties as to remove the excessive hazards inherent in the then existing statutes.

NEW LAWS SPONSORED

The corrective legislation demanded by the surety companies was passed at the 1932 session of the General Assembly, in the form of a revision of section 350 of the Tax Code, and I am satisfied that the surety companies now feel that the risk involved in writing the bonds of the treasurers of the Commonwealth will be kept at a minimum so long as the standards of auditing procedures which have been established are continued and the statutes with respect to the duties of the county treasurers are rigidly enforced.

Section 350 of the Tax Code as revised at the 1932 session of the General Assembly is generally referred to as the County Depository Law. It created for each county a County Finance Board; charged this board with the duty of approving the depositories for the counties' funds and seeing that these funds are secured; required that depositories put up securities in escrow to protect these funds; specified the kind of securities that may be put up; and laid down definite rules as to the manner in which and purposes for which these funds may be withdrawn. This statute, known formally as chapter 400 of the Acts of the General Assembly of 1932, is considered one of the strongest county depositories statutes in existence.

In addition to the county depository bill, we sponsored and obtained the passage of the following other bills at the 1932 session of the General Assembly:

Chapter 153 of the Acts of the General Assembly of 1932—an act to amend and reenact section 349 of the Tax Code of Virginia, relating to the location of the offices of county treasurers;

Chapter 229 of the Acts of the General Assembly of 1932—an act to amend and reenact section 362 of the Tax Code of Virginia, relating to the use by county and city treasurers of public money in their possession, and by other persons handling public money;

Chapter 264 of the Acts of the General Assembly of 1932—an act to amend and reenact section 2724 of the Code of Virginia, and to further amend the Code of Virginia by adding thereto two new sections designated 2724 (a) and 2724 (b), both relating to the duties and powers of the board of supervisors in the allowance and settlement of claims against counties; and to repeal section 2772 of the Code of Virginia; and

Chapter 313 of the Acts of the General Assembly of 1932—an act to amend and reenact section 656 of the Code of Virginia, relating to the duties and powers of county school boards.

In addition to the foregoing bills, which in my judgment will bring about a considerable improvement in the manner in which the fiscal affairs of the counties are conducted, there was a further bill passed known as chapter 167 of the Acts of the General Assembly of 1932, entitled "An act to amend the Tax Code of Virginia by adding thereto a new section, to be numbered section 402 (a), making it a misdemeanor and malfeasance of office for a county or city treasurer knowingly to omit from any delinquent list required by the Tax Code of Virginia to be prepared by him, any taxes or levies which are in fact delinquent, and which should be included in such delinquent list." It is believed, or at least hoped, that this bill will be the means of banishing a practice which not only has been the cause of loss to many counties, but which also has brought distress and financial embarrassment to many of the county treasurers who have been so unwise as to follow it.

You did not underestimate the situation any when you reminded me, in outlining the third objective which I was to accomplish during my incumbency, that I might find myself unable to be as effective in this respect as I would like to be, because of lack of statutory authority. The Auditor of Public Accounts has very little authority in this direction. As a matter of fact, his authority is limited almost entirely to the rendering of auditing and accounting services. However, the work of the department brings the Auditor of Public Accounts into close contact with the officers of the counties, and opportunities to be of real service frequently present themselves, especially with respect to such matters as budget preparation and administration.

Throughout my incumbency I tried to make myself useful in administrative matters of this kind, and I think my efforts were fairly successful. We of course did not force our services upon anyone; as matter of fact, we didn't have to, because the number who sought our assistance required about all the time we could find to devote to this activity. And I feel rather proud of the fact that we showed the authorities of several counties the way to balanced budgets and definitely planned financial programs, and thus established in their counties the basis for efficient administration.

In addition to this we devised and distributed to the counties on January 1st of this year, a County Budget Manual. This manual consists of: (1) a transcript of the county budget laws; (2) a code of the governmental functions of the counties; (3) a code of the items of expense ordinarily incurred by the counties; (4) a specimen budget; (5) a specimen statement of appropriation accounts; and (6) a suggested form of monthly forecast statement. In addition it affords a uniform basis and guide to all the counties for the preparation and administration of their budgets, and, of course, it serves as the medium for coordinating the accounting and budgeting of the counties.

The need for this manual arose from the fact that the old budget forms were very confusing, as a consequence of which careful budget making was practically unknown in the counties. As a matter of fact, only a part of the counties had been making any efforts to make budgets, and only a few of them ever looked at their budgets after they once were made.

There was a perceptible change in the attitude of the county authorities toward the preparation and administration of budgets as soon as this manual was released, and I am convinced that more complete detailed budgets were prepared for the year ending June 30, 1934, than ever were prepared before for any single year. I am convinced also that with proper cooperation from the Commonwealth and the enactment of effective county budget laws, the making of budgets and the administration of county affairs on the basis thereof will become general as a matter of course.

RECOMMENDATIONS AND SUGGESTIONS

From time to time during the course of my incumbency I made various observations, from consideration of which certain suggestions and recommendations have occurred to me. I submit these recommendations and suggestions below for your consideration.

Extension of Policy of Uniform Accounting. Our experience with the uniform system of accounting for the counties and observations that we have made from time to time in connection with the audits made of the accounts and records of county clerks and state institutions have convinced us that there is a positive need for revision and unification of the statutory systems used by the county clerks and the development of a basic system for the State institutions.

The Waring system prescribed by the statutes for the county clerks' offices is no longer adequate, and there is a general demand for a revision thereof. My successor has made a special study of the accounting requirements of the clerks' offices and is prepared to suggest a uniform system for the use of these officers which, in my judgment, will be a considerable improvement over the Waring system. However, repeal of the statute prescribing the Waring system probably will be necessary before a new system can be installed. Besides, it will be the better course to audit the accounts and records of the county clerks first and install the new system later, upon the basis of the results of the audits.

I understand that when the new accounting system of the Commonwealth was installed as one of the changes made pursuant to the Reorganization Act of 1927, the experts who installed it felt that it was sufficiently inclusive to obviate the necessity for the maintenance of complete systems of accounting by the state institutions. As a result of this, the institutions generally do not have adequate accounting systems, and the accounting control between the comptroller's office and the institutions is incomplete and otherwise unsatisfactory.

The most satisfactory way to relieve this situation will be to devise a basic system which will be uniform in its fundamental aspects and flexible enough to meet the special requirements of the individual institutions. I have worked out and left with my successor a plan whereby this can be accomplished, and I shall be more than happy to collaborate with him in any advisory capacity in making the specific applications thereof. In my judgment, the installation of such a system in each institution, with appropriate control accounts to coordinate it with the accounts and records of the Commonwealth in the comptroller's office, is absolutely necessary. The accounting requirements of the institutions are too complicated and voluminous to be met satisfactorily by a central system, installed in the office of the comptroller. I don't say that it can't be done, but I am satisfied that endless confusion would result if it were attempted.

Control of County Indebtedness. The constitution prevents the creation of indebtedness by a county except as a result of the vote of the citizens thereof. This applies to the creation of indebtedness generally, but apparently does not apply to the creation of indebtedness to the Literary Fund. As a matter of fact, it is a matter of record in at least one county that the citizens of the county voted down a bond issue for the construction of a school, and the school board turned around and borrowed the money from the Literary Fund and built the school anyhow. In my judgment, the constitutional provision with respect to the creation of debt ought to apply to the borrowing of money from the Literary Fund as well as to the creation of debt generally.

It is realized, of course, that there is some degree of control over creation of indebtedness to the Literary Fund by reason of the limitations of the fund itself. However, as pointed out in the case cited above, the control is not complete.

Reduction of Interest Burden of Counties. The counties of the Commonwealth are paying out annually approximately $1,500,000 interest on bonds. And as near as we can determine it, the average rate of this interest is about 5%. This is a considerable burden, and one which, in my judgment, is susceptible to a considerable reduction by a very simple process, which I hereby offer for your consideration and that of the General Assembly:

It is suggested that the Commonwealth purchase the outstanding bonds of the counties, raising the money necessary for this purpose by issuing its own bonds secured by the county bonds purchased. It is proposed that this be done by enlargement of the scope of the Literary Fund and the creation of another fund of the same character, the enlarged Literary Fund to be used for the purpose of carrying the school bonds purchased, and the new fund to be used for carrying the road and other bonds acquired.

51

It is believed that under present conditions, at least, the Commonwealth could borrow the money necessary for this undertaking at an average rate of 3%. If this can be done, there would be a differential of two points in the interest rate, which would amount to approximately $600,000 per annum, which saving it is proposed to pass on to the counties—subject, of course, to the deduction of the cost of handling the funds.

I realize, of course, that it is contrary to the present fiscal policy of the Commonwealth to create long term indebtedness, and I assure you that I am a hearty advocate of this policy. However, this proposal does not violate the pay-as-you-go plan, because it does not involve the creation of indebtedness for the purpose of expenditure. On the contrary, the indebtedness is to be created for investment purposes, so that its retirement would be effected not by tax levies, but by the liquidation of the county bonds owned. It seems to me that the possibility of reducing the interest burdens of the counties by this means justifies serious consideration of the plan, especially in view of the fact that there is a definite constitutional control upon the creation of indebtedness by the counties, with the one exception noted in the preceding recommendation, which exception, of course, can be removed easily.

It is not proposed, of course, that this plan is to apply merely to the present indebtedness of the counties. On the contrary, it is proposed that the plan should be a continuing one—that is, that if and when it is adopted, the counties thereafter would not be permitted to issue bonds except through the funds set up to put the plan into operation. This would give a more positive control than we now have over the creation of indebtedness by the counties, and make money available to the counties for their capital needs at the lowest rate obtainable. It probably would be well to make this plan applicable to the incorporated towns of the Commonwealth as well as to the counties.

It would be necessary, of course, for the Commonwealth to have the authority to compel the laying of sufficient levies by the counties to provide for the retirement of the county bonds owned by it. However, in this connection, since local revenues already are being supplemented by the Commonwealth for the administration of certain functions, and since there is a tendency to increase these supplements, it would appear that the Commonwealth probably would be in a position to assure the payment of the county indebtedness owned by it under this plan, just as it now protects the holders of defaulted obligations of the counties by withholding State aid money.

Local Government Commission. It is more and more apparent as time goes on, that a permanent Local Government Commission, clothed with some authority over the administration of the affairs of the local governments, but set up primarily to assist the local governments in the solution of their administrative problems, is necessary. I think the fact that the Commonwealth is such a large contributor to the revenues of the

52

localities would justify this step. Furthermore, it probably is necessary from the standpoint of the credit of the Commonwealth, because it is highly improbable that the Commonwealth can fail to suffer eventually if the present financial situations of some of the localities are not improved. Unless a way is found to clear up these bad situations, the localities that are in good shape are going to be affected first, and eventually the taint will spread to the Commonwealth.

These remarks pertain primarily to the counties, but it is probable that the suggested Local Government Commission should have jurisdiction also over the incorporated towns. For the time being, at least, it does not appear that it would be necessary for the scope of the authority of the suggested Local Government Commission to extend to the cities.

With a Local Government Commission such as that suggested, the localities should be required to file therewith copies of their annual budgets, monthly statements of receipts and expenditures and appropriation accounts, and monthly forecast statements; also applications for the creation of new indebtedness. And the commission should have an executive secretary whose duty it would be to check these budgets, reports and applications, and submit the results thereof to the commission for review and action thereon.

This commission also should take over the duties now performed by the State Fee Commission, and the latter commission should be abolished, not only because all duties with which the latter commission is charged would be a proper subject for the attention of the Local Government Commission, but also because the commission charged with the responsibility of fixing the expenses of the local officers ought not to consist of State officers; it should consist of citizens who hold no other public office.

Compensation of Local Officers. There is no sound reason why the local officers who are still on a fee basis of compensation cannot be put on a salary basis. Nor is there any reason why a definite schedule of salaries for local officers cannot be worked out. The present salary basis for compensating the treasurers and commissioners of revenue is grossly inequitable and should be corrected to a basis that will be more nearly consistent with the amount of work involved in the various offices and thus bring about some degree of uniformity on the compensation of these officers. Furthermore, the Commonwealth should be given concurrent authority, through the Local Government Commission suggested above, with the boards of supervisors of the county, to pass upon the salaries as well as the expenses of the local officers. And in the event of dissatisfaction on the part of any officer with the salary and/or expenses allowed to him by the Local Government Commission and the board of supervisors, his appeal should be to a board of arbitration consisting of three citizens of the officer's county—one member to be selected by the Local Government Commission, one by the board of supervisors, and the third by the officer aggrieved.

One County Administrative Body. With the maintenance of the secondary highways now being taken care of by the Commonwealth, it is difficult to see how it can be successfully argued that there is any necessity for a board of supervisors and a school board in each county. In my judgment, this is the height of administrative luxury, and the counties should be relieved of the unnecessary expense of this excessive superstructure at the earliest possible moment. One board can handle the school and other affairs of the average county and still not be overburdened with duties, provided they will see that the administrative officers of the county perform in a thorough manner the duties required of them by the statutes. Even the admirable optional forms of county government which were authorized at the last session of the General Assembly are obsolete in this respect, and should be amended.

Consolidation of County Functions. It is easy to understand why it is difficult to make any progress with the proposal to reduce the number of counties, but it is very difficult to understand why the consolidation of county functions has made so little progress, especially in view of the success that has been attained in the joint administration of county homes, farms, and schools. There isn't any doubt whatsoever but what considerable savings can be effected through the joint confinement and care of prisoners. Leaving out of consideration entirely the obvious savings available through the establishment and maintenance of prison farms, it is perfectly apparent that the cost of maintaining a large group of prisoners in a concentration camp would be much smaller than the cost of maintaining several small groups of prisoners in separate jails.

Then there is the question of public welfare, not including the matter of maintenance of county homes and farms. We understand that the State Department of Public Welfare repeatedly has demonstrated the fact that this work can be done much more economically on a joint basis.

And so on down the line of county functions. There are opportunities for large savings in expenses, if only the counties will take advantage of them.

Advertisement of County Budgets. We have a statute on the books which requires the advertisement of county budgets. This is an admirable statute, but it doesn't go far enough. It should also require the publication monthly of a summary statement of the receipts and expenditures and of the appropriation accounts of the counties. Many of the controversies that have arisen lately between citizens and county authorities have been due to ignorance on the part of the citizens. The thing that has been lacking is a medium whereby the progress of the affairs of the counties might be interpreted to the citizens. It is my opinion that this medium is to be found in the development of simple summaries of receipts and expenditures and appropriation accounts, whereby the citizens may determine readily how their money is being spent. This would be a very desirable supplement to the published budget estimates, and the whole thing should be concluded with enforced publication at the end of each year of a full statement of the receipts, expenditures, and appropriation accounts.

Coöperation with Security Dealers and Holders of County Bonds. We have observed with some misgivings that the county authorities generally have not been disposed to furnish information with respect to the financial affairs of the counties when requested to do so by security dealers and holders of county bonds. This has had a very bad effect upon local investors. As a matter of fact, until recently there had not been any local interest in the bonds of our counties for quite some time. Knowing that the bonds of many of the counties were excellent investments, we undertook to stimulate local interest in them by bringing them to the attention of the local dealers in securities and supplying these dealers with appropriate data for their guidance. As a result there is considerable local interest in the bonds of the counties, and it is believed that if the policy of cooperation is continued by the department the demand will grow. It is no credit to us that the principal market for the bonds of the counties lies beyond the boundaries of the Commonwealth. The suggested coöperation with security dealers and holders of county bonds, of course, would be a proper function of the Local Government Commission if and when it is established.

Borrowing Money in Anticipation of Revenue and Debt Commitments. Our statutes permitting boards of supervisors and school boards to borrow temporarily in anticipation of revenue are very inadequate. There is no provision, so far as I know, whereby a county may borrow temporarily in anticipation of revenue for the purpose of paying an obligation maturing before taxes are collected, where the payment of the obligation is provided for by a special levy. For instance, a county having bonds maturing on September 1st and payable out of a special levy either must have a surplus sufficient to meet this maturity, or it cannot legally take care of it, although provision for the payment may have been made in the budget for the year in which the maturity falls. Our statutes should permit a county to borrow the amount of money necessary to take care of such a situation, provided, of course, adequate provision is made for it in the budget.

Then there is the situation which develops when improvements are undertaken. For instance, a school board desires to build a school and contracts for a construction loan. Ordinarily the proceeds of such a loan are not available until the building is more than half finished. But the building must be started and work begun in order to get it half finished and so make the construction loan available. There is no provision in the law whereby the county may borrow in anticipation of the proceeds of a construction loan, so there is no way that I know of whereby the county can legally finance the construction of improvements up to the time that the proceeds of a construction loan contracted for the purpose thereof become available.

Abolition of District Lines. I am of the opinion that the division of the counties into districts has been the cause of more inefficiency and waste than any other factor in the administration of county affairs. While the primary purpose of the assumption of the maintenance of the secondary highways by the Commonwealth was to reduce the burden of county taxes, it is a fact that this step also was prompted very largely by the conviction that the Commonwealth could discharge this function of government at a smaller cost than the counties. There is no doubt that such waste as existed when the counties were maintaining their roads was due very largely to the fact that the general policy of the counties was to discharge this function on the district basis. It also is a fact that the principal motive behind the establishment of the unit basis of school operations was largely economic. But when the counties were put on the unit basis for school operating purposes the situation was not entirely corrected, because the district basis for school construction and debt service was continued. As a result of this, unnecessary expenditures for school construction have been substantial and the full benefits of the establishment of the counties on the unit basis for school operations have not been obtained.

A typical illustration of this was brought to our attention recently. The school board of one of the counties found that each of two districts of their county needed a new school in order to take care of the children in those districts. However, after a careful survey they also found that the situation could be taken care of by making an addition to an existing school in still a third district. After careful consideration the school board decided to take matters in their own hands and declare the county on the unit basis for all school purposes. There is some doubt whether the school board's action in this case was within the law, but there is no doubt whatsoever that this action was in the interest of the taxpayers. The only way I know to stop the wastefulness of the present system is to put the counties on the unit basis for all purposes except perhaps for the purpose of representation in the administrative bodies of the counties, which consideration, of course, does not directly involve the question of fiscal operation, which is the principal subject of these recommendations.

The abolition of the districts for all fiscal purposes would do away with the necessity for more than one levy and tremendously simplify the fiscal operations of the counties. Practically all the difficulties that are experienced with the accounting for the counties emanate from the multiplicity of levies that generally is necessary under the present plan of administration. There are counties in the Commonwealth which actually have more than forty separate funds. No wonder some of the treasurers have had difficulty with their account- and record-keeping! One levy for all purposes, and the appropriation therefrom of amounts to cover the requirements of the several functions of government would be far simpler, and it is hoped that the time is not far distant when the unit levy will be used universally throughout the Commonwealth. It has been possible to establish this plan in a number of counties and we have accomplished a great deal in this direction, but a change in the statutes is necessary before universal adoption of it can be effected.

Lobbying Fees. Another source of loss to the counties is to be found in the appropriation and payment of sums for lobbying expenses by the county authorities. The case of this kind which recently was reported by us and taken up by the press was not the only one that we ran across. There were others, and it is little short of a disgrace to the Commonwealth that there is not a law on its statute books making the retention of a lobbyist by the administrative authorities of the county a criminal offense. Such employment is an insult to the General Assembly, and should be so declared by that body and made the subject of criminal prosecution.

Investment of County Road and School Debt Sinking Fund Money. Our statutes permit the investment of road debt sinking fund money in first mortgage bonds, or the deposit thereof in special accounts. There is no provision in the statutes for the investment of school debt sinking fund money. There are three deficiencies here: first, the restriction of the investment of road debt sinking fund money to first mortgage bonds; second, the failure to require road debt sinking fund money to be secured when deposited in special accounts; and third, the absence of any provision at all for the investment of school debt sinking fund money.

The restriction with respect to the investment of road debt sinking fund money is unfortunate. This money should not be invested in any but securities of the highest grade. Many sinking funds are frozen, either in whole or in part, as a result of the present restrictive provisions of the statutes, and the need for a broader and stronger statute is a pressing one.

The existing statute should be revised further, so as to provide that when road debt sinking fund money is taken out of the hands of the county treasurers and deposited in special accounts it should be protected in the same manner that it would be if it were in the hands of the treasurers. Substantial losses have been suffered as a result of the weakness in the present statute.

The same provision should be made with respect to the investment of school debt sinking fund money as is made with respect to the road debt sinking fund money. The situation in each case is the same and there is no reason why the same provisions should not apply in both cases.

In connection with the question of sinking funds, however, I entertain considerable doubt whether it is wise for a county to issue long term bonds. All risk of sinking fund losses can be avoided, and as a rule interest can be saved, by issuing bonds payable in annual installments. Besides, I understand that security dealers generally favor bonds payable in this manner rather than long term bonds. In my judgment, the present situation is a very strong argument in favor of the issuance of bonds requiring annual curtailment of principal as against bonds payable in a lump sum at the end of a long term. And I am strongly inclined toward the opinion that it might be desirable to prohibit the issuance of long term bonds entirely.

County Budget Laws. As they now stand, our county budget laws are grossly weak and ineffective in many respects. To be specific, they haven't any teeth in them. And I do not believe that the administration of the fiscal affairs of the counties upon the basis of carefully prepared budgets can be fully accomplished until our statutes are revised so as not only to require the preparation of budgets, but also the administration of the fiscal affairs of the counties strictly in accordance therewith.

Report on the Comparative Cost of Local Government. The Report on the Comparative Cost of Local Government, which the Auditor of Public Accounts publishes annually, is perhaps one of the most sought after documents that the Commonwealth distributes. However, it is not complete, in that it does not include any data whatsoever with respect to the incorporated towns of the Commonwealth. It is recommended that the statute which requires the compilation of this report be revised so as to provide for the inclusion of data with respect to the incorporated towns, so that the report will show the entire cost of local government in the Commonwealth.

Incidentally, we are about to issue this report for the year ended June 30, 1931. It has been somewhat delayed on account of the difficulties encountered in making the audits for the year ended June 30, 1931, and because of certain changes which we felt should be made in it in order to reduce the size of it and at the same time exhibit the required data in a more convenient form.

Extension of Duties of the Auditor of Public Accounts. The volume of auditing which the Commonwealth is required to do probably exceeds the combined volume of that of all the public accountants and auditors in the Commonwealth. In other words, the Commonwealth itself is perhaps the largest public accounting and auditing agency in the Commonwealth. It not only audits the accounts and records of its own departments, institutions and other agencies, but also those of the counties, clerks of the courts, and other local officers, and those of banks, insurance companies, oil companies, and public utilities as well. In addition to this, the Tax Department does a very considerable amount of auditing of the accounts and records of individuals, firms, and corporations in connection with its checking of income and other tax returns. The Commonwealth, then, is in the accounting and auditing business on a very large scale. But as you are aware, this business is divided up between several departments; namely, the Auditor of Public Accounts, the Banking Department of the State Corporation Commission, the Insurance Department of the State Corporation Commission, the Utilities Department of the State Corporation Commission, the State Tax Commission, and the Division of Motor Vehicles.

Assuming that the Commonwealth is justified in thus being in competition with private business, all the auditing of the Commonwealth, with the exception of that done by the Tax Commission, in my judgment, should be concentrated in one department under the Auditor of Public Accounts. There are many reasons why this should be done, the principal one being, of course, that all activities of the same character should be under one head. It is especially desirable in this case because accounting and auditing are highly technical activities, and it is hardly possible to attain uniform standards of procedure with these activities divided between several departments. There is no doubt about the fact that the creation of a strong department under a skilled technician would enhance the dignity and even the integrity of the audits made by the Commonwealth, because these activities thus organized would attract highly skilled technicians in the field of accounting, auditing, and business administration. This is by no means a novel suggestion; it is being followed in several states with considerable success, and it is earnestly recommended to your consideration.

Auditing of Accounts and Records of Counties by Public Accountants and Auditors. The Auditor of Public Accounts is confronted with a very practical problem in the auditing of the accounts and records of the Commonwealth and its counties. The maximum value is obtained from an audit when it is made and the report thereon delivered promptly after the end of the period for which the audit is made. It is not possible for the Auditor of Public Accounts to complete the auditing of the accounts and records of the Commonwealth and its counties and get out his reports thereon within a reasonable time after the end of each fiscal year. As a matter of fact, in order to be in a position to offer continuous employment to his staff, he has to take a year to make his annual audits. Consequently many of his audits are not made and the reports thereon delivered for a year after the periods covered thereby have ended. This matter has given us a considerable amount of concern, and there seems to be only one solution to it, namely, to permit the public accountants and auditors of the Commonwealth to make the county audits. This, of course, should not be done except under the supervision of and in accordance with specifications as to auditing procedures and report forms laid down by the Auditor of Public Accounts. I think also that if this were done the auditor would be justified in setting up a sort of civil service requirement and extending the right to make county audits only to those public accountants and auditors who meet these requirements. Because of my identification with the public accounting and auditing profession, I offer this suggestion with considerable reluctance. However, I should be disloyal to my convictions were I to fail to offer it, because I am thoroughly convinced that it is the proper thing to do in order to make the department as effective as it should be. So I dare make this suggestion, even at the risk of having my motive misunderstood.

I feel satisfied that since this work comes in the late summer and early fall, the public accountants and auditors of the Commonwealth probably would be disposed to contract for it on a lower basis than their regular charges, and thus make their services available at a very little bit higher cost than that of the Auditor of Public Accounts. It unquestionably would result in the completion and delivery of reports on all county audits within three or four months after the end of each fiscal year, and thus enable the

Auditor of Public Accounts to get out his Report on the Comparative Cost of Local Government within six months after the end of each year. In the meantime, the Auditor of Public Accounts would be free to use his staff for the auditing and certification of the accounts and records of the Comptroller and Treasurer of the Commonwealth promptly after the end of each year, and during the balance of the year occupy himself with the auditing of the accounts and records of the other departments, institutions, and agencies of the Commonwealth. I think there already is sufficient authority in the law to adopt this policy, and I recommend it to your consideration and that of the Auditor of Public Accounts and the General Assembly, for the reasons stated.

The Salary Scale of the Auditor's Office. The salary scale of the Auditor's office, especially for the field auditing staff, is away below what it should be. This situation is made all the worse by the fact that field auditors of no greater training, experience, and skill employed in other departments of the Commonwealth are paid all the way to 50% more than the highest paid men in the Auditor's office. The Commonwealth can get by with this in times like these, but it cannot expect to command indefinitely the services of the high type of men required in the Auditor's office at the salaries now being paid. Unless the scale is increased, the department will have to content itself with mediocre examiners when conditions improve. This is said, of course, with full appreciation of present conditions and without overlooking the fact that the organization of the office of the Auditor of Public Accounts on its present basis has afforded employment to a number of men who otherwise might not have been able to find employment. On the other hand the Commonwealth cannot expect to keep these men at depression wages, especially when employees of the same grade in other departments of the Commonwealth are being paid 50% more.

CONCLUSION

In conclusion I would assure you of my appreciation of the coöperation which I have received from you, the members of the General Assembly—especially the Auditing Committee thereof—and my fellow State officers. The manner in which you have supported the policies followed by me during my incumbency has been a source of encouragement not only to me but also to the employees of the department. And the coöperative attitude of the members of the General Assembly—especially the Auditing Committee thereof—and the other officers of the Commonwealth, has been a source of much assistance and comfort to us.

I desire to say also that I leave office under a considerable debt of gratitude to many of the treasurers and other officers of the counties. These gentlemen gave us many valuable suggestions, and their coöperation generally entitles them to a large portion of the credit for whatever we have accomplished.

Finally, I come to the expression of my appreciation of the fine qualities of the employees of the department. Even under ordinary conditions the circumstances of employment in the department are often trying, and during my incumbency they were especially so because of the pressure under which we labored and the many difficult and often unpleasant situations which we encountered. Notwithstanding this, we enjoyed at all times an esprit de corps and a degree of efficiency and loyalty without which our task might have been a very difficult one. I am very happy to be able to record that never in my experience have I had the pleasure of serving with a finer personnel.

I hesitate to single out any particular employee or group of employees, but I should be ungrateful did I not mention particularly the exceptional services of the field auditors. The circumstances of the employment of these gentlemen are exceptionally trying at times. They are away from their homes practically all the time, and as you know, the accommodations with which they are provided frequently are not as convenient and comfortable as they enjoy at home. Nevertheless they at all times went about their work with enthusiasm and cheerful spirits, which fact no doubt is to be accounted for largely by the fine spirit with which their families accepted the added responsibilities consequent upon their absence from their homes. Upon the field auditors falls very largely the burden of representing the department and the Commonwealth before the county authorities, and I believe it cannot be gainsaid that the manner in which they discharged this particular responsibility was of particularly high order. In my judgment, these men and their families deserve a special degree of appreciation from the people of Virginia for the loyalty and devotion to duty displayed by them under the difficult circumstances of their lives and employment.

I leave now to return to private life, and I extend to you, and through you to the members of the General Assembly, the officers, employees, and other citizens of the Commonwealth, my appreciation of the opportunity for service which you were pleased to afford me.

Very respectfully yours,
T. COLEMAN ANDREWS,
Auditor of Public Accounts.

ACCOUNTING—THE EYE OF MANAGEMENT[†]

by

T. Coleman Andrews

A very eminent citizen recently intimated rather indignantly that the present Federal Administration keeps the government's books not according to sound principles of governmental accounting but according to what they want the people to believe about the state of the nation. Yes, he was certain that they were keeping two sets of books and that any taxpayer who did likewise would probably find himself an involuntary guest at one of the government's houses of detention and reformation.

This obviously was intended as a criticism, but those who have been striving for a proper regard for the importance of adequate accounting for public revenues will be encouraged by the good example of the Federal Government in keeping any books at all. Indeed, if the gentleman had been speaking on governmental accounting, he might have asserted, without fear of successful contradiction, that, if taxpayers generally kept no more or better books than the average units of government to whose support they contribute, we still would be living in the age of barter.

The story of our country's rise to power is a story of industrial and commercial growth. We have developed a highly efficient management technique but we have applied it to such a small extent in the administration of public affairs that the fiscal setups of most of our units of government, particularly those of our local governments, are embarrassingly inferior to those of private business.

A great many factors have been used in the formula from which our remarkable industrial and commercial growth has been wrought, and the interdependence of these factors has been such that perhaps it cannot be asserted that any one of them has influenced the result more than the others. There is no doubt, however, that modern business would be impotent without modern accounting. And it is highly significant that indifference to accounting requirements is one of the most striking characteristics of inefficient administration of public affairs.

Why is this so? Modesty restrains us, but we feel compelled to suggest that it probably is due to the fact that our state and local governments generally have availed themselves of the services of expert accountants and

[†]Reprinted with permission of the Government Finance Officers Association, formerly the Municipal Finance Officers Association, from *Municipal Finance*, February 1935, pp. 2-3.

auditors to such a limited extent that there has been little opportunity for the accounting profession to apply its knowledge and skill to the satisfaction of the requirements of government. At the same time, in fairness to the administrators of public affairs, it is to be said that, when the services of expert accountants and auditors have been employed, the result all too often has been discouragingly complicated.

Nevertheless, it is difficult to escape the conclusion that inadequate accounting is responsible for much of the administrative backwardness with which government may be charged. Accounting is the eye of management, and it is difficult to believe that our public administrators as a class would deliberately and consistently ignore facts that are clearly disclosed to them.

Under the able and aggressive leadership of the Municipal Finance Officers Association of the United States and Canada, a National Committee on Municipal Accounting was organized about a year ago for the purpose of bringing the administration of public affairs up-to-date, insofar as this may be accomplished through the establishment of modern standards of accounting, auditing, and reporting suitable to the requirements of government.

This National Committee is composed of representatives of the national associations of state and local fiscal officers, public accountants, and other technicians. Through various subcommittees, it has been actively at work for months defining the terms used in, and stating the principles of, governmental accounting and auditing, developing forms of statements and reports, classifying revenues and expenditures, and in general compiling a handbook on accounting, auditing, and reporting for government which undoubtedly will advance the technique of these functions for government further than they ever have been advanced for any other field in one effort.

OPENING REMARKS AT BREAKFAST ROUND TABLE DISCUSSION OF THE ANNUAL FINANCIAL REPORT OF A MUNICIPALITY[†]

by

T. Coleman Andrews

AMONG the suggestions passed along to those responsible for the guidance of this meeting was the very appropriate reminder from the executive offices of the Association that the primary purpose of this meeting is to encourage as complete statement as possible of the problems encountered by those present in the preparation of annual financial reports and to bring out, in the discussions following the statements of these problems, the principles that should underlie the preparation of such reports, to the end that satisfactory solutions of the problems stated may be indicated.

You therefore are urged to state any problem of annual financial report preparation that is troubling you. Indeed, we encourage you to go even further. No doubt some of you have encountered and solved vexing problems of this sort, a statement of which and your solutions would be both helpful and interesting to the others present. In such case, give us the benefit of your experience.

There is only one restriction. You are respectfully requested to confine your remarks to the subject under discussion; namely, THE ANNUAL FINANCIAL REPORT OF A MUNICIPALITY. Your chairman has been sternly admonished to keep the meeting on this track because the time allotted to us will not permit digression.

The meeting therefore is yours and the privilege of being heard is subject only to the limitation just stated.

The order of procedure will be a brief general statement of the subject by your chairman, and, following him, there will be specific presentations by Mr. Edward Glick, City Auditor of New Rochelle, New York, and Mr. D. W. McGehee, City Auditor of Jackson, Mississippi, whom your chairman is pleased to have to assist him as discussion leaders. Backed by the cooperation and interest of such able assistants and yourselves, your

---

[†]Presented at a Breakfast Round Table Discussion of the Annual Financial Report of a Municipality (September 10, 1936). Reprinted with permission from the files of the American Institute of Certified Public Accountants.

chairman is encouraged to believe that the purpose of the meeting will be accomplished.

The subject for discussion has especial significance at this time. The first permanent release of the National Committee on Municipal Accounting has been off the press less than ninety days. I refer to the volume entitled *Municipal Accounting Statements* and designated Bulletin No. 6. In this one volume are brought together the results of the thoughts and efforts of the National Committee on Municipal Accounting for the period from the inception of the Committee down to date. In it is presented the majority opinion of municipal accounting and finance officers and specialists in the field of municipal accounting and finance on the subject of fund accounting and reporting. It is divided into five parts, as follows:

Part I: Principles Underlying the Preparation of a
          Municipal Financial Report

Part II: The Report:
          Section 1: Forms of Financial Statements
          Section 2: Forms of Statistical Tables

Part III: A Discussion of Each Fund and Its Statements

Part IV: Explanation of Accounts

Part V: Municipal Accounting Terminology for State,
          Municipal, and Other Local Governments

This report of the National Committee on Municipal Accounting is the answer to the constantly increasing demand for an authoritative statement of the principles of municipal accounting and reporting that finally led to the Committee's creation, under the auspices of the following organizations:

American Accounting Association
American Institute of Accountants
American Municipal Association
American Society of Certified Public Accountants
International City Managers' Association
Municipal Finance Officers Association
National Association of Cost Accountants
National Association of State Auditors, Comptrollers, and
    Treasurers
National Municipal League

The extent to which the importance of adequate accounting for and reporting of the administration of public affairs has been minimized and even disregarded by taxpayers and public officers and employees alike is almost unbelievable. It is actually shocking to citizens of other countries where the responsibilities of public office are taken more seriously than they are in the United States. The power to tax makes revenue come easy in a country as rich as ours has been, and, as with private riches, so also with public revenues: "Easy come, easy go." And whoever heard of the fellow who spends easy money, or even the fellow who supplies it, concerning himself about such trivial matters as rendering an account or making a report of his stewardship? It just isn't done.

But the economic reversal that hit us in 1929 changed our minds about a lot of things. And it brought us face to face with not a few harsh realities which we have considered very little, if at all. Among these was the inescapable fact that we had developed a philosophy of federal, state, and local government, all three, the application of which had resulted in governmental activities which could not be curtailed readily, if at all, in keeping with the curtailment in the income of the taxpayers. Long after we had learned to cut our garments to fit the cloth in all other respects the tax bill was still just as large as it had been before our illusion that we might dance on forever without paying the fiddler was shattered.

And so the taxpayer, the hitherto uncomplaining contributor to our extravagance, became restive. He began to take an interest in the activities which he was being called upon to support. He demanded economy all along the line and curtailment and elimination of activities wherever possible. He had had to cut down; business had had to cut down; why not government? He demanded accurate and sound accounting for, and full report upon, the administration of public affairs. And he demanded and asserted as a definite conviction that public affairs should be run with the same efficiency as business affairs; that those responsible for the administration of public affairs should adopt the administrative principles and methods of business, to the end that the cost to government of any given function or activity might be no greater than it would be to business.

It is to be said to the everlasting credit of the municipal accounting and finance officers of the United States and Canada that they, acting through their joint association, Municipal Finance Officers Association of the United States and Canada, accepted the challenge that rang through these demands, called in as co-workers the members of the several other organizations heretofore named, and set to work through the National Committee on Municipal Accounting to find the answer to the problem.

The National Committee on Municipal Accounting recognized at the outset of its labors that no problem of administration can be solved without full knowledge of the facts of the problem. The Committee recognized too not only that municipal accounting was so inadequate generally that the necessary facts were not available but also that there was such a diversity of principles and methods of accounting and reporting among those municipalities by whom the importance of accounting and reporting was recognized that comparison and reconcilement of the reports of these municipalities would be very difficult in many cases and perhaps even impossible in some. Hence the first objective of the Committee was the development and recommendation of the adoption of uniform principles and methods of accounting and reporting. As heretofore stated, the results of this effort are given in Bulletin No. 6. Let us therefore state briefly some of the highlights of the Committee's recommendations.

ACCOUNTING

The surest basis for adequate reporting of the financial affairs of any municipality is a good accounting system; one which affords readily the information to be reported. It would be incorrect to assert that a satisfactory financial report cannot be prepared for a municipality whose accounting system is inadequate or faulty. In such case, however, the preparation of the financial report usually amounts to little short of a nightmare. How much better it is to have the required information available as a part or by-product of the accounting system. It doesn't cost any more to have it this way; and, what is most important, the report can be made available to the public promptly after the close of the period for which it is rendered. It is an axiom of auditors that their audit procedures should point toward the report to be rendered; that is, that they should first know generally what is to be reported and then lay out their audit program so as to be able not only to assure themselves that all values have been fully and properly accounted for but also to gather as they go along the information required for the report. The accounting system of a municipality should be designed with the same end in view. When it is the preparation of financial reports is a routine matter that requires little more than clerical attention.

SEPARATENESS OF FUNDS

The nature of public business is such that it usually is not feasible or desirable to have a common pot or fund for the support of all activities. Even where it is possible to support all operating functions and activities through one general fund, it usually is desirable and necessary to have a special fund for the retirement of debt. In general, it may be said that the justification for setting up a fund is the necessity, for legal or other reasons, for keeping certain income or other resources and the expenditure thereof separate from all other such items. Each fund therefore is a separate entity and should be displayed as such in financial reports. It is improper to throw all the assets, liabilities, reserves, and surpluses of two or more funds together into one general balance sheet. It also is improper to consolidate the revenues and expenditures of two or more funds into one general statement of revenues and expenditures. Such consolidated statements have no legal significance or standings. A common balance sheet and a common statement of revenues and expenditures may be used for all funds, but in such case the facts as to each fund should be displayed in a separate column. There probably is greater division of opinion on this point among those present than on any other point. It therefore is hoped that there will be frank presentation of views with regard to it.

BASIS OF ACCOUNTING

There always has been and probably always will be some division of opinion as to whether the books of a municipality should be kept on the cash or the accrual basis. The weight of opinion probably is that the accrual basis is preferred to the cash basis; but there is not an inconsiderable number of municipal accounting and finance officers and specialists in the field of municipal accounting and finance who feel that a combination basis of cash for revenue and accrual for expenditures is preferable to either the full accrual basis or the full cash basis. The proneness of members of city councils and county boards of supervisors in my section of the country to overestimate the extent of the collectibility of unrealized revenues has forced us to adopt this combination basis. It is hoped that there will be some discussion of this topic.

THE MEASURE OF WHAT IS AVAILABLE FOR APPROPRIATION

There is a very general tendency on the part of municipal legislative bodies and not a few municipal administrative authorities to regard the cash balance as the measure of what is available for appropriation and expenditure. This is particularly true in those municipalities where the cash basis of accounting is used. This tendency has led to many embarrassing financial situations. It became so general and led to such difficulties in at least one state that laws were enacted making it a misdemeanor and cause for removal from office for any member of a county board of supervisors to vote for an appropriation when the surplus account of the fund for the account of which the appropriation is proposed does not show a balance available for appropriation. Correction of this fallacious conception of the measure of what is available for appropriation probably might well be undertaken as a major objective of the Association. It is hoped that there will be some discussion of this topic.

There are, of course, many other topics that we might discuss with profit; but we cannot hope to get around to all of them within the brief time allotted to us. Your chairman does hope, however, that we may find the opportunity at some point during the discussion to examine Bulletin No. 6 in sufficient detail to enable us to make at least a mental outline of this important document in order that each of us may carry away with us not only the points brought out in the discussions of specific topics but also at least the major requirements of an adequate financial report.

T. COLEMAN ANDREWS, Chairman,
Round Table Discussion of
The Annual Financial Report
of a Municipality.
September 10, 1936

ADDRESS BEFORE ANNUAL MEETING OF NORTH AMERICAN GASOLINE TAX CONFERENCE[†]

by

T. Coleman Andrews

THE first gasoline tax law was adopted by the State of Oregon on February 25, 1919. In the same year gasoline tax laws were adopted also by Colorado, New Mexico, and North Dakota. One by one the states followed suit, until 1929, when New York made it unanimous.

In 1938, I believe it was, the Federal Government adopted a tax of 1¢ per gallon. The rate was later increased to 1½¢ and still later reduced back to 1¢, were it now stands.

Then, in addition to the state and federal levies, there are not a few local levies, as a consequence of which the aggregate of the federal, state, and local levies is as much as 12¢ per gallon in some localities.

Gasoline tax receipts of at least one State account for 80% of that State's total annual revenues, and it appears from such statistics as are available that approximately one-half the total tax receipts of all the states come from the tax on gasoline.

Total taxes of all kinds collected by all the states during the year 1919—the year in which Oregon adopted the first gasoline tax law—amounted to $528,550,000. In 1932, the last year for which published statistics are available, the corresponding total was $1,641,850,000, or $1,113,300,000 more than the total for 1919.

In 1935 the total gasoline taxes collected by all the states—federal and local collections not included—amounted to $616,852,000. Bearing in mind that the first gasoline tax law was not passed until 1919, it perhaps is safe to say that at least one-half the increase in the tax receipts of all the states between 1919 and 1935 came from gasoline taxes.

From 1924 to 1935, federal, state and local gasoline tax receipts increased from $80,442,000 to $801,940,000—approximately ten times, or 1000%. Of the $801,940,000 collected in 1935, $172,262,000 came from the federal levy.

Thus in the short space of seventeen years gasoline has become the source of more state revenue than any other subject of taxation.

[†]Digest of address presented at the Annual Meeting of North American Gasoline Tax Conference, Richmond, Virginia, October 7, 1936. Reprinted with permission from the files of the American Institute of Certified Public Accountants.

The adoption of a tax on gasoline was a natural consequence of the development of the automobile. Condemned at first as an invention of the devil, and a contraption in which only a daredevil or fool would risk his life, and later as a medium for the well-to-do to parade their affluence and vanity, the automobile soon demonstrated its possibilities as a medium of transportation.

But the development of the automobile's full usefulness called for the improvement of the public highways. It was but natural, therefore, that the automobile soon was turned to as a source of revenue for this improvement; and, since all or most of the automobiles derived their power from gasoline, it also was natural that the amount of gasoline used was adopted as the measure of the principal tax to be imposed.

This tax found, and continues to find, favor for other reasons. It is an indirect tax. It comes under the head of painless extraction. It enables the bird to be plucked with a minimum amount of squawking. Then, too, it is regarded as being relatively easy to administer and not difficult to collect, both of which opinions are sound to a degree.

The larger the tax, in both rate and volume of revenue produced, the greater the temptation to evade it. Hence, in spite of the apparent simplicity of administering and collecting this tax, widespread schemes of evasion have arisen.

You have asked me to speak to you about legislation and evasion. I think I perhaps might make my remarks more worthwhile if I should address myself principally to administration and evasion, because it has been my observation that even a poor law can be given strength by effective administration and the best law in the world can be vitiated by poor administration. Let me, therefore, state what I consider to be some of the essentials of effective administration:

(1) *Qualified Administrative Personnel.* Qualified personnel is the most important prerequisite to effective administration of any undertaking. This is as true today with respect to public affairs as it is with respect to private affairs. The business of government is no longer simple; nor is the nature and enforcement of the laws that are enacted to provide the revenue for carrying on this business. For a long time the general property tax was the source of most of the state and local revenues. The administration of this tax was relatively simple at first; but in the transition from a predominantly agricultural to a predominantly industrial economy, highly complex technical problems of administration arose, so that even the general property tax laws lost their simplicity. Along with this came many new forms of taxation, not a few of them as ramified and technical in their application as the conditions which necessitated them. Thus tax administration became a scientific business, requiring the services of technically trained personnel.

Those responsible for organizing the administration of public affairs have not fully recognized the necessity for properly qualified administrative personnel, but the organization of groups of public administrators like your own, and the seriousness with which these groups are studying their problems, are encouraging indications that the situation is being met and that the time is not far distant when the administration of public affairs will catch up with the technical aspects of the laws by which public affairs necessarily are administered. It is an encouraging sign that public administrators are beginning to recognize the fact that political loyalty should be secondary to technical qualification in the selection of public servants.

(2) *Adequate and Liquid Bonds.* The very nature of any gasoline tax law, at least of those thus far conceived, is that there be a substantial lapse of time between the sale of gasoline and the collection of the tax thereon. Hence, it becomes necessary for the states to assure the realization of the revenue from their gasoline taxes by requiring those upon whom the tax is imposed to give bond to assure payment of the tax when it is due. All too often these bonds have been inadequate in amount, the security required has been much less than its stated value, and even the value which reasonably could be placed upon the security could not be readily realized. There seems but one remedy for this situation—namely, that none but corporate surety be accepted.

(3) *Office Auditing of Tax Returns.* Any system of gasoline tax administration should include office auditing of the returns filed by those who become liable for the tax. It goes without saying that these returns should be complete, that is, that they should require all the information that is necessary for a full and correct statement of the number of gallons upon which the tax is to be assessed. Ordinarily this means a complete statement of the gasoline inventory account of the taxpayer.

When these returns are received, they should be checked in detail against corroborative documents, such as reports by transportation companies of gasoline delivered to distributors and interchange reports from other states showing the destination of the shipments on which exemption is claimed. Then, of course, the arithmetical correctness of the returns should be determined.

A very important phase of this auditing of tax returns is the following up of exceptions. We have seen many cases where the auditing of returns was all that could be desired, but the whole system fell down because exceptions were not followed up in such a manner as to assure satisfactory disposition of them.

(4) *Field Auditing of Tax Returns.* It unfortunately has been found to be true that unless returns filed by taxpayers are checked against the taxpayers' books, there will always be some taxpayers who will take advantage of the knowledge of this omission. It therefore becomes necessary to send auditors into the field to compare the returns filed by

taxpayers with the taxpayers' books. This is not just a checking job. It is a job which requires a clear understanding of the principles of modern accounting and auditing. Just as office auditing of returns falls down when exceptions are not definitely disposed of, so also is the entire auditing process jeopardized by unintelligent field auditing. The field auditors of any gasoline tax administrator's office should be real auditors because they have to examine books devised and set up by accountants and auditors who know their business. You cannot expect a person not trained in accounting and auditing to understand and make an intelligent audit of modern books.

(5) *Field Inspection and Laboratory Analysis.* I should say that next in importance comes field inspection and laboratory analysis of the substances reported by the taxpayers. This is necessary not only for the purpose of determining whether the distributors report as such the gasoline they receive, but also to protect the public against adulteration. Some states have carried this to the point of absurdity, in that they have provided an army of inspectors, the vast majority of whom are unnecessary. This phase of gasoline tax administration has been particularly used for the bestowal of political favors. In the average state, a small staff of laboratory technicians with a relatively small number of field inspectors is all that is necessary in the way of personnel.

(6) *Cooperation of State Police.* In the process of enforcement some activity of a police nature is almost invariably necessary. This activity can be best carried on through the established state police, where such officers exist. It ordinarily is not necessary to have special police for this purpose. The same results can be accomplished by giving a selected group of regular state police special instruction in the gasoline tax laws and employing these police temporarily where any situation arises requiring police activity.

(7) *Adequate and Accurate Accounting and Reporting.* Accounting and reporting are the eyes, but not the tools, of management. The purpose of accounting is to record what has happened, and the purpose of reporting is to draw from this record of what has happened a picture of these happenings and a forecast of what is apt to happen in such form as to promote intelligent administrative judgment and action. An accurate accounting system should show not only financial facts, but also such statistical facts as will make possible the determination and reporting of the quantities of gasoline and other petroleum products sold in each community and geographical division of the state. Such information is valuable because it provides a basis for judging the relative consumption of the various kinds of petroleum products imported, and thus lays the basis for the eradication of blending, which is one of the principal forms of evasion in some states.

I should say that the seven requirements I have stated are the essential prerequisites to effective administration. Now let us consider some of the schemes that have been employed in the evasion of gasoline taxes.

It has been said here by at least two gentlemen of long experience in the administration of gasoline tax laws that the number of schemes of evasion are limited only by the extent of the cunning of those who are inclined to circumvent the statutes. I think this is undoubtedly true. A long experience in reviewing the manner in which men and women meet and discharge their financial responsibilities convinces me that most people are honest and that the majority of the embezzlements and defalcations that take place are more often the results of necessity than downright meanness; but I cannot say as much about the tax evader. This type of wrongdoer is seldom impelled by any motive other than malicious selfishness, and he will be with us as long as there is a statute for him to evade.

(1) *Misbilling*. Perhaps one of the most frequently practiced methods of evasion is that of shipping taxable substances under the names of substances which are not taxable. This method has been used quite extensively. It requires collusion between the consignor and the consignee, and it involves the falsification of both the consignor's invoice and the related bill of lading. Whether or not this scheme will work in a particular state depends upon a number of factors which it is not necessary to state here. It is sufficient to observe that it appears to have worked successfully in several states, and it probably is not incorrect to say that the extent to which it has been worked has been limited only by the desire of those who conceived it to reserve the exclusive rights thereto as far as possible.

(2) *Blending*. The results of our investigations have about convinced us that the blending of taxable and non-taxable substances probably has been more frequently practiced than any other method of evasion, and consequently has defeated the collection of more taxes than any other method. It is not necessary for me to explain how this is done, because all of you gentlemen are thoroughly familiar with the methods employed. I might say, however, that although I thought we knew most of what is to be known about this method before we came to this meeting, I am now convinced from some of the discussions that I have heard here that blending is a lot easier than I had previously thought it was.

(3) *Fictitious Exports*. A method often used by evaders in states who have neighbor states who do not exchange information with respect to the movement of gasoline in the claiming of credit for exports to the non-reporting states which were not actually made. You are familiar with this method too, and most of you here have participated in the conference we held yesterday and Monday to work out a system of interchange, at which this particular method was discussed at length.

(4) *False Rejection Reports*. A rather ingenious but not extensively practiced scheme is reporting the rejection of cars that are not actually rejected. The usual method in this case is to report that the car was rejected and returned to the shipper, but what actually takes place is that the car is unloaded, refilled with water, resealed, and sent pack to the refinery.

We have even heard of cases where the car was not refilled with water, but was merely sealed and sent back to the refinery empty.

(5) *Reporting Short.* Another scheme that we have encountered that has been rather widely used has been the reporting of the receipt of less gasoline than was actually received. The usual procedure in this case has been to report a car of 10,000 gallons capacity as having contained 8,000 gallons, or a car of 8,000 gallons capacity as having contained 6,000 gallons.

(6) *Late Reporting.* We have encountered another irregularity which cannot be called an attempt to evade the payment of the tax, but is an attempt to defer the payment of the tax until after the gasoline is sold, and money is made available thereby for the payment of the tax. This method consists simply in reporting cars received in the month following that in which they are actually received. The usual method is to report cars received during the last four or five days of the month as being received during the first two or three days of the following month.

(7) *Undercover Movement.* This category covers movement by media of transportation either not under control of regulatory authority, such as private barges, trucks, etc., or, if under such control, operating in violation of the laws, rules, and regulations to which their movement is subject. Those who use this method of evasion are the bootleggers against whom "eternal vigilance" seems to be the surest defense.

The foregoing are not all the schemes of evasion, of course. They are, however, the schemes which account for most of the tax that is evaded. It is interesting to note, however, that not a single one of these schemes could go on for any appreciable length of time without being detected, if the essentials of effective enforcement heretofore stated are adopted and strictly followed.

Your President, when he asked me to make this address, suggested that I might conclude my remarks with such recommendations as I thought would be helpful. A number of recommendations occurred to me during my preparation of the outline of this address, but most of them would be automatically carried out by the adoption of a uniform gasoline tax law.

I think, therefore, that the greatest need today is a uniform law. Such a law has been developed by the American Petroleum Industries Committee, and I should think that you gentlemen, working from this beginning, could develop a law that would be acceptable, in its main principles, to the different states. It could not be expected that a law acceptable in full detail to all the states could be developed, but one uniform and acceptable as to main principles could be developed, I am sure.

Then I would suggest either a change in the I.C.C. Regulations that will give gasoline a separate classification or a change in the I.C.C. Act that will broaden the prohibition against misbilling so as to make misbilling a crime whether it defeats the rate or not. As the Act now stands misbilling is not a crime unless it defeats the rate; and gasoline is billed at the same weight per gallon and same rate as heavier substances. Consequently the billing of gasoline as one of the heavier substances in the same classification with it is possible, and is actually practiced, with impunity. My own feeling is that both the Act and the Regulations should be changed, but a change in either one would be a great improvement. During the course of a recent conversation with the Chairman of the Interstate Commerce Commission I was encouraged to believe that the Commission would approve and support the suggested change in the Act. In fact, this change was suggested by the Chairman. The Regulations apparently cannot be changed except after petition and hearing.

I think, too, that each state should require a distillation certificate for each car of gasoline or other petroleum product brought in. This requirement would go a long way toward eliminating blending, as well as misbilling, and it would not impose any great hardship on anyone.

Finally as to affirmative measures, I would say that any law that is adopted should have real teeth in it. I believe in fair laws firmly administered, with stiff penalties for violation.

On the negative side, I take advantage of this opportunity to voice my reaction to one suggestion that I have heard expressed several times during this conference, namely, that the solution to the problems of gasoline tax administration lies in putting the matter in the hands of the Federal Government, to be worked out under a uniform statute.

I seriously question the wisdom of this. In the first place, I do not believe that the Federal Government could work out a law and a method of apportionment of the taxes collected thereunder that would meet the requirements of all the states. The minute such a move as this were started, a great many complexities would become evident which I fear that proponents of this plan have not taken into account. In the second place, I dislike very much to see one surrender after another to federal authority. Every time we broaden the cloak of federal authority, we admit that the Federal Government can do the job better than we can.

There are some fields in which this is true, but I very positively do not think it is true in the case of gasoline tax administration. I think this tax is strictly a state tax and should be kept so; and I am convinced that the states can work out satisfactorily any problem of enforcement which presents itself, if they will just remember that through concerted action and cooperation a great many things are possible which are not possible when undertaken alone.

ACCOUNTS OF GOVERNMENTAL AUTHORITIES[†]

by

T. Coleman Andrews

IN spite of the ramifications, size and importance of government, the average citizen seems to be little interested in how its activities are administered and even indifferent as to who does the administering. This seems paradoxical in a country where business growth has been so rapid and where undoubtedly this growth has been due to planning and execution of the most careful sort. The preachers say we have forgotten God in our pursuit of business. It now has become rather painfully clear that we have forgotten our Government too.

INDIFFERENCE OF PUBLIC OPINION

I have been asked to speak on the practical aspects of governmental accounting forms and reports. The consequences of our indifference to the fiscal organization and administration of our Government make this a difficult task. There is little public opinion on the subject, and officialdom has adopted few standards. Until the Municipal Finance Officers Association put the National Committee on Municipal Accounting to work, there were almost as many ideas and practices as there were units of Government. Therefore, such standards as we have are the result, not of critical public opinion, but of devoted professional research.

Undoubtedly many factors account for our civic indifference. Therefore, I should not be so bold as to attribute exclusiveness or conclusiveness to any one factor. Nor is this the time or place to discuss this subject. However, a statement of at least two factors is essential to the matter before us.

My intimate contact with Government dates back only a few years; but this contact has been extensive and voluminous. The more I delve into it, the more I am inclined to the opinion that our indifference is due in some measure, at least, to unnecessary complexity of organization and lack of understandable reports. Perhaps, if we had had understandable reports, our interest would have been stimulated and the complexity of organization

[†]Presented at the 50th Anniversary Celebration and Annual Meeting, American Institute of Accountants, New York, October 18-22, 1937. Reprinted with permission from *Fiftieth Anniversary Celebration* (New York: American Institute of Accountants, 1937), pp. 296-300.

simplified. At any rate, we accountants and auditors know from our experience in changing systems from one form to another that understanding is a prerequisite to interest and coöperation. It is just human nature for us to have no interest in things that are so "clouded all over with obfuscation" as to be outside the range of our understanding.

NEED FOR SIMPLICITY

Governmental organization is complex because we have made almost a fetish of giving individual and separate status to the financing and administering of activities. There are units of Government having less than a million dollars of revenue annually which have as many as half a hundred funds among which this revenue must be allocated. The most expertly prepared financial report of such a unit would be no clearer than a mud fence to the average citizen and a great deal less than a lead pipe cinch for even a very expert accountant.

We need to get away from multiplicity of funds. Much of this multiplicity is the result of legislative enactment and therefore cannot be corrected by administrative order. But no small part of it is due to special treatment of situations which could be handled much more simply and with far more understandable results by following the same principles and rules that apply in similar situations in ordinary commercial and industrial practice.

FIFTIETH ANNIVERSARY CELEBRATION

For instance, a sinking fund that is derived from a general levy is almost invariably reported separately from the general fund. There is no more reason for a municipality to do this than there is for a private enterprise to do it. Moreover, it is common practice to set up a separate fund and report separately the fixed assets of a municipality. Why do this? We don't do it in business and industrial practice. It isn't necessary in municipal practice.

These and other unnecessary practices account for some of the burden of many funds and much of the complexity of organization and administration. There is great need for simplicity.

Some time ago the mayor of one of the best managed cities in the country, in specifying what he expected from a reorganization of the city's government and a revision of its accounting system, demanded a "one-page" monthly report of revenues and expenditures. It looked impossible at first, but such a report was worked out, and the mayor said that it furnished him for the first time with something he could understand. We need more "one-page" reports.

We need, too, to get away from the idea that municipalities have to have two sets of books, one for the so-called "proprietary" accounts and another for the budget accounts. Experience has demonstrated conclusively that this duplication is not necessary for any reason. The surprising thing about it is that it was ever started in the first place. Everything that is accomplished by the dual system is accomplished with much less effort and far more understandable results by a unit system.

REPORTS TO THE PUBLIC

The National Committee on Municipal Accounting has given us a statement of the principles which should be applied and the terms which should be used in municipal accounting and reporting. As in commercial and industrial practice, the accounting system in any given case should be set up so that the kind of reports that will be required may be prepared from the books with a minimum of effort. Reports, in other words, are of primary importance. They illuminate the course of government.

Reports are of two kinds—those designed for the administrative offices and employees and those designed for the public. The former should be as detailed as practicable, in order that the management may have before it full information and so be in position to make sound decisions. In addition, they should be rendered at such intervals as the necessities of effective management require. Reports for the public should be of a more general nature and explained in terms understandable to the public. Reports to the public have been few and in most cases prepared in such a technical form and expressed in such technical terms that the public has not understood them.

The primary reports to the management should give full information with respect to revenues and expenditures. Receipts should be shown in relation to the budget estimates thereof and expenditures should be shown in relation to appropriations. This enables the management to keep track of the progress of the realization of revenues and the momentum of expenditures.

However, these primary reports are by no means sufficient, albeit a great many municipal officials seem to think they are. No type of enterprise engages in so many and such varied activities as a modern municipality. It renders many services never dreamed of by those who founded the republic. If full and complete reporting is necessary to successful operation of private business, which as a rule is expertly manned, it is even more important to public business which is not so manned.

COST ACCOUNTING

There is no enterprise where cost accounting is more essential to good management; yet municipalities have generally only just begun to embrace the benefits of cost finding. Until cost finding is employed where it is necessary, budgeting of expenditures and, to some extent, budgeting of revenues, cannot help being more or less a matter of guess work. It is equally obvious that full and complete recording of revenues and expenditures is essential to any degree of positive and sound budget preparation and control.

If reporting to the management has been inadequate, reporting to the public has been even more so. As already stated, about the only information that the public ever gets about the administration of its affairs comes to it in the form of annual reports of great volume, poorly coordinated and often expressed in terms with which the public is not familiar. There is great need for the development of a form of report that is both informing and simple. The forms of statements and reports which have been worked out by the National Committee on Municipal Accounting are excellent. They have been recognized as constituting the greatest advance in accounting for a particular type of enterprise which has ever been made. But these statements and forms of reports are too technical for public consumption. They were prepared primarily for the use and guidance of administrative officials and employees. We must find a way to develop out of these statements and forms of reports a report for public consumption that will be brief yet comprehensive, well coordinated and expressed in simple terms that Mr. John Citizen can understand. It probably is not an exaggeration to say that the hope of democratic government to some extent hinges upon the accomplishment of this objective. This is undoubtedly true if there is any virtue in the theory that we must have knowledge before we can have interest.

There is need, too, for more frequent reporting to the public. There never was a time when the people of this country had a greater interest in national affairs than they have today. This unquestionably is due to the fact that the President has sat down by the fireside with the public and advised them frequently as to the state of the nation. It is true that these fireside chats have had to do more with social and economic problems than they have with fiscal problems, but they have demonstrated the fact that the interest of the public in the affairs that have been discussed with them has been in proportion to the information that has been given with respect to these affairs. Municipalities should publish a complete annual report and at least a quarterly report, presenting in summary form the progress and condition of its fiscal affairs. There is not a city in the country which would need to buy more than a full page of newspaper space for such a report and none which could not well afford to pay the cost of this space.

Up to this time the accounting profession has not taken a great deal of interest in public affairs. The instances of participation in public affairs by its members have been all too few. Public business undoubtedly has suffered as a result of this, for there is no profession which can contribute more to obtaining the maximum amount of government and public service at the lowest cost.

The challenge is still before us and it is not too late for us to accept it. Indeed, public of officialdom is being made aware of the deficiencies which I have stated through the efforts of the Municipal Finance Officers Association of the United States and Canada. This organization has done one of the finest jobs of a national scope of any organization in the country. It sponsored the National Committee on Municipal Accounting and it welcomes the cooperation of the public accounting profession. We should be unworthy indeed if we did not join in the movement that this organization has started and is carrying on to bring the administration of public affairs up to a high level of accomplishment.

THE TECHNIQUE OF MUNICIPAL ACCOUNTING INSTALLATIONS[†]
by

T. Coleman Andrews

DEVISING and installing an accounting system is like designing and building a house. There is not only the obvious similarity of function between the systematizer and the architect but also the similarity of a common problem. This common problem is to be found in the fact that almost everyone who has anything to do with business administration, whether it be public or private, knows something about accounting. Consequently, the systematizer does not work in a field with which his client is not familiar. Because everybody lives in a house of one kind or another, everybody has some sort of an idea of what kind of a house he would like to have when he gets ready to build. Thus the systematizer and the architect usually get a lot of advice and often a lot of unsound positive instruction from their clients. All of which should make the systematizer and the architect highly envious of the doctor and surgeon, and, to a less degree, envious of the lawyer, because these technicians work in fields not so familiar to their patients and clients and so are in position to do pretty nearly all the directing.

There is still another point of similarity between the systematizer and the architect in that systems, like buildings, often are started and carried through to completion without plans. Consequently, desirable and often times necessary features are not thought of until the structure is complete. The most classic illustration of this occurred in the building of one of the large hotels in Washington. When it was finished or thought to be finished the builder suddenly discovered that no provision had been made for a power plant. There wasn't even a chimney or smokestack. The builder must have thought he was working at Miami, with apologies to our brethren from California.

This may sound facetious and to a certain extent it is intended to be funny but the illustration I have given actually occurred and I cite it to indicate one of the most common deficiencies of system installations, namely, unplanned building.

[†]Presented at the Conference on Municipal Accounting and Finance of the American Institute of Accountants, Chicago, March 28 and 29, 1938. Reprinted with permission from *Addresses Presented at the Conference on Municipal Accounting and Finance* (New York: American Institute of Accountants, 1938), pp. 80-84.

85

Perhaps the next most common deficiency in system installations is the result of the tendency to start at the wrong end. There is little hope for the success of any undertaking that starts at the wrong point. The development and installation of a system, like every other undertaking, should start at a definite point and be prosecuted toward a definite goal. The starting point should be the chart of accounts and the goal should be a system and series of procedures that will assure the final assembling of the accounting facts afforded by the accounts in the reports that are to be prepared therefrom.

The time allotted to me is too short to permit digression but I will take the liberty of digressing at this point for a moment to point out that to provide the accounts necessary for the recording of the transactions of a business is not sufficient. To be really effective an accounting system must be supplemented by reports. Thus, accounting and reporting go hand in hand. They are the Siamese twins of business administration. You can't separate them without endangering the life and usefulness of both. Financial facts are accumulated by accounting and displayed by reporting. It is like motion pictures; the camera isn't worth much without the projector.

But neither accounting nor reporting are capable of cerebration. I cannot too strongly emphasize this statement because accountants have fallen into the error of claiming too much for their systems. They have all too often represented system to be the end of profit making, when, as a matter of fact, it is but the means thereof. Accounting furnishes the instruments by which direction and position are ascertained and financial reports are the charts to which the readings of direction and position are reduced. But neither accounts nor reports can do management's thinking. If management is incapable of using its instruments or reading its charts, the Ship of State just drifts.

This suggests the cause of most of the inefficiency of public administration but this is still another subject and I won't get off on it. I will simply take this opportunity to say regarding it that the problem has been very effectively attacked by the Municipal Finance Officers Association of the United States and Canada and other organizations in the field of public administration including the National Committee on Governmental Accounting, with results to date that warrant the confidence that the time is not far distant when the administration of public affairs undoubtedly will be on a par with the administration of private affairs.

Getting back to where we turned off. The primary objective towards which the systematizer should work is the laying out of forms and the procedures for handling same so that assets, liabilities, revenues, and expenditures will be accumulated as contemplated by the chart of accounts; and I might say also that, as far as possible, the accounts should be listed in the chart of accounts so that the information required by the financial reports may be available from the accounts in at least approximately the same order that this information is called for by the reports.

Nothing is more necessary to the success of a system than well planned and faithfully executed flow of data from the inception thereof to the recording of same in the accounts. Efficient personnel is necessary all along the line but I should say that efficient clerks who handle the paper work required by a system up to the time of actual entry of transactions in the account are more essential to accurate bookkeeping than efficient bookkeepers. As a matter of fact, to put it frankly, a high salaried bookkeeper is not necessary when the documents from which bookkeeping entries are made are properly prepared, since all the bookkeeper has to do when the documents from which entries are made are properly prepared is simply follow instructions. One doesn't have to be a bookkeeper to know where to post an entry if the instructions for the entry are clear.

This is important to accurate and expeditious accounting because overemphasis of the qualifications of bookkeepers and underemphasis of the qualifications of the clerks who handle the paper work leading up to the bookkeeping invariably throws a large amount of the work on the bookkeeper and consequently causes a jam in the bookkeeping department; and a jam in the bookkeeping department means that the bookkeepers have to work under pressures, thereby increasing the possibility of error and delaying the closing of the books and preparation of reports. I say, therefore, that careful planning and efficient execution of the paper work leading up to the recording of transactions on the books is more necessary to an accurate bookkeeping result than the bookkeeping itself.

This brings me to another obvious point, namely, that elaborate manuals of accounting procedure, insofar as they relate to bookkeeping, are a waste of time and money. There isn't an accountant who doesn't look with pride upon the accounting manuals which he furnishes with his systems, but when you get right down to it and consider the matter dispassionately you will find that such manuals seldom are used after they are prepared. However, insofar as these manuals cover the handling of the paper work leading up to the bookkeeping, they are important. Thus, the flow chart becomes of primary importance.

To illustrate what I mean by a flow chart, let us consider the progress of an expenditure from its inception to the recording thereof on the books of account. A department head finds he needs to buy an automobile. He issues a requisition on the Purchasing Agent. The Purchasing Agent receives this requisition and before ordering the automobile he ascertains from the Chief Accounting Officer, usually known as the Comptroller, whether the budget of the department from which the requisition is received carries provision or authority for the purchase of the automobile and whether the appropriation balance to the credit of the department is sufficient to permit the purchase. If the purchase of the automobile has been provided for in the department's budget and there is a sufficient appropriation balance to the credit of the department to permit the expenditure, the Comptroller approves the requisition, notes thereon the appropriation account to which it is to be charged and returns it to the Purchasing Agent. The Purchasing Agent obtains bids and makes the purchase or purchases under a prearranged contract, if such a contract has been executed, and notifies the department from whom the requisition was received. When the automobile is delivered the department for whom it is purchased notifies the Purchasing Agent, the Purchasing Agent then checks the invoice for the automobile and certifies it to the Comptroller along with the requisition and other papers which have been accumulated in connection with the transaction. The Comptroller then approves the invoice for payment and sends it to the disbursing officer. The disbursing officer pays it and the transaction is complete.

In stating the progress of this matter I have purposely omitted all accounting procedure so as to indicate clearly the clerical routine thru which such a transaction normally passes. All this routine is susceptible to reduction to a flow chart showing the origin of the transaction and the different hands thru which it must pass and the different documents that are accumulated as it goes from hand to hand until it is finally complete. All too often the importance of this routine is overlooked. Obviously, if the prescribed routine is faithfully observed, such accounting entries as the transactions necessitate become simple matters.

We come now to the question of machine accounting versus manual accounting. No one in these times thinks of accounting for a large enterprise except in terms of machine operation. It should be remembered, however, that almost any accounting job that can be done by machine can be done by hand and that the question whether a system shall be manually or mechanically kept usually resolves itself into a question of cost. Machine methods ordinarily cost less than manual methods, but there are some operations which can be done at lower cost by hand and still others that can be done at lower cost by joint use of manual and mechanical methods. The latter is particularly true of sorting. This is true in spite of the remarkable progress that has been made in mechanical methods of sorting. However, in view of the increasing use of machines, and since we must necessarily develop this subject in terms of large operations where mechanical methods ordinarily are more efficient than manual methods, we will consider only machine applications.

It may also be said of machine applications that regardless of the difference in cost thereof over manual applications, machines ordinarily accomplish the desired result quicker and with fewer possibilities of error, and, even where the cost of the two methods might be the same, hardly anyone would use manual methods when machine methods will produce the desired result quicker, because there is nothing more disconcerting to management than to have to contend with figures that are produced so long after the transactions have been completed as to make them Ancient History and therefore of somewhat delayed value from the management point of view. At the same time there is something to be said for manual methods in this day of extensive unemployment. I don't subscribe to the idea that we should cling to out-moded methods merely to create employment but there is no inconsiderable school of thought whose thesis is that efficiency alone should not be the goal of management.

There are, of course, all kinds of machines. It would be impossible to cover all of them in the time allotted to me. Therefore, we must leave out of consideration a great many of them. Let us consider, however, for a few moments the modern posting machine. It is perhaps improper to refer to this machine by such a limited title as a posting machine since most of the posting machines on the market can be used for a number of operations other than posting. However, posting is the principal feature of them.

This type of machine has emancipated the accountant and the bookkeeper from at least two irksome jobs. It has obviated the necessity for extensive multi-column books of original entry and in doing so has done much to reduce the month-end jam which formerly caused so much of the delay in closing books and getting out financial statements. In addition it has made possible the production of several accounting records at one operation.

The posting machine has eliminated the necessity for multi-column books of original entry by making it possible to post individual transactions in detail and, as a by-product thereof, obtain automatically the balance of each account posted, so that when the end of the month comes little is left to be done except take off the trial balance and close the books.

By being able to use this type of machine to produce several records at one time, many steps in the process of getting entries on the books have been eliminated. For instance, to use a simple illustration, it is possible to produce on one of these machines, a payroll check and at the same operation post the employee's salary to his earnings account and create a proof sheet which may be used as either the underlying or secondary payroll record.

In the same manner other books of original entry can be created at the same time that the items recorded in these books are posted to the accounts. For instance, the average municipality gathers its receipts and other revenues thru several different offices and employees. The items shown in the daily, weekly or other periodic reports of these officers can be posted direct from the reports to the ledger accounts and at the same time there can be created a proof sheet which may be used as a cash receipts book.

Needless to say simplicity of this kind facilitates not only the account-keeping but also the auditing of the accounts.

Now as to the designing of the accounting forms. Too often this job is left to the representatives of the business machine manufacturers. I don't say that this is not satisfactory in all cases because the business machine manufacturers have some very excellent form designers. I will say, however, that the designing of forms to be used in an accounting system is one for an accountant because the object of a system installation is to accomplish the gathering of financial facts in the manner contemplated by the chart of accounts. It is not just a matter of installing a machine. The representatives of business machine manufacturers are not trained to do this. They are trained to adapt their machines to specified requirements. The accountant, however, should work closely with the representatives of the business machine manufacturers to the end that the most practical adaptation of the machines to be used in any given system may be worked out.

In designing form for an accounting system the designer must know not only what the various accounting machines will do but also something about printing practice. He must know, particularly, the standard sizes and grades of paper so that the forms designed by him may be cut from standard size sheets with a minimum of waste. Also that the right kind of paper may be used for each form. Printers are in the business not only of printing but also of selling paper. Naturally, they are going to try to sell the best job they can, but obviously there is no point in using bond paper where a cheaper grade will serve the same purpose. Also take the matter of the grain of paper. Forms that have to be inserted in machines should be cut so that the grain runs from top to bottom. If the grain runs from side to side the sheet will have a tendency to buckle. This is particularly true of heavy bond papers that are used for ledger accounts.

The system designer also should know something about paper and ink colors so that color combinations may be furnished which will cause a minimum of eyestrain. The contribution of eyestrain to fatigue is very much greater than is usually supposed, and everyone knows that fatigue reduces efficiency. The same may be said about lighting. Scientific studies of lighting have shown that efficiency is substantially reduced when the requisite amount of light is not provided.

Finally, let me urge upon you the importance of simplicity not only in system design but also and more particularly in the designing of financial reports. Let me caution you particularly about trying to put too much information in a single report. There is a great tendency on the part of accountants to try to combine facts and statistics in one report. Usually the effect of this is just the reverse of what is intended. The reader is faced with so many figures that the report is confusing. A busy executive looks for results first and details second. Not long ago the Mayor of one of the most efficiently managed cities in the country specified that the Comptroller's monthly reports to him should be "one page" reports. He said he didn't want to have to wade thru a lot of details to get at a result. This problem was solved by furnishing him a very simple summary report with schedules of details attached.

Nor does a busy executive want his accounting facts and statistics all thrown together in one report. An executive worthy of the name usually is capable of putting accounting and statistical reports together and drawing reliable conclusions therefrom. Any executive who can't integrate separate accounting and statistical reports would be utterly lost with a report which combines accounting and statistics.

INTRODUCTION TO ROUND TABLE DISCUSSION: MUNICIPAL ACCOUNTING SESSION†

by

T. Coleman Andrews

I should like to say, in opening this clinic, that the very excellent program which has been provided was conceived and organized by Lloyd Morey, chairman of the Institute's special committee on governmental accounting. Mr. Morey, as most of you know, is controller of the University of Illinois. It so happens that this is opening week at the university; consequently, it was impossible for Mr. Morey to be here to conduct this meeting.

We start off, therefore, under something of a handicap, but the eminence of our speakers and commentators encourages me to believe that we will be able to do justice to Mr. Morey's plans. Never before in the history of this or any other country has such a program as we are to have here this morning been more timely. From the beginning of organized local, state, and federal government in this country, down to a comparatively few years ago, the necessity for adequate and informative accounting for the public revenues either was not recognized or was deliberately ignored.

When the sources of public revenues and the activities of even the federal, as well as the state and local governments were few and relatively simple, there probably was not any necessity for a great deal of accounting; certainly there wasn't any necessity for anything elaborate. But the activities of the federal, state, and local governments didn't remain few in number and relatively simple very long, and new sources of revenue had to be found and old ones expanded. The trend from a predominantly agricultural economy to a combination of agricultural and industrial economy developed rapidly, once it started. Sleepy villages and towns became bustling cities, beehives of industrial and commercial activity. And so the period of rapid urban development and expansion began, and the era of specialization of effort was under way.

The more our people specialized and became dependent upon the labor of each other, the more they began to look to the federal, state, and local governments to render services not previously required of the several strata

---

†Reprinted with permission from *Papers on Auditing Procedure and Other Accounting Subjects* (New York: American Institute of Accountants, 1939), pp. 199-202.

of government; the more they expected the governments to do for them some of the things they formerly did for themselves.

The carpenter, for instance, employed full time at his trade, found it more convenient and more profitable to have his trash and garbage removed by the community in which he lived than to remove it himself, as he did when spasmodic employment afforded him time to "wait on himself." And so began the rendering, by the federal, state, and local governments, of the multitude of services which everyone now expects as a matter of course—services all, as distinguished from government. And public expenditures began to mount. Then came the World War which ended with a national, state, and local debt and started an era of ten-figure budgets that made everything prior to that look puny and insignificant.

In the recovery which followed the World War it began to look for a time as though we might return to something approaching a normal perspective; but alas and alack, it was but a dream of a new order of things, an economic Utopia, where prosperity would be ever with us, and adversity would never dare raise its head—an era, unfortunately, of wishful thinking and paper profits. Those who thought they had won the war had lost it. Then came the depression and the New Deal, with the dole, otherwise known as relief, piled on top of an already staggering load. And now, with an all-time record of debt and another world war under way, it is difficult to think of our federal, state, and local governments without asking ourselves the question, What next? This is indeed an appropriate time to discuss municipal accounting.

There is another aspect of the situation. All around us we see local government breaking down under the strain, its collapse hastened not infrequently by graft and corruption. Truly, municipal government in America seems to be at the crossroads. The demand for expenditures for the extension of established services, the addition of new services, and the construction of further improvements mounts higher and higher, while staggering sums still remain to be paid to liquidate past expenditures. The cost of education continues to increase despite a declining school population. And those who can't take care of themselves, yes, even those who won't, must be taken care of.

There is bound to be an end to all this somewhere, just as there is a bottom to every pocketbook. The bottom of the taxpayer's pocketbook has just about been reached. Every one of us is putting in entirely too many days each year working for the government. We are not very far from the point where the tail will begin to wag the dog.

Two interesting phenomena feature this situation. One is the fact that the people apparently have been indifferent to the development of it. We evidently have been too busy maintaining our reputation for personal industry or, to put it plainly, too busy maintaining our reputation for chasing the dollar in order that we might enjoy ease and comfort.

There isn't any doubt about the fact that we have become soft and lost our devotion to those principles of government which have given us the freedom to do pretty much as we have been pleased to do. We appear to have become softened to the point of being no longer willing to fight for those things that are worth fighting for, lest the ease of our standards of living be threatened. There is encouraging evidence, however, that we are beginning to recognize that waste, extravagance, mismanagement, graft, and corruption have taken hold as we have lost interest. And there are signs that the people are reawakening to the fact that the privilege of self-government is one which cannot be weaned from the breast of eternal vigilance without great danger of becoming forever lost.

The other interesting phenomena that features this situation is to be found in the fact that those who have capital to invest apparently have completely lost their sense of credit discrimination. In their rush to avoid taxes they have bid the price of municipal bonds up to extravagance-breeding levels, granting credit which was not deserved, thereby denying needed credit to industry and commerce and contributing to the stagnation with which we have been beset.

All these debts will fall due some day, but many of them are not going to be paid. When the defaulting borrowers say "I'm sorry," the bondholders will be able to blame no one more than themselves for the default. Let us hope that we are facing a return to sanity, a return to popular interest in government and a rational basis of financing municipal improvements. Let us hope too that real progress in economic management of public affairs is ahead of us.

It will take the full force of such developments to preserve the Democratic form of government, even under normal conditions. If the war now raging in Europe continues for any appreciable length of time, even these developments may prove insufficient to save us from political and social revolution, whether or not we become a party to this conflict. It seems very doubtful that the principles of government upon which our country is founded and has grown to greatness will withstand the burden of another world war piled upon the sum of the cost of the last one and the cost of the fight we have had to wage against the consequences of the economic collapse of 1929.

We, as accountants, cannot afford to admit, I think, that the present situation would have developed regardless of how well the public books were kept. We should not be justified in any belief that accounting is the *sine qua non* of good management. But we should be justified in the belief, and the assertion, that an informed management is less apt to fall down than an uninformed one, and that when an informed management does fall down it cannot blame its failure upon ignorance.

Is it likely that one will contend that full and correct accounting and an informative reporting of the data afforded by such accounting would not have headed off or at least reduced the degree of loss in the big public steals that we have heard about in recent years? Certainly not. The crook and the unscrupulous politician depend upon concealment of facts for the success of their schemes. Not a one of these steals to which I have alluded could have reached any such proportions as it did if the light of truth had not been dimmed.

Informative accounting is the light by which the path of public administration is illuminated. The only hope that we can have for an interest in the administration of public affairs by the body politic is to keep that light burning brightly. The keeper of the light must never sleep, for, notwithstanding the fact that the public seems at times totally indifferent to the administration of its affairs, it nevertheless is true that an informed person will ask questions. He will want to know the reason why. Accounting tells the reason why.

About fifteen years ago, the finance officers of the municipalities of the United States and Canada organized themselves into the Municipal Finance Officers Association of the United States and Canada, under the leadership of men who saw clearly the consequences of inadequate accounting and realized what advancement could be made in the administration of public affairs by improving this phase of municipal administration. These men relit the lamps, and from year to year have increased their brilliance. Within a few short years, a very complete bibliography on municipal accounting and administration has been created by these men and their supporters.

Just a few years ago, under the leadership of the Municipal Finance Officers Association of the United States and Canada, a National Committee on Municipal Accounting was organized consisting of representatives from a number of national organizations interested in the subject. These bodies included the Institute, which has coöperated wholeheartedly from the beginning through a special committee on governmental accounting, which committee, as heretofore stated, has been headed during the past fiscal year by Lloyd Morey.

The committee has had a very busy year under Mr. Morey's fine leadership. It rendered valuable assistance in the writing of *Municipal Audit Procedure*, a revision of the Municipal Finance Officers Association's *Suggested Procedure for Detailed Municipal Audits*. It collaborated also in the compilation of *A Standard Classification of Municipal Revenues and Expenditures*, another publication of the National Committee.

It prepared a bulletin on local governmental accounting and auditing. This bulletin was published in the April, 1939, issue of *The Journal of Accountancy*.

It prepared a statement dealing with the problems of special examinations as a basis for the licensing of persons to conduct audits of local governments. This statement was published in the April, 1939, issue of *The Certified Public Accountant*. It also prepared a statement dealing with qualifications for public fiscal positions. This statement was published in *The Journal of Accountancy* for September, 1939.

It set up a special subcommittee on federal government accounting and reporting. A statement on this subject was published in the February, 1939, issue of *The Certified Public Accountant*, and important conversations were held with various officials of the Federal Government during the year.

Members of the committee participated in a special session on governmental accounting at the annual meeting of the American Accounting Association at Detroit in December, at the annual meeting of the Michigan Society of Certified Public Accountants at Detroit in May, and at the central states accounting conference at Des Moines, the eastern four-states accounting conference at Atlantic City, and the middle-Atlantic states accounting conference at Richmond, in June.

During recent sessions of state legislatures, legislation was introduced in a number of states affecting audits and financial procedure of local governments. The committee was called on to advise in a number of these cases. Probably the most notable piece of legislation passed was that in Connecticut, the provisions of which were reviewed in the June, 1939, issue of *The Certified Public Accountant*.

The committee has continued its efforts to discourage the use of competitive bidding in auditing engagements for public bodies. The National Committee on Municipal Accounting in its *Municipal Audit Procedure*, and the financial advisory service of the American Council on Education in its *Independent Audits of Colleges and Universities* recommended strongly against such procedure.

The speakers who will address you today and those who will discuss their papers all are gentlemen who have won their spurs in municipal accounting and reporting. They have been among the torchbearers to whom I have alluded.

You will hear of the very excellent work of the uniform accounting committee of California's League of Municipalities. You will hear an explanation of the very excellent systems of the city and county of San Francisco. And in another paper the problems encountered in auditing the books of a municipality will be presented.

These papers will, I am sure, indicate how at least some of the problems to which I have referred are being solved in progressive communities, particularly in the very alert and up-to-date cities of the great state whose guests we are now privileged to be.

97

MUNICIPAL ACCOUNTING[†]

by

T. Coleman Andrews

IT wasn't so very long ago that a check book was about the only accounting record the average municipality maintained. Indeed, a great many municipalities didn't take the trouble to go that far.

The power to tax and impose fines, fees and other charges, afforded an easy means of raising whatever revenue was necessary, usually more than was necessary; the extent of the excess being in proportion to the degree of wastefulness and extravagance present in the particular case. And the average municipal official reasoned that so long as expenditures were kept within receipts, the idea that cities should keep books was a purely academic one.

Indeed, if one is to judge by the few records that were kept under almost all conditions, it is difficult to escape the conclusion that books weren't regarded as necessary, even when expenditures exceeded receipts, which often was the case.

Our Country became great industrially, commercially, and financially, because those to whom credit is due for her greatness in these respects were wise enough to realize that they could not be sure of attaining their objectives unless they kept themselves constantly informed as to "where they were at" and in what direction they were headed.

Constant knowledge of these two factors, the one static and the other dynamic, is essential to the formation of conclusions of the sort that are the *sine qua non* of sound managerial decisions.

Private enterprise in this Country has succeeded largely because private management has not underestimated the value of knowing where it has stood and where it has been headed.

Public administration has lagged behind private enterprise in the character of its organization and the quality of its administration largely because it has failed to recognize the value of what private enterprise considers essential to progress.

But, fortunately for the taxpayer, this condition is being corrected. Public interest, aroused by the mounting of local, state, and federal expenditures, is indeed calling for a new deal, not a new deal of spending, but a new deal of economy and business-like administration.

[†]Reprinted with permission from *Papers on Accounting Procedure and Related Matters*, Middle Atlantic States Accounting Conference, June 16 and 17, 1939, pp. 60-64.

I venture to assert that we are now on the threshold of the final struggle between political administration of public affairs on the one hand and business-like administration of these affairs on the other.

I venture to assert further that if the politician wins this fight the last vestige of self-government will disappear with the gaining of his victory.

Local self-government cannot survive if political administration of local affairs grows. One or the other must go. And, I am not yet ready to admit that a people who have built the greatest nation on earth within the short space of one hundred and fifty years are ready to surrender those principles for which their forefathers poured out their life's blood, and thus ignominiously give up to the political demagogues and other public vultures.

The managerial principles of private enterprise were first applied to the administration of municipal affairs in 1908. This occurred in the City of Staunton, Virginia, which in that year adopted the City-Manager form of government. And it is a rather interesting fact that this type of municipal government was first recommended by none other than George Washington in a paper setting out how he thought the affairs of the Capitol City of the Nation should be administered.

Since the inception of the City-Manager form of government in Staunton in 1908, almost five hundred cities have adopted this form, so that today, after only thirty years of experience with it, the City-Manager form of government is in almost universal use throughout the Country.

With this introduction of business-like management of municipal affairs has come an appreciation on the part of the municipal authorities of the Country of the necessity for keeping complete records of their stewardship, records not only of accounting but records also of costs of operation, sources of revenue, and other details of public finances.

Nearly two centuries ago Pope said—

"For forms of government let fools contest,
That which is best administered is best."

The wisdom of this assertion is not to be denied. It is as true today as it was when Pope uttered it, but Pope never intended that it be narrowly construed. It, therefore, is not inconsistent with Pope's observation to say that the truth of it is proven by the fact that some forms of government are more conducive to low administrative costs than others.

As the movement toward a better type of municipal organization and a higher type of municipal administration developed, the officers in charge of the various phases of municipal administration began to organize and associate themselves together actively for the exchange of ideas. Among these were the finance officers, who have developed one of the finest national organizations in existence, The Municipal Finance Officers Association of the United States and Canada.

This Organization has done a magnificent job of showing the way toward adequate municipal accounting and reporting.

It has accomplished this largely through its sponsorship of the National Committee on Municipal Accounting. This Committee consists of representatives of American Accounting Association; American Institute of Accountants; American Municipal Association; International City Managers' Association; National Association of Cost Accountants; National Association of State Auditors, Comptrollers and Treasurers; National Municipal League, and, of course, Municipal Finance Officers Association of the United States and Canada.

The National Committee has taken its job seriously, so seriously that within a period of approximately just ten years it has brought about more improvement in accounting for municipalities than can be said ever to have been made in any field of accounting in so short a time.

In its various publications it has announced what are deemed to be the correct principles of municipal accounting; given us a manual of municipal auditing procedures; promulgated definitions of words and terms peculiar to municipal accounting and finance; and suggested the forms in which municipal statements should be prepared. Surely, no other organization has done more for its constituents, or rendered a greater public service.

We are concerned today with the principles of municipal accounting promulgated by this Committee. There are fifteen of them. They were made the subject of The Committee's first Bulletin and published in January 1934. This Bulletin is now out of print, but the principles were revised and reprinted in Bulletin No. 6 which contains the suggested forms of financial statements and was published in August 1936. I shall now state these principles as they were promulgated and revised by The National Committee, and comment upon each of them briefly as a basis for the discussion which is to follow:

1. The accounts should be centralized under the direction of one officer. He should be responsible for keeping or supervising all accounts and for preparing and issuing all financial reports.

2. The general accounting system should be on a double-entry basis, with a general ledger in which all financial transactions are recorded in detail or in summary. Additional subsidiary records should be kept when necessary.

3. The accounts should be classified in balanced fund groups. The group for each fund should include all accounts necessary to set forth its operation and condition. All financial statements should follow this classification.

4. A common terminology and classification should be used consistently through the budget, the accounts, and the financial reports.

5. The following classification of funds is recommended: (1) General, (2) Special Revenue, (3) Working Capital, (4) Special Assessment,

(5) Bond, (6) Sinking, (7) Trust and Agency, (8) Utility. Other funds may be established where specific activities require separate accounting. Cash whose ultimate use has not been determined may be included temporarily in the Trust and Agency funds or carried separate in suspense accounts.

6. A clear segregation should be made between the accounts relating to current assets, liabilities, and operations, and those relating to fixed assets and liabilities. Asset accounts for permanent property not available to meet expenditures or obligations should be segregated from other fund assets and the equity represented by them not included in the current surplus of any fund. Revenues should be classified by fund and source; and expenditures by fund, department, activity, character, and object, in accordance with standard classifications.

7. The general accounting system should include budgetary control accounts for both revenues and expenditures.

8. As soon as purchase orders or contracts are signed, the resulting obligations should be entered at once as encumbrances of the funds and appropriations affected.

9. The use of the accrual basis in accounting for revenues and expenditures is recommended so far as practical. Revenues, partially offset by provisions for estimated losses, should be taken into consideration when earned, even though not received in cash. Expenditures should be recorded as soon as liabilities are incurred.

10. Although depreciation on general municipal fixed assets may be omitted in the general accounts and reports, it should be considered in determining unit costs if a cost-accounting system is used.

11. The accounting for municipal business enterprises should follow the standard classifications employed by similar private enterprises. Each college, hospital, library, and other private institution should follow the standard classification applicable to its accounts.

12. Inventories of both consumable and permanent property should be kept in subsidiary records controlled by accounts in the general accounting system. The fixed asset accounts should be maintained on the basis of original cost, or the estimated cost if the original cost is not available, or, in the case of gifts, the appraised value at the time received. The computation of depreciation on general municipal fixed assets is not recommended, except for unit cost purposes, unless cash for replacements can legally be set aside.

13. There should be general uniformity in the financial reports of all municipalities of similar size and type.

14. Financial reports should be prepared monthly or oftener, to show the current condition of the budgetary accounts and other essential information. At least once each year a general financial report should be prepared and published or otherwise made available for public examination.

15. A periodic audit by independent accountants is desirable.

The municipality, which in its account-keeping observes these principles, will make available to those responsible for the management of its affairs the fullest possible financial data.

Observance of these principles affords the fullest possible data as to condition and progress.

No honest and able public officer will object to this; on the contrary, he will welcome it.

The demagogue, the ward politician and others who are more interested in their local government for what they can get out of it than for the help they can be to it will oppose complete accounting and reporting because the last thing they want is to let the public know what's going on.

Modern accounting and auditing are anathema to the self-seeking politician. They are the arch enemies of bad government, corruption, graft and most of the other evils that threaten the ideal of self-government.

Hence, I am not boasting when I say that the accounting profession, more than any other agency, can make itself one of the strongest bulwarks against those evils and forces which undoubtedly will destroy local self-government unless they are checked.

The public is becoming aware of this. They have confidence in the independent accountant and auditor. They know that he can be depended upon to, "Let the chips fall where they may" when he "chops wood." Knowing this, they will insist more and more upon the use of his services.

We, therefore, need to do only two things. First, be sure that we prepare ourselves adequately for this type of service, and second, never permit any consideration to sway us from a firm determination to maintain at all times the position of an independent and unbiased fact-finder, avoiding always alliances and entanglements which might embarrass us in fulfilling our obligations to the public.

Also, let us not be afraid to interest ourselves in public affairs. There is too much tendency on the part of the people to, "Let George do it," and unfortunately George usually is the least able to do it.

Government in this country exists for the benefit of the people. It belongs to the people. Thank God we have not yet become creatures of the state, and I pray that we may never do so.

I urge you, therefore, to take full advantage of your privileges as a citizen of your country, your state, and your locality. There never was a time in our history as a united people when the advice and counsel of thinking people was more needed by all three.

It, therefore, is not only your privilege but your duty to exert every effort at your command towards the defeat of those forces which are constantly striving to deprive us of the privilege which makes life in this country worth living, and which makes our land shine with the brilliance of excelsior in the eyes of the people of every other nation of the earth.

MISTAKES COMMONLY MADE IN THE PREPARATION OF FINANCIAL REPORTS OF STATE AND LOCAL GOVERNMENTS†

by

T. Coleman Andrews

AT first thought the title of these comments may seem to have more technical than practical significance, and this probably would be an accurate impression for normal times. But these are not normal times; they are about as abnormal as one could imagine; the great nations of the earth are at one another's throats in another of those titanic struggles for world-wide political monopoly.

Might and right are locked in what may this time prove to be decisive combat. As usual, both sides are right, for each claims the blessing of Jehovah, and Jehovah is ever right; but somebody has to lose and we may be on the losing side.

Therefore, we might well ask ourselves: What of our side? "Long live Democracy" is a stirring battle cry and an appealing prayer. But will Democracy live on forever? If not, what will destroy it? Obviously something can or might destroy it since nothing is indestructible. Indeed there must be many existing or latent forces which individually or in various combinations could be so manipulated as to bring about its downfall.

We do not have to look far to see proof of this, for has not the power-drunk paperhanger, by show of force and the power of suggestion, convinced not a few of a class of our people who should know better that Democracy has reached the end of its road and that his thus far undefined "new order" is the true way of life?

Something certainly must be wrong when people whose intelligence and judgment have not heretofore been subject to serious question are going off the deep end for such a nebulous philosophy.

---

†Reprinted with permission from *Proceedings, Fourth Accounting Clinic* (Harrisburg, PA: Pennsylvania Institute of Certified Public Accountants—Harrisburg Chapter, 1941), 5 pages. Portions of this article were included in an address at the Down-State Meeting of the Illinois Society of Certified Public Accountants on May 14, 1942. A condensed version of that address was published in the *Illinois Society of Certified Public Accountants Bulletin*, June, 1942, pp. 10-12, 18.

The ideal of personal freedom and liberty, which Democracy was devised to assure, has been attained; state and church have been separated; theoretically, at least, the people make their own laws through their chosen representatives; and trial by a jury of his peers is the right of everyone who transgresses the law. In short, the old rights of man have been established.

But this isn't to say that the ultimate ends of Democracy have been attained. Quite the contrary! Progress is an endless process; for every problem solved a new one is created. Democracy was simple at first; it concerned itself largely with matters of government, the making and adjudication of laws, and the raising and spending of money for those purposes. But all this has passed; the situation is much more complex today.

Now its chief concern, particularly as to states and local governments, is management, management of a variety of services, the scope and cost of which far exceed the scope and cost of government. It is from this job of management that most of the difficult problems of state and local governments arise, and in these problems that the greatest threat to the democratic experiment lies.

We have not yet realized that the average city is far more an aggregate of business activities and service enterprises than it is an agency of government; nor have we yet realized how widely these activities differ in scope and character, what varieties of technical training are required for the management of them, and what unusual ability is required for effective coordination and general management of the aggregate.

Let us consider, for instance the principal activities and enterprises of a well known city of only 200,000 people. There are the usual departments of fire, police, health and public works. The health department not only carries on the ordinary public health activities that are common to practically every city, but also runs a large tuberculosis sanatorium.

Then there is the public school system, with many elementary schools and several junior and senior high schools and, in addition, a public library system. Then there is the public utilities department which impounds, treats and distributes water and manufactures and distributes gas and electricity.

Finally, the public works department, already mentioned, not only maintains the public streets but supervises the construction of new streets, the laying of gutters, curbs and sidewalks and the construction of new buildings, and is responsible for the maintenance and operation of port facilities, toll bridges and other similar activities.

Reflect for a moment upon the variety of the activities and enterprises enumerated, and take notice that not one iota of government is involved in a single one of them. They are business activities and service enterprises, activities and enterprises that require business management.

Many large private enterprises are located within the state in which the city lies whose activities and enterprises have been outlined above. Yet not one of them is engaged in such a variety of activities as that city. That city

106

is the largest aggregation of activities and enterprises within the state and a highly complex mechanism.

But, there's a vast difference between the manner in which the affairs of those private enterprises are managed and the manner in which the affairs of that city are managed. The former are guided by able boards of directors, policy-making groups composed of men with backgrounds, abilities, and points of view equal to the magnitude of their responsibilities, and managed by men selected primarily for their qualifications, men who realize that success doesn't just happen, that it has to be made, that from the financial standpoint, which admittedly is not always the most important aspect, it is measured in terms of money, and that the manager who thinks he can attain success without the help of good accounting records and reports is all but struck out before he starts.

The city, on the other hand, is guided—perhaps I should say misguided—by an unwieldy policy-making body, its council, of whose members so many are incapable of comprehending the thing they are supposed to guide and direct that the two or three members who might otherwise do a constructive job are regularly outvoted. No need even to mention the management in a situation like this, for how could anyone expect it to be above the level of mediocrity. Technicians capable of really effective results simply do not hire themselves out to such masters.

Here lies one of the most serious threats to the success of Democracy, for the management of the business activities and service enterprises of Democracy must be efficient and faithful or it will collapse and carry democracy down with it.

It has been said that democracy moves too slowly. It is undeniable that in dealing with corruption and inefficiency it does move slowly. Seldom is there demand to "turn the rascals out" until practically everything but the city hall is gone; and mere inefficiency often is not only tolerated but condoned.

But there are signs that the people may assume a more critical attitude. They will at least have good reason to do so, for the weight of taxation gets heavier and heavier and the base broader and broader. The more people feel the pinch of taxes the more critical they are apt to become of those to whom the management of public business is entrusted. It will either be that or loss of faith in the whole theory of democracy. If it should be the latter, democracy will go overboard for something else.

My own notion about this is that the people of this country are too accustomed to private enterprise and too well acquainted with the results it has achieved through intelligent application of the principle of delegated management to throw democracy overboard without first trying a wider application of the same principle.

We have said that success doesn't just happen, and we recall that statement at this point for emphasis. Nothing just happens. Everything that happens is caused to happen. And there are direct and indirect causes, and auxiliary factors, behind every happening. Our great private enterprises amply illustrate this. They are the products of man's ingenuity in harnessing the forces and shaping the resources of nature and making them available for consumption.

But each step in the process of the development of these enterprises has been cut with just one tool—the tool of knowledge—knowledge of the past and knowledge of the present, and a forecast of the future based on these two. This knowledge was one of those auxiliary factors to which we alluded above; and insofar as it was expressible in terms of money it was afforded through the processes of accounting and reporting.

It is not claiming too much to assert that the art or science, whichever you choose to call it, of accounting and reporting has contributed as much toward making possible the present magnitude and scope of private enterprise as the discovery of writing did toward the attainment of modern culture or as the wheel did toward the development of industry and transportation. And conversely, it may be asserted with equal confidence that the management of public affairs has lagged as much as it has in comparison with the management of private affairs because public officials until very recently either did not appreciate the value of accounting and reporting or were afraid of the revealing nature of these devices.

People shrink from, object to, and revolt against even beneficial things if they do not understand them. Democracy isn't hard to understand, but the variety and complexity of the activities and services which it embraces are such that their organization and functioning are anything but understandable unless clearly reported. Give the people the facts and they will understand and cooperate, and democracy will be safe. Make the accounting simple and the reporting simpler.

Here are some of the mistakes most commonly made in preparing municipal financial statements. Avoidance of them will promote clarity and understanding.

1. The combining of the assets, liabilities, reserves and surpluses of several dissimilar funds into one so-called "consolidated" or "combined" balance sheet.

2. The "elimination" of inter-fund receivables and payables in the "total" column of a balance sheet showing the assets, liabilities, reserves and surpluses of several funds.

3. The combining of available and unavailable surplus into one unexplained amount.

4. The inclusion of fixed assets and bonds payable in a so-called "Capital Fund" and the showing of the difference between the former and latter as "capital surplus."

5. Failure to reduce receivables by reserves for uncollectibles.

6. Failure to show serial bonds and term bonds separately.

108

7. The combining of the receipts and expenditures of several dissimilar funds into one so-called "consolidated" or "combined" statement of receipts and expenditures.

8. Failure to distinguish between revenue and receipts and between expenditures and disbursements.

9. Failure to classify receipts and expenditures properly.

10. The showing of actual receipts without showing the budget estimates of receipts.

11. The showing of expenditures without showing appropriations.

12. The showing of items in unuseful order such as, for example, the showing of expenditures in alphabetical order when a showing of them by character and object would be more informative.

13. The showing of items in insufficient detail such as, for example, the showing of expenditures by functions without any breakdown as to departments, character and object.

14. The showing of a separate fund for each appropriation.

15. The exclusion of the fixed assets and bonds payable of a utility from the fund maintained for the utility.

16. The exclusion of the sinking fund for a utility's bonds from the fund maintained for the utility.

17. Failure to record depreciation of the fixed assets of a utility and show same in the balance sheet of the utility fund as a deduction from the cost of the fixed assets.

18. The reporting of debt requirements as an expense and the deduction of them from operating revenue in computing the net income of a utility.

19. The intermingling of the accounts of a utility fund with those of the general fund and the reporting of the affairs of the two funds as one.

20. Failure to present the balance sheet of a sinking fund in such a way that the required reserve and surplus or deficit of the fund are clearly indicated.

21. The showing of utility operations on the cash basis.

22. The inclusion of long lists or statements containing details of only routine interest or value.

For a full statement of the principles and terminology underlying the preparation of municipal financial statements see *Municipal Accounting Statements—Revised Edition*, by the National Committee on Municipal Accounting.

FEDERAL GOVERNMENT ACCOUNTING REFORMS: THE GENERAL ACCOUNTING OFFICE

THE WORK OF THE CORPORATION AUDITS DIVISION OF THE GAO[†]

by

T. Coleman Andrews

COMPREHENSIVE auditing of government corporations had its inception in section 5 of Public Law 4 of the Seventy-ninth Congress. This law was originated as the George Bill. It was passed February 24, 1945. On December 6, 1945, a second law was enacted concerning corporations which contained somewhat similar provisions as to auditing but also provided for budgetary and other controls. This was the Government Corporation Control Act. It was officially recorded as Public Law 248 of the Seventy-ninth Congress, and is sometimes familiarly referred to as the Whittington Bill, or Byrd-Butler Bill.

For all practical purposes, the auditing requirements of these two laws are the same. However, the George Bill applies to the fiscal years ended June 30, 1945 and 1946, and the Government Corporation Control Act applies to fiscal years beginning with that ending June 30, 1947.

Following are the portions of the George Bill which are most pertinent to this presentation:

> The financial transactions of all government corporations shall be audited by the General Accounting Office in accordance with the principles and procedures applicable to commercial corporate transactions and under such rules and regulations as may be prescribed by the Comptroller General of the United States....
>
> The audit shall be conducted at the place or places where the accounts of the respective corporations are normally kept....
>
> A report of each such audit for each fiscal year ending on June 30 shall be made by the Comptroller General to the Congress not later than January 15 following the close of the fiscal year for which the audit is made....
>
> The report shall set forth the scope of the audit of each corporation and shall include a statement (showing intercorporate relations) of assets and liabilities; capital and surplus or deficit; a statement of surplus or deficit analysis; a statement of income and expense; and such comments and information as may be deemed necessary to keep Congress informed of the operations and financial condition of

---

[†]Reprinted with permission from *New Developments in Accounting* (New York: American Institute of Accountants, 1946, pp. 165-170. This article, with minor differences, was also published under the title, "Advances in Governmental Accounting," in *The Accounting Review*, January 1947, pp. 23-27.

the several corporations, together with such recommendations with respect thereto as the Comptroller General may deem advisable, including a report of any impairment of capital noted in the audit and recommendations for the return of such government capital or the payment of such dividends as, in his judgment, should be accomplished....

The report shall also show specifically every program, expenditure, or other financial transaction or undertaking which, in the opinion of the Comptroller General, has been carried on or made without authority of law....

The first fiscal year for which audits were to be made was that ended June 30, 1945. Reports are addressed to the Comptroller General and transmitted by him to the Congress, one copy to each house. That to the House of Representatives is sent to the Speaker of the House. That to the Senate is sent to the President of the Senate. Copies go to the President of the United States, the corporations, the Treasury Department, and the Bureau of the Budget.

Each report is printed and a limited number of copies may be obtained from the House Document Room. Whenever there is public demand for as many as 500 additional copies of any report, the Government Printing Office will print an additional supply for sale at from ten cents per copy up, according to the size of the report.

The General Accounting Office is reimbursed by each corporation for the cost of each audit of its affairs. The cost of each audit is determined by the Corporation Audits Division in the same manner that public accounting firms determine the costs of their engagements.

When this activity was created, the Comptroller General determined that it was a job for men educated for and experienced in public accounting; and, having made this determination, he turned to the Institute for advice as to the finding and selection of qualified personnel. This was a hard order to fill in the spring of 1945. The war was still going on in all theaters, and the military services and war agencies and industries had every member of the profession tied up who otherwise might have been available.

But this was no ordinary request. The Comptroller General presented it as a challenge to the profession, and the council of the American Institute of Accountants, to whom it was presented, was quick to recognize and accept it as such. The compilation of a list of members who might be available was started immediately and was ready for the director-to-be when he arrived shortly thereafter. No one on this list could be had immediately, and only a handful could make shift to join us at all; but this handful demonstrated the power of quality over quantity, and with this group the activity was started.

About the time of the Comptroller General's meeting with Institute's council, money to carry on the new activity was provided in the First Deficiency Appropriation Act of 1945. This Act also empowered the Comptroller General to employ ten men outside the General Civil Service Classification Act. These men were to be the director, deputy director, and the assistant directors. This Act also empowered the Comptroller General to employ public accountants and other technicians on the professional basis to audit or otherwise appropriately serve such of the corporations as the Comptroller General might determine.

As a final organizational step, the Comptroller General gave the new activity divisional status in the General Accounting Office by putting the management of it in a new unit of the Office known as the Corporation Audits Division; and to the director of the new Division he gave such authority as the director felt he needed in order to assure doing what was the equivalent of a public accounting job in the manner that public accountants would do it. I am happy to be able to tell you that the Comptroller General has undeviatingly supported the director in his exercise of this authority.

We got under way with a token force in October of last year, and, in spite of discouragements that many times caused us to wonder whether the kind of staff we wanted could ever be assembled, we have succeeded in obtaining to date a total of 210 men. We need 300, and we believe we will have them before too long. Our greatest need at the moment is for men of supervisory grades. These grades carry starting salaries from $7200 to $9000 per annum. We need about twenty men of this grade.

The director, the deputy director, and all of the assistant directors except two, one of whom is not responsible for auditing, are certified public accountants of long experience in public practice. Two-thirds of all our staff from the level of senior up are certified men of varying lengths of experience. Four-fifths of the entire staff are veterans.

We started off with 101 corporations to be audited. The combined resources of these corporations at June 30, 1945, were nearly thirty billions of dollars. Directly and indirectly, their activities ran the whole gamut of industrial, commercial, and financial affairs, and their operations spread over most of the world.

All the audits for the year ended June 30, 1945, have been started. Several have been completed and the reports thereon rendered. Most of those on which reports are still to be rendered are nearing completion. Some audits for the year ended June 30, 1946, also have been begun. We hope to be ready for the audits for the year ending June 30, 1947, when the time to start them arrives.

In the meantime we have undertaken, and either completed or advanced nearly to completion, several complimentary engagements for departments and other non-corporate agencies of the government, including an audit survey of the currency and civil supplies accounts of the Army in Europe, the latter with the very able and highly commended services of two prominent members of the profession, who undertook the engagement at great sacrifice and inconvenience to themselves and their associates.

The organization of the Division is very simple and highly flexible. It is headed by the director, and he is assisted by the deputy director and eight assistant directors. The staff is set up about as is usual with large public accounting offices, consisting of managers, supervisors, seniors, semi-seniors, and juniors, with perhaps more weight in the upper grades and less in the lower than is usual in public practice, since full recognition is given to effective internal control in laying out audit programs and making the audits.

The selection of personnel is done at the directorial level, this being the responsibility of an assistant director. This officer also has the responsibility for all administrative affairs of the Division, although he handles such matters through an assistant known as the administrative officer. Plans are under way which contemplate the establishment of research, economic study, and other needed auxiliary activities.

The deputy director has the over-all responsibility for getting the auditing work of the Division done. An assistant director is made responsible to the deputy director for each audit, including preliminary survey and audit program, the carrying out of the audit in accordance with the program, and the writing of the report. A preliminary survey and the preparation of an audit program is a prerequisite to the beginning of every audit. Reports are reviewed by the deputy director and finally the director, before they go to the Comptroller General for his review and approval.

Our reports have one feature that is unique, if not original. Immediately following the introductory paragraph of submission there follows a summary of the highlights of the auditors' findings. This is done in order to conserve the time of members of Congress and other readers. It apparently has done much to promote general understanding of what otherwise might be clear only to those who have had considerable exposure to the sometimes unavoidable intricacies of auditors' reports.

Another feature is the certificate, which, though common in commercial practice, perhaps might not have been expected in our reports. We do not give certificates freely, and the fact that we have omitted certificates in some cases—always with a statement of our reasons for the omission, of course—has had a salutary effect upon the corporations involved and prompted others to start putting their houses in order.

Our reports also contain statements of the origin, permitted and actual activities, organization, financing, management, and other aspects of the corporations' affairs, these being deemed essential to keeping Congress "informed of the operations and financial condition of the several corporations." Otherwise the members of Congress would have little opportunity to find out independently what the corporations are doing.

I have intimated that the standards of qualifications for employment in the Division are high. We have purposely made them so. A prerequisite of acceptance is a bachelor's degree in accountancy or business administration, or the equivalent in experience in public accounting. This is based upon the conviction that we cannot do a professional accounting job with clerical help. As a result, our staff is well equipped for the job it has to do.

We intend to keep our staff so equipped, of course. To this end we have instituted a program of in-service training, consisting of a course of sixteen lectures, with written problems and periodic review and discussion sessions. This course covers the administrative organization and management of the government, accounting and auditing requirements peculiar to government corporations, and accounting and auditing generally. It is compulsory for all juniors and semi-seniors and voluntary for all other grades; and it is under the direction of a staff member of the highest academic and practical qualifications. These classes will be supplemented by CPA review classes and coaching on CPA problems.

To further assure high standards of performance, we employ a rating system under which each member of the staff is rated on a carefully selected list of characteristics at the end of each quarter and each engagement. Under this system the strong are commended and promoted as fast as possible and the weak are helped, if they can be helped; if they can't be helped, they are let go. To a very large extent the proficiency of the managers and supervisors is judged by their ability to make good accountants and auditors of their assistants. Anybody can fire a poor or mediocre employee. It takes a supervisor who is really good to make a good product out of doubtful material.

We believe that public affairs can be managed with the same effectiveness as the affairs of private enterprise, and while we are not out just to prove this, we believe that strict adherence to the policies I have stated will place and keep the auditing of government corporations on a plane that will do high credit to the accounting profession and the government and warrant the public's unqualified confidence.

This account of the beginning of the Corporation Audits Division, and of the aspirations of its organizers, would not be complete without some acknowledgments. First of all, I want to acknowledge the helpfulness of the Institute. I don't know what we might have done at times but for the sentiments of confidence and encouragement so often and so generously voiced by so many of the Institute's officers and members. I doubt that anyone who ever undertook anything for the profession ever had finer or more nearly unanimous support, and I assure you that never was anyone more grateful. When a fellow is up against a tough problem, there's nothing like the support of his fellows for keeping him going. It's the finest and only safe stimulant in all of man's experience.

Second, I want to acknowledge before you, who are the accounting profession of our nation, the heavy debt of gratitude I feel to the men of the Division who have worked with me. No man ever had a finer group behind him. I should like to name some of them, but I hesitate for fear I might omit one or more who particularly deserve mention. However, I will say, without calling any names, that my deputy and assistant directors, and our

117

managers and supervisors, deserve high praise for whatever we have accomplished. The last thing these men would want me to do would be to pose them as martyrs to any cause, and I do not mean to do this; but I think that we have to admire the high sense of public duty that moved them to brave the rigors and inconveniences of confused, frustrated, and generally fouled-up postwar Washington and that you and I owe them our gratitude for contributing mightily to the advancement of the interests of their profession and their country. The war is over for most of you but it is still going on as far as they are concerned.

Then I'd like to say a word about the firms who have undertaken engagements for us. True enough, they are being paid for their services, and they are getting their usual rates. We did not ask any concessions from them. All we asked was that they do as well by us as they would by anyone else, and I am sure they have done this. But I know that some of them undertook contracts with us when they might well have said they had all they could do and couldn't take on anything else. We are grateful for this and for the very pleasant and helpful manner in which they have worked with us.

We members of the profession to whom the immediate responsibility for the administration of the George Bill and the Government Corporation Control Act has been entrusted regard ourselves as your representatives in this undertaking, and we see in what we are doing the broadest conceivable opportunity to develop the tremendous potentialities of the techniques of our profession as implements of simplification and economy in the organization and management of the public affairs. This, therefore, may be regarded as a report of our stewardship. We hope that the results of our efforts thus far are worthy of your confidence.

Now, if you will indulge me for two or three minutes, I should like to address myself briefly to a more general but by no means unrelated subject. Many of you are aware of the intense ambition I have long had for our profession—of my feeling that we have been slow to develop the degree of influence upon the formulation of important public policies of which we have been potentially capable—of my deep conviction that this influence can he attained only by acts of public service, not merely by high-sounding pronouncements, nor by scattered and uncoordinated individual efforts. If the profession is to have high standing and influence in high places, it must recognize that it, as well as its individual members, has a duty to organize, coordinate, and put to work in the public interest the aggregate of the talents and experience of its membership.

Our way of life is peculiarly one in which all classes must contribute to the common good. But there's a dangerously extensive tendency abroad in the land not merely to neglect our duty as citizens but to leave it to the other fellow. The ultimate consequence of this attitude is obvious, I think. If we persist in it, we are going to wake up one of these days and find ourselves on the short end of an autocracy or absolutism of one kind or another and forever barred from having a voice in the determinations that vitally affect the right of self-determination that was so dearly bought for us by the blood and lives of our forefathers.

It was with intense gratification that I found, upon returning to the homeland from my duties overseas, that during my absence the profession had more frequently brought the weight of its judgment to bear upon matters of public concern on which it was qualified to speak. The characteristically excellent report of the council, which was read at the opening session on Monday, enumerated these activities in heartening detail; so I shall not take up your time with reiteration of them. But I do want to say in passing that I have heard some sentiments expressed in Washington about your participations in the discussions of some of these matters, notably taxation and fiscal control, which have made me immensely proud of our profession.

At the same time I cannot refrain from reminding you that we are but beginning. We have started at the top. Two facts as to the status of our public affairs ought to be sufficient to make us realize that we must go on down to the bottom. It was recently reported that the combined annual federal, state and local tax take of one of the great states of the middle west had reached the point where it is now equal to the assessed value of all property of every description in 44 of the state's 98 counties. And all of us know, I suppose, that the total of the federal, state, and local debt is far in excess of the volume of all the country's known resources.

Thus, our future is heavily mortgaged and we face the greatest challenge of our national existence. Nothing short of the sum total of the finest talent in the land will be required to lick this problem.

So, I say that we must go on down from the federal level to the state and local levels, to the very grass roots, if you please, if the great problems of our time are to be solved and the stability and security of our way of life are to be assured. It is clear, I think, that the state societies and local chapters, as well as the Institute, have their work cut out for them.

These are your problems as much as they are the problems of any other individuals or groups. They are the sort of problems which, if not solved, spawn the confusion, frustration, and grave doubts in the minds of the people that lead ultimately to violent upheavals. They are the sort that give hope and boldness to those who would extend enslaving ideologies to all the rest of the world.

I am convinced by many years of intimate contact with government at all levels, both professionally and as a public official, that there is no more serious threat to the continuity of the way of life to which our government was dedicated by its founders than the inordinate height to which our public expenditures have mounted. I am equally convinced that this is a consequence of failure on our part to keep faith with these champions of the cause of freedom, a failure to realize that democracy and economic security are inseparable, that we cannot leave the preservation of democracy to the other fellow while we go after economic security, without losing both. Someone has said that if we value anything more than we do freedom, we will lose our freedom, and, if it is money we are after, we will lose both. I hold with all the conviction of my being that no group of people in the country is better qualified than you to take the lead in ridding the organization and management of our public affairs of the waste and extravagance that so surely threaten our freedom. The tide is already running strong against the privilege of self-determination. Those who would hold the sacred privilege of freedom must breast the wave together—NOW. Tomorrow may be too late.

AUDIT REPORT ON RECONSTRUCTION FINANCE CORPORATION[†]

Comments by T. Coleman Andrews

Excerpts from the Statement of T. Coleman Andrews, Director of Corporation Audits, General Accounting Office, before the Committee on Expenditures in the Executive Departments, United States House of Representatives, on the Comptroller General's Interim Audit Report on the RFC, July 2, 1946.

I should like to tell you gentlemen enough about our Division to let you see what kind of people are running it and how they have gone about getting the job done that you and the other members of Congress called for.

I believe this is desirable, since ours is a new activity and you gentlemen have not had a previous opportunity to determine with what degree of accuracy or faithfulness we have applied the philosophy of fiscal control which gave rise to the legislation by which this activity was created.

The passage of the George bill on February 24th of last year introduced, for the first time, the application of commercial-auditing techniques in the examination of the affairs of all of a large class of instrumentalities of the government.

The control thus established was substantially broadened by the more extensive Government Corporation Control Act, which was passed last December.

The making of audits "in accordance with the principles applicable to commercial corporate transactions" called for a staff of auditors qualified by education and experience to make commercial-type audits of the very highest professional character. It is highly significant, and very much to the credit of the Comptroller General, I think, that he recognized this and determined to organize the new activity accordingly; and it has been so organized.

The George act was passed, however, at a time when it was by no means certain that the end of the war would come as soon as it did, and there simply were no accountants and auditors to be had who possessed the required qualifications. Selective Service had taken most of the younger men of the profession, and the military services and war agencies and industries had enlisted many of the older and more experienced members.

[†]Reprinted with permission from *The Journal of Accountancy*, September 1946, pp. 265-268.

The outlook for an early beginning of substantial compliance with the requirements of the George bill was dark. Indeed, it was even worse than that; the task seemed impossible.

In this dilemma, the Comptroller General sought the aid of the American Institute of Accountants. This organization recognized the George bill as a challenge to the profession which it represented, pledged its utmost coöperation, furnished a list of more than 100 members of the profession who might make themselves available, and set about doing what it could toward interesting the members on this list in the new activity. The value of the assistance rendered at that time and since by this organization cannot be overestimated.

Fortunately, by the time the new activity was implemented by the First Deficiency Appropriation Act for the fiscal year ending June 30, 1945—this Act was adopted April 25, 1945—the end of the war was in sight; and by the end of June it had begun to appear that at least a token start might be made by fall. This outlook seemed to have enough spark of hope to justify confidence that the job could be done; and so we started to work.

I shall not take up your time with a recitation of the obstacles we had to overcome and the disappointments we suffered in those early days. Suffice it to say that they were legion and that, though our own enthusiasm and determination were great, the example of the Comptroller General's well known high sense of duty and devotion to the public interest, and his unfailing confidence and encouragement, helped greatly to sustain us in many discouraging circumstances.

The Corporation Audits Division was created on July 10th, with a director as its principal officer. The director was appointed and installed on July 19th. Thanks to the military services and some of the war agencies, who coöperated by releasing promptly some of the men whom we sought for managerial positions, we were able to begin operations about October 1st, and I am happy to be able to tell you that several audits for the year ended June 30, 1945, already have been completed; the balance are under way, with a few minor exceptions; and we expect to have those for the year ended June 30, 1946, behind us when the time arrives for starting those for the year ending June 30, 1947. In other words, we expect to be current in our work by the end of fiscal 1947.

Bearing in mind that of necessity we started from scratch three months after the end of the year for which the first audits were to be made, our expectations are that we will complete the staffing of the Division and the first two years' work within twenty-one months. The latter is going to be possible because of the very wise provision in the George bill and the Government Corporation Control Act by which we were permitted to employ public accountants to supplement our staff.

We have not had to make as extensive use of this privilege as we first thought would be necessary, but, to the extent that we have had to use it, it has been a godsend to us. And I think it should be said for the firms who have undertaken contracts for us that their participation has not been motivated by mere material considerations.

The accounting profession was, like most other classes of enterprises, hard hit by the war. There is an unprecedented demand for their services by clients who may be expected to offer continuity of retention, whereas their engagements with us will be for the most part one-year undertakings, and hardly more than a two-year undertaking in any case.

This participation in our work also has been undertaken in spite of an acute shortage of qualified manpower, which shortage is not going to be entirely cured by demobilization, since the demand for public accounting services is far greater than before the war—during which additions to the ranks of the profession were negligible and appears likely to grow from this heightened level rather than revert even partially to the prewar level. We feel, therefore, that these contractors are giving tangible expression to the gesture of coöperation by the national organization of their profession, which already has been acknowledged.... I should like to state the philosophy that underlies our approach to the auditing of the corporations and our attitude toward these agencies.

Our immediate duty is to the Comptroller General, of course. This is an intra-office duty, however. Looking at it from the standpoint of the General Accounting Office, we represent the Congress. We are a fact-finding agency of that body. Our first duty is to it, therefore; and we are required to report to it. Copies of our reports go to the President and the corporations.

However, an audit of the affairs of a corporation is, for the most part, an audit of the performance of the management of the corporation. The auditor accumulates the facts developed by his examination, evaluates their significance, and, of necessity, checks and discusses with the management such matters as should be disposed of at that level.

This procedure accomplishes two ends: first, it enables the auditor to offer constructive suggestions on matters upon which he is qualified to advise the management; second, it saves his report from the inclusion of matters with which the board of directors, stockholders, or other principals should not be bothered and which might tend to obscure or dilute the importance of the matters that should have their attention.

This may sound elementary, as indeed it is; but it is a principle that often is overlooked; and, since it is a fundamental of our policy, I thought it might be well to take advantage of this first opportunity we have had to state it under critical circumstances.

Accounting is a responsibility of management. The primary interest of proprietors in accounting is one of whether the responsibility for it is fully discharged. A finding of faulty or deficient accounting should go no further than the management unless correction is neglected to the point where serious consequences might result, in which case it should be reported to the proprietors.

In the case of Reconstruction Finance Corporation and its subsidiaries and affiliates, important aspects of accounting not only were faulty but also were deficient, and these conditions have persisted for such a period that we feel that the possibility of serious consequences is substantial.

Since accounting is primarily a responsibility of management, and since this was the first time that the situation in the Reconstruction Finance Corporation group had come to our attention, we concluded to take the matter up with the Board of Directors of the Corporation.

But upon considering the finished document, it was at once apparent that the situation was such—in the aggregate, at least—as to clearly dictate that the Comptroller General inform the Congress of it.

We do not derive any pleasure from reporting uncomplimentary or unpleasant facts developed in the course of our examinations. It is strictly an impersonal matter with us. Our only concern is that we scrupulously comply with the Comptroller General's policy that we be as accurate as possible in our findings of fact and as sound as possible in our conclusions and recommendations.

In a letter dated June 20, 1946, the Chairman of the Board of Directors of Reconstruction Finance Corporation addressed the Chairman of the Banking and Currency Committee of the Senate concerning our letter of June 17, 1946, to the Board of Directors of Reconstruction Finance Corporation.... We quote and comment upon the pertinent portions of the Chairman's letter below: ...

> The GAO letter charges that RFC "does not control" certain of its property and income. The word "control" is of course used in a technical accounting sense and the point of the GAO letter is that RFC has not maintained complete centralized accounting records in the manner that GAO feels necessary or desirable.

There are two fundamentally simple groups of problems at issue here. One deals with defense plants, the other with strategic and critical materials; and the particular phases of these problems reported upon in our letter are known as problems of accounting control. The term "accounting control" is one which is quite commonly used and generally understood. It is no mere matter of bookkeeping, and the question of centralization of record-keeping is not involved. Accounting control reduced to simple terms means the maintaining of a system of accounting whereby there is assured an accurate conclusive, and otherwise reliable account of the assets, liabilities, and capital of an enterprise—a system of accounts which will disclose, among other things, what assets the enterprise owns and where they are. Reconstruction Finance Corporation has not maintained such an accounting system as to all of its assets.

In the case of defense plants, as pointed out in our letter. It was necessary that Reconstruction Finance Corporation first effect an accounting with the lessees; second, that it show a satisfactory accounting for the final disposition of the plants and equipment. In effecting an accounting with the lessees, most of whose leases have been terminated, it is necessary for the Reconstruction Finance Corporation organization to determine that all items of physical property for which they are accountable have been returned or that cash settlements have been made for shortages. It also is necessary for them to determine that the rentals paid by the lessees have been correctly computed and fully collected.

The Reconstruction Finance Corporation organization has been woefully deficient in carrying out this responsibility and procrastinating to the point of negligence, even since our audit was begun; this matter was brought to their attention and correction was strongly urged several months ago, but nothing tangible has been done toward correction up to this time. Unless this situation is corrected, there will be no determination of any losses that might have been sustained, and it will be impossible for anyone to state that the defense plant activities have been fully accounted for to the point of termination of the leases.

Finally, it will be necessary for the Reconstruction Finance Corporation organization to show conclusively that all defense plant and equipment have been physically accounted for at the termination of the leases to the point of sale and that all proceeds of sales are positively identified with the disposals. In our letter, we pointed out that the situation with regard to accounting for physical property, as above outlined, is so serious as to make it doubtful that a reasonably conclusive accounting for the physical property can ever be effected.

In accounting for strategic and critical materials purchased and sold, the Reconstruction Finance Corporation management has had the erroneous point of view that it is necessary only to show upon the final conclusion of a given materials program that all or substantially all the materials purchased have been sold or otherwise accounted for. Few programs have been concluded to date; therefore, no conclusive accounting has been rendered on such programs.

No effort had been made prior to June 30, 1946, in the long interval of time during which a given program was carried on, to take a physical measure of the unsold inventory and compare it with the quantity balances shown by the inventory records. Moreover, no effort had been made until June 30, 1946, to make the inventory records reflect all transactions up to any current date short of final disposition of all materials, so that the balance shown on the records would be indicative of the amounts on hand. Further, the inventory records do not show location of materials on hand, which is a prerequisite to use of the records in making a physical check of the amounts actually on hand. An attempt is being made for the first time as of June 30, 1946, at our behest, to effect such an accounting by physical inventory to determine the amount of inventories of materials, if any, that are not accounted for.

We have pointed out that from the standpoint of operating control, the operating organization has been unable to rely on the accounting records for data as to unsold materials on hand and their location from day to day. In the case of United States Commercial Company, we also have pointed out that no attempt was made in many programs to record in the inventory records the quantities of materials purchased and sold. In other words, there was no objective of even determining the final accounting for such materials.

From the viewpoint of auditing, without a physical-inventory check there can be no verification of investment in inventories shown in the balance-sheets of the company nor of the income or loss shown in the income statements. Indeed, it may be assumed, from our knowledge of the condition of the records, that the amounts shown are inaccurate. Just how inaccurate they are cannot be stated until a satisfactory physical inventory is taken.

> The suggestions of the GAO regarding centralized accounting records and controls, desirable as they may be, do not take into account the practicalities of carrying out the corporation's world-wide activities under wartime conditions.

We are not unmindful of the practicalities of carrying on world-wide activities under wartime conditions. On the contrary, we are quite aware of the difficulties presented in such a situation. The problems of communication alone, by which required accounting data would be accumulated, are enormous even under ordinary circumstances. They are multiplied many fold under war conditions. But this is no excuse for neglecting a function of management without the benefits of which management is fogbound.

The whole history of the success of business enterprises is written in the accounts of such enterprises, and accounting for business activities cannot be neglected, without running the risk of serious consequences, merely because it is difficult to achieve. It is a concomitant of the assumption of managerial responsibility for business activities to show in terms of the medium of exchange through which business transactions are expressed, and in other necessary terms, that these responsibilities have been fully discharged.

> In order to meet RFC's wartime responsibilities, to get plants and facilities built and in operation, and to acquire and distribute urgently needed strategic and critical materials, its organization and procedures had to be developed rapidly. Over-all uniform accounting controls and procedures could not have been completely developed and made effective without considerably impeding operations.

This statement is totally inconsistent with the most elementary conception of managerial responsibility. Admittedly, the establishment of a proper accounting system for the tremendous activities that were thrust upon the Reconstruction Finance Corporation organization would have been a very difficult job, but it was a job which should have been done, which could have been done, and whose omission may not be rationalized merely because of the difficulties involved in doing it. Private enterprise did it. They were forced to do it in order to obtain settlements of charges made under their contracts with the government. Surely the government could not well demand full and meticulously accurate accounting from its contractors and be itself grossly delinquent in this respect....

The accounting difficulties of Reconstruction Finance Corporation are the result of a fundamental weakness in the organization of the corporation—a lack of coördination and integration of accounting responsibility. For this reason, we recommended that the Board should appoint a competent controller and give him full authority to execute its policies as to accounting matters, including the authority to reorganize the accounting organization and revise its procedures. We also suggested that perhaps it might be desirable to go even further and draw a clear line of demarcation between policy making on the one hand and management on the other, relieving the board of directors of managerial responsibility, following the American business pattern of making the board of directors a policy-making body and turning over the execution of its policies to a competent management group. The Chairman's letter inclines us even more strongly than heretofore towards the feeling that the latter is highly desirable and perhaps even urgently necessary.

ACCOUNTING AND THE
MANAGEMENT OF PUBLIC AFFAIRS†

by

T. Coleman Andrews

IN an excellent article entitled "The Accounting and Treasury Functions In a Modern Organization," Mr. J. A. Campbell, a prominent accountant of Chicago, made the very sage statement that "the accounting department pays its way by serving the business, not by trying to run it." I doubt that anyone could frame in fewer words a more accurate and inclusive statement of the fundamental purpose of accounting than was thus expressed by Mr. Campbell. It will be my purpose in this paper to indicate at least one important way in which accounting can be made to serve business. But before I start let's be sure we all understand what I mean by the word *"business."*

Most of us, I fear, think of the word *"business"* as connoting only the activities of private enterprise. Even those of us who think of it as encompassing a wider field often use it in the restricted sense. It is by no means a word of narrow application. Business activity is involved at some point in almost every aspect of human life. Government, for instance—one of the most important aspects of living—is business, the biggest business in the world. The late Franklin D. Roosevelt called it not only the biggest, but also the most important business in the world. If government is business—and I agree that it is—there can be no doubt about its relative immensity; and, business or not, the pre-eminence of its importance can not be denied.

For the benefit of those who require the authority of the lexicon, I cite Funk and Wagnall's Modern Dictionary. It defines the word *business* as embracing, among other things, *commercial affairs, a matter or affair, and interest, concern, duty*. The creation, management and servicing—to use a word common to public administration—of an aggregate federal, state and local debt of 272 billion dollars, and the assessing, collecting and spending of 50 billion dollars in one year, certainly involves engagement in *commercial affair*. This also seems to dispose of the second definition, namely, *a matter or affair*. And surely no one will challenge the definition:

---

†Reprinted with permission from *Proceedings of the Ninth Annual Institute on Accounting* (Columbus, OH: College of Commerce and Administration, The Ohio State University, 1947), pp. 5-11. This article was also published in *The Accounting Review*, October 1947, pp. 367-371.

interest, concern, duty, for surely nothing is of more interest to all of us, nothing is of greater concern, especially these days, and nothing imposes a higher duty upon any of us, than government. And so, let's understand that government as well as private enterprise is business, for it is primarily about the use of accounting in our governmental business that I propose to talk from here on out.

On the whole, the administration of public affairs does not require the use of involved accounting systems, procedures, or techniques; except in occasional special situations, the requirements are simple. But many years ago somebody got the idea that the budgeting of income and expenditures called for special methods and techniques, and somehow or other enough public officials fell for the idea to give it a firm foothold; and enough accountants swallowed it to make C.P.A. problems in "municipal accounting" the reef on which the hopes of many a promising aspirant to an accounting career were wrecked. The whole business of governmental accounting became a confusion of fancy terms: estimated receipts, receipts, revenues, appropriations, authorizations, allotments, allocations, encumbrances, obligations, expenditures, unrealized estimates of receipts, unallocated appropriations, unobligated allocations, unencumbered allocations, unexpended balances, and so on. Thus governmental accounting became an end unto itself and utterly useless as a managerial device. As a result, accounting became to the average public administrator just a "necessary evil."

In a paper entitled "Accounting Problems of a Government Agency," read by Eric L. Kohler, C.P.A. of Chicago, at a Conference on Federal Accounting, sponsored by the American Institute of Accountants and held in New York City on December 2 and 3, 1943, the author made this statement:

> From a comparison of governmental operations with those of private business, it is difficult to imagine why Government accounting requirements should offer difficulty. Only simple expenditure accounts seem to be necessary, provided, of course, agreement can be reached on the definition of "expenditure." In practice, involved systems of accounting are the rule rather than the exception; not put to active administrative use, they are frequently badly designed and in arrears. Causes are numerous, the principal one being that accounting needs have been met with concepts that have tended to make accounting an end in itself, rather than a means of information and control useful alike to agency management, supervisory financial agencies, and the Congress.

Mr. Kohler spoke from intimate knowledge of the deficiencies of governmental accounting. He had already put in many years trying to bring order out of some horrible examples of what governmental accounting isn't. He has seen his efforts rewarded in the Tennessee Valley Authority, where he proved the validity of his criticisms by demonstrating that accounting could be made simple in a governmental agency and still be made to satisfy every budgetary requirement. He also had made it popular with, and

130

indispensable to, the management of the Authority. His method was simple. He merely used the principles and techniques of plain everyday accounting. For instance, in the classification and distribution of expenditures, he applied the principles of cost accounting; he provided for the recording of expenditures in such a way that the end result was to show the cost of every activity of the Authority. He made the ascertainment-of-activity costs the primary aim of the system. Objective classification of expenditures was given secondary, if not incidental, importance. Contrast this with the usual practice of putting primary emphasis upon objective classification and the usefulness of the activity approach is at once apparent.

The activities of the Tennessee Valley Authority are somewhat unusual, however; hence, they are not typical of governmental departments and agencies generally. So I will not undertake to explain the Authority's system in detail. Instead, let's apply the principle used there to a familiar setup and see how it would work.

First of all, let us remember what a business organization does and what it is in such an organization that costs money. A business organization establishes and carries on such activities as are necessary to the accomplishment of the purpose or purposes for which it was created. The *activities* that it carries on *are what cost money*.

Then let us remember what an organization's accounting system is supposed to do. It is supposed to be useful to management. If it is to be useful to management, it must present the facts of the business in a manner consistent with management's way of looking at the business. And how does management look at the business? It looks at it as a group of activities which, properly coordinated and managed, will accomplish the over-all objective of the business. It looks upon expenses as what they are and nothing more: as the cost of goods and services acquired for the carrying on of the activities of the business. Whether one kind of goods or services, or some other kind, is used by an activity isn't important of itself. What is important is whether the kind used was needed, whether it was the most appropriate kind to the need, and whether its cost was right. The fact that two or more activities use the same kind of goods or services and that the total cost was so much, is of little value to management.

To illustrate, in a business with two or more departments and several activities, a reliable judgment of whether the total cost of telephone services is in line cannot be formed until it is determined that each department's portion is in line; and no judgment as to any department's portion can be formed until it is determined that each activity's portion is in line. Hence, if expense accounting is to be useful to management, its primary objective must be the accumulation and disclosure of activity costs, and the kinds of things and services a business buys are of importance mainly at the activity level, where the need for them, their appropriateness, and their cost can be adjudged and the benefits derived from the use of them can be appraised.

Now let's go a step further and see how this would work in practice. For the purpose of this demonstration, let's use some ground that will be a bit more familiar to most of us than a department of government. Let's use the accounting department of a private enterprise. The usual activities of such a department are: auditing of income and receipts, auditing of expenses and disbursements, inventory accounting and control, payroll accounting and control, the keeping of vendors' accounts, the keeping of customers' accounts, the keeping of the general books, internal auditing, and so on.

In most businesses the practice as to the classification of expenses is not even to ascertain the expenses of the accounting department as such, let alone the cost of the several activities that constitute the department. The controller's salary probably will be included with those of other executives in both the books of account and the financial statements. The salaries of the employees of the department, generally, probably will be included in a catch-all item, like "Salaries of Office Employees," along with the salaries of clerks, stenographers, and other white-collar employees of other departments. The cost of telephone service probably will be shown as one item for all departments, so also the cost of stationery and other so-called "office expenses." No one in the world would be able to look at the books of account or financial reports and see what the word *office* includes, that is, what departments it includes and what the activities of these departments are. Even the total cost of the accounting department is not indicated, let alone the cost of each of the activities that constitute it. I call this sort of accounting *obfuscation*. Certainly it is not useful information.

Only by classifying the expenses of an organization, whether it be a private enterprise or a division or other unit of government, so that the structure and activities of the organization and the cost thereof will be revealed, can anyone hope to have an understandable basis for judging the necessity for, or reasonableness of, the organization's expenses. By such classification it is possible to compare the cost of the fundamental elements of the organization from month to month, quarter to quarter, and year to year, or any other desirable period. Such classification and comparison also will reveal at a glance any changes that are made in the structure and activities of the organization, as well as the trend of the costs of the continuing departments and activities. Thus, the existence of a new department or activity and its cost are immediately disclosed, as is also the discontinuance of a department or activity.

Now I am fully aware of the fact that a large percentage of business organizations—and let's not forget that we are still talking about governmental, as well as private, business—are too small to warrant a clean-cut separation of every activity, that very often a single person may be found taking part in, or even having sole responsibility for, one or more activities. In such cases one must apply the rules of common sense and practicality. I'm not talking about splitting hairs.

To illustrate the application of activity classification and reporting to public affairs, I'll lift from my memory and experience an actual, though disguised, organization. We'll see how it was set up, how its expenditures were being reported, and how they are being reported on the activity basis.

The various jobs that this organization is charged with doing are divided between twelve bureaus. There are twelve operating "divisions," therefore, to use a common term for operating units of an organization. The office of the head of the organization is divided into three sections, one of which takes care of the organization's general administration, or housekeeping; the other two provide advisory services to the head of the organization. Thus the organization consists of sixteen main sub-organizations: the head man's office, the administrative unit, two service units, and twelve operating units; and each of these sub-organizations engages in at least three activities in the process of carrying out its main function.

All that the public ever saw of the cost of this organization—and it spent a lot of the taxpayers' money—was an over-all statement of its expenditures objectively classified, that is, showing how much was spent for salaries, how much for telephone service, how much for stationery, how much for traveling expenses, and so on. This appeared in the annual budget of the unit of government of which the organization was a part. There was nothing to show the cost of the sub-organizations, let alone the costs of activities.

It was sometimes amusing to see what happened when an inquisitive legislator got hold of the organization's budget requests and started asking questions. Invariably there would be a demand for a breakdown of expenditures by organizational units and activities. It took a lot of digging and no little fancy juggling to answer these questions without disclosing a lot of things the organization didn't want to disclose. The significant thing about this illustration at this point was the point of view of the management—the legislators, members of the board of directors. They wanted to know the costs of activities, but the books hadn't been kept that way. *They weren't responsive to the requirements of management.*

Well, what happened was the usual thing. The legislators finally got tired of being given the run around, and a change was ordered. Today the organization's books and financial reports show the cost of the head man's office, the cost of each section thereof, the cost of each operating division, and the cost of each activity of each of these sixteen units of the organization; and this showing is carried over into the organization's budget request. Hence, when anyone looks at the organization's financial reports or budget, he can see clearly what the structure of the organization is, what activities each organizational unit is engaged in, and what the cost of each activity is. Thus, if he is struck by the character or amount of any object of expenditure, he can appraise it in relation to the activity on which it was spent.

133

Incidentally, this piece of accounting surgery paid a handsome dividend. It led to a tremendous increase in the quality of the work done by this organization and an over-all reduction of 25 percent in the costs of doing it. It also led to the official demise of a gentleman who evidently regarded the holding of a position of high public trust as a warrant to make suckers of the people who have to pay the bill. It disclosed the fact that the head man enjoyed the luxury of an expensive chauffeur-driven automobile that served no purpose other than the satisfaction of his vanity and an exaggerated feeling of importance. Soon after this discovery the name on his door was changed. He was able to cover up this extravagance when there was no breakdown of expenses, but not so after activity accounting was adopted. Did someone say that accounting doesn't pay off? Or was it that accounting is just a "necessary evil"?

Finally, I think I should point out that the placing of emphasis upon the cost of activities runs counter to the hopes of those who seek uniformity of accounting and reporting, particularly the latter, and especially in government, by placing emphasis upon objects of expenditure. However, I do not think this need give anyone concern, because the kind of uniformity that is obtained by putting emphasis upon objects of expenditure was nothing but another commission of the old mistake, so often made, of making accounting an end in itself. The whole idea was doomed to failure from the start because it was a turning of the back upon the fundamental role of accounting for a purely self-serving bit of mechanics.

It is utterly fallacious to believe that anyone but the managers, and possibly the owners, of a small business could get any value out of statements of expenditures that show only the total cost of each kind of goods or services purchased, without regard to how the business covered by the statements is organized and in what activities it engages in order to accomplish its purposes. Such understanding certainly cannot be expected of legislators, who have little time from their legislative duties to gain first-hand acquaintance with such immense and complicated departments, bureaus, institutions, and other agencies of government as exist today. And, if we cannot expect such understanding of our elected representatives, what about us, the poor taxpayers?

The best citizen is one who is interested in his government. The most interested are those who know what is being done with their money. The only way to impart such knowledge is to publish the facts in a manner that clearly discloses the organization of the government—whether it be federal, state or local—the activities in which it is engaged, and their costs.

Let's remember that the products of the ingenuity and efforts of the accountant are not devised for the benefit of the profession; they are devised for the benefit of the owners and managers of business, whether it be public or private, and for the man on the street. If we fail to meet their requirements, we fail in our professional mission.

There is no such thing as uniformity in business organization and management or in human understanding. Instead there is *multiformity*. The requirements of multiformity are what we must meet if we are to have any hope of justifying ourselves.

FEDERAL GOVERNMENT
ACCOUNTING REFORMS:
THE HOOVER COMMISSION

BETTER ACCOUNTING, BETTER GOVERNMENT[†]

by

T. Coleman Andrews

CORPORATE private enterprises are required by edict to be launched in a goldfish bowl, and the business of many of them must be conducted without benefit of the privilege of privacy.

Such regulatory agencies as the Securities and Exchange Commission, the Interstate Commerce Commission, the Federal Power Commission, and the Federal Communications Commission were set up to assure, among other things, that those who do business that materially affects the general welfare do it in the open. The public must be "protected" from the "greedy capitalists," the "iniquities" of corporate finance, and the "evils" of the corporate form of organization generally.

Banks and insurance companies are rigidly regulated and closely watched and examined, the former by the Comptroller of the Currency, the Federal Deposit Insurance Corporation, the Federal Reserve Board and the state banking departments, the latter by the state insurance departments.

Precise bookkeeping and accounting, and "full disclosure" by the great industrial, commercial and financial enterprises of the country are required by law.

Thus the great organizations that have contributed so mightily to the high level of production and the high standard of living that the people have attained are held to a clear showing of faithful discharge of their social responsibility.

Incredible as it may seem, the Government, which now takes and spends not less than a fourth of the people's income, and is twice as large as the first fifty of the greatest corporations in the country, not only does not measure up to the standards of bookkeeping, accounting and disclosure that it requires of private enterprise; it does not even keep a complete set of books! And some of the accounts it gives of the levies it makes upon the people's wages are so inadequate as to be meaningless, if not misleading!

[†]Presented at the Middle Atlantic States Accounting Conference, Myrtle Beach, South Carolina, July 13, 1948. Reprinted with permission from the files of the American Institute of Certified Public Accountants. Portions of this presentation were published under the title, "Where It Goes, Nobody Knows; Some Astonishing Facts about Federal Bookkeeping," in *Tax Outlook*, September 1948, pp. 2-4, and reprinted in *The Virginia Accountant*, March 1949, pp. 14-16.

We shipped billions of dollars of lend-lease goods abroad before, during and after World War II. Some of it, at least, if not much of it, probably never will be conclusively accounted for. Whole convoys of it arrived in one theater with nothing to indicate its value and, therefore, with no basis for billing it to the recipient countries. The prices for the billing of some of these shipments had not been computed as late as a year ago, four years after the shipments were made.

Reconstruction Finance Corporation put billions into war plants that it could not completely account for. Some of these plants were disposed of as war surplus and passed beyond the Government's control without a conclusive accounting for the machinery and equipment that was put into them.

On July 2, 1947, it was announced that the fiscal year ended June 30, 1947 had been closed with a surplus of about three-quarters of a billion dollars. In arriving at this result, only those expenditures were taken into account for which settlement checks had been issued. To start out with, therefore, this statement was inconclusive by the aggregate amount of the checks that had been issued but not presented for payment before the end of the year. But this was not all, and apparently the amount involved was small in comparison with other omissions.

Vast amounts of expenditures by the military services during that year were not taken into account at all; they had not been reported to the Department that announced the surplus. Moreover, no adjustment was made for the expenditures for which checks had *not* been drawn at the beginning and end of the year.

The formula by which the reported surplus was arrived at, clearly did not take into account all the Government's expenditures for the year for which the surplus was claimed; the statement that this year had been closed with a surplus was based upon nothing more than a partial determination of receipts and disbursements.

Such is the degree of reliability, or rather unreliability, that attaches to one of the most important of the Government's annual financial reports to the people!

These deficiencies are merely examples of the inadequacy of the Government's accounting and financial reporting. Many others of equally significant amount and import could be cited if it were necessary to do so and the time available to me permitted.

It has been an amazing phenomenon of public administration at the national level, in this almost incredible country of ours, that the Government—the spender and consumer of so much of the fruits of the people's labor—apparently never has recognized the extent of its obligation to give public account of the money it takes from the people. This obligation is at least equal to the obligation it has imposed upon the enterprises through which so much of the wealth of the country has been produced.

Undoubtedly there is a reason for this paradox; but, whatever the reason is, it never has been clearly identified. Some say it is a carry-over from our royal ancestry of the philosophy that "the King can do no wrong"; therefore, it is not necessary for the King to account for the tribute exacted from his subjects; indeed, it is a part of his "divine right" to omit giving such an account.

This explanation must be rejected as being too imperious to warrant acceptance. Those revolters against royal rule who founded this country never would have been so inconsistent as to have done anything for a reason that was so clearly contrary to their fundamental determination to transfer power from the King to the people; nor is it likely that such inconsistency could be fairly charged to the succeeding generations of lawmakers.

Others suggest that perhaps the activities of the Government are so numerous, complex, and extensive as to be beyond the capacity of the known techniques of accounting and financial reporting. The experience of private enterprise completely refutes this theory.

Still others suggest that perhaps the accounting officers of the Government are not professionally equal to their responsibilities. This could not be true for at least two reasons: First, the Government has no accounting officer as such; no Federal office ever has been created whose holder is required to see that an appropriate plan of accounting is established for every activity in which the Government engages, that qualified persons are employed to carry out the plan, and that the accounting records are kept abreast of operating events; nor has any office ever been created whose holder is required to prepare and make available to the people complete and conclusive statements of, and reports on, the Government's financial affairs. Second, some of the ablest accountants in the country are on the Government's payroll.

Still others say that it is the result of lack of appreciation in Congress after Congress, and in administration after administration, of the need for and value of accounting. Those who hold this view remind us that accounting, after all, is not something that is universally understood and that it has been particularly difficult to envision the accounting needs of so vast and so complex an organization as the Federal Government, let alone the means by which these needs might be satisfied. I suspect that this is about the closest guess that anyone has made. In any event, the Government has fallen far short of discharging its accounting responsibility.

This is not to say, of course, that no one has made any constructive suggestions aimed at curing the deficiency, because some fine suggestions have been made by people both within and without the Government. But nothing substantial ever has been done; some minor improvements have been made, but the major operation has yet to be performed.

Fortunately, two highly authoritative groups have finally come to grips with the problem: First, the Comptroller General of the United States, the

Secretary of the Treasury, and the Director of the Bureau of the Budget have organized a group of their top technicians to tackle the problem from within. Second, the Commission on Organization of the Executive Branch of the Government, under the Chairmanship of former President Herbert Hoover, has organized a group of hand-picked public accountants to tackle it from without.

I am not familiar with the events leading up to the group established by the Comptroller General, the Secretary of the Treasury and the Director of the Bureau of the Budget, and the last thing that I would want to do would be to underestimate the part played by any one of these three distinguished officials in putting their group together. But I suspect that the Comptroller General had a lot to do with this movement and probably sparked it, I say this because ever since this eminent official determined to establish the Corporation Audits Division of the General Accounting Office as a professional accounting organization, he has shown a rapidly growing interest in modern accounting and the application of it to the affairs of the Government; and I am convinced that when he goes out of office, seven or eight years hence, he is going to leave behind him a record of unparalleled contributions to improvement of the handling of the Government's fiscal affairs.

Former President Hoover's zeal for efficient organization and management is well-known. His statement to the American Institute's Committee on Federal Government Accounting, when it began its study and the development of an accounting plan for the Government at his request, showed very clearly that he and his colleagues of the Commission appreciated the important part played by accounting in modern business affairs, that he had long since clearly identified the Government's accounting deficiencies and that the kind of report was wanted from our committee that we would be proud to submit. Naturally, we hope that we are going to be able to live up to the expectations of Mr. Hoover and the other members of his Commission.

The group set up by the Comptroller General of the United States, the Secretary of the Treasury and the Director of the Bureau of the Budget, and the group set up by the Hoover Commission, are working closely together in harmonious cooperation. They will come up with the answer. Nothing more than administrative action will be necessary in order to put some of their recommendations into effect. But the big changes will require Congressional action, since a lot of out-moded ideas about accountability and accounting, that are to be found in the law of the land, will have to be changed; and a lot of new laws will have to be enacted.

No Congress prior to the 79th appears to have recognized the importance and indispensability of accounting, but that Congress declared it to be a *sine qua non* of intelligent and efficient management and one of the management's major responsibilities; and the 80th Congress adopted the Lodge Bill that gave us the Commission on Organization of the Executive

Branch of the Government. The 81st Congress will have an opportunity to bring the Government's accounting and the character of its stewardship reports up to the level that imposes upon private enterprise.

I need not tell you, who are versed in the principles of accounting and skilled in the use of the techniques by which these principles are applied, that the job of developing a plan of accounting for the Federal Government is a tremendous one. Indeed, I am certain that even laymen would at least suspect this to be the case. Nor do I need to tell you that it would take far more than the time allotted to me for this address even to outline what is involved in this undertaking. However, I am sure you will be interested in some of the larger questions that have to be answered in the process of arriving at acceptable conclusions and reducing these conclusions to workable language.

One of the most interesting aspects of the problem is the fact that there are a great many questions of the most elementary nature that have to be answered. Indeed, it is rather surprising, and I suspect that to some it will be unbelievable, that some of these questions were not resolved long ago.

Perhaps the most fundamental of all questions is that of whether the Government should have a chief accounting officer. I believe that professional accountants generally would answer this question affirmatively, without feeling that there would be any necessity whatsoever to discuss it. But there are those who argue, by no means unconvincingly, that the present setup is adequate and that all that is needed is some clarification of the existing statutes. I do not expect that our group will go along with this point of view.

Involved in this question is the collateral one whether the Government's accounting should be centralized. Some say it should. The majority appears to hold the view not only that it should not be centralized but also that it cannot be. And so, you have on one side those who are for centralization and on the other those who are against it. In between there is a highly authoritative group whose members say that there should be centralized control and decentralized operation; and those who take this view generally urge it not as a matter of compromise but as a matter of conviction.

Another collateral question is that of what the title and rank of the chief accounting officer, if there is to be one, should be. Should he be called, as he most often is in private enterprise, the Comptroller of Comptroller General, or should he be called the Accountant General? This question immediately presents a conflict, because it would involve giving the chief accounting officer the title of an existing high officer and changing the title of the latter. It is argued that it would be realistic to take this course, because the officer who presently carries the title of Comptroller General of the United States primarily functions as an auditor, that his title should be more descriptive of his primary duty, and that the chief accounting officer should have the present Comptroller General's title because it would

143

be more descriptive of the accounting officer's primary duty. This presents difficulties, not the least of which is the fact that more than a quarter of a century of usage makes for a high degree of reluctance to adopt the more descriptive title of Auditor General.

Then on the question of rank, or of level at which the chief accounting officer should function, opinion seems to be divided all the way from strong conviction that such an officer should be a member of the cabinet to equally strong conviction that it would be sufficient for him to function at the second level of authority in an existing department or establishment.

These are exceedingly difficult questions to answer, and there isn't any single unqualified answer to any of them.

Then there is the all-important question of terminology. The present terminology is highly complicated and confusing, particularly as to expenditures, the several gradations of which tax the memory of those who work with them daily, utterly confuse many of the top administrative officers of the Government and many members of Congress, and defy the understanding of the layman.

The simple term "expenditure" is a classical example of the confusion of terms that has to be dealt with. As you well know, business people almost universally regard this term as connoting two actions: first, the purchase of something that usually is to be paid for by the disbursement of money; second, disbursement of the money; and accounting for things purchased is one thing, while accounting for cash, of which disbursement is a part, is another. Moreover, accounting for purchases usually is of more significance and usefulness to management than accounting for cash, which, after all, is an incidental aspect of spending and a relatively simple matter.

This is where the Government gets off the track; it uses the term only to demote money paid out; it overlooks the fact that it is just as important to account for the things for which money is exchanged as it is to account for money itself. And so, accounting for purchases receives scant, if any, attention. Accounting for money is important, but it is not all-important; it is only a part of the story.

This emphasis upon accounting for money and neglect of accounting for the things for which money is spent is one reason why the people, many members of Congress, and even some Government officials, become confused by the Government's accounting and financial reports. The solution is simple. Put the Government's accounting on the same basis as that used by the people who compose the Government. The Government is the one that will have to change, because it is the one that is deficient. It stands to reason that if this change were made the Government would be using terms and following a pattern of accounting with which the people would be familiar, and which, therefore, would result in financial reports that the people might understand.

This is but one of the many problems of terminology that confront us. Somehow or other we have to bring order out of the confusion and resulting obfuscation that are inherent in the vast array of terminological devices that have been adopted in order to establish and maintain accounting and financial control. Reduced to its simplest terms, what happens is that the Government takes our money and spends it. It is difficult to understand why, in order to establish and maintain desirable accounting and financial control over these activities, it is necessary to use such a highly complex and confusing array of terms as now confront the Congress, in carrying out its duty of controlling the purse strings of the Government, and the people, in their efforts to understand what is happening to the money they put up for carrying on their national affairs.

Then there is the question of financial responsibility for receipts and expenditures, particularly the latter. Who should be held responsible for the legality and integrity of expenditures? Under what circumstances should an illegal and improper expenditure be recovered? Who should enforce recovery of illegal and otherwise improper expenditures?

These are questions with which public accountants are probably more familiar than they are with any other in the Government's entire complex routine of accounting and financial control, since so many members of the profession served during the war in Government offices, defense plants and military services in capacities that brought them face to face with the difficult job of getting claims against the Government approved and paid.

Here again we are confronted with question whether the Government should go to the expense of attempting to maintain controls that the people who compose the Government regard as wasteful and extravagant and, therefore, would not tolerate in their private affairs—as involving, if you please, far more cost than the losses prevented thereby.

It is argued with unassailable logic that there is no reason whatsoever for the Government to try to avoid the ordinary risks of doing business that the people who compose the Government are ready and willing to take in the conduct of their private affairs, and which they do take with comparatively small risk. Those who take this view insist that it is nothing but wasteful purism to hold a contracting, certifying or disbursing officer responsible for anything other than nonfeasance, misfeasance, malfeasance or fraud. It seems unjust to hold an employee financially accountable for an honest mistake. Vast sums undoubtedly could be cut from the appropriation for administrative expenses if the Government could be induced to accept this point of view.

The foregoing are only a few of the many policy and technical questions as to which our group is expected to make recommendations. A number of the others are equally interesting, and I wish there were time to discuss them; but there isn't, so we must move on.

We hear a lot about world government and about our responsibility to exert ourselves to the utmost in order to bring it about. With its promise of universal brotherhood and peace, this is a consummation devoutly to be desired. It will be a great day when we may stand upon the pinnacle of peace achieved and look back upon the fulfillment of that prophecy so nobly and beautifully expressed by Tennyson, when he said: "Till the war drums throb no longer and the battle flags are furled in the parliament of man, the federation of the world." How wonderful indeed it is even to contemplate its fulfillment.

However, we cannot hope for this, and we cannot hope to be a strong influence in the establishment of world government, until we put our house in order. This is particularly true today when our influence is so great throughout the world, and when, as is true in all the affairs of man, we most assuredly are going to be judged more by our failures and sins than by our virtues.

I don't know of anyone who has put this more aptly than Virginia's Senator Harry F. Byrd, whom we from the Old Dominion admire and respect, and who, we have reason to believe, is generally admired and respected throughout the land as one of the country's most forthright statesmen. Here's the way he put it:

> The most sacred responsibility of every representative of the people in the halls of Congress is to keep America militarily strong, which means military superiority for the preservation of peace, and *at the same time* keep our Government sound and solid. Neither our own people nor those who seek our aid should ever forget that the might of America lies in this strength here at home—our fiscal solvency, our productive capacity under the free enterprise system, and our ability to finance our obligations without crushing taxation. Our financial stability is far more urgent for freedom in the world than any program of international subsidies that would severely strain our economy. Financial instability in the United States would serve the enemies of Democracy far more than any weapon that could be devised. By the same token, our financial soundness is the only hope for those who seek our help. Without it there would be no bulwark against Communism, and freedom could not survive here or elsewhere. If the fiscal stability of America weakens the whole civilized world will follow.

No one, least of all we accountants, who recognize the practicalities of business operations, may say that there is any magic in accounting, because, after all, it is only a means to an end. We may say, however, and it should not be at all difficult to prove by an overwhelming volume of evidence, that successful business operations are almost always characterized by good accounting.

This is so because accounting is the source of the facts as to the origin and use made of funds that are indispensable to intelligent organization and management of business affairs.

I say, therefore, that one thing that our Government must do in order to make itself sound and solid, as Senator Byrd put it, and thereby prepare itself for complete discharge of its world responsibilities, is put its accounting house in order.

In so doing, it will provide itself with the facts as to waste and inefficiency against which no incompetent or self-seeking official can long stand—before which he will sooner or later go down to the oblivion that he deserves. And so I say that the better the accounting, the sooner such unworthy wasters of the people's money will fall and a reasonable degree of economy will be achieved.

That there is waste and extravagance let there be no doubt, for no less an authority than the Comptroller General of the United States has said there is. He has said it over and over again; he is in a position to know whereof he speaks; and he is the kind of man that makes sure that he knows before he speaks. On no occasion did he say it more clearly or more pointedly than he did in the appearance he made at a hearing on the Congressional Reorganization Bill of 1946. This is the way he then put it:

> Our Government is in a mess, ... [a mess that] has been accumulating through administration after administration, Republican and Democratic alike, for years. ... The trouble is that we have developed an extravagant hodge-podge of duplication, inefficiency and inconsistencies. It is an ideal system for the tax eaters and those who wish to keep their snouts in the public trough, but it is bad for those who have to pay the bill.... The Government is full of zealous workers, *but the fact remains that many of them are working in bureaus or agencies that have no earthly reason for further existence.*

Yes, there is waste, there is extravagance, there is inefficiency, and there is duplication; and as surely as these unnecessary burdens upon the people's pocketbooks exist, just as surely will they be revealed in all their evil and certain danger to the continuity of our freedom, if and when the Government's accounting and financial reporting are appropriately revised. I am equally certain that clear revelation will bring positive corrective action.

I have always maintained, and I feel more strongly today than ever, that we accountants have a greater than average obligation of public duty because of the familiarity with the organization and management of business affairs that our daily professional experience gives us. I further feel, therefore, that we are particularly blessed with opportunity to contribute powerfully to the attainment of that destiny of man that a free society alone can bring. And I am happy that we may today honestly assert that our profession is fulfilling its obligation of public duty, that we are indeed contributing powerfully to the attainment of that destiny that is the hope of free men everywhere.

THE ACCOUNTING NEEDS OF THE FEDERAL GOVERNMENT[†]

Report of the Accounting Policy Committee
of the Fiscal, Budgeting and Accounting Project,
T. Coleman Andrews, Chairman

Note of Transmittal

Mr. John W. Hanes,
Director, Fiscal, Budget and Accounting Project,
Commission on Organization of the Executive Branch
    of the Government,
Washington 25, D. C.

Dear Mr. Hanes:

THE Accounting Policy Committee of the Fiscal, Budget, and Accounting Task Force, consisting of the writer as chairman and Messrs. Harry Howell, Edward A. Kracke, Maurice E. Peloubet, Weston Rankin, J. S. Seidman, and Donald F. Stewart, has completed its study of the accounting and auditing of the Federal Government and presents herewith its report. As you are aware, the writer and the other gentlemen named constitute the Committee on Federal Government Accounting of the American Institute of Accountants.

In accordance with the Commission's and your instructions, the Accounting Policy Committee directed its attention primarily to matters of principle and only incidentally to matters of procedure. Specifically, the scope of the undertaking of the Committee has been to determine upon and recommend such a plan of accounting and auditing as will assure, at reasonable costs:

[†]Reprinted representing Part Four, pp. 85-110, of *Fiscal, Budgeting, and Accounting Systems of Federal Government—A Report with Recommendations* prepared for the Commission on Organization of the Executive Branch of the Government (the "Hoover Commission") by John W. Hanes, A. E. Buck, and T. Coleman Andrews and published as Appendix F, *Task Force Report on Fiscal, Budgeting, and Accounting Activities,* to *Budgeting and Accounting—A Report to the Congress* by the Commission (Washington, DC: U.S. Government Printing Office, February 1949). The accounting-related recommendations of the Commission are also included in this report to Congress under the title "Reorganization of Accounting in the Government" and are reprinted in an appendix at the end of this volume.

(a) Ready and timely preparation and issuance of integrated summary financial reports by the Federal Government that will meet the managerial needs of the Executive Branch of the Government and the legislative needs of Congress and afford the people clear and understandable disclosure of the use made of the money they provide for the running of the Government.

(b) A sound basis for development of appropriate accounting (including internal control) and financial reporting within the numerous departments, establishments, agencies, and other organizations of the Government.

(c) Comprehensive auditing of all the accounts of the Government.

Respectfully yours,
T. COLEMAN ANDREWS,
Chairman.
October 21, 1948

ACCOUNTING POLICY

This report contains a number of recommendations. Some of these recommendations have been made before and are given our support because we believe that the interests of the people would be better served if they were adopted. Most of them challenge established and, in some cases, highly cherished traditions of the Executive Board of the Government or the Congress. All of them are aimed at producing a record that will tell promptly, clearly, and conclusively what happens to the money that the people put up for the running of their Government.

The deficiencies that prompted our conclusions and account for our recommendations as to accounting are numerous; but they all have the same root:

1. There is no formal accounting plan for the Government as a whole.
2. No one is charged with the duty of developing such a plan.
3. There is no one who would have power to install such a plan and compel compliance with its provisions if one were developed.
4. The statutes make no provision for either a complete accounting system or a chief accounting officer to direct accounting activities.

Hence, the shortcomings of the Government's accounting are traceable directly to inadequate statutory provisions for the accounting function. One of the most serious results of these deficiencies is that the accounting is not integrated. In spite of much duplication of account-keeping, a complete set of books is not kept anywhere.

Consequently, there is no place in the Government where the whole financial picture can be seen. Another result is that some of the accounts are not kept in accordance with principles whose observance would assure the recording of all essential information. Still another is that the accounts do not afford a ready basis for the preparation of complete, conclusive, and understandable financial reports.

An excellent statement of the objectives of accounting was expressed by the House Committee on Expenditures in the Executive Departments in its report of July 31, 1946—Report No. 2713 of the House of Representatives, Seventy-ninth Congress, second session—as follows:

> Adequacy of accounting implies the establishment of procedures that will assure timely, orderly, and accurate recording, in books of account, of all assets, liabilities, capital, income, and expense, not merely cash receipts and disbursements, and timely preparation of statements from the accounts that show how the corporation's capital is being employed and afford the directors and managers of the corporations and the Congress a clear basis for operating and policy decisions. The Committee recognizes that accounting is not the sole objective of administration, but it believes that the Congress has a right to expect the accounting of the Government's corporations to be equal to, if not better than, the best found in private corporations.

While this statement pertains to the accounting of the Government's corporations, it has general validity as a declaration of some of the important objectives of accounting; and it affords a basis for measuring how far short of required standards the Government's accounting falls.

Incidentally, the Government's standards of accounting and financial disclosure suffer greatly in comparison with those that the Government sets for others. In its regulation of private enterprises the Government not only requires full disclosure of financial transactions but also, in some cases, even imposes highly exacting requirements as to how these enterprises shall keep their books. Thus, there is quite a difference between the Government's own accounting and reporting and what it requires of the enterprises of the people who compose the Government.

Our recommendations as to auditing are, like those as to accounting, prompted by deficiencies that stem from faulty statutes. When the office of Comptroller General of the United States was created, it undoubtedly was intended that the holder of it should function as an independent auditor acting as an arm of Congress. However, the Comptroller General was given not only auditing duties but also accounting and other administrative duties that are inconsistent with his auditing duties in that they make him a party to administrative determinations and decisions of the Executive Branch of the Government that he must later review in his capacity as auditor.

Thus, the Comptroller General has been cast in a dual role. He is both a part of the Government's management and this management's auditor. He also is his own auditor. This involves the Comptroller General in the handling of matters that should be left to the sole discretion of the Executive Branch of the Government and makes it impossible for him to function with complete independence as the Nation's auditor. It also makes the General Accounting Office a party to much of the red tape that precludes prompt dispatch of the Government's business.

In addition, when the office of Comptroller General was created, the statute by which this was accomplished did not require that the holder of the office make audits of broad scope. It appears that as far as auditing was concerned, the framers of this statute apparently had nothing more in mind than that the Comptroller General should check expenditure vouchers in detail. At any rate, this appears to have been the construction put upon the law until World War II, when a broader concept was adopted for the auditing of certain types of war contracts.

Then, shortly before the close of the World War II, the making of "commercial-type" audits of the affairs of the Government corporations was instituted as required by the George bill and has been continued under the Government Corporation Control Act, by which the George bill soon was superseded. Specific statutory requirement that commercial-type audits be made of the departments and organizations other than corporations has not been adopted.

Pending the closing of this gap, it must be said that the Comptroller General's involvement in administrative matters that should be left entirely to the judgment of the Executive Branch of the Government, and the preoccupation of a large part of the Comptroller General's staff with detailed checking of expenditure documents, prevent full development of the potential usefulness of the General Accounting Office as the auditing and investigating agency of the Congress. These duties also prevent full development of the potential influence of Congress, acting through the Comptroller General, upon the promotion of economy, simplification, and prompt dispatch of business throughout the Government.

The principal fiscal officers of the Government are aware of the accounting shortcomings that we have stated, and an effort to correct them recently has been initiated. The Comptroller General has established in the General Accounting Office a new unit known as the Accounting Systems Division for the purpose of developing plans for putting the accounting of the numerous departments and other organizations on an appropriate basis; and he has been joined in this effort by the Secretary of the Treasury and the Director of the Bureau of the Budget. Together these three officers have assembled a group of top-grade technicians to work on the problem.

Thus, it appears that our findings as to accounting are largely confirmed by positive action initiated by the three foremost fiscal officers of the Government. However, as commendable as this action is, we are constrained to say that we do not believe that the shortcomings that we have stated can be satisfactorily overcome in this manner. Our reasons for this opinion are threefold.

First, it involves the Comptroller General still further in the acceptance and discharging of responsibilities that are clearly those of only the Executive Branch of the Government. Second, it is based upon voluntary cooperation between the organizations of the three officials named, and, being only a voluntary undertaking, it does not carry any guarantee of permanence. Correction of the present deficiencies cannot be made overnight. At best, it will be a process of accelerated evolution. It may never be accomplished if it is left to the uncertainties of official harmony. Third, we seriously doubt that a sufficient number of persons of the qualifications required for doing a thorough job of the Government's accounting and auditing can be obtained if these activities are not set up in the manner, and put under the kind of direction, that we shall recommend.

Following is a summary of our recommendations:

1. That a central accounting office be established under the direction of a chief accounting officer of the Government and that the status of this office be made that of an independent establishment in the Executive Office of the President.

2. That the duties of The Comptroller General of the United States be so redefined that there may be full realization of the potential usefulness of this officer as the Government's independent auditor and as the chief investigator for the committees of Congress, especially the appropriations committees; and that there also may be full realization of the potential influence of Congress, acting through the Comptroller General, upon the promotion of economy, simplification, and prompt dispatch of business throughout the Government.

3. That the proposed chief accounting officer be required and empowered to establish and maintain an accounting system appropriate to the Government's needs and to organize the accounting activity on the basis of centralized control and decentralized operation.

4. That the accounts be so kept that they will show currently, fully, and clearly the sources of the funds provided for the running of the Government and for what purposes these funds are spent; specifically, that the accounts be kept on the accrual basis.

5. That accounting terminology be adopted that is specific and free of double and multiple meaning.

6. That positive provision be made in the accounting system for separate accounting for funds that are subject to contractual obligations, restrictions, conditions, or other circumstances that make separate accounting necessary.

7. That accountable officers be relieved of financial liability for expenditures made contrary to law in all cases except those that result from gross negligence or fraud.

8. That the statutes that prescribe the present warrant system be repealed.

9. That the varieties of appropriations be reduced and that the practice of making authorizations to treat expenditures as public debt transactions, the practice of requiring expenditures to be "booked" in years other than those in which they occur, and the practice of writing substantive legislation into appropriation acts, be discontinued.

10. That the practice of attempting to restrict the amount spent for certain classes of expenses by placing limitations thereon in the appropriation acts be discontinued.

11. That the requirement that funds be requisitioned from the Treasury before they may be regarded as being available for disbursement be discontinued.

12. That a thorough study be made of disbursement policy, with particular reference to the fact that the disbursement function never has been completely taken over by the Treasury Department, and to the question whether it is necessary to permit any department to do its own disbursing.

13. That personnel policies be adopted that will assure the attraction and holding of the professional class of accountants and auditors that is necessary to proper carrying out of the Government's accounting and auditing activities.

The Government has been slow to adopt new developments in the field of accounting. Consequently, many of the deficiencies that our recommendations are designed to cure are of long standing. All of them go back beyond World War II and the depression period that preceded it. The manifold increases wrought in the annual budget and the national debt by these challenging misfortunes bring our accounting, auditing, and other fiscal shortcomings into bold relief and make immediate corrective measures imperative to the national welfare.

Before proceeding to the discussion of our recommendations we call attention to a matter of very serious import to both the Government and private business that we were not able to examine but which we recognize as a problem of large proportions. Most businesses are objects of one kind or another of auditing inquiry by Government examiners and investigators. A great number of these businesses are required to submit—some of them regularly—to separate inquiry by agents of several different departments.

Multiple audits are unduly annoying to those who have to endure them and unnecessarily costly to everyone concerned, including the Government. We urgently suggest that this problem be exhaustively studied, with the objective of finding a way, if possible, to make one audit serve all of the Government's needs.

COMMENTS

1. *Accountant General of the United States.*—The first step to be taken toward correction of the present situation is to draw a clear line of demarcation between accounting and auditing. The way to do this is to establish a central accounting office separate from the auditing office and the Treasury Department, head it by a chief accounting officer with undivided responsibility for accounting activities and with final authority in all accounting matters, and require this officer to establish and maintain a system of accounting and financial reporting appropriate to the Government's needs. We further recommend:

a.   That the status of the central accounting office be made that of an Independent establishment within the Executive Office of the President.

b.   That the central accounting officer be designated the Accountant General of the United States.

c.   That one of the qualifications of the Accountant General be that he be a professional accountant of the highest standing and attainments.

d.   That the Accountant General be appointed by the President with the concurrence of the Senate for a term of 15 years without the privilege of reappointment.

e.   That the salary of the Accountant General be not less than $25,000 per year.

We have recommended that a central accounting office be established, and that it be headed by a chief accounting officer with undivided responsibility for accounting activities and with final authority in all accounting matters, because we are convinced that this is what it will take to fill the void that lack of provision for an integrated accounting system makes in the Government's fiscal structure.

If there is to be any hope of developing and establishing an appropriate accounting system, whoever is charged with doing the job must be made free from all chance of being retarded or blocked by unreasoning devotion to tradition and stubborn unwillingness to adopt new ideas, concepts, and methods. He also must be put beyond the possibility of jurisdictional clashes with and between the several fiscal establishments. In short, he must be given a free and unfettered hand.

We are aware that there are those who hold that a new independent establishment should not be created, that there already are more such establishments than the President can possibly keep in touch with. To these we point out that, while the central accounting office would be a new establishment, it would not be engaged in a new activity. It would be engaged in an activity that is as old as the Government itself—one whose proper organization is long overdue.

Moreover, we suggest that a properly organized and directed central accounting office would be the source of information for the guidance of the President that would greatly lessen the time that he would have to devote to the other independent establishments if such information were not available.

We hold, as a matter of conviction, based upon our individual and collective observations and experience, in Government as well as outside of it, that a strong accounting department, set up at the right hand of the chief executive officer, is as necessary to the success of government as it is to the success of private enterprise.

We have recommended that the proposed chief accounting officer be called the Accountant General of the United States because this title would be clearly indicative of the duties of the person bearing it.

We have recommended that one of the qualifications of the Accountant General be that he be a professional accountant of the highest standing and attainments because this officer will have the biggest job of accounting to do that has ever been conceived. We do not subscribe to the idea that an office of this kind can be properly administered by merely a good executive. No executive, no matter how good he is, could fully discharge the duties of the Accountant General of the United States unless he were, in addition to being a good executive, a topnotch accountant.

An executive in this office who lacked the highest accounting qualifications could very easily fail to appreciate the significance of important technical problems and come to thoroughly unsound conclusions as to how these problems should be solved. No one would think of putting anyone but a lawyer at the head of the Department of Justice. It would be equally unthinkable to put anyone but an accountant at the head of the central accounting office.

We have recommended that the Accountant General be appointed for a period of 15 years without the privilege of reappointment because we deem continuity of tenure of office and maximum freedom from political influence to be of paramount importance. Accounting principles are not founded on political considerations; accounting is accounting no matter what the political complexion of the administration happens to be.

We have recommended that the Accountant General be paid not less than $25,000 per year because we regard this as little enough compensation to anyone who assumes and properly discharges the tremendous responsibilities of this office.

The central accounting office should be organized into four main divisions: One to develop accounting systems and procedures; a second to keep those accounts of the Government as a whole that would not be kept by the separate departments and other organizations; a third to receive the reports of the other departments and organizations, combine them with the reports prepared from the accounts kept by the central accounting office, and turn out the ultimate financial statements and reports necessary for the information of the Chief Executive, the Congress, and the people; the fourth, which might be called a field staff, to give the other departments and organizations such assistance as they might need in applying the accounting principles, and making the financial reports, prescribed by the Accountant General.

If it be not deemed feasible or desirable to establish the central accounting office as an independent establishment of the Government in the Executive Office of the President, the alternative would be to make it a division of the Treasury Department. If his establishment is thus located, the Accountant General should have the status of an Assistant Secretary of the Treasury responsible directly to the Secretary of the Treasury.

Assuming that the Treasury Department is to be otherwise continued as at present constituted, we would not favor giving it the central accounting office. Our reasons for this already have been indicated in the statement of our reasons for feeling that the central accounting office should be made a separate establishment in the Executive Office of the President. We also have a further reason, namely, that there always would be the chance of the Treasury Department's own accounting becoming intermingled and confused with that of the Government generally. This is happening today and is one of the reasons for the present unsatisfactory situation.

Therefore, if it should turn out that the central accounting office is located in the Treasury Department, it should be expressly provided that, as to its own accounting, the Treasury Department would be in exactly the same relationship to the central accounting office as every other department and organization of the Government.

Our objection to putting the central accounting office in the Treasury Department might be removed if this Department were stripped of all its nonfiscal functions and converted into a true department of finance, with the central accounting office as a principal subdivision thereof and the Accountant General an Assistant Secretary of the Treasury. There are strong precedents for this type of organization and we might regard it with favor if it were adopted in pure form.

2. *Auditor General of the United States.*—The office of Comptroller General of the United States is one of the most important in the government. Its potentialities as the independent auditing and investigating establishment of Congress, and as the medium through which Congress might influence the promotion of economy, simplification, and prompt dispatch of business throughout the Government, are incalculable. The following recommendations are designed to make full realization of these potentialities possible:

a. That the Comptroller General be relieved of all duties that make him a party to decisions and determinations other than those pertaining to the activities of his own office.

b. That the Comptroller General be required and empowered to broaden the scope of his activities by making commercial-type audits of all the departments and other organizations of the Government.

c. That the auditing of expenditure vouchers in detail by the Comptroller General be discontinued except in cases of gross negligence, fraud, or other circumstances that, in the opinion of the Comptroller General, make detailed examination necessary.

d. That all audits made by the Comptroller General be made on the spot in the offices of the departments and other organizations of the Government.

e. That the designation "The Comptroller General of the United States" be changed to the Auditor General of the United States and that the designation "General Accounting Office" be abolished.

f. That the qualifications and salary of the Auditor General be the same as those of the Accountant General.

We have recommended that the Comptroller General be relieved of all duties that make him a party to decisions and determinations other than those pertaining to the activities of his own office, because these are not proper duties for an independent auditor. When an independent auditor joins management in making determinations and decisions upon matters that he later must review as auditor, he gives up his independence and becomes merely a reviewer of his own acts. Therefore, he never should be required or permitted to share the responsibilities of management.

Accounting is one of the activities for which the Executive Branch of the Government should be held solely responsible but in which the Comptroller General's office nevertheless participates. In its report of July 31, 1946, heretofore cited, the House Committee on Expenditures in the Executive Departments had the following to say about where the responsibility for accounting lies and about the independent auditor's relationship to this activity:

> ... accounting is one of the most important responsibilities of management and it is the duty of auditors to review completed accounting data and no part of their duty to undertake accomplishment of the accounting function or otherwise relieve management of its responsibility therefor.

The usefulness of the Comptroller General's office would be vastly increased, and the full benefits of independent auditing would be realized, if the Comptroller General were relieved of all his present nonauditing duties and allowed to function solely as an independent auditor. The potentialities of his office as the investigating agency for the committees of Congress, particularly the appropriations committees, are enormous.

We have recommended that the Comptroller General be required and empowered to broaden the scope of his activities by making commercial-type audits of all the departments and other organizations of the

Government, because mere checking of the vouchers of these departments and organizations is not enough. The more comprehensive inquiry afforded by the commercial type of audit is as necessary in Government as its is in private enterprise.

The Congress already has required that commercial-type audits be made of the affairs of the Government's corporations, and the adequacy and usefulness of such audits for these corporations has been clearly demonstrated by the Corporation Audits Division of the General Accounting Office. Their use should now be extended to all the other departments and organizations of the Government. This is intended to include the proposed central accounting office. All of the Comptroller General's audits and reports then would be of the same comprehensiveness as those that he now prepares and submits concerning the Government corporations.

As the independent auditor of all the financial affairs of the Government, the Comptroller General also should be empowered and required to report faulty accounting wherever and whenever he encounters it. In addition, he should be empowered and required to report defective organization and poor management, to the extent of his and his staff's qualifications to appraise such deficiencies.

We have recommended that the checking of expenditure vouchers in detail by the Comptroller General be discontinued except in cases of gross negligence, fraud, or other circumstances that, in the opinion of the Comptroller General, make detailed examination necessary, because such checking by an independent auditor rarely is necessary except where there is doubt as to the integrity of the accounts or of those whose stewardship the accounts are supposed to reflect. Moreover, except in such cases, voucher examination of this scope by an independent auditor does not produce results commensurate with its cost. Detailed checking of expenditures is a duty of management and is provided for as a part of the system of internal control that is set up in developing the accounting system.

This is the way private business does it, and experience has shown that it is an unnecessary expense for independent auditors to duplicate this work except where such conditions as indicated above make it desirable or necessary. There is no reason whatsoever to believe that the Government's experience under a proper system of accounting would be different from that of private business.

We have recommended that all audits made by the Comptroller General be made on the spot in the offices of the department and other organizations of the Government, because the records to be audited are in these offices and can be reviewed on the spot with more facility and with greater understanding on the part of the auditors.

There is much more to auditing than mere checking of expenditures documents. In order to get the plus values of an audit, it is necessary that it be made by experienced auditors on the spot, where the workings of the

159

organization under audit can be observed in relation to what the books show.

Witness, for instance, the deplorable state of affairs found in the Reconstruction Finance Corporation, Federal Public Housing Administration, Commodity Credit Corporation, and other corporations, by the Corporation Audits Division of the General Accounting Office. In all these cases the conditions encountered had existed for years, but it took auditing of the broadest scope, as called for by the Government Corporation Control Act, to expose them and get something done about them.

The present requirements that expenditure vouchers and their supporting documents be sent to the General Accounting Office for checking involves a tremendous waste of paper. An even greater waste is involved in the amount of clerical services required for the handling and forwarding of these documents. The cost of transporting them to the General Accounting Office is tremendous. And a very costly storage problem is imposed upon the General Accounting Office. (We are told that the problem of housing voucher auditors and storing copies of expenditure documents were large and costly considerations in the planning of the new housing facilities recently approved for the General Accounting Office.)

Discontinuance of the requirement that the expenditure documents of the departments and other organizations of the Government be sent to the General Accounting Office for checking, and of detailed checking of these documents by the Comptroller General's staff, would greatly reduce the personnel, the housing requirements and, incidentally, the budget, of the General Accounting Office. Substantial savings and other benefits to the forwarding departments and other organizations also would ensue. There would be no reason to expect that this change would cause a material reduction of the amount presently being recovered on account of expenditures made contrary to law, if indeed it would cause any reduction at all.

We have recommended that the designation the "Comptroller General of the United States" be changed to the Auditor General of the United States, because the present designation is a misnomer; it indicates that the person who is so designated is the Government's accounting officer. The title "Auditor General of the United States" would make it clear that the person bearing it is the auditing officer of the Government. The designation "General Accounting Office" should be abolished, because it might be confused with the office of the Accountant General.

We have recommended that the Auditor General should have the same professional qualifications as the Accountant General and that he should be paid the same salary, because the two offices require holders of the same training and experience and impose responsibilities of substantially the same weight.

It is pointed out, however, that our decision to recommend that one of the qualifications of the Auditor General be that he be a professional accountant was not based upon any consideration of the present Comptroller General's performance of his duties; it was based solely upon what we regard as being necessary in order to give maximum assurance that each successive holder of the office will be qualified for the highly professional duties that he must perform.

Finally, we desire to stress the importance of timely and appropriate action upon the Auditor General's reports by Congress. Unless Congress acts promptly upon these reports, it cannot be expected that the Auditor General's audits will have the effect that they should have or that he will be as effective as he should be as the Nation's independent auditor.

The record indicates that many important reports of the Comptroller General to the Congress have not received the attention that they deserved or been acted upon as promptly as they should have been. Not a few of them have gone completely unheeded. The record further indicates that the Comptroller General has repeatedly reminded the Congress of this fact.

Without the backing that would be clearly implied by timely and appropriate action by the Congress upon his reports, the Auditor General could not hope that his office would rise above a minimum of usefulness, no matter how faithfully and efficiently he might manage it.

3. *Basic Elements of the Accounting System.*—The number, dissimilarity and geographical dispersion of the Government's activities make centralization of the Government's accounting impractical. However, it is not only practicable but necessary that this activity be centrally controlled. The basic structure of the accounting activity, therefore, must be one that would provide centralized control and decentralized operation.

On this basis, control would be exercised by the central accounting office, and each department and other organization would keep such accounts as would be necessary for its own purposes and would make periodic reports to the central accounting office. These reports would be in such form that they, along with the reports of the other departments and organizations, could be readily combined to produce reports that would embrace all the activities of the Government in a form that would be useful and informative to the Chief Executive, the Congress, and the people.

There will be some accounts pertaining to the Government as a whole whose keeping could not be decentralized. These accounts would be kept in the central accounting office, appropriate reports would be drawn therefrom, and they would be combined with the reports of all other departments and organizations in making up the over-all reports just mentioned.

As heretofore indicated, it would be one of the duties of the Accountant General to specify the principles of accounting that should be observed by the departments and other organizations in keeping their accounts, and to assist these establishments with the setting up and keeping of their accounts in accordance with these principles. It also would be a duty of the Accountant General to prescribe the form in which the departments and other organizations should prepare their reports to the central accounting office.

Strict compliance with the requirement of the central accounting office by the departments and other organizations, both as to the application of accounting principles and as to the preparation of their reports to the central accounting office, obviously would be essential to the success of the accounting plan. To assure such compliance, it would be desirable and perhaps necessary to give the Accountant General power to enforce his requirements as to the accounting principles to be applied, and as to the reports to be rendered to the central accounting office, by the other departments and organizations.

The accounting of the departments and other organizations, therefore, would be of the utmost importance. Consequently, it would be necessary to put this accounting under the direction of personnel no less qualified professionally, though not necessarily of the same professional attainments, as those charged with the direction of the central accounting office activities. Therefore, we recommend:

a.   That each department and other organization have a controller professionally qualified to discharge the duties of his office.

b.   That he function not only as the accounting officer of his organization but also as its budget officer.

c.   That he be given a permanent appointment, subject, of course, to satisfactory conduct and performance of his duties.

d.   That his salary be made commensurate with the responsibilities that he is required to assume and discharge.

Our recommendation that the accounting officers of the departments and other organizations of the Government function also as their organizations' budget officers is designed to take full advantage of the accounting officers' training and experience. No person should be made the controller of any department who has not successfully managed extensive accounting activities. Such a person will have had intimate contact with the problems of management and ordinarily will have developed comprehensive understanding of managerial policies and operating needs.

Moreover, since the budget is expressed largely in accounting terms, the budget classifications of revenue and appropriations should coincide with the accounting classifications of these elements. Therefore, successful budgetary control of revenues and expenditures is largely dependent upon the appropriateness, adequacy, and accuracy of accounting.

Lack of coordination between accounting and budget administration is one of the most serious defects of the present fiscal situation. We are convinced that a long step toward curing this deficiency would be taken by making the departmental controllers not only the accounting officers but also the budget officers of their organizations.

We believe that the reasons for our other recommendations concerning the departmental controllers are sufficiently obvious to make a statement of them unnecessary.

4. *Basis of Accounting.*—Next in importance to the establishment of an appropriate accounting system and the responsibility therefor is determination of the basis upon which the Government's accounts shall be kept.

There are two bases of accounting. One is the cash basis, the other the accrual basis. The cash basis amounts to little more than the recording of receipts and disbursements. When used in the keeping of governmental books, the cash basis produces little more than an account of revenues collected and money paid out.

Under the accrual basis, income is taken into account when it is earned, and expenditures are taken into account when they are made. Thus, to state it simply, when the accrual basis is used in governmental accounting, revenues are taken into account and put under control when they are assessed or otherwise formally established, controls of expendable supplies, and the investment therein are maintained, and expenses are taken into account as they are incurred. On the budgetary side, the accrual basis affords full current information concerning the realization of the revenue estimates and the expenditure and availability of appropriations.

In government, control of appropriations is especially important. In order to control the use and prevent overexpenditure of appropriations, it is necessary that the available balance of each appropriation account be known at all times. The available balance of an appropriation is the difference between the amount appropriated and the sum of the amounts already withdrawn from it and the amounts that will be withdrawn in settlement of expenditures that have not yet reached the disbursement stage. Therefore, if overexpenditure of an appropriation account is to be prevented, it is necessary that outstanding commitments against the appropriation be known as well as the amounts already paid out in settlement of commitments.

Thus, in budgetary accounting, expenditure occurs when a commitment to buy something is made, and it is imperative that the appropriation accounts be charged at this time. If this is done, the available balance of every appropriation account will be known at all times. If it is not done, commitments might easily be made against appropriations that already have been exhausted.

If something purchased is not immediately consumed when it is received, further accounting usually becomes necessary. To illustrate, if a commitment is made to purchase supplies that may last for considerable time, expense is incurred not at the time that the supplies are received, but later, as they are consumed. For instance, if several months' supply of coal is purchased and received during one fiscal year but will not be completely consumed until the next fiscal year, it would be improper to charge all of

163

the cost of the coal as expense of the year in which it is purchased and received.

Thus, accounting for the expenditure of appropriations is one thing and accounting for the incurrence of expenses is another. But both are necessary, the former to control the consumption of appropriations, the latter to control, among other things, the evil of year end rushing to spend surplus balances of appropriations and the investment in supply inventories as well.

Refinements of accounting such as have been explained above are not afforded by the cash basis of accounting. The Government's accounting is a mixture of the cash basis of accounting and the accrual basis, but it does not include supply accounting.

We think it is obvious that a basis of accounting that never shows the Government's true revenues and expenses for any year, and that does not provide positive control of assets, liabilities, and appropriations, is thoroughly inappropriate to the Government's needs. We suggest, therefore, that the cash basis of accounting be completely ruled out and that the accrual basis be adopted for all of the Government's accounting.

Set up on the accrual basis, the books would show not just cash receipts and disbursements but all essential facts concerning the financial affairs of the Government—assets, liabilities, revenues, the extent to which the budget estimates of the revenues have been realized, appropriations, the rate at which the appropriations have been spent, the true available balance of each appropriation, and the accumulated costs of operation.

Thus, positive control of assets, liabilities, estimates of incomes, appropriations, revenues, and expenses would be maintained, and all data required for the preparation of the regular financial reports would be readily available so that these reports could be prepared as a matter of routine in sufficient time for their contents to be of managerial as well as historical value.

We cannot too strongly urge the establishment of an appropriate integrated system of accounting kept on the accrual basis. If such a system is not adopted, there can be no hope that the Congress ever will be clearly enough informed concerning the financial affairs of the Government to be able to exercise fully intelligent control of the Government's "purse strings."

We say this because Congress obviously must depend upon financial reports as the source of information for its guidance in determining the financial needs of the numerous departments and other organizations, and such reports simply cannot be obtained unless and until an appropriate integrated accounting system is established and maintained.

It is obvious that some of the present financial reports that are prepared for the information and guidance of Congress and others are ponderous, obfuscated and generally unsatisfactory. This is especially true of the budget document.   Some of them are even misleading, though not intentionally so.

For confirmation of this estimate of the principal financial reports, one has only to see the difficulty, as we have seen it at first hand, that members of Congress, even members of the appropriations committees, are trying to understand some of the statements with which they have to work.   Requests for supplemental information and reports are numerous.   An incalculable amount of time is spent by the fiscal departments complying with these requests.   As a result, the routine operations of the fiscal departments are seriously upset.

The reason for all this is that the Government's accounting system simply does not lend itself to preparation of the kind of financial reports that Congress, the people and the administration ought to have.   A proper set of books, accurately kept, would make all such reports more useful; it would make them available more promptly; and it would permit the fiscal departments to function without undue interruption for the preparation of supplemental information.

More important than all this, if Congress were given the right sort of information in the first place, it could approach and dispose of the budget with less annoyance and with freedom from the pressure that having to wait for supplemental information imposes.

5.   *Terminology.*—There is pressing need for adoption of accounting terminology that gives every term the same meaning wherever used.   This would be done as a matter of course as a first step toward the development of an appropriate system of accounting by the Comptroller General, and, therefore, need not be discussed in detail.   We mention it here only to emphasize the need for it, and, to illustrate this need, we call attention to the confusion that surrounds the use of the simple term "expenditure."

As presently used in the Government, the term "expenditure" may mean any one of several things, including the very limited and unusual, if not surprising, connotation that it is the amount paid out in settlement of checks drawn.   In private business this term has definite meaning; the same may be said of it as used in the field of public administration outside the Federal Government.   Obviously, it would be helpful if it were defined by the Government to mean what it means in the administration of public affairs generally; but the important thing is that the Government give it a specific and single definition so that when it is used everyone will know just what it means.

The Government's accounting terminology is characterized not only by other multiple connotations such as this but also by other terminology that is of both obscure and confusing meaning.   This can and should be corrected.

6. *Fund Accounting.*—The accounting of government is characterized by recognition of circumstances and conditions that create fiscal entities known as "funds." In the Federal Government, for instance, there are, among others, the general fund and numerous trust funds.

The National Committee on Governmental Accounting defines a fund as:

> A sum of money or other resources (gross or net) set aside for the purpose carrying on specific activities or attainting certain objectives in accordance with special regulations, restrictions, or limitations and constituting an independent fiscal and accounting entity.

In the keeping of its books, the Federal Government does not give full effect to the necessity for separate accounting for individual funds. It is intended that appropriate recognition of all necessary fund distinctions should be incorporated in the plan of accounting that we have recommended.

7. *Financial Liability of Accountable Officers.*—There are presently on the statute books a great variety of what are known as prohibitory statutes. The compilation of these statutes makes a sizeable volume. Certain officers of the Government known as accountable officers are charged with knowledge of these statutes and are held financially liable for violations of them even though violations may be the result of nothing more than ignorance or poor judgment, sometimes even when the officer held liable does not make the mistake that constitutes the initial violation.

The Comptroller General reports such violations in great detail and volume, but the usual action of Congress is to pass bills waiving the offenders' liabilities. As a matter of fact, the amount or aggregate of such violations usually is of such proportions that recovery is out of the question and the waiving of liability is the only practical way out.

Vast sums of money are spent in checking vouchers for exceptions, in compiling these exceptions as the basis for claims against the accountable officers, and in interminable conferences in which the alleged violators are confronted with their transgressions and heard in justification of their actions. Many of these claims are eventually dropped by the auditors, and the amount recovered on those that are not dropped is of relatively insignificant amount.

As a result of all this procedure—and the policy of the Congress as to recoveries, with which we by no means disagree—it is generally and freely said throughout the Government that, if you're going to make a mistake, make a big one, one too big for the Government to do anything about.

It appears, therefore, that there is little practical value to the policy of holding the accountable officers financially liable for violations of the prohibitory statutes except where gross negligence or fraud is involved. In any event, it seems clear that the amount actually recovered in cases where these elements are not involved is relatively small in proportion to what it costs to develop such cases. Moreover, it seems to us that it is harsh and unfair to the accountable officers to hold them liable in cases where they have acted in good faith and shown reasonable diligence. Besides, to do so is completely contrary to the practice of private business and has the tendency to stifle initiative and put a brake upon efficiency.

We feel that the Government should be willing to take the same risks in conducting its affairs that the people who constitute the Government are willing to take in conducting their private affairs. Moreover, we believe that adoption of this policy would encourage the Government's officers and employees to show more initiative in the discharge of their duties and thereby not only speed the dispatch of the Government's business but also promote economy.

While it may be argued that the present statutes have a deterrent effect, we are convinced that they deter those qualities of management that make for economy and efficiency to a very much greater extent that they deter possible inclinations toward waste and extravagance, so that in the long run they cost the Government far more than they save.

Accordingly, we recommend that the accountable officers be relieved of financial liability in all cases except those that arise from gross negligence or fraud.

8. *The Warrant System.*—The traditional formality of issuing "warrants" as the basis for the recording of receipts, appropriations, accountability of disbursing officers, and other factors in the accounting process is a part of the Government's present accounting procedures. While the warrant system may have had its place in the early development of governmental accounting, later developments in this field rendered it obsolete.

Everything that this system accomplishes now is accomplished without such formality, as a routine part of the system of internal control that is a feature of all modern accounting plans. Therefore, it would be unnecessary to continue this system under such a plan of accounting as we have recommended. To incorporate it in such a plan would be to require a lot of unnecessary paper work and cause those responsible for accounting to go through a lot of motions that would not accomplish any worth-while result.

Moreover, this is one of the points at which the Comptroller General is injected into participation in matters that should be left to the Executive Branch of the Government, since all warrants are required to be submitted to him for review and approval. Obviously, this makes the Comptroller General jointly responsible with the administration for determinations and decisions as to matters which he later must review as the Government's independent auditor.

We recommend, therefore, that the warrant system be abolished.

9. *Appropriations.*—The Bureau of the Budget and the appropriations system were studied by another group. Therefore, we will not make extensive recommendations concerning either. We will make only such recommendations as pertain to accounting and the integrity of the appropriation and expense accounts or that observance of sound financial principles require.

There are, in our opinion, too many varieties of appropriations. We suggest, therefore, that consideration be given to reducing substantially the number of kinds of appropriations. This would greatly simplify the accounting and would make the budget reports more readily understandable.

We also respectfully suggest that authorizations to treat expenditures as public debt transactions are, in effect, detours around the constitutional prohibition against payment of money out of the Treasury except in consequence of an appropriation and that the practice of giving such authorizations weakens congressional as well as administrative control of expenditures.

We also respectfully suggest that the occasional practice of requiring expenditures to be "booked" in years other than those in which they occur be discontinued. This practice casts doubt upon the integrity of the Government's accounting.

We further respectfully suggest that the practice of writing substantive legislation into appropriation acts be discontinued.

10. *Expense Limitations.*—For a number of years Congress has sought to restrict the amounts spent for certain classes of expenses by placing limitations thereon in the appropriate acts. In most cases the amounts involved have been insignificant.

This practice makes unnecessary bookkeeping. In addition, it hamstrings the administrators of the appropriations and leads either to the development of an attitude of fear and frustration and eventually inertia, or prompts the concoction of schemes to find ways to get around the restrictions. So-called "administrative expenses" are a typical example.

It is a common practice to place limitations upon the amount expendable for this class of expense; but no one has ever defined what the term "administrative expense" means. As a result, the restriction has been circumvented time and again by the simple and naturally suggested process of deceptive classification. It has even led to the absurd expedient of inventing the term "nonadministrative expenses."

We respectfully suggest that expenditures cannot be effectively controlled by employment of the expense-limitation device. In the evolution of public administration, experience has shown that the most effective way to control expenditure is to:

a. Make appropriations on the functional basis, that is, for programs, projects and activities.

b.   Hold the spending officials responsible for keeping within the total amounts provided for the separate programs, projects, and activities, but give these officials opportunity to discharge their duties free of depressing and frustrating restrictions based upon the theory that they are not to be trusted until they demonstrate the contrary.

c.   Give the spending officials the help of an accounting system that will call for the keeping of an account for the appropriation made for each program, project, and activity and for procedures that will assure thorough preauditing and proper classification of all charges to the appropriation accounts.

d.   Provide effective independent postauditing, with reports of violations to the legislative body.

e.   Establish a legislative committee that will take timely and effective action upon all reported violations.

It is respectfully suggested that an expense limitation in an appropriation act is a poor substitute for such a plan as that stated above.

11. *Requisition of Funds.*—The law presently requires that funds be requisitioned from the Treasury before they may be regarded as being available for disbursement. Stated simply, this requirement is based upon the concept that it is necessary to keep a separate bank account for each appropriation in order to keep the appropriation from being overspent. This concept is at once one of the fallacies and one of the serious deficiencies of the Government's present accounting system.

In governmental accounting, prevention of the overspending of an appropriation is accomplished by reference to the appropriation account itself, not to the amount of cash on hand. Where the public Treasurer is empowered to provide sufficient funds to meet the appropriations, as is true in the case of the Federal Government, there is no need whatsoever to maintain a cash or deposit account for each appropriation. The important thing is to charge the head of each department and other organization of the Government with the duty of seeing that no appropriation account of his organization is overspent. A proper accounting system under the direction of a qualified departmental controller would make this an easy requirement to meet.

It should be the job of the disbursing officers to pay the vouchers that are approved and certified by the accounting and budget officers as to the availability of the appropriations against which they were charged. Disbursing officers should not be required to assume any part of the responsibility for controlling the expenditure of appropriations.

12. *Disbursement of Funds.*—Certain regular departments and agencies of the Government do their own disbursing, among which are the Armed Services and the United States marshals. We wonder whether this is either necessary or desirable.

We were unable to go into this matter in sufficient detail to justify a definite recommendation concerning it. However, we are of the opinion that the Treasury Department should do all disbursing except under circumstances that make delegation of this function necessary, such as geographical remoteness of an agency from a disbursing center or the need of a business-type activity to do its own disbursing in order to operate on the commercial basis on which it is expected to do business.

We feel that, in general, wherever it is necessary that the disbursing function be carried on within a department or other noncommercial organization, it would be better if the Treasury Department established a disbursing unit in that department or organization.

13. *Accounting Personnel.*—It is obvious, we think that direction of the accounting activities of an organization of such vast proportions and varied activities as those of the Federal Government call for a nucleus of professionally qualified accountants. As heretofore indicated, such personnel will be needed at the departmental level as well as at the central accounting office. The Comptroller (Auditor) General will have need of similar personnel, but he already has a large professional group in his Corporation Audits Division and a good start toward the development of a similar group in his Accounting Systems Division.

On the accounting side, the number of professional personnel will be small in relation to the total staff required, since the handling of most of the accounting detail can be reduced to relatively simple routines. However, the success of the entire accounting activity will depend upon the competence of this relatively small group.

On the auditing side, almost the entire staff, with the exception of administrative personnel, would have to be either experienced professional accountants or men trained for professional accounting careers, such as are now on the present staffs of the Corporation Audits Division and the Accounting Systems Division of the General Accounting Office.

As much as we dislike to have to say so, the plain simple fact is that the Government's civil service is not now attractive to anywhere near enough people of ambition and outstanding competence. This is particularly true of people in the professional fields. The Government cannot hope to attract the kind of professional people it should have unless and until it makes its civil service attractive to such people.

If there is to be any hope of attracting and holding the kind of people needed to direct and manage a real accounting and auditing set-up, the civil-service classification of accountants and auditors must be overhauled and revised to limit classification as accountants and auditors to those who really are accountants and auditors; adequate compensation must be offered;

policies that will assure prompt recognition of outstanding ability must be established; and, in general, policies must be adopted that will enable the Government to compete for such talent with private business, where most of it now is seeking and finding employment.

Respectfully submitted,
T. COLEMAN ANDREWS, Chairman,
Harry E. Howell,
Edward A. Kracke,
Maurice E. Peloubet,
Weston Rankin,
J. S. Seidman,
Donald F. Stewart.
October 20, 1948

HOOVER COMMISSION DISAGREES ON CHANGES IN GOVERNMENT ACCOUNTING[†]

by

T. Coleman Andrews

THE Hoover Commission[1] has made its recommendation to Congress on how accounting in the federal government ought to be reorganized. These recommendations, as finally made, differed substantially from the report of the Accounting Policy Committee[2] which was assigned the task of investigation and recommendation. Seven members of the Commission, including Mr. Hoover, voted not to accept the Committee's recommendations; Dean Acheson agreed in principle with the Committee, but thought legislation giving effect to these principles impracticable at this time; Commissioners McClellan and Manasco disagreed with the Committee in favor of the status quo; Commissioners Pollock and Rowe agreed with the Committee and disagreed with the other ten members of the Commission. The seriousness of this situation is suggested by the fact that

---

[†]Reprinted with permission from *The Journal of Accountancy*, March 1949, pp. 192-199. This article was also published in the *Accounting Seminar*, May 1949, pp. 17-23.

[1]The Commission on Organization of the Executive Branch of the Government.

[2]The Accounting Policy Committee, a part of the Task Force on Fiscal, Budgeting, and Accounting Activities (one of the Hoover Commission's task forces), is composed of members of the Committee on Federal Government Accounting of the American Institute of Accountants.

The members of this committee made their services available to the Commission without compensation as the certified public accountants' contribution to the work of the Commission. Each of the members of this committee is a certified public accountant of wide experience in public practice. Each of them has had extensive experience in the executive branch of the government. The committee's chairman is T. Coleman Andrews, author of the article. Other members of the committee are Harry E. Howell, who is a prominent authority on cost accounting and administrator of UNRRA; Edward A. Kracke, of Haskins & Sells, New York, chairman of the institute's committee on cooperation with Congressional Appropriations Committees which has been very active in analyzing the accounts of certain federal agencies to aid Congress in fiscal planning; Maurice E. Peloubet, of Pogson, Peloubet & Co., New York, a recognized authority on military procurement accounting and editor of a department in *The Journal* on that subject; J. S. Seidman, of Seidman & Seidman, well known accountant and tax practitioner; Weston Rankin of Price, Waterhouse & Co., New York; and Donald F. Stewart, Savannah, Georgia.

this is the first time the Commission has split so widely on any of its proposals on reorganization of the executive branch of the government.

Of present government accounting, the Commission says "The complicated checks and balances employed make for unnecessary inefficiency in every activity, and one of the very first steps toward economy in government operations lies in improving the accounting system. Over the past several years, private business has developed a number of new accounting methods and devices, many of which should be adapted to governmental operations. The situation has not gone unrecognized. Members of the Congress and the executive brand have repeatedly protested at many of the worst features of present budgeting and accounting practices."

The Commission's report points out that accounting must serve the government as a tool in day-to-day management of administrative affairs of the government. Accounting reveals the status of appropriations, the extent to which revenue estimates are realized, the progress of actual expenditures and collections, and comparative operating costs. It provides the basis for summary financial reports which the executive branch sends to the Congress and which are printed for public information. Accounting provides for the fixing of responsibility in the handling of government funds, thus enabling a check of administrative competence and fidelity.

The development of a complete and up-to-date system of accounting for the government comprehends both the fiscal or general accounts and the administrative or departmental accounts. All these systems of accounts, says the Commission, should be prescribed by the same authority in order to have an integrated system. With some prescribed by the Treasury, some by the departments, and others by the Comptroller General, it has not been possible during the last 27 years since the Budget and Accounting Act was passed to work out a satisfactory system. This is how the Commission sums up the present state of federal accounting.

Certain voluntary efforts have been made in the direction of integrating accounting activities and bringing together the Treasury, the Comptroller General, and the Bureau of the Budget. The Hoover Commission says these efforts are in the right direction, but it feels that more than voluntary correctives are needed. A definite system should be established and given more permanence through legislation and organization. The voluntary work already started would be greatly aided, it says, if positive action were taken to establish a responsible official with authority to give continuous motive force to reform in accounting. Since accounting is primarily the responsibility of the Executive Branch, the Commission recommends that "An Accountant General be established under the Secretary of the Treasury with authority to prescribe general accounting methods and enforce accounting procedures. These methods and procedures should be subject to the approval of the Comptroller General within the powers now conferred upon him by the Congress." He "should on a report basis

174

combine agency accounts into the summary accounts of the government and produce financial reports for the information of the Chief Executive, the Congress, and the public."

Thus would be created a single officer of the Treasury with authority to prescribe a single system of fiscal accounts and to represent the Executive Branch in working out an administrative accounting system with the Comptroller General. The Accountant General would further supervise all departmental accounting activities throughout the Executive Branch, and assist departments in performing their accounting duties.

The Commission believes that there is no inherent conflict between the present position of the Comptroller General and their recommendation to create the position of Accountant General.

Section 305 of the Budget and Accounting Act of 1921 has been variously interpreted over a period of years, but under present interpretation, administrative agencies of the Executive Branch are required to submit all expenditure vouchers and supporting documents for every individual transaction to the General Accounting Office for examination and settlement. This is a costly system. It means freight carloads of vouchers from all over the United States hauled to Washington for individual examination in the General Accounting Office. "New arrangements should be made for the examination of vouchers at points mutually agreeable to the Comptroller General and the department heads concerned," says the Commission, and it recommends "that the practice of sending millions of expenditure vouchers and supporting papers to Washington be stopped as far as possible." The Commission further points out that the Comptroller General must obviously continue to determine the adequacy and integrity of administrative fiscal practices to check and make certain that laws governing appropriations are being properly interpreted, to check the efficiency of accounting and other administrative arrangements and to report on these matters to Congress. Therefore the Commission recommends further that "in view of the fantastic growth of detail that a spot sampling process at various places where the expenditure vouchers and papers are administratively checked might be substituted for much of the present procedure of bringing all these documents to Washington."

This recommendation is not intended to weaken legislative control over expenditures, but (1) to free the General Accounting Office from the overwhelming burden of paper work required of the Executive Branch, and (2) to simplify the work of executive agencies in handling expenditure transactions which must be settled by the General Accounting Office.

The Hoover Commission endorses the recommendations of the Accounting Policy Committee that:

(1) The accrual basis of accounting should be applied to both revenues and expenditures.

(2) Simplification or elimination of the present warrant system is necessary.

(3) Uniform departmental practices, procedures, nomenclature, inventory, and public debt accounting are needed, all of which would reduce staff and red tape.

At present 558,000 accountable officers are required to pay from their own pockets for surety bonds provided by private companies at an aggregate annual premium of $2,000,000. Recoveries from these policies average about $230,000 annually. The Commission, endorsing another Task Force recommendation, believes this problem could be solved by the establishment of a fidelity insurance fund in the Treasury to which accountable officers would be required to contribute. The Commission recommends that the Congress continue to study this question in an effort to arrive at a simpler and less expensive procedure.

The foregoing summary covers briefly the recommendations of the Hoover Commission to Congress based upon the vote of seven of the twelve members of the Commission including Mr. Hoover. The foregoing recommendations differ in several important respects from the recommendation to the Commission by the Accounting Policy Committee. Commissioners John L. McClellan and Carter Manasco disagreed with the majority in favor of the status quo. These Commissioners opposed the appointment of an Accountant General, feeling that the Commission has gone afield of its jurisdiction in making recommendations and attempting to change an agency of the Congress. They feel that to follow the report of the majority would be to strip an agency of Congress of effective authority over accounting systems, and they point out that it was on this point that the Reorganization Program of 1937 was defeated. They believe the majority of the Commission is in error in assuming that the Comptroller General has authority only with respect to appropriation and fund accounts and not with respect to property accounts and cost accounts. "The majority's recommendations," say these two Commissioners, "would weaken the participation of the Comptroller General in the development of accounting systems to the point where he would have no authority to require anything." If there is to be any change in basic jurisdiction to prescribe accounting systems, these two Commissioners believe it should be in the direction of strengthening the hand of the Comptroller General.

The vice-chairman of the Commission, Dean Acheson, agrees in principle with the recommendations of the Accounting Policy Committee but believes the present situation of the government is so complex that an attempt to apply the principle to definite legislation would raise almost insoluble jurisdictional questions and would not achieve desired results. He further feels that such changes are not necessary at the present time.

The recommendations of the Accounting Policy Committee were concurred in by Commissioners Pollock and Rowe. In an appendix to the

Commission's report, they expressed general agreement with the committee's recommendations.

Statements of the dissenting Commissioners are published with the text of the report. They make fascinating reading for students of government accounting.

RECOMMENDATIONS OF POLICY COMMITTEE

1.   That a central accounting office be established under the direction of a chief accounting officer of the government and that the status of this office be made that of an independent establishment in the Executive Office of the President.

2.   That the duties of the Comptroller General of the United States be so redefined that there may be full realization of the potential usefulness of this officer as the government's independent auditor and as the chief investigator for the committees of Congress, especially the appropriations committees; and that there also may be full realization of the potential influence of Congress, acting through the Comptroller General, upon the promotion of economy, simplification, and prompt dispatch of business throughout the government.

3.   That the proposed chief accounting officer be required and empowered to establish and maintain an accounting system appropriate to the government's needs and to organize the accounting activity on the basis of centralized control and decentralized operation.

4.   That the accounts be so kept that they will show currently, fully and clearly the sources of the funds provided for the running of the government and for what purposes these funds are spent, and that, to this end, the accounts be kept on the accrual basis.

TERMINOLOGY

5.   That accounting terminology be adopted that is specific and free of double and multiple meaning.

6.   That positive provision be made in the accounting system for "fund accounting," to the extent that contractual obligations, restrictions, conditions, or other circumstance, make segregation of funds, and separate accounting therefor necessary.

7.   That accountable officers be relieved of financial liability for expenditures made contrary to law in all cases except those that result from gross negligence or fraud.

8.   That the statutes that prescribe the present warrant system be repealed.

9.   That the varieties of appropriations be reduced and that the practice of making authorizations to treat expenditures as public debt transactions, the practice of requiring expenditures to be "booked" in years other than

those in which they occur, and the practice of writing substantive legislation into appropriation acts, be discontinued.

EXPENSE LIMITATIONS

10. That the practice of attempting to restrict the amount spent for certain classes of expenses by placing limitations thereon in the appropriation acts be discontinued.

11. That the requirement that funds be requisitioned from the Treasury before they may be regarded as being available for disbursement be discontinued.

DISBURSEMENT OF FUNDS

12. That a thorough study be made of disbursement policy, with particular reference to the fact that the disbursement function never has been completely taken over by the Treasury Department, and to the question whether it is necessary to permit any department to do its own disbursing.

13. That personnel policies be adopted that will assure the attraction and holding of the professional class of accountants and auditors that is necessary to proper carrying out of the government's accounting and auditing activities.

Most of these recommendations will seem conventional enough to certified public accountants and industrial accountants familiar with the practices of business corporations. But in the Federal Government these recommendations are revolutionary.

Thus there are four recommendations for dealing with the problem of present inadequate federal government accounting. They are:

1. The recommendations of the Accounting Policy Committee, summarized immediately above. This represents the considered judgment of experienced public accountants, with wide experience in accounting in the executive branch of the government. These views are concurred in by Commissioners Rowe, and Pollock.

2. The recommendations of the Hoover Commission, seven men of which approved the report sent to Congress, which is summarized in the beginning of this article.

3. Dean Acheson's view that the Committee is right, but that it would be impracticable to do anything about it.

4. The views of Commissioners McClellan and Manasco who claim that the recommendations of both Commission and Committee violate rights of Congress, and that virtually no change should be made from the present procedures.

ACCOUNTANT GENERAL OF THE UNITED STATES

The recommendations of the Accounting Policy Committee are those most like good commercial accounting practice, and the details of these recommendations will be of interest to accountants. Some of the thinking behind these recommendations is discussed here.

The first step to be taken toward correction of the present situation is to draw a clear line of demarcation between accounting and auditing. The way to do this is to establish a central accounting office separate from the auditing office and the Treasury Department, head it by a chief accounting officer with undivided responsibility for accounting activities and with final authority in all accounting matters, and require this officer to establish and maintain a system of accounting and financial reporting appropriate to the government's needs. We further recommend:

(a) That the status of the central accounting office be made that of an independent establishment within the Executive Office of the President.

(b) That the central accounting officer be designated the Accountant General of the United States.

(c) That one of the qualifications of the Accountant General be that he be a professional accountant of the highest standing and attainments.

(d) That the Accountant General be appointed by the President with the concurrence of the Senate for a term of 15 years without the privilege of reappointment.

(e) That the salary of the Accountant General be not less than $25,000 per year.

We hold, as a matter of conviction, based upon our individual and collective observations and experience, in government as well as outside of it, that a strong accounting department, set up at the right hand of the chief executive officer, is as necessary to the success of government as it is to the success of private enterprise.

We have recommended that one of the qualifications of the Accountant General be that he be a professional accountant of the highest standing and attainments because this officer will have the biggest job of accounting to do that has ever been conceived. We do not subscribe to the idea that an office of this kind can be properly administered by merely a good executive. No executive, no matter how good he is, could fully discharge the duties of the Accountant General of the United States unless he were, in addition to being a good executive, a topnotch accountant.

An executive in this office who lacked the highest accounting qualifications could very easily fail to appreciate the significance of important technical problems and come to thoroughly unsound conclusions as to how these problems should be solved.

We have recommended that the Accountant General be appointed for a period of 15 years without the privilege of reappointment because we deem continuity of tenure of office and maximum freedom from political influence to be of paramount importance. Accounting principles are not founded on political considerations; accounting is accounting no matter what the political complexion of the Administration happens to be.

We have recommended that the Accountant General be paid not less than $25,000 per year because we regard this as little enough compensation to anyone who assumes and properly discharges the tremendous responsibilities of this office.

The central accounting office should be organized into four main divisions: one to develop accounting systems and procedures; a second to keep those accounts of the government as a whole that would not be kept by the separate departments and other organizations; a third to receive the reports of the other departments and organizations, combine them with the reports prepared from the accounts kept by the central accounting office, and turn out the ultimate financial statements and reports necessary for the information of the Chief Executive, the Congress, and the people; the fourth, which might be called a field staff, to give the other departments and organizations such assistance as they might need in applying the accounting principles, and making the financial reports, prescribed by the Accountant General.

AUDITOR GENERAL OF THE UNITED STATES

The office of Comptroller General of the United States is one of the most important in the government. Its potentialities as the independent auditing and investigating establishment of Congress, and as the medium through which Congress might influence the promotion of economy, simplification, and prompt dispatch of business throughout the government, are incalculable. The following recommendations are designed to make full realization of these potentialities possible:

(a) That the Comptroller General be relieved of all duties that make him a party to decisions and determinations other than those pertaining to the activities of his own office.

(b) That the Comptroller General be required and empowered to broaden the scope of his activities by making commercial-type audits of all the departments and other organizations of the government.

(c) That the auditing of expenditure vouchers in detail by the Comptroller General be discontinued except in cases of gross negligence, fraud, or other circumstances that, in the opinion of the Comptroller General, make detailed examination necessary.

(d) That all audits made by the Comptroller General be made on the spot in the offices of the departments and other organizations of the government.

(e) That the designation "The Comptroller General of the United States" be changed to "The Auditor General of the United States" and that the designation "General Accounting Office" be abolished.

(f) That the qualifications and salary of the Auditor General be the same as those of the Accountant General.

We have recommended that the Comptroller General be relieved of all duties that make him a party to decisions and determinations other than those pertaining to the activities of his own office, because these are not proper duties for an independent auditor. When an independent auditor joins management in making determinations and decisions upon matters that he later must review as auditor, he gives up his independence and becomes merely a reviewer of his own acts. Therefore, he never should be required or permitted to share the responsibilities of management.

Accounting is one of the activities for which the Executive Branch of the Government should be held solely responsible but in which the Comptroller General's office nevertheless participates. In its report of July 31, 1946, heretofore cited, the House Committee on Expenditures in the Executive Departments had the following to say about where the responsibility for accounting lies and about the independent auditor's relationship to his activity:

> accounting is one of the most important responsibilities of management [and] it is the duty of auditors to review completed accounting data and no part of their duty to undertake accomplishment of the accounting function or otherwise relieve management of its responsibility therefor.

The usefulness of the Comptroller General's office would be vastly increased, and the full benefits of independent auditing would be realized, if the Comptroller General were relieved of all his present non-auditing duties and allowed to function solely as an independent auditor. The potentialities of his office as the investigating agency for the committees of Congress, particularly the appropriations committees, are enormous.

We have recommended that the Comptroller General be required and empowered to broaden the scope of his activities by making commercial-type audits of all the departments and other organizations of the government, because mere checking of the vouchers of these departments and organizations is not enough. The more comprehensive inquiry afforded by the commercial type of audit is as necessary in government as in private enterprise.

The Congress already has required that commercial-type audits be made of the affairs of the Government's corporations, and the adequacy and usefulness of such audits for these corporations has been clearly demonstrated by the Corporation Audits Division of the General Accounting Office. Their use should now be extended to all the other departments and organizations of the Government. This is intended to include the proposed central accounting office. All of the Comptroller General's audits and reports then would be of the same comprehensiveness as those that he now prepares and submits concerning the Government corporations.

As the independent auditor of all the financial affairs of the Government, the Comptroller General also should be empowered and required to report faulty accounting wherever and whenever he encounters it. In addition, he should be empowered and required to report defective organization and poor management, to the extent of his and his staff's qualifications to appraise such deficiencies.

We have recommended that the checking of expenditure vouchers in detail by the Comptroller General be discontinued except in cases of gross negligence, fraud, or other circumstances that, in the opinion of the Comptroller General, make detailed examination necessary, because such checking by an independent auditor rarely is necessary except where there is doubt as to the integrity of the accounts or of those whose stewardship the accounts are supposed to reflect. Moreover, except in such cases, voucher examination of this scope by an independent auditor does not produce results commensurate with its cost. Detailed checking of expenditures is a duty of management and is provided for as a part of the system of internal control that is set up in developing the accounting system.

We have recommended that all audits made by the Comptroller General be made on the spot in the offices of the departments and other organizations of the Government, because the records to be audited are in these offices and can be reviewed on the spot with more facility and with greater understanding.

We have recommended that the designation "The Comptroller General of the United States" be changed to "The Auditor General of the United States," because the present designation is a misnomer; it indicates that the person who is so designated is the Government's accounting officer. The title Auditor General of the United States would make it clear that the person bearing it is the auditing officer of the Government. The designation "General Accounting Office" should be abolished, because it might be confused with the office of the Accountant General.

We have recommended that the Auditor General should have the same professional qualifications as the Accountant General and that he should be paid the same salary, because the two offices require holders of the same training and experience and impose responsibilities of substantially the same weight.

It is pointed out, however, that our decision to recommend that one of the qualifications of the Auditor General be that he be a professional accountant was not based upon any consideration of the present Comptroller

General's performance of his duties; it was based solely upon what we regard as being necessary in order to give maximum assurance that each successive holder of the office will be qualified for his highly professional duties.

ACCOUNTING PERSONNEL

The final recommendation, concerning personnel policies, will, however, be of interest to most accountants. Though stated last, this recommendation is one of the utmost importance. The Government never will have satisfactory accounting and financial reporting unless and until it makes definite provision for it, puts a professionally qualified director in charge of it, and makes Government more attractive to the kind of people that he will need in order to make it what it should be.

It is obvious, we think, that direction of the accounting activities of an organization of such vast proportions and varied activities as those of the Federal Government call for a nucleus of professionally qualified accountants. As heretofore indicated, such personnel will be needed at the departmental level as well as at the central accounting office. The Comptroller (Auditor) General will have need of similar personnel, but he already has a large professional group in his Corporation Audits Division and a good start toward the development of a similar group in his Accounting Systems Division.

On the accounting side, the number of professional personnel will be small in relation to the total staff required, since the handling of most of the accounting detail can be reduced to relatively simple routines. However, the success of the entire accounting activity will depend upon the competence of this relatively small group.

On the auditing side, almost the entire staff, with the exception of administrative personnel, would have to be either experienced professional accountants or men trained for professional accounting careers, such as are now on the present staffs of the Corporation Audits Division and the Accounting Systems Division of the General Accounting Office.

As much as we dislike to have to say so, the plain simple fact is that the Government's Civil Service is not now attractive to anywhere near enough people of ambition and outstanding competence. This is particularly true of people in the professional fields. The Government cannot hope to attract the kind of professional people it should have unless and until it makes its Civil Service attractive to such people.

GOVERNMENT FINANCE AND ECONOMY[†]

by

T. Coleman Andrews

FOR 17 years we have had one emergency after another in our Federal Government, most of them spurious. Each of these emergencies has cost us a lot of money. The cumulative result has been to jump federal spending from 4 billion dollars per year to more than 40 billion dollars.

Now we really have a crisis—the greatest in all our history—one that threatens the very foundation of our system of government—one about which you and I have got to get mad—fighting mad—mad enough to cause us to start throwing our weight around as citizens.

All of you know what the situation is: 256 billions of debt ... surpluses in only two of those 17 years, and those two by accident rather than design ... a deficit of 1.7 billions last year ... an expected deficit of from 5 to 8 billions this year ... another deficit of from 7 to 10 billions in the cards for next year ... as clear a pattern as one could imagine of evolution from government for the benefit of the governed to government for the benefit of the governors—at first a creeping, but now a plunging, return to the tyranny and oppression from which the colonizers of our country fought themselves free only 168 years ago.

What irony, ladies and gentlemen! Less than 200 years of freedom after unreckonable ages of bondage; then back to bondage again! It doesn't seem possible, but that's the way it is. We have given up the vigil. No longer do we have a firm grip on our destiny as individuals and as a people. We have all but lost the will to be free. We are giving up our short-lived freedom. If there is a spark of resistance to slavery left in us it is indeed so dim a one as to be hardly discernible. Or can it be that we merely do not comprehend what is happening to us? Take your choice. We should be as ashamed of one as of the other.

Talk about government finance and economy? Where may we find either today? Our government *has* no financial policy. One day it talks about preventing inflation with deficit financing. The next it talks about using deficit financing to prevent depression. What a miracle-worker spending has become in the minds of the managers of our public affairs,

[†]Address before the Virginia Manufacturers Association, Richmond, Virginia, October 22, 1949. Reprinted with permission from the Virginia Manufacturers Association. In the T. Coleman Andrews Papers (Coll. 119), Special Collections, University of Oregon Library.

and in the minds of all too many of the people as well. And to talk about government economy is farcical, because there isn't any economy in the management of our national affairs. Economy was lost in the shuffle long ago. I repeat, ladies and gentlemen: We are flirting with disaster, and the time has come to do something more than just talk about it.

Perhaps you think that I am just excited. I *am* excited, in all the meaning of the word; and I make no apologies for it. Moreover, I aim to get you excited if I can. One of Richmond's business leaders once told a group of halfhearted workers in an important civic project that they had to get excited about the project if they expected to accomplish what they had set out to do, because nothing worthwhile had ever been accomplished until somebody got excited enough about it to be moved to positive action. I think that there was a lot of wisdom in that statement. I also think that the time has come for us to get excited about the fiscal plight of government in this country, particularly that of the Federal Government.

Thomas Jefferson warned that "to preserve our independence ... we must make a choice between economy and liberty or profusion and servitude." Jefferson and his co-founders of this government saw that down through the ages men had lived by and under the sword, and that the power of the sword was derived from control of the purse. Prior to the founding of this country, the only people who had sufficient funds for ample living were the kings, despots, tyrants and conquerors under whose rule the masses were forced to live. Thus, when the Constitution was written, it was deliberately framed so to limit the powers of the Federal Government that control of the purse strings would be in the hands of the people.

Jefferson and his contemporaries also saw that if the people ever permitted the Federal Government to get control of the economy of the land, individual freedom would disappear and the people would find themselves right back where they were before they won their independence.

This accounts for those provisions of the Constitution and the Bill of Rights whereby the right to acquire and feel secure in the ownership of property was assured. This right is being openly challenged all over America today, but nowhere so vigorously as in Washington.

The Federal Government's gift and estate tax laws were deliberately framed to destroy personal wealth and bring us to the point where every generation would have to start from scratch. The income tax laws make such tremendous exactions that little is left for the accumulation of savings, by which the growth of private enterprise has been traditionally financed.

In England private wealth has been destroyed to the point where it is incapable of further promotion of private enterprise. Of all the 50-odd million people in the British Isles, less than 250 of them have an income of $20,000 per year or more. Think of it, ladies and gentlemen! That's only 1 in every 200,000 people! We are rapidly coming to this point in America, and when it is reached, we will as certainly find ourselves bereft of individual freedom as the people of England are today.

Private enterprise is under attack even by many who profess passionate devotion to our system of government. To be personally successful is to be suspected of fraud, corruption and exploitation of others. Big business, regardless of its virtues, and in spite of any benefits that it confers upon the people as consumers, is regarded as being evil merely because it is big. Yet those who advocate the destruction of big business are the most vociferous advocates of big government, notwithstanding the fact that the government has already reached proportions that take from the people a greater part of their income than any segment of industry or commerce.

Jefferson also left us the priceless observation that he knew of no safe depository of the ultimate powers of society save the people themselves, and that, if we should ever think the people not sufficiently enlightened to exercise their control with a wholesome discretion, the remedy would lie not in taking the people's discretion from them but in informing their discretion by education. Here again was another conviction that led to the establishment of the government of this country as one of limited powers.

Jefferson and his contemporaries foresaw the probability that we would lapse into some degree of acceptance of the kind of illusory propositions with which we presently are toying; and they were convinced that, if we accepted the philosophy of the advocates of these propositions and allowed the government to gain control of the production and distribution of goods, the rights of the individual citizen would disappear and the government would emerge as the master of the people. This already is happening.

There are many who say that the paramount issue of the day is whether the government will be the servant of the people or the people will be the servants of the government. That is the fundamental issue, but it is not the immediate one. We already are far under the yoke of compulsion. We have given up our rights one by one until today the government is so firmly entrenched in control of the factors that determine our destiny that the immediate issue is whether we can save ourselves from ultimate complete loss of self-determination. I think we can, but it is going to take a lot more intestinal fortitude than most of those from whom the people have the right to expect leadership have shown thus far.

We cannot long hold on to what is left of our rights as individuals—and we certainly cannot hope to regain any of those rights that already have been taken from us—if we continue to tolerate a government that not only smiles upon, but brazenly practices, discrimination ... that sets class against class ... that forcibly takes from one class to curry the favor of another ... that claims to be abolishing poorhouses while rapidly qualifying itself to become an inmate ... that makes a myth of social security while squandering the people's substance to such an extent that there can be no security, social or otherwise, worthy of the name ... that essays to save the rest of the world from economic disaster while spending itself into bankruptcy at home.

About three years ago, Congress became sufficiently concerned about the country's financial plight to authorize the appointment of a Commission to study the organization of the Executive Branch of the Government, report its findings, and make such recommendations as it deemed necessary and desirable. The bill creating this Commission provided that it should consist of 12 members—3 members from the House of Representatives, 3 from the Senate, 3 career officials of the government, and 3 citizens. Thus the Commission was to be nonpartisan, and, while it may be, as some have alleged, that some of the dissents from the Commission's findings and recommendations were inspired by political considerations, the Commission nevertheless turned in a thoroughly objective report.

As most of you know, ex-President Herbert Hoover was one of the members of the Commission and became its chairman, and the Commission, officially designated The Commission on Organization of the Executive Branch of the Government, became familiarly known as the Hoover Commission.

Mr. Hoover began the work of the Commission by gathering around him a group of more than 300 business and professional men, each chosen for his knowledge of, or experience in, some particular aspect of the government's affairs. He then divided this group into task forces and made the surveying of one or more departments the responsibility of each task force.

The result was the most thorough and comprehensive inquiry into the executive branch of the government that had ever been made.

After the Commission rendered its report to Congress, it went out of existence, but, in order to make certain that serious attention would be paid to the Commission's recommendations, the Citizens' Committee for the Hoover Report was organized, consisting of men and women from every state in the Union and headed by Dr. Robert L. Johnson, President of Temple University. I will tell you more about the work of the Committee later.

Here are some of the astounding facts that the studies of the Commission's Task Forces disclosed. They indicate beyond question that the Executive Branch of the government is inappropriately organized, that its left hand doesn't know what its right hand is doing, and that an appalling state of confusion exists in the management of our national affairs:

It cost George Washington 4 million dollars a year to run the country.... Abraham Lincoln spent an average of 838 million dollars per year.... William McKinley fought the Spanish-American War and spent only 523 million dollars a year.... Woodrow Wilson spent 5 billion dollars a year during World War 1.... Twenty years ago, the cost of running the Federal Government was about 4 billions a year. Today the cost is about 42 billions.

It is hard to understand a figure like the last one, but here is one that we all can grasp—remember it well, because it affects your life and the future of your youngsters: The Hoover Commission found that in 1948 we wasted—poured down the drain—more money than it cost to run the government in 1928.

Who pays for all this? Every person in the country with any income whatsoever does! America's tax bill averages $371 per year for every man, woman and child in the country—well over $1,000 for the average family. The average citizen works 47 days a year to support the extravagant pandemonium on the Potomac at Washington. These are not just theories or abstractions. They are facts, in terms of hard-earned income.

You pay a federal tax of 20% on theatre tickets, cosmetics, light bulbs, luggage, jewelry and furs; 15% on sporting goods and films, telephone bills and railroad tickets. Then there is the income tax—remember? And next time you buy a pack of cigarettes take a look at them and reflect for a moment upon the significance of the fact that the tobacco man gets only 7 cents and that the rest goes for taxes.

Yes, right here in these United States, 38% of the workingman's income is taken for taxes, and the boys in Washington are falling over each other thinking up new ways to spend money and new taxes; which reminds us that old Comrade Lenin, who, as he lies in the great mausoleum in Red Square at Moscow, is worshipped by all the Communists everywhere, even including this country, gave us fair warning quite a while ago, when he said: "Some day we will force the United States to spend itself to destruction."

Twenty years ago all varieties of government, omitting debt service, cost the average family less than $200 annually. Today, making the same omission, it costs an average family about $1,300. And beyond this is the alarming fact that at this moment executives and legislators are seriously proposing projects which, if enacted, would add one-third more annually to our spending. If these projects were adopted the average family would pay $1,900 of taxes annually.

There is one government employee to every 22 persons in the United States. Worse than this, there is one government employee to every 8 of the working people of the country.

A little more than one person out of every 7 of the population is a regular recipient of government money. If all of those of this group who are of age were married, they would equal one-half of the number of people who voted in the last presidential election.

The Treasury Department has under its jurisdiction 7 agencies, including the Coast Guard and the Bureau of Narcotics, which

189

have nothing to do with finance. On the other hand, fiscal agencies properly belonging to the Treasury, are scattered throughout the Government.

Thousands of tons of obsolete, useless records and documents are kept in steel cabinets on costly office floors at maintenance charges of $29.00 per year when they might be stored in cardboard containers in warehouses at $2.15 a year.

Supervisors are rated and paid according to the number of workers under them. Thus they are encouraged to build up their work forces recklessly.

The appeal of a career in U.S. Government service is so slight that 500,000 persons voluntarily quit annually after a short experience in the work. The government employs more than 2,000,000 civilian employees.

The Post Office, which does a business of $3 billion annually will have a deficit this year of about $500,000,000. Better management and better equipment could save at least $150,000,000.

Two different government agencies surveying construction sites of dams a half mile apart on the same river—at $250,000 per survey—came up with estimated costs $75,000,000 apart.

Some government bureaus maintain supplies of equipment sufficient to last for 50 years. All told the government owns 27 billion dollars of property inventories although no one agency has a record of their nature or whereabouts.

The Bureau of Indian Affairs has 393,000 Indians under its jurisdiction or care. It employs 12,269 persons to administer its program. That's one employee for every 32 Indians.

The Army tore down a camp in Alaska that cost $16,000,000. It shipped the lumber to Seattle, Wash. The Department of the Interior got the lumber in Seattle and shipped it back to a point 10 miles from where it came originally.

A farmer wrote to the Department of Agriculture seeking advice on the best type of fertilizer to use on his soil. He got answers from five separate offices. All the answers were different.

It takes 20 percent more money to operate the Post Office Department's fleet of motor vehicles than it does to operate large-scale private transport fleets.

To turn out its maze of paper work the Federal Government owns 848,567 typewriters. About 235,000 persons on the Federal payroll use typewriters on a part-time or full-time basis. This means that the Government owns 3.6 typewriters for every employee who uses one.

The paper work on 1,500,000 purchase orders each year costs more than $10 per order. And, by the way, half the purchases are for items costing less than $10!

Forty-seven federal agents representing seven different agricultural field services are devoted to the service of 1,500 farmers in a single county in Georgia.

The Army requested budget funds for 829,000 tropical uniforms at $129 apiece—to say nothing of 910 houses for military personnel in Alaska at $58,000 apiece.

The government pays interest on its own money. This happens when government corporations invest their surplus funds in government securities.

The cost of a reservoir was estimated at 44 million dollars in one year and only a few years later at 132 millions.

Forty-five out of the 60-odd top agencies of the Executive Branch today engage in operations affecting foreign policy, and communications among them are so confused that the President and the State Department must sometimes make decisions of the gravest nature without adequate information.

The armed services are split by dissension and threatened by the rule of a military "clique"; and the Army, Navy, and Air Force which together spend 15 billion dollars a year—one-third of the total federal budget—demand twice as much (30 billions) while wasting at least a billion dollars a year.

It takes four times as long for the government to pay a claim made on a veteran's insurance policy as it does a private insurance company. Worse than that, it takes four times as many people to make the payment.

And, perhaps worst of all, it was found that the government never had developed and installed an accounting system as such, and, as a result could not produce a reliable statement of where it stood financially. In one recent year the Secretary reported a surplus of ¾ of a billion dollars when, in fact, there was a deficit of several billions.

Startling as these facts are, they are only a few of the hundreds of similar facts that a study of the Hoover Report reveals. One of the most startling things about them is that they are true of a government of our own choosing—a government of the choosing of a people who may justly claim to be the most efficient in the world in the management of their private affairs.

One end result of the actual and proposed spendings and of the taxes that would have to be raised to cover this spending would be that the government would become the major, if not the only, source of credit and capital for our economic system.

Mr. Hoover has stated publicly that he estimates that adoption of the Commission's recommendations would reduce expenditures at least 3 billion dollars annually and perhaps more. I often have wondered how much he would reduce them if the sole responsibility for eliminating waste and extravagance were given to him. I have no doubt that if this were possible, the reduction would be a great deal *more* than 3 billion dollars per year. At any rate, many of us who worked with the Commission believe that the wastage far exceeds 3 billion dollars a year. Remember that, with the exception of interest on the public debt, there isn't a single item in the Federal budget that cannot be reduced. Remember also THAT THE GOVERNMENT IS LIVING BEYOND OUR INCOME.

The savings estimated by Mr. Hoover aren't great in relation to total expenditures. Indeed, the saving of this amount would not reduce the budget to anywhere near the level that may be regarded as the maximum amount that the Federal Government should spend annually. But remember that the Commission did not deal with the question of elimination of functions and activities. It was authorized to deal only with reorganization of existing functions and activities. If we only had the courage to get out the pruning shears and eliminate every function and activity not necessary to the health, safety and general welfare of the people, the reduction would be several times 3 billion dollars annually.

However, Mr. Hoover's estimate gives us something definite to work on—*right now*. The question is: What are we going to do about it? Are we going to stand by and allow such conditions as those reported by the Commission to perpetuate themselves, as they surely will unless we rise up in our individual and collective might and demand that Congress call a halt on the spenders?

As I have already told you, the Citizens' Committee for the Hoover Report was organized to take over where the Commission left off. Spurred by Mr. Hoover and the Citizens' Committee, the 81st Congress adopted at the session that has just ended five laws based on the Commission's Report. Saving of at least 1¼ billion dollars in the annual cost of government already have been made possible by these laws. This is but the beginning of what can be accomplished if all of us courageously assert our rights as citizens and put our shoulders to the wheel.

The economies inherent in the recommendations yet to be acted upon are not going to be easy to obtain. All manner of opposition has sprung up both within and without the government that presage rough sledding for the advocates of economy. One department head, who unqualifiedly agreed with every recommendation of the Task Force that studied his department, now says that he will resign if a single one of those recommendations is adopted. Obviously the staff and employees of his department have done a thorough job on him.

On the outside, one of the great national organizations has raised its dues by 25 cents per year in order to provide funds to carry on a campaign designed to prevent the adoption of any recommendation that affects the department in which its members are interested.

In addition, there is plenty of that "Yes—But," attitude, also both within and without the government. The average department head agrees that everybody else's department ought to be reorganized, but not his. And on the outside, state and local Chambers of Commerce and other organizations, in discouraging numbers, are willing to go along on everything except those recommendations that affect their pet activities and projects. Obviously nothing will be done if the accumulated local protests are heeded and the general welfare is ignored. Too many of us are thinking in too narrow terms. Too few put the good of all first.

However, there are some encouraging developments. Many national, state and local organizations have pledged themselves to support the Commission's recommendations. Among these is the United States Junior Chamber of Commerce. This virile and enthusiastic organization of the leaders of today and tomorrow has adopted the support of the Commission's recommendations as their No. 1 project for this year. They call it "Operation Economy." I think we can feel especially encouraged that the efforts of the Citizens' Committee are going to have the support of an organization with the energy and vigor that this one and its state and local units have so often demonstrated in the numerous constructive and highly successful projects that they have undertaken in the public interest.

I have had the greatly cherished privilege of working with the Virginia Junior Chamber of Commerce and its local units throughout the State in developing the plans for the support program that they will put on, and I can tell you that it is a real inspiration, and a source of great encouragement, to see the enthusiasm and vigor with which these young men are attacking the job of re-awakening the people's devotion to the principles of thrift and provident living, and to the love of individual freedom, upon which our country was founded.

Until I was made aware of the campaign that these young men propose to put on, I found little to warrant me in feeling that our drift toward some form of totalitarianism would be halted. Oh, there were plenty of people who resented this drift, but there were powerfully few who dared take the risks involved in trying to do something about it.

The Junior Chambers of Commerce will swing into action within the next few days, and I shan't be at all surprised if they make us older men and women somewhat ashamed of our reluctance to stand forth like real men and women and resist in decisive numbers the evil forces that have arrayed themselves against the principles of government that have made our country great.

These young men believe in their country and its system of government. They believe in individual freedom. They believe in private enterprise as the surest route to man's rendezvous with his ultimate destiny. They believe that the qualities of restraint, of integrity, of conscience and

193

of courage still live in the people of America and that it is not too late to summon these qualities into action. Finally, ladies and gentlemen, they aren't afraid.

They are going to do a job that will make the people proud of them and that, I suspect, will cause at least some of their elders to shed their apathy and indifference and get in there and pitch for the cause of sound government. I hope that when the opportunity to cooperate with them and the Citizens' Committee is presented, you will give them your wholehearted support, because they will be carrying the ball for you and me. The least we can do to help is give them our blessing and the encouragement of our moral support.

Now, ladies and gentlemen, I don't know what you think about what I have said to you this morning or about the way I have said it. Maybe some of you regard my presentation as just another speech. However, I hope not, because I assure you that I never was more serious about anything in my life. I very sincerely believe that everything that is precious to us as individuals and as a people is in serious jeopardy.

Perhaps some of you feel, as I have heard many people express themselves, that the American people will never give up their liberty. I tell you that we have already given up a large part of it. More than 25 million people are direct beneficiaries of the philosophy of government that now prevails in Washington, in the form of direct regular receipts of hard cash from the public treasury—cash that has been taken from you and me and others in the form of exorbitant tax levies; and it is the announced intention of the Administration to add millions of others. The most recent objects of the government's grab for power are the schoolteachers.

Can you possibly believe that fair elections are possible when more than half of those who are qualified to vote are made, either directly or indirectly, dependent upon the government for their livelihoods?

Can you possibly believe that those who are made beholden to the government will not support their own *status quo* and other legislation as well that favors other groups at the expense of the majority?

Is it not perfectly clear that a policy of favoring first one minority group after another eventually will put every citizen under the yoke of bondage to a few self-appointed and powerful politicians who regard themselves as endowed with superior wisdom and the "Divine Right of Kings"?

I believe that if you will really search your intellects and your souls for the answers to these questions, you will surely answer every one of them in the affirmative.

Then I think we must consider the morality of the government's present policies. You recall, I am sure, that the Tennessee Valley Authority was established as a flood control and navigation project, with production and distribution of electric power as only an incident to these objectives. No people have ever had a faster one than that put over on them. Even the

194

member of the Senate who sponsored the creation of this organization admitted before he died that it was from the beginning a power project, and that the only reason for calling it a flood control and navigation project was to circumvent the constitutional prohibition against setting the government up in competition with private enterprise.

The Constitution still contains that prohibition, but the advocates of public power no longer bother to wear the mask of flood control and navigation. They espouse their multitudinous power projects with brazen indifference to the Constitution.

Quite a controversy is going on right now over the development at Buggs Island and the proposed development by the Virginia Electric & Power Company at Roanoke Rapids. Do those who obtained approval of the Buggs Island project, and who fight the application of the Virginia Electric & Power Company for the development at Roanoke Rapids, talk about flood control and navigation? They most certainly do not. All they talk about is power development. They are resisting the Virginia Electric & Power Company's proposed development at Roanoke Rapids *not* because it will interfere with flood control and navigation on the Roanoke River but solely because it would interfere, they claim, with the power development at Buggs Island.

This is just one aspect of what I regard as a low degree of morality in the administration of our national affairs. There are plenty of others that could be cited if there were time. Since my time is about running out, I will stop with that one, but before I conclude, I would like to call your attention to one recent series of events that causes one to wonder just how much integrity there is in our government and that rather forcibly suggests how iniquitous and powerful is the policy of government largesse.

I quote from the October 9, 1949 issue of the *New York Times*:

Sept. 30—Edgar F. Kaiser, president of the Kaiser-Frazer Corporation, reported to be in Washington attempting to arrange a loan in excess of $30,000,000 from the Reconstruction Finance Corporation.

Oct. 1—Official of the RFC said the agency had no statement to make on reports that Kaiser-Frazer was seeking a large loan except that "there is no application pending before the board and no loan has been granted" to the motor car manufacturer.

Oct. 5—Henry J. Kaiser's steel company signs a contract with the steel union including the basic recommendations of President Truman's Fact-Finding Board (6 cents an hour for pensions and 4 cents for social insurance, with the employer bearing the full cost of both programs).

Oct. 6—RFC announces a loan of $34,400,000 to Kaiser-Frazer.

In conclusion, ladies and gentlemen, let me say to you with all the earnestness at my command that if the privilege of individual freedom means anything to you, and that if you really believe in the right to acquire and be secure in the ownership of property—in short, if we truly believe in the principles of government upon which this government of ours was founded—then we must conclude that we are faced RIGHT NOW with the choice of either fighting to preserve our rights or accepting the loss of them and a return to the tyranny from which our forefathers saved us.

I assure you that it is later than you think. Rome fell because a hearty race of free men fell for the dreamy idea of a welfare state, where the government was to give everything for nothing. It didn't work in Rome, and it won't work here; and if we don't stop it, we will be as surely engulfed by disaster as were the people of Rome.

A hundred and eighty-four years ago, in little St. John's Church, on the next hill to the east of that on which the meeting place in which we are here assembled is situated, a man whose courage has inspired the world defied no less a tyranny than that by which we ultimately will be faced if we do not strike it down before it attains full maturity. Patrick Henry held liberty dearer than life itself, and he had the courage of his convictions. He dared to defy tyranny publicly.

Can it possibly be that we are to show ourselves unworthy of this glorious and inspiring example of personal courage and thus have to stand before the world unworthy of the priceless heritage of freedom that was bequeathed to us by Henry and the other fearless patriots of his day? Are we going to stand supinely by and permit ourselves and our posterity to become enslaved for want of sufficient courage to resist, at whatever risk might be involved, those who seek to deprive us of the rights with which a kindly providence has endowed us?

God forbid that we should prove ourselves so destitute of simple gratitude.

THE HOOVER COMMISSION'S RECOMMENDATIONS ON FEDERAL GOVERNMENT ACCOUNTING†

by

T. Coleman Andrews

WHEN one begins to consider the government's attitude toward accounting, he is immediately struck by the paradox of a double standard. Though the government imposes precise accounting requirements upon those categories of private enterprise over which it exercises regulatory control, it apparently does not feel that it needs to bother much about accounting for its own affairs, notwithstanding that it is the largest and most complex business in the entire world.

For instance, the Interstate Commerce Commission prescribes exactly how the books of the railroads and other transportation businesses should be kept; the Federal Power Commission decrees how the power companies shall keep their books; and almost no business enterprise could possibly comply with the income tax law without maintaining a complete system of accounts.

Yet, there is not in the government any central accounting department nor any officer solely responsible for seeing that proper accounts are kept and regular understandable reports are submitted by which the people, Congress and the President may be accurately informed as to how the taxes paid by the people for the running of the government are spent.

As an example of faulty reporting, the Treasury Department has regularly reported surpluses and deficits when it has not really known whether there was a surplus or a deficit in terms of the generally accepted definitions of the words "surplus" and "deficit." Its calculations have been based upon figures that have taken no account of great sums of money already spent—sums that usually run into billions of dollars. If the average business concern kept no more appropriate and informative books than the government has kept, it soon would be bankrupt for lack of financial data which management must have in order to do an intelligent job.

The objective of the present government's accounting, auditing, and financial reporting is merely to prevent fraud or to assure detection of it if and when it occurs. The recommendations of the Hoover Commission

†Address given at the annual meeting of the Texas Society of Certified Public Accountants in Dallas on June 12, 1950. Reprinted with permission of the Texas Society of CPAs from *The Texas Accountant*, July and August 1950, pp. 1, 3-5.

would add the important objective of utilizing the techniques of accounting to inform the managers of the government's affairs, the Congress, and the people about what is being done with the people's money, and of enabling these managers to discharge their duties with economy and real benefit to the public.

Accounting, auditing and financial reporting are not ends unto themselves. Yet this is precisely how the government has persisted in using these devices from the days of Alexander Hamilton.

Accounting, auditing and financial reporting are merely means to an end. The end in business is accurately informed management, owners and other interested parties. Only when management has accurate information is it in position to reach sound conclusions. In government, the end should be the same. The result undoubtedly would be a reduction of the burden of the cost of government upon the people. This end cannot be achieved unless and until the government uses accounting, auditing and financial reporting as tools of management.

American industry has enjoyed unparalleled growth. It has reached undreamed-of levels of production. Indeed, the strength of our country lies primarily in the productivity of its industrial plant. So great has been this strength that we were able to fight off and overcome the foes of our way of life twice within the short space of less than 30 years.

There can be no doubt that our economic greatness may be attributed perhaps in large part to the fact that the management of the country's business enterprises has recognized that accounting has been a part of its responsibility ... that it has been incumbent upon management to give a full and accurate account of its stewardship ... and that the accounting profession has kept abreast of management's demands for consistently improved accounting techniques. Management that does not know where its organization stands financially, and what its financial trends are, is doomed to pay the penalty of ignorance sooner or later. This is as true in public affairs as it is in private affairs.

We say, therefore, that the federal government can become the best managed government in the world only if it insures that it is the best informed government in the world as to what is being done with the people's money. The recommendations of the Hoover Commission are designed to make the federal government the best informed government in the world.

Now you ask: "Who is responsible for the government's accounting deficiencies?" I mention this only because I have been asked it many times. Frankly, I don't think it makes much difference who is responsible. The important thing is that there are serious deficiencies in the government's accounting and that we aren't apt to get very far with any effort to reduce the cost of government until the government adopts accounting techniques that will enable us to put our fingers on the points at which waste and extravagance occur. Besides, it cannot be said that any one person or any one group of persons is responsible for the present situation. As a matter of fact, it is clear, I think, that the responsibility lies, in the final analysis, with the people, for their failure to insist, through their representatives in Congress, that those entrusted with the management of their national affairs give a full account of their stewardship.

I have stated this question for another reason; that is, because apparently there have been some who have felt that our recommendations were aimed at individuals. I assure you that not a single one of our recommendations was based upon any personal considerations. In arriving at their conclusions, those who dealt with accounting and auditing had only one thing in mind; namely, to propose the best plan that they could conceive to assure the keeping and rendering of an appropriate and accurate account of the financial affairs of the government. We very sincerely feel that improvidence in the management of our public affairs may well be the most serious threat to continuance of the system of government under which we have lived up to this time, and that proper accounting for these affairs would be one means at least of avoiding excessive cost of government and of saving us from the collapse that seems certain to occur if we continue in ignorance and confusion and court the inevitable penalty of extravagance and waste.

Now, what did we recommend? Here is a summary of our recommendations as it appeared in our report to the Commission:

1.   That a central accounting office be established under the direction of a chief accounting officer of the Government and that the status of this office be made that of an independent establishment in the Executive Office of the President.

2.   That the duties of the Comptroller General of the United States be so redefined that there may be full realization of the potential usefulness of this officer as the Government's independent auditor and as the chief investigator for the committees of Congress, especially the appropriations committees; and that there also may be full realization of the potential influence of Congress, acting through the Comptroller General, upon the promotion of economy, simplification and prompt dispatch of business throughout the Government.

3.   That the proposed chief accounting officer be required and empowered to establish and maintain an accounting system appropriate to the Government's needs and to organize the accounting activity on the basis of centralized control and decentralized operation.

4.   That the accounts be so kept that they will show currently, fully and clearly the sources of the funds provided for the running of the Government and for what purposes these funds are spent; specifically, that the accounts be kept on the accrual basis.

5.   That accounting terminology be adopted that is specific and free of double and multiple meaning.

6. That positive provision be made in the accounting system for separate accounting for funds that are subject to contractual obligations, restrictions, conditions, or other circumstances that make separate accounting necessary.

7. That accountable officers be relieved of financial liability for expenditures made contrary to law in all cases except those that result from gross negligence or fraud.

8. That the statutes that prescribe the present warrant system be repealed.

9. That the varieties of appropriations be reduced and that the practice of making authorizations to treat expenditures as public debt transactions, the practice of requiring expenditures to be "booked" in years other than those in which they occur, and the practice of writing substantive legislation into appropriation acts, be discontinued.

10. That the practice of attempting to restrict the amount spent for certain classes of expenses by placing limitations thereon in the appropriation acts be discontinued.

11. That the requirement that funds be requisitioned from the Treasury before they may be regarded as being available for disbursement be discontinued.

12. That a thorough study be made of disbursement policy, with particular reference to the fact that the disbursement function never has been completely taken over by the Treasury Department, and to the question whether it is necessary to permit any department to do its own disbursing.

13. That personnel policies be adopted that will assure the attraction and holding of the professional class of accountants and auditors that is necessary to proper carrying out of the Government's accounting and auditing activities.

The reasoning behind each of these recommendations was stated in our report, so I shall not comment upon each of them or in detail upon any of them here. However, it is necessary, I think, that I comment briefly upon some aspects of some of them.

As foundation for what I shall say, let me point out and emphasize that inherent in all our recommendations is the absolute conviction that the indispensability of accounting must be recognized. There is no dodging the proposition that in conducting the biggest business in the world, or any business of such a size that the management cannot possibly keep its hands on every detail of operations, accounting becomes indispensable as the source of management's information as to what is going on, and that this is particularly true of public business, the direction of which, after all, assumes the nature of the highest public trust.

ORGANIZATIONAL STATUS OF THE ACCOUNTING FUNCTION

The accounting function should be placed in government where experience in public administration, as well as in private business, has shown that it is best managed. To this end, we recommend that a central accounting office be established under the direction of an officer to be called the Accountant General. We think that this activity should be directly under the President, who, after all, is the general manager of the nation's business. Thus, we envisioned the central accounting office as a unit of the executive office of the President.

The Commission agreed with this recommendation in principle, but in its report to Congress it proposed that the central accounting office be placed in the Treasury Department. We considered this, but rejected it, because the Treasury Department is itself an enormous organization, and its own accounting requirements are prodigious. We feel that, placed in the Treasury Department, the central accounting office would become involved with the accounting of the Treasury Department; and we had good reason for our apprehension, because that is precisely a part of the trouble today.

There are at least three different establishments of the government that today are concerning themselves with the government's accounting, and not one of them can produce a complete and reliable statement of the government's affairs. The Treasury Department is one of these three establishments, and its accounting and that of the government generally are so mixed up together that no one knows where the government generally stands.

Hence, we have no basis for believing that there will be much improvement in the present situation if the central accounting office is made a division of the Treasury Department.

It is a matter of some concern to us that there are some who feel that part of the responsibility of the government's accounting should remain with the General Accounting Office. It has been said to us by one very prominent person who is of this mind that he deemed this necessary because he does not trust the Executive Branch of the government. We suggest that this is not a valid reason for violating a fundamental principle.

It is not necessary for Congress to inject its independent auditor into the government's account-keeping in order to find out what the executive branch of the government does. It not only destroys the effectiveness of the Comptroller General as the independent auditor of Congress to put upon him an important part of the duties and responsibilities of the chief executive; it also carries expediency to indefensible lengths. In our opinion, this is unworthy of a virile and courageous Congress.

QUALIFICATIONS OF THE PROPOSED
ACCOUNTANT GENERAL

Direction of the accounting activities of the government should be put in the hands of a person professionally qualified to discharge the duties and responsibilities of an office of such magnitude and technical complexion as that of the government's chief accountant would be. It is dangerous, we think, to look upon accounting as just a necessary evil and farm it out to someone who has no professional qualifications for directing it. We put doctors in charge of medical affairs. We put engineers in charge of engineering affairs. We put lawyers in charge of legal affairs. We think that an accountant should be put in charge of accounting affairs.

QUALIFICATIONS OF THE STAFF OF THE PROPOSED
CENTRAL ACCOUNTING OFFICE

The personnel of the central accounting office who would have accounting duties should be accountants. There are in the United States today nearly 40,000 certified public accountants and perhaps many more trained but uncertified accountants. Less than 30 years ago there were only 5,000 certified public accountants. Thus, the growth in qualified personnel has been tremendous; and it is continuing.

No other branch of learning has a greater number of students than are to be found in the business schools of the colleges and universities, and on the rolls of business correspondence schools, of the country. The supply is still somewhat behind the demand, but it is rapidly being met. However, attractive careers are available in private enterprise and in the public accounting profession for the best trained and most apt accountants.

If the government is to have any hope of getting its share of this qualified personnel, it simply must offer opportunity to them that will be equal to that which they can find outside the government. The best way for the government to assure itself of getting its share will be to adopt personnel policies that will require that accountants be employed to fill accounting positions and make these positions available under the direction of accountants, with opportunity for advancement equal to that which obtains elsewhere.

The General Accounting Office right now is embarked upon a program in which hundreds of men and women trained as accountants will be needed. The General Accounting Office will not get people of proper qualifications for these positions unless and until the government gives accounting the recognition that it deserves and offers opportunity for those whom it would employ in accounting positions to develop as accountants under the direction of accountants.

BASIS OF PROPOSED ACCOUNTING SET-UP

The government's accounting should be set up on the basis of centralized control and decentralized operation. This proposal recognizes the fact that the government simply is too big for anyone to expect that all its books can be kept in one place. It must be recognized that the bulk of government's accounting work must be done at the department level, sometimes even lower, with a central office where accounting policies would be determined and directed and to which periodical reports would flow from the departments and be turned into over-all reports for the information of the people, the Congress, and the administration.

DISTINCTION BETWEEN ACCOUNTING AND INDEPENDENT AUDITING

There should be clear recognition of the distinction between accounting and independent auditing. Contrary to what many people think, the General Accounting Office is not the government's accounting office. It is primarily the independent auditing office. There is no accounting office as such. The Comptroller General's primary job is that of independent auditor of Congress. He is not the government's accounting officer. But he is, by law, injected into the archaic and confused accounting situation by being made to share with the administration the responsibility for important accounting determinations. Thus he is called upon to review as auditor decisions that he makes as to accounting matters. This obviously is anomalous and improper. The General Accounting Office ought not to have anything at all to do with accounting, except to audit the books and report its findings, opinions and recommendations to the Congress.

Now I wish it distinctly understood that this statement does not emanate from any lack of confidence in or regard for the General Accounting Office or the gentleman who heads it. It is solely a matter of principle. I was privileged to serve under the Comptroller General as organizer and initial director of a division of the General Accounting Office for 2½ years beginning just before World War II ended, and I have nothing but praise for this gentleman. He is truly a consecrated servant of the people, and he occupies a well-deserved position of high respect in the esteem of the administration, the Congress and the people. But we could not bring ourselves to decide such a question of high policy as that of the proper relationship of the accounting and independent auditing functions of the government upon the basis of anyone's admiration for any individual. Such matters may be decided only upon the basis of principle, and the principle here is clear; namely, that an independent auditor of management cannot be made responsible for a part of the executive branch's duties without compromising his position as independent auditor. In public accounting no independent auditor would allow himself to be put in the position where he must audit himself. Nor should the independent auditor of Congress do so or be required to do so.

We have not the slightest doubt that the present occupant of the office of Comptroller General would bend over backwards to keep these two functions separate in carrying out the duties of his office. He has demonstrated this sort of high devotion to duty on many occasions. But we must not forget that the Comptroller's tenure of office is not an unlimited one, and no one can predict at this date who his successor will be or what his successor's attitude toward accounting and independent auditing will be. Moreover, even if the tenure of the Comptroller General were indefinite, and regardless of what the qualifications of his successor may be, it still is wrong, as a matter of principle, to place any part of the responsibility for accounting in the government's independent auditor.

Perhaps I should indicate at this point the meaning of the terms "independent auditing" and "internal auditing," since there are many who seem to be uncertain about them. Internal auditing is a part of the accounting activity. It is the auditing done by management to assure itself that what it becomes responsible for is properly accounted for. In short, it is management's check on itself. Insufficient use of internal auditing has been one of the major deficiencies of the government's accounting.

Independent auditing is the examination of management's account of its stewardship by outside auditors; that is, by auditors who are independent of management and who are free to form and express independent opinion as to whether management has kept its accounts in accordance with generally accepted accounting principles and on a consistent basis, and as to whether management's representations as to its accounting have been fairly stated. The General Accounting Office began this type of auditing with the establishment of its Corporation Audits Division, and we understand that it now is preparing to use it on audits outside the corporate field.

Some of the concern that has been expressed about our recommendation that there be a clear line of demarcation between accounting and independent auditing apparently arises from the fact that a move to improve the government's accounting was initiated by the Comptroller General shortly after our study for the Hoover Commission was started. This move was the result of long consideration by the Comptroller General of the urgings of numerous members of the accounting profession who had observed the deficiencies of the government's accounting and vigorously urged that something be done about it.

The Comptroller General moved to bring the influence of the General Accounting Office to bear upon the situation by creating a new division known as the Accounting Systems Division. A highly skilled accountant was appointed to head this division, and work was begun, in cooperation with the Treasury Department and the Bureau of Budget, on the assembling of a staff and the development of a statement of principles. The new division has attacked the problem with vigor, and we think that up to this time they have done an excellent job. It is a long range project, however, and it isn't going to be completed this year or next year, or the year after. It probably will be at least five years before it is finished.

So, we have no quarrel with what is being done. On the contrary, we think that perhaps it is being done as well as anybody could do it. But we continue firmly of the opinion that the responsibility for the development of a plan of accounting for the government is one of the responsibilities of the executive branch of the government and that the executive branch should not be relieved of this responsibility by permitting an officer of the legislative branch to carry it out. Moreover, we see no guarantee of success in any voluntary undertaking such as that initiated by the Comptroller General. Responsibility for correcting the government's accounting deficiencies should be placed by law upon the executive branch of the government, where it belongs.

Here again we are told by those who insist that the development of accounting systems should be left in the hands of the Comptroller General that this is necessary because the executive branch of the government cannot be depended upon to do it. We do not agree that there is any validity in this reason, and even though such reason were justified, which we are not willing to concede, it would be no excuse for violating the fundamental principle that those who are responsible for accounting should be required to discharge the responsibility for it.

It also is argued that independent public accountants frequently devise and install systems of accounting for their clients and that there is nothing inconsistent about the independent auditor of Congress devising and installing systems for the departments of the governments. Independent public accountants do devise and install systems for their clients, but they don't develop a system and hand it to their client with the power to compel compliance with its provisions.

The responsibility for a private company's accounting system is imposed upon the accounting officer of the company. When independent public accountants devise a system for such a company the system recommended has to satisfy the company's accounting officer, since the responsibility for the system's appropriateness is his rather than the independent public accountant's. In such cases the independent accountant only renders professional service to his client; he has no power to compel adoption of his ideas.

Thus, there is no analogy between the Comptroller General's **prescribing** a system for a department of the government and an independent public accountant's **developing** a system for one of his clients. The latter service is advisory rather than prescriptive, in that the plan recommended by the independent public accountant must be one that squares with the client's accounting officer's ideas as to what is necessary for the proper discharge of his duties and responsibilities. The public accountant must be independent as an auditor. He need not be, and, except in the rare case where demand is made for his approval of a system feature that would prevent full disclosure, he ordinarily is not required to be, independent in the development of systems.

We insist, therefore, that in working out the reorganization of the government's accounting, principle demands that there be recognition of the fundamental requirement that responsibility for the accounting function be placed upon the executive branch of the government. That is where the responsibility for this function properly lies, and that is where it should be placed. No part of it should be imposed upon the independent auditor of the Congress.

THE BUDGET AND AUDITING PROCEDURES ACT OF 1950[†]

by

T. Coleman Andrews

AS most of you know, the Hoover Commission entrusted the study of the Federal government's accounting and auditing to the American Institute of Accountants Committee on Federal Government Accounting, and this Committee found and reported that:

> There is no formal accounting plan for the government as a whole.
> No one is charged with the duty of developing such a plan.
> There is no one who would have power to install such a plan and
>   compel compliance with its provisions if one were developed.
> The statutes make no provision for either a complete accounting
>   system or chief accounting officer to direct accounting activities.

To correct these deficiencies, the accounting and auditing study group made 13 recommendations, among which were the following:

1. That a central accounting office be established under the direction of a Chief Accounting Officer of the government and that the status of this office be made that of an independent establishment in the Executive Office of the President.

2. That the proposed chief accounting officer be called "The Accountant General of the United States."

3. That the proposed chief accounting officer be required and empowered to establish and maintain an accounting system appropriate to the government's needs and to organize the accounting activity on the basis of centralized control and decentralized operation.

4. That the title of the officer now known as "The Comptroller General of the United States" be changed to "The Auditor General of the United States," and that this officer's effectiveness as an independent

---

[†]Presented at the Michigan Accounting Conference sponsored by the Michigan Association of Certified Public Accountants and the University of Michigan School of Business Administration, Ann Arbor, October 14, 1950. Reprinted with permission of the Michigan Association of Certified Public Accountants from *The Michigan Certified Public Accountant*, February 1951, pp. 9-12.

auditor of Congress be enhanced by relieving him of all duties not consistent with those generally required of an independent auditor.

Unfortunately, the 12 members of the Commission split three ways on the recommendations made by the accounting and auditing study group. As a result, the Commission's recommendations to Congress, as to auditing and accounting, represented a compromise of the views of these three groups. This compromise was an unworkable one, as will be later shown.

In due time, a bill designed to carry out the recommendations of the Commission was introduced by Senator McCarthy and referred to the Committee on Expenditures in the Executive Branch of the Government, and shortly thereafter hearings on the bill were begun by this Committee.

At these hearings, the unworkability of the Commission's recommendations soon became apparent since no one could be found, not even of the members of the staff of the Commission, who could in good conscience endorse the provisions of the bill.

This bill was vigorously denounced by your speaker and other members of the accounting and auditing study group on the ground that it was inadequate and would only add to the existing confusion and was opposed by the Comptroller General of the United States largely on the ground that it constituted an attack upon his official competence and integrity.

The Comptroller General had already indicated indignant opposition to the recommendations of the accounting and auditing study group apparently for the same reason; therefore, it was expected that he would oppose any recommendation that the Commission might make.

The Comptroller General apparently got it in his head that someone was gunning for him. In fact, it has been reported to members of the accounting and auditing study group that some of his advisors sold him on the idea that certain members of the accounting and auditing study group actually were after his job.

All of this not only was quite the opposite of the truth, since we actually were trying to increase the importance and effectiveness of his office; it also was absurd, since the Comptroller General is appointed for a term of 15 years, which would not end until 1955 or 1956, and he could not be removed except for cause, not to mention the fact that no members of our group had the slightest ambition to return to Washington as Comptroller General or anything else.

Happily, it was apparent during the hearings that there was considerable unanimity of opinion between the accounting and auditing study group and the Comptroller General as to the need for improvement and as to the situations that required improvement.

In fact, there was no disagreement between the accounting and auditing study group and the Comptroller General except as to how the accounting and auditing functions of the government should be organized and managed.

Indeed, the Comptroller General already had started a program of voluntary cooperation between himself and the Secretary of the Treasury and the Director of the Bureau of the Budget, looking toward eventual correction of the deficiencies that the accounting and auditing study group had reported, which program the Comptroller General explained in detail at the hearings.

The upshot of all this was, I am told, that Senator McClellan, who was Chairman of the Senate Committee on Expenditures in the Executive Branch of the Government, suggested to the Comptroller General that, since everybody agreed that the situation was bad and could be corrected, someone ought to prepare a bill embodying provisions on which there could be more or less general agreement.

The Comptroller General accepted this challenge, and came up with a bill which was registered as H.R. 9038 and which, upon enactment, became known as the "Budgeting and Accounting Procedures Act of 1950."

I think that we accountants ought to be familiar with the provisions of this Act, and in the remaining time at my disposal I shall attempt to outline its principal provisions.

First of all, perhaps it might be well to state the purpose of this Act as it appears of record.

It is as follows:

To authorize the President to determine the form of the national budget and of departmental estimates, to modernize and simplify governmental accounting and auditing methods and procedures, and for other purposes.

Title I relates to budgeting and accounting; Part 1 has to do with budgeting. The portion of Part 1 that is of special interest to us as accountants is the portion that specifies what the Budget shall contain. This is found in Sec. 201 and is as follows:

The Budget shall set forth in such form and detail as the President may determine—
(a) functions and activities of the Government;
(b) any other desirable classifications of data;
(c) a reconciliation of the summary data on expenditures with proposed appropriations;
(d) estimated expenditures and proposed appropriations necessary in his judgment for the support of the Government for the ensuing fiscal year, except that estimated expenditures and proposed appropriations for such year for the legislative branch of the Government and the Supreme Court of the United States shall be transmitted to the President on or before October 15 of each year, and shall be included by him in the Budget without revision;

(e) estimated receipts of the Government during the ensuing fiscal year under (1) laws existing at the time the Budget is transmitted and also (2) under the revenue proposals, if any, contained in the Budget;

(f) actual appropriations, expenditures, and receipts of the Government during the last completed fiscal year;

(g) estimated expenditures and receipts and actual or proposed appropriations of the Government during the fiscal year in progress;

(h) balanced statements of (1) the condition of the Treasury at the end of the last completed fiscal year, (2) the estimated condition of the Treasury at the end of the fiscal year in progress, and (3) the estimated condition of the Treasury at the end of the ensuing fiscal year if the financial proposals contained in the Budget are adopted;

(i) all essential facts regarding the bonded and other indebtedness of the Government; and

(j) such other financial statements and data as in his opinion are necessary or desirable in order to make known in all practicable detail the financial condition of the Government.

This brings us to Part 2 of Title I, which pertains to accounting and auditing. This part of the Act starts out with the provision that it may be cited as the "Accounting and Auditing Act of 1950."

This provision is followed by a declaration of policy, which I think we should quote in detail and which is as follows:

It is the policy of the Congress in enacting this part that—

(a) The accounting of the Government provide full disclosure of the results of financial operations, adequate financial information needed in the management of operations and the formulation and execution of the Budget, and effective control over income, expenditures, funds, property, and other assets.

(b) Full consideration be given to the needs and responsibilities of both the legislative and executive branches in establishment of accounting and reporting systems and requirements.

(c) The maintenance of accounting systems and the producing of financial reports with respect to the operations of executive agencies, including central facilities for bringing together and disclosing information on the results of the financial operations of the Government as a whole, be the responsibility of the executive branch.

(d) The auditing for the Government, conducted by the Comptroller General of the United States as an agent of the Congress be directed at determining the extent to which accounting

210

and related financial reporting fulfill the purposes specified, financial transactions have been consummated in accordance with laws, regulations or other legal requirements, and adequate internal financial control over operations is exercised, and afford an effective basis for the settlement of accounts of accountable officers.

(e) Emphasis be placed on effecting orderly improvements resulting in simplified and more effective accounting, financial reporting, budgeting, and auditing requirements and procedures and on the elimination of those which involve duplication or which do not serve a purpose commensurate with the costs involved.

(f) The Comptroller General of the United States, the Secretary of the Treasury, and the Director of the Bureau of the Budget conduct a continuous program for the improvement of accounting and financial reporting in the Government.

The next provision in which we as accountants should he particularly interested is found in Sec. 112, which starts off as follows:

The Comptroller General of the United States, after consulting the Secretary of the Treasury and the Director of the Bureau of the Budget concerning their accounting, financial reporting, and budgetary needs, and considering the needs of the other executive agencies, shall prescribe the principles, standards, and related requirements for accounting to be observed by each executive agency, including requirements for suitable integration between the accounting processes of each executive agency and the accounting of the Treasury Department.

That provision is then followed by another, further defining the Comptroller General's authority with respect to accounting, as follows:

The General Accounting Office shall cooperate with the executive agencies in the development of their accounting systems, including the Treasury Department, in the development and establishment of the system of central accounting and reporting required by section 114 of this part. [Sec. 114 relates to the Treasurer's part in carrying out the accounting function.] Such accounting system shall be approved by the Comptroller General when deemed by him to be adequate and in conformity with the principles, standards, and related requirements prescribed by him.

That provision is then followed by another which requires periodic review of the accounting systems of the executive agencies by the Comptroller General.

Then comes Section 113, which contains language that is very familiar to all accountants, as follows:

(a) The head of each executive agency shall establish and maintain systems of accounting and internal control designed to provide—
(1) full disclosure of the financial results of the agency's activities;
(2) adequate financial information needed for the agency's management purposes;
(3) effective control over and accountability for all funds, property, and other assets for which the agency is responsible, including appropriate internal audit;
(4) reliable accounting results to serve as the basis for preparation and support of the agency's budget requests, for controlling the execution of its budget, and for providing financial information required by the Bureau of the Budget under section 213 of the Budget and Accounting Act, 1921 (42 Sta. 23);
(5) suitable integration of the accounting of the agency with the accounting of the Treasury Department in connection with the central accounting and reporting responsibilities imposed on the Secretary of the Treasury by section 114 of this part.
(b) The accounting systems of executive agencies shall conform to the principles, standards, and related requirements prescribed by the Comptroller General pursuant to section 112(a) of this part.

After this, we find Sec. 114, which makes what we feel was a rather weak attempt to provide for integration of the accounting. I think I should give you this section in full. It is as follows:

(a) The Secretary of the Treasury shall prepare such reports for the information of the President, the Congress, and the public as will present the results of the financial operations of the Government: PROVIDED, That there shall be included such financial data as the Director of the Bureau of the Budget may require in connection with the preparation of the Budget or for other purposes of the Bureau. Each executive agency shall furnish the Secretary of the Treasury such reports and information relating to its financial condition and operations as the Secretary, by rules and regulations, may require for the effective performance of his responsibilities under this section.
(b) The Secretary of the Treasury is authorized to establish the facilities necessary to produce the financial reports required by subsection (a) of this section. The Secretary is further authorized to reorganize the accounting functions and install, revise, or

eliminate accounting procedures and financial reports of the Treasury Department in order to develop effective and coordinated systems of accounting and financial reporting in the several bureaus and offices of the Department with such concentration of accounting and reporting as is necessary to accomplish integration of accounting results for the activities of the Department and provide the operating center for the consolidation of accounting results of other executive agencies with those of the Department. The authority vested in and the duties imposed upon the Department by sections 10, 15, and 22 of the Act entitled "An Act making appropriations for the legislative, executive, and judicial branches of the Government for the fiscal year ending June thirtieth, eighteen hundred ninety-five, and for other purposes," approved July 31, 1894 (28 Sta. 162, 208-210), may be exercised and performed by the Secretary of the Treasury as a part of his broader authority and duties under this section and in such a manner as to provide a unified system of central accounting and reporting on the most efficient and useful basis.

(c) The system of central accounting and reporting provided for herein shall be consistent with the principles, standards, and related requirements prescribed by the Comptroller General pursuant to section 112 of this part.

It is in this section that we think that the Budget and Accounting Procedures Act of 1950 went far wide of the mark of one of the most fundamental principles in accounting and thus set up what may prove to be an insuperable block against the achievement of the purposes that the Act was designed to accomplish. I will discuss this deficiency later. In the meantime, I would point out that this section also is concluded with the provision that the system of central accounting and reporting that it provides for shall be consistent with the principles, standards and related requirements prescribed by the Comptroller General.

Then come the auditing provisions which are found in Section 117, and which I also think I should give you in detail. This Section is as follows:

(a) Except as otherwise specifically provided by law, the financial transactions of each executive, legislative, and judicial agency, including but not limited to the accounts of accountable officers, shall be audited by the General Accounting Office in accordance with such principles and procedures and under such rules and regulations as may be prescribed by the Comptroller General of the United States. In the determination of auditing procedures to be followed and the extent of examination of vouchers and other documents, the Comptroller General shall give due regard to generally accepted principles of auditing, including consideration of the effectiveness of accounting organizations and systems, internal audit and control, and related administrative practices of the respective agencies.

(b) Whenever the Comptroller General determines that the audit shall be conducted at the place or places where the accounts and other records of an executive agency are normally kept, he may require any executive agency to retain in whole or in part accounts of accountable officers, contracts, vouchers, and other documents, which are required under existing law to be submitted to the General Accounting Office, under such conditions and for such period not exceeding ten years as he may specify, unless a longer period is agreed upon with the executive agency: PROVIDED, That under agreements between the Comptroller General and legislative and judicial agencies the provisions of this sentence may be extended to the accounts and records of such agencies.

Of special interest in this Section is that part which says that "in determination of auditing procedures to be followed and the extent of examination of vouchers and other documents, the Comptroller General shall give due regard to generally accepted principles of auditing, including consideration of the effectiveness of accounting organizations and systems, internal audit and control, and related administrative practices of the respective agencies." Here we find recognition of the effectiveness of internal control upon determination of the extent of the auditor's examination.

And, in the second part of this Section, you will note that permission is given to the Comptroller General to make his audits on the spot "at the place or places where the accounts and other records of an executive agency are normally kept." This gets away from the old idea of requiring all agencies to send their expenditure documents to the General Accounting Office for examination. This undoubtedly will tremendously enhance the effectiveness of the Comptroller General's inquiries.

Now, what is wrong with the Budget and Accounting Procedures Act of 1950? In brief, the trouble with it is that it is like a ship with neither a bridge nor a skipper. To put it another way, it is like a big corporation with a lot of branches and each branch responsible for its accounting, but with no Controller at headquarters to direct and integrate the accounting.

To those of us who studied the situation, it is a forlorn hope, we think, to expect that integration of the government's accounting can be accomplished without a central accounting department headed by a top-flight accountant-executive. Moreover, we think that it is highly inconsistent to make the executive branch responsible for the accounting and then give the independent auditor of Congress the power of veto over everything it proposes to do. This is like giving an independent public accountant the power to disapprove the systems adopted by the chief accounting officers of the enterprises he audits.

Moreover, it isn't sufficient just to say that the accounting will be integrated by some employee or official of undesignated rank and authority in the Treasury Department. The Treasury Department itself is a tremendous establishment; its accounting requirements are prodigious; and one of the most serious deficiencies of the present situation is that the Treasury Department has gotten its own accounting and that of the government generally so mixed up together that no one can make heads or tails of either. This situation has existed for many years. Thus, experience does not justify anyone in believing that the pussyfooting provisions of Sec. 114 would ever accomplish integration of the accounting or timely turning out of financial reports.

As far as the Treasury Department is concerned Sec. 114 merely gives it another job to do without even specifying that the job should be turned over to properly qualified and really responsible people. It is rather difficult to understand how anyone could seriously believe that such a setup as this would accomplish anything but confusion. No one could possibly believe that those who were responsible for this legislation would be satisfied if the accounting of a corporation of which they were directors were organized on such a flimsy and weak-kneed basis.

As to the power given to the Comptroller General to veto the systems worked out by the executive branch, it is equally difficult to believe that those responsible for this provision would, as directors of a corporation, be willing to give the independent auditors of that corporation the power to veto the actions of that corporation's chief accounting officer. Indeed, no independent public accountant would be willing to accept such responsibility, because it would involve him in managerial decisions of the highest importance and destroy the very independence for which he was employed. This provision won't work any more than have those which heretofore have involved the Comptroller General in the managerial decisions of the executive branch.

Thus, we have a situation where the Budget and Accounting Procedures Act of 1950 contains declarations of purposes and policies of the highest order to which anyone could subscribe, but is equally distinguished by omissions and timid provisions that jeopardize the achievement of those purposes and policies.

And so, for want of observance of some of the most fundamental principles that should be observed in determining the organization and management of the accounting and financial reporting, this Act becomes a good example of noble intentions rendered doubtful of achievement by another triumph of expediency over forthrightness.

Time will force correction of these deficiencies, of course, but it is to be hoped that Congress will not take as long to come to realization of the need for correction as it took to get around to the passing of the Budget and Accounting Procedures Act of 1950, as weak as it is.

FREEDOM'S WAR ON WASTE[†]
by
T. Coleman Andrews

WHAT times these are in which we are living! The second world war only six years behind us and the rumblings of the third already audible! Big business—big government! Agricultural and industrial capacity more than twice what they were only twenty eventful years ago.

Remarkable, we say—and so it is. But we need it, for government has become—or rather, it has been made—*eighteen times bigger*, and we stand pitted against vastly greater numbers though fortunately less production capacity, in the threatening struggle for world leadership.

But as colossal, clumsy and inept as it is, this big government is *our* government—yours and mine; whatever happens to it—whether it succeeds or fails—you and I will be responsible. Though not as much so as millions of us would like, it still is a government of free people. It will remain so, however, only as long as you and I—its citizens—recognize and discharge the obligations of freedom as readily and enthusiastically as we avail ourselves of the privileges of it.

The challenge with which we are confronted today is not something new; it has been developing for years. From its first appearance right down to the present moment, the all-important question has been, and is, will we be ready?

WILL WE BE READY?

Congress saw the need and finally moved to do something about it. And so, three years ago, leaders of both political parties agreed that the government must be re-organized to eliminate duplication and overlapping; cut red tape and reduce waste. Unanimously Congress passed the Lodge-Brown Act creating the Commission on Organization of the Executive Branch of the government, The Hoover Commission, consisting of six Democrats and six Republicans.

Three hundred of the nation's foremost experts worked two years. More than 20 task forces dug up 2 million words of facts and figures and made over 300 recommendations to speed up government action, use

[†]Reprinted with permission of the National Association of Credit Management from *Credit and Financial Management*, July 1951, pp. 16-18.

manpower and materials wisely and get ready for every task of peace or war.

THE FINDINGS

The Commission found that we were wasting one dollar of every 10 that we were spending. That was to be expected of a government which in 22 years of depression, war, emergency, and cold war had expanded from 570,000 to 2 million employees; from 100 to 1812 departments, agencies, boards, bureaus and commissions; from a budget of $4 billion in 1928 to $45 billion in 1948 ($71 billion requested for 1951). Yes, even before today's crisis, the cost of the federal government had risen from $240 a year per average American family, to more than $1,200 per year. (Today it is over $500 for every man, woman and child and over $2,000 per family.) One dollar in every 10 was being wasted and could be saved *without eliminating any essential service*. In fact every service actually could be improved. For example, the Commission found:

29 different agencies engaged in making loans;
28 engaged in handling welfare projects;
16 engaged in preservation of wild life;
50 engaged in compiling statistics;
24 supervisors for 25 employees in one unit of the Veterans' Administration;
Post office employees doing the same job, often in the same building, at different rates of pay;
Swarms of overlapping agricultural agents in every U.S. county;
Hidden subsidies;
Interest-free loans of nearly $1 billion to farmers—surplus funds of agencies invested in government bonds;
The Central Arizona Project. Did you ever hear about it? It's hidden away in that $71½ billion-dollar budget we are currently being asked to swallow.

The Citizens Committee for the Hoover Report was organized because popular support of the Commission's Report was essential. There are 300 State and local committees from coast to coast. This Citizens Committee has proved that ordinary and unselfish citizens can get things done in Washington when they really set their minds to it, for

thanks to the unselfish efforts of the membership of the Citizens Committee, about 50% of the Hoover Commission's recommendations have been approved. 20 public laws and 26 presidential re-organization plans were adopted by the 81st Congress. Savings of no less than $2 billion a year—probably much more—will result.

218

More important than that, the government today is operating more smoothly than it was a year ago. Among the chief products of the Commission's work to date are:

1. Strengthened lines of authority and responsibility in 17 major, and many smaller, agencies covering two-thirds of the Executive Branch;
2. True teamwork in the armed services under the Unification Act of 1949;
3. Improved purchasing, storage, records management and building procedures;
4. A modernized budgeting and accounting system;
5. Greatly strengthened internal organization of the State Department;
6. Rebuilding of the Labor Department to cabinet stature.

Scores of lesser improvements also have been adopted.

THE SAVINGS

Though the savings may seem small in relation to present budget figures, "every little bit helps," and see what these savings will buy, even at today's inflated prices:

1,000	medium tanks;
1,000	jet fighters;
25	carriers of the Midway class;
100	heavy bombers;
50	modern submarines;
100	anti-aircraft guns.

In addition, the re-organization already carried out is revealing new extravagances:

93 years' supply of fluorescent light tubes;
247 years' supply of loose-leaf binders;
One major agency did away with 209 inter-departmental committees;
Another changed its review procedure and saved 1,259,488 man-hours
    of work per year.

One authoritative reviewer of the situation says that "If the Military Unification Act of 1949 were its only achievement, the Hoover Commission would have been justified a 100 times."

WHAT DO WE DO NEXT?

Well, that's only a sketchy review, of course; but it's as much as my allotment of time will permit. We're on the 50-yd. line. What do we have to do in order to hold onto the ball and get it over the goal line?

The answer to the first part of that question is that we must keep driving, of course. But let's deal with that later. Let's talk about some of the more important plays that we've got to run from here on in.

1. *Modern personnel management.* This problem we must solve, because it is in manpower that we are inferior to the nation that presently threatens us. We are far superior in agriculture, industry and science, but in sheer number of people the communist countries outweigh us heavily. We cannot waste manpower, therefore. Certainly the government, that is supposed to protect us, should not. There are presently more than 2 million government employees—*more than are on the payrolls of the nation's 50 largest corporations combined*—and the number is growing daily. Most of these people want to do a good job, but they are hampered by red tape in recruiting skilled and specialized workers for key jobs, delay in both hiring capable workers and firing the incompetent, and "empire building" within agencies.

One minor governmental subdivision recently was found to have 17 "sections," 27 "units," 24 "subunits," 13 "groups" and one "inquiry office." Some of them contained only one or two persons, but all had "chiefs," "assistant chiefs," and so on. No wonder 500,000 employees annually become frustrated and quit the government.

2. *Better service for veterans.* The super-duper colossus of waste is the VA. It takes five times as long to pay a death claim to a veteran's widow as a private company does and uses four times as many people to do it. This is the agency where 24 supervisors were found for 25 employees, which explained a 9-page law in 994 pages of regulations and instructions, which wasted big sums on "phoney" educational projects and overpaid $200 million to men who already had left school.

3. *Unified federal hospitals.* Five big, and some 30 smaller, federal hospital systems are set up on a rigidly separate basis. They obtain funds and build hospitals with little knowledge of, and no regard for, the needs of each other. They compete among themselves, and with private hospitals, for desperately scarce physicians and nurses. They fail to utilize manpower fully and efficiently; in other words, they waste it. No one knows how many hospital beds the government maintains.

4. *A modernized post office.* The present system is running at a loss of $500 million a year. It is hampered by an archaic and overcentralized organizational structure, a mass of cumbersome legal regulations and restrictions, outmoded equipment and methods, low morale due to the political appointment of postmasters, and hidden subsidies paid to airlines and other carriers—$120 million a year. One "airline" with total revenue of only $36,000 got $440,000 in subsidy payments.

5. *A check on "pork barrel" public works.* Army Engineers with 40,000 employees and the Bureau of Reclamation of the Department of the Interior between them have projects planned that would cost $52 billion.

They are "brazen and pernicious lobbyists"—both of them. Read their record from "Will We Be Ready?".[1]

6. *An up-to-date department of agriculture.* The present one is ill-organized, riddled with duplication and overlapping, wasteful, creaky and confused. It spent $32 in 1948 for every $1 spent in 1928. The Commission found it a "loose confederation of independent bureaus and agencies" with a score of huge units operating independently and often at cross purposes. In a single county in the State of Washington the Commission found 184 farm agents serving 6,700 farmers—one agent for every 36 farmers.

7. *Other Recommendations.*

(a) Grouping of Social Security, Education and Indian Affairs in a single cabinet department;

(b) Uniform handling of administration of war-created federal jurisdictions overseas;

(c) An attack on the complex relationship of federal and state governments;

(d) Re-organization of the Treasury and other major federal commissions, boards and bureaus.

This program cannot be completed without popular support, for the opposition is strong.

THE CITIZENS COMMITTEE

The surest way to get a job like this done is to join with others and put up a united and powerful front.

Join the Citizens Committee and help form an effective "lobby against lobbies"—a "pressure group against pressure groups." Write to your senators and congressmen often. Tell them you want economy and that you especially want the balance of the Hoover Report adopted.

---

[1]Quotation from "Will We Be Ready?" concerning competition between the Army Engineer Corps and the Bureau of Reclamation.

On tiny Cherry Creek, near Denver, the Army Engineers tore down an existing dam, which local engineers considered adequate, and erected another three miles long and 147 feet high. The Colorado Big Thompson project was estimated to cost $44 millions by the Bureau of Reclamation—but it may eventually cost $200 millions. The $24 million Kendrick Dam in Wyoming was built in 1935—12 long years before any water became available for it. On the Snake River in Hell's Canyon, Idaho, the Engineers and the Bureau surveyed plans for a dam at sites less than two miles apart, spent $250,000 per survey—and came up with cost estimates $75 millions apart.

In conclusion let me quote from a statement by Robert L. Johnson, National Chairman of the Citizens Committee for the Hoover Report:

> We cannot bear the burdens of the world on one shoulder and a burden of waste on the other ... We cannot stand before the world as a symbol of free self-government if we cannot manage our own affairs ... Every dollar, every scrap of material, every bit of human effort we waste is a gift to the enemies of freedom.

·

PROFESSIONAL LEADERSHIP: THE AMERICAN INSTITUTE OF ACCOUNTANTS

ACCEPTANCE ADDRESS OF THE NEW PRESIDENT[†]

by

T. Coleman Andrews

FIRST, I want to thank you for the great honor you have today bestowed upon me. I thank you not only for myself but also for my state and for the entire southeastern part of the country. This is the first time, I believe, that the accounting profession of Virginia and the southeast has been honored by the elevation of one of its members to the presidency of the American Institute of Accountants. Needless to say, you have made this the proudest moment of my life.

I should like to speak briefly about some of the matters that will command our attention as a profession during the coming year. Since you already have received, or will receive, reports on every phase of the Institute activities during the course of this meeting, it is not necessary, and it would not be appropriate, for me to undertake a broad review and discussion of these activities. I merely wish to emphasize some of the matters that seem to me to be of paramount importance.

It must be apparent to everyone that the public accounting profession has outlived its growing pains and now has reached that stage of maturity where it has shed the problems of youth for the responsibilities of manhood. It is no mere boast to say that public accounting has become one of the country's leading professions—not merely because of its numbers, but, rather, because of the magnitude and effectiveness of its contributions to the rapidly expanding economy of the nation.

I think it was natural that the rapid growth and development of our profession should lead to some apparent, if not real, conflict of interests along the way. The measure of seriousness of such conflicts is determined not so much by the heat that they generate as by the wisdom with which they are faced by the parties involved.

One of the principal conflicts that has arisen has grown out of the feeling of our friends of the legal profession that we have encroached upon their prerogatives. Personally, I always have thought that this conflict has been more apparent than real. Nevertheless, the legal profession has openly challenged some of our activities.

[†]Reprinted with permission from *How to Improve Accounting & Tax Service to American Business* (New York: American Institute of Accountants, 1950), pp. 7-10.

I have been proud of the manner in which the American Institute of Accountants has dealt with this matter. We have approached it in a spirit of give and take, through a special task force, and through the National Conference of Lawyers and Certified Public Accountants.

While this conference is not ready to report complete agreement, I believe that agreement is possible. I further believe that it will be achieved, because I am convinced that there is plenty of work to keep both professions busy and that neither profession wants to invade the territory of the other. Joint areas of activity are unavoidable and even desirable. I am satisfied that negotiations will be continued and that mutually satisfactory agreement will be reached.

We have also had basic differences with the uncertified public accountants. It seems to me that we certified public accountants must avoid developing the attitude that the CPA certificate is obtained as a matter of right. This is not the case at all. The certificate is a privilege—one that carries with it heavy responsibilities, not the least of which is the obligation to be alert to the public interest that we serve.

The most rigid tests of fitness to practice public accounting are imposed upon those who seek to call themselves certified public accountants. It is clear that we can take no other position than that those who hold CPA certificates are best qualified for public practice and that this certificate should not be granted to any but those who demonstrate their fitness to enjoy the privilege of public practice by taking and passing appropriate examinations.

Those who demand the privilege of practicing without certification will say that this is a self-serving declaration. This reaction is only natural; so we must expect it. But we must take comfort and courage from our record, and from experience, which clearly shows that the public interest demands that this restriction be imposed.

We have no obligation to those who seek a free ride at the public's expense. We *do* have an obligation to those who aspire to certification to see that the examinations are fair and open to all. We have discharged this obligation with faithfulness in the past, and we will continue to do so in the future.

As public accountants, our principal characteristic is independence. We are, by law, designated "certified public accountants." Thus, the people, in their sovereign capacity, publish to the world that we are possessed of the knowledge and skill required for the examination and formulation of opinions concerning the accuracy and integrity of accounts. More than that, they publish to the world that our characters have been subjected to searching inquiry and not found wanting.

Thus, in effect, the people acting in their sovereign capacity, have satisfied themselves and published that we have demonstrated not only expertness in the examination of accounts but also the strength of character that gives the public the right to rely upon our opinions as to the fairness of the representations of those who have the obligation of giving an account of their stewardships.

These pronouncements impose upon us great and inescapable obligations. From them our independence arises. Deprived of our independence we would be reduced to the status of artisans, and the public would be deprived of a service that has contributed mightily to the unequalled industrial, commercial, and financial eminence that our country has achieved.

There are only two ways by which we can lose this independence. One would be by failure to live up to the standards of skill and integrity that the public has the right to expect of us. I do not fear that this will happen. Our record is too good to warrant anyone's regarding such an eventuality as being even conceivable. Indeed, I think it is little short of remarkable that the instances of lack of skill and integrity are infinitesimal in relation to the vast number of engagements that we handle.

The other way in which we can lose our independence is by bureaucratic usurpation and virtual abolition of our function. This I do fear. The trend of political thinking and action leaves me no alternative. We must, therefore, be alert to the danger that lies in this direction and firmly resolve to resist with all the vigor that we possess any and all proposals that threaten to take away or diminish the mainstay of our usefulness.

This is not just a question of selfish interest. It is much broader than that. It is the age-old question whether as a people we are going to support and control the government or let the government support and control us. There is no middle ground; it is always one way or the other. Man is either completely free or he is not free at all.

Man has no more mortal enemy than autocracy. Hence, in resisting any effort that the government makes to take over our function as a profession, we not only defend our professional independence but also add our strength to the defense of freedom and against the tendency of all government to become absolute, autocratic and tyrannical.

Nor does our duty end there. The public has a high regard for our opinions about management and finance, not only as to private enterprise, but also as to public affairs. The public has a right to look to us for guidance and counsel in the administration of public funds. Today we of the United States stand committed to the expenditure of billions of dollars every year at home and abroad for the sole purpose of protecting ourselves and our friends from the onslaught of communism. Never before in all history has a people taken on such a burden. The people have a right to expect us, as certified public accountants, to cry out when we see these public funds wasted in duplication and thrown away on nonessentials. Time and time again in recent months I have been asked: "Why don't you public accountants speak up?" Now it is our professional duty to speak up. It is our professional duty to help find ways to insure the people of our country that they are getting what they are paying for.

We devoutly hope that the Korean emergency is nearly over. But we are already in a deeper and even more serious emergency which may last for years. We might as well recognize now that "emergency" has become "normal." For the first time in our national history, we are going to have to maintain a large-scale military establishment on a permanent basis. We have not even begun to realize the effects this will have on our national economy and on our daily lives.

When an emergency becomes permanent, it cannot be handled with improvisations and half-measures as the government has been doing for most of the last twenty years.

Unsound fiscal policy will bring about the very collapse the Russians are counting on to win the cold war.

Because we are a very rich country, we have been able to stagger alone under a burden of waste and inefficiency which would have wrecked any other country in the world—which has wrecked some other countries. We cannot afford it any longer.

As an accountant who has devoted a great deal of time to the study of federal government finances, I think I know what I am saying when I tell you that the accounting system of our national government would not be tolerated in any successful business in the United States. There has been a little improvement recently, but not nearly enough. The government does not yet have a budget which tells us what our money will be spent for and how much the various items will cost. We do not have an accounting system which tells us where the money has gone after it has been spent. And it is not merely the people who don't know. Government officials themselves don't know—and can't know, with the system we have now. We need not only improvement in techniques, but a strengthening of the system by separation of auditing and accounting. Unless we get sound accounting for the federal government, and get it soon, we just will not be able to stand the strain of our arms program over the next few years.

This program calls for sacrifice, not only on the battle front, but also on the home front; and I suggest that cold war or hot war, recurring "police actions," or continuing global conflict, we are in for a long period of sacrifice. Let us, therefore, individually and collectively recognize the situation for what it is and *meet* it—not with mere sighs of distress, nor with the whimpering of irresolute weaklings, but with the defiance of courageous and provident men, aware of the priceless benefits of freedom, instantly and bristlingly responsive to every threat to our enjoyment of it.

We are told that we must take in our belts. All right, let's tighten them a notch or two; and let's be prepared to keep on tightening them until our bellies are so thin that fluoroscopes will become useless. But let's demand the same thing of the government.

We also are told that, for a time at least, we may not expect "business as usual." All right, let's cut bark in that department of our lives; and let's be prepared to keep on cutting back until every moment of our time and every ounce of our energy is devoted to defense, if that becomes necessary. But let's demand that those who call upon us to make this sacrifice give up "government as usual" and reconcile themselves to giving up more and more of it until the security of our way of life is assured.

Higher taxes? All right, so be it. But let's demand that public funds be spent for things we really need, without waste or duplication. We cannot carry the burden of defending ourselves and a large part of the rest of the world and carry also the burden of inexcusable waste and extravagance in the organization and management of our nondefense internal affairs without eventually breaking our backs.

Senators and Congressmen of the greatest knowledge and soundest understanding of the nation's fiscal affairs—of untainted devotion to our form of government—and of the highest competence and integrity—assure the people that the budget can be balanced without injury to any essential activity of the government. Many of us of the public accounting profession long have been of this opinion.

With the financial stability of the government now hanging in the balance, and with the survival of modern civilization at stake, it is high time that we and others throughout the land demand that the government cut out the frills, get down to essentials, and devote itself seriously and honestly to the job immediately at hand.

It also is high time for the government to recognize—and we should demand that it recognize—that it cannot continue to make a whipping boy of business in time of peace and expect business to continue to perform the miracles of production that saved our necks in World War I, again in World War II, and yet again in Korea. We should not allow an instrument of defense which, in a matter of days, converted mere blueprints into the rockets and tanks that turned the tide of battle in Korea to be so shabbily and ungratefully treated.

This is not to say that the government alone is sinful and that a brilliant halo encircles the head of business, for business has indeed behaved badly since the Communists struck in Korea on June 25th. Overnight the prices of many commodities were raised to unconscionable and unjustifiable levels. This wasn't just normal operation of the law of supply and demand. It was the old grab game of demanding what the traffic would bear in a seller's market.

Immediately labor began to demand a cut in the take, the spiral of inflation started all over again, and the consumer, who has been taking it on the chin all too long, was again forgotten. Freedom isn't preserved by destroying it. Hence I say that the government should get off of the back of business. But while we are demanding our due from the government, we also should remind business that it is pretty hard to help a fellow who doesn't try to help himself.

If we are faced with a long period of strengthening our defenses, as most certainly we are, let's cut out all the frills and furbelows, tighten up our belts, and get down to the business of defense. Unless matters get a lot worse than they are now, we won't need controls if everyone—the government, business, labor, and you and I—play the game according to the rules of good sportsmanship.

Particularly must we purge ourselves of the sins that we have committed in the name of "social justice," get down to bare essentials, and devote all our resources and energy to defense. There never was a greater miscarriage of justice than our resort to force people to do "good" by law: personal goodness simply cannot be achieved by legislation, and, as Admiral Ben Morrell recently put it, people who advocate this course "lack faith in God and in their fellowmen."

Therefore, let us get down to the basis of "billions for defense, but not one cent for deficits."

ADDRESS AT TAX CLINIC OF THE ALABAMA SOCIETY OF CERTIFIED PUBLIC ACCOUNTANTS AND THE UNIVERSITY OF ALABAMA[†]

by

T. Coleman Andrews

MR. CHAIRMAN, PRESIDENT GALLALEE, DEAN BIDGOOD, DISTINGUISHED GUESTS, FELLOW ACCOUNTANTS, LADIES AND GENTLEMEN.

IT'S a great pleasure to be here tonight to speak to you. The American Institute is very proud of the fact that you have asked its President to come here and address you. We are happy always to meet with our friends of the legal profession and those who are interested in the things we are interested in; and, of course, we are happy to meet with our own people.

Yes, it's a great pleasure to be here, ladies and gentlemen; and it's a great pleasure to be able to see the funny side of life, to enjoy and indulge in a little wit and humor, because, unhappily, this isn't a very funny world that we are living in.

I think most of you know that ever since man emerged from savagery—ever since he organized his first government—he has been trying to escape from one thing ultimately and one thing alone, namely, the tyranny of government. Man has no more mortal enemy than political tyranny and oppression.

We fought quite a big war back in 1776 to 1781 to escape from this tyranny and we have been going pretty well for a hundred and seventy years. In your lifetime and mine—in the past fifteen to twenty years—we have seen nation after nation, people after people, succumb to the tyranny

---

[†]Reprinted with the permission from *Fourth Annual Federal Tax Clinic 1950, University of Alabama Bulletin*, (University, AL: Bureau of Business Research, School of Commerce and Business Administration, University of Alabama, 1951), pp. 73-78.

The following editor's note accompanied the original publication of this article: Readers will understand of course that Mr. Andrews speaks for himself and not for the University of Alabama. In a number of cases he takes quite positive positions on controversial subjects. In fact in several cases this editor finds himself in disagreement with Mr. Andrews' statements, particularly with regard to the ability of the nation to meet present defense needs without controls and the assertion that government produces nothing. In a free country, it is neither probable nor desirable that all of us will agree with the ideas of any one person, and this note is printed only to remind the reader that this publication is attempting only to facilitate the discussion of important problems.

of government; and the battle, the great battle of America today, the great battle of the world today, is the battle between two ideologies—one that would enforce tyranny upon all the people of the world, the other one that would make the people free throughout the world, as you and I have been free here in America during our lifetimes. Jefferson warned at the time the Constitution was being framed that no situation would arise that would so endanger the liberties of the people as would improvident living on the part of the government.

Now, in sounding this warning, Jefferson wasn't worried so much about the mere matter of extravagance and improvidence; that was merely a result, a symptom of something deeper. The thing that Jefferson was worried about—the thing that every one of his contemporaries was worried about—was this enemy that I spoke of, this tyranny of government. Jefferson knew that when government became tyrannical, the next result would be the utter and complete enslavement of the people.

Later on came a man, whom most of you have heard and read about; his name was Karl Marx, the German intellectual, who wrote the philosophy of communism that we hear so much about today; and later on came one of his disciples, one Lenin, who said, "Just give us time and we will force America to spend herself to destruction." That, ladies and gentlemen, is exactly what the enemies of our form of government hope to do—make us spend ourselves to destruction; and I might say that up to this time the communists and other socialists have pretty well succeeded. We are losing the battle today. We are losing it on all fronts. I don't believe, personally, though my opinion perhaps isn't worth very much, that we are going to lose the war. We are going to lose some more battles, but I don't believe that we will lose the war.

Now, let's remember that Marx and Lenin and all of their disciples were not mere wishful thinkers. They were realists of the first water. They had a clearer insight into the nature of man than most of us. They believed, and, therefore, they realized, with ample evidence to back up their convictions, that inherent in the makeup of man is a lust for power; and they saw that this lust manifested itself in acquisitiveness, in a tendency to seek security and power through economic control of one's fellows. Hence, they reasoned that any people who became absorbed primarily in economic pursuit—and the world already was beginning to become preponderantly economic—would so far delegate their political control, and abandon control over their government to political leaders, that their liberty would be forever lost and tyranny would again be firmly established. All this is rapidly coming to pass, and our freedom today teeters on the very brink of oblivion and tyranny.

We accountants are of the business community. We have a stake in the kind of government that we have enjoyed in this country, just as the business people of the country have a stake in it; and, business people have asked me time and time again: "When are you fellows who know so well the economics of the business of America going to say something? Why don't you speak up? Why don't you lend your voices to those that have been raised against extravagance? You know the consequences of it; you see it everyday."

At the annual meeting of the American Institute of Accountants a little over a month ago, we decided that the time had come to speak up, to speak up constructively, if we could, but in any event, to speak up. We have had two world wars and a sickening depression in between, and those two wars have consumed hundreds of thousands of the flower of the youth of this country; and let me say that I put that first among the losses of war because, after all, no resource of our country is more important, more precious, more valuable than the lives of the young people of the country. We lost hundreds of thousands in those two wars. We have already lost nearly twenty thousand in the war in Korea.

On top of that, we have lost a vast portion of our material resources—shot away, burned up, exploded into nothingness; and we have left ourselves with a quarter of a trillion dollars of debt—a mortgage against the future of every man, woman, and child in America today, and of every child that will be born for generations yet to come, because, after all, those dollars represent the future earning or the earnings of the future people of America as well as those of today.

All told, our public and private debt together is twice a quarter of a trillion dollars today, or half a trillion; and this is more than the total value of all our known assets. In other words, to put it plainly, the government is broke and is sustained only by its power to impound the fruits of the people's toil. How much longer that power will sustain us is something that I wouldn't venture to predict.

I am fully aware, of course, that all this public debt is owed to ourselves; but I get no consolation from the fact that a public debt owed to ourselves is not dangerous because it could be wiped clear of the books and still leave us no worse off in the aggregate. That, of course, is just a sample of the specious reasoning that has dictated so many of the policies that have brought us to our present condition. Have you thought what it would mean to wipe off this debt? It would be confiscation. It would be expropriation. It would break every insurance company in America. It would break every bank in America. It would wipe out everything and pauperize almost everybody, especially those who had shown any get-up and go—any ability to produce and make themselves useful members of society.

Now, we have another problem, the war in Korea. This trouble in Korea is but an enlargement of a problem that already existed; it isn't anything new. We could have expected it, and I don't know that we ought to accuse anyone particularly for it. The important question, it seems to me, is whether we will have the wisdom to make the sacrifices that will be necessary in order to save ourselves from the fate that is sure to overtake us if we don't make those sacrifices. We can't pull out of this thing that we are up against now without making sacrifices, especially when you consider the fact that we are now faced with probably a generation—at least that is what everybody in Washington says—of the kind of war we are engaged in at the present time, a generation of enlarged defense expenditures.

Our defense expenditures before Korea were fifteen billion dollars a year. The President asked for eighteen billion more on top of that. He's already spent ten billion. The chances are, apparently, that the rate of expenditure for the kind of war in which we are now engaged is going to be between fifteen and twenty-five billion dollars a year, so that, on top of the fifteen we were spending prior to Korea, we are going to have a budget of almost as much money for defense alone as the forty billion dollars that we had before Korea happened. And, to carry it a step further, it looks like we may have a budget, year after year—not just one year—but maybe for a generation, of somewhere between sixty and seventy-five billion dollars a year. The authority for this estimate is men like Senator Byrd, General Marshall and Mr. Snyder. So we must gird our loins for a higher state of production, one that will sustain and keep stable an economy out of which such a large proportion is apt to be drained off for the wasteful purposes of the government. Now, by that, I don't mean to brand all government expenditures as wasteful; I merely point out to you that the government produces nothing, and that when it takes and spends our income it is spending our production. It contributes nothing to the wealth of the country, except in a few scattered activities. It is a consumer of wealth produced by the people—not a producer.

That's one reason why Jefferson and others were afraid to ever let the government get so big and become so extravagant that it would take too large a portion of the income of the people. The Hoover Commission said that we could save from three to five billion dollars a year by reorganization—not by cutting out anything, mind you; merely by better organization and management of existing activities. This Commission had no authority to consider the advisability, or the desirability, of cutting out any activity in which the government was engaged. Its instructions were to take what it would find and tell us what it thought we could save by organizing and managing it in a more economical way. If we could have gotten into the question of what could have been cut out in addition to what might have been saved by reorganization, three to five billion dollars would have been "chicken feed" compared to what we might have reported could have been saved in the administration of the national affairs. But, let's forget about that part of it. Just from reorganization alone, it was found that we could save from three to five billion dollars a year. Let's split the difference and call it four billion. Do you know what that would buy today in spite of the tremendous increase in prices that has occurred? It would buy two thousand medium tanks, two thousand jet fighters, two thousand antiaircraft guns, two hundred heavy bombers, and a hundred submarines. And that's what we need today. That's what we can use a lot of. That's what we're going to have to buy a lot of.

And so, the great problem that faces America today—a problem in which we accountants have not only a special competence to advise but also a very definite and special obligation to undertake leadership—is to find effective ways to expose and depict the ultimate calamity that is inherent in the government's wastefulness. True enough, the American people seldom have been aroused to action until crisis already had set in. The sixty-four dollar question is: will they wake up and get out this time before the house burns down?

This, I submit, increases our obligation individually and collectively, in our communities, clubs, churches—wherever our influence can be brought to bear—to arouse the people to speedy realization that a government that insists upon inordinate exactions to maintain a vast bureaucracy to enforce its will is a government that thinks it knows better than we what is good for us and that is sure to become tyrannical and oppressive sooner or later. This is a responsibility that I think we accountants, lawyers, businessmen, and educators can assume, and one that I think we should assume now.

The Committee for Economic Development has just released a report that sets forth five specific steps that should be taken at once. Let me read the first two:

1. Curtail government nonmilitary expenditures to the maximum possible extent and achieve the greatest efficiency and coordination in military procurement.
2. (After taking that step—note that, after taking the first step) Raise taxes so that as the military program absorbs production, taxes will withdraw income from private hands.

The other three recommendations are not pertinent to the particular subject of my remarks; so we may skip them. I call your attention to the fact that the C.E.D. people, some of the best brains in the country, have said to us that we have a very definite job to do and that that job is, first of all, to cut expenses.

Now, nobody objects to an increase in taxes so long as expenses are cut down to reasonable proportions. But have any of you heard any suggestions on anybody's part that there be any reduction in expenses? No, not a word. All we hear is: "raise taxes." When taxes are raised to take care of a budget of sixty-five to seventy-five billion dollars, it will be quite an increase. It would take a fifty percent increase in corporation taxes, a thirty percent increase in personal taxes, a twenty-four percent increase in postal rates, and a forty-three percent increase in social security taxes in order to do it. I just don't believe that the people of America can take such additional exactions. I don't believe that the economy of this country can take it. And I think you and I have an obligation to make the people see that they can't take it and why, before it happen.

We aren't in the position we were in before World War II. At that time we had seventeen ships, ocean-going ships, in reserve—seventeen, that's all. Today, we have twenty-two hundred and seventy-seven. So we don't need to worry much about steel. We have got a hundred million tons of steel production as against less than eighty-five million tons before World War II. The engines of war that take the greatest amount of steel are largely already built and waiting. Hence, we don't have to ration steel in order to take care of the kind of war we are in now. But Washington clamors for general controls.

We are turning out today eight million automobiles a year as against three million before World War II. We are producing a hundred and fifty million more barrels of oil. We have a million tons of synthetic rubber production; before Wold War II we had none whatsoever. We are producing a third more food that we produced before World War II. One hundred and twenty-two million more tons of wheat actually are in storage today than before World War II. Three hundred and five million more bushels of corn are on hand. And so on down the line—butter, cheese, and eggs stored away in almost unbelievable quantities.

No, we are not in that unhappy position we were in before World War II; so, we don't need to worry if we will only use our heads and exercise our privileges as citizens. We don't need to strap ourselves to the post of enslavement. All we need to do is just use our economic sense and the things we have.

Now, of course, if by chance tomorrow an atomic bomb should explode over Washington and New York and the world be plunged overnight into a third World War, that is another story. It would be a question, then, of survival for tomorrow or the next day, or whether we would survive at all. We would have to go all out, of course, if total war came; but today we are in a relatively minor engagement. It isn't a police action, but it's not consuming more that ten percent of the productive capacity of the country, and it is not likely to. Therefore, why do we have to raise taxes to sixty-five to seventy billion dollars? Why do we have to keep expenses at that level? Why do we have to strap industry which, after all, is what we depend upon to save this country? Why do we have to put all-out controls upon ourselves in a situation of that kind?

It is your country as well as mine. I think we all have an obligation to see that it is properly organized and run. Most of you, I imagine, came up the hard way, as I did. You probably started in business with nothing and what you have, you earned. Do you want your children to have that same privilege, or do you want the State to tell them where they can work, or whether they work at all? That's the issue. I think your answer will be that you want them to be on their own to pull themselves up by their own ingenuity and efforts. You want them to have that opportunity—that privilege. They don't have it today, not to the extent, at least, that you and I did.

A man came into my office the other day, a manager of one of three branches of the company by which he was employed. The owner had called the three managers in and said, "Look here, boys, I'm ready to quit. I have all the money I want. If you will give me so much money, I will turn my stock over to you." Well, it was a reasonable offer and those men began to figure, and they took an inventory of how much money they could raise. They were able to raise about a third of what it would cost to buy that stock, and after everybody had got through advising them, what was the conclusion? It was simply this: that they could never hope to have enough left after taxes to keep the company properly financed and at the same time pay off the purchase-money obligation. That was not a very happy outlook, was it? Yet, that is the position every one of us is in.

I would like to see a country in which the youth of America will have the same opportunities that you and I had. That is the route by which this country attained its present pre-eminence and power in the world, and I don't think that we should experiment with a substitute for that known and proven method of attaining greatness and power—particularly a substitute that has failed every time it has been tried—that never has succeeded in all the history of the world. No, let us go back to the old virtues and old truths. They are still as good today as they ever were. Benjamin Franklin's *Poor Richard's Almanac* has a lot of good common sense in it for the man that wants to get somewhere in the world, and I further say to you that the Constitution of the United States has more common sense, more justice, and more freedom in it than anything I have heard anybody recently offer as a substitute.

ACCOUNTING PROBLEMS IN A DEFENSE ECONOMY[†]

by

T. Coleman Andrews

ACCOUNTING in a defense economy is something like Winston Churchill's description of Russia—"a riddle wrapped in mystery inside an enigma"—not only because we have comparatively little specific information about the effects defense contracts and defense production will have in the next few years, but also because our program may be changed at any moment by some action of the Soviet Union.

Our problem, therefore, is to be prepared for any eventuality. I do not have to emphasize how much more difficult it is to plan for the unknown than for a definite program which can be counted on with some certainty. Of course, the problems created by this uncertainty will affect all phases of our economy, and I should not like to give the impression that because I speak as a Certified Public Accountant I think the accounting problems are more serious than the others. In some ways, however, the solution of the special accounting problems which will arise for American corporations during the next few years may prove a key to the successful handling of our basic need—the need to mesh the defense program into a civilian economy without serious disruption of either.

Taking the best estimates of government officials about the defense program as they see it, we can contemplate an annual military expenditure of $30 to $40 billion out of a national income which will very probably rise to a rate of at least $300 billion by the end of 1951. In other words, we now expect military expenditures which will amount to between 10 and 15 percent of our national income, and total Federal Government expenditures which ought to be kept below 20 percent of the national income if we exercise rigorous economy in other directions. That compares with government expenditures which rose to about 50 percent of the national income during World War II.

I call your attention to these over-all figures because they indicate that the situation for individual companies under the defense program now

---

[†]Presented at the Financial Management Conference of the American Management Association, Waldorf-Astoria, New York, November 30 - December 1, 1950. Reprinted with permission of the American Management Association from *Financial Planning for Defense Production*, Financial Management Series Number 98 © 1951 (New York: American Management Association, 1951), pp. 13-21. All rights reserved.

contemplated will in most cases be very different from what it was in World War II. At the height of the war, many firms were wholly engaged on war contracts and most of the firms which were doing any war work at all showed a very high proportion of their production in that field.

AN ENTIRELY NEW SITUATION

Obviously, the calculation of costs presents a very different problem for a company working 100 percent on war orders from the problems of calculating the proper allocation of costs to war contracts which may constitute only 20 percent of a company's over-all production. Consequently, the specific lessons of World War II may be of somewhat limited usefulness unless or until the defense program becomes much larger than anything now contemplated. However, our chance of coping successfully with a much graver emergency if it should arise will be considerably improved if we have not only our plans but our books in order.

After Pearl Harbor and during a considerable part of the year 1942, you will remember, the paper problem of letting war contracts created more of a bottleneck than the physical problem of converting plans to war work. Parenthetically, I might remark that American business received a good deal of undeserved criticism in those months for continuing civilian production. The fact of the matter is that thousands of firms were ready and anxious to shift over, but they felt quite properly that it was important to keep their labor force reasonably intact and their assembly lines in operation until the government was ready to give them contracts for war work.

We face a situation which may require us to devote a substantial part of our economic strength to defense for an indefinite number of years. What we used to call "emergency" is likely to become normal. Therefore, the preservation of our American economic system depends not only upon our ability to build up a military establishment strong enough to meet any threat of force, but also on our ability to fit military production into a basically civilian economy. We can accept drastic modifications in our way of life for a relatively short period in a full-scale shooting war, but we cannot preserve our economic system by abandoning it for an indefinite period in the name of national defense.

In this situation, American business faces a new challenge, different from anything we have ever faced before. We claim proudly that American business is the most efficient in the world. Now it must become even more efficient, so that we can successfully combine necessary defense production with a relatively normal civilian economy. We can meet this challenge by working even harder to achieve maximum efficiency and economy. We cannot meet it if we take the attitude that costs are unimportant because the government and the consumer will foot the bill.

That is why I feel justified in my opinion that accounting is one of the keys to the successful management of a defense economy. Never before has it been so vitally important for every business—whether engaged directly in war work or not—to achieve the highest possible output of goods and services with the least possible manpower and materials. Cost control has always been a vital factor in American business success; today it is a patriotic duty.

THE SITUATION IN ACCOUNTING

There is an urgent need for greater efficiency and economy in accounting itself. We cannot afford the luxury of continual duplicating and wasteful audits, first by internal auditors, then by independent certified public accountants, and finally by accountants from half a dozen different federal agencies. We achieved a miracle of production in World War II, but we could have done considerably better had we been able to eliminate unnecessary paper work. So I suggest that one of management's first accounting responsibilities in the defense economy is to insist on a reduction in the duplication of accounting and auditing normally required by the Federal Government.

Of course, the government must protect itself against fraud and the ever-present threat of Congressional investigation. Nevertheless, it just doesn't make sense to have the books of corporations engaged in defense contracts examined over and over by auditors from the SEC, the Treasury Department, the General Accounting Office, the War Department, the Navy Department, the Air Force, and sometimes a few other regulatory commissions. I hope no one will accuse me of prejudice, but in most cases the government would be much better off, in my opinion, to accept the findings of the regular independent auditors, subject to special examination in specific cases for specific purposes.

It is primarily up to business management to set the government on the right track with respect to accounting and auditing. If management just sits back with the observation that "government is like that and there is nothing you can do about it," waste and duplication will go on in the same way it always has.

CURRENT AND FUTURE ACCOUNTING REQUIREMENTS

Now, let me present as much specific information and as many suggestions as I can, drawn from the accounting problems which arose during the last war, and from recent information issued by the Department of Defense.

In appraising an accounting system under current and probably future conditions, it is well to bear in mind that systems of accounting control for purposes of government contracts involve considerations different in some respects from those applying to systems for ordinary management control and regular financial statements. In addition to the information regularly needed by the business, therefore, the accounting system should be set up in a manner to provide the information which contracting agencies need, in appropriate detail and without undue delay or confusion.

There can be little question but that a contractor can make a much better case, both in negotiating government contracts and in subsequent discussions with governmental agencies, if he can support it by specific, detailed figures. The system should be designed to provide such information. Let me illustrate this by discussing some of the phases of the current defense program in which accounting records will play a particularly important part:

Recent statements by persons closely connected with the current procurement program indicate an approach to the setting of prices for defense contracts which differs from that used during World War II. During the war there was a definite tendency to rely upon renegotiation and excess profits taxes to eliminate excessive profits on government contracts. The current approach—so far at least—has emphasized the setting of close prices during the negotiation of the contract.

In so doing, an attempt has been made to set prices which are fair to both government and contractor, and which encourage efficient production. In some instances, contracts provide for price redetermination after a period of experience under the contract. In others, "targets" are established which permit a contractor to share with the government the results of efficient production. To the extent that this approach can be adopted during a stepped-up procurement program now in prospect, renegotiation may become less of a factor than it was during World War II.

Every effort should be exerted to make this approach work. Surely prevention of excessive profits is more to be desired than the forfeit of such profits at a later date. However, it may become very difficult to apply the preventive approach as contracts become more numerous, especially if the defense work involves the production of materials with which the contracting company has had little or no experience. It will prove impossible if the company does not have a system of record-keeping which will furnish reasonable estimates of costs during the negotiation stages or will provide accurate cost data during the time it takes to gain experience under the contract.

I need no more than mention the importance of adequate cost data in the settlement of the cost-plus-fixed-fee type of contract. It is my understanding, however, that this type of contract is being used only where no other type appears to be suitable.

THE STATEMENT OF CONTRACT COST PRINCIPLES

As I have mentioned, the accounting considerations involved in defense contracts are different in some respects from those involved in ordinary accounting control and financial statements. This may be illustrated by brief consideration of the "Statement of Contract Cost Principles" which appears as Section XV of the Armed Services Procurement Regulation. At present, this statement is applicable only to the cost-reimbursement type of contracts. However, it is probable that a similar statement of cost principles will be developed which will be applicable to all types of negotiated contracts; and it seems very likely that the present statement will serve as the basis of any future statement of cost principles. In consequence, it will probably attain the position of the familiar "green book" in the last war as the bible for determining costs for defense contract purposes.

The Statement lists three general tests to be used in determining the allowability of costs. The first two of these are reasonableness and the application generally accepted accounting principles and practices. To that extent, the Statement does not suggest any unusual problems in setting up the accounting records for defense contract purposes. However, the third test listed in the Statement does suggest problems. It relates to any limitations as to the types or amounts of cost items set forth in the Statement or otherwise included in the contract. Let me mention two examples illustrating the importance of adequate and sufficiently detailed accounting records. These are unallowable costs included in the Statement applying to supply and research contracts with commercial organizations.

Advertising, which was the subject of considerable discussion in World War II, is severely restricted. All advertising, except "help wanted" advertising; advertising in connection with the disposition of facilities and of scrap and other waste materials; and advertising in trade and technical journals, is unallowable. Thus in accounting for defense contract purposes it will be necessary to set up the records in such a way as to permit ready segregation of the types of advertising which are allowable from those which are unallowable.

Amortization or depreciation of assets fully amortized or depreciated on the contractor's books of account is also unallowable. However, possible compensation for the utilization of such facilities in the form of a use or rental charge is suggested as a subject which may require special consideration in negotiating the contract. It seems probable that the contracting companies will have to come well fortified with facts and figures of an accounting nature if they are to be able to negotiate fair use or rental charges for the utilization of such facilities.

There is one more point I should like to make which I consider to be of special importance to companies doing defense work. Under the present setup, it is apparent that the contracting parties are expected to be especially alert in anticipating points which should be settled while a contract is in the process of negotiation. Part 5 of the Statement sets forth a check list of "subjects affecting costs which may require special consideration." This list mentions specifically 22 items. Among those mentioned are: the basis for indirect costs; government-furnished property; overtime compensation; and termination expenses.

The negotiation of all these items will in one way or another probably be based upon such accounting data as the contracting company is able to provide. Inclusion in the contract of agreements on these points should go a long way toward preventing disagreement and disappointments at a later date. This in itself is a strong incentive for seeing to it that the accounting system is adequate to provide such information.

PRICE CONTROL

As you will recall, the President issued orders requiring persons who sold or delivered goods or services, or offered them for sale or delivery, in the course of trade or business during the period May 24 to June 24, 1950, to preserve all their records for this period relating to costs and prices. It is not clear at this time just what use will be made of these records, except that they will probably be used in some way to establish price controls should such controls be considered necessary. Possibly they will be used as a basis for establishing price relationships at some selected effective date of control.

If you come within the scope of this order, you have probably taken adequate steps to comply. However, it may be to your advantage to be sure you have the necessary information in rather complete form because of its possible effect on the prices which may be set. For example, there may be a difference between the prices at which you made actual delivery during the base period and the prices at which you made commitments for sales during that period. It may be that in this period some or most of the items you sold were out of season and therefore sold at abnormally low prices. In this cases you should have readily available figures which will indicate what would have been a fair price.

Another factor to be considered might be whether or not your costs during that period were based on inventory acquired during a prior period of lower costs, with replacements at higher figures during May and June. There may also have been instances of special purchases, which would affect any over-all base period figures. The figures should also include all fringe labor costs, such as pension costs, bonuses, and the like. In particular, it will probably be helpful to have detailed figures on your overhead costs. These costs are apt to be the ones most questioned and most difficult to defend unless supported by specific figures. It will be much easier to prepare this kind of information now while the information is relatively current than it will be some months hence.

EXCESS PROFITS TAXES

Let us now turn our attention to another important part of the defense picture—taxes. It is evident that the Federal Government will have to increase its revenues in order to pay for the projected defense program. It is far from clear just what method of raising these additional revenues will finally be adopted, although there has been considerable talk of an excess profits tax. This was recommended by the President in a letter to the chairman of the House Ways and Means Committee about two weeks ago.

Many feel that an excess profits tax is not a proper solution to the problem because, they contend, an excess profits tax tends to encourage waste and has inflationary effects. Some of those who oppose excess profits taxes have suggested that the problem can be met better by the imposition of higher rates. Others have suggested that it be met by imposing a special tax, based on a percentage of the normal and surtax. Still others favor a general sales tax. While it is not clear at this time just what procedure may be adopted or when it may be expected, some sort of excess profits tax legislation may well be passed before the end of 1951. It may or may not be similar to that in effect during World War II. Possibly it will be nothing more than an increase in tax rates, bearing the title, Excess Profits Tax.

The American Institute of Accountants has not taken a stand on the desirability of excess profits taxes compared with other possible methods of raising additional revenues. However, the Institute's committee on federal taxation, through its subcommittee on current tax legislation, has given a great deal of consideration to certain specific points which they feel should be incorporated in any excess profits tax law that is enacted.

Assuming that excess profits tax legislation is enacted in a form substantially the same as that in effect during World War II, one of the most difficult problems is the establishment of a proper base for determining normal profits. This is one of the points which has received study by our subcommittee. Members have suggested that the income credit be 90 percent of the average of the three highest years in the four-year period 1946 to 1949 inclusive, with a minimum of 75 percent of the highest year during that period.

If this plan is adopted, corporations will have quite a bit more flexibility in determining "normal" profits than they had in World War II. Under the subcommittee's plan, a corporation would have a choice between selecting the three most favorable years during the base period or the highest single year during the period. Percentages used in determining the amount of the income credit would be different. If the three-year average were used, the income credit would be 90 percent of the average. If the one highest year were used, the income credit would be 75 percent of that year's earnings.

The subcommittee also proposed that corporations be permitted to elect the use of an invested capital base similar to that permitted during World War II.

The foregoing are only recommendations of the subcommittee, and there is no assurance that they will be adopted if excess profits tax legislation is enacted. Whatever plan is adopted, however, a company's accounting records will play an important part in establishing normal profits. It is none too early to start reviewing operations for the years since the war to determine whether there were any unusual factors involved—factors which should be taken into consideration if and when it becomes necessary to establish figures for normal profits as a base in computing excess profits taxes.

FINANCIAL STATEMENTS

Any discussion of the accounting problems in a defense economy would be incomplete without some consideration of the effects of extensive defense contracting on the preparation of financial statements for stockholder and credit purposes. Let us not overlook the importance of informative and useful financial statements, even in wartime.

In the war period the Institute's committee on accounting procedure issued a number of important bulletins dealing with accounting problems arising out of the war. For the most part they were directed to problems encountered in presenting useful financial statements to stockholders and creditors. We cannot be sure just what conclusions will be reached under the present circumstances because partial mobilization such as is now contemplated poses problems which differ from those arising under the near-total mobilization we had during World War II. In my opinion, however, these bulletins provide much guidance for the present, and I should like to mention briefly some of the problems discussed, which may be helpful.

One of the problems almost sure to be faced in the coming years is that of disclosing contingent liabilities such as those for renegotiation refunds and penalties. The committee issued two bulletins with respect to disclosing possible renegotiation refunds. The first was issued before we had had much experience with renegotiation and was therefore quite general. Primarily its position was that there should he some indication in financial statements as to the possibility of renegotiation of contracts or subcontracts. It suggested that in most cases, particularly at that early stage, a footnote to the financial statement pointing out the possibility of renegotiation refunds was about all that could be given.

The second bulletin, issued after a year's experience with renegotiation, was more specific. It recommended that provision be made for possible renegotiation refunds wherever the amount of such refunds could be reasonably estimated. It also recommended that where such provision was made, there should be disclosure in the financial statement of the basis upon which it was made. In cases where no provision was made, it was suggested that a statement to that effect should be set forth in a footnote, together with appropriate disclosure of the reasons therefor and of the company's renegotiation status. Recommendations were also made as to classification of items, with respect to renegotiation, on the balance sheet and income statement.

Other subjects discussed by the committee in its bulletins during the war included accounting for treasury tax notes, postwar refund of excess profits tax, accounting under cost-plus-fixed-fee contracts, accounting for terminated war contracts, and accounting for postwar reserves. All these pronouncements are worth careful restudy, to determine their applicability in the present situation.

EMERGENCY FACILITIES

The inclusion in the 1950 Revenue Act of a provision for the amortization of the cost of emergency facilities acquired under necessity certificates raises an accounting problem which may need reconsideration. In World War II, numerous companies adopted this tax plan in their accounting procedures and for financial-statement purposes amortized the cost of their emergency facilities over a period of 60 months or less. As a result, many of them started off their peacetime operations using important facilities which had been completely written off for financial statement purposes.

The Institute's committee on accounting procedure discussed this situation in Accounting Research Bulletin No. 27, issued in November, 1946. Broadly speaking, it was the committee's view that financial statements concerning peacetime operations would be more useful if they reflected a portion of the cost of such fully amortized emergency facilities as were in use. It made the following recommendation:

> Where the facts clearly indicate that the accelerated amortization or depreciation of emergency facilities at rates permitted for tax purposes has resulted in a carrying value materially less than that reasonably chargeable to revenues to be derived from the continued use of the facilities, and where such facilities would have a significant effect on the financial statement, the adjustment of accumulated amortization or depreciation of such facilities is appropriate.

There was considerable objection to the bulletin, and this recommendation did not receive widespread application, possibly because of a hesitancy on the part of many to charge off the cost of any facilities twice. There seemed at the time to be sound reasons for writing such facilities off over the shorter period for financial statement purposes as well as for tax purposes, but hindsight lends some support to the belief that more useful financial statements would have resulted had the annual charge for financial statement purposes been limited to the ordinary depreciation charge adjusted for tax differences.

This practice might have been valid, at least to the extent that there were reasonable grounds for believing that the facilities would have continuing use after the war. It may be that this approach will be even more desirable under present conditions because it appears that partial mobilization will be with us for a long time to come. In World War II there was considerable justification for the belief that the war years were abnormal and that they should be considered a period beyond the scope of regular operations.

The present situation, while it is not one of total peace, is not one of total war. Therefore, it is questionable whether emergency facilities should be amortized for financial statement purposes on the same basis as for tax purposes. This question should receive careful consideration if, as may be likely, the amortization of emergency facilities becomes a significant element in financial statements for stockholder and creditor purposes.

CONCLUSION

In conclusion, I should like to emphasize the vital necessity of keeping costs down, both in letting defense contracts and in carrying them out. We don't have to worry much about the disreputable fly-by-night organizations which attempt actual fraud on government contracts. We usually catch up with them sooner or later. But we all know that during World Wars I and II there was a disposition on the part of many honest business men to forget their normal peacetime efforts to keep costs under control and let Uncle Sam pay the bill, no matter what it came to. In all fairness, of course, it must be remembered that we went into both wars relatively unprepared, so that the emphasis *had* to be on production at any cost rather than on dollar efficiency. On the other hand, if we follow this psychology in the period ahead, we will lose the cold war on the home front. Economic disaster can defeat us just as surely as military disaster.

More than that, we have got to foot the bill in the end, and the business which allows unnecessary costs in its government contracts will find the money it makes going right out again in taxes.

If we use our accounting tools as well as our machine tools, we can take the defense program in our stride. If we fail to count costs, we are likely to find ourselves with nothing else left to count.

EMERGENCY IN OUR TIMES HAS NOW BECOME NORMAL[†]

by

T. Coleman Andrews

AT this midpoint of the twentieth century we are faced with a situation that has been termed "emergency." And we are confronted with the obvious task of doing something about it. Emergency, however, is a loose term. It suggests imbalance, a sense of urgency, a temporary condition. Unfortunately, the present situation may be with us for years to come. We must take a hard look at this situation and see exactly how it is reflected in the business community.

The first and most readily apparent symptom is shortage—shortage of the two basic elements of business life: men and materials. A second symptom is an increased demand for the things produced with these scarce items.

The office, nerve center of the business anatomy, will feel the impact of this emergency in many different ways. It will find costs rising to new highs; inexperienced personnel turning out less work; more time being consumed in transportation; government contracts requiring renegotiation; increased paperwork necessitating better filing systems; government taking a fatter slice of income. These are some of the symptoms of emergency in business. The next chore is to prescribe measures to meet this condition we have diagnosed as emergency.

In a word, the prescription is "efficiency." But again we have a term that is all things to all men. To narrow our definition, we can say that business efficiency is the use of labor and material with a minimum of waste.

In the office this efficiency can mean improved mechanical equipment to reduce the manhours required for a job; new systems to cut down on duplication and wasted effort; accelerated training programs. It must mean imagination, initiative and industry.

The office manager, of course, cannot solve all of his problems without assistance. Business efficiency as needed today demands a pooling of knowledge and skills. This means that all of us have a job to do. As certified public accountants, we recognize our responsibility to aid business with systems, procedures, advice, and other aspects within our province. We will welcome every chance to discharge that responsibility.

[†]Reprinted with permission from *The Office*, January 1951, pp. 50-51.

With half of the century now filed under "history," it looks as though the emergency has become normal. It looks as though we have a pretty big job on our hands. But with the combined resources, ability and knowledge of the most efficient business operation in the world, the job will be done.

REPORT TO COUNCIL OF AMERICAN INSTITUTE OF ACCOUNTANTS ON TAX PRACTICE STATEMENT†

by

T. Coleman Andrews

"THE principal purpose [of the Tax Practice Statement] is to indicate the importance of voluntary cooperation between our professions," says the conclusion. It is hoped that the Statement may serve as a basis for settlement of any differences between the two professions by friendly negotiation, rather than by resort to the courts or the legislatures. It is recommended that joint committees representing the local societies of both professions be established. The National Conference of Lawyers and CPA's stands ready to consider any specific problem in the field covered by the Statement of Principles on which agreement cannot be reached by local committees.

The Statement describes itself as "tentative and subject to revision and amplification in the light of future experience." It is necessarily in general terms, and the meaning of many of the words and phrases which it contains can be determined only by the National Conference of Lawyers and Certified Public Accountants in the light of specific factual situations which may arise in the future.

Accordingly, the Statement is not to be regarded as a contract, or formal agreement, but, as its title indicates, as a declaration of broad principles, on the basis of which specific definitions and applications may be developed by the "case method" in the future.

The Statement, therefore, should be considered as a whole, and its various sections should not be subjected to interpretations apart from the general context.

Broadly, it seems to me, the most significant implications of the Statement are as follows:

---

†Reprinted with permission of the Michigan Association of Certified Public Accountants from *The Michigan Certified Public Accountant*, August 1951, pp.4-5. The complete text of the "Statement of Principles Relating to Practice in the Field of Federal Income Taxation Promulgated by the National Conference of Lawyers and Certified Public Accountants" (the "Tax Practice Statement") is reproduced in this volume as an appendix to "The Accountant in Practice and in Public Service."

(1) Each of the professions concerned recognizes the other as maintaining comparable standards, and as engaged in a field which frequently overlaps its own. Each profession recognizes the wisdom of voluntary cooperation with the other in matters in which their joint skills may be utilized to the best interests of the public.

(2) Each profession recognizes that members of the other have a proper and legitimate place in every phase of federal income-tax practice, but that neither should assume the functions peculiar to the other. Common sense will usually indicate what those peculiar functions are, but definitions of these functions will probably be developed as needed by the consideration of specific factual situations.

In approving the Statement, the Council of the Institute did not intend to abrogate or limit any rights or privileges which certified public accountants have properly maintained in federal income-tax practice, nor can I believe that the House of Delegates of the American Bar Association intended to abrogate or limit any rights or privileges of lawyers. The Statement itself says that it is "for the guidance" of members of the two professions, and it may be assumed that this applies both to their daily conduct and to the consideration of any disputes which may arise between them.

In a word, the Statement was written in good faith by men of goodwill in both professions. It may be presumed to mean just what it says, no more and no less.

Since 1932 the American Institute of Accountants has been engaged in more or less continuous negotiations with the committee on unauthorized practice of law of the American Bar Association on questions related to proper scope of tax practice by certified public accountants. The negotiations have been interrupted from time to time by litigation between members of the two professions, or by disputes over proposed legislation affecting tax practice.

The experience of fifteen years demonstrated that no satisfactory solution of this complex controversy was to be expected from the courts or from legislation, and that efforts to seek a solution in these forums would not only breed bitterness between the two professions but might be regarded with distaste and disfavor by the public at large.

The only alternative appeared to be settlement of differences by direct negotiation between representatives of the two professions. Such negotiations, however, cannot be conducted in a vacuum. It is necessary to have some postulates, however broad and general, on which settlement negotiations can be based, and it is with the purpose of providing such postulates, as I understand it, that the Statement of Principles, promulgated by the National Conference of Lawyers and Certified Public Accountants, has been approved.

It is impossible, of course, for the American Institute of Accountants and the American Bar Association to control all the activities of all their members, or even of the local organizations of each profession. In spite of the efforts of the National Conference of Lawyers and Certified Public Accountants, there may be further litigation and legislative proposals in which efforts will be made to limit the scope of practice by certified public accountants in the income tax field. It is recognized that in such event, the Statement of Principles may be quoted and an attempt may be made to interpret its provisions in a manner disadvantageous to the certified public accountant concerned. It is for this reason that I feel it necessary that you understand and have in mind the background of the Statement, as described in this letter, when it is discussed with your clients and with lawyers, in order to avoid the possibility of its being misunderstood.

Yours sincerely,
T. COLEMAN ANDREWS,
President.

WHAT THE ACCOUNTING PROFESSION HAS DONE TO COOPERATE WITH THE BANK CREDIT MAN[†]

by

T. Coleman Andrews

IT is a very great pleasure for me to appear here representing my profession, because I know of no two professions that work closer together and that have more mutuality of interest than do the public accountants and the bankers. In fact, all my life I have been hearing about cooperation between bankers and public accountants, and I wondered whether this was the time when we ought to talk again about what the banker would like to see in our reports. There has been a lot said about that on both sides.

Most accountants know what you want, and most of you know what we want. That subject has been pretty well exhausted. Thus I decided to talk about what the profession actually has done to cooperate, and as a background for that I would like to tell you a little bit about the accounting profession. It has grown over the years to an extent that you probably don't realize. Many things have been done to try to make our services more useful, not only to our clients but to all persons, including the bankers, who have occasion to use the product of what we do.

HISTORICAL NOTE

First of all, I wonder how many of you know that the accounting profession in America originally was British. Up until the latter part of the last century, as most of you know, a large part of the investments in America were held by the British. I remember that as recently as 1919, when the First World War was over, the number of mortgages held by insurance companies in Scotland and England was probably in excess of that held by the insurance companies of America. At that time, some smart Scotsmen came over here and arranged to sell all their mortgages to American interests when the British pound was way down. It fell to my lot as an industrial accountant to handle the accounting on that.

I was impressed with the fact that those Scotsmen showed two traits at that time that struck me as being characteristic. One was the ability to see

---

[†]Reprinted with permission of Robert Morris Associates from the *Bulletin of the Robert Morris Associates*, copyright January 1951, pp. 197-204, 220.

an opportunity to make a dollar. Second, they had great faith in their country. The reasoned that the pound would go back to a normal level, and they figured they could make money. They sold the mortgages to the Americans, and within a matter of a few years the pound did go back and they made themselves a 50 percent profit and started making loans again.

In America the accounting profession started out as an adjunct of the profession in Britain, with the British accountants following the British investments in America and setting up the original accounting firms in this country, firms like Price Waterhouse and others, most of which are well-known now. But I would like to remind you that in the meantime the Americans rose to the occasion, and everyone of those firms today is owned and controlled in this country.

The first C.P.A. law was passed in 1896 in New York. We celebrated the fiftieth anniversary of that event four years ago. In 1921 there were only 5,000 accountants in all the United States. In 1921 I passed the examination in Virginia. As I recall, my certificate was number 52. Now we have several times that many. By 1940, or in nineteen years, the number had increased to 17,500, and in the short space of eight years, from 1940 to 1948, doubled, going up to 35,000. Since 1948 we probably have added another four to five thousand.

Today, there are probably 40,000 certified public accountants in the United States, 16,000 of which are members of the American Institute of Accountants. The other group that are not members are not in practice. There are very few certified public accountants in practice who are not members of their state societies and of the American Institute.

ORGANIZATION OF THE A.I.A.

Just a word about the organization of the profession. We operate very much in the fashion that the American Government is supposed to operate; that is our state societies are autonomous. The aggregate membership of the state societies is perhaps somewhat larger than that of the American Institute, because in the state societies we try to give the fellows who are not certified but who are on the staffs of the certified public accountants an opportunity to find out how the profession operates. Consequently the state societies do have in their memberships many men who are not certified. But the American Institute is the national organization of the certified public accountants, and there are none but certified public accountants in its membership except a few chartered accountants who came into the American Institute in its early days when it was necessary and proper to take in other than certified public accountants. The number of that class is somewhat less than a hundred at the present time.

Each state society is autonomous unto itself, and it operates not only through its state organization but also through numerous chapters. We have five chapters in the State of Virginia, for instance, and that is also true to some extent in other states. Some states have more than one chapter; some of them do not.

The American Institute ties this whole thing together, not in any formal sense, I might say, but rather through a very close cooperation between the state societies and the national headquarters of the profession.

The president of the state society automatically becomes a member of the council or governing body of the American Institute when he becomes president. He serves, for the period of his incumbency as president of his state society, also as a member of the governing body or council of the American Institute.

UNIFORM C.P.A. EXAMINATION

We, of the public accounting profession, owe to the members of the Robert Morris Associates no small debt for their part in achieving recognition of the value of the bankers' criticism of our reports. I would say that perhaps the most effective step that we have taken in the public accountant profession in our program of cooperation with the nation's banks and bankers was one that already had been taken by the profession before I ever got into it. I refer to the move made by the American Institute to make examinations of certified public accountants uniform throughout the United States.

Incidentally, this happens to be a most appropriate time to mention this step, for today, as you and I meet here in the comparative calm and highly pleasant atmosphere of this delightful spot, thousands of applicants for the CPA certificate are beginning at one-thirty this afternoon two and a half days of pencil-chewing, finger-nail-biting and brain-racking in general, in 48 states, in Hawaii, Puerto Rico, Alaska and the District of Columbia. There probably will be somewhere between thirty and forty-five thousand men sitting for this examination. Of course, not a great many of them will pass, for reasons which I will indicate to you later. This is the day, therefore, when the fall examination of the American Institute of Accountants begins throughout the nation.

The only state that does not give that uniform examination is Pennsylvania, and the reason for that is purely legal. Pennsylvania hasn't fallen over itself in any desire to switch over because they do a good job themselves. But there is a question of changing the law in order to give the American Institute examinations. We claim, therefore, that we pretty nearly have uniformity of examination throughout the country.

I regard this as our most effective act of cooperation because it is so true to the American tradition of equal opportunity to all and free and unrestricted competition, thus keeping the profession on its toes and giving you and the public generally higher and higher standards of service and the widest possible choice of those qualified to determine the fairness of the representations of those who must give account of their stewardships.

CODE OF ETHICS

But it is not sufficient merely to assure availability of technical skill. It is also necessary to assure high standards of integrity, which the Institute has done from its very beginning by the adoption and fearless enforcement of a rigid code of ethics. The profession feels that the privilege of membership in the Institute and in the state societies should not remain open to anyone who forfeits his rights to the esteem and respect of his colleagues and the public by failing to live up to the high standards of performance and integrity that the profession imposes upon all its members. I am happy to be able to tell you that malpractice, or rather mispractice—and I hope you will pardon me for coining a term—will seldom occur in the public accounting profession.

PERSONNEL TESTING & SELECTION PROGRAMS

Every year a surprisingly large number of people somehow get the idea that public accounting is at once a highly lucrative and not too difficult field, and they decide to have a go at it. For instance, you would be surprised at how many people still think that because they are actually good at figures or believe that they are, they would make good accountants. As a result, thousands of people sit for the CPA examinations who are doomed before they crack their first books. Aptitude at figures today is a very small part of the necessary qualifications of the accountant. His education has to be a great deal broader than that. As a matter of fact, the growth of the understanding of the requirements for being a CPA has become so great that a lot of fellows like myself who never went to college, have to keep pretty well on our own toes to keep these youngsters from running away with us.

The Institute is trying to do something positive about this matter of so many unqualified people taking and failing the CPA examinations. The laws throughout the country are generally very liberal as to who can sit. It is not like the legal profession; it is not like the medical profession. Almost anybody with a college education and a few years of experience and study can take the CPA examination. We hope that perhaps time will bring us to a more stringent requirement for those who make application, so that this number of failures will not be so high.

Under the direction of the most outstanding experts we could find in the field of aptitude testing, there has been developed a series of tests of interests, aptitudes and achievements designed to guide those who think that accounting might be their field. Centers for giving these tests have been established all over the country, especially in the colleges and universities.

However, development of the testing technique now has reached a point where almost any firm represented in the Institute can give it, although evaluations of the applicant's answers can best be made at evaluation centers. If any bank has an employee that they would like to test for his accounting aptitude, it might be well to look into these tests because it might save you from fitting some round peg into a square hole or vice versa. When there is a question as to whether you will send a man along accounting lines or along some other lines, we might be able to help you determine which route that fellow ought to take.

I am sure I need hardly tell you that these tests are not infallible. We are convinced, however, that they have saved many a person from a career for which he was not suited, and thus have tended to raise the profession's standards of performance.

The selection program comes after the student has completed his academic training and is ready to begin his career. In effect this is a placement service, since it brings to the attention of the Institute's members and others the availability of those who satisfactorily complete those courses. These tests are not given all at one time. The first test is the interest test to determine whether one's interests coincide with those of successful public accountants. Next there is an aptitude test to test his aptitude for accountancy. After he has gone on for a year, he takes another test to show how well he is doing with accounting, and in his final year of study he takes a final achievement test to find out how much he really has learned in the course of his studies.

A great deal of money has been spent and is being spent on this program, and I believe I may say, without appearing to boast, that through these programs the public accounting profession has taken the most progressive step yet taken by any profession to assure the highest possible fitness of its members for the service they are called upon to render.

AUDITING STANDARDS

Let us look at some of the specific things we have done to improve the quality of our services and cooperate with the bankers and others. This takes us back to 1917, when, at the request of the Federal Trade Commission, the Institute prepared a memorandum on balance-sheet audits. That was the title of it. The commission approved it and passed it on to the Federal Reserve Board for its consideration. The Federal Reserve Board, after giving the memorandum provisional endorsement, caused its publication in the Federal Reserve Bulletin of April 1917. Reprints therefrom were widely disseminated for the consideration of banks, bankers, banking associations, merchants, manufacturers, associations of manufacturers, auditors, accountants, associations of accountants, in pamphlet form, under the title "Uniform Accounting—A Tentative Proposal submitted by the Federal Reserve Board."

259

I am sure that most of you here, certainly most of those who are not too young, will remember that early bulletin. That was the beginning, you might say, of our practical efforts to get together and improve our service to banks. In 1918 this pamphlet was reissued under the same sponsorship with the title changed to "Approved Methods for the Preparation of Balance-Sheet Statements," with, however, practically no change from the 1917 issue except that as indicated by the respective titles and corresponding changes in the preface, instead of the early objective of a uniform system of accounting to be adopted by manufacturing and merchandising concerns, the later objective was the preparation of balance-sheet statements for the same business entities.

In 1929 the Institute undertook the revision of the earlier pamphlet in the light of the experience of the decade that had then elapsed. Again, under the auspices of the Federal Reserve Board, this revised pamphlet was promulgated under the title, "Verification of Financial Statements." The preface of the 1929 pamphlet spoke of its predecessors as having been criticized by some accountants for being, on the one hand, more comprehensive than their conception of the so-called balance-sheet audit and, on the other, because the procedure would not bring out all the desired information. This recognition of opposing views evidenced the growing realization of the impracticability of anything becoming a standard procedural pattern to fit the wide variety of situations encountered in actual practice.

Of great significance is the appearance of the following statement in the opening paragraphs of the general instructions of the 1929 publication: "The extent of the verification will be determined by the conditions in each concern. In some cases the auditor may find it necessary to verify a substantial portion of all the transactions recorded upon the books. In others, where the system of internal control is good, tests only may suffice. The responsibility for the extent of the work required must be assumed by the auditor."

Thereafter, in 1936, the American Institute prepared and published a further revision of the earlier pamphlets under the title, "Examination of Financial Statements by Independent Public Accountants."

COMMITTEES ON AUDITING PROCEDURE & ACCOUNTING RESEARCH

One thing I want to point out to you is that in 1939, after all these preliminary steps in dealing with the situation of how we are going to get a better job done so that everybody will be better informed, we organized a committee on auditing procedure of the Institute. In order to make this committee as representative as possible, its members were chosen from all sizes of firms and from all parts of the country, with primary emphasis, of course, upon technical qualifications and professional attainments. The committee this year, as I recall, has 21 members and it is assisted in its work by the Institute's Director of Research. I might mention just a word there about the Director of Research.

We have established in the Institute an accounting research department. It is under the direction of perhaps one of the best qualified accountants in the country, Carman Blough, who served, as you will recall, as the first Chief Accountant of the SEC. Mr. Blough and a highly competent staff devote all their time to questions of accounting research.

The Committee on Auditing Procedure functions pursuant to a body of rules, written as well as unwritten, imposed by the Council of the Institute or self-imposed by itself. These rules are eight or nine in number, and I will not take the time to read them.

What has this Committee on Accounting Research done? It has done a good many tangible things. One thing has been to issue a series of pronouncements with respect to auditing and accounting. We have two series, one the Accounting Series, the other the Auditing Series. The Auditing Series, of course, deals with auditing questions. There have been 24 of these issued from 1939 down to 1949 dealing with various aspects of auditing. I hope that every member of the Robert Morris Associates has a copy of this series on his desk, because it will enable you to check a good many questions that may arise from time to time in your analysis of auditors' reports.

"A TENTATIVE STATEMENT OF AUDITING STANDARDS, THEIR GENERAL SIGNIFICANCE AND SCOPE"

Within the last few years—I think it was in October 1947—we got out what was perhaps the most important release of the Committee on Accounting Procedure. This release was called, "A Tentative Statement of Auditing Standards, Their General Significance and Scope." I should say that every Robert Morris Associate ought to have a copy of that statement in his file. Auditing standards, of course, have to do with several aspects in the business of making audits. We classify the auditing standards in this booklet into three groups: General standards, standards of field work and standards of reporting. I would like to tell you briefly what the main points of these three general standards are.

Under general standards, for instance, the examination is to be performed by a person or persons having adequate technical training and proficiency as an auditor. Second, in all matters relating to the assignment an independence in mental attitude is to be maintained by the auditor or auditors. Third, due professional care is to be exercised in the performance of the examination and the preparation of the report.

Now, as to standards of field work, there are also three. First, the work is to be adequately planned and assistants, if any, are to be properly supervised. Second, there is to be a proper study and evaluation of the existing internal control as a basis for reliance thereon and for the determination of the result and the extent of the test to which auditing procedures are to be restricted. Third, sufficient competent evidential matter is to be obtained through inspection, observation, inquiry and confirmation, to afford a reasonable basis for an opinion regarding the financial statements under examination.

As to standards of reporting, there are also three. First, the report shall state whether the financial statements are presented in accordance with general acceptable principles of accounting. Second, the report shall state whether such principles have been consistently observed in the current period in relation to the preceding period. Third, informative disclosures in the financial statement are to be regarded as reasonably adequate unless otherwise stated in the report.

BULLETIN NO. 23

A great deal has been written, as most of you know, about Auditing Bulletin No. 23. You should speak, probably, of 24 before you speak of 23, because 24 more or less laid down the groundwork for consideration of the important question of what should be the wording of the certificate, and final certificate rules or concepts evolved from that discussion found their expression in bulletin No. 23. That bulletin was issued once. It was later revised, and finally has been revised again, and this time its revision is final. It gets rid of the question of weasel wording in reporting. It makes a clear definite statement of what the scope of it was and whether or not the accountant has an opinion, and if he does not have one and he says so, he gives his reasons.

There are certain rules, as all of you know, that require that if there is any material part of a report that an accountant cannot certify to, then he cannot give an opinion concerning the financial condition of that company.

OTHER PUBLICATIONS

We have developed, as I said, a group of reports in the accounting series. There have been 39 formal accounting series releases for bulletins and 3 special ones. They deal primarily with questions of accounting, and therefore I think we need not necessarily go here to any extent into that content since they are matters more of technique and to a large extent deal with things that have to do with registered statements as well as with the common ordinary run-of-the-mine accounting reports.

The question of internal control became highly important to us, and we began to give some consideration to that. Eventually we came up with a booklet entitled, "Internal Control," in which we explained what internal control was. We went further than that. We made flow charts, a number of them, and put in that report appendices showing exactly what we meant

262

by what we said, so that when an auditor is familiar with what internal control is and applies his knowledge to any particular situation, he is able to tell the extent to which his examination should be carried in order to enable him to give a certificate.

We have gone further than that. In addition to that original booklet on the general subject of internal control, we have now issued three different booklets on internal control as applied to specific industries, and they are, of course, in the nature of case studies. We also have supplemented our audit bulletins with case studies in auditing. Here, again, we have taken the auditing bulletins and gone a step further by developing case studies in auditing in individual industries. Of course, that is a pretty long project. It will take time to develop enough of these case studies on auditing to cover, generally, the industries of America. Of course, you don't have to do that for every single category of business because many categories can be grouped as being so similar that one auditing bulletin or one case-study bulletin will cover all of it finally, although not by any means exclusively.

We recently have gotten out a booklet which I am sure most of you have seen, entitled "Audits by Certified Public Accountants." That booklet is a little red booklet, and I believe most of you have seen it. You will be interested to know we have distributed, gratis 20,000 of those to our members, but the sale of that booklet alone to date runs over 30,000, and it was brought out only about two months ago. There is a very general demand throughout Central and South America for publication of it in Spanish, which is now under way.

CONCLUSION

Gentlemen, I hope you are interested in these things which I have given you. We are proud of the accounting profession. We know we have grown tremendously and we hope we have accepted our responsibility or the responsibilities that have grown out of that growth to the extent that we have been able to keep our techniques and our principles and our policies and our ethics up to date with the progress that the profession has made. The things that I have outlined to you are specific illustrations of the manner in which we have attempted to cooperate, not only with the bankers but also with our clients generally, in improving the technique and the performance of the profession.

At the same time, our Ethics Committee has operated, I think, courageously and fearlessly and has dealt severely with these cases that seemed to require some discipline.

I assure you that the accounting profession will ever be as anxious to cooperate with the members of the Robert Morris Associates as they have been in the past.

TESTIMONY AGAINST S.913
ESTABLISHING A CONGRESSIONAL
JOINT COMMITTEE OF THE BUDGET†

by

T. Coleman Andrews

I am here to speak for myself and as president of the American Institute of Accountants in response to invitations addressed to me in both capacities by your distinguished chairman.

Both the American Institute of Accountants and I appreciate and thank you for your invitation, and we have accepted this invitation because the subject of S.913 is one concerning which we feel that we are in position to speak with some claim to special knowledge, for fiscal problems are the certified public accountants' daily fare.

This is as true of the federal government's fiscal problems as it is of those of private enterprises, for the accounting profession has contributed liberally, in peace as well as in war, not only the rank and file of its membership but also its leaders, toward finding solutions for the government's constant succession of fiscal difficulties.

Being aware of your distinguished chairman's interest in simplification and economy, we are reluctant to raise our voice in opposition to a bill authored by him and intended to help deal more intelligently with the perplexing problem of judging and passing upon appropriation requests. However, we do not believe that S.913 will either simplify the present situation or effect any economy.

We believe, on the contrary, that it will further complicate what appears to us to be an already over-organized, unduly complex, and dangerously obfuscated situation, and, in addition, add substantially to the already intolerable cost of managing the nations' business.

Worse still, if S.913 should have these undesirable effects, it will add to the growing loss of confidence and faith in the government and those who run it that now is apparent to every discerning citizen.

We urgently suggest that there is bound to be a point beyond which the people will not be willing to go in their tolerance of consistently unsuccessful experimentation with the job of gaining and maintaining control of the fiscal aspects of their national affairs. Business, both large

---

†Statement of T. Coleman Andrews, president of the American Institute of Accountants, before the Senate Committee on Expenditures in the Executive Departments, May 15, 1951. Reprinted with permission from *The Journal of Accountancy*, July 1951, pp. 102-106.

and small—even business that is worldwide in its operations—licked the problem of fiscal control long ago. Sooner or later the people will cease to tolerate the government's failure to deal effectively with the aspect of management. We cannot longer afford the "trial-and-error" method of dealing with a problem that is no longer a problem anywhere except in government.

We heartily agree with the declaration by Senator McClellan at the outset of his address to the Senate concerning S.913 on February 19, 1951, that Congressional control over the expenditures of the executive branch of the government is much needed; and we applaud his further declaration that Congress' possession of control over the government's expenditures heightens its duty in times like these "to appropriate only as much (as), but no more than, is actually needed."

We also agree with the Senator's declaration further along in the same address that the budget hearings held by the Appropriations Committees of Congress have become practically "ex parte" proceedings. But, considering the fact that the Appropriations Committees of Congress have had at their elbows a means, established 30 years ago, whereby this deplorable evolution might have been avoided, it is somewhat disappointing that for so long a time the full usefulness of this fine and proven tool not only has not yet been employed but apparently has not even been recognized. More's the pity when we consider that this tool was created by Congress itself, to be its eyes and ears in fiscal matters. But this is getting a little ahead of our story.

At first blush, the idea of having a "Joint Committee on the Budget" sounds like a good one. But on analysis, it becomes clear that, in some of its activities at least, a merry-go-round situation would be created. For instance, we find, beginning in line 16 on page 4 of S.913 that one of the duties of the Joint Committee would be: "(c) to consider all available information relating to estimated revenues, including revenue estimates of the Joint Committee on Internal Revenue Taxation...."

This sounds like hiring auditors to check auditors; the Joint Committee on Internal Revenue Taxation checks the Treasury Department—it just recently reported that the Treasury Department's current revenue estimates were too low—and the Joint Committee on the Budget would check the Joint Committee on Internal Revenue Taxation. This would be duplication of the most inexcusable sort.

The idea of creating a Joint Committee on the Budget from the Appropriations Committees of House and Senate, similar to the Joint Committee on Internal Revenue Taxation, is appealing at first glance. But actually the parallel is misleading.

Under the Constitution all revenue bills must originate in the House of Representatives, and the Senate can in effect originate methods of raising revenue only by the expedient of amending House bills. The Joint Committee on Internal Revenue Taxation was created primarily as a means of avoiding the difficulties and delays which often resulted from this Constitutional provision.

No such special problem justifies the creation of a Joint Committee on the Budget from the Appropriations Committees of the two houses. On the contrary, it might well lead to circumventing the checks and balances on appropriations which now exist through separate consideration of appropriations bills by the House of Representatives and the Senate.

Now to be more specific. On page 3 of his Senate address of February 19, 1951, Senator McClellan called his colleagues' attention to the fact that the Appropriations Committees of the House and Senate had a combined staff of 55 persons, whereas Congress had given the Bureau of the Budget a staff of more than 500.

What the Senator was getting at here is not clear to us. Surely he could not have been suggesting that if the Bureau of the Budget needs a staff of 500 the proposed Joint Committee on the Budget would have to have one of that number. The only clue he gave to the proposed Joint Committee's needs is to be found on page 6 of the same address, where he said that "this Joint Committee would be empowered to employ an adequate expert staff...." An "adequate expert staff" might easily become a full-blown Confessional Bureau of the Budget.

NO ARGUMENT FOR MAINTAINING STATUS QUO

Agreeing, as we said earlier, with your distinguished Chairman's declaration that Congress needs to get control over the expenditures of the executive branch of the government, we would not argue for maintaining the status quo; but we believe that we should say in passing that we think that a good case could be made for the proposition that the better than 1-to-10 ratio of the combined staffs of the Appropriations Committees of Congress to the staff of the Bureau of the Budget is ample. One expert certainly ought to be able to check the finished work of ten others. If what we recommend in place of S.913 is adopted, some of the 55 members of the staffs of the Appropriations Committees of Congress may find themselves hard put to keep busy with budget matters.

In his address of February 19, Senator McClellan pointed out that the Appropriations Committees of the House and Senate have authority under the Legislative Reorganization Act of 1946 to expand their staffs "in order to make a more systematic and intensive analysis of departmental spending requests," but that neither of these committees had fully availed itself of this authority.

He then also pointed out that if these committees should take advantage of their authority to expand their staffs they would create a duplication of service and expense.

Next he asserted that there are only two approaches to solution (of the problem of putting Congress in the saddle with a stout bridle and a bit that would really enable it to control expenditures). "One," he said, "is by having each of the Appropriations Committees adequately expand its staff and confer additional authority and powers on the staffs of the two committees to perform these services. The other ... is the approach made in the bill which I have introduced."

The Senator's reminder that the maintaining of a staff for the same purpose by each of the two Appropriations Committees would be a duplication of both service and expense is not open to question. Nor can there by any doubt that a single staff for review of the administration's proposed and actual expenditures is highly desirable and would be tremendously helpful; such a staff would provide a check on expenditures such as is now provided on revenues by the staff of the Joint Committee on Internal Revenue Taxation.

STAFFS DUPLICATES EACH OTHER TO A DEGREE

But the staffs of the two Appropriations Committees already duplicate each other to a degree, and the past affords no hope that this duplication would be ended by the adoption of S.913. Moreover, there is a better way—a proven one—one that already is at hand and, therefore, makes the creation of a new organization unnecessary. Hence, we disagree with the Senator's statement that the course laid out in S.913 is the only alternative to parallel expansion of staffs of the two Appropriations Committees.

Our suggestion is a very simple one: *Use the Comptroller General and the General Accounting Office.* The arguments in favor of this course are so obvious and compelling that it seems hardly necessary even to state them; but here are a few:

1. The Comptroller General and the staff of the General Accounting Office stand second to none in knowledge of the organization and management of the government. They've been reviewing the government's affairs most meticulously for the past 30 years.

2. They would be moving at full speed before any new organization could get up enough steam to get started.

3. The Comptroller General is a member of the Congressional family. Use him.

4. The services that the staff of the proposed Joint Committee on the Budget would render are among those that the General Accounting Office was created to render to Congress. Let the General Accounting Office render these services.

5. Use of the Comptroller General and the General Accounting Office would give the staffs of the Appropriations Committees the help of people who are out in the front lines of fiscal operations every day and who not only know what's going on but also how to interpret what they see in terms of economical organization and management.

6. Use of the Comptroller General and the General Accounting Office would employ existing personnel and facilities and thus would avoid making things more complicated and costly than they already are.

7. Proper employment of the facilities of the General Accounting Office should reduce substantially the time devoted to budget matters by the staffs of the Appropriations Committees.

What more appropriate organization than the General Accounting Office could possibly be found to provide the Appropriations Committees and Congress with the information they require in order to determine whether the appropriations requested by the administration are necessary and reasonable? The staff of this establishment has been reviewing the revenues and expenditures of the government for the past thirty years.

True enough, the review was on a pretty narrow basis until the Government Corporation Control Act was passed in 1945. But every transaction was reviewed; and since the passage of the Government Corporation Control Act, the basis of the examinations conducted has been steadily broadened until today in every examination the auditors not only inquire into the legality of expenditures but also weigh them from the standpoint of whether they were necessary. They also consider whether the activities that they review are economically organized as well as whether they are economically managed.

But one doesn't have to argue the logic of using the Comptroller General and the General Accounting Office. Congress has already twice said that they shall be used. It did so when it passed the Budget and Accounting Act of 1921. It did it again when it passed the Legislative Reorganization Act of 1946. Unfortunately, however, Congress has never used the tools that it thus provided and has had at hand. Here, for instance, is what section 206 of the Legislative Reorganization Act of 1946 says: "Section 206. The Comptroller General is authorized *and directed* to make an expenditure analysis of each agency in the executive branch of the government (including government corporations), *which, in the opinion of the Comptroller General, will enable Congress to determine whether public funds have been economically and efficiently administered and expended....* " (italics ours)

We suggest that no group is likely to become better qualified to analyze *plans for future expenditures* than those whose business it is to ascertain and report to Congress whether public funds *previously appropriated* have been economically and efficiently administered and expended. Those who know the past are most likely to be the best judges of the future.

So there you have it. *What S.913 would provide already is required by existing law!* Moreover, to a degree it is *being* provided in audits now being made by the General Accounting Office. But Congress isn't using it! Congress is fond of calling the Comptroller General its "right arm" and its "watchdog." The moving finger of that right arm oft has become cramped from its prodigious report-writing, and the watchdog's throat equally as often has been hoarsened by the vigorous warnings it has barked; but Congress seldom has either seen or heard these emanations from the hand and throat of its diligent and faithful servant in the cloistered and crowded depths of the Old Pension Building, or so it has seemed. Often has the Comptroller General been heard to say proudly yet sadly, as he did at a Senate sub-committee hearing on his appropriation requests for the year ended June 30, 1950: "I might say that I have sent more reports to the Congress on waste and extravagance in one year than my predecessors sent during their entire terms office."

I should point out, lest someone get the erroneous impression that I am saying that the Comptroller General has not done his duty under Section 206 of the Legislative Reorganization Act of 1946, that this directive never has been implemented by an appropriation. The record indicates that $1,000,000 was requested for the fiscal year ended June 30, 1948, for initiation of the work called for by this section, but this request was denied by the Independent Offices Subcommittee of the House Appropriations Committee. In reporting on this denial, Congressman Wigglesworth, Chairman of the Independent Offices Subcommittee of the House Appropriations Committee, had this to say:

"The Committee feels that with the assistance already being furnished by the General Accounting Office in its regular reports and otherwise to Congress and to many of its committees, and with the additional help now available in the augmented committee staffs, no additional appropriation to enable the General Accounting Office to begin its new duties under Section 206 of the Legislative Reorganization Act can be justified at this time."[1]

ANALYSES BEST DONE BY ACCOUNTING OFFICE

"The Committee believes that if such expenditures analyses are to be made on such a scale by a permanent staff it should be done by the General Accounting Office. I have discussed this matter with the Comptroller General and he does not object to the elimination of the item of $1,000,000 under all the circumstances involved, provided it is understood that his office cannot begin work pursuant to this new function unless and until an appropriation is made therefor at some later time. I think this, of course, will be clearly understood."[2]

As we understand it, the Senate, in considering the Independent Offices Appropriations Act of 1950, added $800,000 to the General Accounting Office's appropriation for initiating the work required under Section 206 of

---

[1]Congressional Record, Vol. 93, Part 6, Page 7175, June 17, 1947.

[2]*Ibid.* (italics added by *The Journal of Accountancy*).

the Legislative Reorganization Act of 1946, but this $800,000 was striken from the bill in conference and so was not included in the 1950 appropriation as finally approved.

Thus, it is apparent that the General Accounting Office never has been given any money to carry out the directive given to the Comptroller General by Section 206 of the Legislative Reorganization Act of 1946. However, the directive remains on the statute books, and we understand that in spite of not having been given funds to carry it out the Comptroller General has nevertheless so drawn his audit programs that at least some of the expenditure analyses required by this section will be made—in fact, are now being made—in the course of his staff's discharge of its regular auditing duties.

Finally, it must be pointed out that if it were decided to use the Comptroller General and the General Accounting Office to do what is provided by S.913, even this salutary step might duplicate investigative work now being done by staffs of committees of Congress and by the legislative staff located in the Library of Congress. The same would be true, of course, if S.913 were adopted. But Congress can very quickly terminate this duplication by requiring that all investigations of fiscal matters be referred to the Comptroller General and the General Accounting Office, and we strongly urge that this be done. The Comptroller General is Congress' man; he and the staff of the General Accounting Office work for and report to Congress, and their qualifications for making fiscal examinations and investigations are of the very highest order.

To summarize, we heartily concur in the opinion that control of appropriations by the executive branch of the government is dangerous and intolerable and that Congress should move without further delay to cure its surrender of this vital prerogative. But we strongly urge:

a. That creation of a Joint Committee on the Budget is unnecessary and would worsen rather than improve the present situation;

b. That full advantage should be taken of the potentialities of the Comptroller General and the General Accounting Office as the independent auditor and investigator for Congress;

c. That, specifically, the Comptroller General and the General Accounting Office be used to provide the Congress with the services called for by S.913; and

d. That the conducting of all investigations of fiscal matters be entrusted to the Comptroller General and the General Accounting Office.

Last year I testified before this Committee in opposition to a bill that became the Budget and Accounting Procedures Act of 1950. I objected to this bill on several grounds—primarily on the grounds that it failed to provide an accounting department for the government under a qualified director and that it unduly and improperly made the Comptroller General a party to administrative decisions that should never be imposed upon any independent auditor. I pointed out that if the Comptroller General were to be in fact the independent auditor for Congress and as such a member of the Congressional family, he should be used accordingly and should be relieved of his part in the management of those affairs that should be regarded as—and made—the exclusive responsibility of the executive branch of the government.

There were some who chose to assail that testimony as an effort on our part to reduce the importance and prestige of the Comptroller General's office. We hope that what we have recommended here today will dispel this groundless fear, because these recommendations make specific application of the philosophy upon which what we said on that occasion was based. We sought then, and we seek today, to prevail upon the Congress to avail itself of all of the potential usefulness of an officer and of the staff of an organization who are Congress' own, and who could be made not only more useful to Congress than they now are—and their present usefulness is undeniably great—but also the most powerful influence for public thrift at the national level that the country has ever seen.

We say this with the deepest sincerity and with some emotion, because we entertain grave concern about what will happen if the present costly situation is not corrected.

So we say: We already have the man, the organization, and the law that it takes to do what is called for by S.913. Let's not make the mistake of piling more organization on top of the present bewildering colossus and more expense on top of the already inordinate cost of government. What we already have isn't just good enough; it is exceptionally good. All we have to do is use it. So, *let's* use it.

PRESIDENTIAL REPORT DELIVERED TO THE AMERICAN INSTITUTE OF ACCOUNTANTS†

by

T. Coleman Andrews

A year ago—at Boston—we met almost on the eve of the beginning of the second half of this century. Less than three months before the Boston meeting another war against our ideals had broken out—this time in Korea; and already we had begun to feel the pinch of the economic and other restrictions and controls that seem to be inescapable characteristics of armed conflict. Already we had begun to revise our setup and program so that we might assume and fully discharge our obligations as a responsible and essential element of the nation's economic system, and as an important, if not vital, spoke in the wheel of defense.

Our national defense committee had been re-activated in July, and the utmost of our talents and efforts had been pledged to those to whom the primary responsibility for defense had been assigned. This meeting, originally scheduled to be held in Washington, was moved to Atlantic City, lest it inconvenience contractors and others having to be in Washington on defense business. Then, as a climax of our emphasis upon defense, and in order to afford our members the greatest possible exposure to defense policies and plans, we made defense the theme of this meeting, and to that end have been able to bring here as honored guests and speakers perhaps the most distinguished array of government officials that has graced a meeting of any organization up to this time, and certainly the most distinguished group that has ever occupied the platform at a meeting of the Institute. As all of us know, the burden of these gentlemen's duties and responsibilities are so urgent that usually they are at their desks when most everybody else has turned in for the night, and, having taken the time to give us the benefit of their time and intimate knowledge of the nation's defense effort, they will return to their offices to face the added burden of having to increase their exertions in order to dispose of the work that accumulates while they are here. I take this opportunity, therefore, to assure these gentlemen that we are not only honored by their presence but also most grateful to them for coming.

---

†Presented at the Sixty-Fourth Annual Meeting of the American Institute of Accountants, Atlantic City, New Jersey, October 6-10, 1951. Reprinted with permission. In the T. Coleman Andrews Papers (Coll. 119), Special Collections, University of Oregon Library.

Reverting to the outbreak of war in Korea, nations that owed their very existence to our friendship and unreserved aid in earlier conflict formed new alliances and turned against us, just as had happened so often in the past, and that elusive condition of mankind, sometimes called "democracy," became more elusive than ever. Overnight, the hope of peace in our time, already discouragingly dim, became even more so; nor may it be said that the outlook has changed for the better during the year that has passed since then. Indeed, the future seems more uncertain today than ever, and all but the unshakably faithful—of whom, unhappily, all too few remain—seem to have resigned themselves to some undefinable dire inevitability, given up the quest of justice and freedom, repudiated the canons of personal discipline and restraint, and shed their very souls in an orgy of brazen irresponsibility and shameless immorality.

But as dark as the future seems when we try to penetrate the fog of uncertainty that obscures the horizon of our destiny, we must not lose sight of the fact that it has been dark before, and that as surely as the jet-black clouds of uncertainty have been relieved of the weight of their tears before, and been blown away to let in the life-giving and everlasting sun, so will they be lightened and driven away again, that the sun may shine again in all its brilliance and power.

I like to think that it has been in that attitude and spirit of faith and hope that the Institute has ordered its affairs and gone ahead during the year that has just ended, for we have indeed had another year of substantial growth, not only in numbers but also in prestige and influence. Our reaction to the crisis with which the nation became burdened in June of last year reminds me of an observation about people generally that a very wise man once made. This philosopher—and a philosopher he must indeed have been—said that in time of trouble people fall into two categories: those who fly to pieces and those who fly into one piece. I think that the Institute flew into one piece like the defending corpuscles of the blood to fight infection. This was to be expected, of course, of a profession that traditionally has carried its banner high.

To begin with, through the efforts of our very energetic and most capably led membership committee, we gained 2,150 new members and re-instated 36 former ones, making total accretions of 2,186, or 8.44 times the number lost by resignation, death and other causes. Thus we wound up the year with a membership of 17,998, as against 16,071 at the beginning, making a net gain of 1,927.

Second, we successfully met the challenge of two of the three problems that I particularly cited and commented upon in my inaugural address.

These problems were: the achievement of a clear understanding with the bar as to the lawyers' and certified public accountants' respective spheres of practice; the preservation of recognition by Securities and Exchange Commission, in its revision of Regulations SX, of the implications of the certified public accountants' obligation of independence;

274

and the achievement, if possible, of friendly understanding between ourselves and the uncertified public accountants.

A statement of principles was worked out by the National Conference of Lawyers and Certified Public Accountants, and adopted by both the American Bar Association and The Institute, that affords a positive basis for resolving on the case basis such questions of jurisdiction as may arise between the two professions; and the Securities and Exchange Commission issued its revision of Regulations SX in terms that met the needs of the situation as the Commission saw them and at the same time left uninfringed the independence of the certified public accountants as imposed by the states, from which their recognition is gained. I can not recall two more positive examples than these of the virtue of frank but objective across-the-table discussion by parties not in agreement with each other.

There also were meetings during the year with representatives of the uncertified public accountants. These meetings did not produce agreement; but neither did they widen the area of disagreement. I have to report, therefore, that the situation as between the uncertified public accountants and ourselves remains unchanged. This is not going to be an easy problem to solve, because there are many other related problems that must be put behind us before it can be solved; but I have confidence that it will be solved eventually if both parties maintain a tolerant attitude and keep the door of discussion open, and I feel certain that no succeeding administration of ours will deliberately close this door.

Third, the Committee on Accounting Procedure and the Committee on Auditing Procedure not only undertook unusually heavy dockets during the year but also have done outstanding jobs in bringing up to date and codifying their bulletins and statements, respectively, and in carrying to higher levels of excellence the techniques of practice, through additional statements, bulletins, case studies, and other activities.

Fourth, the Committee on National Defense also has had an extremely busy year. You will recall that at its inception this committee was a relatively small one. Need for expansion of its membership and activities already was manifest before the year began. Accordingly, during the year the membership was substantially enlarged and the structure of the committee was changed by dividing it into subcommittees on manpower, renegotiation, procurement auditing, cost principles, price and wage control, and termination. Each of these subcommittees was confronted with very heavy dockets.

Fifth, the promulgation of regulations covering excess profits taxes and the introduction and consideration of a new revenue bill also gave the Committee on Federal Taxation an unusually heavy job to do. By the beginning of the year the growing multiplicity and complexity of federal taxes and the prospect of new legislation already had moved us to divide the Committee on Federal Taxation into subcommittees on current tax legislation, long range tax policy, and tax administration. Developments during the year abundantly confirmed the wisdom of this action, and each of these subcommittees did outstanding work and substantially demonstrated the usefulness of the profession in the development of solutions to the government's tax problems, and, in so doing, rendered a most valuable service to the nation's entire business community.

Sixth, outstanding work also was done in increasing the usefulness of the Institute to the state societies and smaller firms and individual practitioners. Never in the long period of my association with the Institute have I heard as many or more complimentary comments from those whom these committees were set up to serve than I heard during the past year. I shall quote some of these comments to you in my discussion of finances.

Seventh, probably one of the most significant projects ever undertaken by the Institute for the purpose of aiding its members in the solution of their problems, both technical and administrative, was the decision to turn out as a product of the membership itself a publication to be known as *The C.P.A. Handbook.* The writing and publication of such a work is an undertaking of gigantic proportions, and I am sure that all of you will be impressed with the magnitude of the effort that has been made by the committee in charge of this project in order to do a thorough job in the shortest possible time consistent with the turning out of a product of real worth to the membership.

Eighth, undoubtedly one of the most forward steps ever taken by the Institute was the setting up of a committee on public relations and the creation of a department under a qualified director to staff the work of this committee. Several highly valuable and very readable booklets were turned out by this committee during the year, and one sees on every hand abundant evidence that the committee is doing an outstanding job of acquainting the public with the importance of accounting and its application, and of rapidly increasing the prestige of the profession and recognition of the importance of its role in the nation's economy.

Ninth, I am happy also to be able to report that the work of the Business Income Study Group, started in 1947 with a matching grant from the Rockefeller Foundation, has reached the final stage of its studies and deliberations and that it is expected that the Group's report will be published shortly. The work of this Group has been one of major economic significance, and it is believed that its report will be the most authoritative work that has yet been published on the important subject that the Group was formed to explore.

I realize that the foregoing is only a partial report on the activities of the year and that I have spoken only generally about the work of the several committees mentioned and have not even mentioned some of our committees and the important work that they have done. I hope, however, that no committee will feel that any slight was intended by my omission of reference to it and its work, and that none of those mentioned will feel that I have not adequately covered their activities, because the time allotted for

276

my report had to be limited and I could not hope to do more than cover the highlights of the year's activities. If I have been guilty of any serious omission, I apologize for it and call attention to the fact that in accordance with established procedure each committee reported in detail to the Council at its meeting on Saturday and copies of these reports can be had for the asking.

To summarize, we have had a very busy year indeed, and we to whom the responsibility for conducting the Institute's affairs during the year was entrusted hope that you will feel that it has been a year of significant progress. You will permit me, I am sure, the observation in passing that it has seemed to us who have been responsible for carrying on the year's activities that the profession's prestige and usefulness has been substantially enhanced not only at home but also abroad. This is no mere matter of personal boasting, for whatever has been accomplished has not been the work of any single individual or any small group of individuals; on the contrary, it has been the result of the high level of teamwork and personal devotion to the advancement of the profession that long has been characteristic of the Institute's membership. On this subject I should like to say a brief but genuinely sincere word.

I have been connected with many organizations in my time, but never have I seen one where membership participation in the work of the organization has been as broad and devoted as it is in the Institute. The amount of time that individual members are willing to devote to Institute activities, and the amount of personal expense that they are willing to incur in order to make their participation effective, literally amazes me.

Not only have I been tremendously impressed by the prodigious contributions of the members of the committees to the execution of our various programs, activities and projects; I also have reason to be thankful for the cooperation that I have received from all hands—my fellow officers, the members of the various committees, the members generally, and the excellent staff that labors so faithfully and so effectively in our behalf; and I am indeed thankful—deeply so. No one could have asked for more wholehearted cooperation than I have received on every hand and occasion. My year as President, therefore, has been a highly gratifying one—one that has been enriched by the strengthening of old acquaintances and friendships, by the addition of many new acquaintances and friends, and by the incomparable opportunity that it has afforded me to see at first-hand the benefits that flow from inspired and inspiring cooperation by men and women devoted to a common ideal and with the willingness to make heavy personal sacrifices in order to turn that ideal into reality.

I should be remiss if I did not take this opportunity to acknowledge also my gratitude to my wife and partners, whose indulgence and willingness to release me temporarily from my normal duties and obligations made it possible for me to accept and discharge to the best of my ability the responsibilities inherent in the high honor to which you elevated me at Boston.

I do not intend to bore you with statistics, but I do want to give you some idea of what is involved in a normal year of modern Institute activities, in the form of official and staff tours, to meet with and address the members of state societies, local chapters and other national, state and local organizations. During the year there were 138 such appearances covering practically every state in the Union and, of course, most of the larger, as well as many of the smaller, cities. I suppose I should tell you that your President's travels involved official appearances in 22 of the 48 states, the delivery of 45 official addresses and a number of unofficial ones, and more than 52,000 miles of travel.

During the course of the year's travel, so many members have expressed an interest in how the committees of the Institute are appointed that I want to say a word about this subject before discussing the important subject of finances, with which I will wind up my review of the year's activities. Selection of committee members is one of the most difficult jobs that confronts an incoming president, and because of the size to which the Institute has grown and the number of committees that have to be appointed, it is a job that he must get behind him before he takes office. If there are some who think that committee appointments are handed out as plums—and I know that there are some who feel or suspect that this is the case—I want to say here and now that nothing could be farther from the fact. As I have indicated, the Institute has grown because it has had officers and committees who have been willing and able to work hard at the jobs assigned to them, and committee appointments usually go to those who are willing and able to work.

No president can possibly know everyone who is willing and able to take on a committee assignment. For that reason each incoming president requests that state societies, the members of Council and others recommend members for appointment to committees. I urge, therefore, that whenever any of you receives such a request you give it your most careful consideration and be certain that those whom you recommend are particularly qualified for the committees on which you think they might serve and, more important than that, that they are in position to devote the time and incur the expense that a committee member must expect if he is to be really effective.

Now as to the matter of finances. The fact that special contributions were solicited during the year appears to have given rise to the feeling on the part of some of our members that we have been living beyond our income. In asking for these contributions, we tried to make it clear that this was not the case at all; however, our explanation apparently was not as clear as we thought. Evidently this was due to the fact that our supplemental fund-raising activities were related by some of our members to the then current year, whereas the need was for the year ending August 31, 1952, not for the year then in course.

I can tell you positively that we are living within our income, that in spite of rapidly rising prices, we were able to keep expenses for the year ended August 31, 1951, within the revenue of that year and close the year with a small surplus. Since the Institute, like every other organization, has to compete in the open market for everything it buys, including personal services, and since the outbreak of hostilities in Korea was followed by a new upward spiral of prices, what happened was that it became apparent soon after our last annual meeting that by September 1st of the present calendar year we would be faced with the alternative of finding additional revenue or substantially curtailing our activities. The Executive Director promptly reported this outlook to the Budget and Finance Committee and this Committee analyzed the situation and called it to the attention of the Executive Committee.

Thereupon, the Executive Committee instructed the Budget and Finance Committee to go ahead with its preparation of a tentative budget for the year beginning September 1, 1951, for consideration by the Council at the latter's meeting at Colorado Springs in May, in accordance with our established policy of giving the Council a preview of the budget for each year at the spring meeting immediately preceding the beginning of that year.

The Budget and Finance Committee proceeded accordingly, and at Colorado Springs the Executive Committee reported the situation in full to the Council and the matter was discussed at length. In the meantime, the Executive Committee had instructed the Executive Director to cut expenses wherever possible in order to assure our being able to wind up the then current year—that is the year ending August 31, 1951—without a deficit. This was done, with the result that I have already indicated; but it involved reducing the scope of some activities and delaying the initiation of some projects that seemed desirable and had been approved by the Executive Committee.

The Council then approved the expense reductions ordered by the Executive Committee for the balance of the year ending August 31, 1951, went on record as opposing indefinite continuation of the curtailment of activities, programs and projects involved in these reductions, and approved a recommendation of the Executive Committee that a special committee be appointed to study the whole question of income and submit its recommendations for consideration by the Executive Committee in time to permit presentation of a new financial plan for your consideration this morning. The plan agreed upon will be presented as a part of the report of the Council to the membership, which is the next regular item of business on this morning's agenda.

There having been some doubt as to the propriety of making any plan that you might agree upon this morning effective for the year beginning

September 1, 1951, the Council then ordered, upon the recommendation of the Executive Committee, that contributions be sought as a stop-gap means of providing sufficient revenue to enable full resumption of all activities, programs and projects beginning September 1, 1951.

Perhaps this has sounded a bit complicated to you sitting out there in the audience without my manuscript before you, but I hope it has been sufficiently clear to convince everyone that we have not been improvident in the management of our finances, that, on the contrary, we have in fact lived within our means and intend to continue to do so.

Incidentally, the replies to our requests for contributions were replete with expressions of confidence in the manner in which the Institute's affairs have been managed, particularly from the small firms and individual practitioners. There also were expressions in these replies that leave no doubt that those who contributed are overwhelmingly in favor of continuing without curtailment the full range of activities, programs and projects, and of raising the scale of dues, if necessary, to such extent as may be necessary in order to make that possible.

Typical of expressions from the small practitioners was that of one member who said, "I don't know what a small practitioner would do if it were not for the A.I.A." Another said, "From myself and the members of my staff, we extend our appreciation for the wonderful work of the Institute; you are reaching the smaller practitioner and making us feel the thrill of the profession." Still another said, "The Institute should not curtail its operations or activities at this time, but we are of the opinion that dues should be set at a figure calculated to yield sufficient revenue." Yet another said, "To curtail activities at this time would be unthinkable ...; your statement that dues have been raised only $5 in the last 35 years would indicate a possible source of additional revenue." I would not leave you with the impression, however, that there are not some who entertain contrary views, for such is not the case. For instance, one member said that he was "fed up on raises" and obviously thought that we should curtail activities. Another went even further and said, "I hope no business executive outside of the profession sees a copy of your letter; (This referred to the letter from me as President by which the appeal for contributions was initiated) it seems to me a feeble solution of a bad situation brought about by poor planning and management." Still another charged that those responsible for running the Institute's affairs "seem to have absolutely no idea as to what constitutes service to the individual practitioner." And another—obviously a philosopher—contented himself with the simple statement that "He who spends what isn't his'n is very likely to go to prison." However, while we respect these contrary views, they were not representative of the majority of those who contributed, and a proposal to increase dues that the Executive Committee and the Council believe to be equitable will be proposed for your consideration during the course of this morning's session.

In conclusion, I return to the situation that I touched upon only briefly at the outset of this report—namely, the unhappy position in which our country again finds itself so soon after the conclusion of World War II. Not only are we again at war, confronted by an envious and greedy handful of terrorists and tyrants to whom our success as a nation is unpalatable, but also, and more unhappily, we are confronted with a rising repudiation here in our own land of the moral and spiritual principles upon which our system of government was conceived.

It would be useless for me to attempt to deal with our international problems, because even if I were qualified to discuss them there is little that we can do to change that situation. This problem must be left to those in high authority at the seat of government, and we can only pray that they will find a way to peace short of destruction of the civilization and mighty works that a kindly providence has vouchsafed man to erect and of the enslavement of those who have the misfortune to survive such a holocaust. But there is something that we *can* do to help put our own house in order, and that something we must do before it is too late, for no nation, no matter how strong, can long survive on utter lack of responsibility and morals on the part of the official family of its administration. Nor can any nation survive a level of taxation designed to impoverish and destroy its business enterprises and the flower of its citizenry. The one encourages unfaithfulness on the part of lesser officials; the other both destroys the means of acquiring the tools of industry with which the growth of nations is fashioned, and encourages concealment of income, as the only means, short of rebellion, to forestall the leveling of all to the lowest common denominator of the populace. Together these evils lead to destruction of the moral fibre of officials and citizens alike.

This unhappy result already is upon us. It is manifest in the increasing evidences of official corruption, and in the riding tide of crime, that are making headlines in every edition of the newspapers that comes out. One of the latest violations of official corruption is that which has put the Bureau of Internal Revenue under the dark cloud of suspicion. We are shocked at these revelations, because we know from long and intimate dealings with the Bureau that the fine reputation for honesty and integrity that it has heretofore enjoyed has been richly deserved. But we may take comfort from the fact that Commissioner Dunlap, whose reputation for dealing appropriately with wrongdoers, has, with characteristic forthrightness, ordered a full investigation and pledged himself to rid the service of those who have brought discredit upon the Bureau and their innocent fellow officials and employees, to the end that the latter may be vindicated and the Bureau's good reputation may be re-established.

The something that we can do to help put our house in order is join actively and vigorously with those who recognize that as a people we *are* rapidly deteriorating morally and spiritually and that if our achievements in raising the lot of mankind to a higher and nobler level are to be preserved and continued we must avoid at all cost sinking to that ultimate level where we will be complete strangers to the faith and principles in which our system of government was conceived—degraded abdicators of our heritage of freedom and personal dignity—and, like hopeless victims of narcotic addiction, incapable of fashioning the means of our own salvation.

My pride in our profession is well known to all of you. That pride arises largely from the fact that as auditors we are cast by law, and by due sense of professional responsibility, in a role that is second in its implications of virtue to that of no other group that I can think of. This imposes upon us a high obligation, if not a sacred one. As auditors, we are charged with independence; and independent we must be in carrying out our auditing assignments, if we are to have any hope of achieving the eminence as a professional group that we ourselves hope for and that the world will readily accord us if we are worthy of it.

Independence implies faithfulness to truth. As auditors, are we not, therefore, seekers after truth? The world says "Yes," for we have publicized independence as our chief claim to public acceptance, and the public has come to accept the title, "certified public accountant," as the symbol of flawless integrity. And so, we ourselves have erected the pedestal upon which our aspirations are set and determined the cubits of its height. But, as is so often the case, after a group such as ours establishes the premises of its position, and then becomes engrossed in working out the details of its edifice, it is but human for us sometimes to lose sight of these premises, and almost always to take the world's acceptance of them for granted; and herein lies, I think, the only serious threat to firm and enduring establishment of our claim to public confidence.

And so, I suggest that we must be ever mindful of the true nature and significance of the principles upon which we stand, and of the very important fact that these principles have the approval and assured support of a power higher than man. How right was the poet who said:

> Though the cause of evil prosper,
> Yet 'tis truth alone is strong.
> Though her portion be the scaffold,
> And upon the throne be wrong;
> Yet that scaffold sways the future,
> And behind the dim unknown
> Standeth God within the shadow,
> Keeping watch above his own.

In these times, in which the course of evil seems to prosper so abundantly, I find great comfort in the assurance that 'tis truth alone that is strong and that the power that controls the destinies of us all approves the way of the righteous. I suggest, therefore—and strongly recommend—that we must not only continue steadfastly faithful to our obligation of independence, as the characteristic above all others that clinches our claim

282

to existence as a respected profession, but also that we assume and vigorously discharge our full obligation as citizens, for I am convinced that as faithful practitioners of a profession founded upon the rock of high principles we can contribute mightily toward rescuing the nation from the abyss of irresponsibility and moral degradation in which, unhappily, it has fallen.

The power of noble example alone is great, but this is not all that we can contribute. As skilled practitioners and interpreters of the mechanics of the highly complex economy that predominates our time, we not only are exceptionally qualified to help but have a clear and inescapable obligation to do so.

I assure you that this is no mere pious exhortation. Nor do I mean to give you the impression that I have overlooked or under-rated the magnitude of the contributions that have been made by so many of our members toward solution of national problems. What I am saying to you is that this is not enough. This great country of ours was built from the bottom up—not from the top down. If we do not generate at the grassroots more interest in preserving the faith and principles upon which it was founded, the rot that has set in at the top soon will spread through the whole structure and man's nearest and noblest approach to the achievement of freedom and independence will become a rubble heap of lost hopes and a symbol of unworthiness to a world that has put its faith in us and found us wanting in the hour of trial.

We may not "have our cake and eat it too." Enjoyment of the right of self-determination has been the very foundation upon which all of our wondrous accomplishments as individuals, and as a nation, have been achieved. This is a God-given right, and, like most privileges, it is not a one-way street; it has a counterpart of heavy moral and spiritual responsibilities. These responsibilities are individual responsibilities, and they may not be delegated; nor may we sink into habitual neglect of the obligations that they impose, without losing eventually the privileges from which they arise and thus returning to the tyranny of government from which a wiser generation rescued itself in order that it and its posterity might enjoy the blessings of freedom.

ADMINISTRATION OF THE INTERNAL REVENUE SERVICE

SQUARE DEAL FOR TAXPAYER[†]

Interview with T. Coleman Andrews

TO discuss the relations of the taxpayer to the Bureau of Internal Revenue, *U.S. News & World Report* invited Mr. Andrews to its conference room. This interview is the first comprehensive explanation of the Bureau's plans and policies given by the new Commissioner.

Q. Are you changing the attitude of the Bureau of Internal Revenue toward the taxpayer, Mr. Andrews? To many taxpayers it has seemed to be one of hostility—

A. I have been challenged on the question of what the attitude of the Bureau has been toward the taxpayer, and instead of saying that we are changing the attitude to the taxpayers, let's put it this way:

Everybody in the Bureau, and there are 54,000 of us, is an employee of every man and woman whose tax return is filed with us. We are not their bosses; they are ours. We are hired by them to assist them in discharging one of their duties as a citizen. There is no excuse whatsoever for any person in the Bureau of Internal Revenue to take any attitude toward a taxpayer other than one that emanates from a sincere desire to be helpful.

Q. Are you going to give the taxpayer the benefit of the doubt? Some of the Bureau's letters in the past have seemed to some taxpayers to be almost insulting, as though the taxpayer had done something wrong—

A. I have that difficulty with letters that come in to me for signature. I might say that I'm requiring a great many replies to be prepared for my signature—which a few months from now I won't expect to do—just to see what kind of letters our people write. Occasionally I have to send a letter back and say, "For goodness' sake, breathe into it a little bit!" I might say that it isn't that our people don't want to do a better job. As a matter of fact, they seem as anxious about it as I am and they are co-operating enthusiastically.

Q. Are you aware of the popular attitude of the taxpayer toward the Bureau, which is that the Government is interested only in the revenue by any manner that it can collect the revenue, irrespective of the inequities involved?

A. I am very much aware of it.

My feeling about it is that the Bureau has brought this on itself, and that one of our major jobs is to get the people believing in the Bureau again as they used to, to give the Bureau character and standing in the eyes of the public. And I believe that that's a very simple thing to do.

You have mentioned giving the taxpayer a "break"—the benefit of the doubt. Of course, that is what we should do. There should be a square deal for the taxpayer.

We should have the attitude, I think, that we want every cent that's coming to us, but not one cent more, and if there is sufficient doubt we don't want it at all.

I will give you an illustration. A case came up the other day of a dispute with a taxpayer that had arisen over 1943 income when the taxpayer was in the military service. When he came back and his returns were audited, he was told that he owed some $250. He said, "I don't think I owe you $250." And they argued backward and forward, and finally in desperation the taxpayer said, "Well, I'll give you $50 and clean it up," and that compromise was accepted.

Now, I would not have insisted on collecting the $50. Why? Because there was a reasonable doubt as to whether he owed any money or not, and I say that a compromise made in those circumstances is not a compromise at all.

Q. It doesn't prove who was right or wrong, does it?

A. It doesn't prove a thing. If the Government is not satisfied that it is right, then it has two courses open to it. If its doubt is sufficiently strong, it can say, "Well, let's forget it." If it is not strong, then it can say, "Well, let's let the courts decide."

Q. Isn't that the reason for the widespread belief that the Government is collecting nuisance penalties constantly from a public which doesn't want to be bothered with litigation, doesn't want to hire lawyers to defend every minor point? And aren't the sums so small in some cases that the people can't even afford the litigation and would rather pay the penalty then try to have it adjudicated?

A. You are probably right, and I would say that the last thing that any fair tax administrator wants is to have a tax return regarded as an invitation to a lawsuit. Way back in 1927, the Secretary of the Treasury, in a statement to the Joint Committee on Internal Revenue Taxation, stated: "The collection of revenue is primarily an administrative and not a judicial problem. As far as the federal income tax is concerned, a field of administration has been turned into a legal battlefield."

I am afraid that anyone would have to admit that over the years this situation has gotten worse instead of better.

As I see it, the Commissioner of Internal Revenue in his enforcement of the revenue statutes must not only see that every dollar of taxes due under the statutes is collected, but also that not one dollar is collected that shouldn't be. In other words, the Commissioner, in a sense, wears two hats—one as a law enforcement officer, the other as a dispenser of justice—and the appellate procedures provided by the revenue laws were deliberately set up to give the Commissioner the fullest possible opportunity to discharge both of these obligations.

Now, what is that appellate procedure? First, the return is examined, and the taxpayer has an opportunity to voice at that point his disagreement with the revenue agent.

Second, if the taxpayer and the revenue agent don't agree, they can take their differences to the revenue agent's group chief.

Third, if agreement is not reached at this point, the next step is appeal to our Appellate Division.

Fourth, if agreement is not reached at this point, then the next step is the Tax Court. But even at this point there is still another opportunity for informal discussion in the form of a pretrial conference.

Now it should be borne in mind that this procedure is designed to facilitate a meeting of minds across the table by the two people, each of whom must be prepared to give and take—the revenue agent as well as the taxpayer.

Also I call attention to the fact that our Appellate Division is not responsible to the district commissioners in matters of case settlements, but rather is responsible directly to the Commissioner, in Washington. Therefore, while it is the Appellate Division's duty to see that the laws are complied with, it nevertheless to a large extent sits as the representative of the Commissioner, functionally independent of the collecting authorities, to achieve, if possible, a just settlement of the points in controversy.

I have not yet had a meeting with the Appellate people, but I am going to, and I am going to tell them: "Your function is to represent me in my second capacity. My first capacity is to collect taxes. My second capacity is to do it with justice. Your function is to find, if possible, a point at which the Commissioner and the taxpayer can agree. Remember that you are sitting there now in my second capacity to find a just solution to the difficulty if you can, and to settle the case if you can in the manner that any two people willing to give and take can always settle any argument."

Q. What do you think of the Bar Association's plan for a small-claims court for tax collecting?

A. That is a hard question to answer without indicating a negative attitude, which I honestly do not have. But I feel this way about all proposals for any supplementation of the appellate process. I believe—at least, I am strongly inclined to believe after being here now nearly three months—that with a proper attitude from the top the present appellate procedure is sufficient, and that any taxpayer can get justice under it.

Q. And yet there must be millions of dollars collected by the Treasury from people who cannot leave their jobs to go to your tax offices to argue. Rather than argue—whether it's $10 or $15, or whatever it is, and may be a lot of money to them—and lose a day's pay from their job by coming down to the Bureau of Internal Revenue, they just accept the penalty. Now, what procedure have you within the Bureau to review those assessments?

A. The difficulty with that is that if a taxpayer pays without arguing, then there is no system of review that will help him, because the reviewer would never have the taxpayer's side of the case before him—

TAX ARGUMENT VIA MAIL

Q. Could the taxpayer write a letter and try to settle his problem and not take time to come in and argue it?

A. If we could get an adequate letter from the taxpayer stating his position, yes, that could be and would be, and even now is, reviewed if he makes this protest, formal or informal. It is reviewed and given due consideration. But the difficulty with most of those cases is that you can never get all the facts merely by correspondence.

Take, for instance, the question of dependents. There could very easily be a question as to a person's entitlement to an exemption for a dependent which could not possibly be solved by correspondence, but has to be solved on the spot.

There is no reason that I know of, in cases that warrant it, why the revenue agent couldn't go look up the person instead of making the person come to him. As a matter of fact, I have frequently thought it probably would be a lot less expensive in the long run—not to the Government, because it would cost the Government more money, but it would bring about a lot less economic loss—if, instead of making the masses come to the tax collector, the tax collector should try to arrange some way to go to the masses.

I don't know whether this would be practical, but there is such a thing as bringing the mountain to Mohammed when you can't get Mohammed to the mountain. At any rate, such a policy deserves study and we will explore the possibilities of it.

Q. Can a taxpayer, as a practical matter, expect to go to the Appellate Division on his own hook, without a lawyer, without an accountant, and have any real hope for success?

A. Why, certainly—unless there is a complicated question of law or income determination involved. If it is nothing in the world but a question of fact, any taxpayer can do this on his own.

Q. In theory, a taxpayer can take his case to the Tax Court without a lawyer or an accountant—but he doesn't get very far, does he?

A. But that isn't practical at all. And that's why the small-claims-court idea as an adjunct of the Tax Court probably is not the answer. The problem we were talking about is one that never gets to that stage. What we have to do to solve the problem you are talking about is, simply, to do our utmost to develop among the people who deal with us at the lowest level a feeling that the attitude of the Bureau is going to be one of justice, reasonableness, on the part of the agent as well as on the part of the taxpayer—

Q. Might you not lose a great deal of revenue that way?

A. Well, personally I don't believe you would lose any significant amount of revenue, and I think it would be a good investment even if you lost a little revenue by it and achieved the confidence of the American people in their Revenue Bureau.

Q. Do you think you are losing a lot of revenue because people are not reporting all their income?

A. We are losing some, but whether it is a lot I don't know. "Lot" is a relative term.

Q. Do you think some people are not making income tax returns at all who ought to?

A. There is no doubt about that, and we are conducting a survey right now in three cities to find out how many people in those cities who should be filing returns are not filing them. That will be used as a test sample of what we need to do in order to ferret out people who are not now filing income tax returns.

LOOKING FOR CHEATERS

Q. Do you have any indications as to what the answer might be?

A. Not yet.

Q. Did you co-operate with the Census Bureau on that?

A. No. We can do that job through other devices with a whole lot more ease. We can cross-check with the telephone directory and other lists. There are all kinds of simple ways of doing it.

Q. What percentage of the people try to cheat—do you have any idea? Is it high or low?

A. In some categories it is high.

Q. You have some definite plans, haven't you, to make it more convenient for the taxpayer to make out his returns and pay his taxes?

A. Oh, yes. And then, too, I think we may properly say that there really has been substantial change in the public attitude. We're beginning now to get a few letters and telephone calls from people who think we're not too bad. That, of course, is the result of a deliberate effort to improve relations with the public.

Q. How far can you go in helping the taxpayer make out his returns?

A. This year, for instance, we did a rather novel thing. I don't want to claim credit for it myself. What happened was that we were confronted with the problem of getting about 55 million individual returns out of the way in a very short period of time, and what we did was to say: "Now, here, we are going to give the taxpayer every bit of assistance we can, the best assistance we can give them. At the same time, we want to try to hold the line on collections, which have been slipping a bit."

So the plan was to bring into the collection offices in the various cities every person outside of the collection group whom we could make available. For instance, we brought in field agents and other personnel to assist the taxpayer in the actual making out of his returns. Now, there are other things that I will mention later. But that, of course, had a tremendous advantage from both the taxpayer's standpoint and our standpoint, because it put on the job of preparing returns those men who knew most about what the returns should contain.

35 MILLION STANDARD DEDUCTIONS

Q. Don't you find that the general run of people don't know what they can deduct and what they can't deduct?

A. That isn't quite an accurate statement when you stop to consider that there are probably between 35 and 40 million people who never worry about what they can deduct because they use the standard deduction of 10 percent of gross income. So, there is no great problem with all those people. The problem arises with people who have income other than salary—say, rents, interest, profits on sale of property, and that sort of thing—and who may have exceptionally large doctors' bills through the year or whose aggregate deductions will amount to more than the standard deduction of 10 percent. Now, these people have to have help. They are the ones who are most helped in the preparation of the longer form. And so we gave them the best help that's available in the Bureau. That's going to have two effects.

It got them through the line fast. I think the average time that anybody spent waiting was about 20 minutes, which is pretty fast.

Q. Is that here in Washington?

A. That's everywhere, the average for the country.

Q. Can you give us some idea of what the time had been in the past?

A. I couldn't tell you that because I don't think we have any record of it. But I'd say that it must have taken twice as long. As a tax practitioner I can say that 20 minutes is a remarkably short time.

Now, another advantage of that—the unseen advantage, the one that comes later—is that it simplifies our auditing job because we've got more correctly made returns, and that means less need for auditing.

Q. Then you can spend more time on the returns that you have to audit?

A. We will be able to examine more returns that ought to be looked into.

Q. What is the plan we hear you have to relieve 30 or 40 million people of making tax returns?

292

A. That is in its concept a very simple thing, but in its execution it is going to take time. It is this: Every person on a salary has his salary reported to the Social Security Board and the Internal Revenue Bureau. There are two different forms that report the same salary. Our idea is simply to co-ordinate the two.

We know what the man's salary is. And if that's all the income he's gotten, it is a very simple matter to take that information, calculate his tax, deduct it from what was withheld, and send him a refund check or a bill—and he never has to come to the Bureau at all.

Q. He would make no return?

A. None at all. We get the information from the Social Security report and salary-information form filed by his employer.

Q. These are the 30 to 40 million people who have no income other than their salaries or wages?

A. That's right, and who use the standard-deduction form.

Q. Won't he have to sign his withholding receipt?

A. He will probably have to sign his withholding report before the employer sends it in. We will, of course, have to get some change in law to put this plan into operation. It is not something we can do this year, and we may not be able to do it next year. But in another year after that, it ought to—

ONE FORM LESS FOR EMPLOYER

Q. Will it not increase the burden of the employer?

A. It doesn't put any more work on the employer at all. It will save him one form, in fact.

Q. It will put a great deal more burden on the Bureau, though, will it not? And, where the taxpayer frequently calculates his own entitlement to a refund, the Bureau will have to detect each of those cases?

A. We have to audit their calculations in any case, so why not let the auditor do it all in the first place?

Q. Will he get the bill for taxes due at the same time he does now?

A. He will get a receipt for having already paid his tax and a remittance notice. As far as the Bureau is concerned, the handling of a simple thing like that can be done by the least expensive people we have. So, you see, it really boils down to a very low-cost operation at a minimum of trouble to the taxpayer, the employer and the Bureau.

Q. How often would you do this, quarterly?

A. No, it would be done every year, once a year.

Q. Doesn't the employer make the deduction now and turn it in each month?

A. Yes, and they accumulate over the year.

Q. If the taxpayer still owes money, then you send him a bill?

A. Sure. If he gets a refund, we send it to him; if he owes money, then he is called on to pay it.

SPEED WITH REFUNDS

Q. If he has any income other than salary, the plan wouldn't work, would it?

A. No, he would have to file a different type of return. Now, there is another aspect of this taxpayer-help program that I think I ought to mention. By making the move that we did to increase the assistance to the taxpayer and get all this work done and preserving our collection people in their regular job of collection and holding the line in collections, we did something else very important. We got out practically all of our refunds by April 15, and so saved more than 3 million dollars in interest this year.

Q. People are getting earlier refund checks?

A. Oh, yes. There are very few places that I know of where people haven't already received their refunds.

Q. Can you do anything to make it easier for taxpayers to get advance rulings from the Bureau on problems they encounter?

A. Yes, we are already doing something about that. We get about 4,000 requests for rulings a month, and the production reports of the technical divisions of the Bureau indicate that, under a stepped-up program, more rulings are disposed of in each month than we are receiving requests for, so that the backlog of unanswered rulings is being diminished.

Q. Are the rulings worded in such a way so that if the facts change in any way the ruling doesn't constitute approval of what the taxpayer may subsequently do? How do you handle that?

A. Usually you get two different kinds of requests. One will be a request for an application of the statute in a particular situation, with a statement as to what the facts are. We will answer the taxpayer in a case like that by saying to him, "Now if the facts you gave us hold, then this is your answer."

Q. Can anyone write in for this?

A. Sure, and they do, with the questions running all the way from very simple ones to the very complicated. Some rulings take a good deal of legal and other research.

Q. In what sort of fields do these questions come?

A. Every field that we are in.

Q. How can you let the public know what you are doing with respect to these rulings? You may answer 4,000 letters a month, but that information is not available to the public. It's only for the one man who writes the letter. Nobody else knows how you have ruled in particular cases. What can be done to disseminate that information to the public? Could you publish the cases without mentioning the names?

A. What happens is this: We have a great many rulings, of course, that are just duplicates of previous rulings; therefore, to publish every ruling we make would be a tremendous waste of time and money. So, when we get a significant question to answer, we publish the question and our answer in the *Internal Revenue Bulletin*. Also, we are publishing more rulings now. In other words, there are fewer office rulings and more published rulings.

Q. Hasn't that been one of the complaints from the public, that there have been so few public rulings?

A. Yes—let's say that there haven't been enough.

Q. Where does a person write to get these advance rulings?

A. To the Commissioner of Internal Revenue, stating his problem and asking for a ruling.

Q. Who determines whether these rulings are significant or not?

A. That is determined by the technical office. They know. For instance, today we got a question up there on a matter that is almost novel, which probably seems unusual, since we have had an income tax since 1913. But, actually, it was a brand-new question. Well, the ruling on that question will be published so that if it comes up again, and it will come up again because it is a new type of business development, then people can be guided by it.

WHERE RULINGS ARE PRINTED

Q. What is the circulation of this *Internal Revenue Bulletin*?

A. The circulation of the *Bulletin* is available to anybody who wants it. It is not difficult to get. Anyone can write for a copy. The mailing list is handled by the Superintendent of Documents of the Government Printing Office on a subscription basis. The tax practitioners—the lawyers and accountants who actively operate in the tax field—get the *Bulletin* when it comes out.

Q. Is that sent free by the Bureau?

A. There is a small charge, $3.25 a year.

Q. Well, here you have millions of people who may need to know how you are ruling on these cases, but apparently there is no medium by which the general public as a whole can learn what you are doing—unless the newspapers would print that as a service—is there?

A. Under the new policy of the Bureau—if I may call it that—we are releasing a great deal more information to the public through the commercial tax services and the press. Lots of these rulings that apparently nobody heretofore thought of turning loose to the press are now being made available—not that they were ever secret before, but rather we are giving them out on the theory that maybe the newspapers might be interested in them and publish something about them.

The average taxpayer, of course, is not interested in the day-to-day rulings that come out. Even the practitioners aren't! Sometimes they just put them aside and never bother about them until pertinent cases come up; but then they go digging for them.

MAKING THE FACTS KNOWN

Q. Have you any practical suggestion as to how the rulings can be more widely disseminated? Can the newspapers do anything?

A. Well, the newspapers could do a great deal about it, but the question is whether they would find any real reader interest in the vast majority of those cases. I don't think they would—until somebody gets a particular problem.

Q. A few years ago the Bureau prepared a series of articles which were to be published in the press in installments prior to the date for filing income taxes. These daily articles gave the effect of various rulings in a popularized version of what the taxpayer could do, for example, by way of deductions. Couldn't there be something like that again?

A. There is such a publication available for that purpose right now. It is called "Your Federal Income Tax," costs 25 cents and is obtainable at the Government Printing Office. It has a thorough explanation in simple language—as simple as we have been able to develop up to now—though we hope we can make it still simpler.

As a matter of fact, we have tried to make all of our rulings simpler. We've tried to get some human understanding in them. For instance, this morning we had a ruling in which we were more humane than technical. I took the position that it was a situation where we could rule against the taxpayer technically but we should not rule solely on such grounds, but should also be right from a humane standpoint. And I told the man who wrote the decision, "Now, take it back and rewrite it and put it in the language in which you would want to explain it to your 15-year old son." We are trying, in other words, to put a little warmth into these rulings.

Q. This brings up a legal point. You still have a wide discretion, under your regulations, to do a great many things, haven't you?

A. I am told that the Commissioner has pretty wide latitude in some situations. Of course, that means he can be pretty arbitrary if he wants to, or he can be very liberal if he wants to. Now, you have to strike a balance between the two in order to do a good job of tax administration. We hope we are going to do that kind of job.

Q. How many copies of this publication, "Your Federal Income Tax," do you print?

A. During this last filing period it sold about 210,000. It was down because of the fact that there were no appreciable changes in the Internal Revenue laws. With each income tax blank, of course, we give a small pamphlet which runs to about 50 million copies.

What we are trying to do is to make plain the things that taxpayers can deduct so that they can sit down and figure out for themselves whether their legitimate deductions are greater than the standard deductions.

And another thing we have done on the taxpayer-help program, and I think is going to pay big dividends: We went into the high schools of the country last year with a simplified explanation of the income tax law and the preparation of returns. They took a blown-up picture of a return, for instance, and put it up on the wall and explained the various items in the return and how it came down finally to the mathematical calculation of the tax. Then they did the same thing with other forms.

Well, now, that approach has had a great response. The school people like it because it gives them something very practical to teach and adds to their capacity to teach government. Of course, underlying this program is the fundamental idea that, after all, we want to give the next generation an appreciation of why they have to have taxes, and, in addition to that, a knowledge of how to make out a tax return.

Imagine, if you can, the difference in the public understanding of the tax return when all these millions of school children who have been taught about it come up against the problem of making their own tax returns. It is going to simplify our problem tremendously—it's bound to—it just can't miss!

VISUAL EDUCATION ON TAXES

Q. That same method has been applied to voting machines in many States by putting these machines in the high schools when they weren't being used in actual voting. You are doing the very same thing, aren't you?

A. Yes. I call it using visual education to teach two things: respect for and understanding of government and its necessities and, also, a knowledge of how to discharge one's tax responsibility. We think that in the years to come we are going to have a lot less trouble with poorly and inaccurately prepared tax returns.

Q. Are you making real changes in the tax-return blanks and the instructions?

A. We have a group that is constantly working on changes in the wording alone to get it in simple language. One of the duties of the assistant commissioner in charge of administration is to take all tax forms after they have been passed as to their technical correctness and review them completely for language, to see if it is in language that he thinks the average person will understand.

Q. What is the situation with respect to deductions for individuals? There has been a lot in the papers lately about a mother who is employed and goes off to work and has to hire a nurse or someone to take care of the children. And she does not get a deduction for that expense. Whereas, in a business if you hire anybody to do anything, you get a deduction for that expense. What progress has been made in the handling of that issue?

A. There can't be any settlement of it so far as the Bureau is concerned, because the law is very plain on the subject—you can't take that deduction. It is not an ordinary or necessary expense of doing business under the law.

This question involves the matter of what part of income are you going to tax. Now Congress has said you are going to tax a man's gross income, with certain exceptions, and against that he is allowed certain deductions. Unless an act of Congress says that in the case of a working mother we will allow servant hire, the Bureau hasn't any right to allow it, because there is nothing in the law and regulations to justify us in allowing it.

THE WORKING MOTHER'S PROBLEM

Q. How about expenses necessary for production of income—that's allowed. Certainly that is true of a working mother?

A. I don't know that it could be so interpreted under that rule. We've considered it, and I think it has been honestly considered, and I think the only way to solve that problem is by legislation. The question is whether as a matter of principle you want to solve it that way.

It comes down to the whole question, then, of "What are you going to tax?" Are you going to tax an arbitrary amount of income, or rather an amount of income less certain arbitrary deductions, or are you going to tax only net income? If you tax net income, then most people spend all they make and so we wouldn't get much from individuals on that basis.

Q. What is your attitude toward the people who get income in the form of room and board? Lots of servants and hotel employees sleep in, and they get food and lodging. If they were working by the day they would go out and have to have a place to live and they would have to pay for their meals. They might work somewhere else and get increased pay, but they would pay income tax on it. Now, the person who lives in doesn't pay income tax on that income?

A. That is one of those borderline cases that comes under the rule, as I recall it, of whether the room and board is compensatory. This question often is very hard to decide.

Q. Now, if it is part of the employment agreement, is board and room income?

A. Ordinarily, no, where it is a required part of their employment for the convenience of the employer.

Q. Turning now to some of the headaches of business, what does the Bureau think it can do to accelerate the auditing of business returns, so many of which extend over so many years before a business knows whether its returns have been audited or not?

A.   That is a problem that is bothering us a bit. As an accountant, I think I have the answer. No. 1, we regulate our volume of examination of business returns according to the number of auditors we have. In other words, it's almost a mathematical proposition that you need so many auditors for every hundred or every thousand business establishments. There is only so much work that one man can do. Some of the big returns take a number of men. We have one corporation for which there are a dozen men on the job twelve months a year.

But for the average one-man or two-man account, one way we can speed it up is to develop in the revenue agents a greater understanding of the principle which the public-accounting profession has long since adopted, and that is test checking. In other words, no public accountant today ever audits every transaction. He picks a certain number of transactions over the year and examines them thoroughly, and on the basis of his tests he concludes whether everything is generally in order and gives an opinion as to the state of the account. We can apply that principle, the principle of comprehensive auditing on the test-check basis, and considerably speed up the process that way.

Another thing we can do is this: There are a great many auditors now going into some establishments that file more than one kind of return. We propose to wrap up all these returns into one package so that when an auditor comes into your establishment to examine your books, he would examine your income tax return, your Social Security return and, if you have excise taxes, your excise tax returns. Then that is the last time you would see the auditor until the next year.

PLAN FOR SINGLE AUDIT

Q.   You mean that all goes on one return form?

A.   Oh, no—separate returns, but all bundled up in one package for auditing purposes. I think we can speed the process a great deal in that manner.

Q.   Wouldn't you need a change in the law to do that?

A.   No, that could be an administrative determination.   So, by improved auditing methods, which we will get by an intensification of our training program, I think we can probably get our agents finishing their audits faster; also, by cutting out a lot of writing which is now done. One of the things that slows an agent down a lot is that most of them have to write their reports out in longhand. I suspect that a lot of reports don't even need to be written at all. In such cases the agent would say in a simple report form they have examined the return and everything is in order. Or even in those cases where they find something they disagree with, I doubt that the agents have to go through all the gyrations they go through now.

I think the process of developing the agent's reports can be speeded up. I think the process in connection with the papers for appeals can be speeded up. For instance, you usually find in a case where there has been an appeal that practically in every step in the case the facts are completely restated, and they may run for pages and pages and pages. Why not simply incorporate the facts for reference wherever they are first stated, and let it go at that!

FRANKNESS DUE FROM AGENT

Q. In the case of disputes as to items in auditing, do you think that the agent should disclose to the taxpayer that difference of opinion as to an item, or is he justified in saying nothing about it and giving the taxpayer his first notice of a disputed item when he sends him a deficiency letter?

A. The answer to that is that if an auditor examines anybody's returns, the first step in settling the dispute is for the agent to tell him just where he disagrees with him. I never heard of cases where—

Q. But there have been cases—

A. Fraud cases, maybe?

Q. No. The stories we hear are that an agent goes in to a business office and sees a lot of items on the return and he disputes those items. In writing up his report he includes some points that he thinks he can bargain with and writes them up as deficiencies, which he knows he's got to concede. And the impression you hear among businessmen is that some of their experiences with an auditor have been on a bargaining basis, that is, he might take up with the taxpayer eight or nine points, but when he gets back to the office he may find several others and doesn't argue with the taxpayer but simply puts them in—

A. Well, that just isn't cricket. I wouldn't permit that.

Q. Has the Bureau some tax cases that are still there from World War I?

A. I couldn't say.

Q. There are always rumors of cases being there 10, 15, 20 years—

A. They may be excess-profit cases, but I would imagine they are in the courts. I had one case the other day that has been hanging around there since 1928. We are finally getting that cleaned up and out of the way.

Q. Was that in the Tax Court?

A. No. It hadn't even gotten to the point of assessment yet.

Q. That brings us to another question. What about your rules in the various stages in the Bureau before you go to the Tax Court? The average businessman feels, when he goes before some kind of review board, that if he has some evidence or testimony, the Bureau should give weight to that evidence if it comes from competent witnesses. Can he bring in witnesses to support and substantiate his points?

A. Certainly.

Q. At any stage in this review procedure?

A. Sure.

Q. Is the Bureau in any way obligated to give weight to the testimony?

A. They certainly are.

Q. In a good many businesses of a complex nature which could not possibly be understood by the Bureau's personnel, unless, perhaps, a competitor came in and verified it as fact, is there an opportunity to bring in witnesses like this?

A. The taxpayer can bring anybody in that he wants to.

Q. Do any of them do it?

A. Yes.

Q. At what stage? I mean, is this done before it reaches the court?

A. Yes, it is done at any stage of the process, from start to finish. If a taxpayer has a case where he wants to impress the agent with the industry practice, then he may bring somebody else along who can say it is the practice. The Bureau is obligated to listen to that testimony. There is no reason in the world why they shouldn't do it. What we're after is to get the cases settled. We want to stop this pile-up along the line.

TAX COURT DELAY: 2 OR 3 YEARS

Q. Is there much of a jam now?

A. It is pretty bad. It is so bad, in fact, that I am told that Tax Court cases may not get tried for two or three years.

But we are making headway on this. I've given instructions that there must be more concentrated effort to settle.

Q. Wouldn't you get more revenue that way?

A. We get the revenue and get the case out of our way and simplify the thing all along the line. I haven't said that we have to settle a case just to settle it, but I said to these fellows:

"Here, forget about all this business of being scared to death of investigations. Go on and make your decisions. You have the authority to make them. Make every decision you can make within the scope of your authority, and be satisfied that if it is an honest decision you will be defended in it. Now, of course, if you are a person who is not capable of making a good decision as a matter of habit, then we are not going to leave you in that position very long. That is an administrative matter. What we are after is an honest effort to reach agreement with the taxpayer, even if you have to give a little sometimes. If you think it is just to give a little, then do so and get it over with."

Q. Are these pile-up cases mostly individuals or corporations?

A. That I can't answer, but my guess would be that they are business cases.

Q. What do you think of the idea of this 6 percent interest charge which goes on and on and on while a case is unsettled? Do you think it is right or wrong?

A. I think there are some circumstances where the running of interest might be stopped. But just where that point is I don't know. I do believe, though, where there is undue delay on the part of the Government in getting around to the disposition of the case, the Government ought not to expect to collect interest beyond a certain point. But just when that point should be I frankly don't know right now. We'll have to study it. I know that I have seen many cases where I thought the interest should have been stopped at a certain point, and I have had cases where people would pay a certain amount of money in, in order to minimize the interest.

I do think there has to be an interest charge for delay in payment, and there should be, conversely, an interest payment by the Government for delay in refunds.

Q. Why couldn't it be the prevailing interest rate instead of the flat 6 percent?

A. Well, in my own mind there is no particular sanctity in the rate of 6 percent. I don't know that you could defend it on any grounds except that it has the effect of an additional penalty—a penalty that works both ways, however.

REGULATIONS VS. LAW

Q. What is your theory about the discretionary interpretations by the Bureau of statutes in what is called the Treasury Regulations? Do you think the regulations are in conformity with the law?

A. One of the most serious complaints that we have been receiving has been that there is a lot of law in the regulations that Congress never contemplated. As a former tax practitioner, I can say that this complaint is justified, and all of us, at both the Treasury Department level and the Bureau level, are not only conscious of the problem, but are working on it almost feverishly.

We propose to identify, if possible, every such instance and correct it, and we certainly will not consciously allow it to happen in the future.

To give you an illustration, just the other day we were working on a regulation under the 1951 Act, and we found a provision as to which we had doubt concerning its consistency with congressional contemplation, and we changed it. However, let me point out that I didn't think for one minute that the people who wrote that regulation intended to try to do something that Congress didn't intend, so let's not any of us think that the Bureau is headed by people who are using gouges instead of their heads. We must remember that the fact is the Bureau is under the Treasury Department and that in the long run the Bureau reflects Treasury policy. The present

302

Treasury group is as anxious as we in the Bureau to see that the regulations conform to what has been contemplated by Congress.

I think the original motivation was the concept of strict interpretation, with all doubts resolved in favor of the revenue.

TWENTY YEARS OF DIFFERENT VIEW

Q. How far back would you say it goes?

A. It goes back 20 years anyhow. Most of it has happened in that period. I don't want to turn this interview into a discussion of the previous Administration, but I think their attitude was a short-sighted approach for immediate revenue purposes.

Q. How are you going to work with Congress on the matter of the changes in the law? Will you make the recommendations, or is the Secretary's office going to make them?

A. The Secretary's office is going to make them. That is all being handled by the Under Secretary of the Treasury. The Treasury team divides the tax problem between the Under Secretary, as far as legislation is concerned, and the Commissioner, as far as administration is concerned.

Q. Are you going to make some suggestions for administrative provisions?

A. We already have made a great many.

Q. The Administrative provisions in the tax laws haven't been revised for a great many years, have they?

A. No, they haven't, but that whole thing is under consideration, and what we are doing now is this: We have a new policy, it might be said, of dealing with Congress. For instance, we have regular meetings with the Joint Committee on Internal Revenue Taxation, in which the Committee and ourselves sit down and discuss problems of administration and reach conclusions as to what we ought to do. We met with the Committee only last Monday on the question of some of the new regulations that we have coming along.

You see, the regulation process is one of publishing a proposed regulation so that anyone who wishes may get a whack at it. The Committee gets complaints saying we don't like this and we don't like that, and we go up and hash it out. We settled four important points at our meeting last week.

Our attitude is very simple. We say: Congress makes the revenue laws for us to administer; therefore, how can we administer these laws intelligently unless we work closely with Congress and know what it intended. So we've established the closest possible liaison with the Joint Committee and its staff, with the House Ways and Means Committee, the Senate Finance Committee and other committees where the effects of taxation become involved.

Q. What are you going to do about the disclosure to Congress and the public of so-called "compromise" settlements? Do you favor a continuance of the existing practice of disclosing cases where the settlements are compromised due to incapacity to pay?

A. I feel this way about it: When a tax obligation is established by assessment and the liability is agreed to, then at that point any compromise of that tax is entitled to publication. I think the people have a right to know about it. I'm a taxpayer and you're a taxpayer. If you are going to get a special deal on your taxes, for any reason whatsoever, I think I have a right to know it.

Q. Then you would publish the amounts that were "compromised"? Would you publish the facts in the case?

A. We would do what we are doing now. All compromises of income, profits, estate and gift tax cases are now put on a register and are available for anybody who wants to see them.

Q. Those are cases where the taxpayer has claimed his inability to pay?

A. They are for a "compromise" for any reason.

Q. And they are available for anybody to see?

A. Yes. You can go right down there now and see them.

WHAT IS A "COMPROMISE"?

Q. In the previous Administration, Commissioner Dunlap used to say that he would not introduce the other type of settlement. He used the phrase "compromise settlement" for only those instances in which a man was assessed a certain amount of money, say $1,000, and he was unable to pay, and finally the Government would accept $50. All those types of cases he made available to the public. But where there was dispute over an assessment between the taxpayer and the Government, and they finally agreed that all that was owed was X instead of Y—

A. That's not a "compromise." It hasn't even reached the point of assessment because it isn't assessed until that agreement is reached. Now, we are having that every day. We'll have a dispute with a taxpayer over whether he owes X dollars or Y dollars and through the appellate process we finally determine the amount owed. We then bill the taxpayer for that amount.

Q. You call that an "assessment," not a "compromise"?

A. That's right. That is a positive obligation on the taxpayer's part. Now, if at that point he says, "I agree, I owe $100 but I can pay only $50," and offers $50 in payment of his liability, then that is an "offer in compromise."

304

Q. You have much power to make changes in this matter by regulation, haven't you?

A. There is a great deal that can be done administratively, but there is a lot that has to be done by legislation. Take this whole question of disclosure of information as to compromises, or disclosure of information in general, I may have my own ideas about it, but there may be some phases of the thing that could come up sometime where there would be a question of whether under the law I had the right to disclose it. In that case, I would depend upon the advice of counsel.

But, generally speaking, I think that compromise of tax liability, once the liability is firmly agreed to by both sides, is a thing that ought to be a matter of public knowledge if the public wants to know, because then to the extent that the other fellow is being relieved everybody else is being taxed.

Q. That's if he cannot pay his "assessment"?

A. Yes.

Q. What do you do about a case like this:

A business pays its taxes, argues with an Internal Revenue agent, and sometimes with its own accountant about a deduction, and yet that very same moment the Bureau may be allowing that deduction in another case and the taxpayer wouldn't know anything about it. Is there any way a taxpayer can find out what competitors, for example, may be getting in the way of a break in his line of business?

A. Frankly, I don't think you'll find very many cases of that kind, because a good many people in business have pretty good advice as to the preparation of their tax returns.

Q. But there is no publication of the rulings of the Bureau that would guide an industry unless they have this exchange of information among tax practitioners?

A. There would be no way for the Bureau, except at inordinate expense, to be able to publish the fact that deductions made by one business in an industry are different from those made by another business in the industry.

But, frankly, I doubt that we're talking about anything significant here, because through trade-association activity, conferences of tax practitioners and other means business establishments find out pretty well what they can and cannot do taxwise; and I doubt that many of these establishments are missing much that might be to their advantage.

Q. Let me put it another way—is there an obligation on the part of the Bureau, which is aware of its own rulings, to apply that same ruling even though the taxpayer may be unfamiliar with it?

A. Certainly. In other words, there is as much obligation on the part of an agent to give a taxpayer a deduction he is not now claiming as there is for him to disallow an unlawful deduction that he is claiming.

Q. Are there a great many deductions claimed that are not supposed to be claimed?

A. Yes, there are. There are a great many cases of revenue being lost by people claiming exemptions and deductions that are not proper.

Q. Is the expense account itself being abused?

A. It most assuredly is, and the Secretary of the Treasury is taking a close look at this problem from the standpoint of whether the law should be tightened up to prevent the abuse.

Q. How tough is the policy on business-entertainment expenses?

A. Of course, we have to look at it from three standpoints: Is it an ordinary, necessary expense, and is it reasonable? What we try to do is require pretty thorough documentation on entertainment expenses, and, if not documentation, then sufficient explanation to enable us to determine whether or not there is convincing reason to suppose the money was actually spent.

Q. And that is true of individuals as well?

A. Yes.

FORMULAS FOR DEPRECIATION

Q. Can you by an administrative act, by regulation, change the depreciation policy?

A. Many aspects of depreciation can be settled administratively, but there are some that must be dealt with legislatively. Two aspects are presently under consideration. One is the administrative aspect as to, for instance, when shall the determination of depreciation be deemed to be final? I'll come back to that in a minute. The other question is: What formula for depreciation may be adopted? For instance, could we permit a wide-scale switch from the "straight line" method of depreciation to the "diminishing balance" method? Perhaps we could, and the question is being studied by the Treasury staff.

Q. What do you mean by the "straight line" method?

A. It means the depreciation charge obtained by dividing the cost of the property less its probable salvage value by the number of years that the property probably will last. For instance: Cost, $1,000; salvage value, $100; probable life, 10 years; annual depreciation charge, $90.

The main thing that bothers me about depreciation is the fact that as matters now stand an agent can go into a business and say, "I think you've taken too much depreciation. I'm going to cut that down." They argue about it, and, finally, somewhere along the line they compromise. The agent says, for instance, it ought to be 3 percent, and the taxpayer says it ought to be 5 percent, and maybe they settle on 4 percent. But it doesn't end there. The very next agent that comes along may take the position that the previous agent was too liberal, and then the argument starts all over again. Somewhere along the line the taxpayer has a right to expect finality.

WHEN A BUILDING WEARS OUT

Q. Isn't building depreciation fixed at 2 percent a year?

A. No, sir. It shouldn't be.

Q. Is that a matter of administrative determination?

A. There is a regulation on it, T.D. 4422, and a special bulletin, "Bulletin F." In "Bulletin F" a great many categories of property and the applicable rates of depreciation are listed. But that doesn't say that the rates indicated are the only rates that will apply. Special circumstances might change any rate in the regulation.

The position I have taken on depreciation, with the group that we have studying it, is that we should have a regulation that says that once the depreciation on a particular category or type of property is established and the taxpayer and the Bureau agree to it as proper, it should not be changed after that point unless the one who wants to change it takes the burden of proof that the original determination was wrong or no longer applies.

That would save untold annoyance to business organizations and a terrific amount of money to the taxpayers and the Government in a matter which in the final analysis has really cost the Government a lot of money, for the reason that the Government has been beating depreciation charges down, down, down, and taxes have been rising; so that all that has happened has been that the deduction for depreciation has been shoved over to high-tax years and the Government has lost money by it.

Now, regardless of that, I am not just trying to save the Government money. What I am trying to do is get a reasonable policy, save annoyance to everybody and have a rule under which, once a determination is made, there it is going to stay until the Government proves it ought to be lower or the taxpayer proves it ought to be higher.

Q. You hear very frequently among businessmen the idea that a company ought to be allowed to take just about any depreciation it wants and feels is reasonable, providing it is consistent and the Government doesn't lose any money in the long run, because if it fixes too much depreciation it is merely postponing its taxes. What do you think about that?

A. That is not sound accounting to begin with; nor is it good finance.

Q. Once the method has been set, Mr. Commissioner, don't you have to stick to that method in order to prevent distortions of income?

A. Generally speaking, that is true. If you've got the "straight line" method, then you pay on the "straight line" method.

Q. What do you think of the British scheme, which they announced the other day, for a tax rebate on new machinery, and so on?

A. Of course, that was done to encourage investment of risk capital. I doubt that we need to go that far in order to encourage risk capital. In effect, that is similar to the "diminishing balance" method, under which you apply your depreciation rate to the diminishing balance (cost less previous charges for depreciation) of the asset.

For instance, if you've got a piece of property that is estimated to last 10 years, and it costs $1,000, then you take off 10 percent, which is $100, and the next year you take 10 percent off of $900, or $90, and so on.

Q. But you never completely depreciate the property on that basis—

A. No, but you can set the formula so that you can get back in a relatively short time the bulk of the cost of the property, and it is in effect an accelerated-depreciation scheme, and you come down within the estimated life of the property to a residual balance which is approximately equal to its salvage value. But you do it much faster.

Q. Is that allowed now?

A. Oh, yes, there are taxpayers on that basis now.

Q. Can others who are not on it get on it?

A. From the standpoint of optimum application, that is a matter of tax policy and would have to be answered by the Treasury Department. That's why it is being concurrently considered by the Treasury Department.

Q. In other words, broad changes in depreciation policy would probably have to be done by legislation?

A. That approach should always be considered.

SMOOTHER IN BRITAIN

Q. Speaking of the British, have you made any study of their system of tax administration?

A. Not recently, no.

Q. The general impression we have over here is that the British sit down with the taxpayer and work out his indebtedness very promptly, without all this endless litigation. Is that true?

A. Yes. They do a much better job in that respect than we. For instance, I understand that a British chartered accountant can sit down with a taxpayer and work out his tax return, and when he says to the British Government, "I have made this return, I think it's all right," they will examine it, but a great deal of weight is attached to the fact that a British chartered accountant did the job. They don't seem to have as much or as protracted argument as we.

Q. Do you think we have too many disputes?

A. Far too many.

Q. With businesses, or individuals?

A. With business, primarily.

Q. Does the taxpayer in this country have a better chance to get his return approved if he has had it made out by an accountant? Do you take that into consideration in this country as they do in Britain?

A. Let's put it this way: The Bureau doesn't have any policy of accepting a return merely because it is made by an accountant, but I can tell you from my own experience that the taxpayer who keeps good books and has a good accountant make his tax return has very little trouble.

HAZARDS IN "UNREASONABLE" SURPLUS

Q. There is a great deal of interest in Section 102, which prohibits the retention in business of an unreasonable surplus. After the war, many small businesses were alarmed by what they thought was an unfriendly, or rigid attitude—

A. And let me say that I think that those who have been alarmed about it have had good reason to be. Who wouldn't object to having a sword of Damocles hanging over his head?

Q. I wonder whether the attitude has changed—whether or not an ordinary corporation can use its own judgment in retaining income?

A. Within reasonable limits, yes. Of course, no one should be allowed to use unnecessary accumulations of corporate profits as a means of escaping taxes that others have to pay. But I regard Section 102 as a lever, not as a club, and I think that in applying it the Government should assume the burden of proof. As Commissioner of Internal Revenue I'm willing to accept that burden. I do not think that Congress put Section 102 into the law to be used as a pattern for liquidation of the country's traditional enterprise system, to which our people's unparalleled high standard of living is so largely attributable.

Q. The burden should be on the Government?

A. Yes.

Q. By and large, it has been the other way around, though, has it not?

A. I'm afraid it has. In other words, the position of the taxpayer in that situation is just the same as it is with respect to any other question that the Commissioner raises, he has to prove his case. I don't think this should apply in the case of Section 102.

From my point of view, before the Government says to a company that part or all of its profit accumulations are excessive, I think we ought to be ready to prove our case.

Q. At least by indirection, one of your predecessors as Commissioner of Internal Revenue set up a 70 percent rule. The impression was abroad that any small, closely held company that paid out less than 70 percent of its earnings in dividends was suspect under such rule—

A. That's right.

Q. Is that still so—are they still suspect, or is there any reason to believe that they are suspect if they pay out less than 70 percent?

A. I wouldn't say they are suspect, but I think for orderly and common-sense administration of the tax law you've got to have some rule—whether 70 percent distribution is adequate or inadequate, I don't know. I wouldn't want to say. But I say this: You've got to require people to pay out reasonable dividends.

In this question whether accumulations of earnings are necessary in a particular case, you've got to have some standard as a basis to go on. But I don't think it can be any fixed amount—70 percent, or 50 percent, or any other percent.

I think each case has to be considered on its own merits, and when the Commissioner says, "I think you people are taking advantage of a good situation," I think he ought to be able to prove it.

LAW'S POWER TO DESTROY ENTERPRISE

Q. Can that be made policy without a changing of law?

A. I hope so. However, I fear that would require legislation. But as Commissioner, regardless of the legislation, that is one section of the law that I would be very reluctant to be harsh about, for the simple reason that I don't think Congress means to destroy enterprise, and I think that Section 102 in unwise hands can be used to do just that.

Q. Doesn't the Government often spend more in collecting a tax debt than the collection is worth? What can be done about that?

A. In the case of willful and flagrant tax evasion, I don't think anything should be done about it. The time and effort spent in sending a crook to jail often costs more than the revenue that we obtain from him. But that doesn't worry me, for in the long run the deterrent effect of prosecution on would-be evaders nets us revenue far in excess of the costs of a particular prosecution. Moreover, the fellow should be in jail anyway. As between the jailing of a crook and collecting the taxes he owes, I'd rather see him in jail any time.

As to other classes of underpayments, we propose to take all the factors into consideration in each case and use plain common sense. I certainly do not propose to make minor adjustments in the audit of tax returns just to pick up a few dollars here and there; neither do I propose to issue distraint warrants and liens on insignificant amounts of balances due but unpaid. We have the approval of the Comptroller General's office to write off small debit balances.

Q. What is the morale situation in your Bureau? Are you getting much turnover?

A. Well, yes, we are having some turnover; but I think we may say that morale is improving steadily. You see, this is not a spending agency; it is a necessary operating function of the Government. It's always going to be there; therefore, if a man comes to work in the Bureau and keeps his record clean and tends to his business, the chances are he will wind up with a pretty good grade and retire with a fair pension, hence, we don't have as much turnover as some agencies have had. There are a lot of people in the Bureau, and because we are a stable establishment the average age of all the Bureau's people may be a bit high in relation to some of the other agencies.

However, by a different attitude at the top, I think we have considerably restored, or started morale on the way back up.

Q. Fear isn't a dominant factor then?

A. No. We want to get injected into the Bureau, with the approval of the Civil Service Commission, the idea of accelerated recognition of outstanding merit. If we can get that, it will be a great help. Moreover, we think we have to adopt a firm policy as to discipline. We think it has been too lenient in the past.

Q. What are you going to do about gratuities that come toward these employees? Are you going to prohibit them from receiving any?

A. Absolutely.

Q. And what about going to lunch with a taxpayer? Is that a rule of the Bureau?

A. It isn't a rule of mine. I think it is unwise for a man to get too chummy with the taxpayer or his agent, but I don't know whether you can have an ironbound rule on that.

ROTATION FOR AGENTS?

Q. Do you think that agents should be moved from one locality to another occasionally?

A. I think certain types of personnel ought to be rotated. I haven't decided yet exactly where rotation should stop, but there certainly are types of jobs that call for rotation, and I believe it will make for better service to adopt rotation in those cases.

Q. In the past the Bureau has been accused of withholding prosecution where the Department of Justice is ready to prosecute and the Bureau is not, or vice versa. What have you done about that?

A. My feeling about prosecution is that when you find that you have your facts and investigation is finished and prosecution is indicated, the case should go to the Department of Justice promptly with recommendation of prosecution.

Q. There have been a number of cases where they have examined the defendant and found that he supposedly wasn't in good health and so they defer and defer the case, until they finally drop it because the defendant is not well enough to stand trial—

A. That's a matter, I think, to be settled by the Department of Justice and the courts. I don't think it is up to the Bureau to determine that. If the Bureau says to the Department of Justice, "Here's a fraud case. We think it ought to be prosecuted, so we are sending it to you. Whether to prosecute or not is your job." Now if they want to determine that health considerations should delay prosecution or stop it, I think that is a matter between the district attorney and the court.

Q. What proportion of your personnel is under Civil Service now?

A. Every one except me.

REORGANIZING THE BUREAU

Q. What do you do about the deputies that got in at the last minute under the so-called questionable examinations? How are you going to handle those?

A. You mean the district commissioners and the directors of revenue?

As far as the reorganization is concerned—that's what you're talking about, I believe—I have said a number of times that I thought the reorganization of the Bureau was structurally and functionally a sound move. I have considerable reservations about the manner in which it was implemented. My feeling is, however, that nobody is smart enough to walk into an organization as big as that and in a matter of a few weeks, or even a few months, know exactly what he wants to do with it.

You have, moreover, a very serious personnel problem involved there. Suppose I determine tomorrow that half of my district commissioners and half of my directors are unsatisfactory. Where would I get eight district commissioners and 32 directors right quick? Men qualified to hold those jobs aren't running around loose. I'd hope to find them in the Bureau. But in any event it would take time—a good deal of time—to find the right men.

I've asked Congress to let me handle this matter administratively, and I have assured them that, if or to the extent I find I can't handle it that way and need legislation, I'll ask for it. We will not hesitate to replace any officer or employee of the Bureau whom we find not up to his job.

Q. Would you clear up a question about your personal plans? When you took office, didn't you indicate that you were only going to be here for two years?

A. No, I did not. As to this there has been confusion of my personal plans with my official objectives. What I have said has been that as a necessary goal we are shooting at getting the situation in hand within two years. If we did not establish some reasonable deadline for getting our house in order we'd run the risk of wandering aimlessly. It's too early to talk about my personal plans. There's a big job to be done here, we've just started on it, my colleagues in the Bureau are co-operating with me wholeheartedly, and I intend to see it through with them.

TAX UNIT SEPARATE FROM TREASURY?

Q. Have you had any thoughts even before you came into office as to whether the Bureau of Internal Revenue should be divorced from the Treasury and made an independent agency like the Comptroller General's office?

A. I'd rather not get involved in that question. If I advocated independence I'd be accused of empire-building ambitions. If I opposed it, and the Treasury Department happened to be opposed to it, too, I'd be

312

accused of submitting to domination. I do not wish to be put in either position. However, I can discuss the question generally. The important thing, it seems to me, is to settle the question on the basis of what would be best under all conditions.

It so happens that the present Treasury team is a very congenial group. We work together in mutual confidence and complete harmony. Thus, there is no domination of the Bureau; on the contrary, we operate under a grant of broad authority except as to the matters that come under the Chief Counsel of the Bureau, who is functionally responsible to the General Counsel of the Treasury Department.

Obviously, the success of this kind of setup depends largely upon the personalities involved. It seems to me, therefore, that the question is whether from the long-range point of view this is the kind of setup which under all conditions will be most likely to provide administration of the revenue laws that is as directly and as promptly responsive to the intentions of Congress as can be achieved.

So it all boils down to people. The most important thing in the world is people. If I get the right kind of people I can run the Bureau efficiently under any kind of setup.

Q. It has been argued that if you get an independent agency you're liable to get arbitrary action—

A. I believe that experience has shown that that can happen under any kind of setup. It's still a question of people.

Q. Have the previous commissioners been practicing accountants like yourself?

A. No. I believe I am the first certified public accountant ever appointed to the job.

ACCOUNTANTS AND TAXES
Desirable Objectives in Tax Administration[†]
by
T. Coleman Andrews

THERE have been far-reaching changes during the past fifty years in the accounting profession and in the American tax system. In 1903 public accounting in the United States was in its infancy, and the constitutional amendment for a federal income tax was as yet unborn. Today the accounting profession is well established and well organized, and the income tax is a very significant factor in out national economic life.

Unbelievable as it may seem, the next fifty years may well produce equally phenomenal changes. That is beyond the power of any of us to predict, but I should like to describe here some of the change in tax administration toward which we are currently aiming.

The interest of accountants in these changes is obvious. I have practiced as a CPA for many years, and this background has played a large part in forming my own opinions as to desirable objectives in tax administration.

BUREAU PERSONNEL AND OPERATIONS

First of all, I consider that basic honesty and integrity are the indispensable foundation for anything we may try to accomplish in the Bureau of Internal Revenue. The Bureau's personnel is, as a group, as honest and diligent as people come. But there have been betrayers of public trust among them who have let the Bureau and their fellow-workers down. The number of these wrongdoers has not been relatively large, but their misdeeds have been so shameful as to discredit the whole Bureau and handicap its operations. This is being cured by a program of intense self-examination and a policy of prompt and unequivocal disciplinary action. We shall not stop until every malefactor is exposed and weeded out and internal controls are found that will give the greatest assurance possible that absolute integrity will prevail throughout the Bureau. Nothing less will satisfy us, because nothing short of this will assure preservation of the self-assessment system upon which the nation's revenue structure is based.

[†]Reprinted with permission from *The Illinois Certified Public Accountant*, June 1953, pp. 66-67.

315

The second objective is to improve the efficiency of the Bureau's operations. Overhead expense is being carefully studied to reduce the indirect costs, with the hope that the savings thus realized may be applied to extension of the auditing of tax returns. We know that up to a certain point, which we have not yet approached, every dollar spent for auditing will produce many dollars of additional revenue. This naturally will ease the burden on the taxpayer who is already paying his full share.

TAXABLE INCOME AND THE TAXPAYER

Third, and of special interest to the accounting profession, I believe that the government should not require the taxpayer to compute his income by methods that are contrary to generally accepted accounting principles. At the request of the Chairman of the Joint Congressional Committee on Internal Revenue Taxation a special committee of the American Institute of Accountants is preparing a report on this subject, and I think we can expect Congress to move toward a closer relationship between taxable income and income computed in accordance with generally accepted accounting principles. Many present requirements as to income determination came about through regulations of the Bureau. We are re-examining the regulations and making changes wherever we find that they represent a substitution of regulation for legislation.

Fourth, we want to bring about a saving in time and expense for the taxpayer. Means for accomplishing this would include revision of forms, simplification of regulations, and improvement of appeals procedure. I think we can make the preparation of tax returns unnecessary for millions of taxpayers whose whole income is subject to withholding tax. Also, much time of both the Bureau and the taxpayer can be saved by our refraining from unwarranted controversy over the allocation of trifling amounts to one year or another. For instance, the Bureau gains little, if anything, for the government by forcing a taxpayer to change his rate of depreciation, if the rate is reasonable. The amount of tax is not usually affected in the long run to any considerable extent, and the effect may be merely to shift the collection of a certain amount of revenue from one year to another. I don't believe the Bureau should be run on the principle of seizing by hook or crook the maximum revenue for the current year.

Fifth, the necessity for appealing many cases can be eliminated by giving local offices more authority to make decisions. That was one of the primary objectives of the recent reorganization of the Bureau. The government and the taxpayer are more likely to reach agreement on any question if the taxpayer has some reasonable assurance of the finality of a decision reached at an authoritative level. To guard against favoritism under such a system, there must be a high standard of integrity and close supervision. This makes clear again that our first objective of absolute honesty underlies all our other aims.

We are already on the path to fulfillment of these objectives, but much remains to be done. The accounting profession, which is so close to the operation of the Bureau, can contribute much to the success of these efforts. Accountants, together with lawyers and business executives, are represented on a new advisory committee to the Bureau which is helping us find and pin down the Bureau's faults and develop corrective measures. However, individual suggestions from accountants and others will always be welcomed and appreciated by the present management of the Bureau.

SUCCESSFUL ADMINISTRATION OF THE TAX LAWS[†]

by

T. Coleman Andrews

I am going to talk about the present, with, I hope, a minimum of reference to the future, except in terms of high hope.

First, I want to thank everyone for the wonderful testimonial dinner that was given for me in Washington on the 19th of March, exactly one month and a half after I took office. When I saw the great crowd of my colleagues of the profession from all over the country that had gathered there in Washington that night, frankly, I could hardly believe my eyes.

I want to tell you that our guests were just as much impressed by that gathering and by the importance of our profession and the solidarity of its membership as I was. That importance and that solidarity, I can assure you, were manifest on every hand, in the eyes, and in the countenances, and in the demeanor of the hundreds of my colleagues who were there.

The news of that meeting spread around Washington pretty fast. There were some forty or fifty members of the Senate and Congress there, and every one of these men, without exception, called me and expressed the very highest compliments of the accounting profession. Frankly, and I hate to admit this, most of those gentlemen didn't realize what a large profession we are, and the high caliber of the people who are in it. I want to say that the conception, the organization, and the carrying out of that meeting was a masterpiece of effective public relations, and you may be certain that it increased enormously the great pride I already had in our profession and its members.

More important than that, however, was the fact that it gave me a new sense of the increased magnitude of the responsibility to the profession I already felt. I think most of you know how great that pride is, and I am sure that I don't have to tell any of you that I pray constantly that I may be vouchsafed so to discharge that responsibility that, when I reach the end of this assignment, my performance will have warranted the confidence so many of you have so generously expressed in me.

Notwithstanding frequent contacts with members of the profession during the course of my official activities, I have been in a new environment—one that has occasionally not been as friendly as the one I

[†]Reprinted with permission from *Accounting, Auditing, Taxes 1953* (New York: American Institute of Accountants, 1954), pp. 14-23.

was accustomed to when I was in practice. It is therefore mighty pleasant indeed to join you again in annual meeting. I do not want to give the impression that my job is an habitually unpleasant one, for that would really be misrepresenting it. We have had our troubles, of course, but thus far none of them have been too hot to handle.

The fact is that, on the whole, our experience has thus far been very pleasant and satisfying—primarily because we have enjoyed the uninterrupted confidence and support of Secretary Humphrey and Under Secretary Folsom, but also because the job has been an extremely challenging one.

We have heard a lot about Texas since we have been at this meeting. Perhaps I should say that we have heard a lot, as usual, about Texas. Be that as it may, I think that one of our most pleasant and, I might say, amusing experiences was with a gentleman from Texas who had discovered oil and had grown rich. Contrary to the usual custom of employing newfound riches to influence the achievement of a box seat in Heaven, this Texan decided to go to Washington to find out how the government was organized and how his money was being spent.

He arrived in town one morning, came in unannounced, and introduced himself. He said, "Mr. Andrews, I am up here to find out how this government is run."

"Well," I said, "that is a very laudable purpose. I'm delighted to see you, and I hope you will learn a lot. Have you been anywhere else but here?"

"Oh, yes," he said, "I've been here several days now. I've been over to the Department of the Interior and over to the Department of Agriculture," and he named several others. "I decided that I would wait to come to see you last because, after all, you deal in something that is pretty important to me." In the course of my discussion with him, I found out he wasn't kidding.

By his own admission, he had been a tenant farmer a few years ago, and he had lived in a little one-room shack down there on somebody's cotton farm. (I never knew there was something that small in Texas, until he told me.) He had only one chair in the house, he said, and not even a bed to sleep on. Then some oil companies came through there one day and started pecking around and digging, and before he knew it they brought in a gusher on his place, and pretty soon another one, and another one, and the next thing he knew, he was a tremendously rich man. I learned later that his income was now $100,000 a week. I am told that that isn't very much, as incomes go in Texas, but I, having come from a poor but proud state, was greatly impressed by it.

I learned, too, that he had acquired several private airplanes since he had become affluent, that he had chauffeurs and footmen for several cars, that he had sent one of these cars and chauffeurs ahead to Washington to see that he had proper transportation, and under the right sort of circumstances. Then he got into one of his planes and flew on up to Washington.

I shall never forget what the gentleman said to me as he walked out of my office: "Oh, by the way, Mr. Andrews, I haven't asked you how much money you have collected."

I said, "Oh, somewhere between sixty-five and seventy billion dollars a year."

He scratched his head a little bit and looked around and said, "That's a lot of money, ain't it?"

I said, "Yes, that is more money than I can imagine."

He thought for a moment more and, as he went out the door, he said, sort of under his breath, "It's a good thing we don't get all the government we pay for, ain't it?"

Today, I want to tell about some of the things we are doing that, I believe, will be of particular interest to you and your clients. I cannot tell you the whole story because, if I did, you would be here all day. So I will limit myself to a few of the more important aspects and some of the minor things that, with your cooperation, may become major accomplishments for us.

First, let me say that I wasn't merely expressing a pious hope when I announced right after I took office that the new administration would take a fairer attitude toward the nation's taxpayers. The longer I stay in Washington, the more I am convinced that there has been an acute need for improvement in this respect. What is more important, we have already plenty of evidence to prove that a reasonable attitude toward taxpayers pays off richly.

What is our policy in this regard? It is simply this: First, we are in business to help the taxpayers, not to boss them around as though they were our servants. So I said to our people, "Let's get in there and help them and stop acting like a bunch of commissars. The people have done us the honor of employing us to help them determine what taxes their representatives in Congress have said they shall pay and you don't help people by snarling at them and attempting to browbeat them."

Second, our job is, of course, to collect taxes; but it is also our job to be helpful, reasonable, and just. We should not allow spendthrift empire builders to make imperial Shylocks of us. Balancing the budget is not up to us. We merely collect the money; and, if the budget can't be balanced by ordinary processes, it certainly is not to be balanced by the process of getting every feather we can pluck out of the goose, by whatever means we can contrive.

Third, our over-all objective is less litigation and more negotiation. We have been emphasizing these policies and objectives to the Service's personnel almost daily, and I can assure you that it is beginning to seep in and pay off. Of course, we don't want our people to have cold hands, but neither do we want them to have cold hearts.

This problem of getting a proper attitude on the part of our revenue people toward taxpayers is a very difficult one. You don't change people's habits overnight. Every now and then somebody complains bitterly to me that he has had an unsatisfactory experience with our people, and his tone is one of reproof. He is saying to me, in effect, "Why don't you do something about it?" In fact, I am trying to do something about it. We have traveled thousands of miles; we have talked to thousands of our own people, and to thousands of taxpayers; and we always try to impress upon our people the kind of attitude we want them to take. I am glad to be able to tell you that for every one person who says, "Why don't you do something about it?" there are about a hundred who are telling us that they notice the difference.

Of course, we don't expect our people to take insults from anybody. They don't have to. All they have to do is to be sure that they are gracious and just themselves in dealing with taxpayers. The taxpayer, of course, owes the same obligation of reasonableness and courtesy to our people that our people owe to the taxpayer. I think we are making progress in getting a better attitude on the part of our people.

Let's talk about decentralization a bit—what it means to the taxpayer and to the tax practitioners, and what it means to our people in the Internal Revenue Service. But first, let me tell you what the purpose of decentralization is and why we went into it. The purpose of decentralization is to encourage administrative settlements and reduce litigation. That is its primary purpose. Again we want to reduce the formal contest as much as we can, not because I am an accountant, but rather because we were concerned, and are still concerned, about the fact that the Tax Court, when we took office, was confronted with an intolerable backlog of unsettled cases, and that the same was true at the appellate level in our own shop. We soon would have reached an impasse, and it might have seriously affected our whole administration of the tax law.

The fundamental purpose of decentralization is to enable taxpayers to settle their differences with us on their own ballgrounds and across the table, in a spirit of compromise in which each party is willing to give up those things that he can't sustain, to the end that there might be agreement on more positive things.

The same is true in a dispute between business people. We recognize the fact that there has to be litigation of some disputes, and we try to take a reasonable attitude toward it. We do think, however, that the government in dealing with its citizens can very well take the same kind of attitude that those citizens take among themselves in their transactions with each other; for what is government but the people themselves. I don't think that is an unreasonable attitude.

Of course, most of you realize that decentralization was inherent in the whole program of reorganization adopted by Congress last year—a program, incidentally, that, as far as we are concerned, was merely a blueprint we took over. It had not been implemented.

Throughout the country, there were regional offices and chain setups, where the people in charge didn't even know what they were supposed to do. That isn't a criticism of my predecessors. The fact is that they were given a time limit for the institution of the reorganization; a time limit that was so utterly close that there was no chance in the world to make the reorganization effective before the filing season of this present year came around, consequently we had to get through the filing season before we could begin to make this thing work.

One of the first things we decided was that 17 districts were entirely too many to have. They were then called districts; now they are regions. So we cut it down, as you all know, to nine, and we chose nine gentlemen who have distinguished themselves in the Revenue Service to head those districts.

It is men like Mr. Ernest Wright, the Regional Commissioner for the Chicago area, whose entire lives have been spent in the service of their country, who make me proud to be a part of the Internal Revenue organization.

Now, what are some of the criticisms of the decentralization, and what are my answers to them? There are three principal criticisms. Number one is that the people in the field are not capable of assuming the enormous delegations of authority we had to make in order to carry out this decentralization and make it function. Number two is that we have opened a door for corruption on a much wider scale than ever before by giving great discretion to 64 district directors; whereas heretofore most of that discretion had been retained in Washington. The third one we might mention is that there will be no uniformity of rulings and no uniformity of decisions.

Let's discuss these very briefly. As to competence, I look at it this way: Some of the highest rated and highest paid people we have in the field (over 50,000 of the 54,000 employees of the Service are in the field) are the people who are out on the front line of operation, whose entire lives have been spent in that activity. Is it reasonable to suppose that these people are not competent of doing their job? I don't think it is, and I say to you very frankly if that were a valid criticism of the decentralization, then I should have recommended to the Secretary of the Treasury long ago that we wipe out the organization from top to bottom and start all over again.

What about corruption? The fact of the matter is, as all of you know, that there has not been any widespread corruption in the Internal Revenue Service. There have been people in it who have been guilty of some pretty serious indiscretions, yes, but you can count those people on the fingers of your two hands. I do not think that that number of people among 54,000 makes the entire organization corrupt any more than that one bad apple spoils a barrel. Sure, it creates a smell, but it doesn't destroy the rest of the fruit.

In addition, I have never known any organization that was any more corrupt at the bottom than it was at the top. In other words, if those presently in charge of the Internal Revenue Service at Washington are honest and forthright and fair and just in their dealings with taxpayers, I think that everybody else is going to be, right on down the line. To turn it around, I think that the minute we in charge of the Service in Washington prove unfaithful to our trust, and the people down the line know it (and they would find it out before anybody else), we will hear about it. If we in Washington, the Regional Commissioners, and Directors and their staffs give a proper demonstration of integrity and competence, we can expect the same from the people down the line.

As to uniformity of decisions, I think that most of you know that uniformity is a myth anyhow. We know that the Tax Court, which is a single court, has made contrary rulings in similar situations. There is no criticism of the Tax Court. We know that the District Courts have made rulings contrary to each other, and I suspect that those things will continue to happen. We think, however, that we have better control of the situation than the courts, because we have an administrative obligation to seek uniformity as far as it is possible to attain it. I can assure you without going into details that we have not just dumped this thing in the laps of the people in the field and said, "Here it is; it is your baby; go ahead with it." Instead, we have drawn upon our experience as accountants and auditors to install those principles and procedures of internal check and control which will enable us to obtain the highest degree of integrity and competence throughout the organization, and as great a degree of uniformity of decision as is possible to achieve.

I want to point out what we have done to assure the taxpayer a possible opportunity to settle his difference across the table with us. We have set up, as you know, the group-chief conference. Frankly, I don't know whether the group-chief conference is right or wrong; none of us are sure of that yet. A rather strange thing about it is that it seems to work wonderfully in some places and not at all in others. We have to find out why it doesn't work in those places. I can tell you that the policy of the present administration is that nothing we decide to do is sacred in our sight, and that no procedure we may follow is good one minute after we discover a better way to do it.

Next, I should like to tell a little bit about rulings, which are, of course, important to you. This relates, to some extent, to the question of uniformity. Uniformity involves, first of all, the pattern by which all of our field people act under the laws passed by Congress. This pattern has not been decentralized. Then you have the rulings, which have not been decentralized either.

So those fundamental stones in the foundation pattern of applying the law to given situations all emanate from Washington, and will be of course, under the same control as they have been under before. But we are also going to issue more rulings; we already are doing it. As of September 30, we had issued 207 rulings as against 86 for all of last year, and we expect to issue this year more than four times as many rulings as we issued in 1952.

As many of you have observed, these rulings will be more clearly stated, and what is more important, we will get them out faster. Believe it or not, while the general average seems to be 26 days between receipt of request for a ruling and the issuance of a ruling, which is a lot less than it had been, we often get them out in 24 hours. Of course, the more complex the ruling, the longer it takes to get it out, but I can tell you that under the very able direction of Assistant Commissioner Norman Sugarman, the Technical Rulings Division is not dragging its feet. It is doing a wonderful job, and I am delighted to have this opportunity to commend Mr. Sugarman publicly for the very excellent job he is doing.

The purpose of our whole rulings program is to have greater publication. There will be no more of the sort of thing we saw in the past, such as the granting of the deduction of campaign contributions in the guise of bad debts, based on rulings that were never published. This administration is not going to engage in that kind of skulduggery. It is going to publish every ruling we make, except those rulings where the same facts and the same application of law have been published over and over and over again.

I have said that we are striving for simplicity in everything else, even our correspondence. It has been a rather strange revelation to me to receive from a number of people letters telling me that for the first time in their lives they have gotten letters or rulings from the Revenue Service that they could understand. Perhaps some are going out that are not so understandable, but I usually tell Mr. Sugarman when they come up to me, "Norman, make them so I can understand them, because if I can get it, I am sure almost everybody can." I think we have achieved that goal generally, but we still have a long way to go.

We are trying to get all the stilted language out so that you will understand what we are trying to say. We are trying to be responsive to your inquiries. We are trying to make you feel, "Well, these fellows are really human beings; they are just like us, they fight with their wives and they probably get divorces and they do all the things that we do. By gosh, one of these fellows may be our neighbor, who knows?" That is what we want to do.

We want to remove the Revenue Agent and Revenue people from that category of mysterious people who oppress the taxpayers, and I think we can accomplish that largely without ever looking taxpayers in the face by just being attentive to what we say and do.

Of course we are trying to avoid being unnecessarily technical, but I hope that you people will not be led into the error of unduly literal interpretation of what we say in some of these rulings. Please don't misunderstand our simplicity. Don't take us too literally. Let's apply the thing on a reasonable basis.

Finally, I want to mention Circular 230, which, as you know, says who may practice before the Treasury Department, and under what conditions they may practice. This circular is now in the course of revision. There are many who undoubtedly regard this current revision of our rules of practice as just a routine matter, but I want to assure you that, in the final analysis, the very success of our tax system of the voluntary compliance type depends largely upon how broad a participation in the taxpayer-assistance program by persons outside the Service is permitted.

It is a well-established fact of tax administration that compliance with any law depends in large measure upon the public's understanding of the laws and the application to them individually. Meetings such as this afford us the opportunity to show how the laws are applied, to whom they are applied, and in what degree they are applied, but that isn't the whole answer. I think that President Eisenhower indicated the balance of it in a recent speech when he said, and I quote him, "We believe that in judging his own daily welfare, each citizen, however humble, has greater wisdom than any government however great."

This philosophy, when applied to the job that the Internal Revenue Service has to do, means simply that we must allow the taxpayers in choosing who shall represent them in the discussion and settlement of their disputes with us, the broadest possible latitude consistent with sound administrative practices.

I also think that it bars as unthinkable and utterly unworkable the suggestion that anyone save ourselves be permitted to say who may practice before us.

In addition to the basic reasons for allowing taxpayers a wide choice in this matter, there is a very serious immediate reason in our personnel situation. Before I explain that situation, however, let me give you some simple but significant data. In 1939, the total number of tax returns filed in this country was 17,700,000, of which about 10,000,000 were returns other than income-tax returns. Today, there are 93,200,000, of which 60,400,000 are income-tax returns. In 1943, as most of you will recall, our tax base was broadened to bring about this result.

In 1939, the population of our country was 131,000,000. Today it is 29,000,000 greater, or 160,000,000. Bear in mind that that is better than 20 percent increase.

In 1939, there were 45,750,000 employed persons in this country. Today there are 62,300,000, an increase of nearly 20,000,000. Therefore, what do we face in the Internal Revenue Service? We have had an almost tenfold increase in workload since 1939, with the largest increase in the number of returns filed in the income-tax field, where our principal problem lies. In that period of time we have gone through the greatest war the world has ever known, and since 1946 we have been confronted with serious personnel shortages.

When the Korean War broke out the personnel situation became acute again. Employment today is at the highest level (with some slight recent downward trend) it has ever been at in the history of the country; and, in that situation, the Internal Revenue Service has had to defer or abandon many desirable techniques of tax administration, the net result of which is potentially disastrous. What has happened to us is simply this: As of this moment, we are 1200 Revenue Agents short of what is provided for in our budget, and we are not finding it easy to make up that shortage. We must look forward to a normal attrition of about a thousand agents a year. I am referring to agents, not because they are the only problem we have, but merely because we look upon the Revenue Agent as the backbone of our system of enforcement, at least I do, although I am not sure that everybody else does.

We, therefore, are a long way from having all the people that we need to enforce the Revenue laws. Now, don't let me be misunderstood on that. I am not saying that the Congress has acted, toward us, in any penurious manner; quite the contrary. The Congress indicated to us last year, after approving our budget as presented for the first time in the history of the Revenue Service, as far as we know, that if we needed more men, to let them know, and they would give them to us. So we are not in any trouble with Congress. We have the finest possible relationship with Congress and the greatest cooperation that anybody could hope for.

Our problem rather is how many can we get and how fast can we assimilate them? We have an organization which normally is a stable organization, because you are going to have taxes like you are going to have death, and, therefore, you do not have the turnover in our department that you do in other departments of government. In one of the important cities in the Middle West, 70 percent of our top personnel are retiring within the next five years, and a situation almost as bad is to be found in many of our offices.

Therefore, it is absolutely imperative that we do two things: First, provide for a steady increase in the number of our personnel until we get to that point where further additions would not bring in a greater sum than we spend for them, and I can tell you we are a very, very long way from that point. In addition to that we must have just as many people as we can possibly get to help in the administration of the tax law from the outside. The taxpayer must, therefore, be allowed to have all the help that he thinks he requires in accordance with the dictum laid down by President Eisenhower.

The Chinese symbol for disaster is made up of two characters, I am told, one of which is the character meaning crisis; the other the character meaning opportunity. I don't hesitate to state, that we face a crisis, personnelwise, in the Revenue Service, but I also can assure you that we are of that mold and of that frame of mind that we recognize the opportunity and that we intend to seize it. We have a plan for meeting this situation that, in my opinion, will work and will not only give us all the people we need, but will also give us a very much better Revenue Service, a real, true career service.

Only recently Chairman Young of the Civil Service Commission complimented us on this policy of ours, and told a group of government employees that the policies of the Internal Revenue Service will assure, for the first time, one of the great career services of the government.

So, my friends, it all boils down to at least two basic principles: One, successful tax administration cannot be achieved in an atmosphere of mystery as to what the tax laws are all about, who they apply to, and to what extent in each individual case they do apply; and just as it takes all kinds of people to make a world, so also it takes all kinds of people to make a tax system work, especially one as complicated and as varied as ours.

One other thing I would like to mention about Circular 230 is that I frequently have been asked what my attitude is with regard to the publication of disbarment practice. My own feeling is that the taxpayers of America have as much right to know who is disqualified from practice as those who are qualified have the right to publicize that fact. As far as I am concerned, whenever anyone loses his right to practice for cause, it is going to be published. We want the world to know that we are running the Revenue Service on an honest basis, and who the shysters are, if any.

Let me say this to you in conclusion: The question of successful administration of the tax laws of this or any other country boils down to one very simple thing, and that is the question of whether the taxpayer complies willingly and forthrightly, or whether he seeks to evade. Now, I think most of you know that in several countries of the world artfulness and evasion are being more greatly admired than willingness and compliance, and I think all of you know what condition those countries are in. The president of one of these nations said recently that over 90 percent of all the people in that country subject to income taxes were evading them.

Let me point out that there isn't going to be any Marshall Plan for the United States of America if and when it falls upon hard times. One of the best ways I know to keep it from falling upon hard times is that the administration of the tax laws of the country be such that will inspire integrity on the part of those who administer that law, and integrity on the part of the citizens who must comply with it.

I think, very deep down in my heart, that we can draw all the pretty pictures of organization we want, we can write all the fine-sounding procedures for the guidance of our people we want, but that, unless we achieve the situation under which the taxpayer of this country continues to

328

come forward and say voluntarily, "This is my income and this is what I owe you;" unless we can preserve that philosophy of tax compliance in this country, then the time will come when the fiscal system of our country will collapse and carry down with it into the rubble of disgrace everything that you and I hold dear. As the Commissioner of Internal Revenue of the United States, I am dedicated to the attainment of that kind of tax administration.

CURRENT U.S. TAX PROBLEMS[†]
by
T. Coleman Andrews

IT is a very great honor indeed to be invited here to address you ladies and gentlemen of the Bar and of the accounting profession. I have been an accountant most of my life and I have associated long and intimately with members of the Bar—always on the most pleasant basis. I am glad to have this opportunity to discuss with you problems in which we are both interested, because they are common problems of administration for both our countries, and because there is such a close bond between us, the people of your nation and mine.

I suppose it is a bit trite to say so, but certainly after all these years a very pleasant and harmonious relationship exists between you folks and ourselves. Coming here to Canada, anywhere in Canada, is like visiting one of our own cities. As a matter of fact, I don't feel that I'm in a foreign country when I come to Canada, because I have so many good friends here, and you are always so very cordial in the warmth of your welcome.

I am also glad that this is a *joint* meeting of accountants and lawyers, as I always enjoy being with my lawyer friends, especially when I can talk about them and they can't talk back! You know we have had an income tax law in the United States since 1913, and in the 40 years since that "iniquitous" bit of legislation was enacted, the vested interests of the Internal Revenue Service have been presided over by lawyers, with only one possible exception.

You will recall that the "mess in Washington" was an issue in the last election, and probably the worst "mess" of all was in the Internal Revenue Service. Well, after the lawyers spent 40 years getting us into that mess, the accountants took over, and started cleaning up. And we had better do it right, because, goodness knows, the lawyers are certainly watching us closely. Maybe that's the reason we are working as we are.

I'm reminded of the story about a doctor, a lawyer, and an engineer who got into an argument over the antiquity of their respective professions. The doctor said that his profession was the oldest, and to prove it he quoted the Bible, which says that in the beginning God created Man and then, to

---

[†]Address delivered at the closing dinner of the Canadian Tax Foundation's Seventh Annual Tax Conference. Reprinted with permission of the Canadian Tax Foundation from, T. Coleman Andrews: "Current U.S. Tax Problems," in *Report of Proceedings of the Seventh Annual Tax Conference*, 1953 Conference Report (Toronto: Canadian Tax Foundation, 1954), pp. 66-79.

provide a mate, he extracted a rib from the side of Man and created Woman. The engineer, quick to take advantage of an opportunity, pointed out that the Bible also says that God created the heavens, the earth and the seas out of great chaos and confusion. "Now," said the engineer, "that was an engineering job of much more importance than the mere creation of Woman from the rib of Man." The doctor reluctantly agreed that the engineer's profession was older than his. "But," he said, "you still don't win, because, as you pointed out, there was chaos and confusion in the beginning—and who in the world could have created that but the lawyers!"

Now my friends, in order to get a little background for my remarks tonight I would like, if I may, to indicate to you something of the size of the operation which I have the responsibility of administering and a little about the organization for managing that operation. Many of you are interested in what is going on in my country, because you have some contact with tax administration in the United States. I know this because some of you have already been in touch with me about problems that touch the affairs of your clients.

The total number of tax returns of all kinds filed in the fiscal year ending June 30th, 1953, is more than 93 million, of which 60½ million were income tax returns. In other words, that is almost one return for every two people in the country. Of course, everybody does not file the same kind of return. And to further understand the size of the problem I think that perhaps it might be as well to make a little comparison with 1939 when the world got thrown into its latest era of chaos. Enormous things have transpired in our country since 1939, as they have in the rest of the world. At that time there were 45¾ million people employed in the United States. At the present time there are 62 million (62,400,000, I believe by the last count). That's an increase of nearly 17 million since 1939, or about 40 percent.

In 1939, individuals, firms, corporations, and other organizations subject to income tax filed just over 7 million tax returns. With 60½ million filed this past year, that's an increase of about 850 percent. That of course was due largely to the fact that in 1943 Congress in its wisdom decided that the tax base should be broadened so that more people would be brought under the requirements of the income tax law.

There were 10½ million of other types of returns in 1939, compared with 32¾ million at present. Considering *all* tax returns, we had 17¾ million in 1939 compared with 93¼ million filed last fiscal year—an increase of 550 percent, or 5½ times as many. During the same period, our population increased from 131 million to 160 million, an increase of about 23 percent.

Now I think that it will be apparent to all of you that an operation of this size is a stupendous one, certainly beyond the comprehension of any one person. It takes a great deal of organization and a most careful type of management to know what is going on in all departments. I will be very frank in saying that I am not quite sure yet as to what is going on in all departments. This organization, as presently constituted, is headed by the Commissioner, with a Deputy Commissioner acting as his Principal Operations Officer, whose primary duty is to carry out the program, projects and proposals—organizational and management—that the Commissioner approves. Most of these are worked up, I might add, by the Commissioner and the Deputy Commissioner with the advice and assistance of five Assistant Commissioners. You may be interested to know the duties of those five Assistant Commissioners.

One of them we call the Assistant Commissioner in charge of Operations. It is his job to run the day-to-day routine of the Service. He has, in terms of the number of people employed under him, the biggest job among the five Assistant Commissioners. But there are in addition many enormous problems and he also takes an important part in working out new ideas, analyzing them and deciding what should be done.

Then we have an Assistant Commissioner in charge of technical matters. Principally his job is to make rulings on questions that are submitted by taxpayers or by the Internal Revenue organization itself. I might say that there are usually about 4,000 to 5,000 requests for rulings per month. It is also his duty, under the new set-up, to carry on rather an extensive review of the decisions made in the Regional and District offices, in order to see that these decisions, similar in fact and application of the law, are as uniform as possible.

Then we have an Assistant Commissioner in charge of research and planning. We figure that if research and planning are necessary for an organization such as General Motors, Ford Motor Company, Sears-Roebuck, General Electric, or any other nation-wide organization that I might mention, it is equally important that we of the Internal Revenue Service carry on the type of research that will help us improve our organization, our operating methods, and the basis of our dealings with our people.

Another thing which is rather important is that we must try to guess what kind of legislation Congress is apt to adopt three, four, or five years hence, so that when a new law is enacted we may be ready with at least an outline of a plan for administering it. If we are going to know how to cope with problems we have to do some pretty intelligent guessing as to what the problems are going to be, and consequently we regard our research and planning group as an extremely important one. I might say that when I became Commissioner the head of research and planning had not yet been dignified by the title Assistant Commissioner. An operation of that importance ought to have the highest possible rank as far as the question of its head is concerned. Incidently, that same unit deals with refinements of our operations. For instance, we expect in about 18 months to eliminate altogether the necessity for the filing of returns by about half of the 65 million individuals now filing. Technical Planning Division is charged with the task of working out the manner in which this will be done.

I wish that there were time for me to discuss that project with you fully: it is extremely interesting because it involves the newest electronic machines, and for the first time in history the co-ordination of the activities of two of our great Departments of the Government, the Treasury Department and the Department of Health, Education and Welfare. The Social Security Administration of the latter Department, and our own Service, which is a part of the Treasury, will collaborate in bringing together the necessary information to compute the amount of tax liability, deduct the amount withheld, and determine the balance due to either the Government or the taxpayer. The whole plan has been worked out to the point where we know that it is mechanically feasible. All that we have to do now is to complete arrangements with the Social Security people and get the approval of Congress. We don't expect difficulty with either, but it will take another year—at least—before we are able to put the plan into operation. I hope and believe that we can.

The fourth Assistant Commissioner is in charge of our housekeeping. He is the Assistant Commissioner for Administration. His responsibility includes the management of personnel, housing and supply—all matters pertaining to housekeeping within the Service. It is, of course, an extensive job, evidenced by the breadth of our operations. Finally, we have a fifth Assistant Commissioner, whose job is the inspection of our offices, both departmental and field. In accountant's language, his department will be concerned with internal control functions, and will be responsible for the integrity of the Service and of the personnel, for checking on the personnel at all times and also upon the efficiency of the organization. This department will see to it that plan of operation set forth in the Manual is faithfully carried out by all of the officers and personnel of the Service.

Our field organization consists of nine Regional Offices, each with a Regional Commissioner and sixty-four District Offices, headed by Directors. The Regional Commissioners, you might say, are "Deputy Commissioners" too, for they represent me in their respective regions. Their duties, however, are largely administrative, for they do not deal directly with taxpayers, but rather they are charged with seeing that the sixty-four offices of District Directors operate according to plan. I should state, however, that the Regional Commissioners and District Directors have no authority over members of the Inspection Service, who report directly to me.

Now the sixty-four District Directors are what you might call local managers, roughly one to each State—though some States have more than one. Ohio, for instance has four. These Directors are the people who control the organization that deals with the taxpayer. Whereas we used to have a local Collector, a local Revenue Agent and a local Intelligence Chief, each independent of the other, we now have an integrated service

334

with the Director in charge of all of the operations in his area. There are sixty-four of these Directors, and there are 1,400 offices ranging all the way from a one-man outpost to a full-fledged District Director's Office with several hundred employees.

That will give you some idea of the nature of our present organization.

I should like to discuss with you, now, the co-ordination of services within and without our organization. Among the people we look to for help are the tax practitioners. While we have now about 52,000 people in the Internal Revenue Service, and will shortly increase this number, it is not large enough to do all that is required to properly administer the law and provide the assistance taxpayers need. We, therefore, encourage the widest possible practice of such practitioners as can help the taxpayer discharge his tax obligation.

Now you have a very fortunate situation in Canada in which lawyers and accountants constitute the main body of your practitioners. In the United States a lesser percentage of our accountants are certified, and while many of the uncertified accountants render valuable service as tax practitioners, the larger and more complicated cases are handled by the lawyers and chartered accountants.

I am told that, in Canada, you have a very happy working relationship between the two professions. I regret to say that no such relationship exists in the United States. There is a feeling, on the part of the lawyers at least, that practice should be restricted rather than broadened. It is no secret that I do not hold with that point of view. I think, if our system is to work, it is going to have to be upon the basis of the largest possible extension of the right to practice, under such means of control of ethics and behavior as we are able to work out and impose. Furthermore, we have to do what you have learned to do, work out a relationship whereby the lawyers and accountants can function together harmoniously, each realizing that there is plenty of work for both, and not nearly enough people to do it all.

This reminds me of something I discussed yesterday afternoon with some of your folks. We may be coming to a new day and a new outlook of the professions that contributes to the success of business. The lawyer, the accountant, the engineer, and the actuary have begun thinking in much broader terms than we ever thought in before. A business has a right to expect from us, I think, a well-rounded and integrated service. I may shock some of you by even suggesting this, but I am perfectly certain in my own mind that the time will come, how soon I don't know, when there will be integrated professional firms that are able to offer to business *all* of the various kinds of professional service that a business needs...legal service, accounting service, pension service, engineering service and so on. I think that we are going to come to realize some day that it is a narrow point of view for us accountants to say that we may not become members of firms with lawyers and I think it is equally narrow for the lawyer to think that the lawyer should not associate himself in professional transactions with an accountant.

That may shake some of you, but I believe that in the evolution of our economic system, such an integration of professional service will inevitably occur and I should be somewhat inclined, I think, to encourage it.

Let us look at one of the developments, for instance, of one of our own problems there in Washington in the Internal Revenue Service. We have an Advisory Commission—say an Advisory Group—consisting of three lawyers selected from a panel of six that were nominated by the American Bar Association, three accountants taken from a panel of six, nominated by the American Institute of Accountants, and three tax executives taken from a panel of six nominated by the Tax Executives Institute, and then there was another appointed independently, so that there are ten members of that Advisory Group. Three lawyers, three accountants, and three business men, or tax executives.

Now, if in the administration of our law we find it necessary, and I can assure you it was done only because it was found necessary, to bring together professional talent of that kind, it seems only reasonable to me that business itself will someday come to the point where it will expect that kind of integrated service from the professional people. I hope that this may occupy the thoughts of some of you from time to time and that you may find some merit in it.

Now we have a basic philosophy in this new Administration in Washington, that the taxpayer and the tax collector are not natural adversaries. Let us think about that a bit. In all my experiences, there has certainly been a feeling on the part of the taxpayer that there is a natural animosity between the tax collector and the taxpayer. If you will go back to your Bible you will remember that the Publican, the tax gatherer, was a pretty hated man. Nobody liked him. He was just about as low down in the scale of humanity as anyone could be, in the estimation of his contemporaries. This attitude seems to have prevailed through the ages, but I hold that that is wrong. Of course, tax collectors have made themselves unpopular. Let us not forget that because I also hold another fundamental philosophy, and that is that none of us can blame anybody for the impression we make upon others, except ourselves, and if the tax collector has gotten himself in bad it is his own fault.

We are trying to administer the Revenue Law of the United States today in a manner that will correct the impression that taxpayers and tax collectors are adversaries. I admit that it was a pretty tough job to tackle, but we think we are making progress with it. We see the evidence in our daily correspondence. It comes to us now in increasing volume that people are finding a "new look," a new attitude, on the part of the tax collector. He is not giving anything that he should not give, but he is nevertheless giving everything he should: and at the same time whatever the situation, however difficult the problem may be, he is behaving in a reasonable, pleasant manner towards the taxpayer.

Now that may seem very elementary, for I see some of you smiling. I don't blame you because it is rather ludicrous to me that a situation such as I have outlined here already should have ever developed.

Now what does this philosophy mean in terms of action? One other thing, very simply stated, is *negotiation* on tax disputes and less *litigation*.

If any of you have read the recent issue of *Business Week* you'll recall a discussion on the docket of the Tax Court. For many years, the number of cases on the docket of the Tax Court had been increasing steadily. Each year the number of cases on inventory at the end of the year was higher than the year before.

I am happy to be able to tell you, as evidence of progress, that on September 30th of this year for the first time in a decade the Tax Court docket was lower than it was the year before. We are also getting many more cases settled on the Appellate level, and a great many more settled at the Group Chief level—I will explain those two terms to you in a moment—because we are taking a different attitude towards the taxpayer. We want to settle and get these cases out of the way. We no longer believe that "the King comes first" or that he is always right nor do we think it is possible for us always to be right, and the taxpayer always wrong. We figure that we can be wrong sometimes—perhaps we are wrong as often as the taxpayer; and somewhere along the line in our negotiations with the taxpayer, we reach the point where by a little give and take on both sides, we can come to an agreement and, believe me, it's worth it.

This philosophy also means that we get more settlement of tax disputes at the local level, which brings me to something about which there has been a good deal of conflict at home, the *de-centralization* of the Service from Washington.

Without calling any names, there has been for many years in Washington an attitude that all wisdom resides in Washington and on the Potomac. I call it the Pandemonium on the Potomac!

We don't think that all the wisdom of the world is in Washington or that all the wisdom of the United States is in Washington, or that all the wisdom of the Internal Revenue Service is in Washington. On the contrary we look facts squarely in the face, realizing that over 50,000 of our people are in the field, in the front lines of operation, whereas most of the people in the Service in Washington never saw a Revenue Agent's office. We think that the Revenue people in the field are quite capable of solving most of the problems that come up in the day-to-day operations of the Service. Therefore, we are converting the Washington Headquarters into a *Headquarters* and nothing else, making it a planning and control center and putting the responsibility for operating decisions upon the Regional Commissioners and the District Directors. I might turn that around and say upon the District Directors and the Regional Commissioners, because operating decisions are supposed to be made on the local level.

Now that calls for the delegation of a great deal of authority which the people in the field have never before enjoyed. Working on the theory that you cannot expect a man to discharge responsibility imposed upon him unless he has authority equal to that responsibility, we have been very liberal in granting authority to make decisions. We have said to the people in the field, "We don't want you to bring anything to Washington except things so complex or involving such a question of policy that you feel Washington should advise you on it." And so, when you have a tax problem with our people now, in 99 out of 100 cases it will be settled right at the local level.

I happen to be a part of the South, and to do anything that has a flavor of "State's Rights" is as natural for me as eating. Settling our problems at the local level is only natural in my opinion. So let them be settled at the point where they arise, where the people who know most about them are. It certainly seems to me that solutions can be accomplished much more satisfactorily in the field than in Washington where one has to depend almost entirely upon a written record, which—I am sure the great jurist on my right will agree—is never as good as direct evidence.

Our appeals procedure is very extensive. It starts with the Revenue Agent. He goes into a taxpayer's office and presents his credentials, asks for the records he wants and examines them. He compares the record with the return and comes up with his answers; and maybe the answers are not all favorable to the taxpayer. He tells the taxpayer that he thinks there is some income which should have been reported and was not, that there were questionable deductions, and maybe some of his income and expenses are in the wrong period. Therefore, he wants to assess additional taxes, so they sit down to talk it over. This is the first "court of appeal"—the appeal of persuasion through the judgment and understanding of the Agent.

If they can't agree, the case moves on to the Group Chief in the Director's Office. You will understand, of course, that now we are talking about people in the Director's Office. The Group Chief, the Agent, and the taxpayer sit down and the Agent tells his story. The taxpayer tells his. The Group Chief listens, counsels, and when they get all through he says "Well, this is the way I feel about it..." and maybe they are still not in complete agreement. At that point the Group Chief passes the case back to Reviewers who go over the whole thing and if they agree with the Group Chief out goes what we call the 30-day letter.

Now you in Canada don't have the 30-day letter, as I understand it, but you make an immediate assessment if you think more tax is due. Our 30-day letter informs the taxpayer that "On the basis of the following facts, we propose to assess you with $......, penalty and interest" (if indicated). If the taxpayer still thinks the tax is not properly stated, or if he has new facts, he can say to the Group Chief "Well, this is all wrong. You have got

338

the wrong side of this. Let's have another talk." So, they have still another conference, but can't reach settlement. Maybe they get *some* issues settled, but not all.

Then the taxpayer has a right to go to the Appellate Division, and it is at this point that the case leaves the jurisdiction of the District Director and goes to that of the Regional Commissioner, who is my deputy in the Region, and sits as a Judge with specific instructions from me to find a solution—to make a settlement, if at all possible. His job, you see, is more than collecting funds. And so his Appellate Division looks at the case and maybe they get some of the issues settled, but we will say that the case is not completely settled. Then the 90-day letter is issued, which puts the case in line for docket by the Tax Court. But even then, if the taxpayer wishes, he may come in for a pre-trial conference in the hope of settlement: or we may get the taxpayer in and say "We want to try and settle with you out-of-court if we possibly can," and at that point the Appellate Counsel comes into the picture, the man who will have to try the case or recommend whether to try it or not—and we get a whack at him. So, you see, there are five opportunities for the taxpayer to settle his differences with us and for us to settle our differences with him, before a case comes to trial. I say, therefore, it is the people of the Appellate Staff who are responsible for the cases which get to the Tax Court. They can reduce the number considerably. Up till now, the Government has been winning three out of four cases reaching the Tax Court. From now on, with so many opportunities for pre-trial settlement we should win nine out of ten—otherwise I'm going to think that our people are not doing a very good job. Most of you will agree that is a reasonable expectation.

So much for the Appellate procedure—a process through which all appeals must go. I'm not going to talk about the Tax Courts, because I'm sure, you are familiar with the Tax Court situation already.

Something was said, in the preliminary correspondence regarding my appearance here, about hard tax trends. I would like to say that the most important trend in taxes in the United States, certainly the one for which most everyone is looking, is the *downward* trend. And I share the feelings of those who want taxes to come down, because whatever one might say in justification of the present level or against it, the plain fact is that the tax burden of the people of the United States today has reached an all-time high. It is burdensome, extremely so, and should be relieved, if it is humanly possible to find relief.

Now there are some taxes which are going out of existence very soon. You will remember that the Excess Profits Tax was supposed to expire on the 1st of July of this year. There was quite a wrangle over whether it would or not, and it did not. It was allowed to go over with the understanding that it would expire on January 1st, 1954. In addition, the following tax changes will go into effect January 1st, 1954, by operation of law unless, of course, the laws are amended.

Income tax withholding will be reduced from 20 percent to 18 percent.

The maximum tax or ceiling on individual net incomes will be lowered from 88 percent to 87 percent—that is not much more than token reduction. However, it restores the previous limit, and brings us back to what we had before.

Individual income tax rates will, generally speaking, drop about 10 percent, except in the top bracket where the reduction will be slightly less than 2 percent. That is where we fellows with above average incomes get caught in the neck.

The capital gains tax rate for individuals was reduced from 26 percent to 25 percent on November 1st, 1953, by operation of the law. The period for its new tax will begin October 31st, 1953.

Then, in the corporate tax field:

The corporation normal tax will drop from 30 percent to 25 percent on April 1st 1954—about six months from now.

Incorporate capital gains tax will drop from 26 percent to 25 percent.

The tax for settled and accumulated income and regulated investment companies will drop from 30 percent to 25 percent and the normal tax on unrelated business, that is in connection with trust foundations, will drop from 30 percent to 25 percent.

Then there is the great line of excise taxes. We have them too, you know. A great many of them. On the 1st April, 1954, many of them will decline by operation of law. For instance, the tax on a package of cigarettes will drop from 8 to 7 cents: then there is the tax on distilled spirits which will drop from $10.50 to $9.00 per gallon. And the tax on passenger automobiles and motor cycles will come down from 10 percent to 7 percent, and so on. Quite a number of drops there. The greatest reduction percentagewise will be in the gasoline tax which changes from 2 cents per gallon to 1½ cents, a drop of 25 percent in the tax rate.

Now, on the other side there are some impending tax increases. The social security tax is scheduled to go up from 1½ to 2 percent, but there is considerable doubt concerning this move, and considerable opposition. The tax on self-employment income is also supposed to go up from 2 percent to 3 percent. And aside from all that, new tax laws must be prepared and put into effect for the coming year. There is no doubt about the fact that new tax laws will be developed, and will be passed. Now just exactly what those tax laws are going to include I cannot say, but I do know some of the proposals and it is safe to say there will be many changes. Any changes adopted will come as a result of careful study. Representations by innumerable taxpayer groups have been considered by literally hundreds of groups within the Service which looked at various aspects of the law and decided upon the changes that should be made. The new Revenue Code, should be, will be, a great improvement on the old.

Now, in the preliminary work on that law I might say that we borrowed pretty heavily from the experience of your country. For instance, we undoubtedly will ask for a credit on dividend income—not as high as yours, but at least a start in the right direction. Also some changes in depreciation allowance: probably an acceleration by the process of granting a higher rate of depreciation on a declining balance, so that say 65 percent of value might go out during the first half of the life of the property. And the third would be a lower floor on medical expenses.

I don't know why you are laughing at that because I've just that to say—but maybe you don't think that's much relief. I am frequently asked by newspaper men "What do you think of the idea of reducing the 'floor,' that is, the percentage of medical expenses beyond which you begin to allow deductions?" Well, I say, that's fine, but I think it is much more important to know what you are going to do about expenses over and above that level. In other words, long illness and expensive medical care produce a real crisis in the life of an average man, and that's when he needs help most. Somehow it always seemed to me silly to put a ceiling on medical expenses. In my opinion, when a man has the misfortune of a long illness and his expenses pass the 5 percent level, there ought not to be a limit on the amount of his medical deductions.

My friends, today you have been discussing the reconciliation of business income and taxable income. We have that problem too. I brought with me a technical treatise on the subject but I take it that you have already had enough of that sort of thing, so instead, I should like to pose a question. If it seems "revolutionary" to you, don't get excited, because there is nothing unusual about my being revolutionary. Only, don't misquote me.

The question is this: *Is our problem one of the existence of an undesirable gap between business income and tax income?*

I ask that question seriously, because I wonder—isn't the real problem one of Revenue needs? If that is so, can we expect to gain even it we make business income and taxed income synonymous? Think it over.

I have been asked a good many times "What is this tough policy you have on business expense deductions?" We don't have a tough policy, my friends. It is not tough at all. We simply say to those people in the U.S. who are inclined to abuse the privilege of deductions that it isn't possible to allow anybody to unload their tax burdens on someone else, and that we are going to take more pains in the future than in the past to make certain that deductions claimed represent real business expenses. I am speaking more about the deductions of business enterprise than those for personal expenses. We would be false to our oath as officers of the Government if we allowed those who are inclined to cheat a little by claiming deductions to which they are not entitled, to unload the cost of their pleasures and their conveniences on to the shoulders of people less able than themselves to pay.

I addressed a meeting of the American Bankers Association in Boston last August, among other things I said there, "I notice that many of you gentlemen have your wives with you. I think it is a wonderful thing. I always take my wife with me to a convention when I can; but you gentlemen, being familiar with the tax law, know that the cost of bringing your wife here is not deductible, and the ethics of your profession will of course prevent you from deducting these expenses when you get home."

Naturally, I got plenty of razzing about that. I hear a lot about it, even today. In fact one of my friends said to me recently "Coleman, you are changing the *mores* of America." When I looked puzzled over that remark, he went on to explain, "Heretofore, business men have taken their secretaries to conventions and introduced them as their wives, now they are taking their wives and introducing them as their secretaries."

I want to close, if I may, upon a note which seems to me particularly applicable to your country and mine. And that is upon reference to that philosophy, or you might say that attitude of the American people, and by that I mean the people of your country and mine, toward their obligations as citizens. I don't know what the percentage is in Canada, but I am sure it must be quite as high as it is at home, but 97 percent of the people in the United States *freely* and *fairly* pay what they owe in taxes to the Government. They come up to the window of the Tax Collector and say "Here is a statement of my income. This is what I figure I owe you and here's my check for the full amount." 97 percent of them! The people of America have a deep and abiding faith in freedom and fair play. They have confidence in representative government, and a sense of obligation to support their government. They know that our tax system has been successful, and that is why Canada and the United States stand, side-by-side, among the great nations of the world, free and independent.

All countries are not so fortunate. We know one where 40 percent compliance is as much as the Government can claim; another, where 60 percent is the best they can do; and only recently we read in the papers a statement by the President of a nation that 90 percent of the people in his country did not pay income tax at all and frequently cheated on what they did pay. I believe you know what countries I mean.

Tax practitioners, you play an important role in raising the revenues of the land. Though not officially charged by law, you are as much responsible as Mr. Gavsie and his people, as the lawyers of the Dominion, or the Courts system—it's the same as in my country—and I say to you, therefore, that we must regard our work with patriotic zeal. We are not just collectors; it is much bigger than that. We are working to preserve the stability of government by preserving its financial integrity. In so doing, we help to justify the faith of the world in us and, I hope, the faith of free men everywhere. In the final analysis, we are working for peace—for the realization of that glorious dream about which Tennyson wrote so earnestly:

Till the war-drum throbb'd no longer, and the battle flags were furled
In the Parliament of man, the Federation of the world.
There the common sense of most shall hold a fretful realm in awe,
And the kindly earth shall slumber, lapt in universal law.

342

That, my friends, is the high goal of our aspirations.

It is the sublimation of the ideal of service to our fellow-men that guides and directs us in the discharge of our fiscal responsibility. Call it idealism, it you like, but I believe with all my heart that only upon such lofty planes of public service will the public servants of the world acquit themselves worthily in the eyes of their fellow-men, and in the judgment of their Creator.

OUR NEW TAX ADMINISTRATION PROGRAM[†]

by

T. Coleman Andrews

WITH the full support and encouragement of Secretary Humphrey of the Treasury and his staff, we began the job of reordering and realigning this vital Federal service, which, as you may remember, had sunk to pretty low esteem as a result of recently revealed scandals. We made three immediate decisions.

Our first decision was that politics and influence, which had plagued the Service for a long time, were out—that there just could not be a man big enough or strong enough, politically or otherwise, to influence our decisions improperly.

Next, we decided that the Revenue Service should be made a true career service—that every employee would be picked on the basis of merit, promoted on the basis of performance and removed or otherwise disciplined for cause, without equivocation or hesitation—that the day of selecting relatives and friends of the "County Chairman," just because they happened to have "connections," must be ended.

Third, we decided that overhead costs were excessive—that more money should be spent on frontline enforcement work, and that many decisions previously made in Washington should be made in the field.

While much of our effort during these first months has been devoted to stock-taking and planning, we have taken many positive steps forward; and I should remind you that we have had to do this with the plant running full blast. We can't shut down for retooling. Over ninety million tax returns are sent to our "plant" annually, where they are processed into the cash that runs the Government; and decisions by the thousands must be turned out without interruption. Our plant never closes down.

I am happy to be able to report to you that we have almost completed the transition, and that production has *not* decreased. To the contrary, many of the year's annual milestones have been passed in record time. Let me quickly mention a few:

Refunding thirty million overpayments of 1952 taxes was accomplished in record time, with large savings in interest.

[†]Reprinted with permission from *Life Association News*, the official publication of the National Association of Life Underwriters, October 1953, pp. 55-56.

A total of over 3,000,000 man hours was devoted to personal taxpayer assistance during the filing period—five times as much as in any previous years—thus assuring many thousands more correct returns.

The backlog of requests for rulings on tax questions has been greatly reduced; the log-jam of unanswered requests has been broken. It is not at all uncommon for rulings to go out within a matter of a few days after the requests for them are received; not a few have gone out within a matter of hours.

The number of Regional Commissioners has been reduced from 17 to 9, and the Service has been brought closer to the people by giving our field personnel settlement authority commensurate with these responsibilities.

Our field organization is the backbone of our setup, and a large part of the brains of it. We do not subscribe to the idea that Washington has a monopoly on brains. To hold so is to condemn our field force as unfit for its job. To the maximum extent possible, we aim to enable every taxpayer to settle his disputes with us on his home grounds with our District Directors, whom we look upon as our local branch managers.

Other moves of equal importance are in the mill. Naturally, you the "stockholders" in this establishment want to know how much *more money* it will cost you to run this kind of setup.

IT WON'T COST AS MUCH!

The explanation is simple enough: Shortly after we took over the management of the Revenue Service, we surveyed our money needs for the current fiscal year, and whacked the budget submitted to Congress by the previous Administration *a cool six and a half million dollars.* This was accomplished in full by eliminating unnecessary and wasteful administrative operations, much of it at National Headquarters in Washington.

Experience had taught our old-time Revenue men that for every dollar spent in paying the salary and expenses of an examining agent, the Government received from $10 to $15 in return. To a fellow who had been engaged in private business, a proposition of that kind looked *mighty good.* So we continued our search for functions of doubtful value both at National Headquarters and in the Field Service, and we found them—several million dollars worth—right in that big building at 12th Street and Constitution Avenue, Washington, D.C.

It will be our continuing policy—a policy that has the blessing of Congress—to trim overhead in every possible way, and to plow back into enforcement all resultant savings. I think that's good business—*don't you?*

When we talk about tighter enforcement of the Federal revenue laws, we depart sharply from the theme of improved service to those taxpayers who meet their obligations to the Government honestly. We then devote our attention to the small percentage of men and women who fail to pull their share of the load—I mean the cheaters.

Here's the way I feel about *that* matter: If 98 percent of the American taxpayers—and that is just about the proportion—file honest returns, we will not stand by and be a party to encouragement of dishonesty on the part of the other 2 percent. So we intend to use every dollar available to prove to these cheaters that we mean business. And another thing—we don't care what their stations in life happen to be, or to what political party they belong. They'll all be treated alike.

If this plan is displeasing to the American people, they have the wrong man as Commissioner of Internal Revenue, for if I have the correct conception of my responsibilities under the law, I cannot take any other course.

It's hard for me to understand why any person who, year in and year out, files his return and pays his honest taxes should object to us locating, by any reasonable means, a man who has been consistently dodging his tax responsibilities. I'm sure there can't be *many* who object.

Also, our strengthened field enforcement service will examine many more income tax returns than in previous years, and new emphasis will be placed on the collection of past due accounts, and the obtaining of delinquent returns.

Among other things, examining agents have been alerted to watch for abuses in the use of "entertainment expenses," such as country club dues, maintenance of automobiles and yachts, travel for personal reasons, visits to vacation resorts, and similar expenditures claimed as deductions. We want it clearly understood that we have no desire to tell any taxpayer how to spend his money.

We cannot, however, permit expenditures to be deducted for tax purposes where the law does not so provide.

As we intensify our enforcement efforts, no taxpayer who honestly and conscientiously reports his income and proper deductions needs fear arbitrary action by Revenue people. We recognize the fact that we are employees of *all the people*, and we intend to enforce the Federal tax laws in the *interest* of all the people.

Let me add a word in closing: As umpires of this tax-collecting game, we will be fair in our decisions. But here's a warning addressed to both teams—the Revenue personnel and the taxpayers: *Touch all the bases*, or you're apt to be called out.

OUR NEW TAX ADMINISTRATION PROGRAM

Excerpts from an Address before Institute of Newspaper Controllers and Finance Officers[†]

by

T. Coleman Andrews

AT the present time we are changing the composition of our organization. When we went to Washington we felt that there was entirely too much overhead type of expense, and many activities that were unnecessary. One of the first things we felt we had to do was to let some people out of the Service that we felt we did not need. So we have been engaged in the process of reordering our affairs by eliminating overhead and unnecessary operations, and taking the money we've saved in that respect and pushing it over on the enforcement side, so we can get at some of the millions of tax returns that should be examined.

We are only examining about 25 percent of the returns that we know we ought to examine. It will take several thousand additional revenue agents to overcome that deficiency. I deem it my responsibility to lead the way toward attainment of that goal, so we can say that we are examining every return that we think will pay off.

When Congress legislated that the Bureau should be reorganized it made decentralization an inherent part. It would be an omission on our part if we failed to implement that reorganization by decentralizing to the field everything that could be decentralized. I think it particularly important that a taxpayer be able to settle his dispute with us locally, and not have to go to Washington to do it, except perhaps under very complex conditions.

More than 50,000 of the 54,000 people of the Internal Revenue Service are in the field. I think these people in the field are going to be just as honest as the people at the head of the Service are in Washington. I have never seen a corrupt organization in my life that was not corrupt at the top, and I have never seen an honest organization at the top that was corrupt at the bottom. I'm satisfied that we're going to get good decisions, and we're going to get honest decisions. I think we've advanced the Revenue Service

---

[†]Excerpts from a luncheon address presented at the Sixth Annual Meeting of the Institute of Newspaper Controllers and Finance Officers, Louisville, Kentucky, October 26, 1953. Reprinted with permission from the *Institute of Newspaper Controllers and Finance Officers*, Bulletin No. 67, January 1954, pp. 1-2.

to the point where it can no longer be accused of being a political patronage set-up.

Unhappily, there are many people in the Service today who are nearing the retirement age. It is a "must" that we provide immediately some means of assuring succession five years from now, ten years from now, in order that the Service may go on unabated. We have a definite plan for that. We plan to step up our training program so as to make our Service more attractive and afford our men greater opportunities for advancement. We believe that in five years' time we can have more candidates for careers in the Revenue Service than we will be able to accommodate, whereas today we have extreme difficulty getting the required number of qualified people to be revenue agents.

Can you visualize what it would mean to us to have our people better trained to do their jobs more efficiently? Can you visualize what it means to you as taxpayers to have that kind of personnel to deal with you? The money saving is almost beyond comprehension—certainly beyond calculation.

You may have heard of our plans to eliminate the 35 million returns of people whose income is solely derived from salaries and wages, and who want to take the standard deduction. We would save many millions of dollars by that one move alone and eliminate a lot of useless activity.

People say, "Don't take away from the American people the opportunity to know what they're paying." When Congress adopted with-holding, the development of the term "take-home pay" eliminated concern on the part of anyone except those in the high brackets about how much taxes he paid. Eliminating 35 million tax returns is not going to hurt the situation at all. The savings will enable us to put that money into the employment of more enforcement personnel, and thereby enable us to do a better job.

One of the things we are doing to improve collections is the taxpayers' canvass. Rather harsh things were said about us when we started that. The canvass is required by law—Section 3600. It is conducted as a polite inquiry, that and nothing more. Those who said we had adopted Gestapo tactics, and that we were destroying freedom, just didn't know what they were talking about. Not many are doing that any more. It isn't hard to convince even your political enemies that what you are doing is right when you find that 13 percent of the people interviewed were not filing returns. Especially, for instance, when you find one man with a large income who hasn't filed a tax return for sixteen years! Or another who hasn't filed one for seven years, and whose returns for the first year of the seven showed a tax liability of over $30,000, and one which showed another man holding $180,000 on us, and another, $110,000!

I'm not afraid of anybody, in Congress or anywhere else, telling us we should not continue the canvass. On the contrary, we are being urged to continue. It's coming not only from Congress but also from the grassroots of America.

The mail that we receive in support of what we are doing to improve collections and restore the efficiency and dignity and integrity of the Revenue Service is so great that we no longer answer it. It comes from the heart of the people. The average American citizen likes to think when he pays his taxes that everybody else is paying theirs.

We have no desire or intention of disturbing any acceptable and proper commercial practice. We have no desire, or intention, to tell anybody how he shall spend his money. But we do intend to see that expenses deducted by business establishments are in fact expenses of that business—not personal expenses of the officers or employees of that business.

A good deal more than half of the income tax of this country is paid by the man who has a relatively small income and who files a relatively small return. It is the feeling of this Administration that the great mass of the people should not be called upon to subsidize the unwarranted business deductions for the pleasures of the wilful few. That is our policy. We intend to enforce it with equality toward all. It doesn't matter who they are: they all stand in the same light before us.

We are going to keep the racketeer squad. But it is somewhat of a distortion of the fundamental concept of right and wrong for us to assume that the racketeer is any worse criminal, from the standpoint of tax evasion, than anyone else who avoids taxes.

For instance, the man I referred to who had not filed a tax return for sixteen years was a very high-standing man in his community, a man of large income. He had concocted ideas and schemes of evasion that fixed it so that he didn't show any income. Now, just because he had never been caught with anything wrong before, in my figuring, doesn't make him any less of a criminal than the racketeer who has probably been to jail a dozen times.

In my book, they are both evaders of the income tax law and are entitled to the same treatment, good or bad, that we give to everybody else in the same category.

In other words, from my point of view, there will be a de-emphasis on the term "racket squad," and an increased emphasis on proper dealing with evasion.

COMMON-SENSE ADMINISTRATION OF THE INTERNAL REVENUE LAWS†

by

T. Coleman Andrews

YOU know, it is very often said, speaking of my appointment as Commissioner of Internal Revenue, that I am the first certified public accountant who has ever held that job, and that happens to be true.

I like to tell my lawyer friends that we accountants suffered for an awful long time under the income tax, and we certainly are glad to finally get an opportunity to show what we can do with it.

I want to talk to you a little bit about the Bureau of Internal Revenue: the greatest tax collecting agency in the world, of course, because we have the greatest nation in the world.

Considering the ramifications of our activities, I sometimes like to think, when I want to feel sort of expansive, that well, here we are, if we compare our Bureau of Internal Revenue with the great corporations of America, we find that, in the size of its activities, the amount of money that it handles, the number of people it employs, and the extent of its organization, it ranks among the first fifteen of the great corporations of the world.

Government is big business, my friends, and it is extremely important business; and I think it is significant that you of the municipal finance officers' profession have asked me to come here as the representative of the Federal Government, because there is a very close affinity between your problem and mine.

That affinity is very real because you are at the grass roots of democracy and freedom in this country, I say to you that regardless of the Federal Government, whenever the time comes, if ever it should come, that the local government in this country fails at the grass roots, then the Federal Government will have a pretty hard time standing.

And there has to be a time some day when there has to be, I think, an even closer relationship between local government, state governments and the Federal Government, from the standpoint of the proper distribution of taxation, than we have had in the past; and I am very happy to be a part of

---

†Presented at the Annual Conference of the Municipal Finance Officers Association, Miami, Florida, 1953. Reprinted with permission of the Government Finance Officers Association, formerly the Municipal Finance Officers Association, from *Municipal Finance*, November 1953, pp. 63-71.

an administration whose chief executive, the President of the United States, has recognized the necessity for that close relationship, and called together an advisory group to consult with him about how the Federal, state, and local governments should divide up the taxes, because all three governments rely upon the people of the United States.

I would like to call to your attention a matter which you probably had not given too much thought to before, that here in the United Stares we have a very unique situation; namely, what we call the voluntary assessment policy or principle. I would like to impress upon you how tremendously important it is that we maintain that principle. That means nothing in the world but that you and I, as citizens of a great free nation, have agreed that for the purposes of the federal budget we will voluntarily declare to our government the amount of our income, so that the government may assess us with the taxes that we owe.

As a matter of fact, we do more than that. We not only make our declarations, we even compute our own taxes and so give to the government both our own declarations of our incomes and our declarations of what we owe.

Now, my friends, that practice does not exist in any other country in the world, except in our neighboring and, I am almost tempted to say, sister country of Canada, and in the British Empire. I have to tell you that elsewhere in the world where there is an income tax, those who are subject to it often are more distinguished by their skill at evading it than they are by their willingness to comply with it. Whenever there comes the time that there should be a breakdown of our voluntary assessment policy, then I say to you that this government of ours is going to find itself on a very, very shaky foundation indeed.

That is why one person, like the very distinguished lady who tried to defy the tax authorities of the United States—unsuccessfully, I am glad to say—could destroy the entire tax system of the government of this country, if his defiance were successful; and that is why we cannot permit any person, no matter how laudable his aims or how much we might admire his courage, ever to succeed in breaking down this system of voluntary compliance.

Now, what of this organization that collects all of these billions of dollars from the people of America? I have said often, and I don't hesitate to say it again, that taxation in America is burdensome; it is entirely too burdensome, my friends, and without taking the time to go into the reasons why it is so—and I am speaking now from the standpoint of the total tax burden, federal, state and local—without going into the reasons of it at all, I say to you that we have reached a dangerous situation indeed, when as much as thirty percent of the income of the people is required to support the governments under which they live. And, somehow, we must find in America, the means of reducing the cost of maintaining our governmental institutions and activities. I think we are all in agreement on that.

I have been asked since I came here: "What is the prospect for tax reduction?" Well, let me say with regard to that, that of course that is not my job. I don't mean to infer by that that I disclaim responsibility; but the matter of the level of taxation, the kind of taxes we have, the rate of taxes and that sort of thing, is a matter that comes exclusively under the jurisdiction of the Secretary of the Treasury.

My job, as you know, is to collect the taxes that your representatives and mine in Congress say that the American people should pay. I do not attempt to determine tax policy. But I would be less than frank if I did not tell you that I sincerely believe that the level of federal taxation certainly will decline from what it is now, granted that we have a drift or a trend toward more peaceful conditions in the world.

On the other hand, I think we must all recognize the fact that, in terms of what our taxes were in 1939, we, in your lifetime and mine, are still going to have to pay high taxes. The level will be dropped, but it is going to be high in relation to the pre-World War II days.

Now, this bureau that I speak of, this Bureau of Internal Revenue, is headed by a commissioner, a deputy commissioner, five assistant commissioners, and a chief counsel. It has nine districts—regional administrative districts. It has sixty-four local directors and over 1400 officers throughout the United States and its insular possessions, and it collects close to $70,000,000,000 a year. That's a lot of money, even in these days of high prices.

In handling the Bureau of Internal Revenue, with its 54,000 officers and employees, we deal with people; we deal with 54,000 of our own people, which I think you will agree is a sizeable undertaking in itself; and those 54,000 people deal with between 155,000,000 and 160,000,000 fellow Americans—I don't know just what it is now, because I haven't seen the latest statistics. That reminds me that underlying our whole philosophy of managing the Bureau is the very simple and basic principle or conviction that "the most important thing in the world is people."

When I tell you that I could let you go to your rooms right now, if you wanted to do it, and sit down and think for a few minutes, that I am sure you would be able to envisage the whole policy that I am about to unfold to you. "The most important thing in the world is people." Nothing is accomplished in this world except with people. With us, we have no product to sell. The only thing in the world we have to sell is competence and integrity.

We have to convince the people that we are an honest group of their representatives, put in office by them in Washington to do a job for them that they do not have time to do for themselves, to help them, as best as we can, carry out one of the most sacred obligations that every person has as a citizen, namely, to properly determine what his tax liability is, and to make it as easy as possible for him to discharge this liability.

355

That is all our job is—we don't sell anything, we don't make anything—and we do it with people. Therefore, we must do it with an understanding of people, an appreciation of the problems, their trials and their tribulations, and with some understanding of their joys, too, and so on.

Our fundamental policy is to find the way to do this very unpleasant job of taking about twenty-five percent of the people's income, without causing the people to hate and despise us. Now, we don't expect to win any popularity contests, but we do want to get the people's confidence and respect. We know we have lost a lot of it in the past. We want to get back.

Now then, there are a number of things that we can do to accomplish that. One thing we can do is to speed up as much as we can settlement of the disagreements that naturally arise between the taxpayers and the government. You know, income is a very difficult thing to determine. It is easy to say "income" and think you know what you mean by it, but let me tell you that I sat for four years in a group composed of economists, lawyers, accountants, and businessmen, and we tried to define the term—the simple term—"business income"; and, believe it or not, at the end of four years when we wrote our report, there were still some in the group who did not agree.

And so, when we put a tax upon income, my friends, it isn't as simple as it sounds. We have to define income, and the Revenue Bureau's job is to help find what that definition is, to help determine what people should pay taxes on, how they shall determine what their taxable incomes have been.

When these disputes arise, one of the things that we have to do is to find a way to get them behind us quickly. All of you know as well as I do that this world in which we live today is very largely a business world. Sometimes I almost wish it were not so much so, but it happens to be that way, and there is not much that you and I can do about it. It is a consequence of the natural process of economic and social evolution.

When this country was founded, only a hundred and sixty years ago, ours was an agricultural economy. We had very little manufacturing. Today we are so predominantly an industrial or manufacturing nation that we were able twice, within a period of thirty years, to turn back, through the sheer volume of our production machine and our industrial ingenuity, two of the greatest aggregations of oppressive military power that the world had ever seen.

Of course, we did not do it alone, but in concert with our allies. Nevertheless, I think that each of our allies—even the one that has turned against us—would have to admit that it was the industrial production of America, the business world that is largely America, that provided the balance that made it possible for us to triumph in the two wars that you and I have seen in our lifetime.

And so, ours is a business world, and the people who run the business of America are entitled to know, as promptly as is possible for us to tell them, when their tax disputes are ended, so that they may make their plans for tomorrow, next year, and the year after, because, as we all know, business has to plan ahead, and it cannot plan ahead, it cannot make wise decisions, with large unsettled tax disputes hanging over its head.

You have heard quite a lot, I am sure, about dishonesty and corruption in the Bureau of Internal Revenue. I want to tell you something about that, and I am going to be perfectly frank with you. There has been corruption; there has been entirely too much of it. I regret to say that it has stemmed from the very top. The people in the bureau—the 54,000 people that I have talked about—unfortunately, have not had the benefit of the kind of integrity at the top that they should have had. There have been some, therefore, in the lower echelons of the Bureau's activities who undoubtedly have felt, "Well, if the big fellows are doing it, why shouldn't I?" And, likewise, there have been taxpayers who have felt, "Well, evidently somebody is getting away with something, so why don't I cheat a little bit, too?"

So two myths have sprung up in America that I want to explode at this time, if I can. One of those is that the American people are a bunch of crooks—that any American taxpayer who gets the chance to do so will cheat on his tax return. I want to tell you that if we added up the total number of tax returns in which there was a deliberate attempt to cheat—not the government, I remind you, but all the rest of the people of America—we would find that the percentage was so small as to be almost hardly worth mentioning.

The American people are inherently honest people, and they will pay any taxes assessed against them, so long as they are convinced that they are fair and justly assessed, and fairly and justly administered. We proceed on that basic theory.

The other myth that I want to explode is that the Bureau of Internal Revenue, as an organization, is dishonest or corrupt. This Bureau includes about as diligent, hardworking, and honest a group of people as I have ever had the pleasure of working with, and I can tell you that if at any time you want to see how hard they really do work, just come up to Washington and walk down Constitution Avenue between 10th and 12th and look in the windows of the Internal Revenue building some night around eleven or twelve o'clock. You will probably find there on the third floor, every light in every window in front of that building burning, certainly as late as eleven, and maybe later.

They are the people, my friends, with whom I am working, and they are not all new people either. There are some new faces there, but most of them are people who have always been in the bureau, and who have always been honest, and are trying to do a good job.

357

I can assure you, therefore, that the Bureau of Internal Revenue is not a corrupt organization. All they need is the kind of leadership that they are entitled to have, and that you are entitled to have, in order to gain and earn and deserve and keep your respect and your confidence; and it is my purpose to give them that kind of leadership.

I should like to say this to you also: There has been quite a good deal said about influence. I want to tell you that, as far as I know, there is no man or woman in America—there is no business organization in America—that is big enough, rich enough, or otherwise powerful enough, to wield any influence in the Bureau of Internal Revenue as it is now constituted.

We recognize every citizen as standing on the same bottom, and they all get the same treatment, regardless of who they are. That same treatment is simply fair treatment. We do not intend, if I may suggest it, to give away the Treasury of the United States.

There has been a good deal written and said about statements that I have made, to the effect that the taxpayer of the United States is entitled to a fair shake. I mean that, and nothing more. It does not mean that anybody is going to be given anything that your congressmen and senators said they should not have when they adopted the tax laws that we are required to administer. It means that everybody is going to be asked to pay every cent that those laws require of them; but it also means that no one is going to be asked to pay one cent that he does not owe.

There have been policies, frankly, which have been written into the regulatory interpretations of the law, which included law that Congress specifically rejected and did not want in the law. I pledge you a serious effort—and that effort is now well under way—to find every evidence of regulatory law that is now in existence, and to remove it by revising those regulations. We in the bureau and in this administration do not want anything in the way of legislation that is not given to us in the law as passed by Congress. In other words, we will not seek by regulation that which we cannot obtain by legislation.

People ask me, "What are you going to do about the cheaters?" I am frequently asked about the racketeers. Now, of course, we have what we call a racket squad, which has been in existence for some time, and there has been for two years—I believe it has been two years—a drive on the racketeers.

I am happy to report that the dividends have been tremendous; the amount of money gotten as a result of that drive has been many times the cost of putting the drive on.

We are not going to let up on that, but we are going to change our sights a bit, and in this respect: we are going to change our sights by the attitude that anyone who undertakes to cheat and to unload upon the great mass of honest taxpayers a burden which he should be bearing under the law is going to stand before us in exactly the same position as the racketeer.

As far as we are concerned, we see no difference between the so-called good citizen who cheats and the racketeer who cheats. A racketeer is not going to be condemned merely because he is a racketeer.

In my opinion, anyone who cheats, whether he is in an illegal business or not, is just as much an enemy of society as anyone else, and they will all be dealt with accordingly.

What we propose to do is to ferret out every cheater that we can find, and we propose to urge the prosecution of everyone we think can be convicted. We hope—and I may say earnestly hope— that everyone that we can prove is guilty will not just be slapped on the wrist with a suspended sentence or no sentence at all, but will be put in jail for a good length of time. That will teach him that the people of America are not going to put up with those who try to cheat.

I think that policy will succeed. We know, for instance, that the big-time racketeer or gambler or cheater does not care anything about a penalty or a fine or a suspended sentence; but very few people like to be sent to jail, and, frankly, I think that is just where any deliberate cheater belongs. If we have to build more jails in order to accommodate them, then I am perfectly agreeable to building them.

I also want to tell you briefly at this time about a few things we have done which we think are going to improve the service considerably.

You have heard it said that we hope to eliminate the necessity for about 35,000,000 returns. Currently, there are 55,000,000 individuals in America who file income tax returns. Of these taxpayers, 35,000,000 have no income except salaries or wages and claim the standard deduction of 10%. The government gets two reports of salaries and wages paid. One goes to the Social Security Board, the other comes to us. We propose to use these reports, with some revision of forms and procedures, to calculate the tax of the 35,000,000 taxpayers that I have just described, sending a refund or a bill, as each case may require, and thus relieve that 35,000,000 people of having to bother about filing returns.

Some of you may be wondering why we aren't already doing this. Well, my friends, let me tell you something about Washington, in case you don't already know it. Washington is the place where the thing that a person would do ordinarily is the unusual thing; it is the sensational thing. It has always seemed strange to me that when a simple thing like that is mentioned, business people will immediately respond with, "Of course, that's the proper thing to do."

But it is sensational to do it in Washington. It doesn't take any magic to do things simply, the easy way; but it is unusual. And so we think that we will eliminate the filing of these 35,000,000 returns in a couple of years, bearing in mind that we have to have certain legislative clearances and that this will take time.

Now, what will that accomplish? In the first place, it is going to save a tremendous amount of money in administrative costs alone. Think what a difference it will be when we only have to handle 20,000,000 returns instead of 55,000,000. We will be able to take that saving and use it to increase our enforcement effort on the returns that we do have to examine. So you see we are shooting at reducing overhead and increasing our production effort—a very simple thing in business. As we all know, the more overhead you have, the greater your chances of going broke; the less overhead you have, the less you have to get for your product.

So we are merely applying a very simple business principle: that of increasing production effort and reducing overhead. It is just as simple as that.

In addition, we are going to do something else. How many of you have seen those long lines of people every March 15, and shortly before, standing, waiting in line to make their tax returns? I have seen them sometimes three blocks long. We have a very serious situation there, and that situation exists regardless of whether the employer pays those people or the employee stands it.

What we lose there is production, and when we lose production we are losing national income; and when we lose national income, we lose taxable income. So we lose everywhere. Therefore, we feel that it will mean a tremendous economic saving to get rid of those 35,000,000 tax returns. I think there can be little doubt about that.

Here is another program that we are carrying on that I am sure you will be glad to hear about. It is the program of teaching high school children how to prepare tax returns. Maybe you have read something about it in the newspapers. Next year, in the next school season, we are going to give instruction in 30,000 secondary schools in the United States, to the senior classes of those schools, in how to make out tax returns.

How do we know that it is going to work? I'll tell you how. Because we have already tried it, and we know that high school students can be easily and profitably taught the fundamental things about taxation, and particularly how to make out simple returns.

You say that sounds rather peculiar, but let us analyze it for just a minute. What does it accomplish? The most important thing that it accomplishes is that it will be teaching the students of those 30,000 secondary schools something more specific about their civic obligation to pay taxes than they have ever learned before in their lives. We are going to teach them the ABC's, the common sense of being citizens, the economics of being citizens. And those children, and the children that come after them, are going to grow up to be citizens who are going to understand why we have to have taxes, and why everybody should be diligent about paying them.

It is going to do something else, which is also extremely important. It is going to mean that the coming generations of taxpayers are going to be able to make their returns without our having to spend as much money as we now have to spend in order to help taxpayers make their returns. We

360

are going to get more returns, properly made out than we have ever gotten before. That, in turn, is going to reduce the cost of our enforcement operation, our auditing. In other words, it would seem that we are trying to work ourselves out of a job.

We are not going to accomplish that. But we are going to have a lot more people in America, in the years to come, who are going to know how to make out their tax returns, and their returns are going to come to us as good tax returns, on which we are not going to have to spend a lot of money. Don't you think that is a good program? I am sure you do. It makes sense.

I am going to tell you how much sense it makes. We took a sampling of nine thousand such returns that were made out by high school students in our pilot operation, and we brought them in to Washington. We had the same people examine those returns who examine all the other returns that are sent in, so that there would be no doubt as to the similarity of the principles followed in grading the work. And, believe it or not, they were nine thousand of the best-prepared tax returns that we have ever seen in the bureau. Now, that makes sense to us. It makes a lot of sense.

We also have among the 54,000 people who are employed by the bureau, many who go out into the business establishments of America and into the homes of many people, either directly or indirectly, to check tax returns. We know very well that the people who do that work must be well trained; and so we are now thinking in terms of a tremendous intensification of our training program, our in-service training program, so that when we hire a revenue agent, before he comes to you and says, "Mr. Jones or Mr. Smith, I want to check your returns," he will have had three, four, five, or six months of training in a special school.

It may even be that we might establish, as the Army, the Navy, the Marine Corps, and the Coast Guard have done, and the F.B.I. as well, our own academy or institute, perhaps on the campus of one of the great colleges of America, where these people will be taught their job before they go to work, so that when they start, they will know what they are doing.

Don't you folks agree that if such a program as that were established we would soon find ourselves in the position where people would be seeking employment in the bureau—the kind of people that we want—the best young men and women from the graduating classes of the colleges and universities of the country? The end result of a policy like this would be that soon we would have a career service that would be in every sense a career service—one which any young man or woman would be proud to engage in.

But we would not stop there. In order to encourage those who come to the bureau, we would extend that training program to include instruction for those who want to prepare for the job ahead, so that they might always be ready when the opportunity comes. My friends, I think that, too, makes sense.

I think it would be money well spent. I know it would be insofar as greater efficiency and a higher grade of service are concerned.

Then too, and finally, I think we ought to spend more money on research and planning. All of the great corporations of America have their research programs, and they spend a great deal of money on them. We, as I have explained to you, are engaged in one of the big businesses of its kind in the world. We think that we ought to conduct more research. We think we should be two, three, four, or five years ahead of Congress as to the kind of taxes it may perhaps levy, and so know in advance how we could best administer the collection of those taxes.

It is almost catastrophic, certainly chaotic, to wait until Congress passes an income tax law, and then try to decide how to administer it. There is nobody in the world who is smart enough to be able to do it. As a consequence, if you wait until it has happened, you are bound to get off to a bad start, an expensive start, that may never be corrected. So, for that reason we are going to intensify our research and planning program. I saw, just prior to leaving Washington, the big pay-off on that. I saw it in a run-down, or a graphic illustration of how the elimination of the 35,000,000 tax returns is going to work, and it was really one of the simplest things that you could imagine.

It brings together two of the great departments of the government, the Social Security Board and the Bureau of Internal Revenue, in a joint effort, in which the two join forces and get together to pool their resources, to produce a common result. We will save money in that way by eliminating duplication.

Recently I announced that we were reducing the number of our districts from seventeen to nine. That order goes into effect the first of July. That is a managerial shakedown. By that I mean we are streamlining our over-all organization. Instead of having seventeen district commissioners, which is too many for any one commissioner to look after, we are going to have nine; and each one of those nine is going to have more territory than any of the seventeen previously had.

We are going to delegate authority to those district commissioners as deputies of the commissioner to make decisions that heretofore have had to be made in Washington. In other words, we are going back to the old theory of states' rights, to put it in rather simple terms.

We are saying to the citizen in Miami, "It isn't necessary for you to come to Washington to settle your tax problems. We will put the kind of talent in Miami that is needed to give you satisfaction right here in Miami." That is what it amounts to. It does not in any way affect the status of the taxpayer himself, because, just as I say, this is the management level of the bureau. The district commissioner controls the activity in his particular district, to see that everything is going according to plans—to see that the employers in the district are operating properly.

The taxpayer still goes to the same director; he still pays his taxes at the same place; he still talks to the same people when he is in dispute with the bureau, just as he did before.

Again, my friends, we are cutting down overhead, simplifying our organization, and concentrating our effort on enforcement, where we know we get fifteen dollars of revenue for every dollar we spend for salaries and other expenses. Does that make sense? It certainly makes sense to me.

How much do we save by that? We save six million dollars, and that amount will employ 1250 revenue agents. That's a lot of revenue agents, my friends. And what happens? We move out of Washington twenty-five percent of the personnel now there, and we put them in the field, in these districts and in the director's office, to improve our enforcement. Some—those, we won't need—will be dropped.

There is the tangible evidence of getting rid of overhead at the top, cutting down the superstructure, and putting emphasis at the place where you get results, where that fifteen dollars in revenue comes in for every dollar of expense that you put out.

So, my friends, that is the story of the Bureau of Internal Revenue as it is today; not in complete terms, of course, because there is much that I have not told you. But that is the story in as brief a manner as I could give it to you in the little time we had.

We are building for tomorrow. I like to feel that we in the Bureau of Internal Revenue are building for a better tomorrow and a better America for tomorrow. I like to feel that we are putting into effect in government something that I have always believed deep in my heart—and in every public experience I have ever had I have hoped for—that is that it is possible to run government just as efficiently as it is to run private business, and that the same principles apply to both.

Why do we do that? We do it, my friends, because there isn't anything in the world on the outside that can so completely threaten the stability of this government of ours as our own willingness, or our failure, so to order our affairs that it will be possible for the economy of America to carry the cost of the government that the people of America have set up for themselves. Our internal dangers are much greater than any danger from outside; and I believe that it is possible to establish now, nay, that we must establish now, an efficiency of organization and operation that will provide for us the kind of government, insofar as the Bureau is concerned, that I have outlined here tonight.

THE NEW ROLE OF THE TAX COMMISSIONER[†]

by

T. Coleman Andrews

THE Editors of *The Accounting Forum* have been kind enough to ask me to describe the "new role" of the Commissioner of Internal Revenue resulting from recent changes in the Internal Revenue Service.

Basically, the "role" of the Commissioner never changes. In other words, his job is to collect taxes—a painful but necessary adjunct of civilized government. But there are many different ways of collecting taxes, and there are fundamentally separate attitudes which alter the impact of the tax system on the economy and on the citizenry.

It is possible, under the vast powers entrusted to the Commissioner, to interfere seriously with the business and the private activities of the citizens. While tax statutes sometimes seem endlessly detailed, the Commissioner inevitably must supplement the basic law with regulations, interpretations and procedures, and all of these steps can influence very greatly the application and effects of the law.

The first positive policy of our new administration of Internal Revenue has been to insist on *impartiality and reasonableness* in the carrying out of the tax laws.

This policy has been evidenced by the following actions:

a. On May 12, 1953, we issued a policy statement designed to terminate unnecessary controversies over depreciation deductions. The new policy is "generally not to disturb depreciation deductions, and revenue employees shall propose adjustments in the depreciation deduction only where there is a clear and convincing basis for a change."

b. We have established effective liaison with the staff of the Joint Committee on Internal Revenue Taxation in order to assure ourselves that our regulations carry out the intent of the Congress.

c. We have established an Advisory Committee of 10 outstanding citizens to give the Commissioner a balance wheel of independent judgment on policies and procedures affecting the general public. The members are:

Thomas J. Green—New York, New York
Granville S. Borden—San Francisco, California

[†]Reprinted with permission from *The Accounting Forum*, December 1953, pp. 5-7, 46.

Frederick L. Patton—Cambridge, Massachusetts
Frank Olds—Detroit, Michigan
Morris L. Rinehart—New York, New York
Wallace M. Jensen—Detroit, Michigan
J. S. Seidman—New York, New York
Charles D. Post—Boston, Massachusetts
Joseph F. Platt—Columbus, Ohio
Thomas N. Tarleau—New York, New York

Although each man speaks only for himself, these men were drawn mostly from the leadership of the American Institute of Accountants, the American Bar Association, and the Tax Executives Institute.

d. On October 9, 1953, we issued a new policy statement on settlement of disputed cases. This policy is aimed at reducing the congestion of cases in the Tax Court and in the Appellate Division. It calls for more strenuous efforts to effect settlements at the lowest level within the Internal Revenue Service, less review or reopening of agreed issues at higher levels in either the Audit or Appellate Divisions, and more partial settlements in cases where complete settlements cannot be reached (thus reducing the area of controversy on appeal).

There once was an old school of thought in revenue matters which assumed that the natural role of a Commissioner was to be an adversary of the taxpayer. I suppose in some ancient tyrannies there was reason for such belief. But I do not believe that under the American system of government, the tax authority can properly be an adversary of the taxpayer, because the tax official is, after all, only the hired hand of the taxpayers.

The taxpayers obviously would not employ a Commissioner to be their own enemy. The taxpayers want from the Commissioner only impartiality and integrity. They want him to he an enemy only of fraud and favoritism.

Now, this sometimes requires the Commissioner to adopt a hard-boiled role—hard-boiled, that is, toward the offender against the tax law, not against the normal law-abiding taxpayer.

In this aspect of the Commissioner's role, some of our recent actions have been:

1. We have revived with startling success the oldest technique mentioned in our oldest tax laws—canvassing for delinquent returns. A few misinformed people got excited at first thought that our door-to-door canvassers might invade individuals' privacy. However, results in various localities, notably the New England and Denver areas, have shown heavy percentages of delinquent returns picked up by this method, and no improprieties of inquisition.

2. We have alerted our agents to detect and to disallow improper and excessive deductions for entertainment.

3. We are strengthening our audit forces by transferring funds wherever possible from "overhead" activities to the hiring of additional agents.

The foregoing all relates to the Commissioner in his role as the arbiter of the taxes which the statutes prescribe. It is, of course, the most important role of the office. But the Commissioner is also the administrator of a vast complex of men and machines, and he has another role in managing the Internal Revenue Service so that it operates with maximum efficiency and the least cost.

In this role, the Commissioner has an unparalleled opportunity to use imagination and initiative. Here he is not so shackled by tomes of laws and precedents. I think we can do something special in this field.

I have in mind two projects which, although still in the planning stage, show promise of dramatic results. These are:

1. We are devising for consideration of the Congress a plan for eliminating about 35,000,000 of the 55,000,000 income tax returns which are filled out annually. Think of the astronomical quantities of time and paper that go into these 35,000,000 returns. I am referring not only to the personal time of the individuals, but the time lost from productive work. In its present outline, this plan contemplates that a highly mechanized organization will compute the taxes of these individuals from the annual information already supplied by employers (on Form W-2a) supplemented with a minimum of information on exemptions. If and when this plan is put into operation, the 35,000,000 will never have to file tax returns. They will be able to sit back and wait for a bill or refund check to settle up their annual tax liabilities. Naturally this system must exclude taxpayers with itemized deductions and with other special problems or high incomes. The latter would continue to file traditional tax returns.

2. We are designing a new kind of school to produce a new kind of tax official. You might call it a "West Point of Taxation." We'll probably name it the Internal Revenue Academy. Our thought is to place this school under the administration of one of the leading universities of the country—one to be selected particularly for its excellence in accounting and other tax-related subjects. We propose to recruit something like 500 of the best accounting graduates in the country each semester, and give them a post-graduate course in accounting, economics, public administration, and similar subjects, together with indoctrination in the highest ethical standards of our profession. We expect to build from this base the best equipped as well as the most deserving body of tax administrators ever to receive the public's trust.

I mentioned above that some funds were being transferred from "overhead" activities to enforcement work. We have been going over the administrative set-up of the Revenue Service with a fine tooth comb, particularly in the national office, where we have already reduced the force by about 1,000 persons. This has been, in part, an anguishing task, but I believe a necessary one. As fast as we can eliminate unnecessary work in our overhead organization, we have an inescapable duty to do so.

Some reduction of administrative overhead has also been possible outside of Washington. There we have reduced the number of regional offices from 17 to 9, and I believe we have thereby created a more compact and efficient supervisory force.

Another of our administrative aims has been to speed up the decentralization of tax administration which has been going on, by fits and starts, for a generation. I believe, for the convenience of the taxpayers around the country, and for efficient operations, we should strip the national office of all but executive direction, planning, and research activities. I believe the taxpayer, wherever he lives, should be able to obtain authoritative and binding action on his problems close to home.

Such a system necessarily requires inspection safeguards, and these, I can assure you, are receiving proper attention.

We are proud to have in America a system of voluntary self-assessment of taxes which goes beyond the trust placed by any other government in its citizens. This is the American way, and it is the best way. It is conducive of the most justice and the greatest economy of operation.

But a system dependent upon the voluntary actions of the citizens is also dependent upon a tax-collecting organization in which the citizens have confidence.

Therefore, the maintenance of the integrity of our Service is much more a matter than satisfying our personal pride or forestalling public complaint. Integrity is the keystone of our life as tax-collectors. We cannot survive without it. We will not spare any effort to preserve it.

THE PHILOSOPHY OF TAX ADMINISTRATION[†]

by

T. Coleman Andrews

THE philosophy of tax administration starts with people. As one of my friends said, an ex-president of the American Institute of Accountants whom some of the members of this audience would know, the most important thing in the world is people. And I have never known it to be more thoroughly demonstrated or proven than it has been during the now approximately nine months that I have been Commissioner of Internal Revenue.

In a small community, the importance of people is perhaps not as great as in a large undertaking like ours, where we have to deal with the public through a total force of about 54,000 persons, scattered through 1400-odd offices throughout the country. Those offices are directly under the District Directors of Internal Revenue, and those directors, of which there are 64, in turn are supervised and guided at the regional level by nine Regional Commissioners of Internal Revenue. So you see, to us, people are tremendously important, and that's where our philosophy of tax administration begins. I will pass over the employees for a moment, but I do want to come back to them.

I want to mention the fact that we have about 65 million filers of tax returns in this country out of a total population of a little over 160 million. There are 55 million individuals and 10 million corporations, partnerships, trustees, and others who file returns. And, of course, some file returns for more than one tax, so there was a total of something in the neighborhood of 93 million tax returns alone that we handled in the last fiscal year. And of course you can multiply that 93 million several times in order to find out the number of pieces of paper that we handle, and multiply it again by the number of times that all these pieces of paper are handled. By that time you will understand something of the size of the problem with which our people have to cope.

The Government, as you know, does not offer to a person who seeks a career in it the opportunity or the incentive that that person might find in

---

[†]Presented at the Forty-Sixth Annual Conference on Taxation, Louisville, Kentucky, September 28 - October 1, 1953. Reprinted with permission from the *1953 Proceedings of the Forty-Sixth Annual Conference on Taxation*, Ronald B. Welch, ed. (Sacramento, CA: National Tax Association, 1954), pp. 532-539.

private business. In fact, about the only incentive that a person has who decides to pursue his career with the Government is whatever satisfaction he may get out of the achievement of the respect of his fellow citizens and, to a lesser degree, the attainment of whatever ultimate level of authority it is possible for him to reach. The more I see of people in Government—and particularly in this troublesome field of tax administration, where people are so often prone to think you are not the kind of person that you think you are, and sometimes call you even worse—the more I feel that the average person who throws in his lot with the Government is an idealist who is inspired with a desire to be of public service, perhaps somewhat like the professional soldier. At any rate, it is difficult to find any other primary urge that makes people accept government service.

We try to impress that upon the people of the Internal Revenue Service as we go about the country meeting them, because a lot of them, strangely enough, don't know themselves why they are working for the Government. We try to sharpen it up and focus it for them so that they themselves will understand and be inspired to greater effort. We try to get them to understand that they mustn't be disappointed or embarrassed if they see some fellow coming in that is getting a big fee out of a case while they are getting a relatively small salary for working on the other side. We try to bridge that gap between the two sides of the table, and the only way to bridge it, my friends, is in the realm of idealism, by keeping the Bureau employees imbued with a spirit of public service, a feeling that they have an important part in carrying out one of the most important activities of government.

In order to get the most out of Bureau employees or other government employees under the circumstances I have indicated, it's extremely important that there be a personnel policy under which people are employed, promoted, and pushed ahead on the basis of demonstrated performance. Whatever may be the arguments in favor of patronage appointments in the field of tax administration, in my opinion they fall completely when examined by an objective mind. I feel that new employees should be carefully selected and that they should be pushed ahead just as fast as they can take additional responsibility when they demonstrate unusual merit. That is not possible today under the civil service laws, rules, and regulations, but we hope to achieve that policy. I don't believe that we will have the best possible Revenue Service until we get that policy. It is not right to keep a man or a woman standing by for 15 or 20 years to get the promotions in grade and salary that they should have had 15 years before when their ability was demonstrated. In the first place, when you keep a person waiting that long for something he deserves, the chances are he is no longer worthy of it when his turn finally comes because by that time he has lost some of his enthusiasm and vigor. So I feel that any system of tax administration that is to be efficiently operated

370

has to be in the hands of people who operate under a personnel policy that recognizes true merit when it's seen and rewards it promptly according to what it's worth.

I think also—but we needn't dwell on it greatly—that we have to be equally positive in matters of disciplining employees when they do things they shouldn't do. The discipline should be prompt, and it should fit the offense in every case.

So much for the employees. I haven't said anything about pay because I think generally that more or less takes care of itself. At any rate, I am not too concerned about the pay situation at present.

Now let's talk a little about the taxpayer, the fellow who pays the bill, not forgetting, however, that the 54,000 people who work for the Bureau also pay taxes. There are a lot of taxpayers in America who forget that Bureau employees are taxpayers, too, and that it isn't any more pleasant for them to have to pay up than it is for other people.

What is it that the taxpayer wants in order to make him a willing taxpayer—or let's say at least a complying taxpayer who comes up and, in accord with the great American tradition, says to his Government, "This is what my income was, and this is what I owe you, and here it is"? That is the thing that distinguishes the tax system of this country from that of most other countries where the income tax is an important source of revenue. You know as well as I do that there are countries in the world today with income taxes in which the citizen is more distinguished by his ability to get out of paying them than he is by his compliance with them. The president of one of these countries said recently, as reported in the press, that 90 percent of all the people in the country evaded the income tax. That's a pretty high percentage of evasion, isn't it? I wonder why they have an income tax.

We don't have that situation in this country, and we don't want it to happen here. Of course, the tax collector cannot by himself keep it from happening, but he can do a lot to keep it from developing by the attitude that he takes toward the taxpayer, and by the proficiency with which he discharges his job, both directly himself, and indirectly through the people who work under him.

What is it that the taxpayer wants? The average taxpayer wants above everything else to know one simple thing: that there isn't anybody else who can get anything that he can't get. It's as simple as that. Once a taxpayer is convinced that no one can get relieved of something that he can't get relieved of, or, conversely, that he can get relief from anything that anybody else can get relieved from under the same circumstances, then you've got a good taxpayer, and evasion is something that you don't have much trouble with. But once you begin to show favor to any individual or any group of individuals, you get into trouble, and that's when the tax system begins to break down. I have said it before, and I say it again to you now, that there isn't any individual in this country big enough, politically or otherwise, to get any favor out of the present tax administration in Washington. Nobody yet has asked for such a favor, I am glad to say, and I don't think anyone will because I believe it is pretty thoroughly understood that this is not an administration that's going to countenance the granting of favors to anybody.

And so, briefly and specifically, that is our philosophy as far as the taxpayer is concerned—to see that every taxpayer is treated alike, to administer the law in the manner that Congress intended so as to put the burden where it was intended to be put in the proportion that Congress intended, and to follow that policy in any of the disputes with taxpayers which are inevitable under an income tax law. When we have a dispute with a taxpayer, our policy is equally as simple as it is with respect to administration of the law in its broader aspects. We deal with him the same as you would if you were dealing with a customer across the table in a disagreement on a business matter. We meet him on equal terms in a spirit of give and take and of honest effort to arrive at a fair settlement of the dispute, always, of course, within the provisions of the law. No tax administrator can substitute equity completely for the law. He has to observe the law, but in doing so, he can always be reasonable, always be fair, and he doesn't have to have a fight. He doesn't have to operate on the theory that every tax return is the opening of a law suit and that the whole field of tax administration is a legal battleground. Tax administration simply cannot be allowed to get into that condition.

Mr. Sutherland wanted me to discuss a couple of things that may be especially interesting to you. One of these things is my attitude toward fraud.

We have, as you know, in the Internal Revenue Service what we call a "racket squad." The racket squad was set up several years ago to investigate the income tax liability of so-called racketeers, people engaged in genuinely shady occupations. We know that there is a tremendous amount of money that is employed in various forms of gambling. We know that gamblers generally are not good taxpayers; they hide their income; and often they don't even make returns. So the Internal Revenue Service set up a special squad to investigate this kind of fraud. Up to now, it has assessed or proposed for assessment about $200 million at a cost of less than 10 percent of that amount.

Of course, this has been a fruitful field, but in my eyes, as a tax collector, a so-called respectable citizen, one who could parade a dozen or a hundred witnesses before the court to say that prior to his tax evasion he was a great and honorable citizen, is just as crooked as one who has been in jail fifteen times. Anybody who will withhold from his fellow citizens his share of the burden of supporting the Government, especially at a time when the sons and daughters of men are dying abroad in order that freedom may be preserved for us in this country, in my opinion is little short of a traitor. And he ought not to be lightly dealt with. As far as I am concerned, that kind of man, be he racketeer or respected citizen, is a tax evader to whom no deference should be shown.

I know there are those who disagree with that point of view. But my friends, I also know that the law presumes that people intend to do what they do, and when we go into court and show that a taxpayer has deliberately, pursuant to a carefully conceived plan of evasion, done his Government out of taxes and dumped his share of the tax burden into the laps of others, then I say to you that there is in my book no mercy for that kind of man. If he is found guilty, there is just one place for him, and that is a penitentiary, and he should go there for a long enough period to make him realize that this country is not going to tolerate that sort of business. And I am unmovable on that question.

Of course I don't decide the question. The question of prosecution is not determined by the Internal Revenue Service. We recommend prosecution to the Department of Justice, and the Department of Justice has to decide whether to prosecute or not. If the decision is made to prosecute, then the case goes before a grand jury, and there has to be an indictment. We don't control that. After the indictment, there has to be a trial, and we don't control that. And there has to be a decision, and we don't control that. And if found guilty, there has to be a sentence, and we don't control that. So there is a lot of the process with which we don't have anything to do. But I can assure you we have plenty of conviction as to what should be done with those who are found guilty of a carefully conceived and cleverly executed plan of evasion.

Now if I am convinced that a man didn't know how to keep books or made a mistake, that's another story. I am not talking about people who make honest mistakes. I can be just as lenient on a man who makes an honest mistake as the next fellow, and I always will be, I assure you. I believe, Bill, I have said plainly what I think about that.

Also, Bill wanted to know what we are going to do to secure uniformity of decisions, now that we have our operations largely decentralized to the field. Well, first of all, let me say "there ain't no such thing" as absolute uniformity when it comes to matters of human judgment. It's unattainable. You can make a close approach to it, of course, and we aim to make the closest approach possible by the program of organization that we have worked out. Let me explain very briefly how that organization works.

We are turning the Washington headquarters of the Internal Revenue Service into a planning and control organization, in the same manner that the larger corporations of America organize their business, realizing that when the operations are scattered over the face of the United States, nobody is smart enough to sit in a room in Washington or in Detroit or New York or anywhere else and control the day-to-day operation of everything or make all the decisions in that business.

When we decided upon decentralization of the Service, we did so after study of our own problems and of the decentralization plans of some of the greatest industries of America. And we recognized that the reorganization of the Internal Revenue Service, as put through by Congress last year, had inherent in it the idea of decentralization, of giving the people out on the front lines who deal with the taxpayers the power to make decisions, and of giving the taxpayer the right, except in those very complex questions which sometimes arise, to expect his difficulties with the Government to be settled in his own locality so that he would not have to run to Washington to find someone who could tell him what is right and wrong. There is no monopoly in Washington on brains, not even in the Internal Revenue Service.

We have nearly 50,000 of our people in the field, and some of them are the highest rated people we have who are paid as well as the Civil Service Commission will permit. If out of that field organization we can't get decisions that are going to be just and fair to the taxpayers and the Government, then I say to you that the Internal Revenue Service is in a bad way and ought to be abolished. It is not in that shape. We think we have a mighty fine bunch of people in the field, and I don't harbor for one minute any ideas that they are incompetent or that they are incapable of exercising the authority that we have given them.

We have decentralized to the field the right to make decisions that affect the well-being of the taxpayers of America, and we are going to leave it there as long as it works. We think it's going to work, and if it doesn't work, we are going to try to make it work. And I think that's the way Congress wants it, and I think it's the way the people of America want it. I know it's the right thing to do because many people whose judgment I value highly have told me it's the right thing to do.

We are going to have an operation in which our people in the field will enjoy our confidence as long as they are entitled to it, and they are going to have our encouragement and our guidance and our direction to see that they make good decisions more often than they make bad ones. You ask if they are going to make bad ones. Of course they are. They are human. They are going to make mistakes occasionally, and it's my feeling that the United States Government is no different in this respect from anyone else that does business with the people. After all, the people are the United States, and, in the normal transaction of our business, we ought to be willing to take the usual risks of business, the chances that our people who have to do the job will make an error occasionally. That doesn't mean that we have to surrender completely our authority when an error is made. We can still reserve the right to correct an error, and I think as a matter of policy we should do that. And wherever the error is substantial and obviously shouldn't have been made, we should do something about it. We are certainly not going to give up the right to do that. But, by the same token, if we operated on the view that nobody in the Government should ever make a mistake, the taxes you are paying now would be chicken feed compared to what you would have to pay. You wouldn't be able to afford that kind of administration. It just doesn't make sense, and we are not going to operate that way.

We think there will be as much uniformity of decision in these 64 districts and nine regions as there has ever been in Washington. If you wanted to see evidence in support of that opinion, I could show you Tax Court cases on the same point of law and under approximately the same set of facts where the decisions were exactly opposite. And you all know that in the administration of the income tax law we are frequently confronted with decisions of the circuit courts that are contrary to each other. So there isn't complete uniformity in the administration of justice for the simple reason that the right answer is so often a matter of judgment.

Now we are going to try to get more uniformity rather than less. The decisions that are made in the field are going to be reviewed in the field very carefully in a manner that they have never been reviewed before. In addition to that, representatives of the regional commissioner will review the work of the directors' offices in all of its aspects, including decisions made in cases, with such thoroughness as to satisfy any reasonable person that there is a uniform approach within that region. And headquarters in Washington will, by appropriate coordination of the efforts of the nine regions, see that there is a uniformity as among the regions.

For instance, suppose we are particularly concerned, as we might well be, with the attitude in the various parts of the country with respect to Section 102 of the Code. It's a very simple matter for us—and this is precisely what we will do—to pull a selected number of settled cases involving Section 102 from all the regions of the country and see what's being done with them. That's something we never had before. In addition, we propose to go into the settlement of a lot of cases in which there was no change made, no additional tax and no refund. That's something more than we have ever done before. We think it is just as important to see that a case that a revenue agent settled without change has some kind of review as it is to see that one that does involve change is reviewed.

We feel that the control mechanisms we are setting up are going to be sufficient to enable us to be sure that we are getting as near to uniformity of decisions in the same circumstances and under the same section of the law as is humanly possible for us to get. If we don't get that, we will either tighten the system or change it.

We are not just setting up a pretty form of organization, patting ourselves on the back, and saying to ourselves, "This is it and it is going to work beautifully." Anything we do is going to be constantly reviewed and analyzed and weighed and evaluated in accordance with the results that are achieved. And if it doesn't measure up, we will do something to make it measure up.

Now I have given you my philosophy as a tax administrator, which is a very simple one, I am sure. It wasn't at all startling to anybody here, I know, though it may have been said in a fairly positive manner. I have definite ideas, based on experience, and I know that experience has worked, and I know that taxpayers, while sometimes unhappy when such ideas are first put into operation, invariably drop their hostility in a relatively short time and, believing in the fairness of the administration, put their support behind what has been done.

I never will forget my experience as Controller of the City of Richmond. The first man whose water I cut off for not paying his bill was a city councilman, and before I left the City of Richmond he would have given me the city hall if he could have. He was the best supporter we had because he realized that he had no right to that preference, and it pleased him that nobody thereafter was able to get it.

After all, what we want is an administration of the tax laws that assures us that everybody is on the tax rolls who ought to be there, and that everybody, once he has been put on the rolls, will be dealt with in a simple, straightforward, honest manner if he finds himself in dispute with the tax authorities.

Thank you very much.

INTERNAL REVENUE SERVICE
An Address before the Mountain States Accounting Conference[†]

by

T. Coleman Andrews

I want to thank the good folks of this vast Rocky Mountain Empire for the warmth and sincerity of the welcome we have received here in Salt Lake City. It is certainly amazing to me that an audience the size of this one could be rounded up on a busy work day to hear the top tax collector of the country—a fellow who takes a pretty generous bite out of every dollar that reaches the American pocketbook, and conducts no give-away programs on the side—report on the progress made by this Administration in restoring the lost confidence of the people in their Internal Revenue Service.

Frankly, I don't quite know why I was selected as Commissioner of Internal Revenue. I have been asked a number of times how it happened—but I just don't know the answer to that question. In late January of last year I got a telephone call from a New York friend who said that he had heard from a man in Manhattan, who had heard from a man in Chicago, who had heard from a man in Cleveland, who had heard from a man in Minneapolis, that I was going to be appointed Commissioner.

That was completely dumfounding to me, and I just didn't believe it. I knew of no reason why I should be appointed Commissioner—and, when it happened, I was as surprised as anybody else. Anyhow, here I am, after having been down there in Washington for over sixteen months.

I must admit that I have encountered a lot of people who feel that I should have gotten the job cleaned up six months ago; that I should have corrected all the things that were wrong and had been getting wrong over a period of some twenty-odd years; that I should have straightened everything out quickly and been able to say, "Well, now, it's perfect, and every taxpayer can expect justice"—even though he may not expect reduced taxes.

Of course, my friends, it hasn't worked out that way. You don't cure over night a disease that takes years to develop. We have not cured all of the ills of the Revenue Service, and I would not be so bold as to suggest

[†]Reprinted with permission from *Technical Papers Presented at the 1954 Mountain States Accounting Conference* (Salt Lake City, UT: Mountain States Council of Certified Public Accountants, 1954), pp. 23-31.

377

that even when we feel that we have finished our task, we will have cured all of them.

I think we have made progress, and I want to give you folks a sort of progress report today. But I want to be sure at the outset that you all understand that I and the staff of the Revenue Service recognize better than anybody else, better than even our severest critics, that we are a long way from being over the hill with this job; that there is a great deal more to be done and a lot of hurdles still to be cleared. But we do think that we have made progress, and I hope that today I can convince you of that fact.

First of all, though, I should like to say that it's nice to be here. I know that most of you are on the opposite side of the fence from me, but it's comforting to me, my friends, to look into the faces of several hundred people here and realize that every one of you is a good customer—or, at least, should be. One doesn't do business with someone he doesn't like—and therefore I say that you must be my friends. If you are not, I hope to make you my friends before I am finished.

That is one of the great pleasures of going to meetings of this kind and talking to people—because I have more customers than any other man in the United States. Some of them are good, some of them are not so good—but, taken together, they pay in to the Treasury about $65 to $70 billion every year.

Now, of course, I don't know what $65 or $70 billion is. I don't even know what $1 billion is. Rowland Hughes reminded us down in Washington the other day that there are only about a billion minutes in nineteen hundred years. You can take that statistic for what it's worth. I suppose the implication is that, if you wanted to pitch away a dollar a minute, you would have to live nineteen hundred years to get rid of a billion dollars. At any rate, it's a lot of money—a terrible lot of money.

I might say, my friends, that the job I have isn't the most onerous job in the world. Of course, anyone can go to Washington and, in almost any job down there that works a man pretty hard, the way this one does, he can wear himself out in six months' time. It all depends upon what your attitude toward the job is. If you are a worrier, you're doomed before you start, because there's not a moment in the day when you won't have something to worry about.

The doctors tell me that no man ever went crazy or lost his health from doing something that he enjoyed doing. And I confess that I'm enjoying this job. It's a job that I think anyone would enjoy, because it's challenging; there is so much to be done that there isn't a day that goes by when you can't count something accomplished. And that, to me, is perhaps the most important part of living.

Well, I guess you want to hear something about the administration of Federal taxes—what we are doing down there in Washington—so maybe I had better get down to business and tell you about it.

You will probably be a little bit surprised at what I tell you, because I confess, to start out with, that there is nothing miraculous about it. We are not magicians—we have only done what I think any men in this room would have done under the same circumstances, just the usual things that people who have been taught the value of money would do. Of course, one thing you soon learn in Washington is that what is normal and usual in the ordinary affairs of life becomes sensational in Washington—and I rather suspect that before we are through, if we continue to do things in the simple way we are doing them now, I may become some kind of sensation, like the big wind that blew through our town about three years ago.

At any rate, here we were confronted with an organization of 54,000 people, with 64 principal operating offices, and with nine (or, at that time, seventeen) regional offices that acted, as would the regional offices of any business that is doing a nationwide commerce, to tie together, supervise and control the functions of the operating offices within those districts or regions—and, on top of those offices, some 1,500 other installations ranging all the way from one-man stands to organizations of several hundred people.

We had a pretty widespread organization, then—so big that I haven't yet been able to find a map of sufficient size to hold a pin for every office we have.

On top of that, we had 65 million taxpayers to do business with—at least, that is our estimate, and we think it is approximately correct—and those 65 million people filing a total of 95 million tax returns of one kind or another every year. That gives us a paper-load problem of several times that size, because, of course, every tax return gives rise to quite a good deal of paper work. Not a little of this paper work was necessary but some, I admit, was unnecessary, so we have been trying our best to eliminate the unnecessary.

Compared to any other organization of its kind in the world, ours is undoubtedly the largest. Compared to the largest corporation in America, I would say that it certainly falls within the first ten. And since a member of my staff handed me some figures the other day showing that the weight of the forms of one kind or another distributed each year by the Revenue Service is approximately 7,000 tons—enough to burden 260 standard railway freight cars—I'm inclined to a belief that we are perhaps the world's largest purchaser of printed matter. This will give you some idea as to the size of the organization that it became our lot to try to get back on its feet. I say it that way because the Revenue Service was very definitely off its feet, and it wasn't very far from having fallen flat on its face.

In the first place, it had lost the confidence of the people. Actually, that loss of confidence was not quite justified. I am sure that no one realizes better than I, unless it be these gentlemen of the accounting profession, that the Revenue Service was never corrupt as an organization.

Rather, it had developed a few—and I say that advisedly—rotten apples that made the public think, quite naturally, that the whole barrel was rotten.

Now, that was not true. It was not true then, and I can assure you that it is not true today. I believe that the Revenue Service is as honorable, as diligent, as hard-working, as conscientious a group of people as you will find anywhere in the United States. We have our faults, but I don't believe that we can be rated below the average—and in some respects, I think, we could probably be rated above the average.

I say that because I think it is always desirable to let people know that their neighbors of the Revenue Service ought not to be indiscriminately suspected of corrupt actions in the discharge of their official duties. Very few of those 54,000 people deserve that kind of suspicion.

We had a situation, then, involving a loss of public confidence, and public confidence obviously had to be restored. Loss of confidence had, in turn, induced a considerable loss of morale on the part of the people in the Revenue Service. We were losing personnel faster than we were able to hire them. I estimated one day that, at the rate that we were then losing people, the time would probably come within three to four years when there would not be enough personnel left just to man the tellers' cages to take in the cash, let alone to examine returns and carry out enforcement work. Something had to be done about that, too.

We therefore set to work, first of all, to find a way to regain public confidence. I am not going to tell you all the things we have done in order to accomplish that, because I think you have read enough in the papers to know a good deal about it. But I do want you to know that that activity—regaining public confidence—had a No. 1 priority as far as we were concerned.

We started out with the very simple assumption that most people in the United States are honest and that they will believe that other people are honest provided the other people demonstrate it. We backed that up by the further assumption, gained from experience and observation in many years of management work, that usually an organization that is honest and effective at the top is honest and effective all the way through—and, if it stinks at the top, it will stink all the way through.

We therefore determined that the people put in positions of authority in the Revenue Service had to be people of the highest character, and we have tried to adhere to that determination. We believe we have been successful. I am encouraged by the change in tone of the correspondence we receive—a change we began to note shortly after we assumed office. The people of America are beginning to believe that their Revenue Service can be trusted, that they can depend upon us to treat everybody alike and not to show special favors to anyone, and that if, by any chance, an occasional Revenue Service employee should get out of bounds in his dealings with the public, his wrong doing will be promptly and appropriately dealt with.

I would be less than frank if I did not admit to you that there have been cases of that kind. Also, I would be less than human if I did not remind you that, in an organization made up of 54,000 people, you cannot expect them all to be angels. There are going to be some who will stray off the reservation occasionally and who will have to be disciplined.

We think, then, that we have accomplished something in the direction of regaining public confidence, not only in our integrity but also in our determination to deal fairly with people. It has been my experience in tax administration that, when you demonstrate that everyone will be treated alike, the public may not love you, but it will respect you and it will cooperate with you—and your percentage of collections, your realization of the potential of the tax laws, will be high.

To some extent, the morale of the employees rose with the return of public confidence. But we had to do more than that, because we had some gross inequalities and inequities in the treatment of employees. A lot of cliques had developed. You can imagine for yourselves what the political complexion of the service was after twenty years of reign by one party. In a situation of that kind, obviously, promotion often went not to the man who deserved a promotion, but rather to the man who happened to vote the same way as the supervisor. There were other reasons, too, why favoritism was shown to certain employees. We haven't yet corrected it all, but we are making rapid progress.

We found that many people had been required to do work far above the grade that they were getting paid for. We have conducted a complete survey of the classification of every person in the service, and we are now in the process of classifying every person according to the work he is doing or is capable of doing, and paying him accordingly. (When I say "him" in any situation, I mean "her" as well, because, of course, we have a lot of women in the service.) We are now convincing the officials and the employees of the service, I believe, that they can expect to be paid according to the complexity of the duties assigned.

That has done a lot to restore morale. But, again, we still have quite a way to go before we finish that job, because, my friends, it is no easy task to deal with 54,000 individual cases and at the same time run your day-to-day routine operations.

Next to that, our main problem was a problem of manpower. Now, I know what most of you are thinking: "A new broom going in there should have swept clean and got rid of a lot of people, because perhaps there were too many people there." Well, we did have more people than we needed in some areas of our activity, and those we have eliminated—except as we may be able to make further eliminations from time to time by the improvement of our methods.

We have reduced our Washington office—the headquarters office—from about 3,900 people down to about 2,700, so we do not think that the Washington office now has any great amount of excess personnel.

At the same time, another real personnel problem lay in the fact that we had only 7,500 agents to examine all of these returns that we have been talking about, and we weren't examining anywhere near the number that we knew should be examined in order to get the greatest possible revenue yield.

A lot of people said: "Well, what are you going to do about this situation? Are you going to examine every return?" My friends, you don't have to examine every return, but, if you examine enough of them, so that everybody knows that he has a pretty good chance of being questioned, you are going to have many fewer inaccurate returns filed.

Let me say just a word on the question of inaccurate returns. We don't worry about people making mistakes, and we don't worry about their making mistakes deliberately when it's just a matter of deciding an issue in their favor. As I said to an audience the other day, let every taxpayer do what he honestly thinks the law expects of him. If we disagree with him, he will find out about it, and usually (if we get the number of agents we want) we will be able to take care of ourselves all right. Therefore, I am not greatly concerned about the number of errors that are made.

People sometimes say to me: "How is it that you can get so much money out of putting on more agents? Is it because people are trying to cheat?" No, my friends, that isn't the answer. The vast majority of the people who make errors make them because of honest miscalculations, and that doesn't worry us a bit. We will find most of them, and we will get them straightened out.

And so it happens that, by putting on more agents, we can increase the revenue very substantially, in fact at the rate of about $25 to $30 for every dollar that we spend, up to the point where the law of diminishing return sets in—and we do have a law of diminishing return in this matter, just as in other things.

And so there we are. We needed more agents. But the question was: "How do you get them? Do you mean you are going to ask for more appropriations?" The administration wanted to reduce appropriations. We said: "No, we're not going to ask for increased appropriations—certainly not now. As a matter of fact, we will take a cut of $4 million, from $270 million to $266 million, because we see that much in our setup that we can save and still do a lot more enforcement work than is being done." And so we accepted a cut of $4 million—from $270 million, as I have said, to $266 million.

We saved quite a lot of money by reducing those seventeen regional offices to nine and by putting in numerous other reforms that seemed to us to be needed. Overhead with us is just as real as it is with any other business in the country. And so we went after it, and we have cut out a tremendous lot of it.

The only difference between overhead with us and overhead with you is that we live on the power to tax and you have to live on savings. We, therefore, feel that we have a special obligation to see that overhead is brought down to the very lowest possible point. We have people who work on nothing but that all the time, every day bringing in suggestions for reducing overhead.

We also closely watch our enforcement organization and operation, and have succeeded in making substantial reductions in that area. In fact, our savings from reduced overhead and improved operating procedures enabled us to go back to Congress again this year and say: "We still don't want our budget increased. We will take the $266 million. We haven't finished saving money. When we get down to the point where we want to expend further—faster than we can save money—then we will come back to you." Incidentally, we have just recently asked for supplemental funds to greatly increase our over-all enforcement effort.

And so we have operated under a ceiling of total money available, and at the same time we have reduced our operating costs very substantially. I might also say that we have increased the amount of work being done, the number of returns examined, the number of cases settled.

I was told yesterday—I haven't had a chance to fully verify it, but I believe it is correct—that the Tax Court docket is down from a high of 13,500 cases along toward the end of last year to less than 9,000 cases at the present time.

That is a very substantial accomplishment, my friends. We are settling cases faster, and we are getting many more returns examined per man. And we are in a position to judge people's efficiency, because we have sixty-four operating offices—and, when you have sixty-four offices all doing the same thing, you can lay them side by side and tell who is working and who isn't. The same thing goes for the regional offices. Therefore, we are now in a position that we have never been in before, where we can judge efficiency on the simple basis of comparison of one organization with another. And we mean to see that those below the median line raise their production. If they are unable to do so, then the officials responsible will have to give way to others who *can* do the job. In other words, we mean to have an efficient Revenue Service as well as an honorable one.

Those are some of the problems, and I have told you a few of the things that we have done to solve those problems. I should like to go into greater detail if I had the time, because there is big money in some of the things that we are planning to do. One program that we have started will save us close to $25 million a year, nearly 10 percent of our budget. We expect to have that under way by the first of next January. There is another one that we think will reduce the number of erroneous returns to half of what it is now. If we do that, the calculated saving is easily $30 million. We therefore think that in a reasonable time we are going to have things whittled down to as efficient an operation as can be obtained.

And now, my friends, if I may, I should just like to review briefly with you some of the improvements that have happened in the last year—not only in the Revenue Service, but in the management of the Government as a whole.

A short time ago, Budget Director Hughes read a very interesting summary of the fiscal situation as to the time the Eisenhower Administration took over the reins of Government. He attributed this summary to Joe Dodge, whom Mr. Hughes succeeded as Budget Director.

Mr. Dodge compared the status of our fiscal affairs at the beginning of 1953 to the status of a family that had consistently lived well beyond its means, had five years of real adversity related to World War II, had provided itself with more income than it had spent only three times in twenty years, had acquired a debt over four times its yearly income, owed more than a year's income on c.o.d.'s that would have to be paid for on delivery, normally had about one month's living expenses in the bank, had relatively little margin before reaching a fixed limit on its borrowing, was aware of an impending ten percent reduction in its income—and had no immediate plans for changing its habits.

That was the situation seventeen months ago. Since that time, a great deal has been done. A policy has been established—a definite plan to restore economic stability. The essence of that plan is expressed in another statement by Budget Director Hughes, in which he said:

> The Administration is anxious to have taxes reduced as fast as that can be done without building up inflationary deficits and adding still further to the fearsome legacy of debt that we are turning over to our children. Reductions in tax rates need the support of reductions in government expenditures. Expenditure rates govern and determine tax revenue requirements. Expenditures which are not paid for by tax revenues can, in the end, be paid for only by a far more insidious type of taxation, namely, inflation, and it is our determined purpose to make further reductions in taxes only as rapidly as those reductions are justified by prospective revenues and reductions in expenditures.
>
> As President Eisenhower emphasized recently, it is the Administration's conclusion that the budget situation does not justify large additional tax reductions at this time. As we continue in the future, however, to reduce and eliminate the less desirable or the unnecessary government expenditures, it will become possible to turn to other purposes which are the most desirable in terms of their benefits to all the people of the country. These purposes certainly include our twin objectives of balancing the budget and further reducing tax rates.

But there is a much more important thing, my friends, than the mere matter of revenues, expenditures, appropriations, allotments, deficits, surpluses, and so on. All of that is mere dollars—and we can't live on that sort of thing alone. We have to look at the more fundamental aspects of our situation, and look at them from the standpoint of our concept of government—what we want in order to be happy, what we are willing to give up in order to satisfy those wants, what we are willing to do to discipline ourselves properly in order that we may live in peace with the world and attain a reasonable prosperity for ourselves and the maximum amount of help for others who need our help. Let us look back at the situation, then, from that point of view.

A year ago, our government was in serious danger of control by corrupt party machines—yes, even by gangsters—cynical, ruthless, self-seeking grabbers for power. I can tell you—and I think you probably know this without my telling you—that this danger is largely past. As to our Revenue Service, for instance, I can tell you that we are out after the fellow who is trying to unload his burdens upon other people, and we don't intend to let up until we get the last one of them.

Part of our job is to protect the 97 or 98 percent of honest taxpayers in this country against the unscrupulous few—and we take that part of our job most seriously. Why? Because there is a very essential ingredient in our system, and we call that ingredient "voluntary compliance." What it comes down to is that, at tax-filing time each year, every taxpayer comes forward to the collector's window and says: "Here, Mr. Tax Collector—according to my calculations my income was so much, and according to your tables I owe you so much, and here it is."

Contrast that, if you will, with the situation in other parts of the world. In one country, it is openly reported that there is only ten percent compliance; all the rest either pay no taxes at all or fudge on those that they do pay. There is another country where there is only forty percent compliance and where the Finance Minister says openly that there is only one honest rich man in the country as far as taxes are concerned. There is another where the best compliance that can be boasted of is sixty percent.

My friends, we can't afford to get into that situation in this country, and we can well be proud of the fact that we have pretty close to one hundred percent voluntary compliance. Why? Well, it means just one thing: that the American people as taxpayers are traditionally respecters of their obligations as citizens of a great country. They know that they cannot have these great benefits of government that have been achieved by Congress without paying for them. We in the Revenue Service think that they will pay for them loyally and cooperatively—though maybe not without some grumbling when the level of taxes gets terribly high, as it is now—if they believe that everybody else is contributing his share.

Voluntary compliance, my friends! Upon it hangs the destiny of America—and I say that advisedly because, if our revenue system fails, it is inconceivable to me that our economic system can survive. And upon that little ingredient, so simply defined as "voluntary compliance," hangs the hopes of millions of people throughout the world, who want the freedom that we enjoy, but who have not yet tasted its benefits.

People ask me: "What is your job in the Revenue Service? Tax collector?" Oh, no, my friends, that alone isn't my job. We have a much bigger job to do than that. Our job is to make the revenue system of this country work, to make it acceptable to the people of the country, so that voluntary compliance will be preserved, so that evasion of taxes may not become socially acceptable, so that people may not look at the tax collector with a suspicious eye and say: "Well, it looks as though his friends are getting away with something—why should I pay mine?" That is the most dangerous thing that that can ever happen to a nation. We must not let it happen in this country—and we don't intend to, because, once it happens, voluntary compliance will give way to social acceptance of evasion, and eventually we will get down to sixty percent of voluntary compliance, and then forty percent of voluntary compliance, and then our revenue system will go out the window.

If that happens, our economic system will collapse with it, and I am afraid we will get the only alternative to our system of government that anybody ever hears anything about these days.

We don't want that to happen and we don't believe it will happen, because the people have demonstrated clearly to us that they are willing to support their government, that they recognize their obligation to support their internal commitments and the influence of their country abroad, and to maintain that influence so that it may achieve its rightful destiny.

Together with the rest of the administration, we realize that this country cannot grow on any other basis. As a people, we cannot be just coupon clippers on the original investment made by our forefathers, but rather we want to make substantial deposits on which the young people of America—your children and mine, and their children's children—may draw interest tomorrow.

In other words, we look at our job in its most fundamental sense as one that goes far beyond the mere business of tax-collecting. I remember so well the story of the young apprentice mason who was working on a wall of a great cathedral. When he was asked what he was doing, he said: "I am laying bricks." Remembering how far he missed the point, we in the Revenue Service say to you that we are out to make a real contribution to the moral capital of the greatest country we know anything about. All of our policies, all of our plans, all of our activities are aimed in that direction, joining as they do with the inspiring example set from the highest office in the land, which gives assurance to every American that this country today is dedicated to the faith in which it was founded, and to an indomitable will that the affairs of the country shall be administered honestly and efficiently and in the interests of all the people.

VOLUNTARY COMPLIANCE WITH THE TAX LAWS[†]

by

T. Coleman Andrews

I know that some of you want to hear some stories from me this morning. But I am not going to tell you any stories this morning, because I have serious business on my mind. Besides, I have found it a bit difficult to be funny this early in the day.

Before I begin my remarks, I should like to make a request, because this is for the benefit of some of our friends from abroad. It is not a part of the speech. I would like to know whether District Director Ahern of the Upper Manhattan District is in the audience. (Mr. Ahern arose.) There is a gentleman on the outside who would like you to do what you can to speed the tax clearances of our foreign guests, and I should ask you to cooperate with him as much as you can.

DISTRICT DIRECTOR AHERN: It is already taken care of, Commissioner.

COMMISSIONER ANDREWS: Thank you. That is what I call efficiency, ladies and gentlemen, but I assure you that it was not staged; it was spontaneous, and needless to say it was very gratifying to me. I was told that some of our foreign guests were anxious to get away, and they wanted to avoid the red tape of clearance with Internal Revenue. Well, of course, I said there was no red tape in getting out of the United States now, as far as we are concerned, but perhaps we could do something to make it more convenient, and I don't know what they did, but I rather imagine that they brought the mountain to Mohammed and arranged to take care of the clearances here at the hotel.

When we took over, tax clearance for visitors from abroad was taking from three to four hours. As soon as we found this out we did something about it, and now it takes only fifteen or twenty minutes. I think that is speeding it up a bit, don't you? So there would not have been much difficulty anyhow, but I am glad to know that our people have taken care of the situation.

[†]Reprinted with permission from *1954 Annual Meeting Papers* (New York: American Institute of Accountants, 1954), pp. i-x.

It was a little difficult for me to decide what to talk to you about this morning, because so many of you have heard me speak during the past year that I know many of those present would be bored by a reiteration of our aims and ideals and even the things that we have accomplished. So I decided to take a different approach, and leave these distinguished experts all around me here to talk about the technical things that you are interested in. I shall not even mention too much our administrative and organizational problems.

But first I should like to refer here to a recent event at which the well-known Seidman humor was so delightfully exemplified. We were down at the College of William and Mary, which, if you will permit me, being a Virginian, I will brag about as being the second school or college in the English-speaking world to establish a law school—the first having been Oxford, in England.

The first student of this law school at William and Mary was the illustrious John Marshall, the man who brought alive the Constitution of our country, and his professor was one John Wythe, one of the early lawyers of the Colonies in the days just before they became independent.

During the past year, the College of William and Mary decided upon a bold move. Things are moving pretty fast, you know, down in the southern part of the country; we are growing pretty rapidly down there in many ways, and the College wanted to be up to date with everybody else, so it decided to do something new and different, and they established another "first": they established a chair of taxation in the law school, leading to the degree of master of law in taxation, with the idea, of course, of extending it to master of business science in taxation, with perhaps some day a combination of the two.

In my opinion, this is an extremely important development in the field of business education and education for law, because it was, I believe, the first step towards the strong probability that sooner or later we will see integrated professional practices. I know that this might seem like heresy to some people, particularly the members of the legal profession. Some of our friends of that profession probably would look with horror on the idea of being in partnership with accountants. But I can imagine worse things, from both sides, incidentally.

I think that this chair of taxation in the law school of the College of William and Mary is the beginning, the first step, in the development of integrated practice, that is, the type of professional practice that business has to use. Many businessmen have told me they are getting awfully tired of having to pay so many different professional people for the services that they need.

Assembled for the inauguration of the Chair of Taxation was a great delegation of people, including the Chief Justice of the United States, the Lord Chief Justice of England, and the Master of the University College of Oxford. The Chief Justice of the United States unveiled a bust of John

Marshall; the Chief Justice of the Court of Appeals of Virginia unveiled one to Wythe; and the Lord Chief Justice of England unveiled one to Blackstone.

I might say the Lord Chief Justice was an entertaining speaker on such an important occasion, but there was another gentleman there, the Master of the University College at Oxford, an American, by the way, the first one who had ever achieved that distinction. Parenthetically, I discovered yesterday, in addressing a meeting over at the Harvard Club, that he was the uncle of a young man who was there at the meeting and with whom I served in the Pacific. His name was Dr. Goodhart, and Dr. Goodhart brought the greetings of Oxford and the University of Oxford, to this meeting: and it was in Latin, five pages of it. I understand the translation is a very delightful sort of thing, but, of course, nobody understood it. The gentleman read it, however, with learning and obvious knowledge of it himself. But the Lord Chief Justice came to our rescue in his remarks by saying that while he, of course, had studied Latin and there are many Latin phrases in the law, he confessed he didn't understand a word that the good doctor had said.

At this Jack Seidman said to me, "Why have this tax panel that is set up? It doesn't seem to me now to be necessary to say anything about the new Code." Later on, at the panel meeting, I think Jack got off probably the best story of the day, or the best quip, when he observed to his audience: "In this atmosphere I have been thinking what a tremendous part Patrick Henry had in the great fight against taxation without representation; and yet," he said, "I wonder what Mr. Henry would do if he could come across the green today and have a look at the present situation and see the magnitude and the complexity and the burden of what we have acquired with representation."

A very apt expression, and very appropriate to what I want to say to you this morning. I know that most of you are interested in the technical aspects of taxation. That is what you want to hear this morning. But, my friends, having occupied the position of Commissioner for almost two years now—a good twenty months—I get a different point of view from the one you have. I get the point of view of the administrator, the one charged with the responsibility for making the revenue laws of this great country work, and don't forget that the income tax law is not the only tax law we administer; we are concerned with about 70 or 80 different kinds of taxes.

We even have to chase moonshiners and bootleggers—a pursuit which is sometimes rather hazardous and even, on occasion, romantic and venturesome; so much so that not too long ago we came here on one of the great television programs and decorated a gentleman who had singlehandedly gone up into the hills of one of the states down our way and brought in seven armed moonshiners all by himself, even after two of them had taken him and bound him up and stuck his head in the creek and left him to drown. He still brought them in.

Unfortunately, there is no such adventure and romance in the administration of the income tax laws; so there are no decorations of that kind for our people in that part of the Service. But you know, without my having to stress the point, that the administration of the income tax now is, nevertheless, powerfully important.

You have heard me say a lot about the organization and management of the Service since I have been in office, first talking about what we wanted to do, and hoped we could do; and, more recently, talking about some of the things that we have actually accomplished, though guardedly, of course, because we realize that we still have quite a long way to go before we have achieved all of the reform and adjustment that the situation deserved.

The burden of taxation is enormous; let us not make any mistake about it, it is great. The problems of administration are in proportion. The tax burden has been greatly reduced this year; it has been reduced to a greater extent than ever before in all the history of the country in one year—$3.5 billion of personal income taxes, $1.1 billion of excise taxes, and so on, a total of $7.4 billion. But the base is still as broad as before the reductions were made. So we still have the same number of taxpayers, the same amount of administration; and some of the problems of administration are very difficult.

Let me give you just one illustration. Recently I began to be concerned about the question whether the withholding taxes and the Social Security taxes that had been deducted from the paychecks and pay envelopes of the workers of the country were being promptly paid in, and I found some rather disturbing things. I found situations, quite a few of them—and I am speaking relatively—where employers were as much as three to four years in arrears in paying these deductions over to us.

Now, these were not taxes, mind you, that had been levied against the persons who were required to pay them over; but rather were levied against the employees of those people. They represented money held in trust by the people who withheld them, and money which, therefore, should not have been used by the employers; and yet there were many cases of as much as three and four years delinquency.

I need not tell you that a situation of that kind is intolerable. There was over $140,000,000 of such taxes outstanding and, as I recall it, over 250,000 business organizations and other taxpayers who owed them. We cannot permit that sort of thing to continue.

Recently we had one of these cases where the taxpayer felt greatly aggrieved that we had invoked the sanction of law to get the money in. He owed four years' taxes, and he said he thought we were pretty harsh about it.

I said, "Now, let's analyze it. You happen to be in the transportation business. This money was taken from the pay checks of your employees. But," I said, "your employees didn't pay these taxes in the final analysis;

390

the people who did pay them were the people who rode your vehicles, because the fare that you charged them covers every element of expense, including the salaries and wages you paid to your employees, which in turn, of course, include these taxes."

"Now," I said, "if we do not collect this money from you, we are going to be asking the people of this country, including those who rode your vehicles, to pay these taxes again. And," I said, "we can't run the Revenue system of America on that basis."

The gentleman said, "Well, I came here thinking you were a pretty tough customer. I go out feeling that I am a heel."

I said, "I have no intention of making you feel that way, but if I have made you realize your responsibility in this situation, then, of course, I have accomplished a constructive session with you." I wish I could do as well with all of them, but I can't, of course. But I might say that that gentleman has somehow contrived to pay us now half of what he owes us, and we gave him five years to pay the balance.

I might say that one of the reasons why we went after this taxpayer so strongly was that he not only had not shown any interest in paying us but he wouldn't even come in to talk about an extended settlement. Of course, that sort of attitude doesn't sit well with a tax collector, and I think you would understand why.

Now, where do you come into this picture? I'll tell you where you come in. The accountant who had audited the books of that company annually had never once called attention to the fact that those taxes represented trust funds or even to the fact that they were delinquent to the extent of one, two, three, four years. That, I submit to you, was a very serious omission. This didn't worry us, of course, because we didn't issue the reports, but as an accountant I suggest to you that the omission was serious.

Another reason that I am discussing this matter with you is that, whether you like it or not, my friends, you and every other tax practitioner in America are an extension of our Revenue Service. We aren't just a group of 52,500 people engaged in administering the Revenue laws, but rather we are a group of 52,500 people, plus all the people of America who make tax returns and who take part in the handling of disputes with us on behalf of taxpayers in order to get the liabilities of taxpayers honestly and fairly settled.

That is why I have said on numerous occasions that no Commissioner of Internal Revenue, and no Treasury Department having the responsibility for the Commissioner's activities, could ever for one minute agree to any limitation upon the right of taxpayers to choose qualified people, whatever their profession, to help them with the settlement of their disputes with their government over their tax returns.

Now I realize, of course, that there may be some who will call that a prejudiced attitude. If so, they'll just have to make the most of it, because it simply states the situation as I honestly see it from the position of the official who has to make the Revenue system work or else.

I am interested in the success of the Revenue laws of this country, because I think that the success of those laws is a key to the success of our economy and that that in turn is a key to the continuity of the success of the kind of government that you and I think is best for free people. And I do not believe that any public official could for one minute limit and proscribe the right of taxpayers to seek assistance in discharging this obligation to compute and pay in their respective shares of the cost of government without unleashing upon the Congress, and upon his own head, a storm of protest from the people that would soon bring reversing action.

Therefore, I have never been too disturbed about the activities of those who would institute such limitation, and I think that sound reason will prevail in due time and the whole matter will blow over and we will be moving on again shoulder to shoulder in the administration of this high responsibility—the Revenue people, with their primary responsibility, supplemented by the great army of lawyers and accountants and others who assist in the preparation of tax returns, and the other phases of the taxpayers' obligation to make his contribution to the welfare of the nation. I believe that harmony will come and in the not too distant future. We will get these unpleasant disturbances behind us.

In the meantime, of course, I find myself in a very unhappy position, though one that I suppose I can stand. I have been attacked by critics other than those who don't like the fact that I am an accountant. I have even made the pages of the *Daily Worker*, which, I am assured by others who have weathered the fury of the commies and their fellow travelers, is the best recommendation that I could hope for.

Now, I should like to say just a few words, if I may, about the question of evasion, because you have a responsibility here, my friends, that is equal to mine. Just remember that it has been the evasion of taxes that has destroyed the tax systems of nation after nation, and ultimately destroyed the economies of those nations and upset their political structures.

Let me read you some examples to show how public opinion changes on this question of evasion. Here is a rather disturbing statement. It is a letter that went to the President. The gentleman wrote the President at some length, complaining that the Revenue agents were running wild in his area, harassing taxpayers, making them produce records, as he put it, four, six, eight, and ten years old, and that everybody in that area was just about ready to revolt. Well, that disturbed me, because that was just exactly what the situation was in many places when we took over, and when anybody tells me that that is happening again, I get concerned about it. So I began to look around.

In the meantime, I read his letter again, and listen to this. He said, "We all know that since your election and with the return of dignity and fair dealing to the office of President a change has been brought about in the attitude of people toward the Government." Now get that, "the attitude of the people toward the Government." Who is the Government but the people, if you please? But anyhow, that is the way the gentleman put it. To continue, "We all know that many of us skirted pretty close to the law in past administrations, because it seemed to be in keeping with the times."

Well, in my simple and naive way, I must confess that that was the first time that I ever knew that people took their morals, principles, and standards from corrupt politicians.

You might be interested to know that that gentleman was on the verge of becoming an involuntary guest of the United States Government. He wrote the President on the theory, I suppose, that "the best defense is a good offense." Needless to say, he didn't get away with it.

As you know, I am frequently criticized and even abused because I have taken a firm attitude toward the question of evasion. I have held that an evader is, in my book, no better when he comes from the so-called upper strata of society, a man not previously in trouble, one never caught at wrong-doing before, than a racketeer with a long criminal record; and I have insisted that, when people deliberately try to cheat the Government and their fellow taxpayers, then they ought to be put in jail.

I have been accused by some of my friends of the bar of making criminals of these people. It has never been quite clear to me how I could make a criminal of any man who has already made a criminal of himself.

Then I find a rather remarkable statement among the writings of one of my distinguished critics in which he says of the practitioners' relationship to the Revenue Service, "Advocacy requires a certain capacity for insincerity." Drink in those seven words, my friends, and consider, if you will, what would happen to the administration of the Revenue laws of this country if those enrolled to practice before the Treasury Department decided to operate upon the basis that "advocacy requires a certain capacity for insincerity."

When that day comes, I am quite certain that you will find enough Revenue agents to audit everybody and enough determination on the part of the Revenue Service to pay no attention to any person enrolled to practice before the Treasury Department—if, indeed, there are any there to practice—because when you get to that point, then you are asking for autocratic and dictatorial government, and I did not go to Washington to aid in the institution of that kind of government in this country.

Now listen to this one. This is a report on a member of a profession and his wife who cheated you and your fellow citizens out of $81,495 of taxes in four years and in the midst of his trial changed their plea from not guilty to *nolo contendere*, and then were sentenced to eight months and ten months, respectively. I don't know why such leniency to such people. Just listen. This man and his wife operated a hospital as a convalescent home to cover up illegal performance of abortions. Eight months for the man and ten months for his wife! And yet I am accused of making criminals out of people of that kind. Goodness knows I didn't make a criminal out of either of them. I don't know what happened to justice in that case.

Here is another. This man, over a period of three years, cheated us out of $52,000. In the course of the examination of his returns it was found that he had kept inadequate books and records. Therefore it was necessary to make vigorous and extensive examinations of the records of numerous railroad companies, insurance companies, and product service companies involved in damage suits in which this man appeared as attorney. When first interviewed, he said he didn't have any books. We later found some, and we found that even those were faked. In other words, we were dealing with a man of bad character, a man who had no business associating with, or having the benefit of the friendship and favor of, decent people.

What happened? He got 90 days, and wasn't even fined a dollar. Did I make a criminal out of him? What happened to justice there?

Well, finally, my friends, and on this theme of your being a part of an extension of the Revenue Service administration, let me read you what the beloved Justice Jackson, who recently left us, had to say about our system and how important a part it can be shown that you play in this system, you and all your fellow practitioners.

He said, "that the United States has a system of taxation by confession"—that is an interesting way of putting it, and very apt—"where the people, so numerous and so scattered and individualistic, annually are assessed with a tax liability often in highly burdensome amounts, is a reassuring sign of the stability and the vitality of our system of self-government. What surprised me," he said, "in trying to help to administer these laws,"—you remember he was chief counsel of the Revenue Service at one time—"was not to discover examples of fraud or self-serving mistakes in reporting"—I like that; maybe we ought to publish that one, so we don't speak of it so harshly again—"but to discover that such derelictions were so few." And he said then, which I will not discuss this morning, but which I should like to mention, because it is a part of this statement, "It would be a sad thing for the revenues if the good will of the people toward their taxing system were frittered away in efforts to accomplish by taxation moral reforms that cannot be accomplished by direct legislation."

That is kindred to the problem that we have of having to get rid of so much "legislation by regulation." (Incidentally, I understand there is at least one group who wants to ascertain, even before we release our regulations and the Treasury Department has approved them, whether or not we are writing them in the spirit of the new law.)

Then I should like to read to you what was said in a book called *Taxation in the United States*. Interestingly enough, this statement emanated from an old study of taxation in my own state, where I have always thought we had a pretty good tax system. When I read this, it came to me as a surprise, but it is very apropos of the problem dealt with.

"A large segment of the taxpaying public had become acutely tax-conscious, more so than it had ever been, and a substantial minority seemed more determined than ever to avoid taxes.

"This determination on the part of taxpayers had reached shocking proportions and the point at times of bitter defiance and recrimination. Foreign editors spoke of the problem of the United States to 'make its laws proof gainst evasion.' Tax avoidance had developed into a fine art."

The gentlemen who are going to follow me here as experts on this panel are going to talk to you about the problems of framing this new law, about the business of drafting regulations, and so forth under the law, but there is one observation that I would like to make concerning one aspect of the matter.

The other day I was asked by a group of newspaper people if our tax forms this year were going to be more simple than they were last year. Actually, the 1040-A is going to be quite simple; it is going to be a punch card about the size of a check. Form 1040 is going to be a little more complicated in the sense that we have had to take the tax chart off the return itself and move it over to the instruction booklet in order to make way for formulas, statements, and schedules necessary to enable people to calculate some of the new credit allowances by the new laws. But, you see, that is because of things done to *benefit* the taxpayer. It has been my observation, unfortunately, that whenever you set out to plug loopholes achieve more equity, or simplify, you frequently make the end-product more complicated, and I don't know any way to avoid doing so.

You have here this morning a man who worked on the developments of our new law. I personally think that he made one of the greatest contributions to government service of any man of my knowledge, past or present. I know they tried to make it simple, and I think they did simplify the law a great deal, but I am sure he would be the last to claim that it is possible to avoid complications when you throw in new provisions to bring new benefits, or when you try to close this loophole or that. It just seems unavoidable, no matter how hard you work at it. And, of course, there is nothing that any of these gentlemen can do to minimize the problem of evasion.

We believe that 97 to 98 percent of the people of this country try to disclose their true income and pay their taxes: but, of course, we must recognize one thing: that a great deal of petty larceny is probably going on. Almost every one seems to enjoy trying it to some extent. But it can be carried too far, as in my own case when I was a kid, I hopped the steps of an ice wagon to snitch a piece of ice when there was plenty in the ice box at home, fell off in the path of a street car, and nearly lost a leg.

However, we are not worried too much about petty larceny. It is the greater kind that worries me—grand larceny, the sort that destroys the fiber of the taxpayers' character. And why do we worry? I'll tell you. Because we know that when compliance goes out the window, as it has elsewhere in the world, revenue systems fail and national economies falter and collapse.

Seeing and knowing this, we of the Revenue Service realize that we are not just tax collectors and you are not just tax practitioners. You and we are engaged, in the final analysis, in making the Revenue system of our country work, in maintaining the high level of voluntary compliance that enables us to accomplish the great things that we do for ourselves within our country, and to assume those obligations of assistance abroad that enable us to keep the light of freedom burning brightly in this uneasy world.

That, my friends, is the challenge, not only to us of the Internal Revenue Service, but to you as tax practitioners, and to you and all your fellow citizens as taxpayers of the last great stronghold of freedom as you and I understand it. And so, with a challenge of that kind, we—all of us, you and you and you, and all of the people of the country—must realize that we have to meet it, because there won't be any Marshall Plan to save us if our revenue system fails and our economy collapses.

Thus, there rests upon you as tax practitioners, and upon us of the Internal Revenue Service as administrators of the tax laws, a solemn obligation to discharge our respective and very closely related duties in a manner that will raise even the present high level of voluntary compliance, build an effective roadblock against social acceptance of evasion and those who make themselves guilty of it, and make the great experiment in liberty that our forefathers embarked upon in the closing days of 1787 secure against the erosion of time and circumstance and impregnable to the mightiest attacks of those who would assume the political domination of the world and put all people under their feet.

PROPOSED REGULATIONS UNDER 1954 INTERNAL REVENUE CODE[†]
Letter by T. Coleman Andrews
and Response by Allan H. W. Higgins

Mr. Thomas N. Tarleau
Chairman, Section of Taxation
American Bar Association
15 Broad Street
New York, N. Y.

Dear Mr. Tarleau:

AS you know, the enactment of the Internal Revenue Code of 1954 requires the revision of all existing tax regulations. Under our present plans, as soon as the regulations are developed under the various portions of the income tax law, we will issue them as separate Treasury decisions. These Treasury decisions will first be issued in tentative form under the usual notice of rule making procedure, with 30 days allowed for public comments.

The revision of existing regulations is an opportunity, through the notice of rule making procedure, to secure full public consideration of the tax regulations by all members of the public, particularly by the professional groups who as tax practitioners can furnish objective and practical views on the proposed regulations.

I believe the Section of Taxation of the American Bar Association could render a valuable public service if it would, for each of the proposed Treasury decisions, designate one of its members who, during the 30-day period for public comment, would objectively review the proposed regulations and would furnish us his comments. If this can be arranged, we would furnish to the member whom you designate copies of the proposed regulations as soon as they are published in the Federal Register. If possible, we would try to give him some advance notice as to when to expect the document. We would, of course, also consider any comments

---

[†]Mr. Andrews' letter was written as Commissioner of the Internal Revenue Service, and Mr. Higgins' response was written as Chairman of the Section of Taxation of the American Bar Association; Mr. Tarleau was Mr. Higgins' predecessor as Chairman. Reprinted with permission from the American Bar Association, *Section of Taxation Bulletin*, October 1954, pp. 24-36.

on the subject to be covered by the proposed Treasury decision which he might care to send us before we have completed a draft of the proposed regulations for publication in tentative form.

If this arrangement meets with your approval, please furnish us the names and addresses of the members assigned to the various subjects in the attached list.

Very truly yours,
T. COLEMAN ANDREWS,
Commissioner.
August 10, 1954

TENTATIVE LIST

Separate Treasury Decisions to be Issued in Developing Regulations Under the Various Portions of the Income Tax Law

1. Subchapter A and section 116 (Rates and Credits).
2. Subchapter B, Parts I and IV (Definitions and Standard Deduction).
3. Subchapter B, Part II (except 72) (Specific Items).
4. Subchapter B, Sections 72, 101, 1021, 1035 (Annuities and Life Ins.).
5. Subchapter B, Sections 108 and 1017 (Discharge of Indebtedness).
6. Subchapter B, Part III (except 101, 104, 105, 106, 108, 116, 117) (Exclusions from Gross Income).
7. Subchapter B, Section 104, 105, 106 (Compensation for Injuries and Sickness, etc.).
8. Subchapter B, Section 117 (Scholarships and Fellowships).
9. Subchapter B, Part V (Personal Exemption).
10. Subchapter B, Sections 167, 1020 (Depreciation).
11. Subchapter B, Section 172 (Net Operating Loss Deduction).
12. Subchapter B, Section 174 (Research and Experimental).
13. Subchapter B, Section 175 (Soil and Water Conservation).
14. Subchapter B, Sections 163, 164, 165, 166 (Interest, Taxes, Losses, Bad Debts).
15. Subchapter B, Sections 161, 162, 168, 169, 170, 171, 173 (Miscellaneous Itemized Deductions).
16. Subchapter B, Part VII (except 214) (Add'l. Itemized Deductions, Medical Expenses, Etc.).
17. Subchapter B, Section 214 (Child Care).
18. Subchapter B, Part VIII (Special Deductions).
19. Subchapter B, Section 264 (Items not Deductible—Ins. Contracts).
20. Subchapter B, Section 267 (Same—Related Taxpayers' Losses).

21. Subchapter B, Part IX (except 264, 267, 272, and 274) (Items not Deductible).
22. Subchapter C (except Part V) (Corporations Dists. and Adjustments).
23. Subchapter C, Part V (Carryovers).
24. Subchapter D, Part I (Pension Trusts, Etc.).
25. Subchapter D, Part II (Stock Options).
26. Subchapter E, Part I (Accounting Periods).
27. Subchapter E, Parts II and III (except sections 453, 471) (Accounting Methods and Adjustments).
28. Subchapter E, Section 453 (Installment Method).
29. Subchapter E, Sections 471 and 472 (Inventories).
30. Subchapter F (Exempt Organizations).
31. Subchapter G (Corporations Used to Avoid Income Tax on Shareholders).
32. Subchapter H (Banking Institutions).
33. Subchapter I, Parts I and II (Natural Resources—Deductions).
34. Subchapter I, Part III and section 272 (Natural Resources—Exclusions from Gross Income; Sales and Exchanges).
35. Subchapter J, Parts I A, B, C, D and section 683 (Taxation of Estates and Trusts).
36. Subchapter J, Part I, subparts E, F, and section 683 (Clifford Rules, Misc.).
37. Subchapter J, Part II (Income in Payment of Decedents).
38. Subchapter K (Partnerships).
39. Subchapter L (Insurance Comps.).
40. Subchapter M (Regulated Investment Companies).
41. Subchapter N, Parts I and II (Foreign Ins.—Source of Inc., Nonresident Aliens and Foreign Corps.).
42. Subchapter N, Part III, Subpart A (Foreign Tax Credit).
43. Subchapter N, Part III, Subparts B, C, D, E (Misc. Provisions).
44. Subchapter O, Parts IV-VII (Sale or Exchange—Misc. SEC, FCC, Wash Sales, Etc.).
45. Subchapter O, Part III (except 1035) (Common Nontaxable Exchanges).
46. Subchapter O, Parts I and II (except 1017, 1020, 1021) (Recognition and Basis Rules).
47. Subchapter P, Parts I-III (Capital Gains and Losses).
48. Subchapter P, Part IV (except 1233) (Special Rules—Capital Gains).
49. Subchapter P, Section 1233 (Short Sales).
50. Subchapter Q, Part I (Readjustment of Tax Rets. Year—36 month comp.).
51. Subchapter Q, Part II (Mitigation of S L).
52. Subchapter Q, Part III (Involuntary Liquidation Life).
53. Subchapter Q, Parts IV-VI (War Loss Recoveries).
54. Subchapter R (Election as to Taxable Status).

55. Chapter 2 (Self-Employment Income).
56. Chapter 3 (Withholding on Aliens and Tax Free Covenant Bonds).
57. Chapter 4 (Recovery of Excessive Profits—Government Contracts).
58. Chapter 5 (Transfers to Avoid Income Tax).
59. Chapter 6 (Consolidated Returns).
60. Regulations on Subtitle F—Procedure and Administration (Chs. 61-80).

Hon. T. Coleman Andrews
Commissioner
Internal Revenue Service
Washington, D. C.

Dear Commissioner Andrews:

Referring to your letter of August 10, 1954, the members of the Section of Taxation are pleased to cooperate with the Internal Revenue Service with respect to Regulations under the new Internal Revenue Code.

In accordance with the understanding between you and Thomas N. Tarleau, my predecessor, as Chairman of the Section of Taxation of the American Bar Association, I have advised the Chairmen of various Committees of the Section as follows:

> As the new regulations are issued under H. R. 8300 any regulations coming within the scope of the activities of your committee will be promptly referred to you and it will be necessary for you to take immediate action so that a report can be made to the Internal Revenue Service within the thirty day protest period provided for with respect to regulations appearing in the Federal Register.

In some cases this responsibility has been redelegated among Subcommittee Chairmen of the respective Committees. The list of proposed Treasury Decisions enclosed with you letter of August 10, 1954, has been apportioned as set forth in the schedule enclosed, marked "Schedule A."

I have also appointed the following named persons as members of a Policy and Coordinating Committee on Regulations under the Internal Revenue Code of 1954, (for convenience, referred to as the Policy and Coordinating Committee)

Lee I. Park, Chairman, 1000 Shoreham Building, Washington 5, D. C.
Eugene F. Bogan, Vice-Chairman, 1010 Vermont Avenue,
      Washington, D. C.

Walter A. Slowinski, Secretary, Union Trust Bldg.,
Washington, D. C.
Scott P. Crampton, 815-15th Street, N.W., Washington, D. C.
Lincoln Arnold, World Center Building, Washington, D. C.
Seymour Mintz, Colorado Building, Washington, D. C.
F. Cleveland Hedrick, Jr., 1001 Connecticut Avenue, N.W.,
Washington, D. C.

It will be appreciated if, as the proposed Treasury Decisions are issued, you can arrange to have sent to each person named in Schedule A, two copies of the proposed Treasury Decision or Decisions therein assigned to him.

Your attention is invited to footnotes (a) and (b) on Schedule A, which state that the initial responsibility in respect of certain of the proposed T.D.'s has been allocated among Chairmen of Subcommittees of two of the Committees of the Section, namely, the Committee on Federal Income Taxes and the Committee on Special Types of Corporations. You are also requested, therefore, to send to the Chairman of each of those Committees, copies of the T.D.'s which are assigned to his Subcommittee Chairmen in Schedule A, i.e., Nos. 1-7, 9, 10, 12-21, 26, 27, 44-50, and 57 to Charles D. Post, 84 State Street, Boston 9, Massachusetts, and Nos. 32, 39, and 40 to Astin H. Peck, Jr., 830 Statler Center, 900 Wilshire Boulevard, Los Angeles 17, California.

Some of the other Committee Chairmen may also want to allocate their assigned work among Subcommittee Chairmen and, if they do, a supplemental list will be furnished to you.

It is also hoped that a copy of each Treasury Decision can also be sent to each member of the Policy and Coordinating Committee, (at the addresses shown above), and to Allan H. W. Higgins, 1406 M. Street, N.W., Washington, D. C.

The persons designated in Schedule A have been instructed by the Chairman of the Section to send their reports to the Policy and Coordinating Committee. As these are received they will be promptly reviewed by the Committee and all pertinent and constructive suggestions therein contained will be promptly brought to your attention.

In this connection, the initial responsibility for reviewing the reports from the field has been allocated among the members of the Policy and Coordinating Committee as set forth in the Schedule enclosed, marked "Schedule B."*

If you should wish to communicate with the Policy and Coordinating Committee with respect to any proposed Treasury Decision, you will probably find it more satisfactory to communicate directly with the member

---

*Editors' Note: Schedule B was not reprinted in the Section of Taxation Bulletin.

who has the reviewing responsibility as set forth in Schedule B, but you may also feel free to communicate with any member of the Policy and Coordinating Committee at any time on any matter within the scope of the Committee's activities.

You will appreciate, of course, that in submitting any report pursuant to this program, no Committee or member of the Tax Section can speak officially on behalf of the Section or the American Bar Association, as obviously time will not permit compliance with the procedures required by the rules for such official action. It is hoped, however, that the suggestions may, nevertheless, be of help to the Internal Revenue Service in writing the Regulations.

In this connection, I also wish to advise you that at the Annual Meeting of the Association in Chicago in August, Mr. Tarleau urged all members of the Section to send in their views and comments on the proposed Treasury Decisions. It follows, of course, that any such suggestions and comments by members of the Section which may be sent directly to you by members of the Section are also subject to the reservation that they should not be considered as the official views of either the Tax Section or the American Bar Association.

> Respectfully,
> ALLAN H. W. HIGGINS,
> Chairman, Section of Taxation.
> September 23, 1954

AMERICAN BAR ASSOCIATION
SECTION OF TAXATION

Schedule of Members of Section Designated to Review and Make Initial Reports on Proposed Treasury Decisions on Regulations Under the New Code

Numbers in Commis- sioner's List	Title, Subchapter, Part or Section	Section Member Responsible for Report
1. (a)	Subchapter A and section 116 (Rates and Credits)	Walter J. Blum, University of Chicago Law School, Chicago, Illinois
2. (a)	Subchapter B, Parts I and IV (Definitions and Standard Deduction)	Arch M. Cantrall, 701 Goff Bldg., Clarksburg, West Virginia
3. (a)	Subchapter B, Part II (except 72) (Specific Items)	Frank L. Mechem, Central Building, Seattle, Washington
4. (a)	Subchapter B, Section 72, 101, 1021, 1035 (Annuities and Life Insurance)	Joseph B. Brennan, First National Bank Bldg., Atlanta, Georgia
5. (a)	Subchapter B, Sections 108 and 1017 (Discharge of Indebtedness)	Lester M. Ponder, 1313 Merchants Bank Bldg., Indianapolis, Indiana
6. (a)	Subchapter B, Part III (Except 101, 104, 105, 106, 108, 116, 117) (Exclusions from Gross Income)	Alan L. Gormick, 3000 Schaefer Road, Dearborn, Michigan
7. (a)	Subchapter B, Sections 104, 105, 106 (Compensation for Injuries and Sickness, etc.)	Alan L. Gormick, 3000 Schaefer Road, Dearborn, Michigan
8.	Subchapter B, Section 117 (Scholarships and Fellowships)	Harry K. Mansfield, 50 Federal Street, Boston, Massachusetts
9. (a)	Subchapter B, Part V (Personal Exemption)	Martin H. Webster, 215 West 7th Street, Los Angeles, California
10. (a)	Subchapter B, Sections 167, 1020 (Depreciation)	Lester M. Ponder, 1313 Merchants Bank Bldg., Indianapolis, Indiana
11.	Subchapter B, Section 172 (Net Operating Loss Deduction)	William L. Kumler, 523 West 6th Street, Los Angeles, California
12. (a)	Subchapter B, Section 174 (Research and Experimental Expenditures)	Sam H. Field, 2303 Magnolia Building, Dallas, Texas
13. (a)	Subchapter B, Section 175 (Soil and Water Conservation Expenditures)	Harlan T. Moen, 202½ West Main Street, Cherokee, Iowa
14. (a)	Subchapter B, Sections 163, 164, 165, 166 (Interest, Taxes, Losses, Bad Debts)	Barring Coughlin, National City Bank Bldg., Cleveland, Ohio
15. (a)	Subchapter B, Sections 161, 162, 168, 169, 170, 171, 173 (Miscellaneous Itemized Deductions)	Darrell D. Wiles, 408 Olive Street, St. Louis, Missouri

Numbers in Commissioner's List	Title, Subchapter, Part or Section	Section Member Responsible for Report
16. (a)	Subchapter B, Part VII (except 214) (Additional Itemized Deductions, Medical Expenses, etc.)	Martin H. Webster, 215 West 7th Street, Los Angeles, California
17. (a)	Subchapter B, Section 214 (Child Care)	Martin H. Webster, 215 West 7th Street, Los Angeles, California
18. (a)	Subchapter B, Part VIII (Special Deductions)	Henry C. Smith, 15 Broad St., New York, N. Y.
19. (a)	Subchapter B, Section 264 (Items not Deductible—Insurance Contracts)	Joseph B. Brennan, First National Bank Bldg, Atlanta, Georgia
20.(a)	Subchapter B, Section 267 (Items not Deductible—Related Taxpayers' Losses)	Roger L. Shidler, 410 American Bldg., Seattle, Washington
21. (a)	Subchapter B, Part IX (except 264, 267, 272) (Items not Deductible)	R. E. H. Julien, Mills Tower, 220 Bush Street, San Francisco, California
22.	Subchapter C, (except Part V) (Corporate Distributions and Adjustments)	William L. Kumler, 523 West 6th Street, Los Angeles, California
23.	Subchapter C, Part V (Carry-overs)	William L. Kumler, 523 West 6th Street, Los Angeles, California
24.	Subchapter D, Part I (Pension Trusts, etc.)	Frederick A. Ballard, 912 American Security Bldg., Washington 5, D. C.
25.	Subchapter D, Part II (Stock Options)	William L. Kumler, 523 West 6th Street, Los Angeles, California
26. (a)	Subchapter E, Part I (Accounting Periods)	Sam H. Field, 2303 Magnolia Building, Dallas, Texas
27. (a)	Subchapter E, Parts II and III (except sections 453, 471, and 472) (Accounting Methods and Adjustments)	Sam H. Field, 2303 Magnolia Building, Dallas, Texas
28.	Subchapter E, Section 453 (Installment Method)	James K. Polk, 40 Wall St., New York, N. Y.
29.	Subchapter E, Sections 471 and 472 (Inventories)	James K. Polk, 40 Wall St., New York, N. Y.
30.	Subchapter F (Exempt Organizations)	Harry K. Mansfield, 50 Federal Street, Boston, Massachusetts
31.	Subchapter G (Corporations Used to Avoid Income Tax on Shareholders)	William L. Kumler, 523 West 6th Street, Los Angeles, California
32. (b)	Subchapter H (Banking Institutions)	Clair Furlong, 231 South LaSalle Street, Chicago, Illinois
33.	Subchapter I, Parts I and II (Natural Resources—Deductions)	Marvin K. Collie, Niels-Esperson Bldg., Houston, Texas
34.	Subchapter I, Parts III and Section 272 (Natural Resources—Exclusions from Gross Income: Sales and Exchanges)	Marvin K., Collie, Niels-Esperson Bldg., Houston, Texas

Numbers in Commissioner's List	Title, Subchapter, Part or Section	Section Member Responsible for Report
35.	Subchapter J, Parts 1A, B, C, D and Section 683 (Taxation of Estates and Trusts)	William E. Murray, 1 Wall Street, New York, New York
36.	Subchapter J, Part I, Subparts E, F, and Section 683 (Clifford Rules, Misc.)	William E. Murray, 1 Wall Street, New York, New York
37.	Subchapter J, Part II (Income in Respect of Decedents)	William E. Murray, 1 Wall Street, New York, New York
38.	Subchapter K (Partnerships)	Arthur B. Willis, 900 Wilshire Blvd., Los Angeles, California
39. (b)	Subchapter L (Insurance Companies)	I. Jerome O'Connor, 200 Berkeley Street, Boston 17, Massachusetts
40. (b)	Subchapter M (Regulated Investment Companies)	Earl W. Carr, 82 Devonshire Street, Boston 9, Massachusetts
41.	Subchapter N, Parts I and II (Foreign Income—Source of Income, Nonresident Aliens and Foreign Corporations)	Wilson C. Piper, 50 Federal Street, Boston, Massachusetts
42.	Subchapter N, Part III, Subpart A (Foreign Tax Credit)	Wilson C. Piper, 50 Federal Street, Boston, Massachusetts
43.	Subchapter N, Part III, Subparts B, C, D, E (Miscellaneous Provisions)	Wilson C. Piper, 50 Federal Street, Boston, Massachusetts
44. (a)	Subchapter O, Parts IV-VII (Sale or Exchange—Miscl. SEC, FCC, Wash Sales, etc.)	Walter J. Blum, University of Chicago Law School, Chicago, Illinois
45. (a)	Subchapter O, Part III (except 1035) (Common Nontaxable Exchanges)	Walter J. Blum, University of Chicago Law School, Chicago, Illinois
46. (a)	Subchapter O, Parts I and II (except 1017, 1020, 1021) (Recognition and Basis Rules)	Walter J. Blum, University of Chicago Law School, Chicago, Illinois
47. (a)	Subchapter P, Parts I-III (Capital Gains and Losses)	Walter J. Blum, University of Chicago Law School, Chicago, Illinois
48. (a)	Subchapter P, Part IV (except 1233) (Special Rules—Capital Gains)	Walter J. Blum, University of Chicago Law School, Chicago, Illinois
49. (a)	Subchapter P, Section 1233 (Short Sales)	Walter J. Blum, University of Chicago Law School, Chicago, Illinois
50. (a)	Subchapter Q, Part I (Readjustment of Tax Between Years)	Henry C. Smith, 15 Broad Street, New York, New York
51.	Subchapter Q, Part II (Mitigation of Statute of Limitations)	Valentine Brookes, 1720 Mills Tower, San Francisco, California
52.	Subchapter Q, Part III (Involuntary Liquidation—Life)	James K. Polk, 40 Wall Street, New York, New York
53.	Subchapter Q, Parts IV-VI (War Loss Recoveries)	Wilson C. Piper, 50 Federal Street, Boston, Massachusetts

Numbers in Commissioner's List	Title, Subchapter, Part or Section	Section Member Responsible for Report
54.	Subchapter R, (Election as to Taxable Status)	Arthur B. Willis, 900 Wilshire Blvd., Los Angeles, California
55.	Chapter 2 (Self-Employment Income)	F. Cleveland Hedrick, Jr., 1001 Connecticut Ave., Washington 6, D. C.
56.	Chapter 3 (Withholding on Aliens and Tax-Free Covenant Bonds)	Wilson C. Piper, 50 Federal Street, Boston, Massachusetts
57. (a)	Chapter 4 (Recovery of Excessive Profits—Government Contracts)	Numa L. Smith, 1001 Connecticut Ave., N.W., Washington 6, D. C.
58.	Chapter 5 (Transfers to Avoid Income Tax)	Wilson C. Piper, 50 Federal Street, Boston, Massachusetts
59.	Chapter 6 (Consolidated Returns)	C. Rudolf Peterson, 1200 18th Street, N.W., Washington 6, D. C.
60.	Subtitle F, Procedure and Administration	Joseph K. Moyer, 1343 H Street, N.W., Washington 5, D. C.

(a) These come under the Committee on Federal Income Taxes, of which Charles D. Post, (84 State Street, Boston 9, Mass.) is Chairman.

(b) These come under the Committee on Special Types of Corporations, of which Austin H. Peck, Jr., (830 Statler Center, 900 Wilshire Blvd., Los Angeles 17, California) is Chairman.

THE INTERNAL REVENUE CODE
OF 1954[†]

by

T. Coleman Andrews

WITH the enactment of the Internal Revenue Code of 1954, the Internal Revenue Service was confronted with an unprecedented task. This legislation, the most sweeping revision of the Federal tax laws in our Nation's history, makes it necessary to rewrite virtually all of our regulations and revise more that 200 forms used by taxpayers.

When the new Code was signed by the President, we had 40 technicians engaged full time in drafting regulations, and a larger number devoting part of their time to this jobs. In addition, some 20 attorneys in the office of the Chief Counsel were similarly employed.

In using the terms "full time" and "part time" I mean a great deal more in each case, for actually these people are working long past the regular eight-hour business day. For example, one week after the bill was signed, they had completed the first draft of regulations on Subchapter C, dealing with corporate distributions and adjustments and comprising more than 250 pages of manuscript.

This was made possible only because the people working in this particular field had begun the drafting of regulations when the bill was reported out by the Ways and Means Committee. As changes were made by the Finance Committee and the Conference Committee, the regulations were adapted to conform. Similar procedures were followed with respect to other portions of the Code.

An even dozen technical specialists have been working full time in the revision of forms for taxpayers, assisted by an equal number of people who spent part of their time assisting in this effort.

While these activities are taking place in the technical area, our operations people are doing another job that is equally vital. This involves preparation of instructions and devising procedures for our field offices. Many of the new Code provisions required immediate changes in audit and collection procedures. In the more important of these, instructions were issued almost simultaneously with the enactment of the bill. Other procedural changes and amendments to manuals were made rapidly, since

---

[†]Reprinted with permission from *The Tax Executive*, October 1954, pp. x-xi. Copyright © 1954 by the Tax Executives Institute.

the operating staff at the National Office followed development of the Code in the same manner as the technical group.

We will have many problems in administering the new Code. It introduces new concepts and new language which, of course, have not been subject to interpretation by the courts or by the Revenue Service. A great body of precedent rulings has been rendered obsolete, and our rulings division must pioneer in many areas. When the time comes to examine returns filed under new provisions of law contained in the 1954 Code, the audit divisions in the field will be in a similar position.

In outlining the problems that are involved in the transition from the old Code to the new, it is not my intention to suggest that we do not welcome this overdue rewriting of the revenue laws. We have been able, though the office of the Secretary of the Treasury, to bring before the Congress many of our administrative problems, and a significant number of them have been resolved by the changes effected in the 1954 Code.

Substantive changes in the law which remove inequities, clarify issues which have been subjects of dispute and litigation for years, and generally modernize a structure which was beginning to creak with age, will require that we re-orient out thinking in many respects.

All of this is by way of saying that the new Code presents a challenge to the Revenue Service; a challenge to implement and administer its provisions in accordance with the purpose and intent of the Congress which framed it. The efficiency and dispatch with which our people have accomplished the preliminary phases of the change-over gives me confidence we will meet that challenge, and when this has been done the Revenue Service will have marked up one if the finest achievements of its entire history.

SIGNIFICANCE OF THE NEW MASTER
OF LAW AND TAXATION DEGREE[†]

by

T. Coleman Andrews

MR. RECTOR, MR. PRESIDENT, MY LORD, MR. CHIEF JUSTICE, AND DISTINGUISHED MEMBERS OF THE BAR, OF THE FEDERAL COURTS, AND OF THE COMMONWEALTH OF VIRGINIA, AND FRIENDS OF WILLIAM AND MARY.

AS the official whom the President has been pleased to honor with the high responsibility of seeing to it that the Nation's internal revenue laws are administered with integrity, fairness and efficiency, I am greatly impressed and encouraged by the progressive policy which so obviously prompted the creation of a Chair of Taxation here at the College of William and Mary.

Thus William and Mary adds another chapter of high imagination and constructive purpose to its already illustrious record of acceptance of the academician's share of the total responsibility for the success of this nation's dedicated adventure into freedom, in which so many of William and Mary's sons have so brilliantly distinguished themselves.

And so this 25th day of September, 1954, will, I am sure, become a red-letter day in this famed institution's already long and dedicated history and a no less significant day in the annals of higher education.

I am encouraged by this event because I believe that it is a step in the direction of continually re-examining, in its broadest context, the place of taxation in our society—an inquiry the necessity for which I am sure few will dispute.

It is significant that the Chair of Taxation is to be an extension of the College's curricula, not a vehicle for a specialized and limited course. The object will be to turn out educated men and women, not just mechanics—men and women not only with knowledge of the existing tax laws but also with that degree of understanding of the whole problem of how best to finance the cost of government that assures intelligent evolution of method.

[†]An address at the Ceremonies in Celebration of the Beginning of the John Marshall Bicentennial Year and the 175th Anniversary of the First Chair of Law in the United States and the Creation of a Chair of Taxation at the College of William and Mary, September 25, 1954. Reprinted with permission from *Marshall, Wythe, Blackstone Commemoration Ceremonies* (Williamsburg, VA: College of William and Mary, 1954), pp. 31-37. Portions reprinted under the title, "Needed: Higher (Tax) Education," in *Tax Outlook*, December 1954, pp. 2-5.

This broad approach will have a heartening appeal to all who have observed the deplorable abbreviation of social, economic, and political knowledge and understanding that has resulted from trying to meet rapid technological growth with extreme academic specialization.

We have seen trade schools flourish with as short as ninety-day cram courses in a wide range of technical subjects, including the highly-complex and extremely diverse subject of taxation. Corner drug stores carry many pocket editions of college courses which, according to the courses' promoters, can be learned in ten days. I have to say that in my experience as Commissioner of Internal Revenue, I all too often have ended up with a roomful of experts, in addition to the staff member originally called for a discussion, because the matter discussed eventually involved more than one or two sections of the Revenue Code.

Perhaps this kind of highly specialized teaching can afford technical training; but it is *not* education. It is the development of technical skills within narrow horizons. Admittedly, this is all right so far as it goes, and perhaps it constitutes a worthwhile, necessary, and essential service; but seldom does it relate the subject under study to the whole of the co-existing social, economic and political order. Also, it seldom, if ever, makes any lasting contribution to the course of history.

The present management of the Internal Revenue Service holds that, since the Service deals with every aspect of the Nation's economy, those charged with applying the revenue laws, and those charged with reviewing the taxpayers' applications of these laws, must be a great deal more than mere specialists if we are to have any hope of lifting the Service to the high level of functional effectiveness that the people who pay the bill have a right to expect.

We must have men with broad understanding of the tax implications of business policies, practices, and methods. This requires a broader-based background of education than has heretofore been required.

We also must have broad-gauged executives, men with imagination and initiative of the highest order.

Above all, we must have men of high character, whose conduct as men and officials unmistakably stamps them as being well educated in morals and ethics as well as in the material aspects of their jobs.

I am happy to say that with the approval of the Congress we have launched a training program designed to help us achieve these objectives. This program will he carried out at our Advanced Training Center which we recently established at the University of Michigan.

The action being taken today by the College of William and Mary goes a step further by basing its technical study of taxes on the broader foundations of jurisprudence and the liberal arts. This insures a needed philosophical approach to canons, theories, and concepts of taxation in relation to our historic social, economic, and political needs.

This is the type of educational service that is meaningful policy-wise, and it is in line with the high traditions of this College. It is the type on which civilization depends for its progress.

However, while the education of tax officials is essential, it is, after all, only a part of the job. There are those who legislate, those who judicially interpret, those who engage in tax practice; and most important, there are the citizens by whose will taxes are levied and by whose attitudes the effectiveness of tax administration is eventually determined.

Attitudes have varied greatly throughout history. Professor Seligman has attempted to trace their evolution by pointing out six identifiable stages. First, a tax was looked upon as a voluntary gift to the Government. Second, Governments were forced to implore humbly for support. Third, the idea prevailed that a favor was being granted the Government by giving it assistance. Fourth, it was believed that everyone should make a sacrifice to support the Government. Fifth, a national obligation existed to pay taxes. Sixth, there is the current concept that taxation has evolved into a matter of compulsion.

Because the governmental right of compulsion exists today, the Government is more secure in its ability to collect taxes and thus is in better position to protect the citizen who is conscientious about paying his taxes from those who get it in their heads to try to cheat.

But the Government cannot live by compulsion alone. Compulsion is our last-ditch defense, reserved only for that lower order of citizens—thus far relatively few in number, I'm happy to say—who consciously set out to evade their taxes and thus steal from their neighbors.

Our *first* defense lies in the conscious desire of our people to live by the laws of the land, which desire springs largely from the knowledge that in so doing they are abiding by the will of the majority as expressed in the acts of representative government.

Knowledge is the only sound basis for the acts of representative government. The more accurate the knowledge, the better the laws; and the better the laws, the more apt they are to induce voluntary compliance and abolish necessity for invocation of compulsive measures.

It has been said that legislators do not make laws, that they attempt to find them; which suggests the assumption that the more knowledge with which we are possessed, the more apt we are to find those laws which are meet and proper.

Taxation is not something that stands alone in our lives. It is related to our history, to jurisprudence, to the social sciences, and last, but very importantly in today's world, to our economy. If we are to move forward in our concepts of taxation, we must find, accurately evaluate, and take due account of, these basic and ever-changing relationships.

But to thus meet the challenge of taxation requires knowledge far beyond mere ability to prepare tax returns properly. The type of knowledge needed is the type that the College of William and Mary so soundly sets as the goal of its broad-based course of study in the tax field. It is the type of knowledge that will give us better tax laws, better administrators of these laws, and a high level of compliance.

As we move in that direction by the innovation here on this day proclaimed, and by like action which undoubtedly will be taken by other colleges and universities, we can look forward to the day when the inherent justice of our tax laws, the fairness, honesty, and efficiency of our tax administrators, and the well-understood place of taxation in the pattern and fabric of our Nation's existence, will make it socially unacceptable to wilfully evade one's tax obligation. When that day comes, we will have compulsion in tax administration only by the conscience of a freedom-loving people—never by force.

I cannot overstress the need to hasten that day, for I have been shocked during my experiences as Commissioner by the many instances in which deliberate tax evasion clearly had not prompted invocation of social sanctions against the evader, thus making it obvious that in those cases at least evasion had acquired social acceptance.

Acceptance by society of tax dodgers, schemers, connivers, cheats and other malefactors against the law is a sure road to national ruin. No government by law can survive ascendancy and social acceptance of the scofflaw.

Mr. Arthur Weigall, the Egyptian government's late distinguished Inspector General of Antiquities, reminded us that arousing in people a proper attitude of indignation toward the law breaker was a problem even in the days of ancient Greece. "The great lawgiver, Solon, of Athens," said Mr. Weigall, "used to say that to be law-abiding was the secret of prosperity." I would add to this that respect for the law also is one of the important prerequisites to the achievement of successful democratic government.

Continuing, Mr. Weigall said, "When Solon was asked how he proposed to make people respect the law, he replied: 'Those who are *not* injured by a crime must be trained to feel as much indignation as those who *are* injured.' Solon taught the Athenians to hold indignation meetings when crimes were committed, to work themselves up into a passion of anger about them, and to enforce honesty and public-spirited behavior."

Somehow in the short space of one generation we seem to have lost our opposition to sin, particularly sins against the fiscal laws of the Government. Not even the courts have been immune to this lapse, for there are judges who clearly find difficulty in regarding the tax evader as the crook and dangerous threat to our democratic institutions that he is.

The average person's indifference to the moral aspects of tax evasion is well known. I do not know of a single tax evader who has not continued to enjoy the status attributed to an honorable citizen, even after being convicted and serving a prison sentence for his transgression. Yet, these malefactors had, in effect, robbed every other taxpayer in the country, including their mothers, fathers, brothers, sisters, and other relatives and, of course, their neighbors and friends. There is something seriously wrong with a society that does not impose any social sanctions upon such wrongdoers.

We are taught as Christians to forgive the sinner when he truly repents. Seldom have I heard any words, or seen any attitude, of repentance on the part of tax evaders, either before or after they have paid the penalties imposed by law for their crimes. What is worse, we not only seem to have lost our aversion to sin, but there is some evidence that the tax cheat enjoys, in the eyes of some citizens at least, a degree of heroic stature.

It is a part of the duty of the Internal Revenue Service to protect the conscientious taxpayer from those of his fellows who attempt to cheat him by making him pay their taxes. It is difficult for any establishment of the Government to protect any citizen who looks at those who cheat him with admiration rather than indignation and scorn.

Those who are inclined to admire the tax evader, or accept him and his offenses against them without resentment or indignation, might well consider the plight of those Nations where skillfulness at evading taxes has become a mark of distinction and fully voluntary compliance a self-indictment for stupidity.

This country cannot afford any deterioration of its tax system's foundation of voluntary compliance, for it is not likely that any member of the world's family of Nations would be able, or even inclined, to come forward with a Marshall Plan to nurture us back to economic stability if our revenue system and our economy failed.

Nor can the *world* afford failure of our system, considering how much depends upon our prosperity and upon our high level of voluntary compliance with our tax laws in this day of the strongest assaults yet made upon the bastions of freedom by the forces of slavery.

Finally, with knowledge comes understanding, appreciation, and strengthened character. Knowledge, therefore, is our greatest bulwark against decline of national standards and morals. Through knowledge, social acceptability becomes synonymous with the laws by which we govern our conduct.

And so today I am happy to commend the Board of Visitors and the President of the College of William and Mary for having envisioned such a broad-gauged program for the increase of knowledge as is here being instituted. I am proud and happy to have had this part in the exercises commemorative of this trail-blazing event, an event which I am confident will take its place alongside the many other great contributions which this College has made to the course of American history.

Finally, while the Internal Revenue Service could ill afford to lose the man who is to be the first occupant of the Chair of Taxation, we of the Service whom he leaves behind to continue his life of high usefulness and unswerving devotion to public service, in this new and vitally important field are proud that the man needed to inaugurate this history-making undertaking could be found among those upon whom the responsibility for the administration of the Nation's revenue laws rests. When the authorities of William and Mary chose Doctor Thomas C. Atkeson for this assignment, they chose wisely indeed. They could not have done better.

WHY THE INCOME TAX IS BAD[†]

Interview with T. Coleman Andrews

T. Coleman Andrews, who resigned recently after 33 months as Commissioner of Internal Revenue, was interviewed in the conference room of *U.S. News & World Report.*

Q. Mr. Andrews, is it feasible to do away with the income tax? Are there other ways to get income into the Federal Treasury besides taxing the individual?

A. Of course there are. To say otherwise would be to say that we have lost the imagination and ingenuity that have made us leaders among the nations of the earth in so many other fields of human endeavor. Moreover, it would be to resign ourselves to slavery. For absolutism in one form or another is the inevitable end of "steeply graduated" taxes on income and inheritances, and absolutism in any form is slavery.

I am as confident as I ever was of anything in my life that a more just and equitable, and less complicated and expensive, primary source of revenue would be contrived if Congress created the kind of machinery for dealing with the problem that might be regarded as evidence of a sincere desire to find a solution.

In the absence of such machinery, we'll continue to penalize outstanding ability and success until the will to achieve has been destroyed throughout the nation and we've all been reduced to the aimless status of an indifferent conglomerate of bone, tissue and blood.

Q. What do you have in mind, a gross income tax?

A. I'm not going to discuss any particular type of taxation. All that those people want who have a vested interest in the income tax—and there are lots of them—

Q. A vested interest? Do you mean tax lawyers?

A. Now, let's not jump on any single group. There are a lot of people who have a vested interest in maintaining the status quo, and they'd like nothing better than for me to say: "Well, I'd do it this way."

Then they'd start up a great fuss over whether that particular plan made sense, and the idea of creating corrective machinery never would even get a hearing.

Q. What approach do you favor?

415

A. My idea is very simple. There's only one way in the world to change the tax laws. Congress has to do it. Now, you can change the present law—you can amend it, you can extend it, you can contract it, all within the framework of routine legislative procedure and enactment.

But when it comes to getting rid of a form of taxation and putting something in its place, you've got a different problem on your hands. And you haven't got a problem that can be solved at one or two sessions of Congress. Nor do you have a problem that any single Administration can handle, because no Administration could be sure that it would be able within a period of one term to get the answer, polish it up, and get it ready for adoption as legislation. In other words, it's a question of long study and analysis.

What I'd like to see would be a commission appointed by Congress, without any deadline, without any instructions as to what to come up with—except one, and that is that the whole revenue system be thoroughly studied out and that the income tax in particular be given a real going over, with the idea that a substitute be found for it if it cannot be made generally understandable, fair and compatible with our ideals of freedom.

I don't think it can be made even generally understandable, let alone fair and compatible with our tradition of freedom, but I'm willing to await and abide by the verdict of such a group as I have suggested, provided, of course, that it is a clearly honest verdict.

You see, unless that happens, we don't get anywhere. All we get is conversation, and I'm not interested in that, and I don't think other victims of this devouring evil are. I don't know any way to get action except to get machinery set up through which action can be taken.

Q. The income tax law must be written pretty well—it's raising annually about 52 billion dollars of revenue—

A. I'm not saying that the income tax doesn't raise a lot of money, because it does. In fact, I think it can be shown that it raises too much. But what I'm talking about is the damage that it's doing. The minimum rate of 20 percent takes a whale of a slug—$400—out of a taxable income of $2,000. I sure wouldn't want to pay that much if my income were that low. But it hits the people in the middle brackets even harder, and is slowly but surely destroying the middle class.

Q. It's hurting the single man—

A. It's hurting all kinds of people, from top to bottom. Look at the progression. It runs from 20 percent to 91 percent, making a surtax that runs to 71 percent.

Incidentally, the rates above 20 percent raise only a sixth of the total amount of money derived from individuals. The area of the progression is from $2,500 to the $200,000 bracket. But, by the time the $20,000 bracket is reached, half of the progression in rate has taken place.

The $2,000 of taxable income from the $20,000-to-$22,000 bracket is taxed 56 percent—20 percent base rate, plus 36 percent surtax. Thus, half of the progression in added rate is applied by the time only 10 percent of the dollar area of progression is reached.

What this does is sharply illustrated by what happens to a person who correctly answers "the $64,000 question." A married man with two children and *no other income* would have $37,188 left after the tax collector takes his cut. A single person, not the head of a household and with *no other income*, would have $27,808 left. To the extent that either recipient had other income, the tax collector does even worse, according to what bracket the recipient's total income—including the prize money—puts him in.

But hear this! I was talking with a man the other day who said his income was $200,000 in 1954 and that, as a result of improved operating methods and increased sales effort, he got it up to $300,000 in 1955. Then, lo and behold! he discovered to his dismay that he would have only $3,750 left out of the additional $100,000 after settling with the federal and State tax collectors.

"What's the use?" said he. What's the use, indeed! Now, I realize that there would not be any point in getting excited about this case from the purely subjective point of view, and I don't. But I do get excited about it from the standpoint of its iniquitousness as a matter of principle.

Our country's economic growth has been produced with the direct and indirect savings of the people, and those savings have come from the people who have had enough on the ball to do better than just earn a living.

If we keep on at the present rate of taxation, we will come eventually to the point where no one will have anything to invest and the "man on horseback" will be upon us. The Government will own everything, and we'll be forced to do the bidding of commissars imbued with the idea that they know better how to spend our money than we, and vested with the authority to do it.

Q. Haven't you got to do all that, though, to raise revenue?

A. No, not that alone—I disagree with that completely. We've done it for the whole 43 years of the income tax to enforce social reforms—to reduce everybody to the lowest common denominator economically. I don't believe in using tax legislation to force social reforms upon the people or to punish sin.

Q. Shouldn't everybody have the same income? President Franklin Roosevelt said nobody should have more than $25,000—

A. You know I don't subscribe to such socialistic demagoguery as that. I say everybody should have what he can make honestly, with a minimum of taxes. Everyone should be able to keep a much larger share of his income than he can at present, and everyone's right to expect to be protected in his possession of what he makes should be respected, especially by the Government.

Q. That point you make about the purpose of income tax being to destroy the middle class—do you think it was conscious purpose, or was it a result?

A. There was no question in the world about the consciousness of that purpose. Go back to 1894. In that year an income tax was adopted which was part of the Tariff Act of 1894. That was declared unconstitutional about a year later.

That tax was deliberately, avowedly, and unashamedly enacted to get at the "rich" people. There wasn't any apology for it at all. On the contrary its proponent boasted that it was aimed at the rich and would hit only 85,000 out of 65 million people, which according to my arithmetic was about one eighth of 1 percent of the population. And to this day the "soak the rich" purpose prevails. I heard it the other day in a committee hearing in Congress—the whole idea is to get at the rich. It was conceived in vengeance and it has been that way ever since. It has never been anything different.

Q. Well, isn't that a way to do both?

A. True, it's a revenue law. But I cannot accept the proposition that a revenue law ought to be used to penalize success.

Q. Mr. Andrews, granting that the revenue laws are aimed at the rich, do you think they are consciously aimed at the middle class, too?

A. Yes, I do. What do you think the inheritance tax and gift taxes were planned to do? All you've got to do is get the record. It tells you frankly what it's designed to do. It's designed to put every generation back to scratch.

Q. Maybe that's a good thing; they can scratch to get ahead—

A. I don't agree. The best incentive for those who haven't started scratching is the example of those who did and who achieved success by so doing.

TAX LAW'S "INFIRMITY"—

Q. You said a moment ago that it was your own view that this income tax could not be made to work. Did you mean this income tax, or any income tax?

A. Well I was talking about the present one. I am convinced that this law has reached the point of incurable infirmity, and I doubt that any full-scale income tax, rigidly enforced, can be made a primary source of a great nation's income without leading eventually to dictatorship, which I am convinced is happening under the present law.

Q. But it is raising the money the country needs, isn't it?

A. Yes, and I might remind you that an infirm boiler usually holds steam right up to the time when it blows up. You know, it amazes me that so many people seem to accept two assumptions about taxes and expenditures that I believe to be utterly fallacious and indefensible. One is

418

that there is no substitute for the income tax; the other is that the present level of federal expenditures cannot be lowered.

These two assumptions are widely held, even in some pretty high places. If they were valid, we'd be gone goslings. I don't think they are valid. I *do* think that no public official or political leader—there's a difference, you know—and neither of the two political parties could possibly do the people of this country a greater disservice than to accept these assumptions as valid. After all, about one half of all the income taxes collected are paid by individuals and better than five sixths of the part paid by individuals is paid by those individuals whose taxable income is under $6,000.

It's time for somebody to begin thinking about the common folks of this country. Congress can reduce expenditures whenever it really wants to.

Q. For what groups—the middle class?

A. I'm not talking about where you'd cut it. I think everybody is overtaxed, but I think the middle class is being especially discriminated against. And if the public-opinion polls mean anything at all, the very fact that they have had an almost overwhelming response in favor of a limitation of 25 percent in taxes—not once but twice—indicates that the people in the lower brackets don't think that success should be punished and the people in the higher brackets discriminated against.

Q. Let's assume that the amount of money raised or needed for our Government doesn't change, that we need the same large sum, that it's not a question of extravagance but necessity. Is there any other way of raising that same amount of money by any other method?

A. I believe there is.

Q. You really think we could raise the same amount of money?

A. Certainly. We might even raise more.

Q. So that your objection to it is not merely that raising a lot of money is producing extravagance, but that there is a better way to raise a sufficient amount of money even if we wanted to be extravagant?

A. I think there is a simple way. I think there is a better way. I think there is a fairer way.

Q. Why don't you think the income tax is fair?

A. I don't think it's fair because of the manner in which it is applied. I don't think it's fair because I object to invasion of the people's right of property by the Government. I also think the discriminatory manner in which the rates are graduated is unfair.

Q. Do you believe in the principle of the capacity to pay?

A. No, I do not.

Q. You don't believe the man who makes more should pay more?

A. I don't believe he ought to be penalized by being required to pay nearly 50 times more on only 10 times more income, and neither do his fellow citizens, according to the public-opinion polls. I don't believe we

419

ought to take it away from people just because they've earned it. I don't think we ought to use tax legislation to enforce social ends.

Q. But isn't that the principle behind the income tax?

A. Yes.

Q. So your objection is largely to the principle of capacity to pay?

A. That's one of my objections.

"CONFISCATING PROPERTY"—

Q. Don't all taxes have to come out of income unless you're going to confiscate property? The only question, then, is whether you use income itself as a measure of tax liability. If you don't, about all you can do is base it on transactions. Is that essentially a correct conclusion—if you don't use income as the method of measure, then transactions have to be used?

A. Not necessarily. We're confiscating property now. That's one of the reasons why I don't like the income tax.

As I said a while ago, every time we talk about these taxes we get around to the idea of from each according to his capacity and to each according to his needs. That's socialism. It's written into the Communist Manifesto. Maybe we ought to see that every person who gets a tax return receives a copy of the Communist Manifesto with it so he can see what's happening to him.

Q. Would you like to tax everybody equally?

A. You mean at the same percentage?

Q. The same amounts—

A. Of course not. That would merely shift injustice from one class to another. I want to end the "soak the rich" business, because we don't soak the rich—we penalize outstanding ability and ultimately destroy ourselves.

We've been soaking the rich so long that there aren't any rich any more. But there are people with a lot of knowhow, and instead of a tax climate that encourages achievement of one's full potentialities, we have one in which the reward for outstanding performance is forced down as performance goes up. Thus, instead of soaking the nonexistent rich, we penalize high performance and foul the spark plugs of our hopes for sustained and growing leadership. It doesn't make sense, does it?

Q. So a man might just as well take a vacation—

A. Yes, and a lot of them do. And if you don't think so, just go down to Florida and take a look around.

Q. You mean relatively young men?

A. I certainly do.

Q. Do you think that there is a preference between the principle of taxing earned income versus unearned income? Do you think a distinction should be drawn?

A. You mean as between what you earn and what you get on your investments?

Q. Yes—

A. No, I do not. Why penalize investment? We're doing it now by penalizing success, and we're digging our own grave as a nation when we do.

Investment puts people to work. It buys machinery. It takes $12,000 to $15,000 to equip one worker today so he can produce more. I've often heard people speak harshly about other people who apparently were accumulating a little money. The object of the criticism almost invariably was a thrifty man or woman whose money was being put into investment that created tools, that created production, that created work of some kind. Why should that be penalized?

There are only two ways in the world that business activities can be financed. One is through savings. The other is through Government handouts. May the Lord deliver us from the latter.

Q. But while the theory is that you soak the rich because they spend it freely—aren't you really soaking them so that they won't have a chance to invest it?

A. That's exactly what happens. And something else happens, too. Here's an illustration, an estate tax case, but it illustrates a point:

Not too long ago a member of a well-known family died and left 70 million dollars. The "death duties" were 50 million dollars, according to newspaper reports. I don't know whether the figures were right or not, but, whatever the amount, there were millions of dollars invested in American enterprise that the Government took, and, at the rate of spending then prevailing, it was gone in a matter of a few hours.

Q. For unproductive things?

A. Well you certainly can't call Government productive. It might be called necessary, provided it's kept within bounds. But it is not wealth-producing. Incidentally, the Reed-Dirksen resolution, now pending, would abolish estate and gift taxes and leave that field to the States. I don't think that would be good for everybody concerned.

Q. Do you think it is possible, without very sizable reduction in Government spending, to make any major improvement in our taxes?

A. Certainly. Moreover, Congress can reduce expenditures substantially any time it really wants to.

Q. If you have to have this much money and you don't take the larger chunks from big incomes, you're going to have to take more from the smaller incomes, are you not?

A. You've got to take it out of the stream in some way, of course, but I believe that there are ways to take it out that will distribute the load fairly and end the present discrimination against one class.

Q. But without reducing the tax, all you can do is shift the burden—

A. That would not necessarily follow. Under some forms of taxes that have been proposed, there would be a shift from one industry to another. One category of business on its face might appear to pay more taxes than another, but actually it wouldn't. I recognize one thing clearly, and that is that the consumer pays practically all the taxes that are collected. The only taxes I know that the consumer does not pay are the estate and gift taxes, and I'm not sure but what it can be shown that he pays them.

Q. Does he pay the income tax?

A. He sure does. He pays the personal income tax as well as the corporate income tax.

Q. Exactly how?

A. That's simple. The take-home pay is what he's after. For instance, you're running a business—the income tax of everybody you employ is paid by you, and you include it in your cost of operations and shift it to your subscribers or advertisers. Whoever you sell your product to pays the income taxes of your employees. If your customer is a business, it passes along what it pays you, and so on until the consumer ultimately picks up the tab.

And so, when anybody talks about any part of the income tax not being paid by the consumer, he's just water-skiing.

Q. Couldn't that be carried to the ultimate that everybody is paying everybody else's taxes?

A. To a considerable degree that is true, but the important thing is how the burden of tax is made to fall in the first place.

Q. Do you think the Government is permitting some people to escape the income tax?

A. A lot of them are escaping it.

Q. Do you mean evading it?

A. No. I think a whole lot of finagling is going on. Moreover, there are a lot of people who are not paying their taxes because they don't understand the law. That's one of the problems: It's a question of complexity.

The average man today, no matter how much you try to explain the income tax, doesn't even understand the "short form 1040" and he wouldn't know how to start making out the "long form 1040." Perhaps you're saying, "Well, why not simplify the forms?" But you can't make the forms any simpler than the law. Don't forget that.

Q. Mr. Andrews, the Social Security tax on household servants presents quite a problem, too, doesn't it?

A. It sure does. That's a very simple tax, by the way, and, let me remind you, in reality a supplemental income tax.

I made a poll at a social gathering the other night. The results indicated that more than half of the ladies questioned weren't paying the tax. And they weren't deducting it either.

I would be willing to wager that if the number of people necessary for a complete canvass were employed to go around and knock on every door in the United States and inquire about household servants, you would be appalled at what you would find, and, of course, the poor canvassers and the Administration would be swamped with protests not only from the people but also from the ladies and gentlemen on the Hill who passed the law.

Q. In a good many cases wouldn't the servants quit if the employer tried to deduct this tax?

A. I'm pretty certain they would.

Q. And isn't it true that a lot of items that are taken in by merchants aren't counted as receipts, not with the intention of being dishonest, but because the recipients don't know it is income?

A. I think there's a great deal of that, but I doubt that it adds up to a lot of dollars. But let me make crystal-clear, when I say that, that I don't mean for anybody to get the idea that I think the Revenue Service is not doing its job efficiently, because, as a matter of fact, I think they are doing a swell job. At least, I thought they were when I left there, and I know of no reason to assume they are not still doing so.

But time and time again we told Congress that there were not enough agents to examine all the returns that ought to be examined. And perhaps you'll remember that Congress started off giving us 1,000 agents a year and we were to have gone from about 7,300 agents to 15,000 or 16,000, which we figured would have been enough to enable us to do as good a job as possible before the law of diminishing returns would make it unprofitable.

Well, strangely enough, when the control of Congress changed hands at the beginning of last year, someone suddenly decided that we had reached our "optimum level" of employment. I don't know what they've done this year. But there they were, as I said in a recent article, with incontrovertible evidence before them that we could raise about $10 to $20 for every $1 spent for new agents; yet they decided we had reached the "optimum level" of employment of agents.

WHAT CONGRESS FEARS—

Q. Why? Do you think they were afraid?

A. I think Congress is more afraid of a firm and rigid enforcement of the tax law than they are of the loss of revenue. Maybe they think, as many other people do, that if Congress ever gave the Revenue Service enough money to enforce the revenue laws up to the hilt, the income tax would have to be repealed within a year.

Q. Why is that?

A. Because the people just wouldn't stand for it.

Q. You mean they are avoiding taxes in some way?

A. They're just not paying a lot of what's due. Take the farm situation, for instance. The computation of a farmer's tax is a very complicated thing for the simplest kind of farming operation. My blood pressure doesn't rise any over a farmer's not complying fully, because a lot of accounting is involved in making out a farm tax, and a farmer's job is to be a farmer, not a bookkeeper for the Government. The law ought not to be one that the farmer can't comply with without having to employ expensive professional people to help him.

Any kind of a tax system that is as complicated as that is wrong. Any sort of a tax system is wrong when a member of Congress himself finds himself so unacquainted with a law that he has voted for over and over again that he has to resort to the business of getting a special law passed to relieve him of a deficiency that anyone else would have had to pay.

Q. You mean he didn't pay some back taxes?

A. He paid his taxes that he figured he owed, but he deducted something he shouldn't have deducted. He misunderstood it and got a special law passed to save him from the consequences of his error.

Q. Was he caught in some technicality that he thought was unjust?

A. There was nothing technical about it. It was a very simple thing. He just didn't understand the conditions under which the deductions he claimed could be allowed. He failed to satisfy those conditions.

Q. Does that happen very often?

A. The Service is constantly setting up deficiency assessments against taxpayers. I don't know whether there have been other situations that were cured as that one was or not.

When you've got a law that is so difficult to keep up with that a member of Congress has to resort to special legislation to save himself from the normal workings of the collecting arm of the administration, there's something wrong with that tax law.

Q. You spoke of rigid enforcement being unpopular. Would you say that, if we actually required the farmers of this country to pay all the taxes they're obligated to pay under the law, they would almost rebel?

A. I wouldn't apply that to the farmers alone; I'd apply it generally. If complete and rigid enforcement of the tax laws were attempted, I think we would have trouble.

I want it thoroughly understood, however, that I'm no Poujadist. I don't believe in doing anything by rebellion. I don't believe in engendering disrespect for any law. Nor do I believe in teaching or advocating evasion. I believe in doing things according to law—by petition preferably, by ballots if necessary. I'm not advocating rebellion, and I don't mean that anything I have said or will say be so construed.

424

Q. Mr. Andrews, don't you think that the great majority of people pay every dollar of taxes that they owe?

A. They try to, I think, but there are some big holes in the system and, in order to get rigid and complete enforcement there would have to be such an army of functionaries running around the country that I just don't believe the people would stand for it.

Q. Doesn't it breed contempt for all law to leave unenforceable laws on the books?

A. It certainly does.

Q. Doesn't that apply to some degree to income taxes, too?

A. Yes. But one cannot help but wonder whether Congress ever intended that the gambling laws be enforced. It may be argued that, if they did, they would have given the Revenue Service men to do it with. Maybe the members of Congress feel as a lot of other people do, that it's wrong to use the revenue laws to punish offenders against other laws.

Q. Couldn't you eliminate a lot of troubles with the income tax by simply reducing the steep surtax rates and getting more taxable income?

A. It could, and has worked that way in the past. In a subcommittee hearing on the Reed-Dirksen bill the other day, it was argued that lower rates would increase taxable activity to such an extent that there would be a net gain in revenue.

Q. How are people avoiding income taxes? What devices do they use? Are expense accounts the main ones?

A. I have not personally prepared tax returns for others for more than three years, so it would be very difficult for me to answer a question like that categorically. I only know what people are telling me.

Q. What are they telling you?

A. Well, there are all kinds of tricks for getting expenses in that aren't deductible. I'm not so sure, though, that the amount of taxes lost because of this is great. The Revenue Service hasn't been able to do any "doorbell ringing," as they call it, since the first time we tried it with such good results in 1953. They don't have the people to do much of that any more.

Q. Congress probably pulled back when that started—

A. We never pulled back. We gave instructions to do it as often as possible. But getting on top of the terrific accumulation of delinquent taxes that we inherited left little time to do any canvassing for delinquent returns.

Q. Is there an ideal tax system that can be devised which would remove the necessity for a horde of taxes and tax functionaries; that would permit the citizen to compute readily and quickly his taxes so that he wouldn't have to hire attorneys, consultants and accountants to help him; a tax system that would give us all the revenue we need on a simplified basis? Is there such a thing?

A. There isn't one in existence but I believe one could be devised. It seems utterly absurd to me to assume that back in 1913 we found the one and only tax by which this Government can live. That just doesn't make sense. Forty-three years ago, when the country had much more of an agricultural economy than now, we decided that an income tax was the only thing we could live on.

In the meantime, the ingenuity of the people of this country in all the fields that make up American life—science, industry, commerce, finance, anything you could mention—has achieved world leadership. And some people want us to believe that there isn't genius enough in this country to get right down to brass tacks and conceive and develop a better tax system than we were able to dig up 43 years ago. I just don't go along with that idea.

Q. There aren't very many taxes or types of taxes that haven't been tried out either by the Federal Government or the States, are there?

A. No, I don't suppose there are. But at the time Edison invented the electric light, there wasn't any form of light that hadn't been tried out, either. Yet we've found a lot of different light sources since then.

There undoubtedly are tax methods that haven't even been thought of. I think there are others that have been thought of that haven't been given a fair trial or even a hearing.

Q. A few moments ago we asked whether you were objecting to the income tax we now have or to any income tax—

A. I wouldn't say that I'm objecting to any income tax. That's the reason I have declined to say outright, "Abolish the income tax." When there has been a real objective study of this whole problem, I might very well be on the side of those who would want to retain some kind of income tax, but I assure you it would have to be extremely simple for me to agree.

This annual chore of complexity that people are confronted with is, in my opinion, almost as serious as the oppressiveness of the tax itself. It certainly is a shameful waste of time and talent.

"SIMPLICITY" VS. "EQUITY"—

Q. You mentioned that that complexity was the result of the law, which is so complicated. Is it possible under present conditions for Congress to write those laws more simply?

A. I don't think so.

Q. That is one of the basic problems, is it not?

A. One of the basic problems of the income tax is to achieve both simplicity and equity at the same time. Thus far, no one has been able to do both. The more equity you get the greater the complexity becomes.

Q. Would you explain that a little bit?

A. Yes, I can. I'll give you two illustrations:

The dividend credit is one. The present Administration put that through. As it is, it's an insignificant credit. Of course, the original intention was to boost it 5 percent annually, until it got up to be 20 percent. But it doesn't seem to have much chance of going beyond the present 5 percent, what with talk on the Hill about taking away from the "dividend boys" and giving to the "little fellows." More "soak the rich" demagoguery!

In order to provide for that one bit of equity, as small as it was, we had to take half of a page of the return to devote to the computation of it.

Q. Why is this necessary?

A. Because we had to provide a formula for calculation of the credit.

One other illustration is the retirement-income credit. That was changed, too, to make it more equitable. And what happened? The net result was another half-page formula.

Now, to go back to your question, if this Administration couldn't simplify the income tax law with all the talent that it assembled to help it. I don't believe that any Administration could.

In planning its operation on the income tax this Administration had a fine corps of experts in the Secretary's office; it had the finest people we had in our shop, the Revenue Service; it had the staff of the Ways and Means Committee of the House, the Finance Committee of the Senate, the Joint Committee of Internal Revenue Taxation of Congress; it also had representatives of the American Bar Association, the American Institute of Accountants, the Comptroller's Institute, and goodness knows how many more organizations.

It gathered together the finest group of technicians, practitioners, and business people that any Administration had ever assembled before for any purpose. What did it come up with? It achieved simplicity in the sense that the mechanical arrangement of the Code is better. It closed some loopholes. It accomplished more fairness and justice. But it still has a tax bill that is over 1,000 pages long and is so complicated that 18 months already have gone by and all the official interpretations—that is, the regulations based on the law—aren't out yet.

HOW LAW IS "EXPLAINED"—

Q. And what is the importance of those regulations?

A. The importance of those regulations is to explain the law to the people.

Q. And to the staff of the Internal Revenue so that they may interpret the law in individual cases?

A. So that they, too, will understand what Congress meant.

Q. Do you mean that for 18 months the 1954 statute is uninterpreted?

A. Not yet fully interpreted.

Q. Does that mean that all interpretation is stopped?

427

A. No. On the contrary, they are trying to get the regulations out, and they have been working hard at it ever since even before the law was passed and signed; but they are confronted with two problems. First, with the problem of deciding what Congress meant. Don't forget that there are many parts of the law in which Congress did not spell out its intention but instead empowered the Secretary or his delegate to say what was meant.

The Treasury has to find out what Congress meant as to each section. Perhaps you say, "That ought to be easy. Take the committee reports and you can easily tell what they mean." All right, I'll tell you about that.

The committee reports don't always mean a lot because some fellow will be assigned the task of writing a report and it becomes his job to tell what went on in the meeting and what Congress meant by the particular point they were considering. That's all to the good. But no committee report is any better than the understanding of the man assigned to write it. So these boys read and wonder, "What did Congress mean?"

Then, after they decide what Congress meant or should have meant, they are confronted with the problem of expressing their conclusions in writing, and, believe me, that's no easy task. So, they struggle with that one for a while, getting it down in writing after they have decided what was meant.

Q. Isn't there a third step that they have to go through— listening to the protests of the Congressmen: "We didn't mean this at all!"?

A. I skipped that to make it simple. What they do, once they've decided what they think Congress meant and get it down in black and white, is issue what they call notice of rule-making. It's a 30-day notice, published in the Federal Register, that is designed to give all who want to object a chance to do so. Hearings on the objections often are held. Then they come back and try to figure it out again.

Q. And they can't go up to Congress and ask them if they're right about that interpretation—

A. No. They wouldn't get much help there.

Q. Is there any easy way still to explain why the law itself has to be so awfully complicated?

A. Well, principally because the law is based on income and income often is very difficult to ascertain. Following World War II, a group of 25 to 30 economists, lawyers, accountants and businessmen sat for four years trying to define one term, "business income." This group never was able to come to unanimous agreement.

Now you ask about getting help from Congress. Let's be perfectly honest about this thing. I have had members of Congress tell me frankly that they just don't have time to give thorough consideration to a good deal of what comes before them for attention. I'm not going to name any names, but some very important people have said that to me about the Revenue Act.

There are few Congressmen who really understand the income tax law. This is as true of the men who have become important in your mind in the making of income tax legislation as it is of those who haven't. I've had some of those men tell me they had to depend absolutely upon the staffs of their committees for advice as to what to do.

And, we might as well recognize it, our tax laws are not made by members of Congress, the elected representatives of the people, nor by the committees of Congress, who are appointed by the leaders of the Senate and the House, but by the staff members of the tax committees. That's true of all legislation, I suppose. But that's getting it about as far away from the people as you can, and in about the most vital area you can think of—taxes.

I once said to a prominent member of one of the tax committees, "But that's tax legislation by staff members, not by Congress, not even by committees of Congress." He replied sadly, "I realize that, but 1 don't know what we can do about it." My answer was, "Get a simple revenue system. Then everybody will understand it, you'll be in the clear, and the taxpayers will call you blessed."

CONGRESS'S "RESPONSIBILITY"—

Q. But don't these staff members know more about it than even the Congressmen?

A. Maybe they do, but it is Congress's responsibility to pass upon it and understand it, and they don't understand it. Any law that is not understood by the people who pass and impose it upon the people ought not ever to be passed in the first place.

Q. Don't the subcommittees work with them and have a pretty good understanding of the law, though the majority of the committee may not?

A. That may have been true in the early days of the law, but it isn't now. When they began to discover that while the law was simple it was unjust, and they had to do something about it, they began to add on all kinds of fancy gimmicks, gadgets and thou-shalt-nots, until it now adds up to the point where it's so complicated that nobody can understand it. I say to you that any law that isn't understood even by the people who pass it, let alone by those subjected to it, shouldn't be imposed on the body politic.

Now we can come to the question you asked me—if I thought the Revenue Service tries to be fair to people.

"POLICEMAN'S COMPLEX"—

Q. No one in the Service as an individual, but the methods they now use—

A. I can only speak for myself. I have a tremendously high respect for the people in the Service generally. Most of them are career people and those who get up into the high echelon generally are pretty high-minded persons. They will try to carry out any honest orders given to them. If you've got a program that is honest and that gives them some rein, they will do the best they can. But in every organization as big as that you are bound to have an occasional case of "policeman's complex." I didn't see too much of that when I was there; but I wouldn't claim for one minute that we were able to achieve perfection, because every now and then I'd find somebody taking a position in a situation that I thought was unfair and I did something about it.

Unfortunately, there are a lot of people in public office—and I'm not praising myself when I say this—who haven't got the guts to check unfairness because they're afraid somebody will investigate them for doing whatever is right, particularly for deciding anything against the Government. They're afraid of criticism. They don't like to be criticized. An honest official doesn't have to fear criticism; but many honest officials do.

What I am saying is that one of the answers to your question is that the income tax law gives a lot of power to those who have to administer it. It has to. But that's one objection I've got to it. Whenever an inspector in any business sees smoke he doesn't like to admit that there isn't some fire. Then things often begin to happen.

That power can be improperly used in other ways. Consider what happened to taxpayers for several years beginning in the early '40s. Additional revenue was needed, and, not wanting to increase taxes drastically, the Administration made a drive on depreciation. There was hardly a taxpayer who wasn't confronted with a reduction in his depreciation deductions year after year.

I had clients who would have a succession of agents come along and each one would reduce what the other one had reduced, until it finally got to a point where I would say, "Forget about the depreciation. Taxes are going up anyhow, and you'll save money by going along with this campaign of extortion."

Then there was the "blackjack" approach to force the taxpayer to consent to the opening of years closed to examination and deficiency assessment by the expiration of the statute of limitations.

They couldn't get around to everybody in time and what would happen would be that the agent would go to the taxpayer and say, "I want you to give me a waiver for these back years." The statute limit having expired for those years, they couldn't be opened without the taxpayer's consent. The taxpayer usually had no choice but to give an extension of time because the agent was in position to put him to great expense even if he didn't have a valid basis for a deficiency assessment.

Q. In other words, the year that was still open was held as a threat against him, unless he furnished a waiver that permitted the Government to reopen years that had already been closed?

A. That's right.

Q. Was that routine procedure?

A. It seemed that way. Needless to say, I went into office pretty burnt up about that practice and I didn't lose any time making my feelings about it clear. It seemed to me that the staff was pretty happy about the change of policy.

Q. What do you think of the method that has long been used whereby, when a business has closed its taxable year, Congress comes along and passes a law that reopens a year. Do you think that's fair?

A. No, I do not.

Q. It has been done, hasn't it?

A. I understand that it has been tried.

Q. In other words, on many of these complicated matters that you're talking about that have to do with estates and other things, they go back years and change the laws applicable to those years? So you have no certainty—

A. One of the great objections to the present system is that it is almost impossible for taxpayers to get firm assurance as to where they stand taxwise. We improved this situation as much as we could. It can't be completely corrected except at inordinate cost.

ON REDUCING SPENDING—

Q. Well, if you get 35 billion dollars from individual income taxes—which is 15 percent of individual income—in order to modify the gross income tax rate and to reduce the graduation you have to charge a much higher rate on any form of gross income tax than the 15 percent rate—

A. If you're going to replace that income that might be true. But you're working on what I think is an utterly fallacious premise, and that is that the present level of spending cannot be relieved. I don't agree with that any more than I do with the proposition that we can't get along without the income tax. As I've said before, Congress can reduce spending whenever it wants to.

Now, if you've got to raise 35 billion dollars on whatever might be the income of all individuals in the country, the only decision you have to make is how you're going to apply it to the various levels of income. I say that, if you have to do that, then there ought to be some kind of leveling out of this terrific wallop that's given to the people between $6,000 and $20,000.

If anyone wants to see what has happened taxwise since World War II started in 1939, all he has to do is take his gross income for 1939, calculate and deduct his '39 taxes from it, and get his net income after taxes; then take the same gross income, calculate and deduct taxes at current rates, and adjust the net after taxes for the drop in the purchasing power of the dollar since 1939; and finally compare the two results.

Or, do it this way: Calculate how much gross income would be required today to produce as much purchasing power after taxes as was left of his '39 income after he paid his taxes. No one should do this who has a weak heart, because the results will be shockingly startling.

People are kidding themselves. They don't have the buying power they used to have. A lot of the people living today don't know what the buying power of success was before we decided to use excessive income taxes to punish success and estate and gift taxes to force every generation to start from scratch.

Q. You think the middle class is being whacked—the fellow who used to be able to get ahead in the world and save enough to retire on, he now can't do it—

A. The fellow who demonstrates the greatest capacity for leadership—creates things, activity and employment—and contributes most to the growth of the economy and to improvement of our standard of living is the fellow who is getting the most kicking around.

SOCIAL SECURITY: HANDOUT?—

Q. But can't he look forward to Social Security to retire on?

A. He can't do much on that. Besides, that kind of person would rather do his own providing for his retirement and not depend upon a handout, especially one from a system that is already bankrupt.

Q. Eighteen hundred dollars isn't going to be very impressive to him anyway, is it?

A. I don't think so. And that suggests another problem. You should see my mail from people who are on fixed incomes. They're really catching it. It burns me up to see the widow of a successful man robbed of most of her due by the estate tax and then reduced almost to poverty by progressively higher and higher income taxes and mounting inflation.

Q. As a result of the income tax?

A. Largely, yes. Of course, it must be remembered that high taxes come from big spending.

Q. In what way does the income tax hurt the fixed-income widow?

A. Because of inflation—the spending power of the dollar has gone down so terrifically and the taxes have gone up so high that she's caught in the jaws of a vise.

Q. Is there a relationship between the income tax and the diminution of the purchasing power?

A. Certainly. The higher income tax rates go the higher prices are and the less a fellow has left to pay the prices. There's a compound effect.

Q. We come now to the question of deductions. Among the things that people don't understand, I'm sure, is the question of deductions. Do you think the present system of deductions is fair?

A. No, I don't.

Let me give you an illustration. I think that a man ought to be able to deduct every kind of expense over which he has no control. The cost of sickness is a good illustration. Now, we've got a limitation on medical expenses. Why in the world we have it I don't know, for certainly no one is going to get sick if he can help it.

I say that, regardless of any other deductions, a man ought to be allowed to deduct those things over which he has no control. And goodness knows he has no control over sickness.

Q. Are there other things?

A. Yes. Another would be casualty losses. We now get a deduction for casualty losses—some of them. But some of them are meaningless. We had the devil of a time, for instance, with deductions for loss of trees, shrubs, flowers and the like in hurricanes. The way the law was written it usually was hard to permit deduction of what seemed to me the amount of loss suffered.

Then I think it is wrong not to permit deduction of all payments for personal services. For instance, if you hire a servant I think you ought to be permitted to deduct it, because the Government gets it two ways if you don't. You pay it, but you can't deduct it. The servant is supposed to pay on it above $600. Now, that could be easily solved by giving you the deduction on everything above $600 that you pay for a servant. I think that would be only fair.

Q. Take, for instance, a fellow who drives to work—it's no deduction. But if he goes on company business somewhere, the company gets a deduction or he gets a deduction; yet both are related to business—unless he went to work he wouldn't be in business—

A. That's right, but I don't see that one your way.

Q. Commutation fare in New York for all the people who live in the suburbs—

A. That's something that may be regarded as being within the control of the taxpayer. People who work in New York don't have to live in the country. Still, I admit that a good argument can be made for that point of view.

If you happen to be a man who has a pretty good income there are a lot of expenses that you have that are attributable purely to the position in life that your job requires you to maintain; but the law says these are personal expenses and, therefore, not deductible. And as you get penalized not only by being progressively taxed on your success but by being disallowed costs that arise out of your success.

For instance—coming back again to the question of servants—suppose you had a level of income that enabled you to maintain a fairly nice home, not a pretentious but a simple, conservative, modest kind of a garden, and you have a man who washes your automobiles and does your heavy cleaning for you and tries to keep your yard cut. You have to have such

433

a man, because you don't have time to do things you hire him to do, but you can't deduct his salary.

Q. Don't you think if you have a son in college you ought to get more than a $600 deduction?

A. I do, provided he meets reasonable entrance requirements, does good work there, and isn't there just for the sake of appearance.

DEDUCTIONS ARE "ARBITRARY"—

Q. Aren't those deductions an arbitrary thing—they haven't been thought through—

A. Certainly they're arbitrary.

Q. Mr. Andrews, if we were to take care of all these inequities and deductions wouldn't it cost more than the money we have been talking about that could be saved on operation of Government?

A. I doubt that. The things I've been talking about would end a terrific amount of annoyance but I don't believe they would add up to a great loss of revenue.

Q. And probably increase income—

A. Experience says "Yes" to that.

Q. Mr. Andrews, do you think the corporation income tax should be abolished altogether?

A. It should be studied, along with the tax on individuals. I would hope that it could be abolished, because it costs entirely too much to administer and the cost to the corporations of complying with it is pure waste that I am convinced can be eliminated. Moreover, the gap between the individual and the corporation is driving small business right into the maw of big business. At the present rate, we soon won't have anything but big business, and the situation will be just right for the final move to a completely socialistic government.

A U.S. LOTTERY? NO—

Q. A great many countries raise their money by lotteries. Have you any comment on that?

A. Frankly, I guess I would be prejudiced on that. My whole background would revolt against raising public revenue that way. I am not a kill-joy, so I don't care if anybody wants to gamble; but I somehow just cannot bring myself to look favorably upon a lottery as a source of public revenue.

Q. We haven't talked much about complexity as it relates to litigation. Have you any way of estimating the terrific cost of litigation due to the complexity of the income tax, and differences of opinion between the taxpayer and the Government? How much litigation is there?

434

A. That would be hard to draw down to specific terms. But I think I can give you some idea. There are figures, of course that can be supplied. The number of cases that actually go to litigation are remarkably small. Bear in mind that there are some 65 million tax returns filed every year.

My recollection of the last figures I saw on the number of cases that get to the point of adjudication in the courts—in the Tax Court, the Court of Claims or the district courts—is that they total less than 2,000 every year, maybe 1,500. I could be wrong, but I think that's correct.

The main problem that's involved is not in litigation but what happens before litigation begins. It often is long drawn out and extremely costly. The cost of cases to taxpayers sometimes exceed the tax involved. That's one of the very serious indictments against the income tax.

Q. Well, now, apropos of these cases in litigation—is it fair to the taxpayers who have closed their returns, paid their taxes, for past years, suddenly to have the courts decide in the case of a taxpayer who kept his return open by litigation, an important issue which, had it been in effect—that interpretation—at the time he paid his taxes, he would have received the benefit? Is that fair?

A. I don't think it is. But that usually works both ways; that is, sometimes there are decisions against a taxpayer, but the Government can't go back on other taxpayers who have become protected by the running of the statute. Nevertheless, I have always thought that a taxpayer should be made whole who pays taxes that are later found, in the outcome of a disputed issue not to have been due.

As to our own rulings, we followed the policy of applying them prospectively; that is, if we found it necessary to reverse a previous ruling we did not work it retroactively.

Q. That rule was abandoned at least by last year—

A. No, it was the rule up to the time I resigned that changes in previous interpretations of the law were made prospective when to have done otherwise would have been to cause unfairness.

Sometimes, when the circumstances seemed to require it, the effective date was set ahead so that people would get a chance to get themselves squared away. That seemed the fair thing to do, and that was the policy we followed.

Q. Coming to further amplification of the word "complexity," what is to be said on the subject of the various systems of accounting on which taxes are computed with which the taxpayer and the Government differ? Who is the authority on what's the proper way of accounting?

A. The law says generally that the taxpayer's method of accounting shall not be disturbed if it is consistent and correctly reflects the taxpayer's income.

But there often have been rather wide differences of opinion between the Revenue Service and taxpayers as to this. For instance, many publishers account for subscription income on one basis but are required to pay income taxes on another basis. Then you frequently find differences between the way in which regulatory authorities say books shall be kept—Interstate Commerce Commission, for example—and what the Revenue Service thinks is proper. An effort was made to correct such inconsistencies when the 1954 Code was being developed, but it finally came to naught.

"A TRAGIC SITUATION"—

Q. What about the small or medium-sized taxpayer who has neither the time nor the money to take his case to the Tax Court?

A. I regard that as one of the more or less tragic situations caused by the income tax. The fellow who can't afford to spend money for professional help shouldn't have to spend it. It ought to be possible to settle his case without a lot of expense. But, unfortunately, it can't always be done. Any tax that puts that kind of burden upon people who are trying to get ahead is a bad tax.

Let me give you another side of that. I had a letter from an 82-year-old lady the other day, complaining bitterly about having had to spend $275 for experts to assist her in preparing her return. She didn't have a lot of income, but she was a poor bookkeeper and the law was Greek to her. She didn't like having to incur that expense and I don't blame her.

The law is too complicated. Altogether too many people have to have professional help with their returns.

Q. You have a lot of adjectives, I know, up your sleeve; I wonder if you have one or two that would describe this income tax? Would you say it was inequitable, or what?

A. I think the most serious thing about this income tax, frankly, is the ideological objection to it. I don't like to see my country dancing to the tune of slave-makers, which is exactly what I think is happening.

Q. Do you think there is popular resentment to it?

A. My recent mail tells me that there is, and a lot of it.

Q. You really are trying to describe why the income tax is bad?

A. That's right.

Q. What amazes me is that you kept so quiet as a public official while you had in your system this dynamic interest in this inequity of the income tax—

A. That's very simple. My interest in the tax situation has been acute for a great many years, but when I was hired as Commissioner of Internal Revenue I was cast in a very restricted role. My job was to enforce the law, not philosophize about it or try to make new law. It would have been out of order for me to get into the Secretary's field of tax policy. If I had I should have been fired and probably would have been.

436

Q. You couldn't have been very happy, then—

A. I was happy as far as doing a challenging management job was concerned. I often wasn't happy about the way the law worked. I was constantly unhappy about what I saw the income tax doing to us.

WHAT COMMISSIONER DOES—

Q. Is that what built up your feeling about the income tax—what you saw in that job?

A. It did to a large extent. It sharpened my resentment to the tax a great deal. But, as I have said, I wasn't expected to make tax law. Nor was I expected to unmake it. My job was to enforce the law, and that's exactly what I did to the best of my ability. Nobody asked my opinion about the income tax and I didn't express it.

When I got out I began to think about it from this point of view: Now, after all, you've seen it in operation, maybe you've got some obligation to say what you think. Quite a few people urged that point of view upon me. I finally consented to make a couple of speeches, and then I started putting my ideas down on paper, and the further I got into it the more convinced I became that something was amiss.

The idea that we could go along for 43 years with no study or research of any kind, contenting ourselves with just making the primary source of our revenue more and more complicated all the time, without trying to find out whether we had the right primary source—whether there was not something better—struck me as a bit shortsighted for a nation that research had done so much for. As I said to the head of one of our great industries one night recently, "Where would your company be if it hadn't conducted one moment's research in 43 years?"

That's the position the Government is in. We're dealing here with the lifeblood of the nation, and no research.

But there is one thing you haven't mentioned here today and I've been rather surprised that you haven't. There's a curious paradox in the income tax law that somebody mentions every now and then, but which nobody does anything about. I refer to the section that sterilizes so much of the income that is supposed to be the source of the revenue. Take, for instance, foundations. Look at the tremendous quantity of income-producing wealth that is being put out of the reach of the tax collector by the building up of these nontaxable entities. The loss of taxable income here is colossal and this loss is being steadily compounded.

Then, see all the money that's invested in business-type activities by Government. I'm told that the Government has an investment of 60 billion dollars in that type of activity. The Hoover Report says that there are 15 billions of it in 2,500 business activities in the Defense Department alone. Now, that sort of thing tends to grow and expand, and all such business activity is removed from the reach of the tax collector.

437

It's an astounding situation, and it's thoroughly inconsistent with the idea of using an *income* tax as the primary source of revenue. We're sterilizing the very source of our revenue.

Q. Do you think the foundations some day may destroy the economy?

A. Well, I don't know about that, but they sure aren't helping any. Our economy is growing but much of the income that is produced is being kept out of the hands of the tax collector by deliberate legislative action. There is an ever-widening gap between the growth of the economy and the growth of the tax base. The people are bound to get wise to what this absurdity is doing to them one of these days, and, when they do, look out. The people have to make up this loss, you know.

Q. Are you talking now of the sterilization of income through its use by the Government in business activities of its own?

A. I'm talking about sterilization of income, whether it be through Government competition with private business, growth of foundations, or by any other names.

Q. You're getting trusts and foundations—

A. Our economy is growing and we're dependent upon an income tax to finance our growth and our Government expenditures. Yet there is an ever-widening gap between the two, because of the fact that we are depressing the potentiality of income as a source of public revenue by surrender to minority pressures.

Q. Are you saying if we have an income tax we ought to apply it more universally? In other words, apply it to the income of pension trusts and foundations?

A. Yes, I'm saying that. One researcher tells us that the original income tax applied even to churches.

TROUBLE FROM EXEMPTIONS—

Q. You don't advocate that?

A. No. I'm just telling you that all income was taxed, and that, as soon as the tax collector got going, Congress started the process of sterilization by yielding to one pressure group after another, and it has been going on steadily ever since. As a result there is a veritable army of people, organizations and businesses with a powerful vested interest in keeping the noses of the rest of us to the grindstone.

Q. Does that apply to depletion allowances?

A. Yes, it does. But don't take that to mean that I am arguing against depletion allowances. I'm arguing against a form of taxation that Congress evidently thinks we can't maintain without such exemptions. Any tax system that necessitates such extensive shift of burden is unsound and grossly unsuited to the nation's needs. The exemptees naturally think it's wonderful and can't be blamed for wanting to preserve that preferred status, but it sure is rough on the rest of us.

We're playing with dynamite, and I think that if something isn't done about it the result will be to destroy our tradition of freedom and wreck both that tradition and our civilization.

Q. Do you see any immediate prospect of Congress undertaking the study you propose?

A. I don't know about that. I'd say they will if enough people get after them about it, and it looks to me like a lot of people are getting somewhat more than just mildly interested.

But let no one underestimate the power of the opposition. Our only hope for relief is in the greater power of the masses. Sooner or later that power will be asserted.

POLITICAL AND PERSONAL
PHILOSOPHIES

ADDRESS DELIVERED AT MEETING OF LYNCHBURG ROTARY CLUB[†]

by

T. Coleman Andrews

MR. CHAIRMAN AND GENTLEMEN.

UNDERTAKING to gain and hold the attention of an audience like this is a bit unusual for a public accountant. I daresay that if a tabulation were made of the vocations and professions of those who have addressed meetings of civic clubs, the public accountants would be found at the very bottom of the list. Perhaps the reason for this is to be found in the estimate of us that has been attributed to Elbert Hubbard. He described a typical auditor as:

> A man past middle age, spare, wrinkled, intelligent, cold, passive, non-committal, with eyes like a codfish; polite in contact but at the same time unresponsive, calm and damnably composed as a concrete post or a plaster of Paris cast; a human petrification with a heart of feldspar and without charm of the friendly germ, minus bowels, passion or a sense of humour.

Then, as if that weren't enough, and in the manner of the toreador delivering the final thrust, he wound up with this unhappy observation and prediction:

> Happily they never reproduce and all of them finally go to Hell.

Well, gentlemen, if I did not know that at least some of my colleagues here in Lynchburg are living refutations of this gloomy appraisal, I am sure I would be so ill-at-ease that I might easily confirm almost everything that Mr. Hubbard is supposed to have said about us—everything, that is, that can be proved here on earth. I have been told that the devil is going to be my ultimate landlord, and I would be guilty of holding out on you if I did not admit that I probably would be in hell now if some people could have their way—and in the lowest rank of the furnace stokers at that. But I guess that's one bridge none of us can be sure of until we get to it. I am

---

†Presented at a meeting of the Lynchburg (Virginia) Rotary Club, February 24, 1948. Reprinted with permission from the files of the American Institute of Certified Public Accountants.

happy to be able to add also that I was not cursed with the biological deficiency that Mr. Hubbard said is the unhappy lot of most of us.

I believe that disposes of Mr. Hubbard about as far as I can until you have heard what I have to say. For the sake of my colleagues who practice their profession here I hope I may succeed in refuting at least some of his other charges. And, not forgetting that the next 30 minutes of your lives will be irretrievably spent listening to me (I hope), I assure you that I am no less concerned about you.

It's a pleasure, indeed it's a privilege, to address any Lynchburg audience, especially one of such distinction as I am sure the membership of The Lynchburg Rotary Club makes this one. I might also say that it is something of a triumph for me, because a Rotary Club is the only organization to which I was ever proposed for membership that turned me down. They said they couldn't find a classification for me. Considering the range of my activities, that's what I call being exclusive. Never since that happened have I looked out across a speaker's table into the faces of the members of a Rotary Club with anything but the utmost respect for my audience and considerable banging of my knees.

The problem that I shall discuss today is an old one. All of us have discussed it or heard it discussed many times. But that's about as far as we have gotten with it. Like the weather, everybody *talks* about it, but no one ever *does* anything about it. *I* think the time has come *to* do something about it.

Obviously, I could not possibly discuss this problem exhaustively in the time at my disposal. All I can do is hit the high spots, point out some of the most striking facts of it, cite some of its most serious implications, and hope to inspire and stimulate you to individual and collective action. Be assured that if this hope is realized you will find millions of other thoughtful men and women throughout the country with spirit and determination equal to your own. In every state in the Union people are starting on the march for the battle whose outcome will determine whether what we call "our way of life" is to be preserved. If we *lose* this battle, it will be our own fault and the ultimate consequence will be complete loss of everything that we hold dear. Now let's get down to cases.

The people of this country endured *without complaint* the unparalleled cost of World War II and all the restrictions and privations it imposed, not to mention the bereavements that so many of them suffered. Such inspiring patriotism had ever been characteristic of our people. That they would show it in this war could be taken for granted. Nor did anyone expect that victory would bring a return to normal conditions—if indeed conditions ever are normal. Indeed, it was clearly seen, long before the war's end, that peace and normal living might not be established until years after the fighting had ended, and there were dire predictions of widespread unemployment and economic instability generally.

444

Peace has not yet been established. It still is a long way off, and it apparently awaits demonstration, *here in our country*, of all the virtues that are claimed for democracy. But neither have we had the unemployment and generally depressed conditions that the Federal Administration so positively assured us we could expect. With characteristic ingenuity, industry accomplished an unbelievably rapid transition from wartime production to peacetime production. Thus, instead of depression, we have had the greatest prosperity in the country's history.

That's what private enterprise has accomplished! But what of the Federal Government? It continues to plunge madly down the road toward the scrap heap of shattered ships of state and superseded forms of government that it took 15 years ago. And, sad to relate, it looks like many of the states and local governments are determined to take this same road. Unlike private enterprise, the Government has *not* re-adjusted its affairs. IT HAS NOT EVEN *ATTEMPTED* TO DO SO.

For the year that will begin July 1st of this year (almost three years after VJ Day, mind you), the Administration proposes to spend nearly 40 billion dollars. Make the most liberal allowance you wish for increased expenditures for national defense, interest on war debt, all the other expenditures that are in any degree consequences of the war, and for the increase in the cost of what the Government buys, and you will come out with a result that can only be regarded as shameful extravagance when you compare it even with the 8.7 billion dollars spent during the year ended June 30, 1939, which was the last year before hostilities started in Europe—a year, mind you, during which the spend-our-way-to-prosperity program was in full blast. The comparison becomes even more pointed when you recall that the Government's total expenditures for the year ended June 30, 1929, amounted to only 3.3 billion dollars. Even that amount was a lot of money for those days; but it seems small now, doesn't it? The rate of public expenditures reached the supersonic level years before science sent guided missiles and the aeroplane crashing through that barrier. The swing to the left has been far more rapid than most of us have realized. Let's hope we can develop brakes strong enough to stop it before there is a disintegrating crash.

The narcotic effect of wartime patriotism has begun to wear off, and at long last the people seem to be coming out of the hypnotic spell cast upon them by false political prophets, with the connivance of their knavish so-called economic experts. All over the country people are beginning to ask why the cost of government is so high. In some places definite steps have been taken to do something about it. In other places such steps are being considered. There is definite indication that we may be returning to clear understanding that there is no substitute for honest toil and provident living, that the consequence of excessive spending is the same for governments as it is for the individuals who compose governments, [and] that bankruptcy (*not* prosperity) is the fate of the improvident spender.

Let us see where we stand as of today and get some facts and questions out on the table that we can get our teeth into. The cosmic proportions of the public debt frighten *me* more than anything else. What a mortgage we have allowed to be put upon the earnings of generations yet unborn! But before we can do anything about this we must first deal with the wastefulness and extravagance that accounts for it. The several levels of Government that we support are spending between 50 and 55 billion dollars annually. This is in the neighborhood of $400 per person. Whether any individual citizen sees what he is paying or not, he's paying it just the same. It's in the price of everything he buys: bread, meat, shoes, clothing, rent, utility services, and so on.

The national debt amounts to approximately 270 billion dollars. This includes state and local debts, as well as the debt of the Federal Government, and amounts to $2,000 per capita.

Now let us see what this means in terms of our individual incomes. Stated broadly, it means that 33⅓% of the national income is going for the support of Government. This is more than we spend for food. To put it another way, we work a third of every day—every week, every month, every year—for the support of Government. It is almost lunchtime every day before we start working for ourselves. This situation calls to mind the concession to freedom granted to Prussian serfs centuries ago: their masters allowed them to work for themselves two days out of each week.

Let us look at it geographically in terms of Federal expenditures alone. In 1929 Federal expenditures were less than two-thirds of the total income payments to the people of California. By 1938 they were equal to the total income payments to all the people in 11 of the 22 states west of the Mississippi River. In 1946, they were equal to the total income payments to all the people in 19½ of the 22 states west of the Mississippi River. Here it is plotted out on paper. Take a look at it, and you will see that a lengthening shadow of the most ominous import has formed and is spreading rapidly over the country.

Now let us see what all this is doing to us in terms of the buying power of our incomes. In presenting these figures I have taken into account the increased cost of living, because I regard the Government's bungling attempts to control our economy as being largely responsible for this added burden. All comparisons are between 1939 and 1947.[1] In 1939, a net income of $10,000 before tax exemptions had a buying power of $9,657. In 1947 it had a buying power of only $5,055. The buying power of an income of $15,000 dropped from $14,169 to $7,057. That of an income of $25,000 dropped from $22,673 to $10,235. That of an income of $50,000 dropped from $41,379 to $16,080. That of an income of $70,000

---

[1]*The United States News*, Vol XXIII, No. 16.

dropped from $53,895 to $19,545. That of an income of $100,000 dropped from $68,003 to $23,416.

Putting it another way, Dr. G. Rowland Collins, Dean of the Graduate School of Business Administration of New York University said: "Statistically speaking, ... it is entirely possible to establish the fact that the $2,500-per-year income earner in 1939 needs today an income of *$4,511* to match his 1939 position in the market and that the $10,000-a-year man in 1939 needs *$22,483* today to match his earlier position in the market place. Naturally, as we go up the scale of current incomes earned, the multiplier factor of progressive taxation intensifies the need for additional income today. For instance, the $100,000-a-year executive of 1939 needs today *$618,708*, or over six times his 1939 scale of compensation." I'm sure you will agree that these are facts of the utmost significance to employers.

I call your attention to the fact that the higher you go the worse it gets. It is impossible to earn your way to wealth today. I'm sure the significance of these facts already have become obvious to you without my stating it. But in order that there be no doubt about it, let's see what's happening.

This country rose to greatness industrially, commercially and financially under democracy and the free enterprise system, a system that rewards every man according to his capabilities and performance. The highest public office in the land is open to every native-born citizen, and every citizen, regardless of where he was born, may aspire to, and attain, the biggest jobs in private enterprise. But the supply of such talent is being dried up, because the incentive for distinctive accomplishment is being destroyed. Every day we hear of some executive in the prime of his usefulness asking, "What's the use?" and withdrawing himself from the pool of ingenuity that made us great. Moreover, competition for outstanding talent and performance is being stifled. There is no point in a man of demonstrated genius moving from one position to another at a great increase in salary when the net benefit doesn't justify the change. And so, the turnover of executives of the sort who have contributed so largely to the success of private enterprise in this country is being slowed down, and industry is unable to keep on its toes by the introduction of new blood.

At the bottom of all this is an insidious influence—one that seeks to set class against class, one that seeks particularly to set labor against capital. It was expressed no later than two months ago in the Second Annual Report of the President's Council of Economic Advisors in these terms: "The accumulations of capital over the years have in fact involved deprivation (note that word please: DEPRIVATION) of the rank-and-file worker."

There can be no doubt that our present plight may be largely attributed to the presence in high places in the Federal Government of people whose philosophy is aimed at the destruction of capital. Nor is there any doubt that capital and management have been guilty of some pretty reprehensible practices. But there also is no doubt that the unparalleled greatness of this country was accomplished through the wedding of democracy and free enterprise that is fundamental to our way of life.

Therefore, the solution to any problems that our system has created is *not* to destroy capital any more than it would be to destroy democracy. Indeed, if we destroy either, we shall destroy the other. The sensible solution is to be found in working out our difficulties across the conference table with mutual confidence, with our eyes firmly fixed upon the goal of freedom that the founding fathers of the country envisioned for us and with unswerving devotion to the principles that have made us great. We must *preserve* these principles. If we forsake them, we forsake all. With such overwhelming abundance of proof of the superiority of our system all around us—and with not a single instance of a better system in all history, or even of one nearly as good—I never cease to wonder at the determination of those, particularly those of our own people, who persist in trying to foist upon us a system that history shows has failed over and over again and never in a single instance produced a standard of living anywhere near the level of that which we enjoy.

The cost of Government, therefore, and the public debt, have assumed serious proportions and significance in the life of every citizen. The implications of the increasing percentage of our earnings that go to Government are ominously disturbing. I shan't have time to discuss these implications, but I would like to state some of them.

First of all, and most serious, I think is the implicit but dangerous admission that Government is better able to spend our money that we are.

Second, will government ever get around to approaching the job of budget making from the standpoint of "cutting the garment to fit the cloth"? How can anyone possibly justify the raising of taxes before even looking at the requests for appropriations, especially in times like these? This was done on Capitol Hill in Richmond only a few days ago.

Third, at what point in the division of national income between the Government and the individual do we have socialism instead of capitalism? And after socialism, what next?

Fourth, at what level of taxes is individual initiative and enterprise utterly destroyed? Perhaps we already have reached this point, certainly the process of destruction has begun.

Fifth, can we afford so to reduce the rewards of individual effort that it will cease to be forthcoming? For instance, would Henry Ford have been able to perform his mammoth industrial feat under taxes such as we have today? And could we under such a burden of taxation have been able to make the personal promotions that account for the high rate of employment and the high standards of living that the people of this country enjoy?

Sixth, can we afford so to reduce the rewards of capital that it too will cease to be forthcoming? The worker cannot produce without tools. It takes thousands of dollars of capital investment per worker to keep our economy running. The average investment in plant per worker was $4,051 in 1946. One prominent Richmond businessman told me the other day that at his plant the investment was $7,000 per worker. Without production there can be no real income. If the flow of capital is cut off—and it has almost come to a standstill already—there will be no production except of the most elementary sort, for risk and venture capital for machine production are basic in our economy. When we, as individuals, are no longer able to supply funds for the continued growth of industry, the alternative will be to have the Government supply it. When that happens, state socialism will become an accomplished fact; the dream of those whom we allowed to lead us into the mess with which we now are confronted will be realized; and probably we will be unable to return to democracy except by resort to violent measures.

Then I think we must consider the role of the citizen. Should he accept the dictates of his Government without question? Must he submit to the demands of those seeking largesse from the public treasury without any analysis of the need for what they want? Have we reached the point where it is *reactionary* to question the *right* of Government to spend? Or the *level* of its spending? Or the *purposes* for which proposed expenditures are to be made?

Now let's look ahead a little. If the present level of taxation and spending is unbearable, what will it be if and when times become less prosperous than they are now? A recession, or whatever you choose to call it, certainly is a possibility—if indeed it is not a strong probability. Moreover, to mention just one item that looms large on the horizon, old age benefits will begin to exceed the taxes collected for the payment of them by 1960, and the deficiency will go on increasing for many years before it levels off. The cost of this one item alone is going to be staggering. If we don't cut now, tomorrow may be too late.

Now, let me read you an excerpt from an article about one of the millions of Europe's victims of World War II. Its implications add frighteningly to those I already have stated.

> Ten years ago she was young, confident, the beloved wife of a rising attorney. I met husband and wife when they came to New York in 1935, thought them charming and cultured people. After that their daughter was born and then their son, and they sent me pictures of two small, well-bundled babies on a sled in a snowy handsome city street.
>
> The babies are gone now, both of them, one killed suddenly and violently in a raid, one lingering through a long winter of starvation. The handsome clever young husband is dead, too, though she doesn't know how, where or why he died. Even the city has vanished, and when she wrote me three years ago, all she had was a plot of ashy ruins in a waste of rubble and fallen masonry.

Think it over, gentlemen, this can happen to us! With the atom bomb in the hands of an unfriendly nation, it could happen *over night*. The subjects of that story were a family much like the families of most of us—a "rising young attorney," a "young and confident" wife, beloved of her

449

husband, "charming and cultured people," two adorable children, much like your children and mine, the Master's greatest gift to those united in his name, the supreme objects of man's and woman's affection, the final hope for realization of the dreams that we fond parents fail to make come true in our own lives. Yes, it happened *there*, and it can happen *here*.

But I do not believe it has to happen here. Indeed, I am convinced that we can build a sure defense against it—a defense that, paradoxically enough, will *de*crease our public expenditures rather than *in*crease them. All we have to do is make democracy work, *here* in our own country, make it work so well that our friends and potential friends abroad will be unshakably impressed and our enemies will be not only afraid to attack us but even anxious to come to terms with us. Remember, this won't cost us a thing. On the contrary, it will *reduce* our public expenditures and thus *increase* the net income of every one of us, because democracy, like any other form of government, has to be economical and efficient or it will not succeed and endure.

Does it sound too simple? Well, it isn't. Why do men live righteously? Because they see all around them the rewards of good conduct. Why do men strive for business and professional success? Because they see all around them the rewards of successful accomplishment. Success is at once one of the most impressive of all phenomena—and the most contagious. This is as true of government as it is of any phase of man's affairs. Nothing succeeds like success. Make democracy succeed here and it will succeed elsewhere. It still has every virtue that it ever had. *It* hasn't failed. *We* have failed. We are letting it go by default. What a tragedy, and what irony it would be, if we allowed an ideology that was founded upon the ethical tenets of christianity to go by default to one that has no higher aim than inculcation of envy, hate, and destruction in the hearts of men.

We are being called upon to spend billions of dollars in Europe, Asia and elsewhere throughout the world for the propagation of our way of life. *We* call *our* way democracy. *I* believe with all my heart that democracy, like charity, should begin at home. I also believe that the immense investment we are making in efforts to induce other people to embrace democracy will be fruitless unless we make the organization and management of our own affairs, *under* democracy, consistent with the virtues that we claim for our system.

It's all well and good to preach a gospel, but it's quite another thing to live it. *We* aren't *living* the gospel of democracy and free enterprise today. We are merely *preaching* it. We have made only half of the combination work, and we've done that superlatively well. Free enterprise booms. But democracy staggers and reels under oppressive debts and inordinate operating costs—*both* the consequences of political failure, *our* political failure, *yours* and *mine*.

Our enemies are thoroughly aware of this. And in their propaganda they play it up for all it's worth, and more. Is it not reasonable to believe that this creates at least serious doubt in the minds of those at whom it is aimed whether our way is the way to lasting peace and security? Let us not doubt for a moment that it does. Let us not forget that the objects of this propaganda are people who are ill-fed, ill-clothed, ill-housed, financially destitute, sick at heart, and politically disillusioned. No, gentlemen, conversation alone will not win these people to our side. *They* know the horrors of war far more intimately than the people of this country. *They* have been in the middle of it. *They* are sick of privation and want.

I venture the prediction, therefore, that these people will not unreservedly choose our way of life unless and until we demonstrate that democracy can live within its means and thus prove that the security of those who embrace it is not constantly threatened by the possibility of fiscal collapse. Such a demonstration can not be made until we attain the kind of organization and management of our public affairs that we have attained in our private enterprises. If we fail to accomplish this, democracy will fail fiscally; and when it fails fiscally it also will fail politically.

How can we attain such organization and management? We can do it in only one way: By seeing to it that the success of democracy is made as much the business of the business and professional leaders of the country as is the attainment of business and professional success. This means that you and I and every business and professional man in the country must make constructive interest in public affairs a *de*finite part of our daily lives. Anything less is neglect of the duties of citizenship. Is this asking too much? I don't think so.

Let me give you another quotation, this time from a fascinating book by a famous writer. This quotation seems to me to be at once an accurate diagnosis of what is wrong with us and a clear indication of the remedy. In his novel entitled *Lydia Bailey*, Kenneth Roberts, in the characteristic style of his writings, used a narrator whom he called Albion Hamlin. Hamlin was a wise man, and in a discussion of Government with a much younger but no less wise man, Thomas Bailey, he made this observation: "They [he was referring to the founding fathers of our country] held public discussion to be a public duty and inert people to be the greatest menace to a country's freedom." Too many of us today are afraid to enter into public discussion. Even more of us, I fear, have become inert. *This* is not the sort of attitude toward public affairs that brought this country into being. And it is not worthy of those to whom we owe the blessings of freedom that we have enjoyed.

This country would not exist as a land of freedom but for the fact that the immortals who founded it put public duty above life itself and devoted themselves earnestly and seriously to the business of making the system work that they created. But it is not necessary for me to go that far back in history to find a patriot. I need only recall the public service of that

451

great Virginian and citizen of Lynchburg, the late Carter Glass, whose prodigious efforts in the public interest and whose fearless devotion to public duty was no less complete and inspiring than that of any Virginian, past or present. Every sinew of his body fairly teemed with love for his city, his state, and his country, a devotion which, I am told, remained steadfast even in the last moments of his life when the natural consequences of his undying zeal for the principles in which he unshakably believed were sapping the strength of mind and body that made him one of the nation's foremost citizens. He loved and cherished liberty, he saw clearly the consequences of losing it, he burned with the patriotism of Washington, Jefferson and Henry, and the word "fear" was not in his vocabulary. I salute his memory with reverence and profound respect.

We and our country would rise to a new height of influence and power if every citizen firmly resolved to emulate this great and immortal Virginian's inspiring example. "Unreconstructed Rebel," yes. But more important than that, Patriot and Ever Faithful Lover of Liberty, Unrelenting Foe of the Foes of Freedom, who realized, above all else, that improvidence will destroy any government, no matter what its virtues, and that "inert people" are "the greatest menace to a country's freedom."

THE CHALLENGE OF OUR TIME[†]

by

T. Coleman Andrews

SIXTEEN years ago a philosophy of government came into vogue here in our land that holds self-reliance in contempt, regards personal success as a sin, and reverses our traditional concept that government derives its authority from the governed.

Notwithstanding 144 years of glorious and unparalleled achievement under a government of limited powers, and despite history's warning that the people of every form of all-powerful state that ever has been created ultimately lost their freedom, a dangerously large number of our people then accepted in some degree the idea that the individual citizen no longer could cope with the problems of security and that his only hope lay in placing his fate in the hands of bureaucratic planners.

Since that time, despite the fact that this departure from tradition has been a costly failure, the ranks of those who have fallen victim to the tragic illusion that the government can take care of them better than they can take care of themselves have grown to an alarming extent, and the current Federal Administration has announced frankly that it seeks to turn the United States into a "welfare state."

Thus, many of our fellow citizens and the party in power have denied the validity of the cause for which our forefathers fought and have turned back toward the tyranny of government from which man has had to struggle to free himself ever since he emerged from savagery. Clearly, we have relaxed the vigilance that is the price of freedom and are rapidly losing the first two essentials of the character of free men—namely, the will to be free and the willingness to make any individual or collective sacrifice that the ultimate attainment and lasting preservation of freedom might require. We have rejected the scalpel of cure for the opiate of escape and forgetfulness.

[†]Presented at a meeting of the Michigan Association of Certified Public Accountants, January 1950. Reprinted with permission of the Michigan Association of Certified Public Accountants from *The Michigan Certified Public Accountant*, February 1950, pp. 2-4, 9-11. Similar addresses were delivered at the Massachusetts Society of Certified Public Accountants, September 26, 1949, and at the National Affairs Conference of the Virginia State Chamber of Commerce Silver Anniversary Meeting at Roanoke, Virginia, April 15, 1949.

CONSTITUTIONAL FREEDOM

Inherent in our Constitution and Bill of Rights is the tenet that man is completely free or he is not free at all—that he cannot surrender any of the inalienable rights with which nature endows him without ultimately losing all of these rights.

Among the rights guaranteed to us by these heretofore sacred documents is that of acquiring and being secure in the ownership of property. To enable us to acquire property, the framers of the Constitution reserved to the people the privilege of engaging in industry and commerce free of hampering government restrictions. This included the privilege of making a profit commensurate with the risks assumed.

We call this the right of enterprise, and it has been due to the existence and exercise of this right that the nation has grown great, for it has been from the profits of free enterprise and the savings of the people that our matchless industrial plant has been built—a plant so powerful, let us remember, that it saved the world from slavery twice within a generation.

The framers of the Constitution and Bill of Rights foresaw, with prophetic vision, that if the government were permitted to own and control the means of production and distribution the government soon would become the master of the people and freedom would disappear.

Directly and indirectly we have permitted the government to invade the fields of production and distribution to a greater extent than many of us realize, I fear. For instance, large groups of farmers now grow NOT what they WANT to grow, nor AS MUCH as they want to grow, but what and how much the government says they MAY grow. The government subsidizes them and the government is their master. No people can give up their self-reliance for subsidy without eventually suffering their subsidizes to become their masters.

RESIGNATION DANGEROUS

Thus, and in other ways, and in other fields of endeavor, we have gone so far that a dangerously large portion of the population has come to feel that socialism is inevitable. This attitude of resignation is far more threatening to our freedom than those who urge the false virtues of paternalism, for it bespeaks a weakening of the will to be free and of the resistance to tyranny that this will generates.

I suggest that what we have to do in this situation is awaken ourselves to realization of the fact that advocacy of the all-powerful state stems from conviction on the part of those who urge it that the people are incapable of governing themselves. I know of no surer way of accomplishing this awakening than by stimulating the people's pride in what they have accomplished through self-government—in the wonders, I might say, that

454

we have wrought under our present system, without governmental aid and free of undue governmental restraint.

By citation of specific benefits, of which there are endless examples...most of them obscured by forgetfulness, unfortunately, I would start out by recalling what we have made private enterprise mean to us and to others. Let's begin with a few general results.

In population we are outnumbered in the world 14 to 1. In the area of land occupied we are exceeded by 16 to 1. BUT, we have as many radios as all the rest of the people of the world put together ... 1½ times more life insurance ... 1½ times more telephones ... 6 times more automobiles ... 9 times more bathtubs ... ⅓ of all the world's rail transportation ... and so on down through the myriad list of conveniences that give us a standard of living that other people can only dream of: automatic central heating of our homes ... stoves that cook our meals while the housewife shops or the family is at church ... automatic refrigerators ... deep freeze boxes ... automatic washing machines and dishwashers ... vacuum cleaners ... an air transportation system that covers the world ... rail and bus systems that link every community in the land ... the world's highest yields of the products of the soil, with abundant food for all and large surpluses to relieve hunger abroad ... and a host of others too numerous to mention.

PRODUCTS OF FREEDOM

Now, admittedly, all these are material things. But it isn't in the material sense that any of them is important. What DOES make them important ... and of this I remind you with all the earnestness at my command ... is that they are NOT the products of laws and executive orders. They are the products of FREEDOM ... of the opportunity and right that the Constitution and Bill of Rights have given us to develop as individuals, as masters of the state, free of the regimentation and compulsion by which people are restricted when they permit themselves to become servants of the state.

No, my friends, our vastly superior standard of living has not just happened. It is no accident that we who compose only 1/14 of the world's population are able to buy ½ of the world's production of goods. It is because we have had a system of government under which every man has been free to develop to the full the capabilities with which he was endowed. It is because we have been free to compete for the patronage of our fellows in a free market, and to profit therefrom, or, to put it another way, to receive a fair rental for the tools that the investment of our savings has provided ... free to dream dreams ... free to back our dreams with our substance ... free to invest our substance in the expansion of industry, secure in the knowledge that our ownership of property will be respected ... that the process of making more and more and better and better things that people want, at the same or lower costs, might go on and on to the greater and greater enhancement of our standard of living, and to the greater and greater enrichment of our lives. This is free enterprise. It is the cornerstone of our country's greatness.

Now, let us consider briefly the records of some of the segments of our free enterprise system. Fortunately, we are able to see, in this phase of our reflections, not only what kind of jobs some of our important industries have done but also what happens when the government is permitted to engage in business activities. We will start with the railroads.

RAILROAD OPERATIONS

In World War I, government operation of the railroads cost the people of the United States $1,616,000,000—an average of about $2,000,000 a day, ALTHOUGH FREIGHT RATES WERE INCREASED 80% PER TON MILE AND PASSENGER RATES WERE INCREASED 51%.

During World War II, instead of costing the people $2,000,000 a day, the railroads, under private operation, paid $2,500,000 of income taxes per day into the Federal treasury, WITHOUT ANY INCREASE IN FREIGHT RATES ... WITH ONLY A SLIGHT INCREASE IN PASSENGER RATES ... AND DESPITE SUBSTANTIAL INCREASES IN WAGES AND OTHER COSTS. Thus, the Federal Government was nearly $4,500,000 a day better off under private operation in World War II than under Government operation in World War I. And yet there are people who say: "Let the Government own and operate the railroads"!

Now how were the railroads able to do this? They were able to do it because during the period between World War I and World War II they greatly improved their equipment and the methods of railroad transportation. In World War II they were able to carry a freight-traffic load 74% greater than that of the first World War and a volume of passenger traffic 100% greater ... WITH ⅓ FEWER LOCOMOTIVES ... ¼ FEWER FREIGHT CARS ... AND ¼ FEWER PASSENGER CARS. These fewer cars and engines were BETTER CARS AND ENGINES ... they ran on BETTER TRACKS ... their movements were controlled and guided by BETTER SIGNALS AND COMMUNICATIONS ... they had the use of BETTER TERMINALS ... and they were serviced in BETTER SHOPS.

The net result of all these improvements—brought about by the railroads, mind you, *not* by laws and executive orders—was that the average freight car produced twice as much transportation per day during World War II as in the first World War, while the average freight train turned out, during each hour it was on the road, more than twice as much transportation service.

There, in a few words, is one of the epics of American private enterprise, one of the finest examples ever seen of complete fulfillment of the obligation of industry to make more and more and better and better goods and services available at the same or less cost. This is only one example of instance after instance, since the beginning of the industrial era, where this obligation has been honorably and fully met. It is but one example of the blessings of freedom. It was accomplished by the people through their savings, NOT by the government.

AUTOMOBILE INDUSTRY

Now, let's take a look at the record of the automobile industry. The automobile has become so common in our country that we regard it as a commodity. Why? Because private enterprise took the automobile and applied to its manufacture the principles of mass production and made it possible for practically every family to own one. Incidentally, I might mention also that the automobile has become the source of employment for more than 8 million people, or more than 1/7 of the nation's workers.

In 1928, the sum of $1,320 (factory price) would buy a 6-cylinder, 75-horsepower automobile that had a wheel base of 115¾ inches, weighed 3,764 pounds, and would go 65 miles an hour with an engine that gave 14.7 miles per gallon of gas.

In 1948, notwithstanding the tremendous increase in the cost of labor and material that took place in the meantime, $1,280 (factory price), or $40.00 less than in 1928, would buy a 6-cylinder automobile, NOT of 75-horsepower but of 90-horsepower ... that would go NOT 65 miles per hour but 82 ... that would give NOT 14.7 miles per gallon of gas but 22.7 miles.

Here again is complete fulfillment of that obligation of free enterprise to increase steadily the volume and quality of goods and lower their cost. Here again is freedom of opportunity at work for the good of all, accomplished by the people through their savings, NOT by the government. Forget about all the other improvements, if you like; but ponder for a moment that increase of 50% in mileage. That has put money in the pocket of every automobile owner, the same as if he had received an increase in his pay.

The contributions of the railroad and automobile industries to the greatness of our country, and to the high standard of living that you and I enjoy, is a triumph of our system of government—an accomplishment of the people. Why? Because these industries have been built with your savings and those of your friends, neighbors and acquaintances. They aren't owned by a handful of rich people, as the critics of our system would have us believe. They are owned directly by tens of thousands of stockholders—people like you and me—practically every person in the country has an indirect interest in them through their investments in insurance and in pension and retirement funds set up by themselves and their employers.

457

PRIVATE INVESTMENTS

Since almost all of us are investors in insurance, and since many of us are investors in pension and retirement funds, our indirect investment is even more important than our direct investment. Why? The answer is almost articulate in the financial statements of any insurance company, or of any pension and retirement fund. In these statements you find, among other things, that the portfolios of these companies and funds to which they pertain include thousands of shares of the stock of corporations.

The securities of these companies and funds are YOUR securities and MINE, purchased from the savings of income which, under our system, is what our capabilities and diligence make it, NOT what a bureaucratic government says it SHOULD be—income that is sufficient not only to cover the cost of living but also provides some surplus to be laid away for those rainy days that come in the lives of all of us, NOT the puny income of communist and socialist slaves of all-powerful states, where production isn't even sufficient to provide the necessities of life, even if the workers were allowed sufficient income to purchase them. Savings and investment are not permitted in communist and socialist states.

Incidentally, the shares of corporation stocks that are held by our insurance companies, and by our private pension and retirement funds, are in vaults and strong boxes, where we can see them with our own eyes...feel them with our own hands...and take comfort in the feeling of security that they afford for ourselves and our loved ones. How different this is from what happens to the taxes we pay to provide so-called social security benefits. These contributions aren't invested; they are spent as fast as they are received. Hence, before we can get any of them back in the form of benefit payments, we must be taxed again.

Our private insurance companies and our private pension and retirement funds are among our most sacred institutions. Whether we will preserve the integrity of the investments that make these companies and funds sure bulwarks against want is a part of the challenge of the day, for if we give up the free enterprise system, we will perforce put ourselves at the mercy of a still further enlarged bureaucracy that will be less concerned with our security than with its own, and our security will vanish in wasteful and extravagant spending, aimed NOT at making us secure but at preserving the political status of the spenders.

POWER INDUSTRY RECORD

Now let us consider briefly the record of the electric power industry. From 1906 to 1910, the average cost of electricity per kilowatt hour was 10.3 cents. This cost was reduced steadily until in 1947 it was down to 3.2 cents. Thus, ⅔ of what we had to spend for electricity when the power industry was young now is available to be spent for other things.

This record stands out in bold relief against the record of TVA, whose rates, we are told, would have to be 40% higher than those charged by private power companies, if it were required to recover from its customers what you and I are required to pay to subsidize its operations.

We people outside the Tennessee Valley can't have electric furnaces in our basements, because they aren't economical. But the people of the Tennessee Valley have them, NOT because TVA can or does produce and distribute electric power at any lower cost than the private power companies, but because the government can and does use its taxing power to take from us and give to the people of the Tennessee Valley. Here is clear proof that no government can do anything for any group of its people without making all the rest pay for it. No wonder TVA must now begin to build steam plants. It is giving away the margin between its capacity and its consumers' demands.

TVA, mind you, is a GOVERNMENT operation. Its record IS the result of laws and executive orders. The privately owned power industry's record, on the other hand, is the record of free enterprise ... of free men free to dream and build—for their private profit, yes; but also, and of vastly greater importance, for the far greater enrichment of not only the pocketbooks but also the lives of the people, and on the basis of every man paying his own way.

On its face the record of the power companies in bringing the cost of electricity down from 10.3¢ per kilowatt hour to 3.2¢ probably sounds a bit commonplace, and that's exactly what it is. But its implications in terms of better living are incalculable; and therein lies its real significance.

By the mere flick of a switch we turn darkness into light, bringing the voices and music of the world right into our homes, banish the drudgery of housework, preserve our food, cook our meals, and bring within reach a host of other blessings that are yet to come to the vast majority of the rest of the people of the world.

By merely lifting the receiver of our telephone and spinning a dial, we now can bring the far corners of the earth within the sound of our voices. In a matter of moments we can talk to San Francisco. The romance of it is exciting when you think about it. Yet, to most of us the telephone is just another commonplace accessory to our daily lives, and such an inexpensive accessory that we rarely even think of the cost. Just think of it, for a matter of a few dollars a month we make the world our neighbor. Every new installation increases the coverage that this remarkable service affords and thus constantly gives us more and more for the little we pay for it.

The record of the electric power industry is another saga of free enterprise—the saga of another service that is available to us because our system of Government is one that makes it worthwhile to be ambitious ... to find new and better ways to enrich our lives and those of our fellowmen ... and to seek the joy and satisfaction that comes from contemplation of outstanding accomplishment.

459

PRODUCTS OF FREEDOM

All these marvels, my friends, are marvels of freedom—products of the inventive genius, and spirit of enterprise that were unlocked when, here in our land, there was adopted that charter of man's emancipation that we call the Constitution—that charter of freedom under which every citizen was given, as a matter of right, the greatest possible opportunity to develop the talents with which he was by nature endowed, limited only to the extent necessary to protect the body politic from predatory exercise of individual power. These marvels, therefore, are NOT products of bureaucratic compulsion.

Moreover, the examples of the record of free enterprise that I have cited—and I have only scratched the surface of a vast accumulation of such examples—stand out in bold relief against the record of the Government, which, instead of giving us more and more for our money, gives us less and less, and now, four years after the ending of World War II, would take two days of each week of our earnings to meet its largest and ever increasing budget. And for what purpose? For the unthinkable purpose of supporting what has been aptly termed a program of "creeping socialism," the consummation of which would be slavery for all of us.

It may be truly said that the 160 years that have elapsed since the Constitution was adopted have been the golden era of civilization. Our country has made it so. It was OUR forefathers' genius and passion for beneficent government—so firmly and so eloquently expressed in our Constitution and Bill of Rights—that sparked the inspiring march toward man's ultimate rendezvous with freedom that developed in this era and that has produced all the wonders of emancipation from tyranny that we now see all around us.

It is strikingly significant, I think, that down through the ages countless millions, after struggling unsuccessfully to keep body and soul together, have died young in misery and squalor, and that suddenly in one spot on this planet a people found the way to abundant food and banishment of the pangs of hunger. Why has it been, after men died of starvation for 6,000 years, that we in America have never had a famine? It has been because of the vast release of human energy and ingenuity that comes when the individual is set free to work for his own advancement and for the good of his fellowmen.

DEVELOPMENTS UNDER FREEDOM

Consider, for instance, the oil of the Middle East that we've been hearing so much about in recent years. This pool was not recently discovered; its existence has been known for centuries. On his exploration and conquest of the East, Alexander the Great found it oozing out of the ground. That was almost 2,300 years ago—more than 300 years before the beginning of the Christian era. Yet there it lay for more than 20 centuries, undeveloped and unconverted to the good of mankind, in the very path of civilization after civilization—the civilizations of the East, of the Near East, of Greece, of Rome, and of Europe—until a government of free men was established here in the Western hemisphere.

Thus, it was the inventiveness, ingenuity and spirit of enterprise that were born of the incentive given by the new venture into democracy and freedom here in America that opened up the great oil resources of the Middle East and the world.

GOVERNMENTS BY TYRANTS FELL

Remember, my friends, that the governments that rose and fell during all those centuries were NOT governments of the PEOPLE. They were governments of kings, conquerors, despots and tyrants ... governments in which there was not inherent any incentive to individual accomplishment ... governments under which the welfare of the people was subordinated to the philosophy that "the king comes first."

No, until there was established here in this country a government in which the people made themselves the masters of their fate, and gave their government only limited power, was there ever full realization of the boundless potentialities of human freedom.

Thus, it is clear that correction of the imperfections that have shown up in our system lies NOT in enlarging the power of the government and curtailing our rights and freedom as individuals but in jealously safeguarding and extending those rights and that freedom. To enlarge the power of the government is to take a step that all the history of government shows, with telling clarity, to be backward rather than forward ... toward stagnation rather than toward progress ... toward serfdom rather than toward freedom.

A PLAN OF ACTION

Now you undoubtedly are saying to yourselves that in spite of vigorous protests from all over the land against the extension of the government's powers over our lives, the process of whittling down our freedom as individuals and converting the Government to an all-powerful state seems to go on unabated. If so, you are absolutely right. Moreover, you are probably asking yourselves what you, as individuals, can do to stop this trend; and it must be said that this is a natural question. Also, I think that it is incumbent upon me to try to answer this question.

I do not believe that the trend can or will be stopped unless and until the true believers in government of limited powers do something more than merely protest. The time for just talking and passing resolutions, and debating the fine points of economic theory, as forms of protest, is past.

461

Verbal subscription to the principles of liberty that are inherent in our fundamental law is all well and good in its place, but lip service is not going to save private enterprise and all the other rights and privileges that our forefathers thought they were guaranteeing to us for all time. It is going to take something more than that—a good deal more; and I suggest that the burden of responsibility for doing what needs to be done rests upon the country's business leaders, who, after all, are the custodians and practitioners of the private enterprise system.

My suggestion is that you and I, and every one of the millions of people who have the responsibility for making the private enterprise system work, have got to take the time to familiarize ourselves with its benefits and expound these benefits at every possible opportunity. I also think that we have got to familiarize ourselves with our system's imperfections and direct our attention seriously toward finding solutions for these imperfections. Above all, we must admit frankly that there are imperfections and show convincingly that we have a sincere desire, and are really trying, to find corrective measures. Then—and this is the positive action we must take—we have got to start expounding the virtues of individual freedom and private enterprise to everyone who will listen to us.

I would not want to give the impression that the method I have used here today is the best method of selling the private enterprise system, but I suggest that it at least has the virtue of being specific and down to earth, in the sense that it is related to the income of the people. And I would remind you that I have only scratched the surface; the examples that I have used constitute an almost infinitesimal percentage of the number that are available to those who will take the trouble to develop them.

Bear in mind that our job is one of fighting misstatements, misinterpretations, and deliberate falsehood with truth, and that one little grain of truth is always more powerful and more convincing than the most impressive array of contrary representations.

As accountants, you and I know that many of the alleged facts as to the profits of private enterprise and as to industrial, commercial and financial practices and their consequences, have been grossly misrepresented to the people. But we must not be surprised that these misrepresentations have been taken seriously, because there has not been an organization for the dissemination of the facts of our system, whereas those who are bent upon our system's destruction are well organized and stop at nothing in their effort to gain control of our lives. We too must organize; and we must have a positive program for carrying the truth to the people.

If we perfect such an organization, and if we take the time to really work at carrying out the organization's purposes, we are sure to reverse the present trend and get back to sound thinking and action in the management of our public affairs, because right is always more powerful than wrong. That is why a person who is right only half the time usually will succeed.

Moreover, let us not make the mistake of underestimating the intelligence of the American people. True enough, life has become pretty complex, but it still is susceptible of understandable interpretation. The rules of thrift and provident living are as applicable to governments as they are to individuals, and they are just as sound today as they were the day they were discovered and first written. If this were not true, this country would not have attained its present greatness, for it has been by the application of these rules by countless millions that the greatness of our country has been achieved. Make no mistake about it, the people of our country believe as firmly as ever that Goethe was right when he said that "the best government is that which teaches men to govern themselves," and all that the people are waiting for is leadership that will firmly and positively implement this philosophy.

I also would remind you of the warning of Jefferson, to whom we and the world owe so much for his penetrating discourses upon the architecture of free government. He and others of his time foresaw clearly the probability that we would lapse into some degree of acceptance of the very kind of illusory propositions with which we presently are toying. It was he who, for our guidance at such a time as this, warned that he knew of "no safe depository of the ultimate powers of society but the people themselves, and, if we think them not enlightened enough to exercise their control with a wholesome discretion, the remedy is not to take it from them, but to inform their discretion by education."

I suggest that the time has come to heed and act upon this warning—to resist with all our strength the ruinous notion that it is possible for any nation to strengthen itself *or the weak* by weakening the strong. I believe sincerely that the people will follow well organized or sincere leadership devoted to carrying out a program based upon absolute adherence to the principles of government that I have cited. I am convinced of this, because it seems to me that we merely have to make people see the obvious. As Justice Holmes once said, "We need education in the obvious more than investigation of the obscure."

Certainly the time for action is here—militant and courageous action—the kind of action that men take when something really worth while to them is placed in jeopardy, apropos of which I remind you that our form of government is the most priceless possession we own and that its very life is in danger. Our factories—yes, even our cities—could be leveled to the ground and we could rebuild them. But if our government is destroyed, it could not be rebuilt within the foreseeable future, and all that is dearest and most precious to us will be lost forever, so far as we and unreckonable generations to come are concerned.

PEACE FOR THE FUTURE

Tennyson dreamed of the world at peace and of the ultimate ascendancy of the power of common sense. He expressed it in these lines of inspired hope:

> When the war drums throb no longer and battle flags are furled,
> In the parliament of man, the federation of the world;
> When the common sense of most shall hold a fretful realm in awe,
> And the kindly earth shall slumber, lapt in universal law.

I believe that such a consummation is possible of attainment. I also believe that ours is the way of life by which it is most likely to be attained. I further believe that it is within the power of those to achieve it who built the great industrial machine that twice within a generation saved the world from predatory conquest. And I hold that it is our duty to make the effort not only for our own salvation and that of our posterity, but also for the salvation of free men everywhere, and for the salvation of those who yearn to be free, as well.

Our country is the last great stronghold of democracy and freedom—such a haven of refuge as countless millions of oppressed people throughout the world envision as the ultimate sanctuary of those who truly love freedom and aspire to attainment of the ultimate dignity of the individual.

If we restore the light of democracy and freedom to flaming brilliance here, the world may truly be made "safe for democracy." If we allow this light to die out here, the world will again be plunged into the gloom of tyranny and oppression, and another age of darkness will ensue, from which mankind will not again emerge save by bloodshed, starvation and death too global and too horrible to contemplate.

That is the challenge of our time as I see it, and I believe we will accept and conclusively meet it.

SUPERIOR SERVICE, PROFITS AND SAVINGS BUILT AMERICA[†]

by

T. Coleman Andrews

GENTLEMEN, I am greatly flattered to be asked to come here and address you tonight. I am happy to be here, not only because I have come at the request of gentlemen whom I regard as good friends, but also because of the opportunity that it gives me to talk to a group of men who are doing so much to make one of the great basic industries of our country function in an efficient and useful manner. There is no doubt in my mind as to what the future of the railroads is. For a long time I have been hearing people talk about the decrepit old railroads and how they are just one jump ahead of government ownership. But I'm not one who believes that.

I don't think that is apt to occur as long as the railroads continue to do things in a big way and as well as the railroads of America have done. I suppose most of you have read the little piece I wrote some time ago and which Mr. Smith was good enough to circulate. I believe we called it "The Challenge of Our Times." So you know what the accomplishments of the railroads have been, how they have tremendously increased their capacity for doing their job without using more than about half the amount of equipment they used to use. And how they go about their business as the backbone of our whole system of defense in times of crisis, such as we are now in. So I don't have to tell you how the railroads are doing that job. You know better than I because you're doing it.

Last night I spoke here in this same room to the Rotary Club of Roanoke. This great organization's motto, as most of you know, is: "He profits most who serves best." And now, interestingly enough, tonight I am speaking to you who are assembled to discuss Better Service to the customers of the Norfolk and Western Railway. So it seems that this is Service Week as far as I'm concerned—and I'm happy that it is.

If profit were the only aim of Better Service, the purpose of your being here would be a purely material one and, therefore, would be, I would say, largely an ignoble purpose. But I am not so naive as to believe that you don't know which side your bread is buttered on, and that you usually act accordingly. I know several of the men who manage the Norfolk and

---

[†]Presented at the 26th Annual Better Service Conference, Norfolk and Western Railway Company, Roanoke, Virginia, April 13-14, 1951. Reprinted with permission from *Norfolk and Western Magazine*, May 1951, pp. 279-284.

Western and I'm sure that the mere desire to be certain that the Norfolk and Western shows high profits is not their sole purpose as executives of that great railroad. As a matter of fact, tonight, just after I sat down to the table, I asked the president how the railroad was doing; I told him that I had been reading some of the things he said about it recently, and as a very minor stockholder I was happy to see them. "But," I said, "what about that stock? It's not doing so well. I happen to have bought at the highest price it ever went to and never has it gotten back since!"

Well, I got slight comfort from him; his immediate reply was, "Well, after all, there are a good deal more things to running a railroad than merely trying to keep the stock up." (Laughter) Well, it was perfectly obvious that Bob Smith doesn't think always about profits; and I hope that his directors who are here will not be too much influenced by that remark, or at least will take it in the spirit in which it is offered. At any rate, gentlemen, I am certain of one thing, and that is, the gentlemen who run this railroad realize that profit is an incidental result of good service, and that undoubtedly their motto, though unspoken, nevertheless subconsciously is this: "Be sure that the service is good and the profit will come as a matter of course."

It has been my observation all of my life that men who went about their daily business with that dominating philosophy, somehow or another always seemed to be the money-makers of the community. It always is to be found in the background and is the foundation of successful enterprise. And so I would say that the philosophy of these gentlemen exemplifies that beautiful story of the building of the temple, and that their example has gone on to you, that you have acquired also that philosophy and act by it. That is obvious from the spirit of this meeting and from the accomplishments of the road with which your lot is cast.

I would like to tell you that story of the temple; maybe some of you have heard it; but it's a story that always, I think, bears telling. I don't know when it took place, but somewhere back in the past a church was being built in France; and the good Padre who was to be in charge of it one day saw the walls emerging from the foundation. It began to look like the temple would really be an assured fact before too long, and he was happy. So he went among the workmen and stopped at the side of one of the masons, and he said, "Good morning, my son; what are you doing?" The mason replied "I'm laying bricks."

Well, the Padre was a little bit taken aback by that, and he went on down the line and he encountered not a few who had the idea that they were laying bricks. So finally he came to another and asked the same question, and the answer was, "I'm building a wall." Well, that sounded a little better, but it wasn't quite what the Padre wanted to hear. Finally, he came to an old fellow whose hands gave evidence that he had been laying bricks for a long time, they were bony and calloused and hard; but he handled his bricks and his trowel with the deftness of a real artist, and somehow there

466

was in his face a picture of real beauty. And when the Padre asked him, "My son, what are you doing?" this veteran said, without a moment's hesitation, "My good father, I'm building a temple to Almighty God."

That, I think, gentlemen, is the spirit of building, the spirit of doing, that dominates the great and successful industries of America. In my judgment, it has been men, from the beginning of time, who have been building temples who have made the good and the great and the fine things of this world. Unhappily, a deplorably large number of people have lost the motivation of that noble point of view. It is particularly gone from the hearts of those upon whom the mantle of political leadership has fallen. How often, for instance, have you noticed that the national administration—and I'm not here to quarrel with the national administration as such because I'm interested in America, and not in politics—but how often have you noticed that the national administration's reaction to failure of its ill-advised course has been to propose yet another and more costly course? Money, which in this case is just another way of saying "profits," would, by itself solve any problem whatsoever. Failure of our projects all too often is answered by another demand for more money to do it another way. The trouble has been, my friends, that these so-called leaders have just been laying bricks or building a wall; they haven't been building a temple.

Now, our hearts and imaginations have not yet caught the vision of the temple, or if they ever had it, they have lost it; they have not thought in the terms of "Better Service." And so government has come to cost more and more while the cost of everything else has gone down. Now I know some of you will say, "Well, that's a strange statement for you to make. We thought that there was inflation and that prices are up." That's true; in terms of the dollar prices *are* up. But let's go back to that railroad of yours. You are delivering today twice as much freight with the same amount of equipment as you did only a few years ago at a relatively small increase in rates. So, actually, the price of the commodity that you sell has gone down. The other day I picked up the annual report of one of the electric companies, and I was frankly a little bit surprised to find that the curve of their rates to residential consumers showed a gradual and steady stepping down over the last 40 years. Their rates today in units of electricity sold were actually lower than they have ever been in the history of the business. The same thing may be said about your automobile. That automobile costs you more dollars today, but if you will go back only about 20 years you will find that you are getting vastly more automobile for your money than you got 20 years ago—far more than the increase in price that you are paying ... a more powerful engine, an engine that will run more miles on a single gallon of gasoline, tires that will run forty to fifty thousand miles before they're worn out whereas they used to run only ten thousand. And by and large, and all through that wonderful mechanism

467

given to us by the ingenuity of American industry, you get more for your money.

And how I like to think about the wonders electricity has wrought, especially the wonders of the radio and the telephone! You remember the other night, the papers announced that Congressman Martin had talked to General MacArthur on the telephone in Tokyo. Think of it, gentlemen, to be able to walk out into this lobby and pick up the telephone and say to the operator, "I want to talk to my son in Tokyo" and being able to do it in a matter of moments! Think of the radio that brings into your home the most beautiful music of the world; and now the television that brings in the artistry of the world not only through the ear but through the eye! All of these things have been brought to us, mind you, by people who have visions of building temples, not visions of mere profit or of laying bricks or building a wall.

Now where did all these wonder-working things come from? They didn't just happen. How were they paid for; who put up the money? They were paid for, my friends, by profits and savings. Tonight I want to spend just a few minutes discussing profits and savings because there are people in the world who somehow have come to believe that it is sinful to make a profit ... that it is sinful to be in business and to sell your goods or your services for more than you paid for them ... who think that the government ought to control and manage all the means of production and distribution, industrial, agricultural, scientific and all the rest. Are profits and savings synonymous terms? Do they mean the same thing? They do indeed. There is no basic difference between the dollars of profit that the corporation enters upon its books and the savings that you and I put in the bank, as individuals. Let's remember first of all that the corporation is owned by individuals; it is merely an agency that acts for one or two or more individuals. We read recently where the number of stockholders of one corporation was nearly a million—I believe it was the American Telephone and Telegraph Company. Nearly a million people own the American Telephone and Telegraph Company.

Now the difference between what any corporation pays for the thing it sells, whether it be goods or services, and what it gets for those goods and services is profit. And if you happen to work for that corporation and you make $5,000 a year, and you save a thousand dollars, you have made a profit of $1,000. There is no essential difference between your savings and a corporation's profits. And, my friends, it is those profits and those savings that have gone to build the industry of America; it is those profits and those savings that account for everything that you and I see around us of a material nature—not its origin, of course; because, however devoted I may be to the economics of our system, I should be the first to recognize that all of our gifts come from above.

Take the railroad—the Norfolk and Western, for instance, with 650 million dollars of profit invested in your plant and devoted to the public service—where did that 650 million dollars come from? It came from the profits and the savings of this country; from people who had saved their money and had something to invest, who bought stock in the Norfolk and Western Railway Company. Many of you, I presume, are stockholders. Other corporations have bought the stock of the Norfolk and Western Railway out of their profits. The money that has been raised by the Norfolk and Western to build that 650 million dollars of investment has come from the profits that it has made. Where else would it come from? Money doesn't grow on trees; it has to be earned. Oh, the government could print it, surely, but there usually has to be a basis for money as there is in this country; and so the investments of business enterprises in America and elsewhere have been made with profits and savings.

Since 1945 there have been invested in this country 50 billion dollars in expansion of industry and in replacement of worn-out plants. Up to 1948 the investment in all kinds of plants in this country had increased our production nearly 70 percent, and by the end of 1951, unless something unforeseen prevents, that 50 billion dollars of expenditure from '45 down to the end of '51, will have raised the productive capacity of our country to 93 percent more than what it was in 1941. In other words, by the end of 1951 we will be producing in this country twice as much of manufactured goods as we did in 1941. That, my friends, has been possible because there were people in this great country of ours who were building temples, not just laying bricks.

The oil industry is an interesting one; it has written its story recently in the current magazines and, I imagine, most of you have read it. It tells how, since 1945, the oil industry has made some money. The oil people admit they made a profit, and they're not ashamed of it. (Incidentally, I want to digress a moment before summarizing the oil industry to pay tribute to Mr. Ben Fairless, of the United States Steel Corporation, because there's a fellow who isn't afraid to admit that the United States Steel Corporation has been a success. He tells the world that it's been a success and he's proud of it. Why? Well, I suspect it's because he and those who have helped make it a success have been building temples, not just laying bricks.)

In spite of the fact that we went into the last war with the fear that we wouldn't have enough petroleum to see us through, the oil industry now reports that due to exploration since the war began in Europe in 1939, known reserves, discovered by the investment of profits and savings if you please, are now 30 percent greater than they were when the Germans started into Poland in September, 1939. The oil industry has spent enormous sums for the increasing of sources of supply and for increasing refining facilities. Oil leaders tell us that today their capacity for production is 42 percent higher, and their refining capacity is 36 percent higher. And, gentlemen, it was done—86 percent of it—with the profits of the oil business. They didn't ask the government for it; they didn't ask anybody for it—86 percent. The rest of it came from the savings of the people and the profits of us individuals who have faith in America and in the oil business, and in the system of government under which we live. Profits and savings have made the great expansion of the oil business possible. Let us not forget that it is the tremendous productive capacity of the industry of America, gentlemen, that gives us our security; and that's what won for us the victories of 1918 and the victories of 1945.

Sure enough, we had a great Army, a great Navy, a great Air Corps, and last but not least, a great Marine Corps. But did you know that the industrial capacity of America played a very important part in winning that war? Of course you do. Incidentally, 60 percent of all of the materials used in World War II and of all the material handled was petroleum and petroleum products. And I rather suspect the next in quantity was perhaps coal, although I'm not sure.

What is the alternative to growth through profit and savings? Mind you, I said growth through profit and savings. My answer is that it is stagnation under government ownership. And why would we stagnate under government ownership? My answer to that is that we would do so because we would lack the personal incentive to outstanding accomplishment. Oh, there are people who say, "We must take care of these poor unfortunate fellows that can't take care of themselves; we must never let anybody fail." My friends, I don't want to live in a world that takes away from me my right to fail; because if I understand anything at all it is that if you take away from me the right to fail, then you have robbed me of my principal reason to want to succeed. Self-reliance, responsibility under the law, privileges of freedom, yes; but responsibilities too, that go along with those privileges.

And I would like to say as I come towards the end of these remarks, just a few words about the spiritual side of life. Not long ago, one of my sons asked me what it was that made the world go 'round. I had never quite looked at it from that standpoint before, and, of course, I hedged. I said, "Well, son, just what are you getting at?" He said, "Well, everybody seems to be looking for money." I said, "Yes, a good deal of our happiness today comes from the material rewards we get from accomplishment. But," I said, "I think I see what you mean. There is something in the spiritual side of it." He said, "That's exactly what I mean." I said, "Well, let's sit down and talk about it for a minute. First of all, let's see what has happened in the history of the world, and under what conditions it has happened. Let's take those eras of history where you can really say that there has been progress, where civilization has advanced, and then let's see if we can find some answer to why it advanced at that time."

Well, of course, none of us is gifted with the power to search out and find all of the reasons why things happen; but I found these two things, gentlemen: First, I found that the greatest era of advancement in civilization occurred under a race that most of us look upon as filthy and despised, the Saracens, under the Mohammedans and under the philosophy of Mohammed. This fellow, Mohammed, you know, got some ideas that were strange in his time. He got the notion that there was only one God, and that that God was the God of right and truth, and that He was a God of creation, a God who judged men but did not seek to control them; who put them on earth free and exacted of them the penalties of wrong doing. There isn't a great deal of difference between that, my friends, and the philosophy of Christianity to which most of us subscribe.

Under Mohammed, or under the Saracens, beginning back there at Mecca, and from Mecca to Medina, and spreading then over North Africa and up into Europe through what is now Tangiers into Spain, and even on into France, the Saracens grew strong and very nearly controlled most of the world. If they did not actually control it physically, they controlled its thought. Under them trade and commerce began to develop. And would you believe it?—the very cloths on the tables in front of you were given to us by the Mohammedans, the Saracens. Our beds were given to us by them; and when you pronounce such words as mattress and talcum and sugar, you're speaking Arabic. Many of the early advances that were made in scientific fields ... in astronomy, for example ... were made by the Saracens, who discovered things about the universe that man had never known before. They gave us the theories of navigation that made the discovery of America possible. And, believe it or not, they gave us strawberry ice cream, and things as simple as that.

They established the greatest educational system that the world has ever known. The great University at Granada, Spain (which, incidentally, was the site of their last stand in Europe), was probably the greatest university that has ever been on the face of the earth. There was nothing compulsory about life under Mohammedanism. Every man was free and, under that atmosphere of freedom, civilization made one of the greatest advances that it had made prior to that time. When the Mohammedans finally were driven out of Spain, after a hundred years of inquisition, there were one million left. And when they were finally liquidated those that weren't killed were driven back to Africa. It was 300 years before such an era of prosperity and advancement began again. And, gentlemen, it began here in America under a government founded upon the teachings of Jesus Christ. And can anyone doubt that from the time of the discovery of this great country to the present day it has not fulfilled its destiny for the good of man? Has it not reached the very heights of industrial greatness, of intellectual attainment, of advances in religious thought, in the arts and in the sciences?

Is it not significant to you, my friends, that in all of these 6,000 years of recorded history the two great eras in which civilization scored its greatest advances coincided with an era of freedom under which men were allowed to follow their own devices, free to choose their own course, free to do as they pleased, but subject, of course, always, to the obligation of self reliance and the other obligations that freedom imposes upon all of us? And so, my friends, I'd like for you to take away with you tonight the simple thought that after 6,000 years of recorded history—in which man starved, in which he suffered the plagues of famine and pestilence, and in which he died early and never knew the blessings of a long life such as we enjoy, and in which poverty was his common everyday lot (save for that one interlude when the philosophy of freedom allowed the Saracens to give us our first great advance in civilization)—there was established here on the shores of this great country, a system of government under which freedom was the foundation stone. Our people have never known want. Our people, indeed, have been privileged to create such a surplus of things that man needs for his sustenance not only to be able to sustain themselves but also to be able to succor most of the rest of the world and save it from the forces of evil that would reduce it to slavery. Yes, my friends, it is not a sin to make a profit. It is a sin, of course, to exploit anyone in any way; but somehow I'm convinced in my heart that when man sets his spirit at the right level and places his faith where it should be, accepting the full responsibilities that go along with the privileges of freedom, that there is then released that great incentive to accomplishment that has no bounds save the evils of greed that success sometimes can visit upon us. I hope you carry this back to your friends, and back with you to your jobs: You are working not merely for the Norfolk and Western Railway, you are not merely laying track for the Norfolk and Western, you are not merely selling some fellow on the idea of shipping his goods over the Norfolk and Western—oh, no, my friends, if you're doing your job right you're building a temple, not only that you may enjoy the benefits of meditating within the solemn confines of its walls, but that your fellow men may enjoy freedom, that they may enjoy the benefits that you yourself seek, and that you may discharge to your fellow men, that eleventh and greatest of all commandments, "Do unto others as you would have others do unto you." At the same time, you are making the great and noble choice for your children and your children's children, that they shall have in the years ahead of them the same privileges of rising to heights of greater accomplishment that you have enjoyed. You are saving them from the ignominy and all of the evils of slavery that come from those forms of government, those systems of living that say that all must be leveled to a common place in life. Instead, those who are in a position to do a real job and accomplish great things for the world are given an opportunity to rise to the highest potentialities of their capabilities.

ONE MAN'S PHILOSOPHY:
"My Life Is Not My Own"[†]
by
T. Coleman Andrews

T. Coleman Andrews, Richmond accountant, outlined his philosophy of life on a nation-wide broadcast yesterday. The address, broadcast by Station WRVA on the "This I Believe" program with Edward R. Murrow, CBS commentator, follows:

> I believe, as a matter of fundamental conviction, that my life is not my own. That life is of Divine origin and was given to me as a sacred trust to be lived with honor to Him by whom it was given. With the fullest possible usefulness to my fellowman, my community, my State and my country, and with credit to myself, my family and my profession.
>
> This belief implies acceptance of indivisible personal responsibility for my conduct. It opens the door to usefulness to others, which is of paramount importance, for no man can do full justice to himself except to the extent that he helps others do the same.
>
> I am an accountant. I do not think that I would have gotten very far in my profession if I had not decided early in my career that regardless of how good an accountant I might become, my success necessarily would be largely in proportion to the growth of the accounting profession. So I made up my mind at the start that it was up to me to help my profession grow and I have striven earnestly to remain true to that determination.
>
> This philosophy of personal responsibility and usefulness imposes rigid disciplines, in the least of which is that of having frequently to choose between the prestige of respect and the glamour of popularity. A whole new profession, so called, has sprung up to tell me that I am doomed to failure and frustration if I do not seek and achieve influence through popularity. God forbid. What a world this would be if everybody in it were mere back-slapping "yes" men. God entrusted man alone with mental power sufficient to penetrate and solve the mysteries of life.

[†]Reprinted with permission from *The Richmond News Leader*, August 12, 1952, p. 28.

With this power, man has multiplied the span of his life—mastered the sea and the air and the elements—discovered the secret of the atom—annihilated distance and now stands upon the threshold of interplanetary communication. This gift carries with it not only the right, but also the duty to challenge the thoughts and ideas of others and to seek truth ... same in the assurance that straight thinking and forthrightness will have the reward of respect. Through expediency often may we express fruitless silence or compromise.

If I let false doctrine go unchallenged and seek only popularity, having thereby to enhance or protect my selfish interest, I not only delude myself but also condemn myself in the sight of God and my fellow man.

What I seek to protect is certain to be lost in time, and I will stand—if not condemned as a drone—then certainly forgotten in mankind's inexorable progress toward his ultimate achievement of complete fullness of life.

And so this, too, I believe, that we must turn again to the Giver of Life and reassure our obligation of personal responsibility and usefulness, lest we suffer the catastrophic consequences of lost faith that William Penn foresaw when he warned that "people who are not governed by God will be ruled by tyrants."

LET'S GET RID OF THE INCOME TAX![†]

by

T. Coleman Andrews

RECENTLY a 14-year-old boy won $100,000 on a television quiz program. He winds up with about $25,000, after giving the Federal Government its - two-thirds tax share ($67,000) and New York State its $8,000.

Did I say that the young man won? Pardon me, Mr. Tax Collector, as you say, "After me, you come first."

In order to take home a full $100,000, that young man would have had to win a grand prize of roughly $765,000. Taxes would have taken all the rest.

Striking as his case is, it actually represents one of the lesser inequities of our present tax structure. Luck was on the boy's side; he was gambling, and after all he did win a sizable amount.

But what of people of large earning power and often erratic income—high one year, low the next—actors, authors, painters and other artistic or professional people? More than luck and casual knowledge go into the winning of their jackpots. Usually their skill and talent is made to pay off only after long years of study and training. Yet the taxes they have to pay are equally brutal, equally confiscatory. Not being permitted to average their incomes over a period of years, except in special situations, they pay much higher effective rates than people with steady incomes.

The professional athlete fares even worse. Those who manage to break through to the top usually do well incomewise. But the way up is pitifully unrewarding, so much so that those who make the grade more often than not mount the throne of glory head over heels in debt. And their reign usually is short.

These are people with whom the tax collector forms a real heads-I-win-tails-you-lose partnership. For instance, let's see what the income tax does to a boxing champion:

If such a fellow winds up a year having to pay on $200,000—not a high amount for even a not-too-colorful champion—he obviously is 50 times better off incomewise than, let's say, a man paying on $4,000. But—I still gasp at just the thought of this—*his tax is nearly 500 times more!* And before he can get clear financially some challenger polishes him off and

---

[†]Reprinted with permission from *The American Weekly*, April 22, 1956, pp. 6-7, 9, 21-22, 24-25.

475

puts him right back where he started. No averaging for him either. His are indeed the highest effective rates of all.

However, people of irregular earning power are by no means the only sufferers from our income tax laws. Almost everybody has now been gathered under the tent, and the percentage of those taxed leaves few immune to plucking who have enough feathers to notice.

IT'S "LEGALIZED CONFISCATION"

Up to $2,000 of taxable income the tax collector takes 20 percent. That's a mighty big bite for a person at that level of income. But from there he really moves in fast. From $4,000 to $6,000 it's 26 percent. Between $8,000 and $10,000 he takes a third. From $16,000 to $18,000 it's a half. From $32,000 to $38,000 it's two-thirds. From $50,000 to $60,000 it's three-fourths. And so on, until the top rates of 91 percent (more than 9/10ths) is reached at $200,000. This is called "progression," a fancy term which, realistically defined, means "legalized confiscation." But if the term used to define this brigandage is fancy, the results certainly are anything but fancy; they are murderous.

For instance, an executive, professional man or other person with an income of $40,000 pays 47 times more tax than the fellow with an income of $4,000. Ten times more income, 47 times more tax!

But even that isn't the whole of it. To the extent that income is derived from dividends, the government already will have skimmed off more than half (52 percent) before you get yours. Every stockholder should realize by now that while he takes all the risk and responsibility he's just a junior partner when it comes to participating in the profits and must eat at the second table and take what is left.

While the top rate (91 percent) of our "steeply graduated" tax is not reached until taxable income amounts to $200,000, one-half of the graduation above the beginning rate of 20 percent takes place by the time the income level reaches 1/10th of $200,000, or $20,000. This is rank discrimination against the middle-income, "white-collar" class. Is it deliberate?

Well, I'll give you one fact and one observation that ought to answer that question: The *fact* is that the first order of business of every dictatorship is to destroy the middle class. The two simply cannot live together. The masses are not regarded as a problem because dictators figure that the masses can be made to believe anything. The well-to-do don't count because there never are enough of them to be a serious threat.

The *observation* is that I have never known an advocate of statism in any form who did not give me the impression of being either a dupe or, at heart, a dictator. In my book one is as dangerous as the other.

In 1907—12 years after an income tax adopted in 1894 was declared unconstitutional—the late Cordell Hull, then a Congressman, started the ball a-rolling again with a resolution to amend the Constitution so as to permit the levying of an income tax.

In 1909 a similar resolution was offered in the Senate, and on February 3, 1913, the final act of ratification was completed. Then on October 3, 1913, President Wilson signed the first income tax bill under the 16th Amendment, a bill that imposed a tax that Senator Benjamin Harvey Hill many years before warned would enable the government to "make all property and rights, all states and people, and all liberty and hope, its playthings in an hour and its victims forever."

Senator Hill's fears were well founded. Everybody dances to the tune of the tax collector today. Once the government became armed with the income, estate and gift taxes (I'm proud to say that my state, Virginia, never ratified the 16th Amendment; our Senator Byrd's father saw to that) the people ceased to be masters of the government and became its victims.

In a penetrating and prophetic speech against the income tax that was adopted in 1894, Representative William Bourke Cockran of New York warned that "democratic institutions must perish from the face of the earth if they cannot protect the fruits of human industry wherever they are, or in whatever proportion they may be held by the citizens."

Sir William M. F. Petrie, noted archeologist, whose study of the rise and fall of nations and civilization gave him unusual insight into the outcome of man's experiment with government, observed that "democracies consume themselves through excessive and unjust taxation until they collapse and are succeeded by the Man on Horseback or the rank growth of the jungle."

As Commissioner of Internal Revenue I often thought how far we had gone toward consuming ourselves "through excessive and unjust taxation."

We have failed to realize, it seems to me, that through our tax system we have been playing right into the hands of the Marxists, who gleefully hail the income tax as the one sure instrument that will bring capitalism to its knees.

We also have failed utterly to see that Communism is not a political philosophy or plan but rather is a state of impotence to which those marked for subjugation by would-be dictators must be, and are, reduced in order to assure absence of effective resistance.

But there are other reasons for taking a dim view of our tax system, particularly the income tax, that are no less urgent than the fact that the system has become an ideological bombshell. I shall confine my comments primarily to the income tax. That alone is such a monstrous evil that it is hardly necessary to deal with other categories.

IT'S TOO COMPLICATED

One of the strongest and most serious counts in the indictment against the income tax is its complexity. It started out simple enough, but it is not an exaggeration to say that it has become as bewildering, confusing and frustrating a fiscal problem as the people ever had to cope with.

While I was Commissioner we tried everything we could think of to make this tax understandable, and I think we made progress. But we just have to face it: Relatively few people can handle even the short version of Form 1040 without assistance.

That's the nub of the whole problem: The forms have to follow the law; they can't be made any simpler than the law, and anyone who doesn't understand the law can't very well be expected to understand the forms.

Moreover, the unhappy truth is that it seems to be impossible to have simplicity and fairness at the same time. Most of the complexity in the present law came from efforts to achieve simplicity, plug so-called "loopholes," and remove discrimination. The sin of Congress lies in its failure to recognize this weakness of the income tax and do something about it long ago.

The present administration came into power believing it could simplify the situation and make the law more equitable. It had pledged itself to try to do both, and it not only exerted itself to the utmost to make good its pledge but called to its assistance as fine an array of professional and practical talent on a voluntary basis as was ever assembled by any administration to assist it with any problem.

The Treasury and other government people, and the volunteers from outside, all labored long and hard, and on August 16, 1954, after 18 months of the most prodigious effort by all hands, the President signed what has become known as the Internal Revenue Code of 1954.

Was this code an improvement over the old one? In certain mechanical respects it was. It also eliminated some injustices and softened others. But it did not banish the law's complexity. The fact is that many people think it made the situation more complex—and in some respects it did.

Let no one assume that the income tax law is any better understood in official circles than it is by its lay victims. I can't think of anything that would cause a more anguished howl from Capitol Hill than withdrawal of the men whom the Revenue Service assigns there to prepare returns for members of Congress or otherwise assist those ladies and gentlemen with the annual chore that confronts them as well as ordinary citizens.

Congress is not made up of supermen and superwomen. It is a collection of human beings, like the rest of us. Therefore I do not wish to be understood as making any attack on these ladies and gentlemen. But frankness compels me to suggest that just as no one has to understand what dynamite is made of to know that it can blow a person to kingdom come, so also no Representative or Senator has to know how to determine the tax consequences of intricate corporate re-organizations to have found out by now that the income tax is hopelessly complicated and a Trojan Horse.

WHO UNDERSTANDS IT?

Who, if anybody, does really understand this tax? How about the people who write it? The answer is not greatly different. By the time the tax committees and their staffs get through with the grist that is delivered to their mills many undecipherable changes have been wrought. The problem then presented is well illustrated by the struggle the experts in the Treasury Department have been having with the job of getting out regulations to cover the 1954 code.

There is official recognition of the fact that standing alone no revenue law is understandable. So the Treasury Department follows the enactment of each revenue law with an official interpretation of that law. The official interpretations are called regulations. Almost 20 months have elapsed since the Income Tax Code of 1954 became law—but the official interpretation of it isn't out yet!

It isn't that the people in the Treasury Department and the Internal Revenue Service haven't been trying to get these regulations out; quite the contrary. They've been knocking themselves out at it. But it has been extremely difficult for them to reach agreement as to just what Congress meant at many points and equally difficult to agree on how to express the intentions of Congress after they have agreed upon what the intentions were.

No current discussion of the complexity of the law, and who does or does not understand it would be complete without recalling the case of a certain Representative. When he found himself confronted by a substantial proposed deficiency assessment from which there was no other escape, he got himself relieved by a bill applying only to his particular case. And established something of a record for the passage of a bill pertaining to revenue by putting it through the House and the Senate in the remarkable space of four days, including a Saturday and a Sunday.

What's even more remarkable, this bill went through the House without the customary hearing by the House Ways and Means Committee. The record indicates that it *was* considered by the Senate Finance Committee. Because of the private nature of it, it became, when signed, a "private law."

Believe it or not, that happened only last year, and it came as near to making suckers out of all the rest of us as any piece of tax legislation Congress has ever enacted. No need of trying, folks; ordinary citizens just can't get relief that way.

IT'S A 30-YEAR-OLD PROBLEM

While Congress has not done anything effective about the law's complexity, it has been aware of it for at least 30 years and was sufficiently concerned about it in 1926 to include in the Revenue Act of that year a section (120.3). This provided for the establishment of a committee, to be known as the Joint Committee on Internal Revenue Taxation, to investigate and report, among other things, "measures and methods for the simplification" of the federal tax laws.

The Committee was established and is still in operation. It also has the duty of investigating the "operation and effects" of the tax system and the "administration of such taxes" by the Revenue Service.

Like all important Congressional committees, this one set up a staff to do the ground work that would be necessary as the basis for the committee's decisions.

This staff has had the duty, among others, of maintaining the surveillance that would lead to simplification of the revenue laws and keep the Revenue Service honest and efficient.

Has this watch been successful? The answer must be that it has not, for in spite of it the income tax law is infinitely more complex today than it was when the surveillance was established. For the first time in its history the Service was as near administrative collapse as it could be without folding up when the present administration took over in January, 1953, and never before did any administration inherit such a mess of corruption (recently brushed off as a few "fly specks" on the nation's window panes) as the present administration did.

Honest and efficient administration of public affairs cannot be achieved by invasion of the prerogatives and assumption of the responsibilities of executive officials by legislative bodies, committees, individuals, or committee staffs.

There is no basis for assuming that legislators or their staff assistants are more honest, or might be more efficient, than administration officials. Nor can enduring honesty or efficiency be achieved by legislation. Honest and efficient public administration can be achieved only by honest and efficient administrators honestly appointed and free to act only in the interest of the people.

IT COSTS THE GOVERNMENT TOO MUCH

Another count in the indictment against the income tax—and a very serious one—is the high cost of it. There are two categories of this cost: first, what the Government *spends* to administer the law; second, what the taxpayer *pays* to comply with it.

Notice that in identifying the first category of cost I did not speak of it as a cost that the Government "pays." The Government doesn't pay any part of this cost; the taxpayers pay every cent of it—the cost of administration as well as the cost of compliance. The Government never pays anything; it spends and the taxpayers pay.

I am not suggesting that the Internal Revenue Service is wasteful or inefficient, because I know better. After three years of unrelenting war

480

against red tape and unnecessary overhead, and of using the savings thus made to strengthen and expand enforcement and other operating activities, the Service is showing a degree of improvement of which its management and personnel have every right to be proud.

What I am suggesting is that the complexity of the income tax law necessitates the use of a lot more people in the nation's Revenue Department than would be necessary under a simple and better understood revenue system and that, therefore, the cost of administration is a great deal more than it ought to be. We should have a revenue system under which no more than one-half the present revenue force would be required.

The irony of the present situation is that even the 50-odd thousand people presently employed in the Internal Revenue Service are not enough to assure adequate enforcement. The Service is not examining anywhere near as many returns as it should be examining. It's doing a lot better today than it was when the present administration took over, but it still is reviewing no more than one-third of the number of returns that it could examine with profit if it had the people to do it with.

MORE AGENTS NEEDED

In the first two years of this administration Congress showed a disposition to correct this deficiency, and to that end it indicated its approval of a program that would add 1,000 revenue agents a year until the number was doubled. But, when the control of Congress changed at the beginning of 1955, there was a mysterious determination that the Service had reached its "optimum level" of employment. This decision was announced in the face of incontrovertible evidence to the contrary and of equally clear evidence that the Service could expect to collect in revenue from $10 to $20 for every dollar spent on new agents.

The most plausible explanation that we ever got of this curious action was the suggestion that there was more fear that the taxpayers would react adversely to close enforcement of the law than there was concern about the revenue that would be lost by inadequate enforcement.

People don't resent full enforcement of tax laws. They do resent inadequate enforcement, because they know that a lot of people don't pay what they should when enforcement is inadequate.

IT COST *YOU* TOO MUCH

Of the two elements of the cost of the income tax, the part paid by the taxpayers in complying with the tax is by far the larger. One reason for this is that the Internal Revenue Service doesn't have enough top-grade agents and has to spread itself thin in the examination of the complicated tax returns.

This frequently leads to unduly protracted examinations, and the overall results sometimes are appalling in terms of unnecessary and long interruption of the regular duties of taxpayers' accounting and clerical personnel, and of the cost of professional services of one kind or another that are required to satisfy the examiners.

Many taxpayers complained bitterly to me about this situation, and I couldn't honestly disagree with them. All I could do was explain the problem and beg their indulgence. Not one ever refused, but none of them was happy about it—and I didn't blame them.

Many, too, were the taxpayers who asked, "Why should this thing be so complicated that I have to pay big fees to accountants and lawyers to make my returns and argue with your people for me?" I couldn't quarrel with these people either, because I know their complaints were justified.

If a satisfactory substitute for the income tax cannot be found, the only answer to the first complaint is more revenue agents of top grade. But frankness compels me to say that there seems to be good reason to believe that Congress, as presently controlled, will not permit the Service to have all the agents it needs.

IT'S UNSTABLE

At least some of the members of Congress must fear what many knowing outsiders firmly believe, namely, that if Congress ever allowed the Revenue Service to have enough money for all-out enforcement of the income tax the demand for repeal would become so great within a year that it would be irresistible.

As to the complaint about having to employ professional help there is no answer short of wiping the slate clean and starting fresh.

Another count in the indictment is that the income tax is unstable. Being based upon income, it's a low producer in slack times and a high producer in good times. Thus, theoretically, rates must be raised when people are least able to pay, and they may be lowered when everybody is most able to pay.

I am aware, of course, that Congress' practice is to resort to the use of deficit financing in slack times in order to avoid increasing taxes. But this validates my citation of inherent instability. I also am aware of the tendency to hold expenditures at such a level that decreases are seldom effected in good times. I suggest that this only compounds that instability.

After 23 years of deficit financing everyone should be convinced by now that in addition to all the other indictments that may be laid against the income tax it just isn't up to the job that has to be done. And, to paraphrase Virginia's Senator Byrd, if the job can't be done in prosperous times like these—and, I might add, at the outrageously high rates presently in effect—when can it be done?

The man-made deficiencies of the income tax law are to a large extent the consequences of submission to the demands of pressure groups. For instance, tremendous accumulations of income-producing wealth have been removed from the jurisdiction of the income tax law by the exemptions granted to foundations and certain other nonprofit organizations.

Considering the fact that large accumulations of funds such as those segregated for the use of foundations usually compound themselves, it is clear that the effect of this removal of income from the reach of the tax collector is to cause the government a loss of revenue that grows and grows with the passage of time.

Billions of dollars of potential income also are kept out of the reach of the tax collector by the government's engagement in business activities that compete with private enterprise.

The Second Hoover Commission tells us that "More than 2,500 business facilities that provide goods and services are operated by the Defense Department alone," that the investment in these facilities exceeds $15 billion, and that the facilities range all the way from "shoe repair shops to clothing factories, from cement mixing plants to sawmills, from chain stores to tree and garden nurseries."

In all the foregoing ways (and in others as well—space does not permit complete citation) we have by legislative enactment deliberately kept taxable income from keeping pace with economic development and growth, thus precluding realization of the full potentialities of the income tax as a revenue producer and making it more and more unequal to its job. And, sin of all sins, we've made up the loss by taking it out of the hides of the people with the know-how that has so largely accounted for our success as a nation.

Also, the income tax having proven to be an unstable source of revenue, Congress has availed itself of a variety of other taxes. Some, if not many, of these other taxes could be dispensed with if the primary tax were a stable one and could be permitted to produce fully and freely.

WHAT CAN WE DO ABOUT IT?

What then can be done about all this? I suggest that the time has come to take a new and sincerely critical look at our whole tax system. After all, some elements of the present system are as old as the union itself. Even the income tax, which we have been relying upon as our primary source of income ever since shortly after it was adopted, isn't any chicken. It's 43 years old.

Now, clearly, age alone is not a sufficient reason to condemn any particular tax or any tax system. But, as I have shown, there's a lot wrong with the income tax besides its age. Moreover, it isn't just old; it is incurably infirm. If the present administration couldn't give it simplicity and effectiveness, I don't believe anybody can.

483

My proposal is simple. It is that Congress appoint a Hoover-Commission-type group to make a really critical analysis of the income tax in particular and of the tax system in general, and to study such reasonable proposals as may be made with regard to both. Such a study is long overdue. None has been made in 43 years.

There hasn't even been any search for something better in all that time. Incidentally, why hasn't such a search been conducted on a continuing basis? Research pays off handsomely for business as to matters far less important to it than the Government's tax system and its principal source of revenue are to it. It's time the Government got some research started in this important field.

Such a commission as I have in mind should be a nonpartisan one, and all the responsibility for it and its findings should be assumed by Congress. Moreover, it should not be put under the handicap of a deadline. It should have time to do a thorough job, and not be restricted in its inquiry.

No doubt most of my readers have asked by now, "Well, if we get rid of the income tax what would you put in its place?" That's a fair question, and I have some ideas. But that's not the immediate problem. Moreover, if I proposed any substitute tax or plan at this juncture the first step in my proposal would never be taken. The necessity for a commission to go into the whole problem of taxation thoroughly would be lost in an argument over whether my suggestions would be feasible. Those who have a vested interest in maintaining the status quo would see to that. There are many such people, and some of them have tremendous political power.

For the time being I will say only that I believe that a law or system can be contrived that would be simple enough for the average taxpayer to understand. Such a system might be relatively inexpensive for the Government to administer and the taxpayers to comply with and at the same time be a stable source of revenue. Such results have been worked out in at least two very important categories of business enterprise. I believe that the same can be worked out for business generally, and for individuals as well.

IT'S DESTROYING THE MIDDLE CLASS

There isn't any time to lose, ladies and gentlemen of Congress. Whether you believe it or not, everybody is being overtaxed and the middle class is being taxed out of existence and the nation, thereby, is being robbed of its surest guarantee of continued sound economic development and growth and its staunchest bulwark against the ascendency of socialism. We who somehow have managed to hold on finally are beginning to see the shameful extent to which we have been made the special victims of rapacious tax enactments—and we don't like it.

The marvels of television have brought the truth home to us with indelible clarity. The "Big Surprise" to us—and to others as well—has been how little we have left after the "G (Gimmy) Man" has taken his cut. And now that we have seen what a cleaning we've been getting from our "government" our "$64,000 Question" to you is: How long do you think the people are going to let such banditry, compounded by extreme complexity, continue?

Having to accept the short end of the deal in time of emergency is one thing. We do that cheerfully. But having to continue the tax collector as senior partner in peacetime, with annual costly struggles with legislative mystery and getting in return little more than a pyramided bureaucracy, is quite another. It makes us wonder whether we are being represented or sold down the river. We are anything but cheerful about this.

We don't have enough left in our businesses after taxes to keep them abreast of the demands of our customers. And since even more is extracted from us as individuals we can't accumulate anything, and are not able to increase our investment in our businesses and in our country's growth.

Things are mighty serious, ladies and gentlemen. Largely because of the income tax, big business gets bigger and little business and "substantial folks" are beginning to disappear.

We are concerned about the future because we don't believe that we could stand another serious recession, what with the present "good times" founded as largely as they are on defense production, deficit financing and other generators of thin-ice and phony prosperity. And with the tax collector taking the fruits of our labors in "progressive" ratio to our achievements. High rates of tax don't mean anything when there isn't anything to tax.

Time's a-wasting, and the enemies of the way of life that we cherish rejoice as we are obligingly led closer and closer to national suicide.

What are you going to do about it ... and when?

SPEECH AT A RALLY OF STATES' RIGHTS PARTY[†]

by

T. Coleman Andrews

THIS is an honor that I had hoped someone more entitled to receive it and completely free to make the most of it would accept.

There are many fine men and women of long and honorable participation in the affairs of both of the old parties who are no less disillusioned by the ever leftward course of their parties than we who now declare our disillusionment.

These dedicated men and women share our concern over the unhappy fact that their parties, dominated by growing and unyielding socialist factions, now have converged onto the common highway to one-doctrine, one-party dictatorship, under which, as in Russia and her satellite countries, the people are permitted only a choice of men, never a choice of political philosophies.

I had hoped that one of these experienced and nationally known stalwarts of the political scene might be induced to become our standard bearer and lead this our response to the nation-wide and growing demand for restoration of respect for the Constitution and the rights of the states and for return to a genuine two-party system. But none of them was ready to make the break. They all seemed restrained by an understandable reluctance to sever their long-standing party ties.

As disappointing as this reluctance has been, it is indicative of a high sense of loyalty that I believe to be one of our strongest potential assets, for I am certain that many, if not all, of these disillusioned patriots will join us sooner or later; indeed, they *must*, because public resentment of the offenses against our cherished traditions of government by both of the old parties is deep and widespread, and it is going to be expressed in such massive volume on November 6th as to remove all doubt about what vineyard all should labor in who sincerely wish to be faithful to our political heritage.

In the meantime, in response to your insistence, I have agreed to become your standard bearer, and, though conscious of my limitations, I am proud to be the instrumentality, with my distinguished running mate,

---

[†]Speech at a Rally of States' Rights Party in Richmond, Virginia on October 15, 1956. Reprinted with permission. In the T. Coleman Andrews Papers (Coll. 119), Special Collections, University of Oregon Library.

Mr. Werdel, through which those who otherwise would stay at home or go fishing November 6th now will be able to exercise their franchise without being limited to a choice between Socialist Party A and Socialist Party B.

This was not an easy decision, because, for the first time in my life, personal considerations seemed to stand immovably in the way of acceptance of a call to public duty. Having been in my present position for less than a year, I felt that to turn away from it completely to conduct a full-time active campaign might jeopardize accomplishment of the program to which I committed myself when I came to this position and on which we had by that time made a highly promising start.

But I left Washington last October convinced that our right of self-determination had been deteriorated to the danger point; and after seeing the Constitution finally torn up and thrown in the ash can at Chicago, and ignored with an almost audible indifference in the unbecoming and unwarranted atmosphere of self-satisfaction that prevailed at San Francisco, I realized that we'd have to start trying to save the Constitution, the sovereignty of the states, and the rights of the people NOW, or all might be lost. Besides, you insisted, in spite of the restrictions imposed by my personal situation.

So, here I am. And I'm not ashamed to say that I wouldn't have been able to live with myself or ever again be able to look my children and grandchildren, or the children and grandchildren of my fellow citizens, in the face, if I had declined. Needless to say I shall do everything I can within the limits of the restrictions under which I feel my personal obligations require me to labor.

We don't have much time. The two old parties saw to that. Knowing that you would wait and see what kinds of platforms they adopted, they set their conventions a month later this time, with the hope of discouraging and blocking any independent conservative campaign. Nor do we have much money. But here we have two great advantages.

First, we have a vital cause, and there are *real issues* between us and our opponents. So we at least have our *hearts* in our jobs and no lack of basic differences to tempt us into becoming a party to the back-fence quarreling and personal recriminations that thus far have characterized the campaign between the two old parties and added nothing to the people's understanding of the really serious problems that cry for solution.

Second, a truly worthy cause properly led doesn't have to depend primarily upon money for its adoption. Besides, we already are paying a handsome price for this campaign in the form of enforced contributions. I figure this amounts to $4 billion. That's the difference between the amount that reliable sources expect the government to spend this year under the appropriation bills as finally adopted—approximately $70 billion—and the estimate of approximately $66 billion that the President sent to Congress in January. That $4 billion will be included in our tax bills, of course. So everyone will have to contribute to it, whatever his party and whether he likes it or not.

Incidentally, that $4 billion is 40 times the highest amount the two old parties combined ever have been accused of spending for a presidential campaign. So, you see, elections are expensive. They come often, too—every two years for Congressmen and some Senators, every four years for President and Vice President. The price that we taxpayers are made to pay for election-year pork barrel appropriations is staggering.

And what a slick one it is, using *our* money—taxing us, if you please—to get *our* votes! And it's been going on for a long, long time. I wonder if this isn't more corrupt than openly contributing more than $3,000 to a candidate's campaign.

Back in 1944, the keynoter of the Republican National Convention assailed the Democrats in part in these terms:

We believe that the New Deal is destroying the two-party system.... They are using every device and excuse to insinuate themselves into control of the public schools of our states.... They have by-passed the governments of the states in an effort to destroy state effectiveness and compel the people to rely solely upon the New Deal clique at Washington for the solution of all their problems.

You are going to be amazed when I tell you who made that statement, but before I do, let's look at the reason why we are here tonight.

When the Democrats started moving to the left the Republicans abandoned their party philosophy and hollered, "Me, too." That just made the Democrats move farther. But again the Republicans hollered, "Me, too," and the Democrats moved still farther to the left. Thus, the grasshopper race between the two parties was started, with the Democrats always one hop ahead of the Republicans and both winding up, as they have now, so far to the left that neither of them can turn back.

Committed, as both of the old parties are, to uncontrolled spending, oppressive taxation, reduction of the states to the status of political subdivisions of the Union, instead of the Union's controlling elements, as the Constitution provides, and to war-breeding international entanglements, these old parties left millions of their adherents deserted, disfranchised and with no place to go on election day.

It is the purpose of the independents here represented tonight to find a new home for the orphaned members of both the old parties, that there may always be a secure haven for those who believe that preservation of the Union, and achievement of our destiny as a free people, cannot be secured by anything less than faithful adherence to the principles of government upon which the nation was founded.

It also is our belief that we can live in harmony, and enjoy a relationship of mutual helpfulness and goodwill, with the rest of the nations of the world without becoming embroiled in the disputes of others and without undertaking the impossible task of carrying the rest of the world on our shoulders.

Now, who was it who made that statement at the Republican National Convention of 1944? Who was it who said the New Dealers were "using every device and excuse to insinuate themselves into control of the public schools of the states"? Who was it who said that the New Dealers "had by-passed the government of the states in an effort to destroy the state's effectiveness and compel the people to rely solely on Washington for solution of all their problems"? I rather imagine that some of those who don't know have guessed it by now.

It was none other than the Right Honorable "Great Republican Chief Justice" and Integrationist, Earl Warren of California.

If there ever was a case of the "pot calling the kettle black" that's it. Hard to believe, isn't it? Who, pray tell, has ever done more than Mr. Warren and his party to insinuate the Federal government into control of the public schools? Who has done more than Mr. Warren and his party to by-pass the governments of the states in an effort. to destroy state effectiveness and compel the people to rely upon Washington for solution of all their problems? The record being as clear and fresh as it is, I think these questions answer themselves.

CONCERNING EXPENDITURES

Back in February I spoke out publicly in frank criticism of the income tax law for the first time after leaving the post of Commissioner of Internal Revenue. I felt that I owed the people the benefit of what I had seen as the administrator of this law for nearly three years under circumstances that gave me opportunity for observation that a Commissioner holding office under normal conditions would not have had.

Popular approval of my views was nationwide. Official approval, though not openly expressed, was greater than could have been expected. But there was some disapproval, of course, and in every case it took the same line. Each of the dissenters based his objection upon two very curious assumptions.

The first of these assumptions was that the present level of spending couldn't be reduced. The second was that, no matter what the level of spending, we just couldn't get along without the income tax.

These assumptions have become a matter of grave concern to a rapidly growing number of taxpayers. They were adopted by members of both the old political parties, and no spokesman for either of these parties has repudiated them, so far as I know. Indeed, I think it is pretty clear from recent campaign statements that both parties subscribe to them.

Now, let's talk about these assumptions a little. Congress and the present administration appointed the second Hoover Commission and asked it to study the organization and management of the government and come up with recommendations as to where improvements might be made and how much these improvements would reduce the government's annual expenditures. The Commission reported that it had found $7½ billion of annual waste. According to latest reports, legislation affording elimination of only 1/15th of this waste was adopted before Congress adjourned.

About the same time Senator Byrd, who knows more about the federal budget than any man in Washington, reported that his annual review of the budget indicated that the budget for the present year contained $7.8 billions of "new" and "non-essential" spending.

Now, folks, that's $15.3 billion that can be saved. I have said before, and I now repeat, that Congress and the Administration can start saving it any time they really want to. But it is clear from what the Democrats say they *will* spend, and from what the Republicans already *have* been spending, that neither of the old parties has any intention of reducing expenditures.

There is a great deal more that could be saved in addition to that $15.3 billion. But it isn't necessary for the purpose of this discussion to get into that tonight. It is sufficient to point out that $15.3 billion happens to be just about ½ of the amount derived from the income tax on individuals.

It is clear, therefore, that the Administration and Congress could, if they would, give everybody a great deal to be happy about in the form of a really substantial tax reduction. They haven't done this, because their massive domestic programs—both present and projected, notably their designs on education—and their unwarranted and unrewarding generosity abroad, takes a lot of money, creates a lot of power here on the domestic front, and, for those who dish out the money—your money and mine, that is—a lot of prestige on the international front, which neither of them would yield until the people by their vote force them to yield. We propose to provide those votes.

Now, every time we turn around the spenders in Washington are wanting to do something for the poor, impoverished and improvident states and their political subdivisions. My friends, there was a time not so many years ago, when the states could have taken care of the federal government. But since, in 1933, we started creating a kingdom or some kind of dictatorship, and preempting the revenues which the states might have used to keep abreast of the needs of their people, the situation has become reversed and the federal officeholders now want to take care of the states, by which I mean put them out of business.

It is extremely interesting, I think, that that $15.3 billions that the second Hoover Commission and Senator Byrd say can be saved annually also is about ½ of the amount that the states and local governments spend annually for goods and services. Thus, it is clear that if the federal government would turn loose just that $15.3 billion, the states could increase their revenue by ½ that amount and still leave the people a 25% dividend on their federal income tax.

There isn't any doubt in the mind of anyone who knows anything about state government that with that much additional revenue the states could afford to give a lavish farewell party to the field officers and employees of the federal government by whom they are now overrun, pay their railroad fares back to Washington, or to their homes, as the case might be, and become forever free of that fraud known as federal aid and masters of their own fates instead of mendicant pawns of a sprawling and unmanageable bureaucracy.

Let's look at it from another angle. The federal government wound up fiscal 1956 with nearly $2 billion of surplus. That year's revenue collections were the highest in history. Did the Administration and Congress reduce our taxes? They did not.

A recent report from Washington says that collections for the current year will be even greater than those for last year. Do the powers that be hold out any promise of a tax reduction next year? They do not. They say that expenditures must first be reduced.

Well, of course, that's what should be done. So why don't they do it? It is clear that they *can* do it if they want to. The answer is they don't *want* to.

Now, an interesting thing about this surplus of approximately $2 billion is that it wouldn't have cost much more than that to have increased the personal exemption from $600 to $700. And, believe it or not, the top bracket rate could have been reduced from 91% to 34% for approximately the same amount. It wouldn't have taken any straining to reduce expenses enough to have done both.

What shameful indifference it is, my friends, for any government to treat its people so shabbily, when so much could be done for only a fraction of the very minimum amount that could be saved, if only those in authority had the will to save and the interests of the people at heart.

Here's another possibility. It is clear from what I have just said about what could be accomplished with $2 billion that if Congress and the Administration would only reduce expenditures by ⅔rds the total amount that the second Hoover Commission and Senator Byrd said they can reduce them, they could increase the personal exemption by $100, reduce the top rate from 91% to 34%, lower the 20% basic rate to 18% and make a payment of at least 1% on the public debt and still have $5 billion of waste left.

That would be in effect a pay raise for every one of the 60 million people who pay income taxes and would reduce the cost of living for everybody. Mind you this would be only ⅔rds of the minimum consideration for the people's financial welfare that every taxpayer has a right to expect.

So, when somebody tells us that the present level of spending can't be reduced, he either doesn't know what he is talking about or he doesn't want any reduction. And make no mistake about it, folks, there are a lot of people inside and outside the government who have a pretty substantial vested interest in maintaining the status quo and aren't going to let any reduction be made if they can help it.

I think I have made it abundantly clear that spending *can* be reduced. But folks, we aren't faced with the question whether spending *can* be reduced. Our problem is that it *must* be reduced.

We can't afford a budget of $70 billion. That's 17½ times what it was in 1939. But our economy hasn't expanded that much, and no one who works for a living is that much better off. How then can we support a budget of 17½ times as great? We're about $200 billion more in debt, and the interest on the public debt is by itself nearly twice the amount spent by the Federal Government for all purposes in 1939. The amount spent for interest during the past 25 years amounts to $100 billion, and Senator Byrd tells us that the bill that our children will have to pay for this item during the next 20 years will amount to $150 billion.

Now, I'm not suggesting that we can or should go back to 1939, because I realize that we are living in a vastly different world than we were then and that much of the staggering load with which we are now burdened arose from the tragic events—avoidable and unavoidable—of the intervening period. But that's the best reason in the world for taking a hitch in our belt and minimizing our load. This *must* be done.

But what can we expect from the two old parties in the way of action to reduce spending? The answer is nothing, N-O-T-H-I-N-G, nothing. Where there is no will to be frugal there won't be any frugality.

The Democrats, who long ago deserted the states for intense centralization and big government, apparently are quite proud of their spend-tax-borrow-and-elect policy and have been making promises during this campaign that couldn't be met with a budget of twice $70 billion.

The Republicans resent with almost bursting indignation any charge that they too are big spenders. But Senator Byrd told us in his report on his analysis of this year's budget that the present Administration's requests for appropriations in this budget exceeded the appropriation enactments for fiscal 1955 by $9.2 billion or nearly 16⅔%. Senator Byrd called this increase "inexcusable." As I already have pointed out, the ultimate figure was $4 billion more than that.

Incidentally, the Republicans also resent being charged with extending centralization of the power of the Federal Government beyond the point at which they inherited the build-up from the Democrats, and they counter heatedly with the claim to being the champions of giving the people the greatest possible freedom from federal interference in their work and lives.

What a claim! What an amazing claim, with at least three Supreme Court decisions of the past three years that proclaim the absolute contrary—one of them the most brazen usurpation of Congressional prerogative and states' rights in the country's entire history, not to mention a bid for control of the states' school systems by the present Administration that surpassed anything the Democrats ever attempted until their standard bearer nonchalantly tossed in his recent bid of $½ billion.

The Republicans' pretensions, therefore, are considerably at variance with their performance. Unfortunately, our tax bills are based upon cold reality rather than upon fanciful claims of frugality.

The people finally have begun to see so-called Federal aid for the colossal fraud that it has been, and they resent bitterly having been conned into believing that they have been getting something they wouldn't have to pay for, when, in fact, their own money was being used to forever deprive them of their right of self-government. Now that they also are finding out that they often get back no more than 25 cents worth of value for each dollar they put up, they are downright mad about the whole underhanded business.

Federal aid to the states isn't Federal aid at all; it's the exact opposite. It's state aid to the Federal Government! How can there be any aid from the Federal Government to the states when every dollar the Federal Government spends has to come from the people of the states? In simplest terms, Federal aid is an underhanded device by which the Federal Government insinuates itself into affairs of the states that are no part of the Federal Government's responsibility and none of its business.

The only aid involved in Federal aid is the wad that Washington cuts out of the people's contributions for the aid and support of an over-stuffed bureaucracy that arrogantly believes it knows better than we ourselves what is good for us and better how to spend our money. So, it's a case of the states aiding the Federal Government, not one of the Federal Government aiding the states.

But the direct cost of inordinate bureaucracy often is the least costly aspect of it. When uncle puts up our money, he calls the turns; and, having no knowledge of what it means to have to meet a payroll, and no responsibility for such mundane concerns, his commissars set the standards high. Schools, for instance, must be marble palaces. Facilities are more important than product. And so, by the time it's all over, we're lucky if we get 25% of the value we could have gotten had we spent our money ourselves.

Why establish a lot of political fat cats in dominion over us in the District of Confusion and pay them handsomely, if not excessively, for grandiose planning and management of something that we could do a lot better for ourselves? Even if we did it poorly, it is a lot more fun to waste our own money than to let somebody else do it, and that certainly should be our privilege.

494

For instance, what warrant is there for believing that the Federal Government can do a better job of building school houses and educating our children than we can?

We are in many respects the most advanced and powerful nation on earth. In no respect are we exceeded. Yet our country is a relatively young one and we have only about 6% of the world's population.

Many, if not most, of the men who have figured so prominently in the industrial revolution from which our material might grow, and many of those who expanded and solidified the spiritual faith upon which the nation was founded, were products of either self-education or the old state or locally supported one-room school houses. Many of the outstanding men of this very day are self-educated men.

Yet, the big-government boys say that our school system is all wrong. Indeed they say that our system of government itself is all wrong. Everything is all wrong, according to these power-seeking, self-nominated wise men. The real trouble with these men is that they are afraid of the established order, because they know that as long as that order stands they will never be able to establish the socialist dictatorship over which they secretly hope some day to preside.

Now, I'm not advocating a return to one-room schools or to the era in which they made their magnificent contributions to the achievement of our unparalleled greatness. But there wasn't any Federal aid in those days, my friends. Washington didn't have any Federal aid. Jefferson didn't have any. Lincoln didn't have any. Ford didn't have any. The Wright Brothers didn't have any. None of the greats who started America on the road to glory had any.

But I'll tell you what they did have. They had F-R-E-E-D-O-M—freedom to dream and freedom to do and achieve, unhampered by ruinous taxation and bureaucratic interference.

These are the freedoms that have really been taken away from us while we've been soothed into insensibility to the touch of the filching fingers of the pied-piping hucksters of other freedoms.

No, my friends, we don't need any Federal aid for our schools. We know what kind of education to give our children. We know how much to give them. Above all, we know in what environment it should be given them.

We don't need any Federal aid for any activity that is best done by, and that the founders of this country intended to be done by, ourselves at the state and local levels.

In short, we know how to manage our affairs better than anybody in Washington, and all we need to prove this is access to sources of revenue that never should have been preempted by the Federal Government in the first place.

Before leaving the subject of Federal aid, there's an aspect of it in relationship to the present Administration that must be mentioned.

The present Administration is largely composed of businessmen. I have no quarrel with this. But I do quarrel with their failure, where there has been failure, to apply business principles to the management of activities that come under these men's jurisdiction, especially in the field of Federal aid.

The way this Federal aid works is that the Federal Government injects itself into state and local affairs and sets up an organization to control these affairs which must be financed by levies against the people of the states.

Now, if these were activities that the people of the states were incapable of carrying on for themselves, this might be understandable. But they are not such activities.

Hence, we have a situation where we're going all around our thumb to get to our finger, and spending a lot of money unnecessarily in the process.

There are in the present Administration some of the nation's top business executives. These men wouldn't tolerate for a minute an unnecessary and wasteful stratum of administrative expense in their own businesses. What I don't understand is why they tolerate it in the government.

The fact that they do tolerate it causes many people to think that the businessmen of the present administration must feel that the people can afford waste that these men's businesses can't afford.

Now, what do we independents propose? We propose that the Federal Government must save the money that it is now wasting, reduce taxes accordingly, and thus enable the states to pick up where they were cast aside in 1933 and finance their own affairs.

In this way only can we restore the rights and sovereignty of the states and the freedom of the people from the enslaving consequences of overpowering centralization. In this way only can we prevent the triumph of socialism and assure a government of limited powers based upon the constitutional concept of a true union of states. And the sum total of all government—federal, state, and local—would be greatly reduced in the process.

And may I say that if there is any one thing that the people of this country are more concerned about than they are by the usurpation of the powers of the states through the iniquitous device of so-called federal aid, and the presumptuousness of a Supreme Court that has discarded its law books for communist novels, it is the fact that they are being surtaxed—not just taxed, mind you, but surtaxed—to support backward or decadent foreign countries and their people.

Yes, we are spending for foreign aid just about the amount of money that is derived from the surtaxes that start at 22% and end at 91%. That amount is between $5 billion and $6 billion.

The people of this country are not happy about the fact that they have been taxed to give vanquished enemies and other people the finest and most modern machinery in existence to be used along with slave labor to destroy domestic businesses and deprive the employees of these businesses of their jobs.

We don't have to go far, my friends, to find instances of the disastrous results of our misguided generosity to foreign nations and people. I'll cite a few. The famous Camperdown Mill in Greenville, South Carolina has been closed and all its people thrown out of work by competition from Japanese manufacturers equipped with machinery of the most modern type that those dispossessed employees of Camperdown and we were taxed to pay for and that child labor at 11¢ an hour operates. This famous old mill was established in 1874.

Another mill in South Carolina, one of the largest in the industry, has been forced to postpone indefinitely a multi-million dollar expansion program because of this foreign competition created by our own government—with our money.

In North Adams, Massachusetts, the Windsor Print Works has been forced to close down, sell out and add its workers to that distressed area's army of unemployed. One of the great textile manufacturers of Alabama has been forced to cut production 20%, so there, too, many have lost their jobs.

The same sort of thing has happened to the plywood industry. In 1955 the importations of Japanese plywood were 25 times as much as they were in 1952. Again, competition from 11¢-an-hour labor and machinery that you and I and the people in the plywood industry helped pay for.

In Ohio the sewing machine industry, one of the great old standbys of our economy, stands faced with ruinous competition from both the Far East and Europe.

On the Pacific Coast half the tuna fleet lies rusting and rotting away in idleness. Canneries are closed, and half the people employed in the fishcanning industry are out of work. Again, competition from Japan, one of our vanquished enemies.

Did somebody say something about "Peace and Prosperity"? I'm sure the jobless ex-employees of Camperdown and other closed factories wouldn't call it that.

In Tennessee the employees of one textile mill addressed a communication to their Senators and Congressman beseeching these gentlemen "who represent us in Congress to protect us against the loss of our jobs, which are now threatened because of the uncontrolled flow of Japanese low-cost cotton textiles into this country" and went on to point out that "the government is using *our* income taxes to provide Japan with cotton eight to ten cents a pound cheaper than American textile mills have to pay" and that "Japan is taking this cheap cotton, paying wages about one-tenth of our wages and threatening our means of livelihood by flooding this country with cheap cloth and garments."

A resolution was introduced in the Senate proposing an amendment to the Foreign Aid Authorization Bill for 1956 which would have required the

President to apply quotas on excessive Japanese imports into the American market. Not only has this administration turned a deaf ear to pleas such as this from people already out of work or threatened with unemployment; worse than that, the Democratic candidate for Vice-President and his senatorial colleague named in the petition opposed the amendment that I have just mentioned.

There isn't any difference between the Republicans and Democrats on this question of foreign policy, which includes the intolerable trade situation that I have just discussed. President Eisenhower says there isn't. In his press conference of last Wednesday, he is reported to have said that there are no basic policy differences between the Republicans and Democrats on foreign policy. So we can't expect any improvement from either of the old parties in the deplorable situation that I have described.

This "tragedy of errors" has been happening under a foreign involvement which the Democrats started in 1947 and which is known as General Agreement on Tariffs and Trade, generally referred to as GATT. The closings and curtailments of production that I have referred to occurred earlier in the present year.

Under the GATT set-up a team of as many as 75 members sit behind closed doors in Geneva and work out, on behalf of the Secretary of State, tariffs and trade agreements with representatives of 30-odd other countries, parties to the agreement. A very curious facet of this disastrous business is that the Secretary of State acts in the name of the President to whom the system delegates the authority to set tariffs, which authority the Constitution vests in Congress.

It's all a very queer set-up. But, then, for more years than most of us can remember, the Federal Government seems somehow to have been able to make the Constitution mean what it has wanted it to mean.

Both parties laud the GATT program and say, "Sure, in programs of this kind some industry is bound to get hurt, but on balance we'll come out way ahead." But I can tell you that it has not worked that way. The value of our exports in 1955 was almost exactly what it was in 1947—approximately $15 billion. Considering the fact that prices have gone up substantially since 1947, it is obvious that our 1955 exports actually were less than those of 1947. So, from the export standpoint, we have lost ground under the GATT set-up.

The story is even worse on the import side, for, whereas our imports in 1947 were $5⅔ billion, they were double that figure in 1955, or $11⅓ billion.

So, obviously, GATT has worked out fine for everybody but us.

Isn't all of that a shocking story of a government that is supposed to be "of the people, by the people and for the people"? Could it possibly be that there are still some traitors on the payroll? There are those who strongly suspect that there are.

And what a shocking thing it also is that the current budget included appropriations for further aid to Communist Dictator Tito, who had turned against us! Strong objections to continuing this aid has been raised because this dictator, who never dresses in anything but full military regalia, has been especially chummy with Moscow's head man recently. But the latest word from Washington is that the Administration will continue to woo this fickle and probably completely treacherous revolutionary with *our* money.

Let us examine this foreign aid business briefly from the philosophical point of view. Having driven the stakes of socialist philosophy deep into the soil of our beloved country, both parties have moved into the highly explosive international field to dabble into smoldering resentments of a hate-filled world in which no nation is more hated than we ourselves, in spite of our unprecedented generosity and good intentions. Friendship just can't be bought. What's that old ditty?

I once had money and a friend
I loaned my money to my friend
I lost my money and my friend.

We seem to lose even when we *give* our money away.

We spend huge sums trying to persuade the world to our philosophy. We tell them that socialism, communism and dictatorship in any form whatsoever are wrong. But, bless Pat, we practice the very things in our own government that we tell the world we abhor; and the world laughs at us. Well ... shouldn't they?

Freedom isn't something that people suddenly make up their minds they must have. It isn't something that can be bought. Oh, no, it's something that has to evolve out of long years of suffering the lack of it until the need for it becomes a burning passion—a passion so intense that those who experience it are willing to die to satisfy it.

Freedom cannot be brought to all the world at once, either. It comes nation by nation. It has to be this way because the history of every nation is different.

Hence not every nation is ready for freedom as we understand it. Some of them may never be.

Our way is not the only way, and no amount of our money can make it so or bring any kind of freedom to any nation until that nation is ready for freedom. Indeed, I venture to suggest that our so-called foreign aid has had a softening effect and has in fact set the cause of freedom back in most countries to which it has been dispensed.

Nor is every nation ready for our standard of living.

We didn't get where we are by aid from abroad. We got here because we wanted better than we had ... because we were willing to work hard to get it ... because for some reason the Supreme Architect of the Universe, in His infinite and inscrutable wisdom, chose to bless us with the ingenuity

499

that it took to figure out *how* to get it. And so we may not expect to bring other nations to our standard of living merely by surfeiting them with our money.

Not every nation is ready for automobiles, televisions, or even modern housing with telephones and all the wondrous appliances that we enjoy. In short, not every nation is ready for all the myriad conveniences and luxuries that make up the abundance that is ours.

Most of those nations that don't have such things will have them in time, but not, in any case, until they are ready for them. And we can't force these nations up to our standards. In the meantime, they aren't missing them, and to try to carry our standard of living to any people before they are ready for it does more harm than good. It's an ill-advised gesture of misguided generosity.

There's a lot more to living than automobiles, television and modern appliances. And people who do not yet have such conveniences and luxuries have to change a lot of habits, customs and environmental points of view before they will be ready for such modern miracles.

The sooner we learn that we can't carry the rest of the world on our shoulders without wrecking ourselves and creating confusion, frustration and unrest, rather than peace, in the world, the better off we will be.

CONCERNING THE INCOME TAX

As for the income tax being the only tax capable of providing the Federal Government with the vast amount of money that it needs to carry on its manifold and far-flung activities, there isn't a person in the United States who can say with absolute assurance that we can not get along without this tax. The reason for this is very simple. No one in Washington ever has tried to find out whether there might be something better.

Of *course* there is a better way. To say otherwise is to hold that we have lost the ingenuity that made us the greatest nation on earth in practically every field of human endeavor and that we do not have the capacity and good sense to work out a tax system that is compatible with the priceless tradition of freedom that is our heritage.

Now, I am not suggesting that the income tax should be peremptorily repealed. I know that such precipitate action would be ill-advised. What I *am* saying is that having had the income tax for 43 years without any search whatsoever for something better, and having come up against the cold reality that it is a vicious and lethal levy, the time has come to take a thorough-going and open-minded new look at it.

As a matter of fact, I am convinced that there never has been any popular demand for the income tax and that it would be voted down by an overwhelming majority if the people ever were given a chance to decide its fate at the polls.

Recently, a thoughtful young man who had come up against the disappointing discovery that the income tax probably would keep him from realizing his ambitions asked me with understandable concern if I didn't think that every generation ought to be given an opportunity to vote upon the laws that affect its livelihood and well-being. I am not so sure but what this young man had a good idea.

It will be *difficult* but *not* impossible to find a new tax system; and I am satisfied that if we independents are successful in pulling the Federal Government off the backs of the states and their people, and taking it out of those activities that the central government never should have gotten into in the first place, the federal need for revenue will be so reduced that the problem of developing a well-balanced and just tax system will become not too difficult to solve.

Now, what's wrong with the income tax? Well, there are a lot of things wrong with it. It started out wrong, because it began as an instrument of vengeance. It was frankly and unashamedly aimed at the rich. And I say to you that whatever might have been the justification for destroying those at whom the 16th Amendment was aimed, it was one of the biggest mistakes the country ever made to allow its tax system to be used as a punitive device.

I sincerely believe that the income tax is the worst thing that ever happened to our Country; first, because it invaded the privacy and property rights of the people in violation of Article IV of the Bill of Rights, just as Senator Byrd's distinguished father said it would do, when, as Speaker of the Virginia House of Delegates, he led the fight to keep Virginia from ratifying the 16th Amendment, in which fight Virginians can be proud to say he was successful, for Virginia did not ratify it; second, because it preempted sources of income that rightfully belonged to the states, and which, if they had been left to the states, would have enabled the states to meet every reasonable need of their people and keep the Federal Government from usurping one after another of the rights guaranteed to the states by the Constitution.

Yes, my friends, the income tax has been the bonanza that has financed every boondoggling usurpation of the rights of the states and every something-for-nothing fraud against the people that the perverted minds of the New Dealers, Fair Dealers and Raw Dealers have conceived and foisted upon us since we were started down the road to socialistic ruin in 1933.

It has been the wherewithal with which a mushrooming and arrogant bureaucracy has been built to destroy the balanced separation of the powers of the three branches of the Federal Government that the founders of the Republic set up to protect the people and the states against concentration of power in Washington.

It is a sad spectacle to see, as a result of what has happened because of the income tax, a proud Congress literally cringing before the overpowering administrative monster that it has created and a Supreme

Court forsaking the Constitution and its law books for the teachings of foreign sociologists to turn itself into a Super Congress, imposing its presumptuous will upon the people and destroying the rights of the states.

This tax has been the meal ticket that financed the bloated bureaus that made possible the infiltration of the Federal Government by the Hisses, the Rosenbergs, the Harry Dexter Whites, and all the myriad company of shadowy plotters against the freedom that we enjoy.

It has been the irresistible temptress that has lead Congress to preempt the most fruitful sources of public revenue and reduce the states to tin-cupping their way up and down Pennsylvania Avenue from the Capitol to the Treasury in order to meet the bare minimum needs of their people. Give the states back these sources of revenue and they won't need any aid from the Federal Government.

There are many other counts in the indictment against the income tax. It is the most confiscatory tax in our history, and I wasn't the first to say this. Our President said it four years ago, and it has been said by other important officials of this Administration since then. Any tax is confiscatory that takes from 20% to 30% of the taxable income of persons in the low income brackets, from 30% to more than 50% of the taxable income of persons in the middle brackets, and from more than 50% to 91% of the taxable income of persons in the upper brackets.

Incidentally, I should mention that while the income tax was originally designed to soak the rich, and although some politicians would still like the people to believe that it does, it actually soaks everybody, for 5/6ths of all the revenue derived from the tax on personal income is derived from the basic rate of 20%. There is progressive, and finally rank, discrimination above that rate. But everybody gets hit and HARD. So, the idea that the income tax hits only the rich has become a pure myth.

The income tax and its running mates, the estate and gift taxes, are right out of the *Communist Manifesto*. They are the rankest kind of poison for a free country like ours. In the *Communist Manifesto*, which was published 108 years ago, Karl Marx listed ten essentials to assurance of the triumph of communism. For our purposes we need refer only to essentials 2 and 3.

No. 2: "A heavy, progressive or graduated income tax." The income tax today starts at a basic rate of 20% and is graduated on up to 91%. And I might say that there is nothing in the 16th Amendment to keep Congress from taking all of everybody's income if they wanted to. They don't even have to allow any deductions. So the stage is all set for total confiscation; and if anyone complained, Congress could reply quite honestly that it was all done strictly in accordance with the Constitution.

Now, don't say this can't happen, because it can. The rate of the original income tax was 2%, and the proponents of this tax stood aghast at the suggestion that if Congress could make it 2% they could make it as high as 10%. Look at it now. The top rate is 91%!

502

No. 3: "Abolition of all right of inheritance." Under the estate tax laws, the government can now confiscate as much as 75% of the value of an estate.

The more I see of the history and the Federal Government's use of the income, estate and gift taxes, the more difficult I find it to believe that these taxes are not a part of a shrewd plot to destroy our freedom and turn out Country into a socialist dictatorship.

What chance have our children got under such an array of exorbitant exactions as these? Indeed, my friends, what chance does our Country have of achieving its destiny as a land of freedom under such levies?

The income tax also is shamefully discriminating, because it puts a heavy penalty upon success. A very troubled young man recently put two questions to me. "Is it true," he asked, "that when I get to making 10 times more than the salary I start at I'll have to pay 47 times more tax?" This young man obviously was ambitious and knew what he wanted and expected to get it. His second question was, "Is it true that if I should be successful enough to earn some day 50 times more than the salary I start at I would have to pay the government 500 times more income tax?"

I had to say, "Yes, my young friend, that's right. That's the way the law is written, and there won't be any way you can escape it."

Let me say to every mother and father who is listening to me tonight that this, in my opinion, is one of the saddest evils of the income tax and that if you vote for either the Democratic Party or the Republican Party you will be voting to commit your children and grandchildren to political bondage.

Let's look for a moment at what inflation and the income tax, which has been one of the causes of inflation, have done to us. The figures that I am now about to give should be a matter of grave concern to every man, woman and child in this Country.

A $2,000 job in 1939 has to pay $4,600 now, or the holder of it has less buying power after taxes than the job afforded in 1939; a $3,000 job has to pay $7,100; a $5,000 job has to pay $12,500; a $7,500 job has to pay $20,250; a $10,000 job has to pay $29,500; a $15,000 job has to pay $51,500; a $25,000 job has to pay $113,000; a $40,000 job has to pay $235,000; a $60,000 job has to pay $395,000. Those are the figures for single people. Married persons fare a little better when one member of the family receives all or most all of the family income.

Do any of you people know of any $5,000 jobs in 1939 that pay $12,500 now? Or of any $10,000 jobs in 1939 that pay $29,500 now? Or of any $15,000 jobs in 1939 that pay $51,500 now? The rest are too astronomical to warrant asking about.

That, my friends, is what your children and grandchildren face. And it is a very gloomy outlook indeed, considering the fact that neither the Democratic Party nor the Republican Party seems to be concerned about it, let alone having any intention of making the reduction in spending that would make it possible to do something about the problem.

The income tax is a terribly complex and confusing thing, too. Not even the Congressmen who vote for it understand it. The present law was signed by the President more than two years ago, but such is its complexity that the complete official interpretation of it isn't out yet. More than 15 million people had to have help with the preparation of the returns filed this year. The cost of administration is inordinate; the cost of compliance is even greater; and remember, we taxpayers pay the cost of administration as well as the cost of compliance.

And, oh, what fraud and corruption this law has engendered! And what a nation of liars many say it is making of us! I know something about these evils, because I was appointed Commissioner of Internal Revenue to clean up probably the greatest accumulation of corruption that the Federal Government ever experienced. I will not dwell on what I found, however, because it was all thoroughly publicized and I am sure that everyone is as familiar with it as I.

Finally, one of the most serious counts in this indictment, though by no means the last that I might mention, is that the income tax law carries within itself the seeds of its own collapse. Notwithstanding that we have placed our reliance upon income as the principal source of revenue, Congress has, by one enactment after another, exempted group after group from the law's provisions. Thus, enormous aggregates of income have been put completely beyond the reach of the tax collector by deliberate legislative action.

Untold amounts of income-producing wealth are held by foundations, welfare funds and other exempt organizations; and vast untaxed activities are carried on by the government in competition with private enterprise. The second Hoover Commission reported that the Department of Defense alone has $30 billion invested in over 2,500 activities that compete with private business.

Thus, an ever-widening gap has been created between the amount of income produced by our economy and the amount subject to the income tax. How can we expect anything but oppressive, confiscatory and discriminatory taxation when those who work and labor to be good and useful citizens and contribute what they can to the economy of the Country are made to assume the massive burden of those who enjoy exemption from the burdens of the law? The question answers itself.

There is another compelling economic reason why something has to be done about the income tax. Experts tell us that the day is not far distant when the social security system is going to be requiring staggering sums of money to meet its obligations. These experts doubt that anything can be done to avoid disaster when that time comes. Apparently the least that can be said is that there are an awful lot of good folks in this Country who are expecting something from the social security laws that they aren't going to get—and at the time in their lives when they will need it most. It is of the utmost importance, therefore, that we do the best we possibly can with the income tax and the revenue system generally while there is a chance.

And so I say, as I have said so many times before, that it isn't a question whether we can get along *without* the income tax. The real question is: Can we *keep* it and survive as a free people?

Both the Republicans and Democrats say, "Elect us and we will see that the government is turned back to the people." Now, my friends, that is a very curious sort of appeal. For who took the government away from the people in the first place. Why, the Democrats, of course. And who has been heading it further away from the people during the past 4 years? The Republicans.

I say to both of these groups, "Now, don't you worry about giving the government back to the people, because the people aren't going to wait for you to give it back; they are going to take it back. And when they take it back, they are going to take the Federal Government out of all of the activities that are prerogatives of the states and recoup for the states the revenues of which they have been robbed by the Federal Government. And with these revenues they will manage their own affairs at far less cost than the Federal Government could possibly manage them. And in the process of doing all this, they are going to restore the rights and sovereignty of the states and the dignity and freedom of the people and thus put the Federal Government back in its place as a government of limited powers.

Some of the Democrats who find themselves without a place to go November 6th have asked us if it would not help to elect the candidate of the Republican party if they voted for us. Republicans in the same fix ask us if it would not help the candidate of the Democratic party if they voted for us.

I don't know the answer to these questions. But I do know that it wouldn't make any difference which of the two old parties won because we would have a continuation of socialistic government in either case. I also know that whenever anyone votes for a choice of evils he still votes for evil. I know further that the only hope for those who have been abandoned and disfranchised by their parties is to vote for something they believe in. Such people cannot expect ever to develop any respect for their points of view by voting for "Tweedle-dum" or "Tweedle-dee." After all, the longest journey begins with a single step.

Now, in conclusion, I want to offer the hospitality of our home to some mighty fine Americans. I note that the President, Mr. Paul Hoffman, The Fund for the Republic and others are talking about writing off many loyal Americans as members of the Republican party. The news stories indicate that these include Senators Jenner, Malone, Welker, Dworshak, Schoeppel and McCarthy and Governor Bracken Lee of Utah.

I want to say to these unyielding patriots that our door is open to them and that we can assure them that with us they will be safe from purge or liquidation. We welcome to our cause *all* who love their Country and sincerely seek return to Constitutional government and a genuine two-party system.

RIPENING FRUIT[†]
by
T. Coleman Andrews

MOST Americans, when they contemplate the bewildering and seemingly inescapable predicament in which we find ourselves at home and abroad, appear to think that it all just happened. Yet the blueprint for putting an end to our "noble experiment" in freedom was drawn many years ago:

> First we will take Eastern Europe; next the masses of Asia; then we shall encircle the last bastion of capitalism, The United States of America. We shall not have to attack; it will fall like an overripe fruit into our hands.

Thus boasted Lenin in his plan for the conquest of the world by the Communists. And what an unbelievable degree of success Lenin and those who have followed him have had in making good that boast!

Take a look around: Eastern Europe is gone, and most of Asia, including China with its 600 Million souls; and the anchor point of the prophesied encirclement of us has been established within rocket seconds of our shores, in Cuba.

In the meantime a growing army of subversive agents and dupes has inveigled our government into a piece-by-piece pattern of continuing socialistic spending that has brought us to the brink of economic disaster and political upheaval. And the enemy waits in drooling confidence that sooner or later the dying stem of our freedom will release its overripened fruit into his hands.

From Communism's small beginning in the backward Russia of 1917, it has spread over every part of the world, until it now holds in bondage a third of the earth's people and a fourth of its land area. This is a tragedy of the first magnitude. Sad to say, it could not have happened had not persons entrusted with the destiny of the American people given the Communists the strength needed for its survival. We—our own people—saved the Communists!

Under Roosevelt, our government recognized Communist Russia as a worthy member in the family of nations. Then our money was given to

---

[†]Speech before the Sales Executives' Club, Milwaukee, Wisconsin, January 19, 1961; published by The Patrick Henry Group, Richmond, Virginia, 1961; in the T. Coleman Andrews Papers (Coll. 119), Special Collections, University of Oregon Library. Reprinted with permission from *The Louisiana Certified Public Accountant*, October 1963, pp. 16-31.

them—money extracted from each of us through confiscatory taxation. Without these two essentials Lenin's prophesy would have remained a futile declaration of hope.

We shouldn't forget that.

And as we saved Mother Russia, so have we "saved" her daughters-in-slavery. Time after time, over the years, we have put up the money to establish new countries only to see the leaders whom we helped put in power ally themselves with Moscow—Nkruma of Ghana and Sukarno of Indonesia, for example. We have given great sums to Tito of Yugoslavia, and to Poland, and to other countries hostile to us. And now, Castro, just off our shores. We made Castro!

JOHN BULL

We have spent billions upon billions building and establishing defense bases abroad. We have done so though it has been apparent, even to the layman, that a number of these installations would become neutralized by fear of Russia on the part of the countries in which they had been established. Even worse, we knew that some would wind up in the hands of Russia and thus give the Communists, without a penny of cost to them, ready-made, close-at-hand bases for attack on us.

We can't even be sure today of our once-staunch ally, England, the country we twice saved from oblivion. True, John Bull allows us to have air bases in the British Isles, but if we see an attack coming we must obtain the approval of the Prime Minister before sending aloft a retaliatory force.

One must wonder, therefore, whether our air installations in England are not as useless as those in other countries. And if *those* bases are of doubtful value, what of our Polaris-Submarine base recently established in a British port (Holy Loch)? Why should this *naval* base be any more effective than our *air* bases? It, too, must operate under similar hampering restrictions?

THEN THERE IS MOROCCO

When Morocco was a French colony, we were given permission to build four air bases there. And we did so—at a cost of more than a billion dollars.

In proportion to Morocco's population and economy our aid to this North African country has been generous. In addition, the amount of money spent by our military and civilian personnel has been great.

When the Crown Prince of now-independent Morocco visited The United States a year or so ago, he was lavishly entertained and given still more aid. Then, upon his return to Morocco, his country accepted Red jet fighters, Red advisers and Red technicians.

Subsequently, at the Moroccan government's request, we agreed to abandon our bases there by 1963. But now we are being asked to leave sooner—as quickly as possible!

And so, our billion-dollar bases in Morocco are to be given up and turned over to the Communists, bases that are closer to The United States than is Europe.

Is this chance?

A new philosophy took hold of the world after World War II. Its essence is this: No matter what guilt may attach to a country that provokes war and upsets the peace of the world, loss of the war is punishment enough and the victors somehow have a moral obligation to put the vanquished back on their feet.

Generous America swallowed this philosophy, and multi-billion dollar gifts were made right and left. From the rubble of war beautiful new plants, equipped with the most modern machinery and equipment—all paid for by taxing you and me—sprang into being.

This was a magnanimous thing for us to do; but it played havoc with many of our home industries and seriously weakened our domestic and world position. As a result of our generosity more than a score of American industries are hard hit and unemployment is at its highest since 1940; in the textile industry alone more than 800 factories have been closed.

American factory owners, paying many times the wages paid by their foreign competitors, simply can not compete with the low wages and up-to-the-minute facilities of their foreign competitors. There is a good reason for this. Burdened as our people are by unjust taxes—used to build these foreign plants—they cannot afford new plants of their own. What irony!

GIVE AWAY

To add insult to injury, there sits in Geneva—well out of range of its victims—a creature of our making known as GATT. This organization, though completely without legal authority is, however, armed with an arbitrary delegation of bureaucratic power. And it dispenses tariff concessions to foreign manufacturers with utter indifference to the effect its generosity has upon the economy of America.

Thus, in giving relief to depressed areas abroad we have created depressed areas at home. And if the new administration is to fulfill one of its most-often-repeated campaign promises—relief to depressed areas—it must tax us even more to palliate our self-induced domestic distress.

The foregoing but opens the door to the foreign aspects of our helpfulness to the Communists in carrying out their blueprint for world conquest. We have, wittingly or unwittingly, aided the enemy that waits for us to drop, as overripe fruit, into his hands.

Such is the brought-home meaning of Foreign Aid, begun in 1949, and to have ended, with the Marshall Plan. But it did not end there; nor is there any plan to stop it. In all, we have given away the astronomical sum of $80 billion. In giving this sum we have given away the equivalent of our country's 32 largest cities.

Give this a moment's thought. We have given to foreigners the equivalent worth of New York, Chicago, Los Angeles, Philadelphia, Detroit, Boston, San Francisco, Pittsburgh, St. Louis, Cleveland, Washington, Baltimore, Minneapolis-St. Paul, Buffalo, Cincinnati, Milwaukee, Kansas City, Houston, Providence, Seattle, Portland (Oregon), New Orleans, Atlanta, Dallas, Louisville, Denver, Birmingham, San Diego, Indianapolis, Youngstown, Albany and Columbus, Ohio. All this we have given away, just given it away.

Isn't it a fair question to ask what we have received in return? What, other than hatred abroad and peril at home?

When Lenin boasted that it would not be necessary to defeat The United States in battle in order to attain the Communist goal (world-wide dictatorship) he was not saying that the Communists had changed their minds about using force whenever they might deem force necessary. Nor was he saying that they would not use force against The United States.

He was saying, rather, that he saw an easier way than fighting to bring about our end as a free people—that there were others who would do the job for them. Communists are realists, you know; they never fight for something that can be had without fighting. The Cardinal Mindszenty Foundation puts it this way:

> The Communist apparatus in America faithfully follows the dictum laid down by Dimitorv at the Lenin School of Political Warfare: "Let our friends do the work. We must always remember that one sympathizer is generally worth more than a dozen militant communists."

And who are the Communists' friends in America? Among their most effective friends are the Fabian Socialists—a growing cult of economists, sociologists, and other "thinkers" and masters of "gradualism." For more than a quarter of a century these borers from within have been so skillfully conditioning us for delivery into the Communist orbit that probably not one-in-ten of us has ever heard the name, Fabian Socialism, let alone become aware of the poison that its practitioners have been feeding us.

SAFE WAY

There is something ironic in this, for it is indeed these people, these Fabians, who are actually pulling us apart. The Communists also are working, of course. But for each Communist there are many Fabians. We haven't become aware of them, one supposes, simply because we have had our eyes so glued to the Communist rat hole that we have failed to pay proper heed to the mice, the Fabians, gnawing away behind us.

But these skulking cowards are worth our notice. They have a stripe only slightly different from that of their bullyboy brothers; they abhor violence. For all of that, they are no less dedicated to the destruction of Capitalism than are the Communists. And today, they, the Fabians, are everywhere around us—in growing numbers and strength. And the Communists chortle as they progress, for the Fabians are their allies. As these "gradualists" whittle away our freedom and soften us sufficiently to be taken over without fighting, they perform yeoman work for Moscow.

The Fabian way may take a little longer than the coup d'etat, the Communists reason, but there is no doubt in the Communist mind that "gradualism" is the better way. There is no reason to be in a hurry about a "sure thing." So let the Fabians do it. As day slowly turns to dusk, so dusk will turn to night. Therefore, have patience, the Commies say. Then, when our destruction is complete, all the Communist need do, in relation to the Fabians, is flex their muscles and the trophy will be theirs.

The pattern has been clear, and it has always been the same: The Fabian Socialists plow the ground, plant the seeds and tend the crop, and the Communists reap the harvest of another disillusioned people! Thus the tyranny of ruthless dictatorship has been planned, developed and established throughout the world.

Yesterday it was Cuba. Tomorrow, we are told it will be Spain and Portugal. In the meantime the fruit continues to ripen!

FABIAN SOCIALISM

Fabian Socialism was founded in the early 1880's in England. Its originators were men who resented the fact that doers—those who do things—derive greater reward from their accomplishments than do those who prefer to think about how things should be done.

In other words, Fabian Socialists don't like to work; they just like to think. Wherefore, goes the Fabian mind, the thinkers should be exalted and the doers cast down; and Capitalism, which treats the doers well and doesn't appreciate the thinkers, must be destroyed and replaced by Communism. Listen to George Bernard Shaw, one of the early leaders of the Fabian movement. He said that Fabian Socialists

> were the first to see that Capitalism was reducing their own class to the condition of a proletariat and that the only chance of securing anything more than a slave's share in the national income for anyone but the biggest capitalists or the cleverest professional or business men lay in a combination of all the proletarians, *without distinction of class or country, to put an end of capitalism by developing the communistic side of our civilization until communism became the dominant principle in society*, and mere owing, profiteering, and genteel idling were disabled and discredited.

511

There you have it! The Fabian Socialists are malcontents and haters. They are destroyers, not builders. They hate capitalism and Capitalists. Therefore, capitalism and Capitalists must be destroyed and a classless, one-world society must be established under a communistic form of government—classless, that is, as to everybody but themselves; they would be the ruling class.

THE COVER

The pioneers who developed the strategy and the tactics by which Fabian objectives were to be achieved included "a very high proportion of people who combined remarkable intellectual ability with a strong sense of practical possibilities."

The Veritas Society recently told their story. In "Keynes at Harvard," an excellent and extensively documented exposure of Fabian socialism, the society listed the following as the first of five outstanding characteristics of the Fabian Socialists:

> A cover of respectability and good manners as a means of gaining entry into all social activities, while avoiding use of the label "socialism," (but) promoting socialism continuously by coloring such activities with new terms *so as to attain socialism by stealth*.

Roger Baldwin (Harvard, 1905) is reported in "Keynes at Harvard" to have been pursuing the methods of Fabian Socialists in The United States for more than 55 years, and to have said in "an advisory to a socialist agitator":

> Do steer away from making it look like a Socialist enterprise.... We want also to look patriots in everything we do. We want to get a good lot of flags, talk a good deal about the Constitution and what our forefathers wanted to make of this country, and to show that we are really the folks that really stand for the spirit of our institutions.

The Fabian Socialists' paramount rule, therefore, is this: "Never admit you are a Socialist; pretend to be anything else; never show your hand."

Does it begin to come home to you who in our government these people are?

The drudgery of work is beneath them; they think and scheme, and their chief weapons are stealth and deception. You'll find them everywhere in government except in the uniform of their country. They don't like military service any more than they like work.

John Maynard Keynes, about whom the Fabian book was written, was one of the shining stars of British Fabianism. Typifying his breed, he tried every ruse his scheming mind could conceive to escape military service and finally declared himself a "conscientious objector." His own mother was so ashamed of him that she called his stand "unpatriotic."

HALLMARK

Fabians are experts at infiltration, and patience is their hallmark. Their plan is to ease us into socialism by indiscernible steps—"to put an end (to) capitalism by developing the communistic side of our civilization until communism (becomes) the dominant principle in society."

Fabianism is like slow murder with arsenic; each dose is so small that it cannot be tasted; but accumulation eventually kills the unsuspecting victim. As Keynes once put it: "The trick is to get control of the government. Then the road to socialism is automatically assured."

The Fabian Socialists call their method of operation "gradualism."

Therein lies the primary difference between Fabian socialism and Communism. The Fabian Socialists' formula is infiltration and peaceful evolution. The Communists' formula is infiltration, coalition, revolution and forceful takeover. The end of both is destruction of Capitalism and personal liberty and the attainment of dictatorial power.

The first significant achievement of the Fabian Socialists was their destruction of the Liberal Party of Great Britain. By infiltration, deception and stealth, the Fabians first corrupted, then destroyed, the character of this once-great party. At the same time they prepared the ground for the organization of the present Labor Party which came to power following World War II. In the opinion of many, the Fabians would have completely socialized the government and economy of Great Britain except for one thing: In victory, they pushed their nationalization (Socialist) program with such excessive zeal as to frighten many of their own half-educated members. They are not apt to repeat that earlier mistake.

As might have been expected, Fabian Socialism spread to The United States. But its adherents didn't gain perceptible political power here until after Franklin Delano Roosevelt became President. With his predilection for people whose political inclination was to the left, Roosevelt was completely taken in by Keynes. Consequently, not long after Roosevelt's first inauguration left-wing professors and brain washed students began to descend upon Washington. They came from every direction, principally from the northeast.

ALIEN LIGHT

Professors with enthusiasm for Fabian socialism or outright communism had a field day. These professors, serving as incubator tenders, delivered into Washington a host of young men, most of whom were without experience in anything except their incubator, going to school. These callow kids, eyes aglow with an alien light, were placed in government positions that called for the handling of matters of the utmost importance. In time Washington was over-run with "bright young men" willing and anxious to follow the left-wing lead of their professorial Svengalis.

In relatively short order after their installation by Roosevelt, the Fabian Socialists and the Communists scored their first big triumph: Diplomatic recognition was extended to Russia!

That did it. Russia was down and all but out. Had the new administration refused to recognize Russia, communism would have suffered a serious, perhaps fatal, blow. But the Roosevelt administration did recognize Communist Russia and, as we know, Russia lost no time in making herself an increasing threat to the peace of the world. Communist infiltration of our government in many important aspects of our nation's life became an ever-increasing problem. It remains so today.

Thus the fruit began to ripen! And now we face a mounting peril that no citizen can afford to ignore.

For nearly 30 years, the Fabian-inspired philosophy that has determined our decisions has been based on the notion that money will cure any ill. We have been taught to believe that when we have failed in matters that have involved the spending of money it has been because we did not spend enough—tax, tax, tax; spend, spend, spend!

A classic example of this notion was seen recently in the report filed by the President's Commission on National Goals. Success, it seemed to say, will be assured if we just spend more. This, despite the fact, as a people, we are more in debt than all the rest of the world—ONE TRILLION, THREE HUNDRED AND FIFTY BILLIONS of debt. TRILLION! And now our gold reserve—the heartbeat of our economy—is nearly defunct. Still, they want to spend more.

The drain on our gold supply started with the adoption of the Marshall Plan in the late 40's and it has been going on ever since.

Now, $80 billion later, we are reduced to seeking the aid of others, and except for a gesture by West Germany there is no hand extended in our direction.

Nevertheless, our dollar still remains the principal reserve currency of the free world. But it does so only because a better currency, a more secure base, is not available. Without our dollar as their base the currencies of those countries tied to it would have little value. The managers of the monetary affairs of other nations know this and they don't dare withdraw their deposits from our treasury now, lest they precipitate a world-wide monetary debacle. We are all in it together; America has been sucked into a vortex that promises destruction to us all. Such is the result of not living up to the obligation of prudence and good faith that was inherent in our assumption of world financial leadership.

The combination of Fabian Socialism and Communism, the one-two punch, has done its work!

For all of their effectiveness, neither the Fabian Socialists nor the Communists maintain political parties in this country—not as such. Their grand strategy is to infiltrate and covertly control the established parties. Were they to organize, maintain and work through political parties honestly identified as their own they would expose their hands, and that is the last thing they want to do.

THE DONKEY

For an example of their strategy of infiltration and covert control, consider the plight of the Democratic Party. Their conquest of the party of Jackson is all but complete and is identical to their conquest of England's Liberal Party. What's more, an impressive start has been made on the Republican Party. The GOP is not nearly so impervious to Fabian infiltration as it would like to think.

It isn't that the Democratic Party sought either the Communists or the Fabians. The opposite is true. The Communists and the Fabians sought the Democratic Party, and for a very good reason. The Democratic Party has the reputation of being the "party of the people," and the manipulation of people is what interests the Socialists and Communists. Moreover, they hate Capitalists, although they are not averse to adding the Republican Party, the "party of the Capitalists," to their bag. Everything is grist for their mill.

Just how far have they gone in infiltrating both parties? Hear what Congressman Utt of California says:

> We are rapidly coming to a point where a complete change of elected officials, including Congress and the White House, can mean little change in policy. You are governed more and more by people for whom you have never voted, for whom you never will vote, whom you have never seen, and whom you cannot recall by your vote. They are entrenched in the boards, bureaus and commissions, even at the policy level.

Reading between the lines of this patriot's statement, one would have to be strangely naive to think Congressman Utt was talking only about the protection thrown around government employees by the Civil Service Commission.

To be specific, what was behind the fight that destroyed the effectiveness of the House Rules Committee?

I have reason to believe—and I do believe—it was an outright effort to make Congress a rubber-stamp for the Fabian-manipulated executive branch. This being so, what could be finer for those who control the infiltrators than to have Congress dancing to the Executive's tunes?

ALL THREE

And what of the Supreme Court? It is hard to see how anyone may accept some of the court's decisions as nothing more than high-minded interpretations of law, particularly those decisions that have dealt with Communism, Communists, Civil Rights, Sedition and other controversial matters and persons. What sinister influences were behind these decisions?

Read what one of the nation's greatest newspapers, *The Indianapolis Star*, has to say in this regard:

> The (Supreme) Court is engaged in a race which, if persisted in, can be won only by destroying the governmental system we revere. It is competing against time to enforce new doctrines before nebulous public resentment becomes hardened public resentment.

There can be no question about it: Subversive influences are at work in all three branches of the government! How else to account for the likes of Harry Dexter White, for the long list of traitors that we have been fortunate enough to catch and expose.

Did this all "just happen"?

Who is to believe that the people who manage our government, having worked themselves to the top, are stupid? True, government is terribly big and bewilderingly complex; and mistakes are to be expected. But when wrong decisions become the rule rather than the exception, what conclusion should a reasonable person make?

How else do you account for an occurrence such as this, for example, which was reported by Mr. Fred C. Koch in his extraordinary treatise, "A Businessman Looks at Communism":

> The Judge Advocate General of the U.S. Navy, an Admiral, told me that he had addressed the Naval War College on communism a few years ago. At the conclusion of his address, a Harvard professor arose and excoriated him as a Fascist and a reactionary. Since that event he has never been asked to address the War College again.

On January 1, 1959, one of the largest newspapers in the country quoted a State Department expert on Latin American affairs as having told the Subcommittee for Inter-American Affairs of the Senate Foreign Relations Committee that

> there was no evidence of any organized Communist element within the Castro movement or that Senor Castro himself was under Communist influence.

Quite to the contrary, there was voluminous evidence that Castro himself had been a Communist since 1948, and probably before then. This evidence is of a character that only a State Department that has been fast asleep would not have had. It begins with reports from Bogota, Colombia, in April of that year, when Colombian detectives took correspondence from Castro that showed him to be a member of the Communist Party in Cuba.

516

Castro was in Colombia to participate in (perhaps to direct) the Bogota uprising of 1948. Nathaniel Weyl, in his extensively-documented book, *"Red Star Over Cuba,"* published by Devin-Adair, says that "this uprising was directed chiefly against the United States" and that one of its purposes was "probably, but not certainly, to engineer the assassination of the (then) U. S. Secretary of State, General of the Armies George C. Marshall."

That was but the beginning of Castro's Communist record. Was the State Department asleep from April, 1948, until the end of 1958? How could it, as late as January, 1959, have permitted its expert on Latin American Affairs to assure the Senate Subcommittee that there was no evidence Senor Castro was under Communist influence?

With these facts in hand, can there be any question in the mind of anyone, whether subversives are established widely and in strength in the government? Can anyone possibly believe that our danger is due to nothing more than somnambulant civil servants? Has Rip Van Winkle, been, in fact, our Secretary of State. If you are inclined to believe there is nothing "rotten in Denmark," try answering these questions:

Do you believe that Bang-Jensen, the United Nations official, committed suicide?

Do you believe that the riots by college and university students in South America, Japan, England and other countries were no more than impulsive outbursts of local political dissatisfaction?

Do you believe that the San Francisco riot of university students against the House Committee on Un-American Activities was not inspired ... that it was nothing more than an impulsive blowing off of steam by the students?

If you do, have you seen the documented movie of this riot entitled, "Operation Abolition," filmed by news-reel cameramen and released by the Committee? If you haven't, you should. You also should read J. Edgar Hoover's report, "Communist Target—Youth," an official report on the same outrage. Copies of this report may be obtained from the House Committee on Un-American Activities.

Have you read Committee Chairman Francis E. Walter's statement of the Communist Party's reaction to the outcome of the San Francisco riot? This is what he has reported:

The Communist Party was so elated over its success in San Francisco that at Communist rallies and cell meetings since that time party members have been instructed that such behavior now is to become common practice whenever the Committee "dares" to stray outside the protection of the Federal buildings in Washington. A Student Communist group in New York City has already promised that they will do ten times as well as the students in San Francisco should the committee come to that city.

Do you believe it is mere chance that American history has been de-emphasized in our schools and that our economic system is derided? Do you believe this is "just happening"?

Do you believe that the glorification of socialism that began in our schools in the early 30's has caused a deterioration in the character and moral fibre of those who have been exposed to it?

If not, how do you account for the estimate by the Communist Chief of Intelligence relating to American soldiers taken prisoner in Korea? This estimate was found in a captured enemy document and was reported by BABSON'S WASHINGTON FORECAST of January 9, 1961 as stating that

The American soldier
(1) has weak loyalties to his family, community, religion, country and fellow soldiers;
(2) has hazy and ill-formed concepts of right and wrong;
(3) when by himself feels frightened and insecure;
(4) underestimates his own worth, strength and ability to survive;
(5) is ignorant of social values and has little real knowledge of his own country and its system or philosophy of government;
(6) fails to appreciate the meaning of or necessity for military service, organization, or discipline.

Do you believe that the ministers, churches and church organizations that become involved in controversial political questions do so only in response to sincere feelings of compassion and are not unwitting victims of subversive propaganda?

Do you believe that the tendency of so much of the working press to be socialistic is a development that has taken place without subversive inspiration?

Have you considered what is the significance of the fact that conservative authors are largely ignored by the book reviewers and their publishers find it almost impossible to get conservative books on store shelves, while the most trivial musings of left-wing authors get rave reviews and their books get preferred display in the stores?

Do you believe that the labor leader who says, "To hell with National Defense; I'm for Labor," is merely asserting that he knows which side his bread is buttered on? Or, do you believe that he has been stripped of his loyalty to his country by propaganda or subversion?

And what of the president of a great tax-exempt foundation who said to a congressional investigator, "My job is to change the economic climate of the U.S.A. so that it can be comfortably merged with that of the Soviet Union, and you aren't going to stand in my way"?

What about the star of the late evening chit-chat and trivia show who made a one-night stand in Havana and came back praising Castro as a great deliverer?... Or the impresario of the variety show who also got into the act, visited Castro in his hideout in the Sierra Maestra Mountains and went so far as to call the bearded killer "the George Washington of Cuba"?... Or of the television reporter of news and weather who stages leftward-slanted, quickie interviews on highly controversial subjects and who makes a great show of emotion over his one-sided approach to man's inhumanity to man? "Peace," indeed.... Or the pseudo pundit who with a wrinkled-brow affectation of profundity slants his so-called "documentaries" so far to the left that even his sponsors complain of his bias?

Are these men merely giving vent to the ego that is so much a part of successful showmanship? Or have they fallen victims to subversive propaganda?

Finally, what of the flood of immoral filth and left-wing propaganda that is coming out of Hollywood again, now that the Commies have been put back on the payroll? And of the equally immoral glut of filth that presently befouls Broadway. Worse still, what of us, the American people? Are the authors and producers of what passes today for dramatic art only pandering to the lust of a people who are no longer worthy of their heritage of decency and freedom?

These are but a few of the myriad areas in which the forces of subversion are at work in our land, ripening us as fruit.

Lenin called our country "the last bastion of Capitalism." A truly great man called it the "last great hope on earth."

Which is it? Which are we—today?

Tom Anderson, that towering giant of loyalty and steadfast devotion to all that the Founding Fathers intended America to stand for, said in a recent editorial:

If the lamp of freedom is blown out in America, the world will be thrown into darkness.

That is the meaning of it all: A world to save—from our folly.

GOD'S PLAN?

Perhaps, as the Archbishop of Canterbury has said, it is a part of God's plan that we pay the price of our waywardness and go the way of all peoples who have wearied of keeping the vigil that liberty demands.

From the bottom of my heart, I hope it isn't. But know that a deadly peril exists, and, as President Eisenhower made abundantly clear in his farewell message, that neither people nor nations avoid disaster by doing nothing.

Some mighty knowledgeable people who understand this peril better than I feel that time is running out on us. One of these has put it this way:

> At first I worried about my grandchildren. Then I began to worry about my children. Now I wonder whether I will live out my own life in freedom.

I know, too, that some people already are talking surrender. For example, Dr. Donald Soper, Methodist Minister, West End Mission, London, the 1960 Lyman Beecher, Lecturer at Yale, has said:

> The West must search for world government, and we must face the fact that Krushchev will be the first president.

We must realize that we have already passed the time when we could afford the luxury of doing nothing about all this. We're in a war, a war as real as any the world has ever known, a subtle, stealthy, creeping war to the death; and we face a fanatically determined enemy. What is worse, the tide of battle is running in that enemy's favor, not ours. That kind of enemy in that kind of situation doesn't quit; he has to be defeated! Any person who thinks that we can have "business—or anything else—as usual" and win this war, is deceiving himself. Wars are won by *people—fighting people*.

EACH MAN'S JOB

Let no one think that his congressman or his senators can do the job without guidance and help. These men will do only what they think their constituents want them to do. Even if they were willing to do all the fighting, to expect or to allow them to do it would be the same as using mercenaries; and mercenaries don't win wars; nor do free men worthy of the name expect other men to do their fighting.

Anyone, then, who thinks that he can be neutral in this fight for control of our government is deluding himself. It should be remembered that if the Socialists and Communists one day attain such a degree of power that they become our masters, even those who did not oppose them will share the fate of those who did. For it is axiomatic that when revolutionaries triumph neutrals get the same treatment as active enemies. As they reason, if you are not for them, now, before they win, you will be listed as having been against them.

The plight of neutrals is never a happy one. Recall Dante's dictum: "The hottest fires of hell are reserved for those who, in a period of moral crisis, maintain neutrality."

Busy yourselves, then, by putting your congressmen and your senators on notice that you want those responsible for our plight thrown out of the government, that you want your government purged of every enemy who made possible the spread of communism in our land. Pick out a specific subversive instance and let your congressman know your convictions. Write him—today.

Make it clear that you mean it and do not intend to let up until the job is done. Don't wait until the situation has reached the point where the conspirators are in irrevocable control, for by then the shoe will be on the other foot—*you* will have become the *conspirators* and they the "loyalists." In the Spanish Civil War of the mid-30's it was the Communists, you may remember, who were called "The Loyalists."

Above all, urge everyone who will listen to you to do the same thing. Whether our officials are loyal but dumb, or smart and subversive, those who have failed us must be thrown out—every one of them, not just some of them. A token clean-up will not accomplish anything lasting; the job must be a thorough one.

Begin today; for *you and all your loved ones are the ripening fruit.*

Appendix
REORGANIZATION OF ACCOUNTING IN THE GOVERNMENT†

*Report to the Congress by the Commission on Organization of the
Executive Branch of the Government*

THE conduct of the accounting system of the Government affects all other administrative problems.

The financial operations of the Government must be controlled even more rigorously than those of private business. Maintenance of financial integrity affects the confidence of the Nation in itself and the moral standards of all the people. A failure of such integrity in private business affects the pocketbooks and slackens the morals of a few, but its failure in public business affects the morals of all.

Policies and methods in the handling of governmental funds must be clearly defined and responsibilities firmly fixed.

Nevertheless, the complicated checks and balances employed make for unnecessary inefficiency in every activity and one of the very first steps toward economy in governmental operations lies in improving the accounting system.

Over the past several years private business has developed a number of new accounting methods and devices, many of which should be adapted to governmental operations.

The situation has not gone unrecognized. Members of the Congress and the executive branch have repeatedly protested at many of the worst features of present budgeting and accounting practices.

ACCOUNTING OBJECTIVES

Governmental accounting must serve several purposes. It is an indispensable tool in the day-to-day management of the administrative affairs of the Government. It reveals the status of appropriations, the extent that revenue estimates are realized, the progress of actual expenditures and

---

†Reprinted from *Budgeting and Accounting—A Report to the Congress* by the Commission on Organization of the Executive Branch of the Government (Washington, DC: U.S. Government Printing Office, February 1949), Part Three, pp. 35-44. The recommendations contained in this, the Hoover Commission's final report to Congress, differed materially from those made by the Accounting Policy Committee of the Fiscal, Budgeting, and Accounting Task Force chaired by T. Coleman Andrews, whose recommendations are reprinted in this collection under the title "The Accounting Needs of the Federal Government."

collections, and comparative operating and other costs. It provides the basis for the summary financial reports which the executive branch sends to the Congress and which are printed for public information. Last but not least, accounting provides for the fixing of responsibility in the handling and use of Government funds, thus enabling a check of administrative competence and fidelity to be made by a representative of the legislative branch, the Comptroller General.

THE PRESENT ACCOUNTING SYSTEM

The accounting system of the Government, as it now exists, consists of two general types of accounts—fiscal accounts and administrative accounts.

The fiscal accounts are the over-all or general accounts which are kept mainly in the Treasury Department. These accounts comprehend the fiscal operations relating to revenues, custody of funds, disbursements, public debt, and currency. The Comptroller General does not ordinarily concern himself with the form of these accounts or the contents of the reports which are made from them. Nor is he concerned with property or cost accounts.

Section 309 of the Budget and Accounting Act of June 10, 1921, provides ...

> ... The Comptroller General shall prescribe the forms, systems, and procedure for administrative appropriation and fund accounting in the several departments and establishments, and for the administrative examination of fiscal officers' accounts and claims against the United States. (31 U.S.C. sec. 49.)

The authority of the Comptroller General is thus, by law, limited to prescribing administrative accounts. He does not now have any authority over fiscal or other accounts.

He has from time to time issued regulations prescribing in detail the form of these accounts—the latest issue being "Regulation 100" of a few years ago. But the Comptroller General has not been particularly concerned with property accounts or with cost accounts. They have been developed chiefly by the departments with the assistance of the Treasury.

The development of a complete and up-to-date system of accounting for the Government comprehends both the fiscal or general accounts and the administrative or departmental accounts. All these systems of accounts should be prescribed by the same authority in order to have an integrated system. With some prescribed by the Treasury, some by the departments, and others by the Comptroller General, it has not been possible during the last 27 years, since the Budget and Accounting Act was passed, to work out a satisfactory system.

The present unsatisfactory situation has been recognized by the organization of a voluntary committee, comprising the Secretary of the Treasury, the Comptroller General, and the Director of the Bureau of the Budget, to arrive at mutually agreeable reforms in the accounting system.

The Comptroller General emphasized this situation in a letter of October 20, 1948, to the Government departments and agencies. In this letter he announced a broad program which ...

> ... contemplates the full development of sound accounting within each agency, as a working arm of management, in terms of financial information and control. At the same time it envisions an integrated pattern of accounting and financial reporting for the Government as a whole responsive to executive and legislative needs. Balanced recognition will be given to the need for a flexible basis for accounting development within agencies in the light of varying types of operations and management problems and to over-all fiscal reporting, and audit responsibilities.

The Comptroller General further states:

> I wish to deal with the concept of my responsibility in the prescribing of accounting systems. I believe this function should be exercised so as to provide all possible encouragement to the agencies to exercise their own initiative and responsibility in the solution of their accounting function. In line with this, it will be my objective as the program progresses to prescribe requirements largely in terms of standards, principles, and basic forms, procedures, and terminology.

These efforts are in the right direction. But this Commission feels that more than voluntary correctives are needed. A definite system should be established and given more permanence through legislation and organization. Indeed, the admirable work of the Secretary of the Treasury, the Comptroller General, and the Director of the Bureau of the Budget will be greatly aided if positive action be taken to establish a responsible official with authority to give continuous motive force to reform in accounting. Since accounting is primarily the responsibility of the executive branch, it is proposed that this official should be an Accountant General in charge of a new Accounting Service in the Treasury Department.

*Recommendation No. 10**

Therefore, the Commission recommends that:

a. An Accountant General be established under the Secretary of the Treasury with authority to prescribe general accounting methods and enforce accounting procedures. These methods and procedures should be subject to the approval of the Comptroller General within the powers now conferred upon him by the Congress.

Editors' Note: Five of the twelve members of the Hoover Commission dissented from this recommendation. Their comments were referenced here and printed in separate sections of the Commission's report.

b. The Accountant General should, on a report basis, combine agency accounts into the summary accounts of the Government and produce financial reports for the information of the Chief Executive, the Congress, and the public. (See chart.)

Our recommendation would create a single officer in the Treasury Department with authority to prescribe a single system of fiscal accounts and to represent the executive branch in working out an administrative accounting system with the Comptroller General. The Accountant General would further supervise all departmental accounting activities throughout the executive branch and assist departments in performing their accounting duties.

We believe there is no inherent conflict between the present position of the Comptroller General and our recommendation to create the position of Accountant General.

SETTLEMENT OF ACCOUNTS AND CLAIMS

Section 305 of the Budget and Accounting Act of 1921 provides that:

... All claims and demands whatever by the Government of the United States or against it, and all accounts whatever in which the Government of the United States is concerned, either as debtor or creditor, shall be settled and adjusted in the General Accounting Office. (31 U.S.C. sec. 71.)

The meaning of this language has been determined over a period of years by various opinions and decisions of the Comptroller General. In fulfilling his responsibilities under this section the Comptroller General now requires administrative agencies of the executive branch to submit all expenditure vouchers and supporting documents for every individual transaction to the General Accounting Office for examination and "settlement." This is a costly system. It means freight carloads of vouchers from all over the United States hauled to Washington for individual examination in the General Accounting Office.

The office now labors under a deluge of paper work of all kinds which requires about 10,000 people to examine. Over $30,000,000 is needed a year to operate the General Accounting Office on its present scale, and a whole new building is required to house personnel and papers. Of this number of persons and of these total costs, about half result from the central examination of individual expenditure vouchers and documents.

New arrangements should be made for the examination of vouchers at points mutually agreeable to the Comptroller General and the department heads concerned. This was done during the war in the case of the War Department.

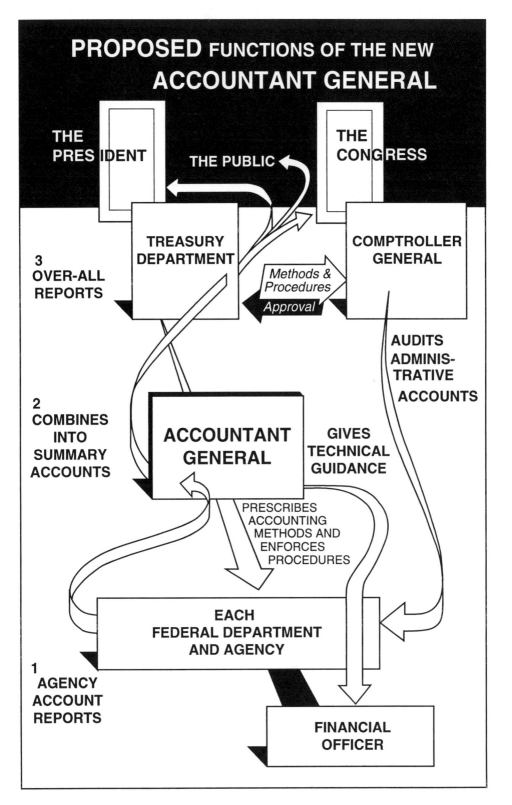

PROPOSED FUNCTIONS OF THE NEW
ACCOUNTANT GENERAL

THE PRESIDENT

THE PUBLIC

THE CONGRESS

3 OVER-ALL REPORTS

TREASURY DEPARTMENT

Methods & Procedures

Approval

COMPTROLLER GENERAL

AUDITS ADMINIS-TRATIVE ACCOUNTS

2 COMBINES INTO SUMMARY ACCOUNTS

ACCOUNTANT GENERAL

GIVES TECHNICAL GUIDANCE

PRESCRIBES ACCOUNTING METHODS AND ENFORCES PROCEDURES

EACH FEDERAL DEPARTMENT AND AGENCY

1 AGENCY ACCOUNT REPORTS

FINANCIAL OFFICER

Therefore, the Commission recommends:

a. That the practice of sending millions of expenditure vouchers and supporting papers to Washington be stopped as far as possible.

The Comptroller General must obviously continue to determine the adequacy and integrity of administrative fiscal practices; to check and make certain that laws governing appropriations are being properly interpreted; to check the efficiency of accounting and other administrative arrangements; and to report on these matters to the Congress.

b. But this Commission recommends, in view of the fantastic growth of detail, that a spot sampling process at various places where the expenditure vouchers and papers are administratively checked might be substituted for much of the present procedure of bringing all these documents to Washington.

This recommendation is not intended to weaken legislative control over expenditures, but (1) to free the General Accounting Office from the overwhelming burden of paper work required of the executive branch and (2) to simplify the work of executive agencies in handling expenditure transactions which must be "settled" by the General Accounting Office.

OTHER RECOMMENDATIONS

Our task force on accounting recommends that the accrual basis of accounting should be applied to both revenues and expenditures. It recommends simplification or elimination of the present warrant system. It proposes uniform departmental practices, procedures, nomenclature, better inventory and public debt accounting, which would greatly reduce staff and red tape.

Recommendation No. 12

The Commission endorses these recommendations.

Surety bonding, as at present practiced, adds greatly to departmental red tape and cost, especially in the Treasury Department where lists of bonding companies and surety bonds in force are maintained.

Under the present procedure about 558,000 accountable officers are required to pay for their own surety bonds provided by private companies at an aggregate annual premium cost of about $2,000,000, while recoveries average only about $230,000 annually.

The problem, it seems, could be better solved by establishing a fidelity insurance fund in the Treasury to which accountable officers would be required to contribute.

Recommendation No. 13

We further recommend that the Congress continue its study of the whole question of fidelity insurance for the accountable officers of the Government in order to arrive at a simpler and less expensive procedure.

T. COLEMAN ANDREWS:
A BIBLIOGRAPHY†

"The Profession of Accountancy: Its Problems and Its Ideals." *The Accounting and Business Quarterly* (September 1923): 3-5.

"International Accountants Congress." *The Certified Public Accountant* 7 (January 1927): 18-20. *

"Reorganization of Virginia Accounts." *The Certified Public Accountant* 13 (November 1933): 677-689.

"Accounting—The Eye of Management." *Municipal Finance* 7 (February 1935): 2-3.

"Opening Remarks at Breakfast Round Table Discussion of the Annual Financial Report of a Municipality" (September 10, 1936). In the files of the American Institute of Certified Public Accountants. 4 typewritten pages.

"Address before Annual Meeting of North American Gasoline Tax Conference," Richmond, Virginia, October 7, 1936. In the files of the American Institute of Certified Public Accountants. 15 typewritten pages.

"Future of Professional Accountancy." *The Journal of Accountancy* 63 (March 1937): 220. *

"Accounts of Governmental Authorities." (Address at the 50th Anniversary Celebration and Annual Meeting, American Institute of Accountants, Waldorf-Astoria Hotel, New York, October 18-22, 1937.) In *Fiftieth Anniversary Celebration.* New York: American Institute of Accountants, 1937, 296-300.

---

†This bibliography includes several papers that are representative of Andrews' political and personal philosophies, but does not represent a complete listing of his political writings and speeches.

Items followed by an asterisk were not reprinted in this volume.

"The Technique of Municipal Accounting Installations." In *Addresses Presented at the Conference on Municipal Accounting and Finance*, Chicago, March 28 and 29, 1938. New York: American Institute of Accountants, 1938, 80-84.

"Introduction to Round Table Discussion: Municipal Accounting Session." In *Papers on Auditing Procedure and Other Accounting Subjects* (Presented at the Fifty-Second Annual Meeting, American Institute of Accountants). New York: American Institute of Accountants, 1939, 199-202.

"Municipal Accounting." (In Middle Atlantic States Accounting Conference. *Papers on Accounting Procedure and Related Matters*, June 16 and 17, 1939, 60-64.)

"Accounting for Reserves." [June 1941] In the files of the American Institute of Certified Public Accountants. 9 typewritten pages. *

"Constructive Accounting." *The Accounting Forum* 12 (June 1941): 52-55, 62.

"Cooperation with Bar Association." (Presented at the Meeting of the Advisory Council of State Society Presidents, Detroit, Michigan, September 15, 1941.) In the files of the American Institute of Certified Public Accountants. 7 typewritten pages.

"Mistakes Commonly Made in the Preparation of Financial Reports of State and Local Governments." In *Proceedings, Fourth Accounting Clinic*. Harrisburg, PA: Pennsylvania Institute of Certified Public Accountants—Harrisburg Chapter, 1941, 6 pages. *Illinois Society of Certified Public Accountants Bulletin* 4 (June 1942): 10-12, 18 (condensed).

"National Debt and Taxation Equity" (Letter by T. Coleman Andrews). *The Journal of Accountancy* 74 (September 1942): 257-258. *

"Audit Report on Reconstruction Finance Corporation." Statement before the Committee on Expenditures in the Executive Departments, United States House of Representatives, on the Comptroller General's Interim Audit Report on the RFC, July 2, 1946; *The Journal of Accountancy* 82 (September 1946): 265-268 (excerpts).

"Shall We Cut or Cut Out? That is the Question!" [February 3, 1947] In the files of the American Institute of Certified Public Accountants. 9 typewritten pages. *

"The Work of the Corporation Audits Division of the GAO." In *New Developments in Accounting* (Papers Presented at the Fifty-Ninth Annual Meeting, American Institute of Accountants). New York: American Institute of Accountants, 1946, 165-170. Also published under title "Advances in Governmental Accounting." *The Accounting Review* 22 (January 1947): 23-27.

"Accounting and the Management of Public Affairs." In *Proceedings of the Ninth Annual Institute on Accounting*. Columbus, OH: College of Commerce and Administration, The Ohio State University, 1947, 5-11. *The Accounting Review* 22 (October 1947): 367-371.

"The Accounting Needs of the Federal Government." Report of the Accounting Policy Committee of the Fiscal, Budgeting and Accounting Project, Part Four of *Fiscal, Budgeting, and Accounting Systems of Federal Government—A Report with Recommendations*; Prepared for the Commission on Organization of the Executive Branch of the Government, by John W. Hanes, A. E. Buck, and T. Coleman Andrews, 110 pages. Published as Appendix F, *Task Force Report on Fiscal, Budgeting, and Accounting Activities*, to *Budgeting and Accounting—A Report to the Congress* by the Commission on Organization of the Executive Branch of the Government. Washington, DC: U.S. Government Printing Office, February 1949.

"Address Delivered at Meeting of Lynchburg Rotary Club." February 24, 1948. In the files of the American Institute of Certified Public Accountants. 16 typewritten pages.

"Better Accounting, Better Government." (Address at the Middle Atlantic States Accounting Conference, Myrtle Beach, South Carolina, July 13, 1948.) In the files of the American Institute of Certified Public Accountants, 12 typewritten pages. Also published in part as "Where It Goes, Nobody Knows; Some Astonishing Facts About Federal Bookkeeping." *Tax Outlook* 3 (September 1948): 2-4. *The Virginia Accountant* 2 (March 1949): 14-16.

"Hoover Commission Disagrees on Changes in Government Accounting." *The Journal of Accountancy* 87 (March 1949): 192-199. *Accounting Seminar* 3 (May 1949): 17-23.

"Audit Procedure in the United States." In *Summer Course 1949—Proceedings at Christ Church, Oxford, from 14th to 19th July, 1949.* London, England: Institute of Chartered Accountants in England and Wales, 141-168. *The Accountant* (England) 121 (September 17, 1949): 288-291; (September 24, 1949): 315-318; (October 8, 1949): 386-390. *

"Government Finance and Economy." (Address before the Virginia Manufacturers Association, Richmond, Virginia, October 22, 1949.) In the T. Coleman Andrews Papers (Coll. 119), Special Collections, University of Oregon Library. 14 printed pages.

"Acceptance Address of the New President." In *How to Improve Accounting & Tax Service to American Business* (Papers Presented at the Sixty-Third Annual Meeting, American Institute of Accountants). New York: American Institute of Accountants, 1950, 7-10.

"The Challenge of Our Time." *The Michigan Certified Public Accountant* 1 (February 1950): 2-4, 9-11. Similar addresses delivered at the Massachusetts Society of Certified Public Accountants, September 26, 1949 (in the files of the American Institute of Certified Public Accountants, 18 typewritten pages) and at the National Affairs Conference of the Virginia State Chamber of Commerce Silver Anniversary Meeting at Roanoke, Virginia, April 15, 1949 (published by the Committee on National Affairs of the Virginia State Chamber of Commerce, in the files of the Virginia Historical Society, 15 printed pages).

"The Hoover Commission's Recommendations on Federal Government Accounting." *The Texas Accountant* 22 (July and August 1950): 1, 3-5.

"Accounting Problems in a Defense Economy." In *Financial Planning for Defense Production*, Financial Management Series Number 98 (Papers Presented at the Financial Management Conference, American Management Association, Waldorf-Astoria, New York, November 30 - December 1, 1950). New York: American Management Association, 1951, 13-21.

"Address at Tax Clinic of the Alabama Society of Certified Public Accountants and The University of Alabama." In *Fourth Annual Federal Tax Clinic 1950, University of Alabama Bulletin.* University, AL: Bureau of Business Research, School of Commerce and Business Administration, University of Alabama, 1951, 73-78.

"Emergency in Our Times has Now Become Normal." *The Office* 33 (January 1951): 50-51.

"What the Accounting Profession has Done to Cooperate with the Bank Credit Man." *Bulletin of the Robert Morris Associates* 34 (January 1951): 197-204, 220.

"The Budget and Auditing Procedures Act of 1950." (Talk given before the Michigan Accounting Conference at Ann Arbor on October 14, 1950.) *The Michigan Certified Public Accountant* 2 (February 1951): 9-12.

"Superior Service, Profits and Savings Built America." *Norfolk and Western Magazine* 29 (May 1951): 279-284.

"Testimony Against S.913 Establishing a Congressional Joint Committee of the Budget." *The Journal of Accountancy* 92 (July 1951): 102-106.

"Freedom's War on Waste." *Credit and Financial Management* 53 (July 1951): 16-18.

"Report to Council of American Institute of Accountants on Tax Practice Statement." *The Michigan Certified Public Accountant* 3 (August 1951): 4-5.

"Presidential Report Delivered to the American Institute of Accountants." Atlantic City, New Jersey, October 9, 1951. In the T. Coleman Andrews Papers (Coll. 119), Special Collections, University of Oregon Library. 18 typewritten pages.

"The Accountant in Practice and in Public Service." In *The Sixth International Congress on Accounting*. London, England: Institute of Chartered Accountants in England and Wales, 1952, 402-418. *The Accountant* (England) 127 (September 27, 1952): 346-355. Also published under the title "The American Accountant in Practice." *The Canadian Chartered Accountant* 61 (December 1952): 229-242 (excludes Appendix A). An article covering similar topics was published under the title "The History, Growth and Organization of Public Accounting in America," in *Memoria de la Primera Conferencia Interamericana de Contabilidad, Mayo 17 al 22, 1949*. San Juan, Puerto Rico: Instituto de Contadores de Puerto Rico, 1950, 137-149.

"One Man's Philosophy: 'My Life is Not My Own.'" *The Richmond News Leader* (August 12, 1952): 28.

"Current U.S. Tax Problems." In *Report of Proceedings of the Seventh Annual Tax Conference*, 1953 Conference Report. Toronto, Canada: Canadian Tax Foundation, 1954, 66-79.

"Square Deal for Taxpayer—Interview with T. Coleman Andrews." *U.S. News & World Report* 34 (May 8, 1953): 28-41.

"Accountants and Taxes: Desirable Objectives in Tax Administration." *The Illinois Certified Public Accountant* 15 (June 1953): 66-67.

"Our New Tax Administration Program." *Life Association News* 48 (October 1953): 55-56.

"Common-Sense Administration of the Internal Revenue Laws." *Municipal Finance* 26 (November 1953): 63-71.

"The Internal Revenue Service." *The Illinois Certified Public Accountant* 16 (December 1953): 42-43. *

"The New Role of the Tax Commissioner." *The Accounting Forum* 24 (December 1953): 5-7, 46.

"The Philosophy of Tax Administration." In *1953 Proceedings of the Forty-Sixth Annual Conference on Taxation*, Ronald B. Welch, ed. Sacramento, CA: National Tax Association, 1954, 532-539.

"Successful Administration of the Tax Laws." In *Accounting, Auditing, Taxes 1953* (Papers Presented at the Sixty-Sixth Annual Meeting, American Institute of Accountants). New York: American Institute of Accountants, 1954, 14-23.

"Internal Revenue Service: An Address before the Mountain States Accounting Conference." In *Technical Papers Presented at the 1954 Mountain States Accounting Conference.* Salt Lake City, UT: Mountain States Council of Certified Public Accountants, 1954, 23-31.

"Voluntary Compliance with the Tax Laws." In *1954 Annual Meeting Papers* (Papers Presented at the Sixty-Seventh Annual Meeting, American Institute of Accountants). New York: American Institute of Accountants, 1954, i-x.

"Our New Tax Administration Program: Excerpts from an Address before Institute of Newspaper Controllers and Finance Officers." *Institute of Newspaper Controllers and Finance Officers*, Bulletin No. 67 (January 1954): 1-2.

"The Internal Revenue Code of 1954." *The Tax Executive* 7 (October 1954): x-xi.

"Proposed Regulations Under 1954 Internal Revenue Code" (Letter by T. Coleman Andrews for the Internal Revenue Service and Response by Allan H. W. Higgins for Section of Taxation of the American Bar Association). American Bar Association, *Section of Taxation Bulletin* (October 1954): 24-36.

"Significance of the New Master of Law and Taxation Degree." (Address at the College of William and Mary, September 25, 1954.) *Marshall, Wythe, Blackstone Commemoration Ceremonies*. Williamsburg, VA: College of William and Mary, 1954, 31-37. Portions reprinted under the title "Needed: Higher (Tax) Education." *Tax Outlook* 9 (December 1954): 2-5.

"Let's Get Rid of the Income Tax!" *The American Weekly* (April 22, 1956): 6-7, 9, 21-22, 24-25.

"Why the Income Tax is Bad—Interview with T. Coleman Andrews." *U.S. News & World Report* 40 (May 25, 1956): 62-73.

"Speech at a Rally of States' Rights Party." Richmond, Virginia, October 15, 1956. In the T. Coleman Andrews Papers (Coll. 119), Special Collections, University of Oregon Library. 40 typewritten pages.

"Ripening Fruit." *The Louisiana Certified Public Accountant* 23 (October 1963): 16-31. An Address before the Sales Executives' Club, Milwaukee, Wisconsin, January 19, 1961; published by The Patrick Henry Group, Richmond, Virginia, 1961; in the T. Coleman Andrews Papers (Coll. 119), Special Collections, University of Oregon Library.

THE ACCOUNTING HALL OF FAME

THE Accounting Hall of Fame was established at The Ohio State University in 1950 for the purpose of honoring accountants who have or are making significant contributions to the advancement of accounting since the twentieth century. Through 1995, 55 leading American and foreign accountants have been elected to the Hall of Fame. There were no selections to the Hall for the years 1962, 1966, 1967, and 1969 through 1973.

While selection to the Hall of Fame is intended to honor the people so chosen, it is also intended to be a recognition of a distinguished service contribution to the progress of accounting in any of its various fields. Evidence of such service includes contributions to accounting research and literature, significant service to professional accounting organizations, wide recognition as an authority in some field of accounting, advancement of accounting education, and public service. Obviously, a member has reached a position of eminence from which the nature of his or her contributions may be judged.

Elections to the Hall of Fame are made by a Board of Nominations consisting of up to 45 eminent accountants from each of the following three fields: public accountants, educators, and industrial and governmental accountants. Each Board member serves a fixed term. Starting in 1973, Board membership became international. In addition to members from the United States, the Board has included members from Australia, Canada, England, Japan, Mexico, and other countries.

Nominations and the election to the Accounting Hall of Fame by the Board are made annually by mail in two steps. Individual members of the Board are asked to nominate a living or deceased accountant for possible selection to the Hall of Fame. From these preliminary nominations, a ballot is prepared containing the name alphabetically listed of not more than four candidates who have been nominated most frequently. The members of the Board of Nominations then cast their votes for one of the four nominees. The single candidate receiving the most votes on the ballot is entered into the Hall.

Evidence of election to the Accounting Hall of Fame takes three forms. A certificate issued under the seal of The Ohio State University and signed by the President of the University and a representative of the Board of Nominations is presented to each person elected (or to the person's representative when the person elected is deceased). The names of the elected persons are inscribed on a scroll, and a photographic portrait of each person elected and the citation attesting to the election are permanently displayed, together with the scroll, in the corridors of Hagerty Hall on The Ohio State University campus. The photographic portraits and citations are currently being replaced by large bronze plaques for each member. Each plaque contains an engraved likeness and a biographic sketch. Presentation of the certificate usually takes place at the American Accounting Association annual convention. Members of The Ohio State University faculty are not eligible for election to the Accounting Hall of Fame.

THE ACCOUNTING HALL OF FAME
MEMBERSHIP

1950
George Oliver May
Robert Hiester Montgomery
William Andrew Paton

1951
Arthur Lowes Dickinson
Henry Rand Hatfield

1952
Elijah Watt Sells
Victor Hermann Stempf

1953
Arthur Edward Andersen
Thomas Coleman Andrews
Charles Ezra Sprague
Joseph Edmund Sterrett

1954
Carman George Blough
Samuel John Broad
Thomas Henry Sanders
Hiram Thompson Scovill

1955
Percival Flack Brundage

1956
Ananias Charles Littleton

1957
Roy Bernard Kester
Hermann Clinton Miller

1958
Harry Anson Finney
Arthur Bevins Foye
Donald Putnam Perry

1959
Marquis George Eaton

1960
Maurice Hubert Stans

1961
Eric Louis Kohler

1963
Andrew Barr
Lloyd Morey

1964
Paul Franklin Grady
Perry Empey Mason

1965
James Loring Peirce

1968
George Davis Bailey
John Lansing Carey
William Welling Werntz

1974
Robert Martin Trueblood

1975
Leonard Paul Spacek

1976
John William Queenan

1977
Howard Irwin Ross

1978
Robert Kuhn Mautz

1979
Maurice Moonitz

1980
Marshall Smith Armstrong

1981
Elmer Boyd Staats

1982
Herbert Elmer Miller

1983
Sidney Davidson

1984
Henry Alexander Benson

1985
Oscar Strand Gellein

1986
Robert Newton Anthony

1987
Philip Leroy Defliese

1988
Norton Moore Bedford

1989
Yuji Ijiri

1990
Charles Thomas Horngren

1991
Raymond John Chambers

1992
David Solomons

1993
Richard T. Baker

1994
Robert T. Sprouse

1995
William W. Cooper